Ava Gardner

Also by Lee Server

Robert Mitchum: "Baby, I Don't Care"
Asian Pop Cinema: Bombay to Tokyo
The Big Book of Noir
Over My Dead Body
Sam Fuller: Film Is a Battleground
Danger Is My Business
Screenwriter: Words Become Pictures

Ava Gardner

Love is Nothing

LEE SERVER

BLOOMSBURY

First published in Great Britain 2006
This paperback edition published 2007

Copyright © 2006 by Lee Server

The moral right of the author has been asserted

Bloomsbury Publishing Plc,
36 Soho Square,
London, W1D 3QY

First published by St. Martin's Press,
175 Fifth Avenue, New York, N.Y. 10010.

A CIP catalogue record for this book is available from the British Library

ISBN 9780747580829

All papers used by Bloomsbury Publishing are natural, recyclable products
made from wood grown in well-managed forests. The manufacturing
processes conform to the environmental regulations of the country of origin.

10 9 8 7 6 5 4 3 2 1

Printed in Great Britain by Clays Ltd, St Ives plc

www.bloomsbury.com

For Terri

CONTENTS

PROLOGUE

Ava

Some who knew their old movies said it was all just like the one of hers with the funeral at the beginning and the end and the blue-gray clouds and the black umbrellas and the mourners in the rain.

Sunset Memorial Park lay at the western edge of Smithfield in a small, flat expanse of trimmed lawn and looping drive open to the main street below and to the surrounding houses and mobile homes. An assembly of five hundred or so stood silently in the rain—local people and old acquaintances and fans and the ones who had read about it in their morning news and come out to have a look.

There were people who had known her long ago but not since who remembered her with proprietary fondness, and there were others who had known her only on the big screen or on the late show on TV but were pleased and proud that she had come home to her birthplace after so long a time away. There were some in the crowd who were there in the hope of seeing a celebrated face or two, one or another of the famous woman's famous friends. A stretch limousine had rolled up the gravel driveway and stopped close by the grave and no one had come out and people had looked through the smoked glass windows, eager to know who was inside. (It was a hairdresser from Raleigh.)

At the grave site those who could claim more direct ties to the deceased sat on folding chairs within a roped-off enclosure, randomly protected from the weather by a leaking black canopy. In the front row was sister

Myra with her children and their kin, and among them a stranger to Smithfield, the raven-haired South American woman who had come with the body from another country far away, now sitting with head bowed and weeping without pause. Great bundles of red and pink roses and tulips surrounded the cherrywood casket. The largest and most extravagant of the floral arrangements had been ordered from a local flower shop by a former husband of the dead woman; the check that came from California carried the signature of the man himself, and the florist would regret not keeping it as a souvenir, but it had been a very large order and a very big check.

Presiding at the grave was the Reverend Francis Bradshaw of the nearby Centenary United Methodist Church. He had not known the deceased personally (she had not lived in Smithfield for nearly fifty years), but he was a friend of her family, and it was to their world that she had now returned. The eulogy was brief—for a woman about whom a few million words had been written in her lifetime. She was authentic, genuine, said the Reverend Bradshaw, but no saint. She was who she was. In the movie there had been more to go on. It was Humphrey Bogart then remembering a dead star as he stood in the rainy Italian cemetery, with the good lines by Joe Mankiewicz, the lighting by Jack Cardiff, and the color by Technicolor.

She was who she was: Ava Gardner. Actress, love goddess. Resident of London, Madrid, Hollywood, and Grabtown. She liked jazz and driving too fast and nights that went on forever. She loved gin and dogs and four-letter words and Frank Sinatra. Once upon a time she was thought to be the most beautiful woman in the world. She had luminescent white skin, eyes like Andean emeralds, eminent cheekbones, a wide, sensuous crescent mouth, a sleek, strong body that moved with a feline insolence, and a dancer's grace. She played temptresses, adventurers, restless women, in the movies and in private life. On the silver screen she conveyed a powerful image of dark desirability. To see her in the flesh was said to have made the blood race, the hair on the arms stand up. To know her more intimately was to surrender to mad passions, to risk all. "I'm a plain simple girl off the farm," she liked to say, "and I've never pretended to be anything else."

Hers was the old rags-to-riches story, a Cinderella rewrite, the barefoot country girl who became a reluctant movie queen. Fate or luck or genetic coding had given her an extraordinary appearance and the brains, style, and whatever were the incalculable ingredients for stardom (whether you were born with it or caught it from a public drinking cup, like the man said, she had it). As an unknowing teenager, she had gone direct from small town to the picture capital, drafted by the mightiest of the dream factories. At first it was not at all certain what she had to offer beyond her youthful beauty. A reluctant performer, she was modest and self-conscious, nervous to the point of illness before a camera. Coaches, publicists, and photographers set to work revising her to the studio's standards, doing away with her backwoods accent, unpolished movements, and uncouth manners, trying to make her into someone else before she was quite sure who she was. She felt humbled, full of resentment. She nurtured a defiant rebelliousness that would drive her forever after.

In the beginning her social life—not her acting—got all the attention. She was famous if at all for her famous admirers, movie stars, swinging bandleaders, mad millionaires. Her mother far away would see the pictures and the stories in the gossip columns and wonder what her little girl was getting up to, but Ava could take care of herself (and the millionaire had the stitches on his face to prove it). She married for love, no matter what anyone said to the contrary, once and then again, and again after that. The first husband was too young at heart, the second one too cold. Love became her terrible habit, something hopeless to resist, impossible to get right. In the end she would find it, the one that she knew was forever, but that one became the most impossible of all.

She had been around a lifetime in starlet years when her break finally came. It was in one of those pictures that began to appear at the end of the war: dark, spiritually ravaged stories for a grim, wised-up populace that no longer believed in happy-ever-after, only lust and temptation and doom. A carnal, dangerous angel in the chiaroscuro dreamscape of film noir, she was a success at last. Smoldering in black satin, she loomed over Broadway, eight stories larger than life.

She became at once the principal sex symbol for the movies' new dark age. Audiences responded to her style, an impudent, provocative blend of sweater girl and spider woman, the all-American accessibility of Lana Turner and the dark exoticism of Dietrich or Lamarr. Her cynical demeanor and sometimes less than wholesome glamour made her fit company for the new generation of male stars, Lancaster, Mitchum, Mason, Peck (in his surly early years), the corps of unsmiling, morally ambiguous men of postwar cinema. She played noir temptresses and big-city vamps and a statue of Venus sprung to succulent life, but never the girl next door. Audiences tuned in to her private persona as well, the one that seemed not so different from her screen image, the playgirl who lived for kicks, the denizen of nightclubs, the temptress who brought powerful men to their knees. Her popularity soared. Her acting grew in assurance, charisma, and variety. The studio execs dragged their feet—skeptical of her talent, fearful of her independence—still gave her the utility parts as the leading man's bland leading lady, but in between there would come unusual projects and distinctive roles to which she would bring unique presence, elements of style, personality, and personal history. Her greatest films are hard to imagine without her.

She took no pride in her career, saw acting as an embarrassing ordeal. Psychiatrists wrestled with her issues of self-esteem. Friends called her a dedicated contrarian, someone you could depend on to do whatever she was asked not to do. She cursed the burdens of stardom, the prying of the press, the studio's hypocritical codes of moral conduct, as she reveled in her privileges and pursued a scandalous romance with a married man. The affair demonized her as a home wrecker but fed her status as a symbol of sexual allure, made her more famous and popular than before. She would rise above the strata of movie stardom to some even more rarefied atmosphere, on the cover of every magazine everywhere, one of the handful of pop deities who made the whole world want to follow their every move.

The illicit romance became legit, but even in marriage the couple remained a scandal. They loved each other as if love were a battle to the death. When the obsession, the jealousy, and the destruction became too much she ran away, kissed off a husband and the industry town she despised in one flight, left America for new horizons, and never looked back. She was searching for something in her new surroundings, without and within, but finding it was something else.

In Europe and in adventures around the world she became the glittering expatriate, her life a hotly reported tale of glamour and sex and mad love. Existence became a daily contradiction as she craved her privacy and dignity but lived in headline type for the world to see, complete with front-page-worthy love affairs, drinking binges, public spectacles, and violence. She became first the prototype and then the caricature of jet-set decadence, a founding mother of *la dolce vita*, queen of the night, in constant flight from the paparazzi. Pleasure took the place of love, and love became something to be feared or at best enjoyed at a distance and in memories of what had or might have been.

Along the way she had turned into a good actress. Not that she wanted to hear about it. Professional compliments still made her uncomfortable and shy. You must be thinking of some other dame, she would tell people when they said something nice. She worked only for the loot, she would say, only to finance her extravagant devotion to fun and forgetting. Deep down, she would say, I'm very superficial.

The clock ticked toward midnight, and the face that had once awed the world began to go away, lost to age and assorted excesses. She escaped again, another new beginning. A quiet life at last, a return to common sense. There was peace in this but regret as well, time to look back and think about choices made and things gone wrong.

Screen goddesses, if they lived long enough, became Dorian Grays in reverse, placing themselves out of sight, hidden from the public in their cloisters in Paris, Los Angeles, New York, London, ravaged by time as their celluloid faces remained on view around the world, always the same, never growing old. Reclusive, she would watch herself on television late at night; see the films like moving scrapbooks, animated memories of amazing places and extraordinary people, touchstones for experiences, some that had been all but forgotten. She would look at her image of forty and nearly fifty years before and ask herself—not immodestly but with uncertainty and a sense of wonder—if anyone had ever been so young or so beautiful.

Life every now and then behaved as if it had seen too many bad movies, Bogart said, at the funeral in the rain. She was who she was, said the Reverend Bradshaw. The camera craning forward, Spanish guitar on the sound track, slow dissolve.

PART ONE

ONE

Goddess Country

She was born in Johnston County in the red-dirt heartland of North Carolina, beyond Smithfield, at the western bend of the old Grabtown Road. The baby was delivered from her mother at ten o'clock that December 24, 1922, healthy, noisy as hell. In the morning family and friends gathered around a candlelit Christmas tree and cheered the new arrival and everyone had a look at the infant girl and listened to her yell. Two cakes—one chocolate and one white coconut—were baked to honor a twice-blessed day—a Christmas/birthday ritual forever after. Though one cake was intended to honor the baby Jesus, the girl would come to think of them both as tribute to her alone. They named her Ava Lavinia Gardner, the first after a beautiful maiden aunt, and the second because it sounded so pretty.

Her people were from the Piedmont plateau, the wide central strip of rolling hills between the Allegheny Mountains and the low-lying coastal plain and wind-whipped barrier isles to the east. Her bloodlines were a composite of the Piedmont's migrant herds: English, Irish, Scotch-Irish, a drop or two of French Huguenot. They had come to North Carolina over the previous century and a half, come down the Pioneer Road, down the Great Valley Road in the era of European settlement of the Carolina backcountry that started in the 1750s. Few whites lived in the region before that time. Neighboring Virginia and South Carolina were settled and prospered, but North Carolina long resisted greater colonization due to its hazardous Atlantic harbors and the lingering stigma of Roanoke Island, the death-cursed lost colony where English America had falteringly begun. The land was as it had been since its creation, granite mountain, forest and foothill, ancient seabed plain, home to wildlife and for ten thousand years to scattered tribes of Amerindians: the Bear River, Cape Fear, Catawba, Cheraw, Cherokee, Coree, Chowan, Eno Hatteras, Kajawee, Meherin, Nachapunga, Neuse River, Occaneechi, Pamlico, Saponi, Secotin, Sissipahaw, Sugaree, Tuscarora, Waccamaw, Wateree, Waxhau, Weopomeoc. A young London-born naturalist and Crown surveyor named John Lawson would make the first formal exploration of the interior lands, traveling far along the upper reaches of the Neuse and beyond, visiting the tribal settlements and recording the unspoiled terrain and abundant natural resources. He would publish an avid account of his experiences in a volume titled *A New Voyage to Carolina*, producing much interest in the forgotten colony and helping set off a wave of migration to inland North Carolina that would last for more than a hundred years. Now arrived newcomers by the thousands from Virginia, Pennsylvania, England, Wales, Ireland, half a million from the ports of Ulster alone. The wilderness was cleared for farmland, the hills and valleys echoed with English drinking songs, Scottish reels, and Goidelic hymns, and the Native American tribes were all but eliminated by war, smallpox, and syphilis. Some years after the publication of *A New Voyage to Carolina*, and in thanks for spreading the good word about their homeland, some Tuscarora Indians would find John Lawson and stick his body full of sharpened splinters of kindling and set them on fire.

The backcountry settlers were scattered across a rural landscape in a region without cities and only primitive transportation routes before the railroad came, limiting trade with the outside world. The residents of the Piedmont were simple farmers, most of them, working fifty acres or less. They were known as plainspoken, self-reliant, ornery, blessed with an innate suspicion of government, politics, and religion (at least until the irresistible hegemony of the Baptists). On the subject of slavery—the explosive national issue that would one day be settled in an apocalyptic conflict, state against state—North Carolinians of the central and western counties were widely if not deeply ambivalent. Few farmers in the region owned slaves—few could afford to—but the wealthy planters who did owned enough to bring the black population in the Piedmont up to 30 percent and the culture of slavery thrived openly. In Smithfield, the county seat, there was a large slave market (not far from the present site of the Ava Gardner Museum) where as many as three hundred humans were sold on the block in a single day. "Dey uster strip dem niggers stark naked," said former slave Josephine Smith of Johnston County recalling activities in the Smithfield market, "an' gallop 'em ober de square so dat de buyers could see dat dey warn't scarred or deformed." Family on Ava Gardner's mother's side were slave owners, with modest stock, at the time of the Civil War; her mother's mother, Elizabeth Forbes Baker, then of Edgecombe County, was willed the ownership of two adult slaves in her father's possession—"1 woman Maryann and 1 man Jim"—though with the outcome of the war she was not to collect on this inheritance. A flesh-and-blood link with the time of slavery remained well into the twentieth century. Growing up in Johnston County in the 1920s and '30s, Ava Gardner would cross the path of many an elderly African American who had been born and sold as human property.

North Carolina seceded from the Union in 1861, giving some 150,000 troops to the Southern cause, one in three never to return alive. A farmer from Wilson County, James Bailey Gardner was among those North Carolinians who would wear the Confederate gray and he would be one of the lucky ones who came back alive and unharmed. He was a farmer, as his father had been before him, working a parcel of land his father had cleared in western Wilson County. Since 1853, James Bailey had been married to Peninah Batts, a planter's daughter, whose American roots went back nearly two hundred years to the first Atlantic colonies. Their union would be blessed with seven offspring before Peninah's untimely death in 1867. That same year Gardner claimed a new bride, the teenage Mary Dilda, twenty-two years his junior. With her his issue would grow by another half dozen: Cynthia, Benjamin, Charles, Warren, and in 1878, Jonas Bailey, and two years after that their last, a daughter named Ava Virginia.

James Bailey Gardner was a disagreeable man, prone to black moods, drunkenness, and violence, increasingly so as the years went on. He was a chronic imbiber of moonshine, and when his black moods and his corn liquor converged he was a menace to all. At those times it was the designated job of the youngest child, Ava Virginia, to run into the house and find the old man's gun and hide it. Gardner and his second family lived on the farm his wife had inherited from her father, and the main cash crop there, as on any farm in the Piedmont that could sustain it, was tobacco, the bright-leaf tobacco that grew best—and for a time almost exclusively—on the rolling red-clay hills of north-central North Carolina. Tobacco had been grown in the region for hundreds of years, but it was only in the 1830s that the secrets of bright leaf had come to be known, a male slave of Catawba County credited as the first to create the flue-cure process that began a revolution in the tobacco industry. Carefully cured, the golden leaves of the Piedmont were so mild that their smoke could be inhaled and held deep within the lungs, thus delivering to the bloodstream a quicker and more addictive nicotine kick. The worldwide cigarette industry—and habit—was born, and quality "yellacured" bright leaf became about the most desired vegetable on earth. Its cultivation remained specialized and painstaking, however, and while the heirs of Washington Duke and others made incalculable fortunes from processing and selling Piedmont tobacco, they would leave the growing to the small farmers who did the difficult and dirty work for far more moderate profit.

Tobacco farmers passed their skill from father to son, and James Bailey's son Jonas had begun to learn the intricate cultivation of the bright-leaf plant by the time he could walk—the long process from January to late summer, seeding, plowing, cropping off, killing out, grading, sometimes literally making your bed in the barn with the tobacco so you could watch the temperature in the furnace all night long, and finally in August or September preparing the big juicy golden leaves for market. Given his father's penchant for disappearing off the farm after every drunken dispute, usually holing up for days at the house of one of his older children, Jonas had run a good portion of the farm from the age of ten or eleven. He had little formal schooling, but he was a very learned farmer and he could tell you the story of twelve kinds of dirt just by running them through his fingers.

He was long and lean, hawkish and handsome with green eyes and a cleft chin, brown-skinned on his face, neck, and forearms from the years spent working outdoors. He was a good man, temperate, loyal, hardworking. In his early twenties he found a girl, Mary Elizabeth "Molly" Baker, from Saratoga in Wilson County, the daughter of David and Elizabeth Forbes Baker, a red-haired, red-faced Scottish father and a mother who had died when her girl was very young. Molly was pretty, with dark eyes, skin as white and smooth as cream, and a soft rounded figure. She had a strongly maternal nature, ached to produce children, and was a diligent homemaker and a glorious cook. In January 1903, Jonas and Molly were married in the parlor of the Baker house in Saratoga.

They were opposites in many ways. Molly warm, outgoing, and emotional, Jonas introspective and shy of strangers. But they loved each other, and that love would last with few interruptions till the day that each one died. Nine months and some days from the hour of their nuptials a daughter was born, Beatrice Elizabeth, followed, at nine- and twenty-four-month intervals, by two more girls, Elsie Mae and Edith Inez.

Soon after his wedding Jonas began to search for land, a place to farm that would be his own, that he could cultivate and make flourish and that would become his legacy to his family and to those who came after them. He found such a place in the area of Boon Hill to the west of Johnston County, making a down payment for the purchase of two large parcels of rural land southeast of the town of Smithfield.

For three years he traveled to and from the homesite, building the wooden frame house where his family would live. He hauled the wood and he dug the well and he dug the outhouse. In 1907 they moved in, Jonas, Molly, and the three little girls. The house was on the old back road that ran through the area known as Grabtown. The derivation of the nickname is now only speculation: Some say it was after the way the local kids always hungrily "grabbed" at a traveling peddler's gewgaws from the outside world. Their excitement was understandable: The residents, the children especially, lived in a near-complete isolation. Smithfield, the county seat, was just eight miles away, but it could seem like a hundred when bad weather turned the dirt road into mud. It was a region of modest family farms, the poorer ones no better than small clearings in the woods. Many in the 1900s still existed outside the cash economy, growing what they lived on. Some farmers owned their land, passed down over generations, but many were tenant farmers, kicking back a portion of their crops in royalties and fees to the landowner; mortgaged landowners like the Gardners worked to pay the bank and hoped for profits or at least enough to make ends meet. Like all of the greater Brogden area, Grabtown had no running water or electricity (and none to come until the 1940s). Children attended a little one-room schoolhouse along the road until it closed with the opening of the Brogden School a mile away. Like much of the American South, Johnston County was racially segregated. The black sharecroppers and fieldworkers had their own neighborhoods, their own churches and schools. Racialist views were common enough in the county, but among many of the struggling rural farmers there was said to have been a live-and-let-live attitude toward the black minority, with less of the overt antagonism and sense of entitlement of whites in the eastern counties where blacks in fact outnumbered the whites by a considerable margin.

On December 5, 1908, Molly Gardner gave birth to her fourth child, the first to be born in their new home, and the first boy: They named him Raymond. A family photo shows a delighted, sandy-haired kid in a straw hat. One early winter morning, two-year-old Raymond was standing near the warming fireplace amid the hustle and confusion of a new workday. A stray dynamite cap from the supply Jonas kept for use in clearing boulders had fallen in transit through the front room and been brushed into the roaring fireplace. The cap ignited in the flames. The explosion hit Raymond in the face and chest. He died on the way to the hospital in Smithfield.

The brutal random death of their baby boy would leave a permanently unhealed wound in the hearts of Jonas and Molly Gardner. Jonas was a practical man whose only propensity for the occult was an unswayable belief in the *Farmer's Almanac*, yet he would sometimes in the years ahead come to think that a darkness had entered their lives with Raymond's dying and remained, a black cloud of hovering bad luck. The farm would fall prey to natural disasters and to man-made ones as well. His land would not remain his own.

Pregnant at the time of Raymond's death, Molly would give birth to a second boy, Jonas "Jack" Gardner, and four years later in 1914 another daughter, Myra, their sixth child—and, they assumed, with growing conviction as the years went by, their last.

At first they all called her "Liz," in deference to Aunt Ava, her father's unmarried sister who had come to live with them in Grabtown. She was
made much of and spoiled by everybody. She was a beautiful baby, everyone said so, though for a time she was curiously deficient in hair; at last, in
her second year, she began to sprout a layer of soft blond curls. She was a
restless child, no sooner placed in her crib than she was standing at the
bars and demanding to be let out. She was walking at eight months, ready
to see the world. She once climbed through an open second-floor window
and was on her way into midair when her brother, Jack, caught her by the
drawers at the last instant.

Though her later success in Hollywood would bring the stretch of land
called Grabtown a degree of lasting fame, Ava's time there was brief.
When she was not yet three, the family was forced to move on. Jonas
could not make the farm thrive, expenses always increasing, profits always
slim, and now the whole region plagued by an economic downturn. Jack's
liability for property destroyed in a fire (sneaking a cigarette, he'd
dropped a match and burned the seed barn to the ground) didn't help
much. What options there might have been ran out suddenly and the
house and the land were lost.

Someone at the county school board came to the Gardner family's aid
with a well-timed offer that combined employment with a place to live.
Down the road in Brogden next to the new redbrick schoolhouse, the
old school—the clapboard building a few steps away—was being used
as a dormitory for the young lady teachers. In recent years Johnston
County had begun an ambitious program to consolidate and raise the
standards of primary education in the rural districts. Modern, multi-
story buildings were being constructed in a number of communities
across the county, in many cases replacing primitive one-room school-
houses where country children learned the "three Rs" and often not
much else. For each new school the county supplied certified school-
teachers and provided "school trucks" to transport the children. The
upgraded facilities had proved controversial: Some farmers and back-
woodsmen suspected any intervention at all by government outsiders,
even if they were only as far outside as the county seat, and the construction of one of the new brick schools, at Corinth-Holder, was delayed by local saboteurs who blew it apart with dynamite. The school at
Brogden, happily, opened without incident. The faculty was by edict

made up of unmarried (white) women, and the county provided them room and board at a Teacherage, a secular novitiate where they could live safely and away from temptation. The Gardners would manage the Brogden Teacherage and be given a portion of the house for themselves, with Molly serving as cook and housekeeper.

Molly took to the job at once. With her domestic skills and maternal warmth, she made the boardinghouse into a home, not just for her family—her husband and son and the girls—but for the young ladies who lived there with them, some very young and away from their own mothers for the first time in their lives. For a while Jonas Gardner sharecropped, working a landlord's farm. He hoped to turn things around for himself and regain some portion of his own property, a dream that would not come true. The makeshift job and lodgings they shared at the county's expense drifted into an unplanned permanence. They would stay for nearly ten years, and the Teacherage would be the setting of Ava Gardner's young life, the big clapboard house, the school, and the fields and orchards and dirt roads of Brogden.

Of her earliest years at the Teacherage she would remember mostly her mother and the whirl of excitement around Molly's long day of work, cooking and cleaning from early to late, moving through the halls and from room to room, never at rest, Ava toddling behind, trying to keep up, a hand on her mother's apron. She would remember the wonderful smells and tastes in her mother's kitchen, something steaming, baking, or frying, it seemed, every hour of the day. She would remember the lady teachers who shared her home, another whirl of activity in the morning, the floorboards creaking as all of them went from bedrooms to bath to dining room, getting themselves ready for school in the morning; and then all of them together again from the late afternoon, generating quieter sounds, relaxing on the porch or in the parlor in the evening, working on their school papers, reading books and newspapers, chatting together. The young lady teachers doted on Ava, talked with her and played with her and held her on their laps, many of them looking at her longingly, daydreaming of being finished with their single, working lives and having husbands and children of their own.

When she was old enough she went to school in the redbrick building across the lawn, joining a hundred or so kids who arrived each morning from all over and poured out of the school bus in screaming droves. Knowing all the teachers for so long and living right next door reduced the trauma of leaving her mother and going among the strange children. It was odd fun to be at school with the ladies and see them made up for classes and behaving with such formality—she'd seen them at home for so long, chattering and running around in their bathrobes, their faces smeared with cold cream. Her favorite teacher was Mrs. Williams, who taught her to read and write. Ava would remember a sweet, tolerant woman, who ran her classes with a "wonderful serenity." Maggie Williams had the distinction of being the only married teacher at Brogden, an exception made because her husband was to be away for a very long time, in prison for murder. (Many years later, in 1952, his curious life story became the subject of a movie, *Carbine Williams*, filmed at MGM, Ava's place of employment by then, with James Stewart in the title role and Jean Hagen playing Maggie.)

At school there was a brief portent, a glimpse of future events in miniature, her acting debut, and a lead role no less, as the narcoleptic fantast in the school production of something called *A Rose Dream*. It had less to do with any instinct for performing on the girl's part than it did with her glowing prettiness and how everyone knew that she would look wonderful under the lights on the little Brogden school stage. At five and six she was already attracting attention for her appearance. Her hair was long, blond, and curled in those early years, oddly almost unique among her classmates—a photo of the children in her class posing together at the school shows row upon row of girls with dark hair and the popular but severe Colleen Moore cut (after the silent movie gamine, a short, straight bob with bangs) surrounding little Ava and her untamed golden locks.*

School captivated her in the beginning. She was filled with curiosity for the knowledge contained in her schoolbooks and in her teachers' words, exploring the new worlds of history, geography, literature. She was a smart little girl, her teachers said. She studied, asked questions. But the time would come by the fifth or sixth grade when her excitement for learning would fade, replaced by new interests and urges. The gaps in her

---

*In adolescence her hair would darken to a reddish brown.

knowledge and her lack of education were things about which she would feel great regret and embarrassment in her adult life.

In the summers she helped her father with the tobacco crop. She would remember standing barefoot in the fields of tobacco, picking off worms, hauling the heavy leaves, helping to hang them out to dry and tie them together in great bundles. She would remember how the sticky black sap oozed from the tobacco and coated your hands and everything stuck to them like to flypaper, and you couldn't get them clean till you washed them with a lye soap that was so strong it could take your skin right off. Rough work for a little girl and sometimes dangerous (nearly losing an eye once when her sister swiped at her with a hoe), but she enjoyed being outdoors—in the field you didn't have to keep your hair combed and your shoes on your feet—and she loved being near her father, collecting an occasional word of praise. Jonas spoke so tersely that just to hear him say, "Good morning, Daughter," thrilled her no end.

"She thought of her childhood as a very happy time," said Spoli Mills, Ava's close friend for the last thirty years of her life. "It was a time when she had her mother and father together, and she adored them both. And they gave her, I think, a great deal of freedom. Not in the way of being unconcerned but in letting her think for herself, make up her own mind about things. She never had any racial prejudice, for example, not at all."

Her memories of those times would be mostly fond, of a Tom Sawyerish childhood: barefoot days, hot summers, the swimming hole in the woods, her friendship and adventures with a black migrant worker named Shine, the nights camped out with her father as they nursed the curing tobacco. She grew up under opposing influences—within the Teacherage the warm femininity and domesticity of her mother and the dignified, disciplined lady boarders; and outside, the allure of mischief, dirt, and adventure. It seemed clear early on which influence had the stronger pull. "She was a real tomboy back then," Clarence Woodell would remember. He was a neighbor and a classmate in Brogden. "She liked to act just like the boys did," he remembered, thinking back to a time nearly eighty years before. "You know, shoot marbles and climb trees, get down in the dirt. I remember one time she climbed the water tower out back of the school, maybe sixty feet up and hanging off a little ladder. You just didn't see many girls doing things like that in those days. She was the prettiest thing and sweet when you got to know her, but she was a little tomboy, oh my.

Feisty. If you were playing and said something she didn't like she came right at you; didn't matter if it was somebody bigger, she wasn't afraid."

Her immediate hero was her scrappy brother, Jack, and some thought she was trying to emulate him, the boy who'd burned down the seed barn, who was always finding trouble, and who once as a youngster had a business peddling a near-lethal version of moonshine whiskey until his father caught him (in later life Jack became a politician). At school she made friends with sweet, smart girls like Clara Whitley, but on the weekends she would tag along with Jack and with some of the toughest of the local farm kids. They mucked around, smoked cigarettes (fresh tobacco rolled up in a piece of newspaper), broke a few windows, stole watermelons in harvest season (not an easy crime for a little girl to commit, with Piedmont watermelons sometimes weighing twice what she did). Boys taught her a rich vocabulary of four-letter words and obscene phrases, and she enjoyed using them as often and as inappropriately as possible (but never around Mama). She loved the way they gave a "satisfying jolt" to a conversation, making her daintier classmates at school drop their jaws when out of her little-girl mouth would come the words "goddamn," "shit," or "fuck."

She had a natural-born laziness. She loved to sleep late, hated to do the daily chores her mother gave her, always slipped away when she was supposed to help with the cooking or wash the dishes. She loved having nothing to do but lie across the porch steps and chew gum and play with her dog and daydream, or gorge on one of her mother's succulent Southern dinners. When she did rise out of her happy indolence it was often to seek out excitement, emotional release. Her family's Baptist church was too sedate for her, and she liked to go sneaking into one of the passionate Pentecostal assemblages where the preacher shouted and the people would begin to shake and cry and dance in the aisles. She'd wait for the feeling to come and shake her up like that, too, and she would raise her voice to an angry God and shout and sing wildly with the other sinners.

Ava loved music of any kind and responded deeply to it. She loved to dance, feeling the rhythms of the music deep in her bones, and she ran to music wherever she heard it playing. There were guitar pickers and fiddle players to be heard on many a front porch in those days, putting out the old Southern melodies and folk songs. And there were the songs of the black laborers heard from the fields, their sinuous laments. If she came near a radio or a record player she was thrilled. Wind-up phonographs could play the thick black platters they sold at the store in Smithfield: "Lovesick Blues," recorded over in Asheville, North Carolina, or one of the new "hillbilly" stringband recordings coming out of Winston-Salem, not far away. There was a piano in the parlor of the Teacherage, and if anyone got near the keys the girl was sure to be there to gyrate to the sound. Teenage Myra Gardner was once awarded a series of piano lessons, and Ava was so eaten with jealousy that her sister would learn the secrets of making music before she did that she angrily ran up to the piano and bit a chunk out of it. She could find a beat in anything, and even "Nearer My God to Thee" might be accompanied by Ava's shimmy.

She discovered the movies when she was eight or nine. The talkies had come in by then, and a teacher with an automobile began taking Ava and her mother into Smithfield on the weekends to see pictures at the new stucco art deco movie theater. They were soon movie mad like everyone else. Ava loved romances and high adventures, the beautiful sad face of Greta Garbo and the working-girl struggles of Joan Crawford, and if she liked a picture a lot she would beg her mother to sit through it twice. Ava's and Molly's instant favorite was Clark Gable, when they saw him in *Red Dust*, the steamy melodrama of lust and rubber—years later a bittersweet memory for Ava, who would know Clark so well and remake the picture with him; she'd go back in her mind sometimes to that Saturday coming out of the old Howell Theater with her mother and think of Mama's pleasure and the unimaginableness of the future that was to be. She did for a while nurse a daydream of becoming a movie star, a common fantasy for American girls in the 1930s, but one to which she gave some elaborate consideration. When she saw the Bing Crosby film *Going Hollywood* late in 1933 it seemed to her like a dream snatched from within her own head. There was her own future as she imagined it: Marion Davies as a starstruck fan who breaks into pictures, becomes famous, and winds up with the love of a famous sexy crooner. She went with the black girl who worked for her mother, and for some time afterward they enacted scenes from the movie. "I was Marion Davies and Bing's part was taken by the colored girl," she would recall. "We were acting this thing for weeks!"

Molly had thrived at the Teacherage. Much loved by the lady boarders, generations of them as the years went on, she treated them as warmly as

her own children. Ava's daddy had not fared so well. Jonas had given up
the dream of regaining his land, his dream of a legacy for his family. He
had taken various jobs through the years, but farming was what he knew
and all he wanted to do. The years of sharecropping had meant dawn-to-
dusk work and little to show for it. As the 1920s came to a close, tobacco
farming was no longer the sure, steady business it had been ten and
twenty years before. As the cigarette business had grown more competi-
tive and the desire for greater profits increased, the companies in the big
cities—where they could no more grow the bright leaf than they could
smoke the red dirt in which it prospered—had repeatedly lowered the
price they would pay for the "yellacured" crop. The farmers, with their
special skills, who had nurtured the prized tobacco for the better part of a
year, would go begging for a decent price at the auction house; oblivious
to their potential collective power, they took what they could get. At one
auction Jonas Gardner attended the price the buyers offered was one
penny more per pound than it had been thirty-odd years before. Some
farmers could not afford to go on when even subsistence living was uncertain (in the same period, falling prices would cut cotton farming in Johnston County by half). Conditions would only become worse with the
ravages of the Great Depression. Jonas Gardner, like many rural farmers,
blamed many of the country's problems on the malevolent schemes of the
wealthy manufacturers and speculators. He did not have the temperament
to indulge in angry political bluster even if he had been articulate enough to
do so, but he would follow with stoic, bitter interest the events that came to
pass on Wall Street in 1929 and the black tide of economic disaster that
rolled across the country in the years to follow. Other farmers may have
expressed their frustration and resentment more aggressively: In 1932 two
of Smithfield's tobacco warehouses were burned to the ground under suspicion of arson. In the autumn of 1932 Johnston County would vote overwhelmingly for Franklin Roosevelt in the presidential election, desperate
with the hope of reforms and relief to come for the beleaguered farmer.

Help did not come in time to save the Brogden Teacherage. In the fall of
1934 the Board of Education, suffering from reduced revenues, determined that the county could no longer afford the luxury of providing a
boardinghouse for its teachers; with thirty days' notice the ladies would

have to find meals and respectable lodging on their own. The Teacherage would be closed down indefinitely. The Gardners were out of a job and a home. They had no savings, and Jonas's uncertain income could not be depended upon to support them.

Molly had an old friend who now ran a boardinghouse up in Newport News, Virginia. There were many such places there, catering to the shipyard workers and the merchant seamen. The friend knew of one that needed a manager, and perhaps when they came there Jonas might find work in the shipyard.

And so they left Brogden, left Johnston County, and left the state of North Carolina, where they had all lived their entire lives.

Ava was leaving her whole world behind, friends and familiar surroundings, heading off to a strange place and unknown prospects, but she did not complain or cry about the move. She had seen it at first as a great adventure. Newport News was not New York or New Orleans or Hollywood or other places she had heard about and wanted to see, but it was the world beyond the mud roads and farmhouses of Brogden. When they rolled out of Johnston County, she looked at the road ahead and not behind at the scenes of her past.

Newport News was a noisy, intimidating place after bucolic Brogden. The Gardners' new home was a run-down house on West Avenue in a harsh neighborhood near the docks. In place of the genteel ladies of the Teacherage there were sullen stevedores with red eyes, stale clothes, and stale breath. School was no longer the inviting brick building with her mother's kitchen always within view and the teachers all friends from her parlor. In Newport News on the first day the teacher teased her about her country drawl, and the children mocked her backwoods background.

"The teacher said, right in front of all the people, 'What does your father do?'" Ava would recall. "I said, 'A farmer.' Some big horrible jerk laughed. My eyes filled with tears."

The self-confidence of the adventurous country girl drained away. A painful shyness began to inhabit and to inhibit her. She huddled in her seat at school, afraid to be noticed, afraid to speak and let them hear her accent and see the teacher's disdain and the other kids laughing. At Brogden the children were all farm kids, and there were few great economic differences between them. But at Newport News she was conscious of the gap between herself and many of the other children, whose parents came from different walks of life. It was painful to go among the girls at school, Ava in her mostly homemade wardrobe, the others in their store-bought outfits in the latest styles. Her own school clothes numbered two, the way she recalled it, "one always in the wash while the other was on my back." She would remember wearing her coat indoors when she could so that no one at school would see she was always wearing the same skirt. She felt isolated, demeaned. "Mother told me that clothes don't make you beautiful," she would recall, "but at that age you need material things to make you feel secure."

Along with the social pressures causing her anxiety, there were physical and emotional changes to be dealt with—sprouting breasts, menstruation, romantic impulses, each stage of maturation carrying its own enigmas and embarrassments. Matters weren't made easier by the awkwardness that her parents showed around the subject—anything to do with sexuality had always been forbidden and fraught with discomfort in the Gardner household. In her parents' shame-filled view of sex, a woman could be only one of two things, "a prude or a prostitute." When her first period arrived and the flowing blood had her on the edge of panic she turned for help not to her mother but to the hired woman who did the sweeping-up.

She charted her body's developments—widening hips, pubic hair, a bustline—with a mixture of awe and dread. Others were noting the changes too, and she was increasingly sensitive to such scrutiny. Her baptism at the local church became a ritual humiliation when the pastor submerged her in the concrete bath at the altar before the entire congregation and she saw the water turn her baptismal shift transparent. She nurtured a distaste for the church from that time (organized religion would come to have little place in her adult life). At home there was more discomfort, covetous looks from her mother's boarders, "revolting old men" as she remembered them, disgustingly flirting with a thirteen-year-old girl. She felt ashamed of where she had to live and the men there lying around with their rank smells and with their ugly alligator eyes following her, and she felt she could never invite a friend home to visit her in such a place. Trying to cope with the murky facts of life left her in a tizzy. "Even before I knew what sex was, I was afraid of it," she would remember. "I had a child's normal curiosity about 'it' but every time the subject came up in conversation with other girls I felt I should hide my head and not listen. If I did listen I went home with guilt complexes tearing at my mind."

But what to do? She grew prettier every year, and boys grew more alluring. She would see them at school or on the street looking her over and smiling, and she would want to smile back and then become afraid and want to again and not know what to do. She was fourteen and wanted to talk to boys and know what they thought of her and know what they were like. But she worried about what her mother would say and worried about what the boys would want to do with her. One day it happened: She had a date. It happened so suddenly she was not sure it had really occurred. He was a good-looking football player three years older than she was, and when he came up to her in the hallway at school and asked her out she impulsively—"in one second I was in love"—said yes. The hours before he arrived to pick her up she spent sick with fear that her mother would see him or that he would see the men who lived there in her home. They went out for hamburgers and Cokes. She was a nervous wreck. "Couldn't open my mouth," she would remember. "A bump on a log. Bored him to death." He took her home early and never spoke to her again. Other boys tried flirting with her, but she was plagued by insecurities. She was dying to go to the school dances but couldn't bear to be seen in her poor clothes when all the other girls would be dressed in their finest.

She suffered through the years at school in Newport News—"I hate it more each day," she wrote to her friend Clara in 1936—and with the seedy conditions at home, surrounded by the lecherous longshoremen, she felt a tremendous relief when her mother agreed to let her go away in the summers, to stay with her sister Inez and family in Raleigh and then for many weeks with Elsie Mae and her family at their home back in Brogden. She felt instantly more comfortable on her old home soil. The change seemed to happen as she crossed the state border from Virginia, the feelings of shame and self-consciousness left behind like a larval enclosure. By the time of her second summer in North Carolina she had blossomed to startling effect. As a little girl her looks had often drawn compliments, but the person who returned to Johnston County that summer was a young woman glowing with beauty, with a radiance to her eyes and smile and flesh; in alliance with the ripe contours of her body the effect was both lovely to look at and unsettlingly erotic.

The transformation of the tomboy from the tobacco fields did not go unnoticed at her seasonal homecoming, and that summer would become for her a kind of unofficial down-home debut. M. W. "Mokie" Stancil was a Smithfield boy who knew her during those teenage visits. "She was a very attractive young lady," Mokie Stancil would remember. "Y'know, in those days—you don't know this—but in those days girls just weren't nearly as attractive. They didn't have all this eye makeup and things they have today. And Ava was attractive without having all that stuff. There wasn't anyone in these parts had anything like the look she had. So pure, her skin so beautiful and smooth and such. She was a really beautiful girl then, she was fourteen, fifteen.

"She wasn't a person of any depth or any consequence to talk to at that time," Mokie recalled. "She had some small talk, that was all, and she had a sense of humor. But she was a very attractive person. You were pleased to have her along with you. We'd get together at someone's house in those days on a Friday and Saturday night. We had what we called our crowd, all the same age, but Ava was a couple of years younger. We sort of adopted her.

"In those days there was a pavilion out at the lake, Holt Lake, where they had a jukebox, and we all went out there to listen to some music and to dance, and Ava came with us. Boys and girls were there, and when Ava walked in everybody just stopped dancing and just looked at her, she was so pretty. They just stopped, I remember, and then the music stopped and no one fed the jukebox right off, they just stood around looking at her."

There were other nights at the Holt Lake pavilion, and Mokie remembered how the boys would crowd around Ava, lining up to dance with her as the jukebox played Tommy Dorsey and then Artie Shaw and then Jimmy Dorsey. "Somebody would dance with her, and then somebody would break on in," he remembered. "Nobody really had a conversation or found out much from her because there was always another boy behind him. She might ask the boy something about himself, and no sooner'd he try to answer than somebody'd tap him on the shoulder want to break in. I remember one of those boys crying to me that he didn't think he was gonna ever get to dance with her, there were so many waiting."

Boys wanted to take her out, and Ava's mother didn't think much of the idea, she and Ava's sisters and brother, Jack, all fretted over it. In the end Jack said, "Mama, I'm watching her and nothing's gonna happen to her, she's a good girl," and they thought it would be all right to let her go on one date since it was Smithfield and so long as there were chaperones and it was a nice boy. Mokie Stancil, who was a friend of Jack's, went on a double date with his girl and Ava and the boy who asked her out. "And you could see she hadn't done much dating before. And she was shy with someone she didn't know. She was shy and he was shy and hardly a word was exchanged between them. He wanted to keep dating her, but she said to me, 'I just don't want to date him again.'"

But there were many others waiting. Ava's mother remained very concerned and particular about whom Ava saw, and she told Mokie she was happy he was kind of looking after her daughter. As time went on he found himself with the job of screening the boys who asked Ava out. "The boys back then, we called them 'wolves' if they were fast, want to kiss the girl on the first date or something like that. And if she asked me about one of the boys here in town who was sort of fast with girls, I would tell her not to go with him. And o' course this was all just between us or I would have been a dirt bomb with those boys. So she kept it strictly confidential, and it worked out fine."

Boys who made the cut would submit to Mokie's questioning. "I'd tell 'em you can't try any of this kissing-on-the-first-date business 'cause she's not going for that. And some of 'em said, 'Can I hold her hand?' and I'd say, 'Well, I think you can do that. Just don't try to be too fresh with her 'cause she's not gonna like it.'"

And there were boys who wanted a date but had a problem with their own mothers: "A lot of times the town people just looked down on some of those country people. I don't think any of the boys ever made Ava feel like that, but some of the mothers of some of the boys might look a little askance at her, at their boy dating her, thinking that she was a little beneath them or something."

Screening all those boys, Mokie sometimes thought that he would have liked to date Ava himself, but he had a girl and that would not have worked out at all, although one time at the lake his girl had to go back to town and Ava said, "How about we go on a rowboat? I've never been rowed around the lake." And Mokie told her he would be glad to do it. And they rowed around Holt Lake on a warm blue-sky afternoon, an hour or two he had not forgotten in sixty-seven years.

"Those were good times in the summers," Mokie Stancil remembered. "Nobody hated nobody, and everybody had fun and enjoyed life."

Like his youngest girl, Jonas Gardner had not found much happiness living in Newport News. He had not fit in with city life. He was a farmer and that was all he knew, and now he lived in a boardinghouse in a city with ships. A sickness came upon him. Perhaps it had been there even back in Brogden, just a plain smoker's cough then, and nothing he would ever have given a second thought. It had gotten worse in Virginia and never gone away, a heavy, choking cough that brought up thick viscous scrap from deep in his lungs. Like any sensible male Jonas hated doctors, and for many months he made do with bottles of drugstore cough syrup. He caught a chest cold in the winter, and the sickness in his lungs got very bad. When he went into the hospital and the doctors found a serious infection in his bronchial tubes, there was no money to keep him in the hospital for as long as he needed. He returned home, and Molly cared for him in their room on the second floor of the boardinghouse. It started to seem as if he would never get better. Sometimes it went on all day and all night, the strangled, agonized coughing. Molly had to move him to another room so the boarders could sleep. She had to work and take care of the house and nurse him. It wore her down. Once Ava saw her break down and cry, the only time she could remember seeing her mother like that, just crying from weariness and hopelessness. Ava would come home from school each day and sit beside her father as he lay propped up in bed and read him the newspaper. He liked to hear about politics and listened with pleasure when she read to him the latest doings of his man, President Roosevelt. He called her "Daughter," as he always did, in happiness or in consternation, his only name for her since she'd been a little girl. Sometimes he would just look at her and hold her hand and tighten his grip when she smiled at him. Pain would come to him with the hard, deep cough that felt as if his insides were being flayed, but he would never complain or curse his fate to anyone. It would be many years later that Ava would look back at that time and really comprehend what she had witnessed, her father's modest and undefeated courage in those worst months of his illness. And she would come to remember with a terrible regret her own sometimes selfish thoughts and behavior as she sat at her father's bedside wanting to be out with her friends and she would think of the things not said then that should have been said and the moments thrown away that could never be regained.

He was buried in Smithfield, in the Sunset Memorial Park cemetery at the edge of town. Family comforted the mother and daughter, urged them to stay on awhile, but Molly told them that the house on West Avenue had to be managed; Ava had to get back to school. Molly forced herself to be strong. You could not fall apart—you had to hold on, keep going, and survive. Molly went back to her cooking and her chores and taking care of her boarders. She tried to go on. But nothing could be the way it used to be. She had always treated the scruffy, lonely men who lived there just as she had the bright young lady teachers at Brogden, with kindness and concern, whether they deserved it or not. But try as she did, her enthusiasm for her work had drained away. She felt useless, vulnerable. Jonas was no longer in the house, but she still felt his suffering every day. "My mother never got over his death," Ava would say years later. "She was never the same person again."

Molly and Ava would sit together in the evenings, and Molly would ask her if she was happy, and Ava would not know what to say, afraid to make her mother feel worse. But Molly did not want to stay where they were anymore, and Ava agreed with her that North Carolina was their real home and that maybe the time had come for them to go back.

That summer of 1938 Molly heard of a job opening down in Rock Ridge, a small town with surrounding rural community in Wilson County, thirty miles or so to the northeast of Smithfield. The situation was just about identical to the one she'd had at Brogden; she applied and was hired, and late in the summer Molly and Ava moved into the Teacherage adjacent to the fifty-year-old brickwork Rock Ridge School.

The school opened in the fall, eleventh grade for Ava, graduation year back then. She went not knowing what to expect; it was North Carolina and it was Rock Ridge, only a short ride from where she was born, but she was a stranger again, everything new. That first day, though, a teacher she knew from the boardinghouse made her welcome at once, and best of all she had her meet one of the other girls in that graduating class, a genial and beautiful girl named Alberta Cooney. "The teacher, who was a favorite of mine, introduced us," Alberta Cooney would say, sixty-four years later, "and asked me to show her around and introduce her to some of the classmates. First thing I saw was how pretty she was. Then she spoke, and she had a very husky voice, and I thought she had a cold. And I didn't realize that was her natural voice. And a lot of people who met her would say, 'Oh, do you have a cold?' But that was how she spoke. We talked some and I showed her around, and we found that we got along and had things in common and just became the very best of friends."

The two girls had a special bond right off: Alberta had lost her father, too. "You had to take it one day at a time," Alberta would remember telling Ava. "That was all you could do. She was handling it well, but she spoke of him often. She said she loved her dad very much, and she missed him a lot."

Ava invited Alberta over to the Teacherage for lunch. "Ava's mother gave me a piece of cake she had baked, and she served whipped cream on it and I had never had that before! She was the best cook. But Ava thought my mother was the best cook, too. . . . We used to spend the weekends with each other. I would go to her house, and she would come to my house. The Teacherage was right on the same street as the school, and they had an apartment, a kitchen, a living room, two bedrooms that I can recall, and we would sleep in one and her mom in the other bedroom. Her mother was such a loving person. When I stayed the night there she'd always come and tuck us in and kiss us good night. And I was not used to that. My mother loved me, I know that, but it just didn't happen in my house. I had never been kissed good night by my mom."

Alberta Cooney lived out in the countryside at Spring Hill. She felt abashed the first time she brought Ava out to visit, what was she going to think—it was real simple living then, no inside plumbing, and not even an outhouse. But Alberta relaxed soon enough—Ava was more country than she was. "Ava had to go to the bathroom, and my stepfather drove up while Ava was outside doing her business, and she just popped right up when she saw him and shouted 'Hey!' and then popped back down. We all laughed. She was just a plain old country gal. Soon as she came to our house she was always barefoot. In the summertime as soon as she got off the bus at my house she'd take off her shoes and put them in the mailbox. Not me; I never went barefoot, but she did. Our street was not paved at that time and she just loved it, the dirt and the grass in her feet. We would walk down to my uncle's house; they had babies, and she loved to play with the babies. And every time she took her shoes and stuck them in the mailbox till she had to go home."

Ava and Alberta went on double dates together. Ava enjoyed going out, but she never ended up with a steady boyfriend in high school. Alberta believed that many boys were standoffish around Ava because she was so good-looking. And if Ava didn't intimidate them, then her mother did. On New Year's Eve, when she saw Ava and her date come home from a school dance and the boy gave Ava a hug and a brief kiss, Molly came charging out, chased the boy back to his car, and then followed a mortified Ava into the house, shouting imprecations in her ear. It was Molly's blind spot, the one subject that made her lose her temper and her common sense. With Jonas gone, she felt an even stronger compulsion to guard her daughter from temptation. "If you know a man before you're married," she told her more than once, "I'll see you in your grave."

"She would say to me that her mother tried to make her terrified of boys," Ava's friend Spoli Mills recalled. "She was very strict about that one thing. It was something a lot of mothers of that generation did. You know, keep close watch, make sure they don't get into trouble."

On that New Year's Eve, Ava said, she ran into the bathroom, scrubbing her face with soap, trying to "wash off the dirt I was sure I had contracted from that kiss."

As a student, Alberta Cooney would recall, "Ava was about mediocre. Like me." In class the two girls were easy to distract from their lessons, preferring to exchange whispered funny remarks or work on each other's nails. Ava enjoyed singing, dancing, and music but at school showed no interest in the performing-arts programs—though once in English Lit. she did stand before the class with a few others and act a part in an old play. According to Alberta, "She just wasn't so good. We all laughed at her, you know how kids will do."

Neither girl had much of a plan for the future. One time they were double-dating and had the boys take them to a fortune-teller who operated on the outskirts of Wilson. The fortune-teller looked at her crystal ball and told Ava she was destined to go far away across the water. "We giggled about it," said Alberta, "but I don't think Ava gave it much thought. . . . We figured we might get jobs as secretaries. That was about all we could imagine."

Graduation time was nearly upon them when the school burned down.

No one was hurt, but it caused no end of confusion, finding temporary accommodations for the classes and then revising the graduation ceremonies. In the end they were held outdoors on the ball field on a hot humid day. The graduates sweated in their robes, and when they got up to get their diplomas the robes stuck to the chairs. Then came the time to hand out the annual "Superlative" awards that every senior class voted itself. It was widely understood that the "Most Beautiful" award was a two-girl contest, that it would have to go to either Ava or Alberta. It was hard for the two good friends, waiting to hear the announcement. In the end an extra award was created and Ava won Most Beautiful and Alberta Most Attractive. Ava said it was really a tie, but Alberta had always known she had never seen anyone prettier than her friend.

"The first time I ever met her I thought that. She would stay overnight with me, and this sounds sick, but she would stay overnight with me and I would wake up in the morning and I'd look over at her in the bed and I just never saw anyone so perfectly made as she was, just a beautiful young woman."

One night in Rock Ridge there appeared a visitor from faraway New York City. She appeared out of the night like a glamorous phantasm, standing in the doorway of the Teacherage in a Broadway hairdo and neon red lips and wide-shouldered fox-collared coat and high heels and a fog of attar from the perfume counter at Macy's. Considering the incongruity and extravagance of such a presence in the doorway of a boardinghouse in Wilson County, North Carolina, she might just as well have come from Oz, Glinda the Good Witch with a permanent wave.

Beatrice Gardner was the eldest of the five daughters, born late in 1903, the year in which Jonas and Molly were wed. Growing up, she had been known as a lively, smart, and sharp-tongued child. She was pretty like all the Gardner girls, although as a young woman Beatrice tended to give what she had an extra spin—the word to describe her would not have been openly applied in those days, but Beatrice was sexy. The girl had an independent streak, and at an early age she had eagerly gotten out of the house in Grabtown and put the tobacco fields behind her, moving to Smithfield and finding herself a job. In town she would meet a handsome law student named Bill Godwin and at the age of nineteen she married him, the same year that Ava was born. When Beatrice would come to visit her family the baby sister could never seem to get her name right. Ava called her "Bappie" and it stuck. It was Ava's name for her forever after.

The marriage to Bill Godwin was not to last. There were accusations of infidelities. Divorce was not at all common in that time and place, and Godwin tried to patch things up, but Beatrice became determined to be free of him. The bonds were sundered and Bea, wanting to be away from the furtive looks of Smithfield gossips, left to seek her fortune elsewhere.* One day Beatrice would arrive in New York City, finding work as a department store salesclerk. Though her Carolina drawl drew a few cracks from her Brooklyn-accented coworkers in the handbags and gloves department (they nicknamed her "Dixie"), everyone soon warmed up to the ebullient Southerner. She came to feel right at home in the bustling metropolis, and in due time she shed her Piedmont style for the manners and dress of a sophisticated 1930s Manhattanite—or at least a drawling handbag shopgirl's version of one. She met lots of men and fell in love with some of them, broke some hearts and had hers broken. One day at lunchtime she stepped into a portrait photo studio on Fifth Avenue, hoping to get a picture taken to give to a boyfriend who was going out of town. The photographer and manager of the place (one of several his family owned in the city) was a short, brash, fast-talking New Yorker named Larry Tarr. He took one look at Bea, and before she knew what was happening they were drinking cocktails across the street, and before she knew what was happening after that they were living together.

And now, after many years in New York, in a swirl of glamour, Beatrice/Bappie descended on the house in Rock Ridge, bearing presents and fabulous tales of life in the big city. She found her little sister even more beautiful than the last time she had seen her. Although Bappie was old enough to be Ava's mother and they had never even lived under the same roof, the two had through the years formed a special bond that did not exist with their other siblings. Perhaps Beatrice, the daring divorcée who had gone off to live in exotic New York, sensed some common affinity for

---

*Godwin much later became a judge and then the mayor of Selma, North Carolina.

adventure or unconventionality in her youngest sister. Or perhaps, near-ing forty and—unlike Inez, Elsie Mae, or Myra—childless, she simply saw in the girl the closest thing to a daughter of her own. She had often behaved as a self-appointed liaison between Ava and Molly, a generational intercept saving the pubescent girl from her mother's decidedly antique country ways—as when Ava had first developed a need for a brassiere, and Bea swooped in with a new store-bought model before Molly could employ the rural method of binding the young 'un's breasts with a diaper closed in the back with a safety pin.

Now, in Rock Ridge, Bappie came bearing presents from the Big Apple, and like Glinda awarding Dorothy the ruby slippers, she gave Ava a very special pair of shoes—made of lustrous green satin, they had been hand-crafted for movie actress Irene Dunne (who had recently starred in the screen version of *Show Boat*) and had ended up being sold at a charity auction where Bappie had made the highest bid.

"Put those on, sugar," Bappie said, "and maybe they'll walk you right to Hollywood."

Ava would take them from their box and unwrap them and gaze at the fabulous movie-star footwear; later she would carefully rewrap them and close the box and then place them out of harm's way on the top of the tall dresser in her bedroom. Despite what Bappie said, Ava thought they were far too special for her ever to put them on her feet. There was also the fact that she hated wearing shoes.

If Ava had felt any sense of achievement on her graduation from high school it faded fast, soon replaced by feelings of aimlessness and bore-dom. She looked for a job without success. The Great Depression still hung over the region, and there had never been many opportunities for women in the best of times. Alberta and another classmate had gone off to Washington, D.C., to find work as secretaries. Another friend—who had wanted to go on to college and learn a profession but had no money for it and was discouraged by her parents—found a job at the local five-and-dime. For most of the girls Ava's age in that time, in that part of the world, the course of your life, even if you pretended for a little while to have some control over it, was preordained—a man to be found, marriage, home, kids, grandkids, death, all of it in the same county.

She had little else to do that summer but help her mother at the Teacherage, something she never did with great enthusiasm. She hated the domestic chores that were her mother's life (with the exception of ironing clothes, which she found satisfying, therapeutic, a task she continued to enjoy even years later when there were maids and personal assistants at hand). She learned how to cook some of her mother's dishes almost as well as her mother did—her fried chicken with all the trimmings best of all—but Ava had none of Molly's devotion or discipline in the kitchen. She would cook up some food, leave a great mess everywhere, then slip away when it came time to clean or do the dishes.

Her social life was active, if demure. Molly had reconciled herself to the fact that her daughter was reaching marrying age and had to be available to meet the right fellow when he came along. Which didn't mean, though, that she couldn't continue to instill the fear of God in Ava about sex. She remained a vigilant presence even when her child was alone with a guy in the front seat of his car. Ava saw other girls kissing up a storm with their dates—right in front of her for everyone to see, but she held back, terrified of getting a reputation, of Molly finding out.

To this becalmed setting one day came a letter from New York City. Bappie wrote that she was lonely and invited Ava to come visit. To tempt her—as if she needed tempting—Bappie told her she might find a job in the city as there were hundreds of them advertised in the papers. With Molly's permission reluctantly given, Ava packed a bag and took the bus to New York. As it turned out, there were not so many jobs available after all, but for a couple of days she made the rounds of employment agencies. "I didn't land anything except aching feet," Ava said.

Larry Tarr made much of Bea's nearly seventeen-year-old sister. "She was such a beauty," he would recall years later. "Skin like peaches and cream, those green eyes and that little cleft chin. And I never saw a happier kid." He had his camera out during much of her stay, eagerly trying to capture her glowing looks on film. She would be plopped in a chair at the end of the day, exhausted, she remembered, and Larry would be buzzing around her with his big Speed Graphic saying, "I want to take your picture just that way, with your eyes half shut," and the pop of the flashbulb nearly scaring her to death every time. He took some formal portrait shots, too. They decided a pretty studio portrait of Ava would make a nice gift to bring back to her mother. She wore a sleeveless print dress she borrowed from Bappie and a straw bonnet with a ribbon tied under her chin. She smiled at the camera with a sweet yet guarded smile. It was the photo that would change everything.

Back in North Carolina, brother Jack, who was doing well as a businessman in Smithfield, decided to do his bit to help his little sister find a career. Jack said if she enrolled herself in the secretarial course at Atlantic Christian College in Wilson, he was willing to bankroll her tuition. So she went back to school, in the autumn of 1940, learning to speed-type and take shorthand.

Atlantic Christian was a small but well-appointed college with an assortment of campus activities and social events. Ava's physical appearance again did not go unnoticed. She was voted Campus Beauty and found many male admirers (and among the coeds pockets of simmering enmity). For a brief while she dated the son of Atlantic Christian's president, Steve Hilliard. Nan McGlohon, for many years the wife of Loonis McGlohon, the North Carolina musician and composer, would recall double-dating with Loonis, Hilliard, and Ava; she remembered a quiet, very beautiful girl with a gorgeous face, and quite oblivious to that beauty and the strong effect it had on people. You found her pretty or you didn't, but it wasn't something in which the girl herself seemed to show much interest. One night they were out together and Ava was encouraged to enter a Cotton Queen beauty pageant being held in Tarboro. "Loonis played for the pageant," Nan McGlohon recalled. "And Ava didn't even get an honorable mention. And the little girl that won that night . . . it was just pitiful. She must have known one of the judges. But Ava didn't give losing the contest a thought because Glenn Miller and his band were playing over in Wilson that night at the Center Brick Warehouse, the tobacco warehouse, and she didn't care about the contest—she just wanted to go and hear Glenn Miller and dance."

Another night, another boy, another dance hall, this one over in Rocky Mount. An imported swing band played loud up on the stand, and the hall was filled with frenetic young people. Ava's arrival had its usual palpable effect on the stag line. A date, if he had any sense, took her to the dance floor fast and got in a few spins before the competition moved up. One of those who wanted a dance with Ava that night was a tall, self-assured man in his midtwenties, a wealthy man-about-town from Goldsboro named J. M. "Ace" Fordham.

"I thought she was pretty, and any girl who was pretty was all right with me," Ace Fordham recalled, sixty-three years later. "She had a fellow took her there, a large fellow, larger than I was, and I'm six foot. I don't know if he didn't like me or he did; I wasn't worried. Down here if somebody breaks on you you don't say a word you just give up the girl and go on and break on somebody else. You don't do that in New York, do you? Well, it used to be that way here. I haven't been to a dance in a long time."

Ava was a good dancer, Ace Fordham remembered, knew all the tunes. "She was a real jitterbug. She told me she was going to college at ACC— A Country College, we used to call that. And I said I'd like to see her again, and I told her more or less I'd be calling her. She was living with her mother then, in a house close to Wilson, where they took care of the teachers. They had a two-room apartment, and the teachers lived upstairs. It was not a first-class house by any means. Her mother was a very nice woman. Ava and her mother got along beautifully. On our first date we went to the Paramount Theater in Goldsboro. To the movies. We saw a Mickey Rooney picture."

When they got back to the Teacherage that night, Fordham walked up on the porch with her to say good night. "She was about to go inside, and then she said, 'I bet you can't do this!' And she bent over backwards on the porch and put the palms of her hands on the floor behind her. Stretched all the way back and put her hands on the floor. I call that double-jointed. Not many people can do that."

Ava and Ace saw each other again and then began going together all the time. Fordham could offer her many new experiences, took her horseback riding at his ranch on the lower Neuse River, took her flying. "I'd been a pilot since 1935. We rented a plane out at the Rocky Mount airport, a five-seater, and I flew her around for about an hour. I think it was her first time in the air. Was she excited? She didn't get excited about anything. I remember she asked me to buzz over the college."

They had been going together awhile, and Ava wanted to visit her sister in New York, so Fordham agreed to take her in his car and spend a few days. They took turns driving, a twelve-hour ride in those times before the Interstate. In Manhattan, Fordham got a hotel room and took Ava to stay with her sister. Fordham found Larry Tarr to be all he had ever heard about "nervy" New Yorkers. "The first thing, he made some remark about my coat being too short. He told me I was out of fashion. My coat was from Edwards Young Men's Shop back home."

They went out every night, to restaurants and nightclubs, stayed out late, the later the better Ava liked it—New York was an all-night town, just the idea of which thrilled her. They went to the racetrack. She was so pretty she caught attention wherever they went, sometimes unwanted attention: At the track she was felt up by a pair of turf bums; her violent response sent them running in fear. At a restaurant she went to with Ace and her sister, she saw Henry Fonda sitting five tables away; he was the first movie star she had ever seen. "I've got to get his autograph," she said, and when she went to his table Fonda's glamorous female companion reacted to Ava as if she were the star. "Sweetie, you're so pretty you should go to Hollywood," the woman told her. Bappie and Larry Tarr thought the same thing. They watched in amusement and amazement the impact the girl had—she created more stir than two Henry Fondas. Years later Tarr told a reporter, "We kept saying to each other, 'We gotta do something about the kid.' " But what to do? Ace Fordham said he had a friend who had backed a movie one time ("and lost his shirt") and now worked in the theater, and he gave him a call and told him about the real pretty girl he knew who ought to be in the movies. The friend said, "Forget it. Pretty girls are a dime a dozen."

The last night before they were to drive back to North Carolina, they were at a club to hear some music. Fordham and Ava were at the bar, and the bartender, taking a fancy to the good-looking girl, got schmoozing with the two out-of-towners. Ava told him, yes, she liked to sing, loved music, all the bands, and so on. As the talking went on the bartender told them that he knew a bandleader who was looking for a girl singer and that—well, if she had a voice half as good as she looked and if she was interested in something like that, being the girl singer in a hot swing band, how did that sound to her?

Ava, in her posthumously constructed memoir *Ava: My Story*—recalling slightly different circumstances, eliminating her wealthy boyfriend from the scene, and remembering the bartender in the conversation as the bandleader himself—reckoned that "the hope of my life was to stand in front of a big-band orchestra and have a crack at the microphone."

Next day they waited in Bappie's apartment for the guy to call, delaying their departure for home. "We waited," said Fordham, "and he didn't call and we were fixing to leave and get on the road when at the last minute he finally called and he gave her the appointment." They went to an address, an office suite in a building in midtown, Ava, Ace, and her sister. Ace and Bappie sat outside while Ava was taken into the next room. In her memoir Ava wrote that she made a demonstration record, singing "Amapola" (a hit that year for Jimmy Dorsey) with a piano accompanist, and sending the record on to the bandleader, but Ace Fordham recollected it as more of a live audition, Ava singing for a few minutes while a couple of guys listened. "They had her sing a song. We sat outside, and we could just hear her through the walls a little bit. Then she came out, and we left there. She was very calm about it. She was always cool about everything she did unless you got her mad. She just said, 'I think they'll sign me up.' But then on the drive back she said something like, 'I hope I get it.' So she wasn't so sure."

Back in Rock Ridge she waited for word from the bandleader telling her she was his new songbird and she was going on tour. She checked the mail each day. Nothing ever came.

But back in New York someone else had taken an interest in her.

Like the speck of grit, insignificant and unwitting, which in a chance encounter with the oyster makes possible the rarest pearl, so is the brief, random, and yet decisive appearance of Barney Duhan in the story of Ava Gardner. Although he would never know her, never even see her in the flesh but for a momentary introduction some decades later, his significance to the course of her life was such that without him little else in her future would have happened as it did, and the words on these pages, in the nature of commercial endeavor, would likely be about somebody else.

Barney Duhan worked as a runner in the New York legal department of Loew's Inc., the worldwide theatrical organization and corporate parent of the Metro-Goldwyn-Mayer motion picture studio. Duhan had little interest in the picture business himself—he saw his future in the law—but he was not unaware of the allure of the movies to other people, especially females, and he was not above using his tangential connection to the fabled MGM to impress attractive young women. "I'm Duhan from MGM/Loew's," he might say to some lovely he would encounter. "Baby, have you given any thought to being in the movies?" It was a bit as old as Edison's Black Mariah, but still very effective.

One day in late spring 1941, Barney Duhan was making his way down Manhattan's Fifth Avenue when his glance caught on an image he found arresting. It lay behind the display window of Larry Tarr's photo shop, exhibited to the passing parade—artfully framed and matted, a blown-up print of the portrait photograph Tarr had taken of Ava as a gift for her mother, the black-and-white head-and-shoulders shot of the teenage girl in her print dress and bonnet.

Barney Duhan stood still amid the hustle and noise of the busy avenue, and for a moment or two he studied the girl in the photograph: the wide-eyed gaze, the lush dark curls, the full lips, the tentative Mona Lisa smile. He decided that this was a young woman he would like to meet. Exactly what happened after this, who did or said what, varies according to the teller of the tale. In Duhan's version: "I was running late for a party, and thought what lousy luck it was with my looks and my income that I didn't have a date for the party. I saw the picture and said out loud, 'Maybe I can get her telephone number!' "

He called the shop from a corner phone booth.

"I'm Duhan from MGM/Loew's," he said, and I'm interested in that girl in the picture in your window. What's her name and where can I find her?"

The person on the phone informed him that the girl had gone home to North Carolina.

Duhan's ardor cooled. It might have ended right there. But Bappie and Larry Tarr, excited by a movie company's supposed interest, pursued the connection. Tarr printed up his best pictures of the girl in his window. He packaged them nicely and he delivered them personally to Metro-Goldwyn-Mayer's office in Times Square.

After the excitement of her New York sojourn and the dashed dream of a job with a big band, Ava resumed an ordinary life in Rock Ridge—now more ordinary-seeming than ever. She would help her mother during the day—perfunctorily—and sit with her listening to the radio in the evening or sometimes go with her to the movies (singing cowboy Gene Autry was Molly's new favorite).

She began now to contemplate the real, modest possibilities for her future. When she completed her courses at Atlantic Christian she could more than likely look forward to finding a job as a secretary. She could be a good one maybe. Her shorthand was 130 words a minute, her typing 60 to 65 per minute for accuracy. That was what it looked like she might do, she thought then, eight, nine hours a day of typing and dictation, five and a half days a week. What else was there? Marriage at last came up for consideration. Her high school best friend, Alberta, who had not seen much of her since graduation, remembered her coming by one night and telling her of a local boy she intended to wed. Was it a passing whim or something more serious—and who was her intended? Sixty-some years later Alberta could not recall. If it was Fordham, then the notion remained secret and one-sided. A friend of Ava's spoke to him, slyly perhaps. "So when are you two going to get married?" Fordham replied, "We'll see about that." He never found out if it was something Ava had put her up to asking. "But back then I was young and I wouldn't have married the Queen of Sheba. I was looking to know pretty girls but not to marry them."

In that summer of 1941, as Ava pondered her future prospects, her mother began to show signs of chronic health problems. She suffered recurrent stomach pains, sudden vaginal bleeding. Stubbornly indomitable, she refused to seek outside attention for her ailments—she had never seen a doctor in her life for anything but to aid her in childbirth and once or twice when the kids themselves had been ill—she went on working without complaint, masking her pain as best she could with increasing doses of aspirin. Ava would later write that Molly and Ava's older sisters shielded her from any details of Mama's "women's complaints." It seems a curiously protective attitude toward a young adult, perhaps a convenient rationale for what might have been inattention to Molly's growing ill health. Ava loved her mother with all her heart, but like many spoiled children she had always enjoyed receiving more attention than she gave, with little reflection or guilt.

In July a call came from Bappie in New York. She recounted for Ava the tale of the desirous messenger boy and the picture in the window and the photos sent to the movie company—it was all very fast and confusing over the crackling long-distance line.

"They want you to come in, hon."

What for?

"They want to meet you!"

Who does?

"MGM."

Where?

"Where Clark Gable works, baby!"

Another pipe dream, like the big-band job. Why go all that way for another disappointment? She could be stubborn when her feelings were hurt. But Bappie didn't let up. Bappie said she had to get her *be-hind* up there to New York and not even think about letting a chance like this get away.

Molly agreed. Ava went to Ace Fordham and told him what was up. He thought again about what his friend in the theater business had told him about girls like her being a dime a dozen. "So I wasn't too excited. I didn't put much stock in her getting into the movies. She asked me did I want to go to New York again, and I said no."

Ava went to Smithfield to catch the bus, sat by herself at the station with her suitcase. Ace Fordham figured he would be hearing from her in New York one day soon, saying, "Come and get me!" But he never did. "Maybe . . . I should have had an idea what would happen . . . as pretty as she was."

The next time he saw her it was her picture in the newspaper, with the story all about the Tobacco Road girl who had made good.

TWO

Zombies at the Beachcomber

To many who worked for Metro-Goldwyn-Mayer in what they called the home office at 1540 Broadway, New York City, Hollywood was a provincial wasteland and the fabled West Coast studio a mere adjunct to a vast international enterprise. The movies were made "out there" in California, but their fate was largely determined in the Loew's State Building on Times Square. At 1540 they approved scripts, casting, budgets, and production schedules; designed publicity and advertising campaigns; controlled print orders and worldwide distribution; and signed Clark Gable's checks. And it was at 1540 Broadway that many of the biggest stars in Hollywood had their first contact with the movie business.

From early on a critical division of the New York office was the talent department, whose assignment was the contractual capture of potential effective film actors and actresses and, most important, potential stars. Originally the department was intended to go after only performers who were already established—on Broadway or the European stage, in vaudeville or nightclubs—luring them to their motion picture debuts. But with the success of Metro's Joan Crawford, plucked from the back row of a New York chorus line, the studio realized that a discerning talent scout might find stars—unique and great and profitable stars like Crawford—in people without experience. These persons might even be without discernible talent but with some special quality that could connect with an audience in the dark of a movie theater and in doing so make lots more money for MGM and Loew's Inc. It was an idea born in the early years of the picture business, when "legitimate" stars had often refused to work in the primitive new medium, but adapted by studio chief Louis B. Mayer to the industrial age of moviemaking: Find him the raw talent and he could process and package it like any other manufactured merchandise.

And so it came to be that the talent department in New York devoted much of its time to scrutinizing unknown, unproved individuals for signs, however embryonic, of that special, profitable star quality, stalking small theater productions, beauty pageants, sporting events, modeling agencies, and billboards and leaving their doors at least partly open to the solicitations of people straight off the Broadway sidewalk.

Early summer, 1941, Ava arrived at the Metro office on Broadway. The activities inside 1540 showed few connections to the glamour and mystery of the movies, and as she sat and waited to be interviewed it might have been for a job as a secretary. Someone led her to the office of a man named Ben Jacobsen, a specialist in talent, who sat and stared at her for some time without saying a word. At last he handed her a few stapled pages, with strangely spaced words on each one. She read to him as he asked her to, and the man folded his hands and smiled and after a minute or two he asked her to stop. Jacobsen would one day recall that the beautiful teenager had sounded nearly incomprehensible to his New York ears, everything drawled vowels that seemed to last forever and "gs" that dropped "like shattered magnolia blossoms." It didn't matter. She could have been speaking Chinese—he couldn't take his eyes off her.

Jacobsen escorted her out of his office and down the hall to see his boss, a department head named Marvin Schenck, a relative of the Loew's Inc. president, Nicholas M. Schenck. A sequence of events followed that was much like what had occurred in the first room. She answered questions, she read pages, she looked left and right and straight ahead. Schenck and Jacobsen huddled. They whispered. They stared.

Schenck said: "Test her."

Al Altman is an underappreciated auteur of the American cinema. His films, short, sometimes experimental in nature, never seen by more than a small, select audience, were nonetheless highly influential and frequently featured some of the biggest names in movie history. Altman was MGM's New York screen test director. A Massachusetts accountant and amateur magician (a pal of Harry Houdini's) when he met Louis B. Mayer in the 1920s, he had been sent to New York to sign up Broadway talent when Mayer relocated to California. It was Altman who, in 1924, had discovered Joan Crawford. She had been hoofing in a speakeasy when Altman put her before a camera; MGM saw the test and turned her down, but Altman persisted, shooting her twice more before the studio finally signed her. It was the kind of story that brought tears to Louis Mayer's eyes— how close they had come to losing that gold mine!

Altman's ability to spot potential screen talent became one of the studio's most valued assets. In later years he concentrated his efforts on directing tests, an art of his own invention. Altman used a variety of methods to bring out the best in his subjects on-camera, including interviews and improvisations, sometimes whipping up psychodramas, sometimes barking out odd, surreal instructions to a startled actor ("A large horse is coming at you—now it's going up the wall!"), sometimes reshooting several times if he thought someone had something special that wasn't coming across, trying to let the performer show off his or her range within a few minutes of screen time and to give them their best shot at a studio contract. He then often worked at editing the test reel to a perfected final cut, as diligent as any director aiming for an Academy Award, though Altman's film would never be seen by more than a handful of executives on both coasts. Among those whom Al Altman introduced to the movie camera were James Stewart, Bob Hope, Henry Fonda, Franchot Tone, and, in preparation for *The Wizard of Oz*, an entire diminution of Munchkins.

Through the years Al Altman had interviewed or tested hundreds of pretty girls, some of them the "special friends" of executives, known as "must-tests," some of them very pretty indeed, but he had seen few women in all those years he had ever chosen to describe as beautiful. It was an arbitrarily high standard, but by Altman's definition a beautiful girl was a true rarity—a "freak." And the teenage girl from North Carolina he met at the Loew's Building that summer in 1941 he would identify as one of these rare creatures. "My father was not someone who often talked about women's looks or anything like that," his daughter, Diana Altman, would recall, "but he always said that Ava Gardner was the most beautiful woman he had ever seen."

They did the test over in Hell's Kitchen at the Fox Movietone News studio, on the cramped soundstage on the first floor. Ava wore a long flared print dress with a lacey scooped neck, a pair of high-heeled shoes she borrowed from her sister, and her favorite chain necklace with a little stone. Her long hair was combed up high and back in the fashion of 1941. Al Altman brought her to the small set they had created—a sitting room with a cane chair, a table, a curtained window. They escorted her onto the wooden-platformed set, and she stood there for what seemed forever as the men fixed the blindingly bright lights and others adjusted the big movie camera and a couple of others did things she couldn't see, moving around in the darkness beyond. At last the camera turned and a man stepped in front of her with a board with her name and those of the director, cameraman, and soundman written in chalk. Also chalked in was her height, five feet six, and her weight (118 pounds), held right up to the camera lens (how embarrassing! she thought). The slate was cracked, and Al Altman asked Ava to tell them her name, where she was from, what she did back there—who her favorite movie stars were. Then Altman came over to her on the living room set, told her that they wanted to show how she moved, and guided her through a simple piece of action. Ava walked across the small set holding a vase of flowers, which she placed on the table. She swiveled, turned her head. Her upper lip seemed to fold under as she tried to smile, her mouth gone very dry with nerves and the heat of the lights. They did it again, maybe three or four times, then switched to a medium shot, Ava holding the vase in her hands and staring at it, looking away. They moved over to stand her before some plain backdrop paper and posed her for close shots, Ava moving her head and eyes at Al's direction, looking left, looking right, looking at last directly at the camera.

Then it was done.

Al Altman said, "Thank you very much, Miss Gardner."

Ava stepped out on the hot pavement on Tenth Avenue. She stood in front of the building in the summer sun, began to breathe again. And that was that. She had been terrible, she knew, the way she must have looked, mouth dry, lips sticking together, holding those terrible flowers. No one would ever put anybody into the movies after seeing a routine like that. The heck with it. She had been given a screen test by Metro-Goldwyn-Mayer, and not many people could say that, it would be a little story she could tell her grandkids someday. She was sure she would hear nothing more from anybody.

"My father described that test as a disaster," Diana Altman remembered. "He just thought the whole thing was a mess. She had been so awkward, could hardly move or look up, couldn't talk."

Al Altman had three choices after shooting a test: Ship it to the studio in California, shoot the person again and try and improve the results, or shelve it. To go as far as testing a person on film was already an investment by the studio, so Altman did not dismiss anyone out of hand, no matter how unpromising. And film, he had learned from nearly twenty years of experience, was a tricky medium: Sometimes it captured something you did not know was there. That evening Altman and some others from 1540 went to the Fox Movietone screening room to watch what they had done that day (in addition to Ava, Altman had shot tests of singers Vaughan Monroe and Hazel Scott).

Ava's test began. Al Altman's daughter, Diana, remembered him telling the story many times: "He said that when Ava's face came on that screen every guy in the room fell madly in love with her."

In the portion of the test—now presumed lost—when Ava spoke her responses to Al Altman's prompts, she was said to have been awkward and difficult to understand. In the moments of her moving across the screen in the long homespun dress with flowers in hand she appeared tall and lean with a small bust and a long torso, pretty but not inordinately appealing. The silent close shots, though, head and shoulders and then a facial close-up, almost spectral against the blank backdrop, were something else, alive and alluring, a glimpse and no more, but a flash of something the stiff body movements and requested expressions and awkward speech had seemingly tried to deny. The large, shadowed eyes especially, for a moment looking straight into the lens, were filled with a flash of hypnotic fire, as if some other presence within had suddenly revealed itself. It was in those few seconds, a hundred frames of film perhaps, that her future was decided.

Al Altman eliminated the sound elements from the test and edited together the best shots, less than two minutes altogether.

Altman said, "Ship it."

Ten days later someone called Ava from New York and told her they had liked what they saw in Hollywood and had a contract for her to sign. "Will you be ready to go to Hollywood within a week?"

Molly Gardner had gone with her daughter Inez to see a doctor in Raleigh. The pains and bleeding that had plagued her for a long time had continued, gotten worse. The doctor's diagnosis was cancer of the uterus, inoperable. Nothing could be done. She had to stop working and just take it easy, the best thing for her now. It was decided that Molly would move in with Inez and her husband.

And what about California and MGM?

That was decided, too. Of course Ava had to go. Molly wouldn't hear of Ava not going, such an opportunity. And Bappie would go with her, an eager volunteer.

"Somebody has to see that you drink your milk and eat your vegetables," Bappie said. (Larry Tarr would be left to find nourishment unaided.)

The contract ran for seven years, with one-way clauses that allowed the studio alone to abrogate the deal almost at will (many "seven-year contracts" were severed within a year). Salary was fifty dollars a week, with periodic raises to the end of the contractual term. Ava looked through the pages of small type and strange phrases, shrugged, signed.

In New York, Ava and Bappie boarded the Twentieth Century Limited for the journey to Los Angeles, three days' travel with a change to the Super Chief in Chicago. A young Metro publicity man named Milton Weiss traveled with them, assigned to make sure no harm came to the new employee before the West Coast boys got a closer look at her. Ava sat by the window, looked out at the people on the platform gliding away, at her reflection in the blackened tunnel, at the meadows and factories and homes going by. She didn't show much excitement, Bappie would remember. She was an odd girl, her baby sister, not like other girls her age. Bappie herself could hardly hold on to her own enthusiasm, heading for Hollywood, and a free ticket to boot.

Later that first evening, Milton Weiss came back to the compartment with news. On the same train with them was MGM's latest star, Hungarian import Hedy Lamarr. People were falling over one another trying to get a look. And could you blame them? She was gorgeous.

Bappie said, "That makes two movie queens on board!"

Ava stared out the window, and the train rushed on into the Midwestern night.

They arrived in Los Angeles on August 23. The sun was shining. In the station courtyard there were palm trees, and there were fragrant red roses whose color seemed amplified as if by electricity. A company car brought them to the stately Plaza Hotel on Vine Street in Hollywood. Bappie plopped down on a bed, saying she would sleep for the next twenty-four hours. Ava had to get herself ready to go out almost right away. Milton Weiss was coming back to take her to a party at the home of journalist Ruth Waterbury, where there would be other press people, a chance to show off the studio's latest purchase and maybe get her name into the papers and fan mags. Weiss drove a slow scenic route, pausing on a hillside curve so Ava could watch the sunset. In those days before the war, before the freeways, and before the skies became copper with soot, Los Angeles was among the more pleasant places on earth, with endless clear vistas and the air smelling not of industry and exhaust but of sage and wildflowers and ocean.

At the party the men, many of them reporters and studio publicists, began to congregate around the new arrival. "Like tomcats in heat," Ruth Waterbury would remember. This was supposed to be the place, the movie capital, where pretty girls were a dime a dozen, but it was just like Holt Lake all over again.

In the morning Ava saw her new place of employment for the first time. Behind high walls, imperious sandstone buildings fronted a sprawling complex that stretched across 117 acres of Culver City, a city in itself, though in places it more resembled a storybook kingdom. There were offices, cottages, laboratories, barnlike soundstages big enough to house zeppelins, a barber shop, a hospital, a schoolhouse, a Western Union office, a stable, an artificial lake, a stretch of railroad track, a street of New York tenements, a vaguely medieval castle, and a portion of African jungle. This was MGM, the dream factory supreme, the most celebrated and successful purveyor of filmed entertainment in the world. Approximately four thousand people worked there, from horse wranglers to linguists. One hundred or so at a given time were contracted actors, a roster divided among stars like Gable, Garbo, and Crawford; featured players and character actors like Marjorie Main, Frank Morgan, and Reginald Owen; and an assortment of presumably promising newcomers who could be put to work in insignificant parts while being groomed for bigger things.

Milton Weiss gave her the guided tour. He took her around to the various departments, to makeup, hair, and costume, places she would be coming back to every day, Weiss told her. They went past dressing rooms with the embedded names of cinema legend and Weiss told her maybe she would have one of those one day (she would, Norma Shearer's, the largest dressing room of all—one day). They strolled up the cavernous driveways between the great soundstages, passing the costumed extras looking like Arizona ranch hands or South Sea cannibals. Weiss wanted to show her a working set, maybe give her a chance to watch a scene being filmed, and though many of these were closed to visitors they found one open—it was a Busby Berkeley picture, a "youth musical," they were calling *Babes on Broadway*. They entered the soundstage and moved toward the set where the unit was in rehearsal for a scene, a raucous comic turn, a parody of Carmen Miranda, the exuberant Brazilian entertainer, singing "Mama, Yo Quiero." Impersonating Carmen Miranda was the star of the picture, and in the summer of 1941 the twenty-year-old man who ranked—for the third year in a row—the most popular star in the movies: Mickey Rooney. He was wearing at this time a spangled bra and skirt, a fruited turban, had rouged cheeks, and his lips bore a thick coating of red lipstick. A famously short young man, he stood now on high platform heels favored by Miss Miranda. You know who that is, don't you? Weiss whispered in Ava's ear. She stared in wonder at the person Weiss identified as Rooney: She had last seen him as an impish boy on a big screen in North Carolina. Not that he looked much like a girl now (or anything else she had ever imagined). For a brief while they stood at the edge of the busy film set. Then Weiss nudged her; they had better be getting along.

All at once there was a parting of bodies and a sudden spangly, fruited rush in their direction, Mickey Rooney clomping over in his high heels. The introductions were made, Ava smiling shyly. Rooney shifting his turban to a rakish tilt.

They spoke for a few moments only, then he had to go, and Weiss led Ava away. Rooney glanced back at his departing visitor. Then he glanced back again.

When she came back to the studio the following day it was no longer to sightsee but to work. A new test had been scheduled. She had to be made ready, moved as on an assembly line from department to department. Wardrobe ladies charted her five-foot-six-inch height and her measurements—thirty-four–twenty–thirty-six, then handed her over to the wizards of hair and makeup. The cosmeticians and hairdressers circled around, studying, touching, mumbling with enthusiasm or often dismay, delineating what needed to be done with her numerous previously undetected flaws. Ava seldom wore makeup, only a layer of Tangee Red on her lips; now she became masked in pancake and blush, and her mouth turned into a smear of glowing scarlet.

Ann Rutherford, an MGM ingenue best known as Andy Hardy's perky girlfriend, Polly Benedict, remembered seeing Ava on her first day in the makeup chair. "We were introduced and she was lovely, just darling. And I saw them getting her made up, and the makeup man was busily attempting, against his better judgment, to fill that dimple in her chin. Some brainless producer thought she would look better without that 'defect,' and the makeup man was filling it in with mortician's wax!"

Ava—for the time being—succumbed to everything except an attempt to pluck her eyebrows in advance of penciling them back in. She objected with a violent squawk. The thick dark eyebrows would remain more or less intact.

The director of her new test was George Sidney, a savvy show-business veteran at twenty-five (he had acted in a movie opposite Tom Mix when he was four), the son of Metro executive L. K. Sidney, and a highly regarded troubleshooter at the studio, writer and director of award-winning short subjects, experimenter in stroboscopic and 3-D cinematography, and since April, a director of feature films (his work, in the years ahead, would include *The Harvey Girls, Show Boat, Scaramouche,* and *Kiss Me Kate*). He was considered a discerning judge, especially of young talent, directed numerous in-house tests, and was one of those who regularly weighed in on the screen tests from New York. Sidney had seen Ava Gardner in her silent debut and advised the studio to sign her.

Sidney: "She was a sexy gal. You can't believe what a sexy gal she was. What was she, seventeen, eighteen? She had great skin, great eyes. She was from a small-town country background. And I think she found the whole thing very strange. And I think she thought we were all a little crazy. She would give you a look as if to say, Are you sure you have the right girl? She didn't think she belonged there, but it was plain that she had something. There is a spark, a glow that comes off certain performers; they don't even know they have it sometimes."

He shot a simple test. Ava was seated in a swivel chair so he could film her from every angle. She read some lines of dialogue and answered a few simple questions about herself. She looked sensational, but it was clear to the director she was not ready for the big leagues yet. Her self-consciousness was almost painful to see. And the voice had to be trained. It was a beautiful, sexy speaking voice that Sidney heard, a sexy, Southern accent with a low, throaty tone and a raucous laugh; but you couldn't have that regional accent then in a Hollywood movie, this despite the phenomenal success of *Gone With the Wind* two years before. (The general consensus then was that actors had to sound as if they were from nowhere in particular. It would have presented the same problem if she had come to them with a strongly regional accent of any sort.)

Together Sidney and Louis Mayer looked at the new test. The girl, it was decided, might work out. Yes. Maybe. It was too soon to tell. "At the studio under Mr. Mayer at that time they could train you if they were interested in you," George Sidney would recall. "They didn't just give up on you. They had an incredible program for young talent. They had almost a university within the studio walls. And I showed the test to Mr. Mayer and he saw that she had something." Mayer, said Sidney, had an ability to see talent that didn't even exist yet. A terrific feeling for talent. And Mayer said, "Let's get her some coaching and see what happens."

Ava's MGM education began with a speech coach, Gertrude Fogler, a plump, seventyish woman who worked out of a tiny office on a distant lot.

She was a relic of the coming of sound, when experts were first recruited to teach silent stars not to speak through the nose and to overarticulate all vowels, a job ridiculed mercilessly in *Singin' in the Rain*. But Fogler was actually an innovative teacher whose methods included mental imaging and yoga breathing exercises. A grateful Ava Gardner remembered her as kindly and helpful in a confusing time. Many years later Gertrude Fogler would recall Ava's first visit: "In walked this timid, self-effacing, miserable, beautiful child. She wore horrid old clothes, no makeup, and her hair was all awry, yet she was so eager to learn."

To gauge the girl's manner of speech Fogler had her read a story out loud. Ava's unspoiled soul was manifest: When she reached an unhappy passage in the story, she choked up with sadness. For an hour each day they worked on losing her Carolina accent. To change her "ahs" to "ers," Ava read pages of applicable words, deliberating over each final syllable. Fogler gave her exercises to alter her vocal style, trying to change her slow-rippling, honey-coated drawl to something faster, flatter, and more Midwestern, something more acceptable in the deracinated, common-denominator universe of MGM characters.*

To teach her how to act, Ava was sent to Lillian Burns. Admitted to the Metro family in the mid-thirties with vague credentials and an abundance of pep, Lilly Burns was another member of Mayer's personal team of trusted advisers. She was a small, sultry-looking woman with a theatrical personality, the intense air and slashing gestures of a tiny Bette Davis. Some who received her coaching swore by her ability to mold a performer and nurture fledgling talent; others found her rigid and self-absorbed. She had a tendency to instruct everyone with the same "grande dame" movements and facial gestures, and some thought her goal was to make every actor resemble a version of herself. Her greatest success story, as far as Mayer was concerned, was Lana Turner, the studio's reigning sex symbol, whose early star performances were considered to have been completely mimetic, every single facial gesture, body movement, and line

---

*There were, of course, numerous exceptions to the studio's "middle American" rule, including Garbo, the cast of Anglophiliac productions like *Mrs. Miniver*, and scattered character players with comic twangs and Noo Yawkisms, but the typical MGM screen talent tended to be non-region-specific American: A look at the contract roster from one year in the 1940s shows that just eleven out of eighty stars and featured players were foreign, and some of these were musical specialty performers like pianist José Iturbi.

reading slavishly copied from Burns (adding only a crucial 1,000 percent more sex appeal). Gene Reynolds, a child actor and in 1941 a juvenile lead at Metro (later the producer of the acclaimed television series *M*A*S*H*), recalled, "Lillian Burns was a lovely woman, but very vain. In her office—which was kind of a living room setup with some soft chairs and a coffee table—she had a couple of large mirrors, and while she was showing you how to play a scene or read some lines she was often looking right past you and looking at herself in the mirror. She loved to look at herself in the mirror! But she was very talented, and she helped a lot of people enormously. If you knew something about acting, then she would just make suggestions and go over a scene with you. And it was really only if you didn't have a clue what you were doing that she made you give these manufactured performances."

Lillian Burns assessed Ava's ability. She told George Sidney (the two married later that same year) that Gardner had extraordinary natural presence but turned wooden with self-consciousness when she had to "act." Burns would have her read a few lines and then read them herself, demonstrating what to do, complete with pauses, raised eyebrows, flared nostrils. It was the Lana Turner routine again, making the student learn by imitation, gesture by gesture. Ava found Lillian's exemplary style corny, but she did what she was told. Sometimes Ava would be paired off to run lines with one of the other new starlets-in-training, such as Donna Reed or Leatrice Gilbert. Seventeen-year-old Leatrice Gilbert was there on a minimum-wage novice contract like Ava, but their backgrounds could not have been more different. Leatrice was the daughter of silent-screen actors Leatrice Joy and John Gilbert, the legendary romantic idol of the 1920s, one of MGM's first and greatest stars, lover of Garbo and Dietrich, tragically gone at the age of thirty-six. "We met in Lillian Burns's office," Leatrice Gilbert (now Fountain) remembered. "We read a scene together. I liked her very much. She was not sophisticated at all, but she was very bright. Very matter-of-fact about everything, nothing drippy or saccharine about her at all, a real no-nonsense kind of girl. We just got along right away.

"One day they sent us off together to the beach to do a photo shoot. This was what you did when you were under contract and you were a nobody. They took your picture with a firecracker for the fourth of July, and maybe one of the magazines or newspapers printed it and mentioned your name or at least mentioned the studio. They were always sending you out to do publicity photographs and pinups. They took us out to the beach, early in the morning before anyone else was there. I was told to put on this kind of two-piece tigerskin bathing suit. Now, I was skinny as a rail, and I had just had a very short haircut, so there I was with a boy's haircut and no bosoms whatever. And Ava came out with her lovely long hair, which was kind of reddish brown and down around her shoulders, and wearing this beautiful white spandex bathing suit that showed every curve, and those greenish eyes flashing, and we were supposed to toss a ball back and forth on the beach. And she would catch the ball, and the photographer would snap. And she looked like a sexy goddess, and I never felt so totally embarrassed in my life. I said to her, 'Oh my God, I look terrible next to you!' And she was so sweet about it. She said, 'No, no, no, we're just different types. You're the Katharine Hepburn type.'"

Ava and Bappie had moved almost immediately from their costly hotel room to cheaper lodgings they found at the Hollywood Wilcox, renting by the week an efficiency apartment with a pull-down bed and small kitchen facilities. Bappie got herself a salesclerk job at one of the big stores on Wilshire Boulevard. Ava followed a wearying routine: up and out by dawn for the three-bus transit to Culver City. Classes in speech, drama, and soon dance and singing lessons too. It really was like going back to school. Except that at Rock Ridge High or Atlantic Christian you weren't likely to come within a few yards of Clark Gable arriving for work—as she did one morning and was struck dumb with awe—Clark Gable on a motorcycle and wearing big goggles and looking grimly hungover, but otherwise as dazzling a sight as he had been in *Red Dust* or *Gone With the Wind*.

Nearly every day she spent some hours posing for photographers: sometimes long, formal sessions in the portrait studio, other times improvised work around the back lots or on the beach at Malibu or by a hotel swimming pool or anywhere else a bathing suit or short skirt might conceivably be worn. There were "cheesecake" shots meant to show off her figure—personality and holiday and gimmick and gag shots, photos of her swinging a tennis racket, milking cows, and feeding chickens. For one image, reflecting the dog days of summer, she held a thermometer in one hand, an ice-cream cone in the other, and perched her swimsuited bottom on a giant block of ice. It had not been easy at first, being the object of such direct attention from strangers, the photographers and assistants posing her, guiding her body this way and that, fingers bluntly rearranging her clothes as if she were a department store mannequin. The swimsuits were tighter, thinner, more revealing than anything she or any other girl had ever worn at Holt Lake. Inevitably, as the work became routine, her ingrained reserve began to lessen, although there would still be uncomfortable moments when the man behind the camera seemed to want more than she was willing to give, wanting her to lean her cleavage still lower or arch her buttocks higher in the air. She would hear Molly's voice in her head at such moments, or see her reproving gaze and go cold. Nevertheless the figure in the printed results no longer showed much in common with the tentative girl in a straw bonnet in Larry Tarr's shopwindow. In the cheesecake photos she was youthful sexiness personified, a sprightly dazzler of an American teen. In the formal portraits, some by veteran masters of light and shadow like Clarence Sinclair Bull, she was something else again: enticing, mysterious, and erotic, a dark dream of succulent desirability.

"She came up to my office one day," recalled Berdie Abrams, then in her second year in the studio publicity department. "She came in very quietly, almost snuck in, because this was when she first started and was afraid of everything. And she says, 'I know I'm not supposed to be here, but I'm really curious to see what my pictures look like.' So I said, 'Well, c'mon.' And I went and pulled out the drawer of her stuff they had taken. And I spread the pictures out for her to look at, and she studied them. And you want to know something? Those were some *stunning* photos of her. She was the most beautiful woman on the lot, absolutely, nobody compared to her. But not only that, she couldn't take a bad picture. And that was rare, y'know; everybody has a bad side. And she looked at the pictures for a little while, and when she was done she straightened up and kind of shrugged, and she said, 'Jeez,' she said, 'From the way people went on so, I thought I was better-looking than that. . . .' "

The studio contract Ava had signed included what was generally known as a "morals clause," a turgid proscription of any activity that would "shock, insult or offend" the community or public decency or otherwise bring shame upon the motion picture industry. Any violation meant instant dismissal. The clause was reflective of the high standards of MGM. Wasn't Louis B. Mayer the man who did more than anyone to fight the stereotype of a licentious Hollywood, presenting to the world an upright, stern corporate image (his three-piece suits were emblematic in a land of plaid blazers and tennis shorts) and in his films a cinematic espousal of prudence, patriotism, and good clean living? Ava, in time, would come to jeer at this presumption of moral superiority. She would learn to see Metro's aura of rectitude as a front like those propped-up facade movie sets behind which was a great deal of dirt and garbage.

A newcomer like Ava Gardner learned from the grapevine or, less fortunately, from experience, that bad behavior among the Culver City hierarchy was endemic. One heard the stories passed around at lunch or whispered in the makeup room. There was Eddie Mannix, the studio's bulldoglike general manager and longtime Mayer confidant who had beaten his mistress so violently that she required multiple abdominal surgeries. And Ben Thau, the stone-faced executive of whom it was said that he "pissed ice water," another notorious serial predator in the hallways and offices of MGM. And Arthur Freed, the producer of *The Wizard of Oz*, *Babes on Broadway*, and most of the classic Metro musicals, who, in a meeting in his office with Shirley Temple in 1941, exposed his penis to the then-twelve-year-old child.

Mayer himself was a recurrent if often inept lecher, offering the casting couch to select actresses, especially faded stars in need of a comeback and a paternalistic spanking. Judy Garland, a Metro employee from the age of thirteen, would recall Mayer, in his office, routinely groping her adolescent breasts. These men—most of them short, middle-aged, and ugly, surrounded by young and spectacular-looking women (some of these admittedly with more ambition than scruples)—regularly traded a key to the kingdom in return for physical pleasures, and what they couldn't get by trade they were often raring to grab.

"A young woman starting out on her own was in a very vulnerable position at the studio," recalled Leatrice Gilbert. "There was a lot of lechery and abuse." One evening, she would remember, Ben Thau had lured her to his house on the pretext of giving her some mementos that had belonged to her late father, John Gilbert. Thau answered the door in a bathrobe and nothing else. "And suddenly he made the big move on me. I was seventeen and a virgin and scared to death and I just ran out of there. . . . But you heard of bad things happening to girls at the studio all the time."

Ava would have her own close encounter with one of the squat wolves from the executive floor during her first week at work. An exec had invited her to see a new movie in his projection room, and the moment they were alone the man groped and tried to kiss her while growling some mixture of job offers, sweet talk, and vague threats. She got away and hid herself in someone's office in the publicity department and later told the tale to publicity chief Howard Strickling, who was known to be a decent guy. He told her he would have a talk with the man and make sure he would never do anything like that again. Ava was upset and Strickling told her to hold on, he was sure she was going to be a big star and she couldn't let one unfortunate incident ruin her great future. Then he told her not to tell anybody what happened.

Ava willed herself to forget about it, though it was not easy, and sometimes the memory would come back and she would flare up in anger and want to find the man and do what she should have done instead of running and hiding—do something with her shoe that he would have a damned hard time forgetting. What made it worse, she thought, was how hard she had tried not to draw the wrong sort of attention. There was gossip about some girls at the studio that did not bear thinking about, and Ava had pointedly tried to not let anyone get the wrong idea about her. She turned away from men who attempted to flirt and turned down invitations to parties and after work get-togethers. It was tempting to mingle or go out with a boy, but it was intimidating, too, when you didn't know what you were getting into (it didn't help matters that she was shy of speaking at will, aware that her Carolina accent struck some people with horror).

She had even turned down a date with a movie star.

When they met that first day on the *Babes on Broadway* set, he in his eye-catching Carmen Miranda costume, Mickey Rooney had beamed from ear to ear, looking upon the newly arrived starlet like a boy contemplating the world's largest ice-cream sundae. "Everything in me stopped," he would write in *I.E.*, his 1965 memoir. "My heart. My breathing. My thinking." In another minute he was called back to the set and Ava had gone on her way. But Rooney had not been able to put her out of his mind. He sent one of his hangers-on to talk to Weiss the publicist, find out her story. With new female contract players you never knew if they were already the special interest of someone higher up (in Rooney's words, "potential pussy for the executives"). He saw her for the second time in the studio commissary; they chatted, he fawned over her, asked her to come out to dinner that night. She said no.

He crept back to his cronies at the lunch table, hurting but elated and told them that was the girl he was going to marry.

Mickey Rooney: born Joe Yule, Jr., in 1920, in a boardinghouse in Brooklyn, New York. The son of small-time vaudevillians, he grew up a nomad amid the seedy glamour of variety and burlesque houses, surrounded by jugglers, baggy-pants comics, and long-legged showgirls. His cradle was a drawer in his parents' backstage dressing room. Almost literally born a performer, he was said to have stolen his first scene at the age of one and a half when he crawled onto a stage in the middle of an actor's monologue and brought the house down. Not much later he was doing his own act, singing, drumming, telling jokes in a custom-made tuxedo. When welfare workers in one city came investigating a possible violation of the child-labor laws, he had to pretend to be an adult midget. His parents split up when he was four, and his mother, Nell, settled with her boy in Los Angeles. She spent much of her time foisting him on movie producers. In one picture he got to play a midget again. His big break came at the age of six: He won the title role of "Mickey McGuire" in a new series of cheap two-reelers based around the character of the tough little urchin in the popular Toonerville Trolley comic strip. After a while the producers came up with a scheme to "do away" with licensing payments to the creator of the comic strip by making their little star change his name legally to that of the character he played, which he did (Joe Junior's mother, for consistency, changed her name to McGuire, too). The series ran its course after fifty two-reelers, while the cartoonist finally won a lawsuit that incidentally required the young actor to stop calling himself Mickey McGuire on screen or off. The boy was at once out of a job and out of a name, a has-been at twelve.

It was around that time, too, he stopped growing. They tried stretching exercises and mechanical devices—nothing worked. He would top out at a hair over sixty inches, the size of a boy for life.

A publicist at Universal came up with his new name, this one with no legal injunctions against it. David O. Selznick saw him cutting up at a charity Ping-Pong match and, knocked out by his energy and talent, elbowed him into his new production, *Manhattan Melodrama*. Mickey played Clark Gable's character as a child. The picture was a hit, helped along by all the free publicity when John Dillinger went to see it and got shot to death by G-men on his way out of the theater. Metro signed the fourteen-year-old to a long-term contract. For a while he simmered, stealing scenes from the edge of the frame (it was said that his on-screen energy could take the spotlight even from "a cooing baby playing with a forlorn puppy"). Then in 1937 he appeared in the first of what would be known as the Hardy Family series, enormously popular, gentle comedy-dramas about the household of a small-town judge. Mickey Rooney played Judge Hardy's son, Andrew—a rambunctious, lovelorn American teenager—and following the audience's response, he was soon made the focus of the series. The diminutive, not particularly handsome young man (his face was cruelly reckoned by one critic to resemble a squeezed grapefruit) became Metro's hottest property, rushed into films that in their variety (comedies, dark dramas, musicals) revealed the scope of a phenomenal performing talent. By 1939, with the regular Hardy installments and stand-alone hits like *Boys Town* and *Babes in Arms*, he was the box-office champion of the world.

"He was just one of the most gifted people, just amazing," remembered Gene Reynolds, a fellow Metro child actor and a supporting player in several Rooney vehicles. "No education to speak of . . . at the Little Red Schoolhouse there at MGM they could never find him, they were always chasing him down for a lesson. . . . I think he could barely read . . . but he was just naturally talented, intuitively smart: He taught himself to play piano, write music, dance, a great golfer. Anything. On those musical numbers everyone would rehearse all day, all week, from Monday to Friday. And Mickey would not show up. No one could find him all week. He would be off at the track or somewhere. He would come in on Friday morning—everybody else had been working on the number all week long—and he'd say, 'Okay, show me what I do.' They would walk him through the damn thing, do this, now it's a time step, then this—by noon he had the whole thing and be gone, hop in his car, and drive off to the races. It was all too easy for him."

Rooney was strong evidence of the gulf that existed between MGM's wholesome public image and the often rough reality of the place. To moviegoers he was the grinning Everyboy of the Hardy movies, puckish yet decent, earnest, innocent. But Mickey Rooney in real life was no Andy Hardy, no naive small-town boy whose interest in the opposite sex could be sated by a kiss and an ice-cream soda with two straws. Mickey Rooney in life was a wised-up Hollywood playboy. "I was about three years younger than Mickey," said Gene Reynolds. "But I was like *thirty* years younger. Are you kidding? Mickey at fifteen, sixteen, he would get off work and pop open a beer and then go off and get laid. There would be some party with all the young ladies from the studio, and Mickey would be saying 'You see that one over there, the redhead? I've had her. . . . see that blond over there? I've balled her.' He would meet them and charm them and so forth, and the next thing you knew they were in bed. He could even get laid on the Great Plains of Omaha, Nebraska, when we were out there for *Boys Town*."

Rooney, said an article in the *Saturday Evening Post*, "had studio watchdogs assigned to bail him out of scrapes. He was a belligerent kid with no inhibitions . . . a confirmed wolf, junior grade. When he wasn't smoking cigars or driving cars too fast the big boss had him on the carpet constantly for lectures, and Rooney displayed his best acting at such sessions. He wept, beat his breast and swore to reform, then promptly cased the horizon for personable females."

After the ravishing young contract player's cool dismissal of him in the studio commissary, Mickey Rooney's interest in Ava had only increased. Get me that Southern babe's phone number, he told one of his flunkies, and that evening he called her at home.

"Miss Gardner, won't you reconsider? I would love to take you out to dinner."

"No, I'm sorry. I can't."

He called her again the next night.

"Miss Gardner . . . Ava."

"No, thanks all the same."

The next night the same thing, and the next.

"No, I'm awful tired."

"No, I . . . G'bye."

It drove him a little crazy. Once he really set his sights on a girl, it was not normal for him to get the brush-off like that. It was a blow to the ego, not a pleasant sensation at all. It caused one to question oneself, equally unpleasant. He was single, twenty years old, with a very large paycheck forty-eight weeks a year. He was used to having girls fall into his lap, wait in hiding, beg him for a date, even if it was only a run up to the top of Mulholland Drive and a few minutes in the backseat of his car. "Ava didn't give a damn who I was or what I was or what I could do for her," he would recall. Her face and body were unsettling enough, but her intransigence went under his skin, touched a raw nerve of vulnerability that lay beneath his often unbearably brash surface. He was the most popular movie star in the world, wasn't he? What was wrong with him? Was it because he was short?

At the studio he sent another minion to find her and plead his case, tell her all she was missing. Dick Paxton, Mickey's stand-in, found her in the "shooting gallery" getting some pictures taken. Mickey's a great guy, Ava, he told her. Mickey can do a lot for your career. Go out to dinner with him, willya? What have you got to lose?

Bappie said the same thing, back in their little room at the Hollywood Wilcox. Every night they ate hamburgers across the street, played rummy, listened to the radio, and went to bed at nine. She was bored stiff with her baby sister the movie queen. Bappie said, "Why don't you let him take you to dinner, sugar? I bet he goes to some real nice joints. A helluva lot better than that hamburger stand."

Ava said she didn't want to get people talking about her the way they did some of the other new females at the studio. And Mickey had a reputation. He'd been with a million girls. Who knew what a movie star expected you to do on a date? And Ava told her again how small he was the time she saw him at the lunchroom and he wasn't wearing his Carmen Miranda platform heels. He had barely come up to her breasts.

"Well, give me the phone next time," said Bappie. "I'll go out with him."

In the end Ava gave in. And Bappie did come. Ava said she couldn't leave her sister behind, and Mickey, not about to lose his opening, said, "I'll pick you both up at seven!"

He picked them up in a new red convertible that glistened like wet rubber. They roared up Sunset Boulevard. At every red light people stared, waved, shouted: "Hiya, Mickey!" "That's Mickey Rooney!" And Rooney glowed with an infectious comic ecstasy. It was like sitting next to the boy-king of the universe. They went to Chasen's, an expensive industry hangout. He plied them with cocktails, champagne, filet mignon, crêpes suzettes for dessert. The room was spinning, from booze and from Mickey Rooney—he dazzled them, an exploding pinwheel. The sisters were gasping for breath, no letup.

He urged Ava out of their booth at one point and glided her over to one table and then another, all of them filled with friends and boosters, some of them recognizable faces from the screen and from fan magazines, but she was too dizzy to remember who was who.

"Fellas, this is Ava Gardner and she's new in Hollywood. Isn't she gorgeous?!"

Later they went dancing. And Mickey was a great dancer. Everyone in the club watched them and grinned and applauded. His spirit lifted the whole place higher, like a round bought for the house. It was nearly two in the morning when they pulled up at the Wilcox. Bappie stumbled along ahead and let her baby sister say their good nights. They went up and Mickey clung to her, escorting her down the hallway of the tatty hotel. She looked down at him and he beamed up at her, held her arm tighter.

"Ava," he said. "Will you marry me?"

She pulled her arm away, took one more startled look back, and ran into her room.

And so it began. He called her in the morning to tell her how much he had enjoyed the evening. He tracked her down at lunchtime, took her out that night. Ava told Bappie, "He's not my type at all!" And Bappie said, "Baby, just go out and have fun and don't worry about it. Mickey's a great guy."

They went out that night, just the two of them. The next night too.

They had zombies at the Beachcomber, caviar at Romanoff's. Went dancing at the Trocadero. He introduced her to movie stars they met along the way: Uncle Spence, Uncle Wally. They looked older and drunker than they did in pictures. He showed her everything he had—fame, charm, money—and then he showed her again.

He knew she didn't want him. Her disinterest only increased his desire. He would later reflect that if she had only felt about him what he felt for her, the romance would have ended like all those before it had—"on the spot . . . or on some other spot a few weeks later," lust gratified and replaced with "instant boredom."

He began picking her up in the mornings and driving her to the studio. He would keep the car top down even on cold mornings so everyone could see what he had in the passenger seat. Sidney Miller, a young actor and part of Rooney's retinue, would recall to Rooney's biographer Arthur Marx how Mickey would drive slowly along the studio streets shouting to passersby, "Hey, this is my new girl. She's going to be a big star!" and Miller would remember Ava sitting there, embarrassed as hell.

He took her around to meet people at the studio, producers, directors, casually but with intent, partly to help her along, partly perhaps to let them know to keep their hands off. Sid Luft, a friend of Rooney's then working for Metro star Eleanor Powell (and later to marry Rooney's favorite costar, Judy Garland) remembered being introduced to Ava in those early days of the relationship: "Mickey was completely gone for her, like I'd never seen him act before. I met her and we talked a little. She was a very beautiful girl but very, very naive. She seemed like she had just walked in out of the woods."

Other than her two screen tests, Ava had yet to work in front of a camera. One day Mickey went up to the office that produced Metro's short subjects, the one- and two-reelers that ran between feature films.

"I was running the shorts department at that time; I was executive producer," remembered Richard Goldstone. "And Mickey Rooney just came in to see us, very friendly, and said he had a favor to ask. He said that he had found this lovely girl and asked us did we think we could find her a spot in one of the shorts. She was new, he said, and he just wanted to get her a start. And I think . . . I mean, obviously he wanted to impress her. This wasn't something he had ever done before to my knowledge, and he was a big star at Metro, and he was a very nice guy so we obliged him. I okayed it. We were making about seventy shorts a year back then, and we had one we were shooting, and we put her in it. I believe it was the first thing she ever did."

It was titled *Strange Testament,* part of the Passing Parade series of one-reelers dramatizing odd but true historical anecdotes, with narration written and delivered by journalist John Nesbit. The short was filmed silent, with an ex–vaudeville dancer named Sammy Lee directing. "It was a restaurant set," said Goldstone. "Ava played a waitress. I think she walked over to the table and poured a cup of coffee. She looked beautiful. And that was it."

That was it: She was in the movies now. Mickey beamed at her: "I'm telling you, kid, you're gonna be big!"

Suddenly—it felt like overnight, with the tornado that Mickey kicked up, never a moment to stop and think what was happening—suddenly they were a couple. She had looked away, and when she looked back she was "Mickey Rooney's girl," and strangers in public places were popping flashbulbs in their eyes. She was on his arm at the hottest nightspots, at the prizefights, at a movie premiere at the Chinese with a red carpet laid out before them. The press took note. Louella Parsons, the queen of the Hollywood columnists, wrote: "Mickey Rooney's latest is Ava Gardner, brunette stock actress at MGM." Jimmie Fidler announced that she looked like Hedy Lamarr, only better, and Sidney Skolsky reported to his readers that Rooney's new interest was "a North Carolina beauty . . . who is much taller."

On October 3 the *Smithfield Herald* ran an entire feature on the hometown girl: PRETTY AVA GARDNER IN LIMELIGHT AS MICKEY ROONEY'S "LATEST" GIRL FRIEND. It read, "Ava Gardner, recently of Johnston County . . . doing all right at the movie capital . . . a glimmer of stardust in Ava's hair . . . box-office smasher Mickey Rooney chasing after her. . . . It shouldn't be long before the folks back home can be seeing Ava at their local theater."

Pictures appeared of the two of them dancing at the Mocambo. In her spike-heeled shoes she stood ten inches taller; in the pictures it looked as if she were in a different latitude. Towering over him and wearing her MGM makeup and hairstyle and the chic clothes Mickey bought for her, she looked more sophisticated and in control than she was. Rooney was the driving force in everything they did and Ava the mostly passive object of desire, but some people saw the pictures of the towering gorgeous woman and the short, boyish, excited Mickey and figured her for a gold digger, figured that she had hit town and craftily latched on to Mickey Rooney as a career move. Ava was too unsure of herself and too indifferent and surprised by each day's events to hatch as calculated a scheme as that. The farthest she could think ahead was to the evening's necking session in the convertible and how she was going to keep Mickey from going too far.

He was feverish to possess her. She would squirm on the front seat and tell him, "I can't do . . . that . . . before I'm a married woman!"

And then he would propose marriage.

He later calculated that he asked her twenty-five times.

"Ava and I and Dorothy Morris, another actress, would go eat lunch at a drugstore on the corner," recalled Berdie Abrams. "We would go there because it was more peaceful than the studio cafeteria. And we'd sit in the little booths and talk. And she wanted our opinion about Mickey. And we'd say, 'Oh, he's adorable. Everybody loves Mickey.' And we did. He used to call me 'Legs' because I won a contest for best legs at the studio. And she would ask some more about him, and we'd say he was cute and nice. And one day she said, 'Mickey asked me to marry him. What do you think?' And I said, 'Well, that's a big question. You shouldn't ask anybody else. You have to know that for yourself.' But she wasn't sure what she felt about him. And he was just wild about her."

People at the studio—spies from the studio, like Mickey's assigned caretaker, Les Petersen—began to sniff around, ask what was going on with the brunette dame, why he was tying himself down like this instead of playing the field. Which had the effect of making Rooney—who hated the studio's dictates and its attempts to run his life—more determined than ever. Ava's turning him down was a challenge and a rebuke. He could sell more movie tickets than Clark Gable; surely he could win over one virgin from North Carolina. He employed what he called an "all-court press," not letting her do anything without him, overwhelming her with sheer Mickey Rooneyness. He worked on Bappie as well, charming her onto his side. "He's awful sweet, Ava, don't you think?" she would say to her sister. "Isn't he funny? Did he do his Lionel Barrymore imitation for you? And when are you two gonna get hitched?"

December came. And on the seventh the Japanese attacked Pearl Harbor, and the United States was at war. Clouds of uncertainty, fear, and panic hung over Los Angeles. There were rumors of imminent invasions. At enlistment offices young men lined up around the block, eager for battle, revenge. There was tension and drama in everything now. No one knew where it was all going to lead, only that there would be more blood and horror in the times ahead. On the evening of the ninth they had been out to dinner. Later that night the two of them had gotten into his car to head back to the Wilcox. Mickey didn't start the car right away, and for a time they sat there in silence in the dark.

"Ava," he said then. "Will you marry me?"

Maybe it had something to do with being far from home during such a terrible week; maybe she had been feeling somber and vulnerable as so many people did in those first days of the country at war; or maybe he had just won her over at last. Fifty million moviegoers couldn't be wrong.

She said, "All right, Mickey."

She imagined a big wedding. Not because she was marrying the biggest star in Hollywood, but because a big wedding was supposed to be the dream of every girl who was getting married. She called long distance to tell her mother about it, and Molly was so happy for her and yet a little unbelieving. It was all such a strange thing, her child in Hollywood, now to be the bride of a famous young man. Ava wanted to make arrangements for her mother to come out to California. They would pick out a nice wedding dress and all the rest. Molly was so happy for her, and Ava said yes, she was happy, too. Mickey was a great guy. They were going to be very happy. He was so talented and so crazy about her.

Mickey had said they had better keep their intentions a secret for the moment, but then he had been ready to burst with it and broke the news himself. He called the Hollywood columnist Hedda Hopper and gave her the scoop on his engagement. But then Hedda called up MGM for confirmation, and they told her the story wasn't true, and of course she believed MGM. She wondered what had gotten into the boy, making up a thing like that.

Soon came a message from Culver City, from the third floor. Mr. Mayer would like to see Mickey and his . . . friend. Right away.

They arrived arm in arm, Ava parroting her fiancé's subdued demeanor as they neared the mogul's lair. White-haired Ida Koverman, Mayer's stern, devoted executive secretary, looked at them with open reproof as she would at anyone or anything that caused her employer distress. They entered the colossal private office, the size of a tobacco warehouse but considerably more plush (regal-modernist design courtesy of Academy Award–winning Metro staffer Cedric Gibbons). And now Ava looked upon the fifty-six-year-old former junk dealer from Minsk who was the highest-paid executive in the world and one of the handful of men who had invented the motion picture industry. Short and unhandsome, with a heavy, bespectacled head set upon a thick, powerful torso, he looked like an owl made of pig iron. He gave *her* no greeting at all but launched into Rooney with a righteous fury.

"How dare you do this to me! Who has been like a father to you! To this studio that has been your family who has raised you to great success!"

Mayer fumed behind his colossal desk. Behind and to his side were Bennie Thau and Howard Strickling, silently hovering, ominously observing, like two henchmen backing up the big boss in a gangster movie. Mayer went on with his rage. He was known for his temper tantrums when those under contract disappointed him, but for Rooney he always reserved a particularly savage exasperation. To Mayer the Hardy series was not only an incredible moneymaker but a profound cinematic expression of the studio's Main Street values—Mayer's much-vaunted personal values—a veneration of family, home, innocence. And Rooney, to Mayer, was forever doing something to threaten that pristine image. Mickey's own mother had once come to the office to complain that her son was throwing all his money away on hookers. And there was the time a year or two ago—it had nearly given Louis B. cardiac arrest—when he received the news that the teenage Rooney was having an affair with Norma Shearer, the Queen of the Lot—*shtup*ping the thirty-eight-year-old widow of Irving Thalberg the length and breadth of her *Marie Antoinette* trailer! ("She was hotter than a half-fucked fox in a forest fire," Mickey would recall appreciatively in his memoir.) And now this—Mayer treated Rooney's "engagement" as just another transgression, no more honorable than the others. Where did he get the temerity to go off and get engaged? Engaged to be married? Did he know what the public would think when they heard that America's favorite high-school-boy virgin was planning to marry some hotsy showgirl? Had he even considered how such an action might damage the box-office potential of the next Hardy picture or the next one with Judy? Were people going to believe he was still a sixteen-year-old dating the girl next door when there were pictures of him with a sexpot wife?

Mickey told Mayer he and Ava were in love. He was a grown man now. The public would have to understand.

Mayer growled, "You won't listen to reason? All right. I simply forbid it. That's all. I forbid it."

Then Rooney, with a look of cheerless resolve, explained that he was going to marry the woman he loved and if Mr. Mayer could not respect that and did not think they should continue their working relationship, then he would have to see if there was some other studio that wanted him.

Few in the world of the movies had contradicted the wishes of Louis B. Mayer and thrived. Mickey Rooney's box-office standing would mean nothing if Mayer became determined to destroy him. There would be no "other studio"; they could keep the boy in litigation and off the screen for years (that was the whole point of the studio system, to make sure no one was more powerful than the studio they worked for). Rooney, despite his youthful impulsiveness, had to understand all this. But his determination was fanatic. This was Ava's allure at nineteen: The biggest movie star in the world was ready to risk professional annihilation rather than give up the girl he had known for fifteen or sixteen weeks. He had diligently (and God knew celibately) courted her for all that time, and now that her charms in full lay almost within his grasp, nothing—not even the great and powerful Mayer—was going to stop him from getting what he had to have.

Mayer, face-to-face with such grotesque defiance, gave perhaps his first serious thought to the root cause of the commotion, suddenly conscious of a heretofore barely-acknowledged fifty-dollar-a-week contract hopeful with a hopeless hillbilly accent. Ava Gardner? That had to be one of Strickling's concoctions. What was her real name? Lulubelle? And here she was out of nowhere threatening the future of one of Metro-Goldwyn-Mayer's most valuable assets?!

The tension in the big room grew, peaked—ebbed. Mickey Rooney was, after all, a very valuable asset indeed. However much Mayer might have wanted to call his bluff it was not in the interests of the studio to risk the loss of such a uniquely talented moneymaker. New York would not understand such a decision. It would not be good business to punish Mr. Rooney at this time. Better to wait for a day that would surely come—perhaps not for many years but one day—when the willful boy's value would be less and he could be made to regret his arrogant behavior (Mayer had a long memory). For now, let the boy have his hillbilly.

The mogul's mouth became a chilling smile.

"Mickey . . . you know it would break my heart to see you unhappy."

The studio would handle all the arrangements. It was decided. Ava waited for details, daydreaming with Bappie about the fantastic ceremony MGM was bound to produce. But Metro's wedding planners up on the third floor felt the best thing was to get it over with quickly and without a fuss, minimizing the publicity and cutting their losses. Ava was told not to bother asking any of her Carolina relatives to come out. And an elaborate wedding dress was deemed to be out of place and an unnecessary expenditure. Ava was disappointed, angry, and embarrassed, but shared her feelings only with Bappie. Mickey had already gone out on a limb with the studio, and now they were supposed to keep their mouths shut and follow orders. She found solace in a friendship with Judy Garland and her musician husband, David Rose. Like Mickey (and probably bolstering his own resolve), Judy had defied the studio in the name of love. Like Ava she was nineteen years old. In the previous summer—during the filming of *Babes on Broadway*, just before Ava and Mickey had met—Garland and Rose eloped to Las Vegas. Judy had asked for a couple of days off for a honeymoon, and Mayer and Arthur Freed furiously demanded she return to the studio that very day, and she did (but with a simmering resentment). Ava and Mickey visited the Roses at their house in Bel Air. Judy was hilariously caustic about her bosses. Ava was nervous about the wedding and Judy, for laughs, got them to rehearse the ceremony in the den. Judy wanted to take a picture of the couple and send it to Louis B. and the rest of them—"You were cordially not invited"— inscribed with an obscenity.

They went into January with the wedding in a holding pattern. Mickey had to finish the new Hardy picture. A date was set for the end of the week and then had to be canceled: Mickey was needed for a few retakes. "If the picture is out of the way on Saturday," reported Louella Parsons, "the wedding can take place," Ava wanted to thank Louella for the news. The studio at last gave the nod. On January 10, a small wedding party drove out of Los Angeles in two cars. There were Ava and Mickey; Bappie (who would be maid of honor); Mickey's mother, Nell (a tough old bird whose first words upon meeting Ava were, "Well, I guess he ain't been into your pants yet"), and his stepfather, Fred Pankey; his father, Joe Yule, Sr. (who was currently working in a strip joint in downtown LA), and Dad's new wife, Theota; Les Petersen, Mickey's appointed "keeper" from the studio (and self-appointed best man); Eleanor Stewart, an actress in Hopalong Cassidy Westerns and Petersen's wife; and a staff photographer from the studio. They picked up a marriage license in Montecito near Santa Barbara and then continued on to the small village of Ballard and the obscure Santa Ynez Valley Presbyterian Church. Petersen had chosen the location and quietly reserved the Santa Ynez, although Ava was a Baptist and Rooney a Christian Scientist; the joke was that Petersen picked it because Andy Hardy was a Presbyterian.

The group gathered inside the church at a few minutes before eleven. Ava wore a feathered hat, a plain blue outfit, and a corsage (she still brooded over being denied a fancy white gown). Rooney wore a sedate dark suit. Both the bride and the groom looked grim and distracted. Ava's uncertain mood was understandable: There had been little that could be called normal in the past half-year, and this least of all, a wedding to a movie star among a group of strangers (only Bappie had known her as long as six months ago), thousands of miles from home. The Reverend Glen H. Lutz performed the ceremony; his wife pumped out the wedding march on a wheezy organ. Mickey slipped a platinum ring onto Ava's finger; the ring bore the inscription, "Love Forever." Les Petersen had picked it out. Lutz pronounced them man and wife. Ava leaned down to kiss her husband. The Metro photographer prepared to take the official wedding portrait, and Petersen scurried up ahead of him with the little stool he had brought from the studio, plopped it on the floor, and helped Mickey to stand on it, bringing him up to Ava's height for the picture.

One car took the guests back to Los Angeles. Mickey, Ava, and Les got into Mickey's convertible and headed up the Monterey coast to the place Les had chosen for them to stay for the next four days, the sprawling Del Monte Hotel near Pebble Beach.

"You're married now, doll, how does it feel?"

Ava looked at her husband. Then she turned and looked at the other man in the car, the publicist and minder from MGM.

"Are you coming on the honeymoon, Les?"

"Sure. I go where you kids go."

He was joking, sort of. He checked the couple in to the hotel and joined them in the suite for some iced champagne, then dinner; at last he left them to themselves. As the night came on, the prospect of facing her matrimonial bed left Ava visibly disconcerted, which in turn spooked Mickey, and they both drank too much. Ava would give a discreet, vaguely satisfied account of the night in her memoir, but Rooney's recollection would be blunt: An evening-long booze-up had diminished his resources; while the bride was locked away in the bathroom he rolled over in bed and passed out. Ava, fully primped for her ordeal, came out to find her husband sleeping. The night of bliss he had risked so much to enjoy was his for the having, and he'd let it slip away.

On day two of the marriage, Mickey said they were going to play golf, or Mickey was going to play and Ava could watch. With the wedding night having passed uneventfully—anyway, without the main event taking place—and the morning proceeding briskly to breakfast, Ava might have wondered when exactly her husband was going to claim the prize for which he had so long feverishly clamored. For most of that day, however, the object of Rooney's pleasure was not the breaching of his bride but of the eighteen holes on Pebble Beach's legendary course.

In the evening, though, his attention returned to her in full.

She was tense, skittish to his touch. Why couldn't it be like in the movies? A kiss, some pretty music, and a fade to black, not this embarrassing intimate grapple. Mickey, by his reckoning, was contrastingly confident, attentive, and then "tremendous." Her body gave proof of what for months her words and the prohibitive snap of her thighs had declared: She was a virgin. He made love to her, and Ava, "agreeably surprised" by the thing her mother had taught her to fear, soon opened herself to it absolutely. They made love all night long. A "sexual symphony," said Mickey Rooney.

In the morning, more golf. Ava followed him around the course with a puppyish devotion, euphoric from the night before, and when the time came to return to their suite she rushed them along in eager anticipation. Another symphony was performed. Ava would much later rave to intimates about Mickey's expertise in bed. "Don't let the little guy fool you," she told Ann Miller. "He knew every trick in the book." According to journalist Radie Harris, Ava said she had been so ignorant of sex in the beginning that for a time she completely surrendered herself to Mickey's domination, but that her enthusiasm for the activity was such that she quickly developed a more active and aggressive approach, "such a technique," as Harris reported, "that no man would ever dominate her in bed again."

It was good that Ava was so pleased and consumed by their sexual encounters because Mickey paid little attention to her away from the mattress. "It was an ideal honeymoon," he wrote. "Sex and golf and sex and golf." After the first couple of traipses around the course, though, Ava had had enough and spent her remaining mornings at the hotel lying in bed; she would have lunch with Mickey in the clubhouse, then play cards and get treated to a chocolate milk shake with Les Petersen, then dinner and back into bed for the next course in her sexual education.

After four days they drove to San Francisco. Metro had decided to make it a working honeymoon from there on and tie the star's travels to various public appearances and publicity events, some connected to the war effort, some to the promotion of their new release, *Life Begins for Andy Hardy*. From San Francisco they took the train east. They stayed a night in Chicago, promoting, then caught the Twentieth Century Limited for New York. Putting them up in a suite at the New Yorker Hotel near Penn Station, Les coordinated a meeting with press and photographers at the hotel. The Metro man scurried about making sure the poses looked proper—Ava seated in a deep chair and Mickey on the arm so that he loomed above her. Bappie arrived from Los Angeles by train, and the sisters were loosed on the Manhattan stores with a blank check from Mickey. They went to Boston and attended a charity function hosted by the mayor and attended by a contingent of area blue bloods. Ava was overwhelmed by the pomp and could barely function for fear of picking up the wrong piece of silverware.

She had naturally wished to include a stop to see her mother and family while they were in the East, and so the MGM planners, not wanting to waste their boy on a strictly personal side trip, booked him to make a morale-boosting visit to North Carolina's Fort Bragg. Mickey shook hands with some generals and fired a machine gun as flashbulbs popped, then went with Ava to Raleigh, where Molly was living with Inez and her husband, John Grimes, at their small but comfortable house on Fairview Road. Everyone in the Gardner family who could make it arrived for a big welcome-home-and-meet-Mickey party. Molly's illness had taken an evident physical toll, but she rose to this joyous occasion, delighted by the return of her beautiful daughter and the chance to know her famous son-in-law. Mickey lavished Ava's mom with attention, poured on his legendary personality, joking, dancing, trying out a song from his new picture, leaving the crowd of young and old laughing and applauding, Molly most of all. Ava watched, almost in tears with appreciation for her new husband.

The next and last stop of the tour was Washington, D.C., and for Ava the most impossible experience of an unreal six months. They were to be among the star-studded Hollywood contingent attending Franklin Roosevelt's sixtieth birthday party at the White House. The president and first lady greeted them on their arrival, and Ava, curtsying nervously, could not stop imagining her father's expression if he could have seen this moment—his daughter meeting the man he had always spoken of as a kind of god. Ava, Mickey, Bappie, and Les Petersen sat together in the vast dining room, Ava causing much attention, the radiantly beautiful newly-wed, stunningly turned out, the regal sweep of her shoulders highlighted by a strapless black gown. The protocol for the event was for FDR to sit at a different table for each course, and soon the time came when he was wheeled up to his place at the table with Ava, Mickey, and the others. They were allowed a few minutes of small talk between bites, though Ava was too nervous to speak or eat. FDR, too, seemed to be distracted. Some would recall that President Roosevelt could not take his eyes off the dazzling young woman at his side.

The honeymoon ended. Married life, real life, began.

Rooney owned a big house in Encino where his mother and stepfather had been living with him, and it was decided to let Ma stay there and let the newlyweds get a place of their own. Les Petersen found them an apartment in Westwood. Right away, Rooney was needed back at the studio, a new slate of films waiting to be made. No longer the unattained object of obsession she had been for the previous six months, Ava found herself faded into an adjunct position in her husband's life. He was often too busy to see her at the studio—he was starring in as many as four movies a year—and many of his free hours he returned to spending as he always had, handicapping horses, playing golf, and joyriding with his gang of buddies and sycophants. Mustering little interest in an ordinary married home life, he only seemed bored by Ava's initial assumption of a wife's traditional activities of keeping house and making home-cooked meals. He much preferred to spend every night at Chasen's or Romanoff's, with the noise and the smoke and the visible fealty and the glad-handing between courses. Day by day Ava became more aware of how little they seemed to have in common. Mickey, as everyone said, was always "on." He liked performing, noise, fun, crowds; he had a manic mind that seemed to fear quiet and calm as if they were death. Ava liked to be "off"—to laze around in bed till the sun was halfway across the sky; shuffle around barefoot and aimless; eat long, lingering meals; and lie on the floor for hours listening to records. Like her father, she was wary of strangers. Mickey greeted every stranger's gaze like the warm caress of a spotlight.

One thing seemed to sustain their mutual interest: Rooney was the happy beneficiary of his wife's recently uncaged sensuality. Back in Monterey nineteen years of trepidation had evaporated in a night of pleasure. Now Ava approached the sex act with an animal enthusiasm, wanted to make love all the time, in all ways. She would signal her need with a smoldering look or a provocatively raised eyebrow or come to greet him in a pair of panties and nothing else. Or dispense with subtleties altogether, growling at him: "Let's fuck!" By Rooney's reckoning, she was custom designed for intercourse. Her body seemed to possess something "extra"—something wonderful. He'd had a wealth of experience behind him for comparison, from good-time girls to horny widows, and, he would write in his memoir, there had never been anyone like Ava "down there"—it seemed to have a life of its own, as supple and expressive as "a little warm mouth."

One night Ava began screaming from shooting pains in her abdomen. It reminded her of her mother's cancer and the painful spasms she had seen Molly suffering, and she screamed as much in terror as in pain. Mickey got an ambulance that rushed her to the hospital. She was operated on for acute appendicitis and remained at Hollywood Hospital for a week of convalescence. Mickey had come to the hospital repeatedly, full of gifts and affection, but when she returned home Ava found what she believed to be telltale evidence that her husband had been entertaining one or more other women while she was away. Rooney denied it—then and in later recollections (which did not often fail to reveal regretted behavior)—but Ava erupted with jealous fury.

They would kiss, make up, and go on, but the relationship had been exposed to serious discord—and in Ava's version to betrayal. From now on each disagreement and every suspicion she felt accrued a greater and lasting weight. It was a downhill turn from which the marriage would never recover.

Since Ava's debut before a camera the previous autumn, her career had moved at a very modest pace. She had gotten more bit parts in short subjects and then the same in feature films, most in the B or low-budget unit but a couple of A productions as well, including *We Were Dancing*, starring faded Metro diva (and Mickey Rooney's former flame) Norma Shearer. She was nervous and unsure of herself on the film sets, and on some of those early jobs Mickey had been there to help her. For a bit she did as a movie cashier in an Our Gang short called *Mighty Lak a Goat*, Robert Blake—then a boy actor playing a member of the gang—remembered Rooney bringing her to the set and privately directing her through the very brief performance. She told journalist Adela Rogers St. John, "Mickey was so patient, so kind . . . when I got my first parts he showed me how to walk, to stand, what to do with my hands, how to ignore the camera. If I ever do anything big, I'll owe a lot of it to Mickey, bless him." Her memoir, curiously, contained a much less generous recollection, saying Mickey had never taught her anything and never gotten her an acting job. It was more likely that he had gotten her not only her first part but some of the other early work as well. But his influence was somehow not great enough to land her a more substantial job, even on an Andy Hardy picture. When he asked producer Carey Wilson to give Ava a role in the latest installment, *The Courtship of Andy Hardy*, Wilson refused, saying she was not ready for it (the part went to Donna Reed). (The Andy Hardy films had made a tradition of introducing the studio's newest ingenues, including Lana Turner, Esther Williams, and Kathryn Grayson.)

All of Ava's earliest appearances were uncredited, nonspeaking parts, hardly more than extra work, some virtually incorporeal. "We did a lot of those together," said Leatrice Gilbert. "You didn't know what the film was half the time. You'd get in and get your hair and makeup done, and then you hung around the set for hours, and then you did your scene. And sometimes you weren't even in the sight of the camera. And we'd go down to the commissary for lunch and say, laughingly, though we wanted to believe it, 'We're actresses!' There was one Ava and I did together called *Hitler's Hangman* [the film was released as *Hitler's Madman*] and we were dressed up as little Czechoslovakian girls in the village where the Nazi Heydrich was hanging everyone. Neither of us had anything to do, really; we just stood around all day looking like mournful refugees."

After some months of silence Ava was at last entrusted with speaking parts. Her brief first chance occurred one day when she was plucked out of a group of starlets playing students at Miss Hope's Finishing School in *Calling Dr. Gillespie*, shooting from early February. In the final scene of the movie, she sits outside with four other young women, laughing with surprise at the romantic advice of the geriatric, wheelchair-bound Lionel Barrymore. Ava's laugh, throaty and real, is heard above the tittering of the other girls. In a moment she is sharing a two-shot with the film's leading lady and, startlingly so, making the lovely Donna Reed look like she is playing the ugly duckling sister. Then her voice, low and melodious, devoid of accent. "Can it really be a happy marriage," she asks, of all things, "if a girl deliberately goes after a man?" Barrymore harrumphs: "No marriage was ever spoiled by the trivial question of who started it." She will remember him fondly, the old actor kind and patient with the nervous newcomer. A boy comes for her, she leans toward the camera, whispers in Dr. Gillespie's ear: "I'll let you know in ten minutes whether your advice was any good or not." And she glides away, breathtaking. It is a sudden glimpse of the celestial in an earthbound programmer. A star's presence is clear in the half-a-minute of celluloid, the radiant face, the voice, the floating movement. For MGM it ought to have been the moment of elucidation, bells and whistles sounding: let's do something with that girl! But no one noticed. Uncredited bit parts and a few more lines were her only reward.

Her first officially assigned dialogue, and the public debut of the voice that had once caused Metro so much consternation, was to be heard in the film *Kid Glove Killer*, previewed at the Ritz in Los Angeles on March 10, 1942. *Kid Glove Killer* was a B movie with a three-week shooting schedule under producer Jack Chertok's supervision, a small-scale mystery about a crime-solving police lab technician. The movie marked the graduation from the shorts department to feature directing for a man who would later become one of the more artful and acclaimed of postwar filmmakers, Fred Zinnemann. Ava's bit was efficiently staged in two shots on a soundstage set representing the exterior of a drive-up diner. She played a carhop paying call on leading lady Marsha Hunt and second lead Lee Bowman in their convertible, stopping first to leave a tray on the door of a jalopy and suddenly kissing the young man behind the wheel.

To Bowman and Hunt she spoke her first line of two, "Anything for dessert, folks?"

Bowman, gesturing to the scene of the kiss, says, "I don't see that on the menu. . . ." Ava replies, "Oh, him? Well, he's my husband."

Cut.

The appearance lasted all of twenty-five seconds on screen, and was not extraordinary but was not bad either: Eye-catching in her twenty-five seconds, with a beautiful smile and the sleek sexiness and precise movements of a fashion model (in her snug sort-of-paramilitary carhop uniform looking unexpectedly chic), she gave the otherwise homely film its only moment of glamour.

Proof that it was acting was the fact there was no sign of the great anxiety the work had caused. For the entire time it took to complete the scene she was wretchedly nervous, queasy, close to vomiting. "So unhappy was she about the awful job she thought she had done," Fred Zinnemann remembered, "that she wanted to go back to North Carolina immediately."

Other speaking parts followed, but the studio had no coherent plan for her career, and she experienced no clear hierarchical advancement—she continued for some time to be used as needed in silent walk-ons. Her anxiety when she had to perform remained, though along the way she discovered that a slug or two of booze before a take did wonders; she found that if you befriended certain of the prop men they could be depended on to have available a little liquid encouragement, poured into a paper cup. She hated the taste of straight liquor and took it down like an awful medicine, but she was becoming increasingly fond of its relaxing effect. It relaxed her on the set and it relaxed her at social gatherings, parties where she had often found herself sulking on a chair in a corner while Mickey and the other Hollywood extroverts held court.

The marriage had continued to deteriorate. By summer the arguing and recriminations were an almost daily occurrence. There were good days, and they continued to have sexual relations—now that she had been introduced to that pleasing aspect of married life she was reluctant to give it up. But the dream of love and marriage had dissolved for Ava, and she now increasingly saw only disappointment and betrayal where there had been hope and trust. Her husband was immature, selfish, and, she believed, chronically unfaithful. She disliked his friends, was distressed about his endless gambling losses, suspicious of his frequent late-night disappearances. One night she was with him at a drunken party at the Ambassador when some of his pals began teasing him about his "little black book" of girlfriends' numbers. A new friend of Ava's at the studio, the young Peter Lawford—suave, shallow English playboy actor ever on the make—whispered to her that Mickey had a new dolly he was meeting daily at his country club. She looked for signs of his infidelity, pondered evidence of unexplained activities, looked for lies on his lips and in his eyes.

Thinking that they could use a change of scene and more breathing room, Mickey moved them to a large rented house on Stone Canyon Drive in Bel Air. It solved nothing. They simply no longer got along. They fought when they were alone, they fought in public. She had been drinking more and more. It had helped her nerves at the studio, relaxed her at parties. Now it briefly erased some of the pain of a crumbling marriage and gave her courage to complain. As drinking became an increasing component in her social life, it was also becoming clear that she was chemically ill-equipped for the amount she might consume, one of those who with sufficient alcohol in her system could become startlingly transformed, prone to emotional imbalance, paranoia, even violent outbursts, a Jekyll-and-Hyde syndrome, as some would come to describe it.

Rooney had to wonder: Where was the bashful farm girl he had helped down off the hay wagon nine or ten months before? She would tear into him, obscenity-laced complaints; she once threw a heavy inkwell at his head during an argument; at a party—"juiced on martinis"—she flirted and danced intimately with other men, intent on provoking or humiliating him. Where was the girl? he would wonder. *He* was still the same, fun-loving guy she had married.

One weekend that summer they had gone down across the Mexican border to Tijuana, to the races. They had had a good day, watching the horses, drinking chilled tequila with lime. They drove back to California, a beautiful summer day with a flaming orange sunset at the end. They got back to Los Angeles and had a late dinner at Chasen's. Ava said she was tired and wanted to go home after they ate, but Mickey was caught up in his usual whirlwind with a hundred admirers. Ava drank too much, brooded, became angry, stormed out of the restaurant, and had a taxi drive her home. Raging from the liquor and mounting dissatisfactions, she took a carving knife from the kitchen and went around the living room stabbing and tearing at the sofa cushions and the upholstered chairs, leaving clouds of cotton batting floating in the air. Then Ava went upstairs and got into bed, knowing her marriage was over.

Mickey returned, less than sober himself, finding everything shredded and overturned. What the hell?

She left. The next day or the day after she returned to the apartment in Westwood Village, still under lease. She had a brief falling out with Bappie—now living at her own place on Fountain Avenue—who sounded to Ava as if she was taking her husband's side. Mickey was after her at once, calling, pleading with her to come home. Leatrice Gilbert stayed with her for a while to keep her company. "She didn't want to talk about it much," Leatrice recalled. "She said she was done with him and she felt like she was breathing free for the first time in months."

If Mickey had often taken her for granted in their time together, her sudden absence from his life, from his bed, made it painfully apparent how much she meant to him. The thought that he would never again touch her glorious body or hear her hoarse whispers of appreciation left him shaken, desperate. He called all day long, pursued her at the studio, sent presents. He sent a messenger to deliver a ten-thousand-dollar mink coat. One night, frantic with desire, he showed up at the apartment and demanded she take him back. Leatrice Gilbert recalled the night: "She was terrified. He had driven up on a motorcycle, as I remember it. She wouldn't let him in. He was crying for her. He so wanted to be back with her that it made him crazy."

Ava called the studio and told them what was happening and threatened to go to Louella Parsons or maybe the police if they didn't help her, and Metro, holding its corporate head at the prospect of the bad publicity, revised the schedule for the picture Rooney was shooting, *A Yank at Eton*, and sent him at once across the country to some locations in Connecticut. He called every night, but Ava refused the calls or hung up on him. In September the press reported the separation. In the *Smithfield Herald* it was written that "Johnston County's glamorous Ava Gardner admitted . . . that her marriage to filmdom's greatest box office attraction had ended in failure."

"We just couldn't seem to hit it off," Ava told a reporter, "things just weren't happy around home and we decided to call it quits. As things stand now I'll ask for a divorce later."

Now MGM stepped up. In August, Mickey Rooney had been classified 1-A by the Draft Board and was eligible for induction into the army in September. MGM intended to fight with everything they had against their valuable employee's being drafted. Eddie Mannix, Mayer's bulldog, requested the actor be given an "occupational deferment." In an affidavit Mannix explained that Rooney in his movie stardom was an asset to the war effort, and that in the next Andy Hardy movie Rooney's character would propagandize for American boys to volunteer for service, and further that Andy and the Hardys represented to the public "the highest type" of the American family. Mannix could be damn sure that headline stories of a pending divorce were not going to help them make their case for Mickey/Andy's moral standing, not in an America where many considered divorce a sin and a scandal. He called the couple in and pleaded with them to reconcile, for their own sake, of course, in the name of true love.

And so she took him back. But it was not a happy reunion. It was clear that the romance had outlived its expiration date. The dynamics had changed, the sense of dependence had reversed, and Ava seemed at times to be pursuing a cruel payback for Mickey's real or imagined offenses. Now she was the one to aggravate him, disappear, come home late without a good excuse. She had pals from the studio, some of them with a reputation, party girls, hard drinkers. How could a guy know what his wife was doing out there?

Ava had acquiesced to the urgings of the Metro executives—intimidated, uncertain of the future—but she resented it at once. It felt intolerable to have them managing her private life. At times she felt not much happier with her own behavior. The dissolution of the marriage often haunted her. It was how people behaved in Hollywood: Love and marriage were what you did until the next romance came along. But it was not how it was supposed to be. She thought of her mother and father, never wavering, together to the end. She struggled with uncertainty, disappointment, and apprehension, questions of right and wrong, what she was doing in that town, what she was becoming.

In December, Ava and Bappie went to Raleigh to be with their mother for the Christmas season. Ava had planned on a January visit, but Molly had become very ill early in December and no one knew how bad it might get. They arrived at the Grimes house on Fairview Road on the eighteenth. Molly was tucked under blankets on the living room couch. It seemed she had aged a dozen years since Ava had seen her the previous January. Molly beamed and cried with happiness at the embrace of her glamorous daughter. They sat together and talked and laughed. They exchanged gossip about Hollywood and Smithfield and Rock Ridge. They celebrated Ava's birthday, and they celebrated Christmas. Bappie and Inez baked the chocolate and the white coconut cakes as one or another in the family had done since Ava was born. There were presents for everyone from the fancy stores on Wilshire Boulevard.

Ava departed on the twenty-eighth. The newspaper in Raleigh reported that she was eagerly returning to her husband in anticipation of their first wedding anniversary.

In reality the marriage was over. On January 15, after four months of ambivalent reconciliation, Ava filed for a formal separation.

Mickey surrendered to her wishes, succumbed to the legal fact of it. But her loss obsessed him. He was full of self-recriminations, abstract jealousies. Why hadn't he done better? Who would be taking his place? There were some people at the studio who said you could see his distress on film; he looked older than Judge Hardy. What a dame could do to you! Some nights he drove around her apartment house and made himself crazy thinking about her: "Ava in the shower. Ava in bed . . . Ava with a parade of guys, singly and in bunches." It was impossible to accept that he could not have her again.

Ava waited to see what the reaction would be. Would the studio turn against her, despite Mickey's assurances to the contrary? Would she be shunned at the nightspots and restaurants where Mickey's patronage was valued and frequent? She decided to stay away from them rather than have an unpleasant time. Instead, she would try to do something less frivolous and contribute her presence to the local USO, bringing good cheer to the servicemen on leave. Once in a while someone from Johnston County would turn up, an old schoolmate or a relative, now in uniform, bound for overseas and the fighting. She would chat and dance with them, introduce them to some stars, take them out to dinner or home for hot dogs and beers.

Metro did keep her on. Mickey, certainly, had done nothing to impede her employment. And when a friend eventually persuaded her to go back to Romanoff's one night for dinner, Mike Romanoff himself came to greet her and escort her to one of the better tables. For better or worse, it seemed Hollywood was not ready to send her back where she came from.

On a morning in January in Los Angeles, Howard Hughes read with interest the newspaper item about the breakup of Mickey Rooney and wife. He looked with even greater interest at the photograph of the sumptuous brunette pictured standing beside her diminutive husband.

Hughes twisted the page with the photo in the direction of a nearby underling and with a thin smile said, "The little runt couldn't satisfy her."

Hughes, a busy man, often looked for new friends in the newspaper, also in magazines, new movies he privately screened, and in pictorial calendars of the sort that hung on the walls of barbershops. He liked very young girls, very sexy and especially sexy and bosomy girls, and he liked movie stars, who were often in possession of those first-named enticing characteristics as well as offering in their renown proof of his power to attain what other men imagined unattainable. Hughes was also particularly enthused about dating young women who were freshly separated or divorced and therefore he imagined in a state of great sexual avidity.

Hughes left the initial contact with Ava to an operative named Johnny Meyer, his press aide, fixer, and liaison with the female gender. Meyer was a man of many talents, and could schmooze up a date for his boss with a beauty contest winner and bribe a United States senator in the same afternoon. He went to Ava to "size her up" and reported back with a ringing endorsement. She was gorgeous, friendly, just what the doctor ordered. Hughes then called and asked her out to dinner and she agreed, at least in part because Meyer had implied that Hughes might be on the lookout for a new star for one of his pictures. She felt no great new compulsion about her career, if that was what it was called, but she had to pay some mind to her future; it was a tentative time with MGM, they had not gotten rid of her, but their intentions were not clear.

The man who came to her door for their dinner date was tall, rail thin, with the lined, rawboned face of a cowboy or a leathery farmer. At once he reminded her of her father. He behaved with a confidence bordering on the arrogant, but in his manner there was also something shy, boyish, and absentminded, something like the diffident charm of Gary Cooper.

Howard Hughes was, in 1943, not yet forty years old and the most legendary and flamboyant rich man in America. The son of a Texas tycoon, orphaned and an inheritor of millions as a teenager, he had lived an impossibly colorful life, at once a powerful businessman, highly independent filmmaker, and reckless, wildcat adventurer. He was an inventor, a record-

setting aviator, the majority owner of Trans World Airlines, and a celebrated ladies' man whose string of famous girlfriends had already included Jean Harlow, Billie Dove, Ginger Rogers, Katharine Hepburn, and
Bette Davis.

Ava, for most of her first, perfectly pleasant evening with the man, gave
no thought to his wealth, his legend, or anything else, having come out on
the mistaken understanding that she was with movie director Howard
Hawks. Hughes took the mixup with modest amusement (oddly, Hughes
had recently fired Hawks and taken his place on his latest film production
The Outlaw). Ava found him at the outset a charming fellow, quirkily
funny, interesting. They were fellow Capricorns, in fact shared the same
Christmas Eve birthday. When he asked her out again she agreed readily,
and soon they were seeing each other several times a week and more.

Though he was often crude and lustfully chauvinistic about women to
the aides who helped him manage his social life, Hughes played it modest
to a fault with his new companion. For the first few weeks he pressed to be
allowed to kiss her on the cheek, but nothing more, which was all to the
good, as Ava did not find him an appealing prospect as a lover. As she re-
lated to friends then and through the years ahead, for all the affection she
came to feel for the man as their friendship progressed, they were sexually
incompatible as far as she was concerned. She simply could not relate to
him that way. In time, she would have more specific reasons for avoiding
his bed: he was too strange, had an offensive body odor, and there were
rumors from reliable sources that he was infected with a venereal disease.
Hughes pursued her with patience, certain of his ultimate victory. He was
crazily generous with her. She would later complain that you had to watch
yourself not to say anything nice about anything or glance too long at
something in a store window or Howard would rush off and buy it for
you. Ava's sister and her girlfriends at the studio would listen to this complaint and not sympathize.

But it was not all fur coats and baubles he bestowed. Some of his gifts
were of a more personal and humane sort and were received much more
warmly by Ava. He learned that she was a dog lover and had not had a dog
since she was a child (the family pet had been lost on the road when they
moved from North Carolina to Virginia) and one day Howard presented
her with a young Belgian sheepdog. Of course, the pooch was exceptional,
trained by the top performing-animal trainer in Hollywood; the dog could

walk itself and practically make its own dinner. There was another time, a day she had called back east to talk to her mother and Molly had been in a lot of pain and could not come to the phone. And Ava was distraught, and Hughes arrived and asked what was wrong. She told him about her mother and he said he wanted to help and a few days later one of the country's top cancer specialists arrived at Molly's home in Raleigh. It had seemed to Ava the most generous and the most amazing thing anyone had ever done.

He moved in on her life. He seemed to know what she was doing, what she needed, at any given time, and he or an underling was there at once to provide it. He would book her for dates weeks into the future, and if his business called him away he had John Meyer drop whatever he was doing—probably corrupting a government employee—and hurry around to be Ava's surrogate date at Ciro's or the Mocambo. When she was looking for a doctor for herself Howard arranged for her to see one of his, Dr. William Smith. "She was a wonderful girl, still a small-town girl in many ways then," Dr. Smith recalled. "She came for a routine checkup when I first saw her. At the time I was taking care of Howard Hughes, and he would send me all his young ladies. I guess he and Ava were an item at the time. But he had a lot of items then."

For a time Hughes seemed content with their flirtatious but platonic friendship. A kiss good night at the doorway, a brief squeeze of her hand at the wrist. Then one evening, over dinner at Preston Sturges's Players Club, Hughes produced a little velvet box and slid it over to Ava, instructing her to open it. The box contained a substantial square-cut emerald ring.

"Howard, what is this?"

"It's an engagement ring."

"And who's supposed to be getting engaged?"

"We are. I want you to marry me."

"Don't be silly, Howard."

"Yes. Yes, you will."

"No, I won't."

"Well . . . I don't much like that."

Ava thought it was ridiculous. They weren't in love. She didn't love him. He had never hinted at such a thing before, and now he acted surprised when she turned him down. For Pete's sake, she was still married to

Mickey Rooney! But Hughes was only following his standard procedure, in romance as in business. He had plied many women with proposals and engagement rings in the past and would do so in the years to come. In fact the emerald ring he offered Ava had already spent time on the finger of Ginger Rogers. Hughes looked upon such utterances and such offerings with the dispassionate eye of an Indian trader. They were made in simple exchange for something he wanted and that apparently could not be gotten cheaper. It was thought by those who would make a study of his psychological makeup that Hughes, due to the peculiarities of his childhood and the probable presence of an undetected mental illness, was without normal interpersonal guidelines and was incapable of feelings of love. His relationships were fueled by lust and curiosity and sustained by a cold-blooded obsessiveness. The "sanctity of marriage," the sacredness of love, meant nothing to him. He was capable of plighting his troth almost at will and without a trace of guilt. He was once engaged at the same time to both Lana Turner and Linda Darnell. When he first proposed marriage to Ava, Hughes was simultaneously pursuing an interest in a teenage Jane Greer (in time to come the noir vixen of *Out of the Past*), while at his mansion in Los Angeles he was keeping a seventeen-year-old mistress, and at the same time he had scattered around the city other females in various stages of "cultivation." Nevertheless in the months ahead he pursued Ava Gardner with an appearance of righteous single-mindedness, for all the world as if she were the only girl in the world. He told John Meyer and others he had found in her the ultimate beauty: "I can do no better."

Meanwhile a humble development occurred in the slow professional ascent of the actress Ava Gardner. Ben Thau informed her that she was being given a featured role in a movie. Whether the assignment was somehow connected to alimony negotiations with Rooney or to the fact that she was now making a hundred dollars a week on her contract and there was more reason to seek a return on MGM's money is not clear. In either case it was no proof of their faith in her talent, since the breakthrough role was to be done on loan-out to another and considerably less prestigious studio. Monogram was a small B-picture factory that specialized in three- and five-day Westerns, cheap serials, and the like. Ava's assignment was a quickie called *Ghosts on the Loose,* the latest entry in the

East Side Kids series, starring Leo Gorcey, Huntz Hall, Bobby Jordan, and so on, the continuing adventures of the juvenile delinquents introduced on film in *Dead End* in 1937 and now grown into knuckleheaded adults. Playing the sister of Hall's "Glimpy Williams," Ava in the film gets married and heads with her new husband for their honeymoon cottage only to find it is being used by Nazi propagandists led by Bela Lugosi; the East Side Kids come to a noisy rescue. Shot in a week at Monogram's tiny redbrick base, the production startled the actress with its shoddiness and haste. There was no time to rehearse anything, and when cues were missed or props dropped, they just kept on going. The conditions on the set were too hurried and rough-hewn for her to feel her usual butterflies, not enough attention was paid her to allow her to become self-conscious. You went to your mark on the dirty, scuffed floor and did what you were told; and by the time you did it the people behind the camera were already paying attention to something else. Director William Beaudine shot everything in the primitive, unblinking style of Edwin Porter's *The Great Train Robbery* of 1903; the camera turned and the actors shouted and bumped into one another, and you moved on. Ava's part called for a few lines spoken, a few expressions of bemusement, and a lot of affectionate gazing upon her bridegroom. She found Bela Lugosi to be a sweet old man, and she went on a dinner date with her lumpish and unskilled leading man, Rick Vallin. For Ava there was one satisfaction derived from the assignment, an unexpected thrill a few months later when she and Bappie were walking in Hollywood and came upon a grindhouse marquee that read: *GHOSTS ON THE LOOSE* STARRING AVA GARDNER, the first such recognition she had ever received.*

Howard Hughes continued his pursuit, plying Ava with gifts and increasingly fantastic offers, most of which she met with indifference or annoyance. The more he tried, the more she would feel he was trying to buy her favors. Did he think she was a courtesan? That he simply had to find the

---

*The movie had a brief cult following among teenage doofuses who caught repeat screenings in the belief that you could hear Bela Lugosi screaming the word *Shit* during an on-screen sneeze, a wild transgression in 1940s cinema; on examining the footage my guess is that the inscrutable Hungarian merely mispronounced the word *Ah-choo!*

right price and she could be bought? She wished he could relax and enjoy their companionship as she was doing. Why couldn't they just be friends? Howard was fun and crazily exciting. Mickey was a star with money to burn and had shown her a big-spending life she had never known, but Hughes made Mickey seem like a boy who had just gotten paid from his paper route. Howard was a kind of wizard, capable of breathtaking acts of magic. Did you want to fly to the desert at Palm Springs for dinner? Or to Acapulco for the weekend? Did you crave a quart of barbecue from Scott's in Goldsboro (her favorite—the secret sauce had come to the Reverend Scott in a dream—)? You had only to ask; Howard had only to snap his fingers. Of course she enjoyed it. But then Howard would go too far, expect too much, and she would have to put her foot down, sometimes a stiletto-heeled foot right on his instep. It became a kind of game, a teasing, sometimes torturous game at which she was becoming increasingly adept. Hughes took it and came back for more, though there were times when his patience would snap. One weekend he had taken her on a trip to San Francisco—planned an elaborate, grand weekend that seems to have been intended to lead up to another proposal of marriage. Ava had grown bored and was reading the comic strips just when Hughes had expected her to be eating out of his palm. He slapped the paper away in a sudden rage, and Ava's temper flared back twice as fast and hot.

As Mickey Rooney had done, Hughes went to work making Bappie an ally. It didn't take much effort. Bappie would repeatedly growl at her in disbelief. "You've got the goddamn richest man in the goddamn country wants to marry you and you turn him down?"

Ava tried to tell her of the man's eccentricities, weirdnesses, hygiene problems. He ate exactly the same meal every day of the year (steak and peas, the latter numbered exactly twenty-five). He hatched million-dollar deals at gas station pay phones like a cheap traveling salesman, afraid that the government had his office telephones tapped. He wore dirty old clothes and tennis sneakers unless he was forced to wear a presentable or formal outfit. Then he put on something out of a box direct from the nearest clothes store, or on one memorable occasion a Roaring Twenties vintage linen suit and celluloid collar that looked like wardrobe from a revival of *Good News*. Ava harbored a growing suspicion that he was certifiably crazy.

To all that Bappie said, So what? Then Ava would say that anyway she wasn't in love with him. And then Bappie would tell her that *she* was crazy.

Once Ava and Howard were fighting and Ava refused to make up, and Hughes summoned Bappie to act as mediator. She came running to her sister with news of Howard's peace offerings: rings and bracelets, diamonds and rubies, piled in a heap like a sultan's treasure, waiting for her. Bappie was orgasmic. Ava said: "Tell him to fuck off!"

In the second week of May 1943, Howard took Ava and Bappie to Las Vegas, Nevada, piloting them himself. They took a suite at the El Rancho, one of the few resort lodgings in a town that had not yet found its fame. On the morning of May 16, Hughes left Ava and Bappie to breakfast and the swimming pool and drove out to Lake Mead, where he was flying some test runs in his beloved Sikorsky amphibian before handing the aircraft over to the government for military use in the war. Hughes took the controls, with his mechanic and flight engineer and two representatives of the Civil Aeronautics Administration (CAA) sitting beside and behind him. The plane went up in the bright desert sky, banked around Hoover Dam, and after a short scenic cruise descended again on the lake's Vegas Wash. On touching the water the plane spun out of control. It tore and split in several places and one of the propellers shot loose and flew at the cockpit, and sliced away half of mechanic Richard Felt's head. The ravaged parts of the aircraft churned in the water and then began to sink to the bottom of the lake, taking along the body of one of the men from the CAA who was trapped in his seat. Hughes, the other aeronautics man, and the flight engineer, clutching Felt's blood-slicked body, managed to swim away and were rescued by an approaching boat.

Hughes had a gash in his forehead but was otherwise physically unharmed. He returned to Las Vegas in the afternoon. He had had to discard his waterlogged clothes and someone got him a cheap pair of pants and shirt to put on, both several inches too small for his six-foot-plus frame, leaving his pale belly and calves exposed. When he walked in on Ava and Bappie at the hotel, Ava burst out laughing.

Hughes said, "I've killed two men."

On May 21, Ava was granted an interlocutory decree for divorce from Mickey Rooney. She had asked for no alimony, accepting a cash settlement of twenty-five thousand dollars (approximately ten weeks of Rooney's salary), plus the fur coat and jewels she had accumulated from her husband, a fraction of what she might have gotten if she had wanted to fight for it; MGM promised to be grateful in return for her not taking their boy to the cleaners. The divorce decree would be final in one year.

On the same day she received the news that she had been expecting and dreading for months. Her mother was gone. She had been taken to the hospital at Raleigh, and in the morning just after sunup she passed away. Molly was fifty-nine years old (the same age at which her husband, Jonas, had died).

It was wartime, and flights east were perpetually, totally booked, but Howard Hughes did what was necessary (that is, canceling other passengers' reservations) and Ava and Bappie flew out to arrive for the Sunday funeral in Smithfield. A connection to Raleigh-Durham was missed or a flight cancelled—they arrived too late. For the sake of the two sisters a special graveside service was conducted on the following day.

Ava remained in town till the end of the week, grieving.

She went out by herself to the Teacherage and some of the other places where her mother had lived her life. She stood in her mother's kitchen, imagining it as it had been and the swirl of activity when Molly had cooked her glorious meals, and she thought about how happy it had made her mother to make other people happy.

She couldn't be sure when they had begun spying on her. At first it was just a feeling on the back of her neck. They came in shifts to her apartment house, sat in their cars across the street. Then sometimes she saw one of them outside a restaurant or a nightclub, the same cars, the same guys sitting in the dark watching her. It took a while longer to find out that Howard was responsible, that he had her under twenty-four-hour surveillance. When she confronted him about it he said he was just looking out for her. Howard said he had secret sources in Washington who told him that Nazi spies might be trying to get to him through the people he cared about. She had no idea—not yet, anyway—that Howard had all his girls followed and watched, that photographs were taken and reports filed, that he had his own spy ring that the Nazis would have envied.

Though he seemed to Ava to have become a major presence in her life, she was severely compartmentalized in his. When they were together he spoke only elliptically of his day's events, and she had only the vaguest knowledge of the many other facets of his eventful existence, his responsibilities to business interests like TWA and Hughes Oil, his overseeing the fulfillment of huge military contracts and his other complex and often nefarious dealings with the American government, his legal and public relations battles with censors over the release and exploitation of *The Outlaw*, his controversial "sex Western." And at first she knew just as little about the variety and duplicitousness of his romantic pursuits.

One night Hughes had taken Ava to see singer Frances Langford at the Cocoanut Grove. At the end of the evening they were driving back to Westwood, headed west on Santa Monica Boulevard. Stopped at a red light, Hughes looked across the street at the facing traffic and saw a familiar convertible roadster paused there waiting for the green. The light changed, the two cars moved past each other, and for a moment Hughes's eyes locked with those of the driver of the sports car, the haunting, dark, sensuous eyes of Hughes's seventeen-year-old "fiancée," Faith Domergue.

Faith: just fifteen—but a disconcertingly sultry fifteen—when she had come aboard Hughes's 320-foot private yacht Southern Cross *for a Warner Bros. publicity event. With the wary blessings of her parents—who were quickly put on the company payroll—she was moved into Hughes's Los Angeles estate, becoming his protégée, his special project, privately groomed for stardom, and along the way—and sometime before the statutes of California allowed it— becoming his lover. She had been carefully nurtured and adored by this man old enough to be her father and in Faith Domergue's teenage mind she and Howard were deeply in love, betrothed, and destined to be wed sometime soon after her next birthday. He called her his "Little Baby." For much of their time together, Hughes had kept her locked away like a caged butterfly. Like a lonely Beauty to his Texas Beast, she lived a strange fairy-tale existence, alone most of every day, roaming the halls of a palatial aerie at the peak of Sorbonne Road. Now, at seventeen, and in receipt of a shiny new sports car from her patron, Faith did on occasion get out of the house.*

There was a squealing of rubber behind them as the roadster did a sudden U-turn. Hughes looked up to the rearview to see the sports car following them. He turned down a side street and then another, trying to lose her. Ava, languidly resting beside him, felt the surge in speed and glanced up to see Howard twisting his head front and back, and then to see through the car window a flashy convertible coming up as if to pass them in the oncoming lane.

"Christ, what is she doing?!" he said.

Ava saw the young woman behind the wheel. For a moment a streetlamp flashed by at an angle to light up her face, and her eyes seemed to be glaring past Howard and directly at Ava.

Now there were cars coming from the other direction, aimed for a head-on collision with the convertible. Howard took a sharp, sudden right turn into a deserted parking lot on Fairfax.

"What the fuck was that about?" Ava yelled, pulling herself back into her seat.

Then the sports car was in the parking lot with them and arcing around them till it was pointed at the passenger side of the car.

Howard Hughes cried out, "Holy hell!" as Faith Domergue's car shot forward at Ava's passenger side door. The impact was only enough to leave the sedan trembling against its springs. Faith quickly backed up, returned to position like a bull about to charge, gunned her engine, and sped forward. Ava screamed and Hughes pulled her over him as the roadster crashed against the passenger door, backed up, tires squealing, came forward again—*shhbooom*!, the metal of the sedan door crumpling inward and the big car heaving in a giant convulsion. Domergue's car stopped moving. The front grille of Faith's vehicle was smeared against the crumpled passenger door and the hood spurted steam.

Another car had pulled up, and the driver got out, having witnessed the entire spectacle, and rushed over to see what could be done. Hughes urged him to get Ava away from there, take her home, and let him deal with the rest. Faith Domergue sat inside her steaming car and looked unhappy. Ava, too shocked to ask questions, made her way to the other man's vehicle and was driven away.

Howard called her the day after, explaining why she had nearly been killed by a crazed beautiful girl, how the girl was a bit delusional, an aspiring actress and so on, who had come to him for help with her career, a sad case, really, but he was going to make sure she got the proper medical help. To help her forget the upsetting night in the parking lot, he sent Ava with Bappie to Mexico City for a weekend shopping spree. He had every faith that Bappie, with his line of credit in hand, would help Ava think well of him again. One of his operatives, Charlie Guest, accompanied the sisters to Mexico and reported back on their every move.

Bappie became very fond of Charlie. He had started out as Howard's golf instructor. Soon he was being useful for a variety of odd labors, graduating to become one of the inner circle managing Hughes's romantic interests, keeping track of many of the actresses and models and young beauties; he made introductions, handled surveillance, took care of a lot of the details of housing and transportation. He was a nice guy, a quiet drunk when he wasn't working, with a world-weary, beaten-by-life style that Bappie seemed to find attractive. They began sleeping together. When Ava moved with Bappie to a two-bedroom bungalow in Bel Air, Charlie moved in with them. For Howard it was a bonus, having his own man right inside the henhouse. On the other hand, Charlie, in his cups, would eventually let Ava in on many of the details of Hughes's busy personal life—the different girls stashed away, the relationship with Faith Domergue, the constant trawl for new prospects. It had all been a game with Howard, she realized. She was one of the pieces—perhaps, it was nice to think, the most valuable and desired of all of them—on Howard's game board. From Charlie she would learn the extent of Howard's spy network, the way he would send his teams to stake out a girl's life—Ava's included—taking photos, logging reports (she did not yet hear about the even more invasive room bugs and phone taps Hughes would put in place). She would confront him with her knowledge, Howard would apologize, say he was only trying to make sure she was safe. In time, of course, he would return to his sneaky ways, the snoops, the surveillance, and the intimate reports. It made you a little crazy yourself, being with Howard. She thought Charlie Guest had it right when he said that

Howard did with his relationships just what he did with his airplanes, pushed to see how much they could take before they crashed.

Their odd alliance continued. To keep Howard in her life was a great, luxurious advantage. She had been honest with him, made it clear there would be no romance and no marriage in their future. If he wanted to continue to offer his friendship and all the perquisites that went with it, she could have worse friends. There was as well an element of perverse play in what they had together. As Hughes seemed willfully, masochistically to punish himself in pursuit of her, so was there cruel pleasure to be derived in withholding herself from the man who could have everything.

Hughes carried on, obsessed with her, determined to possess her body and soul. It didn't help matters that she was still not officially free of her husband. Aware that Mickey Rooney had been sniffing around her of late, looking to make a reentry in his almost-ex-wife's life, Hughes urged her to go to Las Vegas and finalize her divorce with a six-weeks' residence rather than waiting the entire year for the California decree (since 1931 the renegade state of Nevada had offered streamlined marriage and divorce laws in addition to legal gambling).

It was a good idea, Ava thought, to get it done with Mickey and move on with her life. And so, at the end of July 1943, with Howard's blessing and financing and with one of his minions to fetch for her, Ava headed into the desert. "She just wants to get it over with," Bappie told a reporter.

She checked into the Last Frontier and remained there for much of the next six weeks. Even the isolated resort showed the tumult of the war. Soldiers were everywhere, and all across the lobby and up and down the halls were stressed families and straggling kids come to visit their husbands and fathers stationed at the training camps outside town. Many of these camp followers, to the dismay of the management, had turned the swank lodging into something more like a hobo jungle, cooking on little burners in their rooms, hanging laundry from the windows. There were young lovers on a last weekend together, tearful girls saying good-bye to their soldier boyfriends about to go off to the unknown. Ava Gardner—there to divorce a movie star, enjoying the patronage of a millionaire twice her age—could only look upon it all as upon a scene from another world. Each morning after breakfast she lay by the pool in one of her hundred-dollar swimsuits from I. Magnin, oiled and glistening in the 115-degree summer heat, under the Nevada sun. Each day went by like the last. On the forty-second day her divorce was granted, and she returned to Los Angeles a single woman again.

The funny thing was, she went looking for Mickey and not the other way around. The studio had given her a nice part, a funny part. One of the casting guys said, "This is a cute piece. You could do something with this if you wanted."

It was another in the Dr. Gillespie series (until 1942 the Dr. Kildare series, when Lew Ayres, in the title role, had refused military service as a conscientious objector and the names Ayres and Kildare became anathema to Louis B. Mayer), hospital dramas starring Lionel Barrymore and now a newcomer, Van Johnson. The innocent yet tawdry plot of *Three Men in White* concerned Gillespie's attempts to test the resolve of Dr. Van. Ava was to play, along with blond starlet Marilyn Maxwell, a tongue-in-cheek temptress. There was in the part a little sex, a little romance, and a touch of comedy. She rehearsed at home, but the rehearsals would end with a cry of despair.

"I can't act! I can't do this fucking thing!" she would scream to Bappie, who was blandly feeding her Van Johnson's lines.

Mickey had been her greatest acting coach by far. Whatever his faults, he was a brilliant actor, and when he talked her through a performance and told her how to feel and the technical tricks he knew by the million, she could understand and know what she was doing and make it work. She called her ex-husband. "Mick, can you help me?"

Baby, anything.

They went to a quiet place for dinner and went over the dialogue, and Mickey was a great help. He showed her which lines she wanted to throw away and which ones to really sell. How to use her eyes to let the camera know she had something on her mind but didn't want to come right out and say it. They went over the lines, and they finished dinner and had a drink, and then they went to bed.

She hadn't intended anything like that to happen. But the evening had been so nice, he had been charming, she had been horny. What could you do?

It became a little thing they had. It wasn't every night or even every week. But now and again he would call and say, "How about dinner tonight, Ava?" Or, "How'd you like to go see Dorsey tonight at the Palladium?" and now and then they would end up spending the night together.

They would sometimes make a game of Hughes's spying, Ava said, and evade the pursuit cars and the detectives staked out on the street. What Ava didn't know was that Hughes had her home bugged with recording devices, devices in every room. One day when he returned to LA from business in the East, Hughes was brought up to date with his surveillance agents, and when it came to the report on Ava Gardner he learned that she had not always been alone, that the tapes from her bedroom had recorded evidence of sexual activity, and that some of the recordings were very loud.

One night Ava had come home after dinner out and gone right to bed. She was tired, had to be at the studio by dawn the next morning, and made it an early night. She had been asleep for a while when the lights suddenly came on and she awoke to see Howard Hughes standing over her and glowering like an irate vampire.

"Howard! What are you doing here?"

"I want to talk to you!"

"Get out of my room at once!"

Hughes, disconcerted, admitted he had expected to find her in bed with a man. His spies had screwed up their report, Ava decided, and Howard had come running to expose her. She was shaking with anger. The damned man had gone too far. She pulled on her clothes, stormed outside, screaming at the richest man in the world.

"I won't be fucking spied on! I'm not your goddamn property, you son-of-a-bitch!"

Hughes reddened, opened his mouth to speak. Words seemed no good. His hand lashed out at her as hard as he could, straight at the face, knocking her backward across the couch. The slap had caught her on the eye, stung badly.

Howard stepped back and turned away in instant dismay at what he had done. It was too late. She gave a cry of rage, reached for something, anything, finding a heavy ornamental bronze bell. As Howard came toward her she launched it at him right between the eyes. The bell emitted one flat, echoless ring as it met with flesh, bone, and teeth.

Howard stumbled, blood running from his face. Ava scrambled around again and found a wooden desk chair, dragging it along the carpet and then swinging it into the air. As Ava remembered it, the housemaid tackled her and stopped her from crashing the chair down on his head and neck and killing Howard Hughes. She was dragged back while Bappie and Charlie Guest rushed over and knelt to help the injured aviator. Trails of blood ran down from his nose and mouth.

"Oh, honey, look what you did to poor Howard!" Bappie said.

"Fuck poor Howard!" Ava said. "He'll never hit me again."

The maid came with a steak to put on Ava's swollen eye, and an ambulance came for Howard Hughes.

In a diary Faith Domergue kept in the 1940s, she made this entry: "There is a strange quirk in Howard, stranger than all of his other peculiarities. Once he has become involved with a project or a person, he cannot let them get away from his control. Once owning something he has to own it for always. . . . And it is the most self-destroying element of his character."

Hughes would not let a few stitches or a lost tooth get in the way of his obsession with Ava Gardner. "He stuck to me like molasses," she complained. His men continued to follow her, continued to file their reports, photographs, telephone transcripts. How did you get rid of the man? She insulted him, ignored him. On the inauguration of his new Constellation aircraft, meant to be a well-oiled publicity event, he kept a planeload of VIPs waiting at the gate for hours while he tracked her down on the telephone and begged her to come along. He paced among the celebrities, fuming, "Damn her, damn her. . . ." He called again, begged some more.

Ava was one more difficulty in what seemed to Hughes a vast sea of difficulties to be encountered throughout 1944. Potentially disastrous unraveling business deals with the government put him in a state of constant duress. A car accident that shot him through the windshield was one more blow to a head that had already sustained the impact of numerous airplane crashes (and one bronze bell). There was increasing evidence of brain damage, inherited biological flaw or chemical imbalance, a severe obsessive-compulsive disorder. Hughes himself believed he was having a nervous breakdown.

One day in October he disappeared without a trace. No one connected with his various businesses had any clue where he was hiding (or did not admit it if they did).

Ava had no more idea what had happened to him than did anyone else.

After years of the Metro executives struggling to keep him out of uniform, Mickey Rooney had at last been called into service. On June 13, 1944, he would begin a new career as a buck private. Mickey was proud to go. He had not been happy with the way the studio had made him look as if he were evading his duty. Now he was in, a soldier for the war, and whatever happened happened.

Mickey called and asked Ava to go out with him the night before his induction, and she agreed. It was a sad, sweet evening. They went to the Palladium as they had so many times before, from the first weeks they had known each other, and they talked only of the good times they had known. Full of sentiment and pride and vodka, she told Mickey she would be waiting for him when he got out.

They wrote to each other. Ava's letters were affectionate, Mickey's full of passion and plans for the future. When he had not received word from her for some time he tried to phone her at home, but Bappie or the maid fielded every call. Ava was out or working late or they just weren't sure where she was right then. He would try again many times.

One late night in the barracks somebody woke him up and said he had a long-distance call.

It was Ava. Mickey gushed, but she stopped him at once, said he would have to stop writing to her, stop calling. She said it was over between them. She had someone else. Mickey told her how he felt. It couldn't end. He loved her too much.

They spoke, but there was nothing more to be said. And after a while he realized that the line had gone dead. He found himself crying, alone in the corridor by the public phone. He cried for a while, and then, when he had pulled himself together, he went back to the room with the other GIs and went to sleep.

THREE

Femme Fatale

She was introduced to him at a party by her high-spirited, flame-haired good friend Frances (Mrs. Van) Heflin. Fran told each the other's name, but she needn't have bothered as Ava knew who he was and he—Artie Shaw—was probably not listening anyway. The two locked eyes, the grinning Frances Heflin got out of the way, and the thing began.

She had been listening to his music, loving his music, since she was sixteen or so; danced to his records a thousand times, lain before the amber glow of the Philco for a thousand nights, hearing that fantastic sound, "Begin the Beguine" and "Moonglow" and "Frenesi," the melodic swing and the soaring spirals of the leader's clarinet. No longer a starstruck kid, she had married a movie star and knew many of the famous faces of Hollywood, but this was something else, like meeting a god.

Shaw, too, in his own way, was mightily impressed. He had never heard of Ava Gardner—if he had even bothered to hear Frances say the name—didn't know what she did and most likely did not care, but the impact of her face and body was staggering. "She was," he would later say, "the most beautiful creature you ever saw."

They chatted, or Artie talked and Ava listened, and basked. She had never heard such talk, so many words, so many big words, but even if she didn't know what the hell he was talking about she gave herself over to it till it sounded as rich and enveloping as his music. Though she felt intimidated by the evident gulf in their intellectual capacities, she was pleased to feel that he liked her enough to share with her his complex and never-ending views of the world. After a while Ava said she thought she would like to get away from the crowd, get a drink somewhere, and did Artie want to come?

Shaw said that he did. (Fifty years later: "What are you going to say, No? You'd have to be an idiot.")

They went somewhere. And then the next night and the next. They went to intimate places, sat in booths over candlelight, and drank wine and talked. She would tell him how much his music had meant to her. And he would say something she would find exciting and dramatic, telling her how it was to make an ugly piece of wood come to life and how when you were really playing well it was better than anything, even sex.

She had until then known of him only as a musician and a notorious lady-killer, husband of Lana Turner, among others. She found him a brilliant, complicated man. The fact that he so clearly didn't give a shit what other people thought of him made his intimate revelations to her seem then all the more privileged. He told her how she had found him at the end of a terrible time, returning into the light from the most anguished and despairing time of his life. The war had come. There had been a line in *Time* magazine: It had read that to the average German, America meant "skyscrapers, Clark Gable, and Artie Shaw." It sounded like a special responsibility. A few months after Pearl Harbor, he enlisted in the navy. He spent his first months in service on a minesweeper. Sailors would come up to him with mocking admiration: "Can I shake the hand that held Lana Turner's tit?" Then the navy decided they wanted to use him in his natural habitat and let him lead a military band. He put together a first-rate group of guys—the Rangers—and they went off to the Pacific to entertain the troops, ferried from island to island, tramping into the jungles. They came under attack by Japanese bombers. They were on Guadalcanal during some of the worst fighting. People were wounded and killed all around them. The homesick soldiers wept when they heard Shaw and his band playing the old hit songs in the jungle ten thousand miles from home. The strain was enormous. He returned to America an emotional wreck. He lay in his bed and couldn't leave it, so depressed and disgusted with the world that he couldn't find a reason to get up. A friend led him to May Romm, a famed, unconventional psychotherapist, a European refugee then living in Los Angeles. Months of work brought him back to the world. He was finding his music again, he was playing again, he was forming a new band.

For the first weeks they went together there was no talk of bed. Surprising; she knew from the gossip columns and from friends of Artie's love-'em-and-leave-'em reputation, and at the age of thirty-four he'd already had four wives, including Lana Turner. But Artie dealt with her as a comrade, and seemed to be enjoying her company and their time together for what it was, not just as a necessary prelude to something under the sheets. His cool approach became its own form of seduction. When was he going to make his move? Didn't she appeal to him in that way? It was like the early months with Mickey or the times with Howard, only the roles were reversed. She was the one with the growing impatience for the big event. One evening, in the middle of a discussion of the mathematics of Chopin or nuclear fusion or something, he had looked at her and abruptly told her that she was in all ways the most perfect woman he had ever met and further that he would marry her in a minute if he hadn't already done that too many times, which in its perfectly Shavian way contained at the same time a boast ("Artie took it for granted that everyone was panting to marry Artie Shaw"), a put-down (he didn't think enough of her to marry her), and a great compliment (he spoke as a connoisseur of perfect women). One night they went back to Artie's Tudor mansion in Beverly Hills, and it happened and it was good.

Shaw was putting together his new group, with fresh personnel—the expressive Barney Kessel on guitar, innovative pianist Dodo "the Moose" Marmarosa, the spectacular trumpeter Roy Eldridge—and was full of new ideas and creative goals. For Ava to be there on the inside of Artie's music as it was being created was like living in a joyous dream, exciting and satisfying in ways that moviemaking had never been. Artie took his new seventeen-piece band on the road, and Ava went with him. She was the band's number one fan, cheering at every rehearsal, dancing on the sidelines of every one-night stand—"sipping bourbon, listening to the music, and having a ball." It was likely that Ava had a better time than Artie. Shaw hated touring, not the playing of the music but the people he played it for, the hoi polloi of jitterbugging teenagers. He felt he was creating for a serious form, a revolutionary American music to take the place of European classical, stomps the new sonatas, and here he was giving this greatness to pimpled jerks in bobby socks. He would be playing, soaring solo, his eyes closed, in communion with the infinite, then open his eyes and see some kid popping his bubble gum. The horror! Unlike the leaders of some other popular bands, Shaw had always refused to pander to audiences with funny hats and novelty numbers, and he added strings, even a harpsichord, to his lineup, as if to distance his music from the simple needs of the saddle-shoed hordes. His less-than-inviting attitude was evident in his chosen theme song (all the big bands had an identifying theme, usually something pleasant and hummable); Shaw's theme was "Nightmare," a film noir bad trip set to music. Still, the crowds would not be turned away, and Shaw continued to suffer as a king of swing. The new tour was a hit, though Artie refused to enlarge it to the kind of endless cross-country ordeal he had felt forced to do in the past.

Somewhere in this period Shaw suggested that Ava become the band's vocalist. He had heard her singing to herself in the shower, probably heard from her about the time she had auditioned in New York. She sounded good enough, and she looked great. He said they would rehearse until she felt ready, put a chorus behind her, the works.

"You'll look gorgeous up there," he told her. "Better than all of them combined."

It would be her great fantasy fulfilled, but she sensed that it would never work. Already aware of Artie's demand for perfection in his music, she could foresee the trouble it was bound to bring to their relationship. He kept at her about it for a while, but she refused even to sit in some night for a single tune.

They were on the road for her birthday and for New Year's Eve. In New York City on January 9 the band made their first recordings together. One of Artie's new compositions was a tribute to Ava he was titling "The Grabtown Grapple." He cut the track with his chamber jazz spinoff known as the Gramercy Five (a septet on this occasion). It was a raucous jive paean to their sex life, a pumping nonstop beat interrupted by eruptions of wailing pleasure.

They traveled to Chicago and then back to California for a series of shows up and down the West Coast. On tour, Ava became friends with the band's show-stealer, Roy Eldridge—aka "Little Jazz"—the trumpeter and charismatic performer late of the Gene Krupa Band (his vocal duet with Anita O'Day, "Let Me Off Uptown," was one of the high-water marks in the history of hip). Eldridge was black and a dynamic and funny guy, but he had been scarred by his encounters with racism. It was as trivial as the amount of stage space that had to be placed between Roy and the white Anita when they were performing, and as serious as threats of castration from a gang of ofay thugs. Ava, Artie, and Roy would sit at a table having drinks after a show, and Ava would feel the perturbed glances of passing strangers. Ava had never understood it, had never been a part of it even as a kid who didn't know any better, the atavistic color hatred that came so easily to so many people. Artie didn't understand her confusion: The explanation was simple, the world was chock-full of assholes.

One night they were playing somewhere in California, and Eldridge didn't show. It turned out he had gotten caught up in a fight with a bigoted doorman outside the hall. Artie became enraged, called for the manager, and demanded he "fire that cocksucker." Eldridge was so shaken up—he quit the band shortly thereafter—that he spent much of the evening in tears. Ava commiserated, held his hand. "Ava Gardner was great," Little Jazz would say many years later. "A very fine person."

To move around with Artie, Ava had all but abandoned her movie career. She was living now in the night, not on the dawn-to-dusk cycle of the studios. Shaw—who hated MGM from his conflicts with them over Lana Turner (Mayer had once lectured him on the birth control he should use so as not to impregnate their sexy star)—did not discourage her from playing hooky. The question was whether Metro cared. They appeared to have lost any real interest in developing her as a star. She had stalled at the level of supporting player in the B category. By the end of 1945, after nearly five years at the studio, she would rate no better than an eighth-billed part in the low-budget comedy *She Went to the Races*, supporting the less-than-stellar leads, James Craig and Frances Gifford. Her only encouragement at this time came from an outside source, independent producer Seymour Nebenzal, who negotiated with Metro to borrow her for the female lead in a project titled *Whistle Stop*. It was her biggest part to date, and by comparison with anything else she had done, a part with background and emotional complexity.

Whistle Stop was ostensibly an adaptation of a best-selling novel of the same name by Maritta M. Wolff, a book that had caused a bit of a sensation for its provocative sexual content. Nebenzal was an important figure in the prewar German cinema—his credits included Fritz Lang's *M*—now working in the haphazard world of the Hollywood independent. He had, in fact, produced a film (*Hitler's Madman*) in which Ava had done a few days' extra work, but it was *Whistle Stop*'s screenwriter and associate producer Philip Yordan who claimed to have introduced him to the actress one night at the Mocambo and suggested she was perfect for the female lead in their film.

Yordan, a lawyer-turned-writer with a colorful and sometimes brilliant career ahead of him, would recall a friendship with Ava Gardner that pre-dated the production. "I came to her apartment in Westwood or Beverly Hills, somewhere, it was a small party, I went with some other people. Someone—an actress who had passed out from drinking—started a fire, I don't know, she dropped a cigarette on the couch, and that was a big commotion. I met Ava that night, and we had a good time. She was a very sweet girl then. She was not a heavy drinker yet. I had to work with her later in Spain, and that was a different story."

Yordan once claimed to have had a sexual fling with the actress. Asked about this again many years later Yordan would only say, more ambiguously, "We went out. Who can remember what we did?"

Yordan's screenplay had to make considerable changes from the source material. "The book was full of stuff that could not be put into a movie," he recalled. "The brother and sister were fucking each other. The girl was a hooker. I used a very small portion of the actual book and developed the story from there. My script was very good. But Nebenzal made some poor choices. He put George Raft into this thing because he was a big name around the world and he was on the skids and we could afford him, but he looked like hell and who wanted to see this old man with Ava Gardner? It should have been a young guy like a Burt Lancaster."

Yordan maintained the opening setup of the novel—the return of a beautiful young woman from the big city to her small hometown and the uncertain rekindling of an old love affair, and the script made surprisingly explicit that the girl, Mary, had been living as a prostitute and kept woman during her Chicago sojourn. But the book's old love affair was an incestuous one between two siblings, which was of course entirely taboo in forties cinema, and so for the screen Mary's love interest went from an alluring ne'er-do-well young brother to a jowly ne'er-do-well ex-boyfriend who for some reason or other lives in Mary's home with his mother. It still felt like incest: George Raft looked old enough to be her father. After some passionate sparring between girl and ex-, the script veered off on its own in the direction of noir skullduggery, with a thwarted robbery, a murder, and a frame-up before a happy ending and the girl and the middle-aged boy walking off into the murky horizon.

Nebenzal put together a first-rate package on a constrained budget. The cast included Raft, Victor McLaglen, and George Sanders's dessicated brother Tom Conway. Cinematography was by Russell Metty (whose future work would include Orson Welles's *Touch of Evil*). The production design was by another skilled German refugee, Rudi Feld. The director assigned was Leonide Moguy, a Russian who had worked in the Soviet film industry in the years after the revolution, then fled to France and worked as a director there until the arrival of the German army, at which time he fled again and settled in Hollywood.

Whistle Stop was a mildly creditable effort in the subset genre of forties lowlife melodrama, an atmospheric evocation of a sordid small midwestern city made up entirely of bars and cocktail lounges and pool halls (even the barber shop is part of a saloon). Ava had largely risen to the occasion of her first full-bodied part, though it was obvious she was not yet in control of the instrument of her voice and she evidently had difficulties with the longer stretches of dialogue (Yordan would recall that both Ava and the veteran Raft needed to have an entire scene rewritten on the set to a manageable monosyllabic simplicity). Moguy's English was said to have been very poor, and though he treated Ava with sympathy, he could not offer her much help with her performance. He was, though, successful in capturing her nonverbal presence. She was posed, lit, and dressed to striking erotic effect. And Moguy would be the first director to imagine her as more than a utility performer, staging her mink-coated, high-heeled arrival on-screen in arresting backlit and silhouetted images that gave her the mythic aura of a presumed star.

Artie Shaw had, predictably, grown bored with touring and dissatisfied with his return to public life. He put the new band on hold and went home to ponder his future and to consider worthier endeavors. Artie and Ava lived together now in his big faux Tudor mansion on Bedford Drive. Word was not long in getting to the third floor at MGM that one of their contractees was shacked up with the—to them—notorious bandleader. Ava was warned by one of the execs that her domestic arrangements were going to lead to bad publicity and scandal. Ava ignored the advice and the veiled threats. She was in mad love, she would choose life with Artie whatever the consequences.

But time passed and they more obviously settled down as a couple. The war ended, victory over Japan declared on September 5. There was in the air then a feeling of new beginnings, everyone with fresh plans for the future. Whatever the inspiration, the idea of marriage began to seem more relevant. And Artie came around to it or didn't give a fuck—tie the knot one more time? Why not? Perhaps it would be fifth time lucky.

In the evening on October 17, 1945, they were married in the Beverly Hills home of Judge Stanley Mosk. Frances Heflin attended the bride and Artie's friend Hy Craft was best man. With Bappie, Artie's mother, Van Heflin, and a few others they went out to celebrate afterward. Artie and the new Mrs. Shaw drove to Lake Tahoe for a honeymoon, spending much of the time there in bed.

The marriage did not turn out to be such a great idea after all. Something became lost—not to be recovered—in the transition from girlfriend/mistress to wife. Ava couldn't figure it, she was the same crazy in love with him but sometimes Artie acted as if he had been sold a bill of goods. She had never, for instance, claimed any qualification for the role of conventional hausfrau, but Shaw nonetheless began to assess her in this role and not surprisingly found her wanting. One evening, as Artie told it, she had come home happy and glowing from a tennis lesson, walked in on her husband in the bedroom, and asked him, "What's for dinner?"

Said Shaw, "Ava, I do certain things for you, do I not?"

"Darling," she replied, "you do everything."

"No, wait, not everything. But certainly some things."

"Oh, darling, I know you do—"

"And, Ava, what do you do?"

"What do I do? I love you, baby."

"You love me. I love you. We're even. But I own the house. I pay the maid, the butler. I own the cars. I buy the food. What do you do? Can't you at least go down and tell *me* what we're having for dinner?"

It sometimes seemed as though the wedding had devalued her in Shaw's eyes. No longer the ravishing bauble of before, the creature of glamour and sex and freedom, she seemed now an official responsibility, like his mother, like family.

Artie Shaw could be . . . a difficult man. In the opinion of many he was arrogant and contemptuous. He had little patience for the imperfect, the banal, the obvious. The existence of the mediocre nagged at him like a bleeding ulcer. He was no less hard on himself, cursing particularly the precious time he had squandered on the mindless pursuit of attractive females. "What was I doing with those women I was living with?" he would reflect in later years. "I was thinking with my groin, that's all. I had no connection with those people. Lana Turner might as well have been a Martian."

It was no different with Ava. He was, certainly, not dismissive of the value of simple human beauty, as appreciative of his wife's physical splendor as everyone else. "She was a goddess," he would say. "I would stare at her, literally stare in wonder." But it was not enough. He would become dismayed—even angered—by her lack of education, by her lack of interest in the world beyond the latest records, fashions, the gossip from her damnable movie studio. He would try to educate her on a subject that interested him—science, history, literature—and then wait to gauge the result, which was usually to his mind disappointing. He was abrasive by nature—his father had been a rough, unpleasant fellow, and his mother could be infuriating, they bickered his whole childhood—and was prone to respond to disappointment with stinging rebukes and outright insults.

Some women—Lana, for instance—were lured by the surface attraction of the handsome, dapper, supercool music star, and then fled when the egocentric posturing began to surface (quoth Lana: "The most conceited, unpleasant man I ever met"). But Ava had fallen head over heels, and in concert with (what the analysts would now call) her own issues of low self-esteem, she accepted Artie's rising tide of arrogance and rebukes, commiserated with his disappointment in her. She was a hick, dumb, lazy, had never put heart and soul into anything, hadn't even kept up with her tutorials at MGM—Artie was right on the money. From the beginning of their relationship, she remembered, in their first conversations, she had felt such a sense of inferiority that she shaved a couple of years off her age, thinking that a dumb nineteen-year-old didn't seem as bad as a dumb twenty-one-year-old.

Once, changing trains in Chicago, Ava had gone off to buy a book, and Artie had been horrified when she came back with a copy of the bodice-ripping best seller *Forever Amber*—trash! (Ava liked to tell that story for its coda: that Artie later married Kathleen Winsor, *Forever Amber*'s author.) Ava had sheepishly admitted that she never read anything, hated to read, that the last book she had finished was *Gone With the Wind* many years ago and that was only because she was not going to be the only person in North Carolina who hadn't read it. Artie gave her a syllabus for her lost soul. She went to the bookstore in Beverly Hills with the list: *Babbitt* by his friend Red Lewis, *Buddenbrooks*, *The Brothers Karamazov*, *Madame Bovary*, *The Magic Mountain*. She said Artie had made her bring a copy of Darwin's *Origin of Species* on their honeymoon.*

"Artie Shaw and his mental domination," wrote Lena Horne, who had known him earlier and became a good friend of Ava's, ". . . he liked his women to read a lot of books. And he'd pick the books. But she wasn't ready for them. It's kind of like a child of nature being shut up in a room to study." Shaw, wrote Pete Martin in the *Saturday Evening Post*, "resembled a man determined to teach a willing but unweaned kitten how to drink milk from a saucer."

Screenwriter and novelist Budd Schulberg was one of Artie's writer friends in this period. He would recall, "The trouble with Artie, he really was a male chauvinist. The only sort of thing he could think to say about her was what a beautiful ass she had. He would praise her physically but never showed much interest in her as a person, treated her like a dumbbell. He'd ask her a question and he'd say, 'Oh, just forget it, you wouldn't understand!' He looked down at her mentally. She was unknowing about pol-

---

*Ava once met Darwin's great-grandson Francis at a Greek restaurant in New York and mentioned her honeymoon reading matter; after their encounter, Young Darwin, who had been drinking retsina, said—adjusting his spectacles—that Ava Gardner was "the highest specimen of the human species."

itics of the time, things that might have been of interest to Artie. But she was not dumb. She was just very uneducated. She didn't know much.

"I don't remember her ever giving it back to Artie. She just kind of took it. And it made her feel bad."

Ruth Rosenthal, the wife of Ava's lawyer, remembered a time a group of people had been sitting around talking and Ava had typically slipped off her shoes and tucked her bare feet under her on the chair. She told writer Charles Higham, "Artie looked at her coldly and said in front of everyone, 'For God's sake, what are you doing? Do you think you're still in a tobacco field?' Well, she went white, she trembled, she cried. It was ghastly." Rosenthal would say it was in this period that Ava first began to drink in earnest, not for pleasure but for escape. "I think it eased her pain, and she stuck with it after that."

One drunken night of arguing, needling, and tears, she stormed out of the house, into her car, tearing through the streets of Beverly Hills, trying with a mind spinning from too many insults and shots of Wild Turkey to remember the way to Van and Frances Heflin's house. The police spotted her speeding and weaving and gave chase. They roared through the posh, sleeping neighborhood, the cops catching up only when she braked her car on the Heflins' lawn. Van came to the doorway and found Ava Gardner crouched on his porch with a policeman aiming a revolver at her forehead.

"I was so much in love," she would write of her second husband. "I adored and worshipped him, and I don't think he ever really understood the damage he did."

She became, inevitably, a convert to Shaw's religion, psychiatry. She began seeing doctors and therapists from May Romm's circle of Freudians. One administered, at Ava's own pleading, an intelligence test. With great relief she learned that she was not an idiot, was in fact high above average in intelligence, though the doctor suggested that her perfectly good mind had yet to be taken out of the box that it came in.

Less reassuring: Her therapy sessions pried open a vast array of supposed subconscious repressions and psychosomatic disorders. She would now be led to believe that the chronic abdominal pains she had suffered for years and that no physician could diagnose were caused by guilt for abandoning her mother to die in North Carolina while she fulfilled a frivolous destiny in Hollywood; that her anxiety about having children was rooted in a fear of the cancer that had attacked her mother's womb and had done the same to her grandmother. (Ava would often speak of a desire to have kids and doted on young relatives and the children of friends, but there is no evidence to suggest she ever deliberately sought to become pregnant. Mickey Rooney claimed that after sex with him one night—although in the declining days of the marriage—she had said, "If you ever knock me up I'll kill you." Ava would later reprove Artie for not wanting to have a child, but Shaw denied it and told her it had been entirely her decision always to run to the bathroom and insert a diaphragm before they made love.)

In her memoir she would recall her time in analysis without regret. "I found it," she wrote, "a great help." But observers of Ava in this period and after, and her own early comments, describe a more complicated and largely negative response. To more than one friend she would say, "The head shrinkers made me crazy."

In the spring, without warning, Artie told her they were moving. He was selling his Tudor mansion on Bedford Drive, and they were off to live at a more modest house he had leased in Burbank, near Warner Bros. The family that had rented them the Burbank place found themselves unable to occupy their own new home right away as planned, and so for a time Ava and Artie were unlikely housemates with a middle-class suburban family with two young teenage kids (one of them fond of playing records by the dreaded Guy Lombardo at top volume). The move was a giant drop in their comfort level, and Ava claimed that Artie gave her no reasonable explanation for it. They seemed to argue about everything now, and she was frequently in tears. Their sex life had gradually declined in frequency and intensity. She began to believe that he no longer loved her.

Ava had hardly worked a day in the seven months since finishing *Whistle Stop*. She had gone to a preview screening and had wanted to walk out; the picture and her performance seemed to her equally bad. She was twenty-three and she felt faded, her opportunities slipping behind her and nothing ahead. Her studio did not know what to do with her after five years. Her husband seemed to be tiring of her. Instead of making movies she was taking extension courses at UCLA, trying to improve her mind, trying to impress Artie that he had not married a dunce. They were living in a crummy little house now, and she didn't understand why. Her stomach pains had returned, and she often felt the need to vomit. She lost weight. Three times a week she saw her psychiatrist. She couldn't bear to read another page of *Buddenbrooks*. She drank.

One day Metro called. It wasn't a part, only someone who wanted to talk to her about a part. And of course it was nobody at MGM. His name was Mark Hellinger, and he was making a picture at Universal called *The Killers*.

Hellinger: one of the great reporter-mythologists of New York City, a rival and comrade of Walter Winchell and Damon Runyon, a son of Orthodox Jews become the caricature of a Broadway sharpie, perennially dressed like a comic-strip gangster, with his dark serge suits and dark blue shirts and white ties. He drove around Hollywood in a bulletproof Isotta Fraschini limousine that had belonged to the racketeer Chink Sherman (whose body would be found in a Catskills lime pit). His wife was Gladys Glad, a legendary showgirl from the Ziegfeld Follies. He wrote wry and sentimental columns and short stories about the Manhattan demimonde, the same guys and dolls as Runyon, but Hellinger was a nicer guy. Prohibition ended, the Depression began, and New York lost some of its Arabian Nights luster, so Hellinger went West to write movies. He had a flair for pictures and became an associate producer at Warner Bros., working with production chief Hal Wallis, overseeing such Warner's hits as *The Roaring Twenties, They Drive by Night,* and *High Sierra.* Then, not wanting to miss out on the biggest story of the century, Hellinger left town, sending himself to the South Pacific as a war reporter. Back in Hollywood in 1945 he refused to return to work with the unbearable Jack Warner, who fully recognized Hellinger's special talent for moviemaking and still treated him as if he had just caught him stealing his wallet. Instead Hellinger formed his own company in a production and distribution alliance with Universal-International, and in the summer of '45 he was ready to make his first picture.

Hellinger wanted to make an impact with that first one. He wanted it to be a sensation, to make a fortune, and to put him on the map as the new big name in town, the postwar David O. Selznick, only a snappier dresser. He gave Universal a few ideas. They were ready to move ahead with an adaptation of a play called *The Hero*, and a script was being prepared. It was a cynical character study ultimately produced and released under the title *Swell Guy*, starring Sonny Tufts, and it was Hellinger's only failure as a producer. Soon, though, he realized that *The Hero* was not going to put anybody on the map, and he turned back to an idea he had been nursing since before he left Warner Bros.: an adaptation of Ernest Hemingway's 1927 short story "The Killers." Hellinger's experience and strength had always been in tough-guy melodrama, and Hemingway's famous story was one of the touchstones in the history of hard-boiled literature, the brief, brutal account of two hired gunmen terrorizing the occupants of a small-town diner in their attempt to locate and murder a local resident known as "the Swede." As strict narrative—leaving aside the haunting overlay—it was no more than a single situation, the scope of a two-reeler in Hollywoodspeak. But Hellinger saw it as a springboard, Hemingway's compelling scene out of which a feature-length story could be drawn. Plus it was Hemingway, and a famous and memorable title. "The exploitation values," Hellinger told Universal executive Bob Sparks in September 1945, "are little short of gigantic."

Hemingway hated Hollywood, but Hellinger fancied himself an old pal of the great writer, and when he wrote to ask about the price of screen rights for the famous story, he wondered if Hem might extend him the courtesy of a discount. Hemingway's lawyer, Maurice J. Speiser, wrote back saying that Hemingway had "withdrawn all contact with the outside world" and was working on his tan, but because Hellinger was such a close and very old friend, the author was willing to sell him "The Killers" for fifty grand (which in 1945 dollars was no favor for twelve pages of prose). Beseeching cables were dispatched to Idaho, to Cuba, to New York. Hemingway jerked him around. RKO wanted to buy it, maybe Hemingway didn't want to sell it to anybody, and so on. At last a deal was struck: Hellinger would pay $36,750 but agreed to say for the public record that he had paid the fifty grand, and then Hellinger went and said he had paid seventy-five grand, since that would get even more press (even the real figure made it the most expensive short story in Hollywood history). Late in October the contract was signed, granting motion picture rights to the Property known as *The Killers,* complete with various (and odd) restrictions, such as: "Owner agrees no version thereof shall ever be presented in vaudeville." On November 24, 1945, Universal officially agreed to proceed with Hellinger's project.

The exact genesis of the story line, the expansion of a vignette to a feature-film narrative, would be inexact, an amalgam of spitballed ideas, random conversations, scotch-and-water lunches at the Brown Derby, all in advance of the serious business of writing something down. Hellinger held to the notion that Hemingway's enigmatic sketch revolved around a robbery gone wrong, a double-cross by one member of the gang, making off with the loot, and how the killers finally tracked him down and he was tired of running. Writer Richard Brooks, back from the war and having written the novel that would become the controversial noir thriller *Crossfire,* had come on the payroll to adapt *The Hero* (and would later write Hellinger's prison drama, *Brute Force*). "Hellinger worshipped writers," Brooks recalled to interviewer Pat McGilligan. "At the end of the day you'd gather in his office for a drink. . . . He liked nothing more than to sit with a writer and have a drink. Hellinger was a good man." Hellinger pumped Brooks for ideas, and Brooks came up with some, like making the protagonist a determined insurance investigator and the story line in part a chase after the missing money. Brooks claimed he had also tracked down Hemingway and asked him what was the rest of the story, and Hemingway said, "How the hell do I know?"

Hellinger tried to give the screenplay assignment to Irwin Shaw, a consciously Hemingwayesque writer and author of the first big novel of the war, *The Young Lions.* Then Hellinger renewed an acquaintance with a colleague from Warner Bros., John Huston, who had coauthored the script of the Hellinger-produced gangster picture, *High Sierra.* Huston was a magnetic and mercurial personality and a dynamically creative talent, whose directorial debut four years before, *The Maltese Falcon,* had been a groundbreaker in style and attitude, a reinvention of the crime drama that set the course for the genre that came to be known as film noir. An ex-boxer, newsman, now a veteran of battle (his filming of the San Pietro attack, under fire, was perhaps the most remarkable cinematic product of the war), Huston was another "son of Hemingway" type and, Hellinger was sure, the perfect man for the job at hand. Huston had formed a loose writing partnership with Tony Veiller, a skilled Holly-wood veteran, the son of playwright Bayard Veiller and actress Margaret Wycherley (Cagney's malevolent mom in *White Heat*). Huston and Veiller had worked together on a *Why We Fight* propaganda film for Frank Capra's unit and had hit it off. But Huston was still in uniform, and after that he was tied by contract to Warners, so his part in the job had to be done on the QT. Veiller was first to be demobilized from the army and would take sole credit for the script. The only indication of Huston's sub rosa involvement was a clause in the contract allowing Veiller to employ a collaborator to advise him in the writing and to assist in research. Veiller took Hellinger's money and handed half to Huston, and in two months in the winter of '45–'46 they wrote the screen story and script of *The Killers*.

Working mostly in New York, at Huston's rooms in the Weylin Hotel in the east Fifties, Veiller's mother's apartment at 10 Perry Street, and at various watering holes in between, they worked up first the elaborate, complex flashback structure moving back and forth between the present and the past and in effect unfolding two stories at once. The "theory we have evolved for telling the story," Veiller told Hellinger on December 2, afforded "tremendous possibilities for something really off the beaten track." The storytelling method was clearly influenced by the innovative screenplay of Herman Mankiewicz and Orson Welles for the film most ad-mired by every ambitious movie writer and director in 1940s Hollywood: *Citizen Kane*. Huston and Veiller may also have been thinking about the much-admired Eric Ambler thriller *A Coffin for Dimitrios*, filmed in '44 as *Mask of Dimitrios*, with its multiple narrators and in which past and pres-ent stories ultimately, violently dovetail.

By early February the first draft of the script was turned in. Hellinger requested a number of revisions and added a few touches of his own. He eliminated some of the "trick names" of the gangsters, which struck him as too much Runyon cliché. He decided that the killers should arrive by automobile and not, as in the script, by train (generally, unless one is very good with a schedule, not a practical method for making a quick getaway after a murder). The Huston and Veiller screenplay kept the Swede unseen in the opening sequence, but Hellinger felt it would be more effective to show the audience the hopeless look on the face of the man who knows he is about to be killed. Hellinger added a few more touches from his own re-porter's notebook: For instance, he wanted Blinkie's deathbed confession to take off on the surrealistic ramblings he had heard from the dying lips of gangster Dutch Schultz, shot down in a Newark chophouse.

But this was a great screenplay, more than Hellinger could have hoped for: Hemingway's short story nearly intact in the first reel, then opening up in a brilliantly "off the beaten track" way, first a detective mystery, then a gangster story, a love story, and in the end the detective story again tying everything together. Taking off from the prologue of the Swede's murder, the script introduced Riordan, the dogged insurance man, following a trail that uncovers the secret history behind the killing, revealed in a series of flashbacks: the corruption of a washed-up boxer mixed up with a gang and a gorgeous moll, a spectacular robbery, a double- and then a triple-cross over the girl and the loot, a final retribution for the remaining bad guys (and girl). Hemingway's existentialist tease became Huston/Veiller's grandly elaborated thematic question: What could bring a man so low that he would surrender himself to violent death? The scripted answer was above all a woman, a slinky underworld Circe whom Huston and Veiller had named Kitty Collins.

A beautiful script, Hellinger thought, and a ballsy one. He sent it off to the movie industry's independent censoring body, the Breen Office, for approval, and hoped it would not come back gelded. On March 5, the response from the censors arrived:

First, [they suggested] remove as much as possible the present overemphasis on violence and murder [underlined]. Also emphasis on illicit sex. These will meet with bad public reaction.

Detailed showing of the robbery should be omitted.

Furthermore . . . (page 8) there should be no showing of sawed-off shotguns in hands of criminals. Also (page 13) change showing of gun blasting straight into camera.

Page 21 There should be nothing offensive about the showing of the corpse.

Page 30 Swede should not be shown stripped to the waist. Furthermore, even though he is drunk, please omit any liquor or drinking in scene.

Page 32 Please get technical advice as to Queenie's use of the Hail Marys.

Page 41 Make this prizefight less brutal.

Page 45 There must be no exposure of Swede in this scene in the shower. Also omit liquor and drinking.

Page 51 Omit drinking.

Page 52 Care will be needed with this low-cut gown worn by Kitty.

Page 59 Avoid disrespect in burial sequence.

Page 60 Omit the liquor.

Page 64 Omit liquor.

Page 65 Avoid showing unmade bed.

Page 68 Liquor.

Page 70 Omit reference to Candy having been a drug addict. Too much crime and violence already present.

Page 76 Omit detailed method of payroll robbery.

Page 91 No sawed-off shotgun for criminals.

Page 92 No flaunting of loot.

Page 102 No use of dum-dum bullet, illegal missile.

Page 106 Avoid undue brutality.

Page 115 Change line "she and Swede shacked up together in an Atlantic City hotel."

Page 119 Liquor.

Page 124 Liquor.

Page 125 Should be played elsewhere than bedroom. Kitty and Swede should be fully clothed and end of sequence should be no suggestion of sex.

Page 130 Sign should read "Ladies Lounge" and no sawed-off shotguns with criminals.

Page 132 Kitty dialogue beginning "Aren't I, Swede?" and ending "Break every bone in my body" and succeeding dissolve too pointedly suggestive of sex.

Page 131 Riordan in Ladies Lounge looking for Kitty permissible only if there are no women present and of course no implication whatever of toilet activities, only powder room. Omit any indication of a toilet room beyond.

Breen—knowing that clever filmmakers sometimes tried to slip their transgressive material between the lines of a script and think they could get away with it—reminded Hellinger that approval was not given until the viewing of the completed film.

Hellinger read the letter, then carefully placed it in a file labeled "Fuck You," and went back to work.

With shooting to begin at the end of April, Hellinger had much to do.

The choice of director seemed almost inevitable:* Universal had under contract Robert Siodmak, the man who was then deemed the most talented specialist in suspense films since Alfred Hitchcock. The German Siodmak had entered the Berlin film industry in the mid-1920s as a title writer for silent pictures, then a cutter, and in 1929 he made his first film as a director, *Menschen am Sonntag* (*People on Sunday*), a film whose adventurous, improvisatory spirit resembled in advance the New Wave efforts of Godard and Truffaut. In the thirties Siodmak, a Jew, had been forced to leave Germany—Joseph Goebbels railed against him by name as a decadent influence—and worked for some years in France. Robert's younger brother, the novelist and screenwriter Curt Siodmak, had immigrated to the United States and to Hollywood in the late thirties, and eventually Robert followed. A specialist in horror pictures at Universal, Curt got his older brother hired to direct his screenplay for *Son of Dracula* (and Robert immediately replaced his brother with another writer, "a sibling rivalry," said Curt philosophically). Thrilled with Siodmak's handling of the material, Universal put him under long-term contract, and he was soon turning out a series of thrillers and murder stories with a psychological element, some of the best in the new style of dark suspense the French were to dub film noir: *Phantom Lady*, *Christmas Holiday*, *The Suspect*, *Uncle Harry*, and *The Spiral Staircase*. Siodmak's cinematic characteristics included mordant humor, vivid delineations of the perverse and the pathological, and a highly wrought visual sense in the symbolist, nightmare style of golden-age German expressionism (critic Andrew Sarris wrote that Siodmak's American films were far more German than his German ones). Hellinger screened some of Siodmak's recent pictures (including, perhaps, *Christmas Holiday*, with its own flashback structure). He felt that the style he wanted for *The Killers* was reflected in particular in *Phantom Lady*, with its lush nocturnal atmosphere and dazzling set pieces (a pursuit through empty Manhattan streets, an orgasmic midnight jam session, and so on). In addition, though this was probably unknown to Hellinger, one of Siodmak's acclaimed German films, the 1932 *Stürme der*

---

*I could find no substantiation for the idea that Huston was considered for the directing job or the claim of future action ace Don Siegel that Hellinger wanted him to direct the film; Siegel would direct a quasi-remake of *The Killers* in the 1960s in an entirely different style from the original.

Leidenschaft (*Storms of Passion*), had explored material quite similar to *The Killers* in a tale of criminals, obsessive love, and a treacherous femme fatale. Hellinger hired both Siodmak and—to ensure he wasn't backing the wrong horse—*Phantom Lady*'s skilled and fast-moving cinematographer, Elwood "Woody" Bredell.

Once Siodmak was signed on, Hellinger "kicked the story around" with him. The director suggested ways of streamlining scenes and a few places that could be adjusted to increase the potential for visual excitement. He also weighed in on the characters and dialogue. Siodmak felt that Hellinger-Huston-Veiller overexplained some things that were better left unexplained and particularly sought to eliminate some of Hellinger's interjections in the dialogue, which he saw as too sentimental: a few wisecracking lines by the Swede that tried to make him a more likable and humorous character, to temper his obsessive passion and anger; and some dialogue for Kitty that similarly sought to give her a more sympathetic backstory, a nice girl who had just fallen in with the wrong people. Siodmak preferred a pitiless view of both characters.

Casting was next: three leads, several strong supporting roles, and bits to be filled in a matter of weeks. Bucking the conventional wisdom, Hellinger had no interest in big names. He figured that the star of his picture was Ernest Hemingway, and if there was another star it was going to be himself. The film would feature fresh faces like Charles McGraw, William Conrad (Al and Max, the drily ferocious hit men), Jack Lambert (previously mostly employed as an ax- and gun-wielding cover model for true-crime magazines) and Burt Lancaster as the Swede, making his motion picture debut (for a time Hellinger had been set on giving the part to Wayne Morris, the athletic, inconsequential leading man of numerous Warner B movies, but Jack Warner vindictively nixed it). Other parts would be taken by the more familiar mugs of iconic character players, Sam Levene, Vince Barnett, and as villain Colfax the veteran tough-yet-urbane bad guy Albert Dekker (just then concluding a term as state assemblyman from Hollywood's Fifty-seventh District and considering a run for mayor of Los Angeles). As with the writers Hellinger hired, the producer looked favorably upon actors who had been in the war, feeling they would carry with them a certain quality of hard experience, a grim authenticity that would work well for his tale of tough guys, bloodshed, and double cross. Lancaster had been a part of the Army Service Forces entertaining troops at the battle lines through the North African and Italian campaigns. Edmond O'Brien, cast as Riordan the insurance man, had been three years in uniform. Jeff Corey, cast as Blinkie, was a navy combat photographer on the carrier *Yorktown* and a few months before returning to Hollywood had filmed a Japanese kamikaze plane as it crashed practically at his feet.

For the role of Kitty Collins, Hellinger fielded suggestions from every agent, talent department, and casting director in town. Two who came under close consideration were Audrey Totter and Leslie Brooks, both blonds with a hard edge. Hellinger thought the "blond bombshell" type was a cliché, and Siodmak agreed. But time was running out. Hellinger had shared the casting dilemma with fellow producer Walter Wanger, who operated out of the next-door bungalow on the Universal lot. One morning Wanger called him. He had just been to a screening of *Whistle Stop*.

Wanger said, "You better go see this girl."

Hellinger went to see *Whistle Stop*. The next morning he called MGM to arrange an interview with Ava Gardner.

Hellinger later as much as said that she had nabbed the part the moment he saw her in person. "It was sex-two-and-even," he joked to the press. But her erotic impact was serious business. Hellinger was no slouch as a judge of female attractiveness: he had married his ex-showgirl spouse when she was known as "the most beautiful woman on Broadway." He believed at once that Ava Gardner could convince audiences a man would steal, go to prison, die for her.

In the meeting with Hellinger, Ava behaved the way she always did when directors or producers talked to her about a part: She acted as if they must have the wrong person. But she listened to Hellinger explain about the character of Kitty Collins—he gave her his vision of Kitty, with some of that sentimental *Scheisse* that Siodmak complained about—and there were things about the girl that could not but draw her interest. Kitty was a nice girl, Hellinger figured, but she'd allowed herself to accept the easy way of life. She came from a good family "but linked up with the wrong type of people who supply her with the wrong cues in life." The romance between Kitty and the Swede, Hellinger posited, "is one of frustration.

They both know it is too bad they hadn't met before both of them were tangled up in their present situation. They might have married and had a full and happy life. As is, they are both destined for a short and unhappy one."

Ava thought, yes, there were maybe some things she could respond to in the character of Kitty Collins.

On April 26, a few days before filming of *The Killers* was to begin, an agreement was signed between Mark Hellinger Productions and Loew's Incorporated. The agreement called for "use of the Artist to begin not later than May 8 and continue for the period necessary to complete the portrayal of her role but not beyond June 24." Ava's on-screen and advertisement billing were specified in convoluted legalese. Since it had not been decided if Edmond O'Brien or Burt Lancaster or both would be given star billing, Ava's credit was specified under a series of contingencies, guaranteeing her either first featured credit below one of them as star or third starring credit below both. In the end the release-print credits gave her more than the contract called for, an indication of Hellinger's satisfaction: O'Brien was reduced to first featured and Burt Lancaster and Ava Gardner in that order were billed on screen as the twin stars of *Ernest Hemingway's The Killers*.

In compensation for her services the payment was to be $1,000 per week for a minimum of seven weeks, money to be delivered each week to Loew's at Culver City. Ava herself would, of course, get only her regular MGM payment, netting Metro a 700 percent return on the deal. It was standard studio practice, but when she realized the extent of the inequity on this and the *Whistle Stop* deal, she was furious. Artie told her, "Screw 'em. Go on strike." Eventually, Shaw claimed, he went in to sort things out with Metro, an assignment he must have relished; he hadn't seen his friend Louis B. Mayer since the Lana marriage, when Mayer gave him instructions on how not to knock up his wife. Shaw said he gave them a take-it-or-leave-it offer, and Metro, sensing by then that Ava was at last a probable hot property, agreed to raise her salary to $1,250 a week with a $10,000 bonus at the end of the third year.

Among the aesthetic decisions made by Hellinger, Siodmak, and Bredell in the weeks leading up to the first day of shooting was a determination to avoid anything resembling what they saw as typical Hollywood glamorization and overlit "unreality." Hellinger told Bredell he wanted all scenes to be lit "exactly as they would be seen in real life." Enthusing to *American Cinematographer* magazine, Bredell said, "The Hemingway story was a perfect chance for me because I had always wanted to take a crack at a show where nothing had to be beautiful." In scenes like the opening arrival of the killers that would have ordinarily been flooded with fifty arc lights, Bredell would use four. The scene of the robbers gathered around a poker table was illuminated with a single dangling overhead light as it would have been in life, with no correcting fill light when the actors' eyes became shadowed. (It is remarkable how many of the creators of classic film noir images now perceived as highly stylized and phantasmagoric, believed they were working in the name of "realism.") As for Ava, however alluring and irresistible *The Killers* man-killer star was meant to appear, she was not exempt from the filmmakers' pursuit of reality. Coming to the set at Universal for the first day of test shooting, Ava had gotten made up in the heavy MGM style that was considered mandatory for working under her home studio's standard blast of heavy arc lighting.

"Ava, darling, what iss wiz all zis face?" said the bald, pop-eyed director. "Please, you are going and washing off and bringing back face alone!"

Ava shrugged, went back to the makeup room and returned unadorned. Siodmak and Bredell enthused. Bredell would long after speak of Ava Gardner as the first adult actress who had ever agreed to be filmed without makeup: "All we did was rub a little Vaseline into her skin for a sheen effect."

The look of Ava's flesh on test footage, lit only with Bredell's simple setups, would influence the visual style of the entire film. The smooth ivory tone of her skin produced such a pure white image that Bredell based his whole lighting treatment around it. His "out of balance lighting," created in many scenes an extreme form of contrast, the whitest whites, deepest blacks and eliminating as much as possible all gray halftones.

To see how the movie's chosen lovers looked together Ava was also tested in a love scene with her fledgling costar. The intensely masculine ex–circus acrobat Burt Lancaster was still new to that sort of intimacy on a soundstage and gave a less than professional response to the demands of the scene. Some years later, asked by a French filmmaker what it was like the first time he kissed Ava Gardner for the camera, Lancaster said proudly, "I got an erection." Apparently such a rampant hard-on that the entire crew broke up over it. Ava good-naturedly accepted it as a compliment.

She liked Lancaster. He had a great, charismatic enthusiasm for life. At the age of thirty, after many years of struggling on the obscure fringes of show business, he now seemed to be inescapably bound for sudden success—in the first week of his first acting job onstage he had received seven offers to work in movies. He was amusing company, still carefree, not the sometimes-pompous know-it-all to come. She learned that his "discovery" was as much a fluke as her own, a story he told her with hilarious insouciance. Going up in an elevator to see a friend about some crummy job, he said, another fellow in the elevator kept staring at him. "We got out on the same floor, and the guy is still eyeing me up and down like he can't get enough. I walk away but he comes up behind me so I grab him by the necktie and tell him, 'Listen you pansy keep it up and I'll beat the shit out of you!' I go to my job interview and the phone rings and it's this guy from the elevator, and my friend tells me the guy is casting a play and all he wanted was to ask me to audition. That play got me to Hollywood. And I almost blew my chance 'cause I thought the guy was queer for me!"

Hellinger had Ava and Burt taken off to Malibu to pose for some innocuous promotional photographs, filler for the newspapers to start the drum beating about the leads in his coming release. While the photographer snapped away the pair frolicked across the beach, he in swim trunks, she in summery white shorts and T-shirt. Lancaster showed off some of the skill that had kept him employed by various circuses a few years before, tossing and spinning her in the air. Ava got into the spirit of it, doing a remarkable full handstand balanced only by Lancaster's grip on her shoulders, and then carrying the brawny six-foot-two actor down to the waves on her back. They looked like the healthiest, sexiest circus act there ever was.

On May 8 Ava recorded the song Miklos Rosza and lyricist Jack Brooks had written for the film, "The More I Know of Love." It would be the song Kitty Collins sings at the piano just after the Swede first sees her and becomes hooked—ensnared—forever. It was typical of the integrity and vision Hellinger showed toward the production: Universal higher-ups thought it ought to be a little irrelevant musical interlude as in every other movie, a pop tune their song-publishing company might subsequently get Bing Crosby or the Andrew Sisters to record. Instead Hellinger stuck with Rosza's downbeat wisp of a composition and the lyrics that reflected the bitter pleasure and delusions of love. Ava loved to sing, but when Hellinger scheduled the recording session she predictably resisted. The producer enthused and insisted. She credited him with getting her to relax enough finally to do it. She sang in a small but very sultry voice that had the effect of an erotic whisper in the listener's ear.

On May 10, Ava went to work on Stage 6 at Universal, shooting the party scene that served as her introduction in the film. Hellinger's zest and positive reinforcement kept the company in high spirits, and Siodmak and Bredell worked with such speed and creative energy that there was little time to be bored or nervous, Ava's normal conditions on a film set. Phil Brown, who played Nick Adams, the young man in the diner who runs to warn the Swede of his impending murder, and speaks the first line in the movie ("Ketchup!"), recalled, "Siodmak always knew what he wanted and worked very quickly. There was no rehearsal before the actual shooting began. Siodmak's interest was in staging and camera placement. He did not discuss motivation with the actors or give line readings. Everything went smoothly. The only difficulty I had was in trying to jump all those fences—it was shot in one take—and not break my neck."

It was not that the director was unconcerned with motivation or psychological subtext, but Siodmak was entirely a man of the cinema and he masterfully understood the plastic nature of film to express depth through surface means. In the case of Ava Gardner, Siodmak's functional directions and concern for the pace, movement, and gesture within each frame rather than a more overarching and motivational instruction seemed to be just what she needed to sidestep her often fatal nervousness and consequent woodenness before the camera. In the way of Mamoulian or von Sternberg, who could direct Garbo or Dietrich to stare into space and count to twenty and yet make an audience read profound contemplation on their faces, so Siodmak helped Ava to create a coherent characterization and a haunting erotic presence out of such things as the shift of her eyes, the turn of her lips, and the feline sprawl of her exquisite body. He wanted her to act not more but less: She would say a line or give an expression and Siodmak would tell her to do it again but "half as much." Other actors remembered Siodmak's fascination with the actress, moving her around to try different poses, excited by the heat and mystery she brought to his compositions. For the scene when the gang first meets around the poker table, Edmond O'Brien told writer Charles Higham, "He focused the camera entirely on her boredom and restlessness, which she most subtly conveyed."

Ava's only difficulty was in pulling off the histrionic breakdown at the film's climax, as Kitty pleads for a way out from the mortally wounded Colfax, a phony alibi to save her from jail ("Don't ask a dying man to lie his soul into Hell," Sam Levene memorably tells her). She did not have sufficient technique to reach the emotional pitch called for in the scene, and so Siodmak chose to bully her into approximating in real life Kitty's distraught state of being. For that day the usually puckish director became the stereotypical sadistic Teutonic auteur, barking that if she did not do the scene right he would hit her, shouting at her for take after take until the acting of the scene became a release for her mass of jangled nerves and anger.

It was for the rest a pleasant and stimulating experience, for Ava the first time she had felt a real part of a creative enterprise. "It was a very happy set," recalled Bob Rains, a U-I publicist who became attached to the production. "Of all the movie sets I have been on, it was one of the most friendly. No prima donnas, no problems or arguments. Everyone seemed to be enjoying their work. Burt was very enthusiastic, and Ava was very friendly. The crew loved her. She insisted everybody call her Ava, not 'Miss Gardner', just a regular gal. Hellinger made sure everyone was happy. He was that kind of guy. If a studio guard showed him where to park his car, the next day he sent the guard a big basket of liquor."

With Hellinger, Ava had found the sort of patron she had never had in five years at MGM. He was confident in her ability and determined to make her a star. There was not a day that went by from her signing through the film's wide release that he did not try to promote her somewhere: publicity photos to specific editors and news desks, on-set interviews with journalists, plants with columnists, guest appearances on radio shows, and any other possible interaction that promised at least to spell her name right. Hellinger's efforts included an "Ava Gardner Celebration

Week" in Wilson, North Carolina, timed to the local release of the film in the fall, and the naming of Ava—or part of her, anyway—as "The Most Beautiful and Healthy Legs in America," the climax of the National Association of Chiropodists' Foot Health Week.

The Killers was marvelous entertainment, a summit of Hollywood art and craft, a film of narrative intricacy and aesthetic splendor. The script by Huston and Veiller marshaled a sprawling series of events and changing relationships, unfolding them as an interlocking series of dramatic high points. The characterizations and dialogue had a vivid and yet matter-of-fact toughness that at the least matched Hemingway for authenticity and hard-boiled poetry. The photography by Woody Bredell was equally tough yet poetic, the harsh, single-source lighting that somehow became beautiful, full of inky blacks and flaring white whites that challenged the "invisible" imagery (that is to say, undistracting for the audience) commercial Hollywood cameramen were generally ordered to create; Bredell's powerful chiaroscuro effects bore comparison with the legendarily elaborate work of *Citizen Kane*'s Gregg Toland. Siodmak made these elements congruent with inspired direction, from the first glimpse of the killers posed on the shadowed roadside like emissaries from hell, to the vividly inhabited milieus of boxing arena, flashy hotel suites, creaking rooming houses, and small-town diner, and the awesome set piece of the payroll robbery, filmed in one traveling crane shot following the action from the entrance of the crooks through the company gate (actually a Universal studio side entrance), the robbery itself, and the chaotic getaway (the sweeping, floating camera somehow another proclaimed attempt at "realism," with the voice-over narration supposedly meant to sound like that of a documentary). Throughout, Siodmak constructed thrilling moments from the choreographed interaction of camera and performers, cinematic frissons, as in the bookend appearances of murderous Max and Al—the contrapuntal movement in the lingering opening shot of the two men as they approach the diner, and the breathtaking seconds before the shoot-out in the Green Cat Club with the relentless boogie-woogie piano background suddenly joined in neurotic dissonance with Rosza's memorable four-note motif (the "dum-dah-dum-dum" theme later used on *Dragnet*). The influence of *The Killers*—the script, the style, the music and more—would be seen in countless films to come, from *Out of the Past* to *Once Upon a Time in the West*.

Ava Gardner's work in the film might as well have been, like Lancaster's, her debut in motion pictures. She seemed born again for the film. What *Whistle Stop* had crudely hinted at *The Killers* revealed in full. She shone in a sophisticated and attention-getting production. Her actual screen time was brief and contained relatively little activity but she haunts the entire film with her compelling presence and in the end, the last man standing so to speak, she is revealed as the film's black heart. Truly alluring, she draws attention even when placed in the background of a shot and with her back to the camera as in the first glimpse of her, in the party scene, the light glowing on her broad, bare shoulders. It is not the consummate performance of a great actress but neither is she a mannequin: In the way of pure film actors, she had used a minimalist technique that yet enlarged her screen space and left a lingering impact; the viewer stays riveted, watchful of a revealing gesture: Her every smile seems to convey a variety of corruptions. It is a controlled, teasing performance, never giving up Kitty's secrets. She floats through the film as a kind of dream image, fever inducing, as much talked about—thought about—as seen.

Ava had joined what in the brief history of film noir was already a sizable sisterhood of memorable femmes fatales, duplicitous dames, and lethal spider women. Some have seen in the wartime/postwar onslaught of these fatal females a psychosocial metaphor: Were they a lurid embodiment of the wives and girlfriends on the home front whose increased independence, presence in the workforce, and sexual liberation during the war left their returning men in states of anxiety and suspicion? Pointedly, Kitty betrays both Colfax and the Swede when they are away—not in uniform overseas but in prison (like Ava Gardner's words to GI Mickey Rooney, Kitty's promise to wait for her man's return is not kept). Whatever the metaphoric meaning, among the ranks of the film noir femme fatale, few had captured anything like the almost supernatural quality in the deadly allure of Ava's killer creation. Villainesses Mary Astor (*The Maltese Falcon*), Barbara Stanwyck (*Double Indemnity*), and Joan Bennett (*Scarlet Street*) were matronly by comparison, and the lovely-in-Technicolor Gene Tierney (in *Leave Her to Heaven*) could barely keep her dithering screen husband interested. Even Rita Hayworth, Ava's most ravishing noir rival, could not compare as an evil beauty: Rita's Gilda was essentially a good girl waiting to be redeemed by love, not Kitty's calmly treacherous temptress. If there was a possible filmic comparison to Ava's amoral, enigmatic, and super-erotic young bad girl it might be the Lulu of Louise Brooks in *Pandora's Box,* another nonblond with a fateful allure and perverse sexuality. (There was more to this: *The Killers* script had contained hints—ultimately censored—of a strongly sadomasochistic element in the lovemaking of Kitty and the Swede.)

The Killers had its New York opening on August 28, exactly two months after the production had wrapped in June. Through the summer, a giant Manhattan billboard heralded the film's coming, as did nearly every columnist and radio host, Hellinger calling in favors from his friends cultivated over the past twenty years. Preview screenings were met with great enthusiasm, and when the response cards showed particular interest in Ava Gardner, Hellinger increased the focus of his advertising campaign on his female star, though the new ads threatened to spoil the film's denouement ("Some guys never find out . . . WOMEN can be KILLERS too"). Reviews were almost unanimous in their praise. *Life* magazine claimed, "there is not a dull moment," and the critic for the *New York Post* called it "the best picture of its kind ever made." Ava Gardner was frequently singled out for approval, hailed for her extreme beauty and for her effective embodiment of the femme fatale. Only Bosley Crowther of the *New York Times* voiced disdain for the film as "depressing rough stuff." In a Sunday Theater Section feature he decried both *The Killers* and *The Big Sleep,* the new Bogart private-eye thriller, as "perverse," "unprogressive," "reflective of impoverished thought in Hollywood and a distorted taste of the public," and reminiscent, he grimly recalled, of German films in the period leading up to Nazism (Crowther's antiviolence screeds were eternal: Twenty-some years later *Bonnie and Clyde* would give him another case of the vapors). Hellinger probably uncorked more bottles of champagne, as it was almost a given that a piece attacking a film for its sensationalism increased audience attendance.

Word of mouth was tremendous, and by the middle of opening day there were lines down the block waiting to see Hellinger's production. Walter Winchell, tossing a bouquet to his old tabloid pal, told a national radio audience in his signature teletype style: "Dateline New York . . .

probably the heaviest one day's box office receipts were recorded this week by *The Killers*. . . . This is the new Mark Hellinger moving picture hit sensation. . . . $10,000 the opening day at the Winter Garden."

In the first week *The Killers* broke every box-office record at the thirteen-hundred-seat theater. Universal had put up signage eight stories high on two sides of a corner Broadway building—"TENSE! TAUT! TER-RIFIC! Told the untamed Hemingway way!"—with three stories' worth of Ava as the center image, and across the entrance of the Winter Garden was an elaborate three-dimensional poster and cutout display. Hellinger had photographers document the crowd: There they are, a sea of mid-1940s New Yorkers, many of them looking not unlike some of the tough mugs in the movie, the line snaking along in front of the Singapore Restaurant ("Chinese and Island Eats . . . Ladies Served"), past Pennyland, past the Original Glori-Fried Ham 'n' Eggs, and the triangular marquee for the Havana Madrid nightclub, where Carlos Varele and his Orchestra played rhumbas each night, and up to the Winter Garden's brass box office (ALL SEATS $.70), where a sumptuous, larger-than-life, painted Ava Gardner in her black satin dress lured the customers to the ticket vendor just as irresistibly as she did Burt Lancaster to his doom.

As the moment was coming to unveil her as one of the great screen temptresses of the age, Ava Gardner was struggling with the breakdown of her marriage to Artie Shaw, seemingly unable to tempt the one person in the world she wanted. She continued to lose weight—down to 108 pounds that summer—and wrestle with the stomach pains that still plagued her in times of stress. Who can say but that these domestic circumstances contributed to her playing of Kitty Collins, giving her a vivid sense of the potentially poisonous nature of love, only at home she was playing the Burt Lancaster role. For a woman who caused people to stumble over themselves when they saw her, now the lead in a major production, she was full of self-disparagement. On the set of *The Killers* she mentioned that Artie had a film project he was considering producing. Someone asked if she would be the star. "No," Ava said. "I'd probably just louse it up." She had stopped going out. After work, she said, she went home and read. On the set she talked in earnest of her UCLA courses, of the education she so desired. She talked so much of her woeful ignorance that others picked up on the theme, joked about her. Siodmak said she called champagne shampoo.

The arguments and the icy standoffs back home got so that Ava had begun sleeping on the couch. After one quarrel she ran off and stayed several days with her attorney's family. The press started sniffing around. Late in June a reporter caught up with Shaw, asked if he and his wife were having problems. The clarinetist was evasive.

"We're living together in this house. And it's a small house."

The reporter raised an eyebrow. "Do you mean you're living together but not living together as man and wife?"

"I don't see how you could do that," said Shaw, shifting to the pedantic. "Not in a house this size."

Artie reckoned that he and Ava had their difficulties and blamed them, for the record, on their different working hours. He was up all night, and she went to the studio at 6:00 A.M. "Makes for domestic friction," he said.

A few days later, the friction having apparently increased, Ava left home again. She took up an open invitation to stay at the house of agent Minna Wallis, who had cultivated Ava's friendship (she was not Ava's agent, Charles Feldman having taken up that position) since not long after her arrival in California. Minna, the middle-aged sister of producer Hal Wallis, and bearing an unfortunate resemblance to him (neither sibling was easy on the eyes), doted on the beautiful young actress. Through the years Ava had occasionally turned to her as a maternal figure for advice and comfort, but some said that the lesbian Minna's interest was less wholesome than that. When Ava first came to work at MGM, recalled people who knew her then, she had been ignorant even of the concept of homosexuality. There had been a curious incident with one of the girls from the costuming department, a flirtation or a come-on of some sort, and when Ava spoke of it to some friends at lunch she was apprised for apparently the first time that there existed girls who were attracted to other girls and that as a result the two girls did certain things with each other that did not involve men. Ava cackled in disbelief. Five years later she was much more knowing about the varieties of human nature and routinely tippled cocktails and had friendships with homosexual men working at Metro, some of those whom historian William Mann called the studio's "behind the scenes queens," the more ebullient of them giving her detailed accounts of their latest sexual escapades, stories that would have made the eighteen-year-old Ava Gardner pass out cold. As for Minna Wallis, there is no evidence that she offered more than Platonic affection to her houseguest, but still there were gossips who voiced bitchy speculation, as well as witnesses to the relationship who believed Minna was romantically smitten with the young actress, and lavished her with unusual concern and affection.

Ava's departure from the house she shared with Artie had been impulsive, never intended to be permanent. But that was how it turned out.

"I must be very difficult to live with," Shaw would reflect many years later. "I have to assume that. Although, of course, none of the women I've known ever proved they were any easier."

In Ava's view of things she had somewhere in their time together lost Artie's love, and it was not coming back. Bored, tired of her, he had set about disengaging himself from their life. Shaw didn't buy that. He believed that their breakup was by no means inevitable. They had started to drift apart, it was true, but it was Ava, he felt, who had chosen Hollywood over him, siding with the Philistines. He had told her that he wanted to move to New York for a while, get away from Hollywood's half-wit palm-tree-and-nutburger culture; who knew, maybe relocate for good. It was natural that he expected she was coming too, but she had not wanted to go with him, feeling that her big chance had come at last, saying, "They'll forget me if I leave."

Shaw thought it sad. He wanted to tell her that they would forget her anyway. In the beauty business the merchandise got shopworn fast; gravity was going to have its way on even the fairest flesh, and one day the next eighteen-year-old would be there to take her place.

She was still crazy about him, for all that she felt she had suffered for it. And hey, he loved her too. But when a thing like a marriage started to crumble, man, there was nothing for it but to get on your way, get moving before something fell on your head. The only thing was to call a cab, Shaw would say. Pack your bag, call a cab, and get in it and go away. That was fundamental.

"Artie Shaw was no good for her at all," said Ava's friend Kathryn Grayson. Ann Miller, another of the MGM sorority, said, "It was Artie, and all those head doctors, and becoming a big star, I guess it was too much to handle, it made her a little coo-coo, I guess. She became quite a wild child."

She made up her mind to be more cautious in the future. If a man knew you loved him, he took advantage, treated you badly. She wouldn't go through it again.

"I don't trust love anymore," Ava Gardner said. "It has led me astray."

FOUR

Venus in Furs

When you talk to Ava Gardner you are always in for a double-barreled dent. That true glamour of hers gives you the first wallop . . . At conversational closeness, her face and figure are genuine dream stuff. Further, Ava is deliciously neither too old nor too young, and she was born with the rare knack of being fascinatingly feminine. In person, not merely on screen. When Ava goes to a premiere or to Ciro's she lands in all the columns the morning after. Her behavior is invariably genteel but her appearance is completely sock.

Obviously, Ava is developing her acting ability out Culver City way and is now destined to climb to her very own niche in Hollywood's history. But the generally unappreciated fact I think worth bringing out is this: away from her studio she is already in full bloom—as a human being.

—"Human Side of a Heavenly Body," *Screenland* magazine

She prefers informal clothes, but since she must as part of the Hollywood game attend diverse formal functions, she owns four evening gowns, the most expensive of which cost $200. Her entire wardrobe is insured for $8,000; $5,000 of it covers a mink coat she bought several years ago. . . . She wears black, white and blue lingerie—"never pink"—and green is her favorite color for outer garments. She has a simple taste in jewelry. Her ears were pierced last spring for earrings. She is near-sighted and often wears shell-rimmed glasses, which is one reason why few fans recognize her on the street.

—"The Girl Who Learned Too Much Too Late," *Redbook*

The thing you've got to understand about this girl is that she isn't easy to understand. You expect her to be a slinky siren, and she turns up talking badminton. It doesn't prove anything. She can still slink, and if you've ever seen her in the middle of a rhumba, you know. She doesn't remind you of your mother.

She went through a time when she was miserable, and she got too thin, and she stayed out too late, with too many people. That's over now. From the way Ava tells it, she's become a happy-medium addict.

—"Honey Chile," *Modern Screen*

Being a star is a responsibility. It means I have to go forward or go back; I can't stand still. Sometimes I shiver and shake at the idea. Me. Who never had a nerve in her body!

What puckers my alabaster brow is whether or not I'll keep up full steam ahead or revert to type. As I said, I'm an old-fashioned girl. Hoot all you like, but what I really want is a home and kids. I'm not completely sure yet whether I'm going to be Forever Ambitious or not. One thing is a cinch, though. I won't be Forever Promising anymore!

—"Confessions of an Ex-Playgirl," Ava Gardner

"What did you eat today?"

"It's been said of you that you have the most graceful walk in Hollywood. How did you achieve it?"

"Do you have pancake makeup on now?"

—Questions for Ava Gardner, *Screen Guide*

"I must have a Dr. Jekyll and Mr. Hyde split personality because I photograph so differently from my real character. Men seem to expect to see the femme-fatale sultry Jezebel dripping orchids and mink. When they see, instead, a skirt, sweater and saddle-shoe girl, with no make-up, it's a great let-down."

—Ava Gardner, *Screen Guide*

"I know that keeping the lips slightly parted and wetting them occasionally with the tongue makes them appear fresh and appealing. So I do it."

—Ava Gardner, *Screen Guide*

There had been a preview screening of *The Killers* in early August. Everyone went; everyone was excited. That weekend Jules Buck, Hellinger's assistant, invited Ava to come with him and his wife and some friends going out to visit John Huston at his rambling ranch property in the wilds of the Valley. Huston had been at the preview and was lustfully enchanted by the woman he had seen on-screen embodying the duplicitous bitch of his own invention. He greeted her with a tipsy extravagance, a tall, wiry man with an oddly simian handsomeness. They liked each other at once. He had a dazzling mind, a courtly charm, a compelling, theatrical manner of speech—and, she would soon learn, an anarchic, dangerous streak he fueled with gallons of liquor. And she was gorgeous. In time Huston would come to know and to enjoy and admire more about the woman whose stardom he had helped to create: what he recognized as a reckless engagement with life that made her very much a kindred spirit.

In the evening Huston showed off his postwar parlor trick, hypnotism, learned from the army psychiatrists treating soldiers for mental disorders. Jules Buck went into a deep trance, but Ava, perhaps wary of revealing the sort of stuff she gave to her psychiatrists, resisted, and Huston decided to ply her with more scotch instead. Everyone drank too much, or enough, whatever you called it. Ava remembered Huston becoming active with desire for her and chasing her out of the house and through the woods until she leaped into his swimming pool to get away. Eloise Hardt, who had been a starlet at MGM and first met Ava during her time with Mickey Rooney, was a friend of Huston's and came by the ranch often to work with his horses. "I was feeding the horses, and I went to the house to speak to John because one of the horses was kicking in the stall. John loved to get girls to fuss over him and he knew how to convince every woman that she was the greatest thing on earth. I went into the house and Burgess Meredith was there somewhere, wandering around, completely out of it, and John was in bed with Ava and some other man, a New York actor. I don't know if there was any sex. But that's where I found them."

Everyone had blearily decided to sleep at Huston's and drive back into Los Angeles in the morning, but the chase to the pool, Huston's inebriated attentions, had been enough for one visit, and sometime near dawn Ava had come bounding up to the snoozing Bucks and asked to be driven home. The sun was just coming up as Jules Buck tried to navigate the car to the dirt road, and Huston was on his verandah "waving . . . an alcoholic goodbye."

They would see each other again, but their professional reunion, after *The Killers,* would be many years in coming. The next evening Huston went to dinner with his then-regular date, actress Evelyn Keyes, and on a whim they left their table at Romanoff's for Las Vegas and that night they were married (and some years later Keyes would wed Artie Shaw).

The period after the breakup with Artie in the summer of '46 was filled with restlessness, randomness, impulses followed then denied. Ava moved frequently, from apartment to apartment, leaving each on a sudden whim. She lived alone much of the time; she and Bappie remained apart after Ava and Artie separated, though Bappie was ever ready to come running back into Ava's life as needed. The places Ava rented were often never fully furnished, never fully inhabited either, her bags left partially unpacked, clothes strewn around as if in a hotel room taken for a night. Her personality seemed equally transient. Different people knew different Avas: sweet, down-home, acerbic, or outrageous, the barefoot tomboy playing volleyball and football and roasting hot dogs at the beach, the big sister baby-sitting and doting on the kids of married friends like the Heflins and the Rosenthals, and the lover of the night, habitué of the glitzy Mocambo and Ciro's, all the boites of Hollywood and the jazz joints of Central Avenue. "She was just a country girl, and she wasn't sure what she wanted out of her life," said Eloise Hardt. "She didn't have a plan. None of us did. You just got pushed along and hoped you would land on your feet. But she was in the fast lane, and that was trickier to maneuver."

For a time after leaving Minna Wallis's place Ava lived in a small two-family house on Olympic Boulevard at the edge of Beverly Hills. She rented the second-floor "penthouse"; on the ground floor lived Candy Toxton, actress, former girlfriend of Tommy Dorsey, and later the first wife of Mel Tormé. "I paid $175 a month and she paid a little more because she had the upstairs, better apartment. Charlie Feldman was my agent and was also her agent, and he found the apartments for us; he may have owned the building, I'm not sure. He was a very charming and so-phisticated man. He and Ava, if they had something going on, it was for a short time. Charlie was married, but he had a history of going on the make for every woman he represented. He was married to Jean Howard and cheated on her. Anyway, it was nothing serious.

"She played a lot of Artie Shaw records, I remember that, and that was a bit of a pain in the ass to hear all the time. I guess she had just busted up with him—I had met Artie when I was dating Tommy Dorsey, and Tommy didn't like him at all. And I remember her place was filled with yellow roses. Somebody was always sending her all these fresh yellow roses.

"We'd borrow a cup of sugar from each other now and then. And she knew some of the men I was dating, and I knew some of the men she was dating. But we were neighbors, not best friends, and I did not know any of her inner thoughts. She seemed content when I knew her, and I never sensed any great unhappiness about her. She was a very free person, it seemed to me, and she was not embarrassed about anything. If a man stayed overnight with her she didn't try to hide it; she would just say, 'Oh, he stayed overnight.'

"She was *very free*, I mean, nothing embarrassed her. She was very comfortable with her body, I know. I remember going up to her apartment one day, she was getting ready to go out, and she wanted to borrow a pair of earrings. Her door was open, I don't know if she was expecting some-body. And, I mean, things weren't as crazy as they are today, but her front door was open and I tapped and she yelled, 'Come on in.' And she was in front of the mirror putting some makeup on, and she was standing there nude. It was rather shocking for me. And she had the *most* gorgeous body, and the complexion and the hair, I mean, she was just *beautiful*. And she was quite comfortable being like that . . . and it made me very uncomfort-able because I felt quite *ugly* next to her."

Ava went out three or four nights a week; after her cloistered, devotional years with Shaw, she returned to nightlife with a vengeance, dancing, din-ing, drinking. She had always said she felt "more alive" when the sun went down, and now she proved it. Herman Hover, the boss of Ciro's, the ne plus ultra of forties Hollywood niteries, recalled her as "the most constant and the most intense customer" he ever had. She went to parties, she went out with dates or with groups of friends and—rare for young women of the time—she went out alone, enjoying the music at one club or another, buying rounds for the musicians, moving on. From the summer after *The Killers* had concluded filming until the end of the year she had few professional obligations beside publicity work, and so there was no having to get up at dawn and report to the studio. Her evenings out might last past sunup, and she sometimes scheduled two separate outings with different friends or two different dates in a single night, going home after eleven to freshen up or to meet her late-shift caller. Ava often complained that she suffered from insomnia, and that this made her reluctant to go home, but some recalled that she often expressed a kind of childlike fear of going to bed or of the lonely moments on the pillow before sleep came. She had a habit, when there was no Bappie or husband or boyfriend about, of asking people, females and males alike, some she had just met, to come home with her and even to share her bed with her while she fell asleep. It was a provocative habit that would on occasion lead to misunderstandings.

Some nights if she found herself alone and restless, she liked to call in to one of the radio stations and chat with the all-night disc jockey. She would ask the dj to play one of her favorites. The song she most frequently requested was Gershwin's wistful "Someone to Watch Over Me"—in later years it would be "Lush Life," Billy Strayhorn's world-weary ode to a life of "jazz and cocktails." Sometimes she would go to the station and sit in the studio and just quietly listen to the music. "She did that a lot," recalled Johnny Grant, a North Carolina native and in the period a top disc jockey in Hollywood, for a time broadcasting live from a booth at Ciro's. "She absolutely loved music, and she would just come by and sit while you played the records. She didn't want to talk on the air or anything or have you mention she was there. You'd have a little chitchat during a break, but she just liked to come and listen to the music. I played the regular stuff, Dorsey, Artie Shaw and all, but she liked to hear a lot of the harder jazz, and there was another guy, a disc jockey named Don Otis she liked to drop in on quite a bit because he played a lot of the music she liked. They had a very good friendship. It wasn't a romance or anything, as far as I know—well, it could have been, who knows?"

In October she went to court to divorce Artie Shaw. Until then she had not done anything to finalize things, keeping the marriage alive if only on paper. But Artie had already found someone to replace her and had called her into his office to tell her and to ask that they get the split in the works as soon as possible, would she be so kind—as simple and as bland as that. It hurt but it made her laugh: She was already ancient history in Artie's autobiography. Someone had introduced him to the glamorous-looking novelist Kathleen Winsor, whose notoriously sexy novel *Forever Amber* he had once chastised Ava for buying. She was married too. They had known each other for only a couple of weeks but had decided to tie the knot. Ava numbly agreed to Artie's businesslike request for her cooperation. Shaw and Winsor then went across the border to Juarez, Mexico, to get a pair of quickie divorces, staying for five days at a small hotel where they registered as Mr. and Mrs. Arthur Sanders "to avoid newspaper comment." The divorce decrees from their spouses were granted, and they were immediately wed, returning to Los Angeles at the end of the month. But it turned out to be a little messier than anyone had expected. The district attorney's office took exception to the circumstances of the Shaw-Winsor Mexican union, and the couple was forced to flee the state at once to avoid "the probability of bigamy charges and the threat of jail." It would take more than a year to disentangle the embarrassing mess, and newspaper comment was not avoided. By the time Artie and his best-selling bride were fully and legally recognized as married they were ready for a divorce. In court, Shaw said his wife tried to force him to be sterilized, and Winsor claimed Shaw threatened her with violence when she refused to join the Communist Party, an accusation that made the papers and resulted in Shaw being subpoenaed and humiliated at length by the House Un-American Activities Committee.

Naturally there were men waiting to take Artie's place with Ava Gardner. There were many men ready and willing. She was not going to let them do that. *Baby, I have had it with love*, she would say. She enjoyed the attentions, the affections, of men, she couldn't help that; and she was fond of sex, no denying it, that cat was out of the bag now; but she was giving no man access to her heart, not for a long time to come.

"She was so beautiful," said Candy Toxton, "that every man wanted her, they all fell for her. But I felt she didn't really care what they thought. If they liked her, if they didn't like her, she didn't really care. It was like she didn't take them seriously, all these men. If they loved her or not, she was just not going to work that hard at a relationship with a man."

There were dates who were in the way of buddies she had known for a while, fun-loving hunks like Peter Lawford and Turhan Bey, with whom she could have random nights on the town and no strings attached. "She was a wonderful free spirit," recalled Turhan Bey of a time when he was the handsome young Austro-Turkish actor (born Turhan Gilbert Selahettin Sahultavy), best known for his bare-chested appearances in the delirious adventure films of Maria Montez. "I have such wonderful memories of her as a dear friend, some of them quite humorous and some of them not printable. She was very easygoing when I knew her. She took things for what they were. She knew that she was beautiful and she didn't pretend otherwise. But she was okay. I liked what her agent, Charlie Feldman, would say, 'Ava is an okay dame.' She was very real. She said what she felt, did what she wanted, and you knew where you stood. She was 100 percent okay. She was one of the best.

"We were very social. She was invited everyplace, of course, but sometimes she would get stood up or needed someone to take her to a party, and she would drag me out of the darkroom and take me along. A couple of times she brought me to some big event at Louis B. Mayer's, which was great for me because I was at Universal and I would have never met such important guys.

"We got along so well. I don't know who made a pass at who. The romance was interesting; sex was not what was most interesting. To me that was always the beginning of the end. Did I want things to become more serious? Yes, I think we both felt that way, but somehow it never happened. Maybe we became too friendly, liked each other too much."

There was sometimes a taunting quality to the way Ava dealt with men, the way she made herself almost indiscriminately available and yet unreachable and easily distracted by the next interested male to come along. Her habit of booking two dates in a night seemed part of the same game. She sometimes had two suitors crossing paths in her hallway, like a changing of the guard. "There was a place behind the steps leading to the second floor," Candy Toxton recalled of the Olympic Boulevard house she shared with Ava. "And that was where she would tell a guy to wait until the first date left. . . . I think that was fun on her part. I think she liked that playing one against the other. I don't think she was *mean* about it, she just enjoyed it. She liked men . . . but she knew how to handle her men."

She began seeing Howard Hughes again. It was late in the summer just after she had separated from Artie. Howard had fallen out of the sky once more, his closest brush with death yet.

After his year of peripatetic hiding, nursing what he believed was a nervous breakdown, he returned to public life. Immediately he had tried to renew his friendship with Ava, but she was deeply under Shaw's spell by then and refused to talk to him. On July 7, 1946 Hughes had taken off from his aircraft plant in Culver City for a test run in the prototype XF-11 reconnaissance plane. Toward the scheduled end of the test the aircraft lost power in the right wing and began to descend rapidly. The XF-11 came crashing through a residential street in Beverly Hills at 155 miles per hour, tearing through the tops of palm trees, a wall, a rooftop. The plane exploded. Hughes had confidently put twice the legal amount of fuel in the plane's tank, and now the explosion sent fire a hundred feet into the air. Hughes should have been incinerated but somehow managed to get free of the cockpit and was dragged through the flames to safety by a fearless marine who happened to be at the scene. The fire blazed for hours. Hughes arrived at the hospital with burns to his hands and face, broken bones, concussion, and multiple lung punctures. He was given a 50–50 chance of survival.

Ava got a call from John Meyer. "You heard what happened to Howard? He asked for you, kid. Can you come over to Good Samaritan and just let him see you? Might be the last thing he ever does."

Ava still felt an odd affection for the man and could not turn down such a request. She hurried to the hospital, but when she got there she found that Howard was not permitted visitors. Reporters, however, were on hand to take note of Hughes's harem. Ava, Jean Peters, Linda Darnell, Jane Russell, and other filmland beauties gathered in Hughes's name. Howard had orchestrated the scene through Meyer and a couple of flacks for his own amusement, as well as dictating a press release to downplay the story about the young marine who claimed to have saved his life.

In September he was largely recovered and ready to get back in the game. But he had changed much since Ava last saw him two years before. He seemed many years older, slower, less vibrant. His hair appeared badly dyed, and he now wore a mustache (apparently to hide a burn scar above his upper lip). On September 17 Howard piloted them both to New York for a long weekend trip. They went dining and shopping and attended the Joe Louis–Tami Mauriello fight at Yankee Stadium. She enjoyed their time together, but soon Howard was back to his exasperating habits: nightly requests that she marry him, outlandish gift giving (she did accept, with minimal complaint, the Cadillac convertible he presented to her), and the return of his cadres of spies staking her out and following her every move. Her temper would flare up at some of the liberties he took with her, but she seemed now to have a less personal concern for his deep-rooted eccentricities. She would keep him as a friend, occasionally enjoying the things he could do for her, and at times playing with his infatuation for her, but always keeping him at arm's length.

Often in those bachelor-girl days Ava went out and about with other females, part of a floating group of uninhibited girlfriends known for their love of the high life, a coterie of Hollywood-bred playgirls. There were friends of long standing from her starlet days like Marilyn Maxwell and Peggy Maley, two lush bottle blonds still waiting for their big break in pictures (Maley's moment of glory would come in 1954, in *The Wild One*, feeding Marlon Brando the famous straight line: "What are you rebelling against?" to which biker Brando replies, "Whaddaya got?"). And now with Ava's newfound status after *The Killers*, there were bigger names in her circle, too, such as Ann Sheridan and Lana Turner. Turner and Ava had much in common: They had both been teenagers plucked from nowhere without experience or education, Lana was Metro's previous hot sex symbol, and she and Ava seemed to fall for many of the same guys. Some of them, like Artie and Frank Sinatra, had been Lana's first; others, like Howard Hughes and the racketeer Mickey Cohen's sleek thug Johnny Stompanato, were Ava's castoffs. Ava liked Lana, but she found her a bit of a bore at times, humorless except unintentionally funny as when, with the manner of an accountant she reviewed the genital size and ability of her various lovers. Texan Ann Sheridan, eight years older than Ava, was another straight-shooter about men and romance. Ava met Sheridan, the

Warner Bros. "Oomph Girl," through local radio star Johnny Grant. "That was one of the great days in my life, listening to these wild chicks. They could drink and mix it up just like guys," Grant remembered. "To hear Ava and Sheridan talking together was like being in a navy boat with a crew of horny guys. Ann was a gal who would greet you saying, 'Hello, you *cocksucker*!' And Ava was just as bawdy. They loved guys and they were both insomniacs, too, so they never went to sleep. These were great ladies who in those days you could say were real 'broads,' and they took it as a compliment."

Peggy Maley was Ava's occasional roommate, when Peggy was between residences or when Ava was feeling lonely or blue. Peggy, said Ava, "was into everything," and the two had many adventures together, including smoking pot for the first time, some reefer they had scored from one of Artie Shaw's jazz brothers. They enjoyed putting people on and amusing each other with private jokes. There was one bit Ava did, aimed at the particular sort of dullard who might pester one of the girls while they were out together. Singer Mel Tormé recalled sitting with Ava and Peggy at the studio commissary: Ava trying to eat her lunch and an English actor, pompous and newly arrived, trying to charm her into going on a date; at the end of the man's long and flowery offer, Ava looked up from her soup at him and impassively asked, "Do you eat pussy?" After a moment's silence, said Tormé, Peggy burst out laughing, while Ava went back to her soup.

"She had some friends like Marilyn Maxwell who were the drinking, partying kind of girls," said Candy Toxton. "Very good-looking in a very cheap sort of way. . . . Anything went with a girl like that. You know, drink and sleep around. She was Bob Hope's mistress and this one and that. A girl like that was sort of what Ava *became* . . . later. Ava had a mind of her own, but I think she was exposed to certain behavior. I don't think that was her nature; I think she let certain people become an influence on her. I think friends like that hardened her a little."

She was by now a strong, steady drinker. In the beginning it had been a remedy for her great shyness; she had been so painfully withdrawn and tongue-tied among all those clever and self-assured people; then, during two dissolving marriages, it was an escape from hurt and hopelessness. Now it was just there, like eating or driving, one of the things you just did.

Everyone drank then, and many drank too much, but she had a fierce capacity even by the high standards of 1940s America. She had never stopped hating the taste, like an awful medicine every sip (for many years she would drink with the booze in one hand and a bottle of Coca-Cola in the other to drown it), but through the years in Hollywood she had come to crave the effects. She preferred the speed and certainty of spirits and pure alcohol cocktails to wine and diluted drinks, but she would drink almost anything offered and sometimes everything—there was her habit at parties of taking every bottle of hard liquor available—gin, vodka, scotch, tequila—and pouring it all into a single mixer or punch bowl and drinking up the fiery, revolting concoction whose only purpose was to knock a person through the floor.

She was still very young and had the recuperative powers of youth, and so for a long time the drinking was seen as a reflection of her energy and a love of life, not as a harbinger, nothing negative at all. A girl showing indications of desperation or self-destructiveness would be the last things on the mind of anyone who gazed upon the glorious sight of of a twenty-three-year-old Ava Gardner crossing the floor of a Hollywood nightclub on an autumn evening in 1946. Still, there was no denying booze had crept up, taken its prominent place in her existence. Many of her friends were heavy drinkers, and liquor was sometimes used as a litmus test for further social interaction. Mitch Miller, the musician and record producer, recalled seeing Ava at the bar at Chasen's with singer Vic Damone: "It was the first time I saw her in person. She was pushing a drink on him, and he said, 'I don't drink,' and finally she said, '*You're too square for me,*' and she got up and left."

Ava Gardner saw off 1946 at a series of New Year's Eve parties in the company of Peter Lawford. She began 1947 on an impromptu date with Mel Tormé, a 3:00 A.M. manic drive through the night in the convertible Howard Hughes had given her, ending up on the beach at Santa Barbara in the blood orange light of dawn.

At last she was making another movie. The powers at Metro had stood by while another studio had turned their girl into a star, Hellinger and Universal doing in the course of sixteen weeks or so what MGM's vastly greater resources had been unable and mostly unwilling to do in nearly six years. And now Metro stood to gain considerably from Ava's success.

She had been requested to come to a meeting with Louis Mayer. Gone was the contempt he had expressed on their first get-together, when she was going to marry Mickey Rooney. Now he was Uncle Louis or Papa Louis, full of benevolent condescension, an enthusiasm that nonetheless managed to sound like a threat.

"You've done it, Ava, just as I always knew that you would. And now a new life has begun for you. You must realize that a star has great responsibilities. You must assume those responsibilities now. There is no escaping them. Your time has come, young lady."

She was told that the studio would be looking for wonderful properties for her, important roles, and to get this renewed relationship off to a good start they were going to put her in a featured part opposite "the King" himself, Clark Gable. *The Hucksters* was based on a popular novel by Frederick Wakeman, a satiric exposé of radio and advertising. Gable had vetoed the project at first, declaring, "The novel is filthy and it isn't entertainment." Metro put its writing department to work excising the filth and trying to make what was left a bit more entertaining. Gable okayed the adaptation, and the production came to life. Metro's great male star had not worked in nearly two years, remarkable for the sort of assembly-line schedule the studio usually kept. But his previous film, his comeback after military service, had been the disastrous *Adventure*, with Greer Garson, and Gable had decided he would not work again until they found the right material. One might have thought a rip-roaring adventure film or a serious war movie would be the sort of thing to restore Gable's prewar status, not a satire about radio jingles. And after zero chemistry with Greer Garson in the last film, one would have expected Metro to avoid pairing him with another well-bred British actress, this time Deborah Kerr in her American debut. Ava Gardner's feistiness and overt sexuality could be seen in the tradition of Jean Harlow and Lana Turner, two of Gable's past big box-office team ups. She might have been just the hot female costar to light a fire under the veteran male sex symbol, a Gable-Gardner pairing to compete with Warner's Bogart-Bacall team—but no, Metro would take another five years to put something like that together for the two very compatible performers. For *The Hucksters* Ava's role as nightclub thrush Jean Ogilvie was not the female lead or love interest (she played Gable's former flame), and Metro would reward her newly won stardom out of *The Killers* with fifth billing, below Gable, Kerr, and character actors Sydney Greenstreet and Adolph Menjou.

Ava had come down with her usual case of heebie-jeebies when it was time to go back before the cameras. She had even tried to get out of the assignment, feeling the pressure of being in a big Metro project with their biggest star. Working with the unknown Burt Lancaster and a company of character actors was not the same thing. Then Gable called her one night, said, "I'm supposed to talk you into doing this thing. But I'm not going to. I hated it when they did that to me. But I hope you change your mind, kid, I think it would be fun to work together."

Ava liked Gable. She had some time ago been introduced to him at a party at Minna Wallis's and they remained friendly passing acquaintances. He was an uncomplicated man with a vast natural charisma that he never sought to analyze; he drank himself to sleep, got to work on time, and never took himself too seriously; wore his crown, as Louise Brooks said, "at a humorously apologetic angle." Ava found him solid as a rock. It *was* fun to work with him. Gable's easygoing attitude kept her calm throughout the production. He was relaxed, reassuring, funny. On one occasion shooting was halted while some adjustments were made to a gown Ava was wearing in the scene; because of the way the low-cut top was revealing too much, the costume person had to take her aside and fasten her breasts down with some invisible tape, and Gable cracked, "That's the same stuff they use to pin back my ears."

Kissing him in a scene, and in another singing a song directly to him (her voice dubbed by Eileen Wilson), Ava's biggest problem was getting lost, distracted by the strangeness of it, of doing these things with the man she and her mother had both idolized so many years ago. "I had been in love with Clark Gable since I was a little girl," she would recall. "And every once in a while I'd think, 'It's CLARK GABLE!' and I'd go to pieces."

They became good friends and would make two more films together in the years ahead. The pair developed an easy, kidding rapport, and most believed it was no more than that, a sisterly/big brotherly sort of relationship. Ava refuted any rumors outright: "There was never anything between us—ever." Some speculated that at forty-six Gable was too old to attract Ava as a sexual partner, and others said Gable never pursued her because he had an aversion to brunettes—although the truth was Gable in his time had gone to bed with women of every hair color and probably a few bald ones too, so that couldn't have been it. If they were never more than friends, it seems that the friendship may have come to be a particularly intimate one. Ruth Waterbury, the veteran Hollywood journalist whose party Ava had attended on her first day in California, recalled a visit to Ava's residence in London circa 1953, about the time the actress was completing the movie *Mogambo*. Arriving at Ava's flat in the morning for a breakfast appointment, she found the actress in the kitchen making eggs and bacon. Waterbury said that from the back room she heard a familiar voice, and a moment later Clark Gable walked out, "wearing nothing but a grin."

In *The Hucksters* they proved to be a wonderful pairing, with an on-screen spark between them that revealed their genuine amusement and easy pleasure in each other's company. In the film Gable's charisma was more weary and rueful than in the past but he had never seemed more urbane or so wise. Gardner was ebullient, radiant; she lit up every scene she was in; it was a glowing performance. The film itself was handsome, well-crafted, and entertaining, a seemingly knowing look at a little-known subculture, the first of what would become a minor genre of films exposing and mocking the banality of advertising and the "media." In the hands of a Joe Mankiewicz or Billy Wilder the material might have found another level, but director Jack Conway, an old Metro reliable and one of Gable's favorites, put it all together with his usual middle-of-the-road competence. It was well received by the critics, Ava Gardner was given many positive reviews, and the film made money.

She was still filming *The Hucksters* in late February 1947, when she began working in her next movie, *Singapore,* starring opposite Fred Mac-Murray. Universal had had a last-minute problem with their scheduled female lead and needed a "name" actress immediately. Metro agreed to loan Ava for five thousand dollars per week for a minimum of ten weeks, and for a while she had to divide her time between Culver City and the Universal lot north of Hollywood. The film was a hodgepodge of elements from *Casablanca*—an American adventurer separated from his lover by war, reunited in an exotic city ridden with intrigue and nightclubs—and the film noir staples of shadows, looming ceilings (tropical subdivision: ceilings with languidly turning fans), time-tripping narrative, and a case of amnesia (noir's version of the common cold). The story was not a good one, and the dialogue was often less than riveting:

MacMurray to amnesiac Ava: "Look, Linda. . . . What's the matter, what's happened to you?"

Ava: "My name isn't Linda."

MacMurray: "Linda Grahame! With an *e* on the end."

MacMurray, whom French filmmaker Jean-Pierre Melville once enigmatically called "the inventor of underplaying,"* having left his jaunty Paramount years behind, had entered his stolid freelance phase; he was unconvincing as an adventurer and uninspired as a passionate lover, his scenes with Ava having a very low wattage (though the two got along fine, and Ava called him "great"). Ava appeared—yes—gorgeous, shimmering under a soft overhead spotlight, the Asiatic cast of her eyes perfect for this sort of hothouse orientalism atmosphere. Her physical perfection was challenged only by a few moments in a bathing suit, an unflattering glimpse of heavy thighs that showed she had at least been eating more regularly since the breakup with Artie Shaw. The director, John Brahm, a sort of poor man's Robert Siodmak, was another German exile who had just hit his stride in darkly atmospheric crime melodramas, the remarkable vehicles for the corpulent Laird Cregar, *Hangover Square* and *The Lodger*, and the crazed-with-flashbacks noir *The Locket*. *Singapore* signaled the end of his brief surge of artistic glory, obscure films and television lay ahead. Of Ava, Brahm said, "She has the makings of an excellent actress and a very big star. However, so far she hasn't played enough important roles to gain confidence in herself. She is apt to approach a scene full of the fear of doing it wrong. Consequently, to get the best performance out of her I explain how the scene should be played, how the character would feel, speak and react in such a situation. Once she knows all that is expected she can do it very well. A great deal of the time she could figure things out for herself if she only had confidence in her own judgment."

---

*Melville: "You can't help being astonished by the economy of means with which he achieves his effects. . . ."

Ava was not bad in the end, but like everything else in the film, just not very interesting, and *Singapore* proved a step backward after the professional achievements of her performances in *The Killers* and *The Hucksters*.

Her private life remained free-floating. In romance she followed the whims of the moment, working perhaps too diligently at not being harmed by her emotions. "She was sexually uninhibited, wild, all kinds of goodies and quick," Jo Carroll Silvers, wife of comedian Phil Silvers, told writer Kitty Kelley. "She was gone and off with somebody else before you knew where you were." Ava took on lovers and discarded them with a seemingly deliberate carelessness, sometimes with what seemed deliberate cruelty. She ended a two-month relationship with Mel Tormé (then at MGM working in *Good News* while Ava was shooting *The Hucksters*) after he broke a date with her to attend a sneak preview of some new movie, and lied about it. She summoned him to her apartment without letting him know she had found him out, smiling, said Tormé, as she told him, "We're through, Melvin. Finished. You lied to me and I won't take that from anyone. Out!"

Through the spring she had again been seeing much of Turhan Bey. They made a glamorous and sexy couple, photographed together at parties and premieres. One night they went on a double date. "Ava was my date. And Ava's friend Peggy Maley, a wonderful girl with the most beautiful breasts in Hollywood, she was with her date, David Niven. The four of us were out and as the night went on David began to hit it off with Ava. She liked to laugh and David made her laugh, he had a great sense of humor. And he was good-looking. She was out with me, you know, but what could I do? Now she was getting along so well with David I did not have the heart to interrupt them. When you were with Ava and somebody came along that she liked, you had to bow away. And there was poor Peggy, stuck with me. Finally, I took Peggy home, and David took Ava home. Niven said to me, 'You're a man after my own heart.'"

There followed a short-lived affair. Niven was a recent widower, his beloved wife, Primmie, killed in a grotesque accident during a game of lights-out hide-and-seek, falling headfirst down a flight of stone steps. Niven suffered the loss deeply, no doubt, though he claimed a rather odd manifestation of his grief was an extended period of satyriasis, a near-perpetual erection, relief from which he found in the procreative recesses of all the alluring Hollywood females who would have him. Ava did not give much thought to Niven's peculiar grieving process but simply enjoyed a few scattered days and nights with the suave, jocose Brit. When they later costarred in two movies—*The Little Hut* (1957) and *55 Days at Peking* (1963)—she seemed hardly to remember their brief period of intimacy.

Extraordinarily, to those taken with the JFK mythos, Ava's time spent with a young John Kennedy left even less of a lasting impact. Her agent, Charlie Feldman, had made the introduction, at Kennedy's request (his visits to Los Angeles were for the express purpose of meeting the latest screen beauties). The "ambassador's son," as he was then known in the press, had put "quite a rush" on Ava, so heard columnist Louella Parsons. When Parsons cornered her for a scoop, Ava told her Kennedy was "very nice, sweet," and Louella, in private notes to herself, concluded "not any great thing as far as I can see." When her relationship with Kennedy came up in conversation many years afterward, Ava claimed to no longer remember anything about it. Bappie, ever Ava's archivist, would gleefully remind her of the juicy details.

Another brief encounter was with Kirk Douglas, then a fairly recent arrival in Hollywood. They met during an appearance on a radio program, went out together, and had, according to Douglas, a very lusty liaison. This apparently coincided with a High Holiday, taxing his endurance, as Kirk would chivalrously recall: "Being a Jew I always fasted on Yom Kippur. And let me tell you, it's not easy to make love to Ava Gardner on an empty stomach."

She had an equally short fling with Vinicius de Moraes, the Brazilian vice consul to Los Angeles (later the co-composer of an ode to another emerald-eyed beauty, "The Girl from Ipanema"). One night at a party, according to Moraes, Ava turned to him and said, apropos of nothing and with a weary amusement: "Yes, I am very beautiful, but morally, I stink."

Ava's longest-lasting relationship in this period was with another promising young actor new to the movies, Howard Duff. He was twenty-nine when she met him, a good-looking, athletic guy with soft eyes and a deep, expressively resonant voice. Before the war, he had been a disc jockey and regional theater actor. His career began to fall into place after he got out of the service in 1945: He landed the title role on the *Sam Spade* radio series, playing the Dashiell Hammett detective hero with a self-mocking brio. Then Mark Hellinger discovered him for the movies, putting him in a featured role in *Brute Force*, Hellinger's prison drama follow-up to *The Killers*. He and Ava had first met on the set of *Brute Force*, where Ava had come to visit Burt Lancaster, the film's star. Duff was then in the middle of a love affair with Yvonne De Carlo, another luscious postwar temptress (Howard Hughes would come after her, too), but Ava would become an instant infatuation, the most beautiful thing he had ever seen. He told himself, *"I have to have her if it kills me."*

They did not meet again until several months later, in New York, where Duff was making *Naked City*, again for Hellinger.*

Ava joined Mark and several people from the film at their table at the 21 Club. She and Duff chatted, paired off, headed to Greenwich Village for a lobster dinner. They consumed their crustaceans, and, already loaded on champagne, they went on a downtown bar crawl, drinking their way from Bleecker Street to Chinatown. Ava had an iron constitution and an insatiable thirst, and the drunker she got, Duff saw, the more restless she became, rushing them from place to place, inexhaustible, her temper racing up and down the scale from angry hellcat to purring pussy, with little or no motive for each mood change. Duff on that first night out with her gave some grave wonder to what he was getting himself into, but not enough to step away.

"We hit it off at once," Ava would say. "He was warm and generous, fun to be with, and it wasn't long before we were sharing the same bed."

It was in many ways the first serious relationship she had ever had in which she could call herself a full and equal partner. Neither the naive teenager who married Mickey nor the walking inferiority complex of her years with Artie Shaw, with Howard Duff she felt evenly matched. If she was a bigger star, he was a well-paid performer with a rising profile, some finding in his good-humored swagger and deep voice the qualities of a new Gable (a potential that, as it happened, was not to be reached). For a

---

*Mark Hellinger would not live to see the release of this last great film of his career; in December he dropped dead of a heart attack at the age of forty-four.

while they seemed perfectly in sync: physically, sexually, emotionally, alcoholically. By day they ran around in T-shirts and blue jeans, wolfing down burgers and shakes at Dolores' drive-in, playing volleyball at the beach, arriving unannounced to skinny-dip in their friends' swimming pools; by night they were one of the town's beautiful couples, well-dressed, one hundred proof; in bed they were dynamite. There was one problem and it only grew: Howard fell in love with Ava, and Ava did not want to be in love. The more he began to need her, the farther she would pull away. The early unalloyed pleasure that they had taken in each other's company became compromised by frustration, jealousy. They would fight, split up, heatedly reunite. She would refuse to see him for weeks at a time. And so love became anger became hate became pain became love again. There were public spectacles: squabbling at the Beachcomber, their favorite restaurant, and suddenly the air filled with four-letter words and with almond duck and chicken chow mein.

"She treats me like a dog," Duff would cry to all who would listen.

In January 1948, Ava began work on yet another loan-out to Universal. This made the third out of her last four films to be made for the rival studio. The projects Metro had promised to develop for her had yet to come to anything. A part she had voiced an actual interest in, that of the young bride in *Cass Timberlane*, from the Sinclair Lewis novel, which Louis Mayer had hinted might be hers, went instead to Lana Turner. It was as it had been since her arrival at the studio—MGM had one sex symbol and they did not not know what to do with another one.

Universal was being charged $75,000 for fifteen weeks of Ava's services in *One Touch of Venus*. The production was based on the Broadway musical by Ogden Nash, S. J. Perelman, and Kurt Weill, as adapted for the screen by Harry Kurnitz and Frank Tashlin, with most of the songs excised, the story of a statue of Venus that springs to life when kissed by a department store clerk. While Metro stubbornly resisted exploiting Ava's rising public profile, Universal confirmed it in the most literal way, casting her as the goddess of love and beauty. Studio flacks announced this ultimate typecasting and press releases made much of Ava Gardner's mythic beauty, positing her physical superiority to all previous depictions of the deity, with the inclusion of her measurements for the benefit of Greco-Roman scholars:

Bust: 35¾
Waist: 23¼
Hips: 34
Neck: 12½
Thighs: 19 inches
Calves: 13
Ankles: 7½

To help in the creation of a proper life-size statue to be used in the film, Ava was sent to pose for New York sculptor Joseph Nicolosi. Several hours each day for two weeks she assumed a position in the studio at Nicolosi's Malibu home. At first clad in a two-piece bathing suit, she saw the sculptor repeatedly stop work to approach her and stare with concern at the swimming costume. It seemed that the fabric disturbed him as an interruption of the body's natural line; the Anatolian Venus, Nicolosi sighed dramatically, had worn no such garment.

"Would you like the bra off?" Ava asked.

Nicolosi averred that it would surely aid the cause of art, and so Ava, after a steady stream of what she described as "hot drinks," unhooked the swimsuit top and resumed her stance with breasts bared. Further sighs of dissatisfaction from Nicolosi eventually resulted in her rolling the bottom of the bathing suit to just below the pubic mound (the mons veneris, indeed). Sometime later, prompted by a reporter and sculpture enthusiast eager to hear more details of these modeling sessions, Nicolosi said, "Miss Gardner gives an appearance of slenderness but possesses the roundness and fullness in the necessary places which set her apart from the emaciated female whose cadaverous outlines most American women seem determined to achieve."

In early February the sculptor proudly unveiled his finished work to producer Lester Cowan and was met with a torrent of invective.

"Are you crazy? *Her tits are showing!* How are we gonna put that in a movie?"

The sculptor had to go back and create a more modest goddess.

Another piece of art was created, a small souvenir knockoff of the Nicolosi statue, an idea cooked up by the Universal publicity department, to be sent to select members of the press as a promotional giveaway. Someone in the art department created the eight-inch clay version of Venus, and before it was sent out for casting, publicist Bob Rains decided that as a courtesy they should show it to Ava first. "I took the clay model over to her dressing room. I said, 'Ava, you want to take a look at this? What do you think?' She looked it over and laughed. She said, 'That's not my figure.' And then with a cute smile on her face she pinched off some of the clay from the chest area and stuck it to the rear end. She smoothed it on with her finger and made the fanny bigger. She said, 'That's more like *my* ass.' I was startled but amused. I took it back to the department and told them what happened and everyone broke into hysterics."

The film's flesh-and-blood Venus needed her own bodily adjustments. For most of her scenes Ava wore a chiffon drape, a classic Grecian "goddess gown" designed by Orry Kelly, the silk material too flimsy to hide the effect of a cold spring on the actress's breasts. Many good takes had to be discarded because of the prominent visibility of her erect nipples, a problem that eventually dissipated after prop man Roy Neal was assigned to follow Ava everywhere with a portable heater.

The film was originally scheduled to be directed by Irving Reis, a man Ava had gone out with on several occasions. Whether his dropping out of the production suddenly and leaving for New York had anything to do with their personal connection is not clear. He was replaced by veteran William Seiter, who had begun working in Hollywood as a Keystone Kop and had directed more than one hundred movies since 1919, an underrated moviemaker with a deft touch for comic romance. He got Ava to give her most relaxed and confident performance to date. Not a demanding part and not a complex performance, but one of simply radiant charm: funny and cute and sexy. Ava exuded a happy-go-lucky eroticism, like a Vargas girl come to glorious life, looking more spectacularly beautiful than ever in this, her first real star vehicle, a production virtually designed around her personal charisma and physical appeal.

The male lead in *Venus* was Robert Walker, the winsome MGM star of *See Here Private Hargrove* and *The Clock* with Judy Garland, in the war years the movies' representative of all the shy, small-town nice boys who had gone away to fight. For all that he played mostly comic parts there was a sad vulnerability to Walker on screen, and even more so in real life. He was a deeply troubled man, probably a schizophrenic, and at the least dangerously depressed and alcoholic (Metro would eventually force him to undergo psychiatric treatment at the Menninger Clinic). When the woman he had loved since they had met as teenagers at college, the woman who had since become known as movie star Jennifer Jones, had left him to be with producer David Selznick, Walker had plunged into a very dark despair from which he would never really escape. His personal life was in such disarray at the time of *One Touch of Venus* that he had moved into his trailer at the studio to cut himself off from the outside world.

Tentatively he had come to befriend his beautiful, flimsily clothed costar, and soon enough after that he was under her spell, entranced by her looks, delighted by her attitude. Walker professed to hate the movie business and most of the people in it and found in Ava a seeming soul mate. After what he saw as his betrayal by a success-obsessed Jones, Walker melted over Ava's lack of ambition. Making goo-goo eyes at her at lunch one day, Walker said, "You know, it isn't fair; you should get top billing in this picture."

Ava laughed. She said, *"Who wants it?"*

Walker had tried to remain sober for the picture, but when Ava had invited him out, he went, and when the drinks started coming, he drank them. Ava had had one of her periodic breakups with Howard Duff, and Bob Walker seemed eager to fill the empty place. Many nights they went out together, Walker drinking till he was insensible. Ava, for the record, denied they were ever lovers, saying only that when he had gotten drunk after dinner she had taken him to her place to sleep it off. Others, including David Hanna, Ava's future manager, and Walker's biographer, Beverly Linet, who would speak to Walker's best friend and right-hand man, and to Howard Duff, revealed evidence of a more intense relationship of some sort, however much the intensity was one-sided.

One day Walker knocked on Ava's dressing room door, and the baritone voice of radio's Sam Spade said, "Yes, this is Ava," followed by the sound of two people laughing inside. Ava and Howard had evidently made up. Walker paced around the area until Duff left, then confronted his costar in jealous fury. The two screamed at each other, and Walker suddenly grabbed her and slapped her across the face. Ava knocked him out of the way and ran from the room.

She refused to speak to him again for the rest of the filming. Duff had wanted to go and have it out with the guy, but Ava had said to forget it. Walker became contrite, begging her for forgiveness. She refused. One day she returned to her dressing room and found scrawled across the door a single word. CUNT.

Filming ended. She left the studio. Walker continued to call her until she had her number changed.*

Nearly two years after Ava's breakthrough in *The Killers,* MGM had finally come up with a starring part for their star at her own studio. *The Bribe* was another tropical-exotic thriller like *Singapore,* this one set in a fictitious Caribbean republic populated by smugglers, expat derelicts, and the usual extraordinarily beautiful nightclub singer, another hodgepodge of bits and pieces of other, better movies, *To Have and Have Not, The Lady from Shanghai,* with the hard-boiled voice-over of *Double Indemnity,* and a variation on Kitty Collins's little black dress. The poor, unfocused script by Marguerite Roberts left the viewer constantly feeling as if he had walked in at the middle of the picture. It was, though, a handsome production with outstanding deep-contrast cinematography by Joseph Ruttenberg, and a stylishly filmed action climax during a raucous street carnival. The cast was a strong one, with Robert Taylor as the romantic lead opposite Ava, Charles Laughton, John Hodiak, and Vincent Price. Laughton was pleased to know the young actress, offering her tips on the phrasing of her lines, advising her as well to read out loud from the Bible as an exercise in speech and cadence. Vincent Price recalled Ava as the one Hollywood actress who fully lived up to her rep as a sex symbol. "My god she was sexy, let me tell ya."

Taylor thought so too. A mutual attraction sparked. She found him a "warm, generous, intelligent human being." Like Gable, Taylor—born Spangler Arlington Brugh—was a diligent pro, doing the job of movie star like a reliable factory worker, fueled by a never-ending intake of black coffee and cigarettes, an outdoorsman away from the studio, happier ranching or flying his airplane than attending parties and premieres. Since 1939 he had been married to Barbara Stanwyck, though he assured Ava

---

*Three years later, aged thirty-three, the actor was dead from a reaction to a dose of sodium amytal administered as a sedative during an emotional crisis, though exactly what occurred in the last hours of Walker's life remains something of a mystery.

that the marriage was on the rocks. Taylor was a careerist of the old school and not a troublemaker (his would end up the longest unbroken star contract in Metro's history). He feared negative gossip, scandal, and the application of the dreaded "morals clause"—and perhaps even more he feared the wrath of his ball-busting wife (who, when his desire for her had waned, spread word that he was impotent, adding fire to an already floating rumor that he was homosexual); an affair had to be carried out in the strictest secrecy. Ava herself enjoyed provoking the town's decency watchdogs, but she agreed to Bob's undercover conditions. Oddly, Taylor's "safe house" for their sexual encounters was the home of his mother, Ruth. One night, postcoital, Taylor had slipped out of bed and run straight into the woman, who had words with him. Ava, wrapped in the sheets, heard Taylor pleading: "Mother, would you rather I go to a cheap hotel?"

For two months or so they enjoyed their secret love affair. By day on the banana republic sets of *The Bribe* they would plot intrigue and mime an adulterous passion, and by night they would do it again for real.

Ten months later Ava would be working in a film with Barbara Stanwyck. Originally Ava had been intended to play the lead role in *East Side, West Side*, but the veteran star had become available and Metro had simply decided to make a switch. "So they moved me into the smaller role. It was a much better part. Metro always treated me like that, but that time it worked to my advantage."

East Side, West Side was a glossy look at love and jealousy among the Manhattan elite, with Ava displayed more erotically and sumptuously than ever in strapless evening wear by studio costume designer Helen Rose. As the melodrama piles up and a homicide plot kicks in, her playgirl character becomes the victim of a deadly rival, the Amazonian blond Beverly Michaels. Among the cast it was Stanwyck who more likely harbored murderous designs on Ava; despite their best efforts, word of her affair with Robert Taylor did reach Stanwyck's ear, and she had placed Gardner on her enemies list forever. Filming *East Side, West Side* she avoided even being introduced to the younger actress. Although Taylor and Ava were never again intimate, Stanwyck suspected them for years, and once sent an emissary to Rome with her husband with orders to keep an eye out for "that Gardner girl," who was also in Europe—though in another country, a thousand miles away (as it happened, Taylor's spare time in Rome would be taken up, this time, with an Italian starlet).

The Great Sinner began as an adaptation of Dostoyevsky's *The Gambler*. The produced screenplay was something both more and less, a confabulation of the Russian writer's life and work with a bit of *Crime and Punishment* thrown in for good measure. "I thought it was a pretty interesting idea," said Christopher Isherwood, co-credited with the screenplay. "Rather than simply film the book, to see how it came to be written. Well, there had been a writer on it for a long time before me, a Hungarian. And I never really had the time to work on all the ideas that I might have had. I rather think the film had too much MGM and not enough Dostoyevsky. I would have liked to make it the other way round.

"I met Ava Gardner at the studio, and of course she was most beautiful. Was she good in the film? I don't think I ever saw it."

The film explored the world of gamblers winning and mostly losing around the tables of the luxurious casino at the Wiesbaden spa in the 1860s. Gregory Peck was the visiting Russian writer, finding material for his next book the hard way by nearly killing himself with a newfound gambling addiction. Ava took the role of a Russian general's daughter, Pauline Ostrovski, a hedonist and adventuress whom Peck's Fedor calls "one of the most corrupt women I've ever met." Pauline's corruption would ultimately be tempered by love, and she becomes his muse, at least in the final cut, nursing him out of the casino and onto the bestseller list.

Sinner reunited Ava with Robert Siodmak, but this would not be the swift, stimulating experience that *The Killers* had been. There was a doorstopper of a screenplay to begin with, which Siodmak complained would run eight hours as written, though producer Gottfried Reinhardt insisted he shoot it all. The great number of scenes within the turbulent casino, filled with extras and incidental movement, caused endless delays and retakes. Siodmak seemed strained, only adding to the problems with a seemingly uncertain perfectionism. The long, tedious shooting and the continual repetitions drove everyone to distraction and exhaustion. Peck, for a scene in which he was supposed to be lying unconscious with fever, spent so much time in the sickbed that he fell asleep for real. George

Folsey, the cinematographer, recalled one simple scene being shot and shot again. "After sixty-some takes, in front of everyone Ava Gardner asked sweetly, 'Bob, may I go to the bathroom after the eighty-first take?' " Siodmak was to be found for long periods of time on the camera crane, raised high up to the rafters, and some members of the cast believed he was not planning shots but simply hiding out.

Some of the many European émigrés who had small parts in the film often gathered around a chessboard during the long wait between setups. Ava would sometimes hover over the players with interest and was finally asked if she wanted to play. She wouldn't mind, she said, and to everyone's pleasure she played a very good game. Ava explained that when she had been married to Artie Shaw he had wanted to play chess with her, so he had hired the Russian grand master Stepan Vronsky to give her lessons. Eventually she and Artie played their first game, she won, and he had never asked her to play again.

The Great Sinner struggled through postproduction. "We cut and cut until it came down to three hours," Siodmak would recall. "But it was still too long, terribly slow, and with the additional disadvantage that now the story didn't even make sense." The director washed his hands of it, leaving others to whittle away another hour and shoot a new, happy ending. The finished film was certainly imperfect, but it was also unique, in part a result of a quirky blend of opposing intentions—Reinhardt's pompous desire for a highbrow literary adaptation running head-on into Siodmak's zesty, sardonic take on degeneracy. Though middlebrow critics would be put off by its perceived middlebrow pretensions, for some there was great fun to be had in seeing all those expensive production values and Metro tradition of quality supporting a tale of vice, addiction, and gambling psychos. For Ava Gardner *The Great Sinner* was a watershed, a professional advancement or at least a revelation. Her smooth, convincing performance in the part of a worldly nineteenth-century Russian aristocrat would have been inconceivable just twenty-four months earlier. Her uncertainties about her abilities and her ambivalence about acting in movies remained, but there was no doubt now that she was up to the job.

Gregory Peck, who would become a lifelong friend, gave her an inspiring pep talk about her need to gain some experience on the live stage. Ava said she had not tried out for a play since high school, and that then she had been eliminated at the first audition. Peck rhapsodized about the theater, and Ava reckoned that she was terrified at the thought of being in front of a live audience but that perhaps in that terror was a challenge she needed to confront. Peck spoke to his connections at the La Jolla Playhouse, and an invitation was extended. Ava nervously agreed to get her feet wet with a very small part. Relaying the invitation to the bosses at MGM she was told, "Of course you can't do that." Ben Thau explained that it just would not do to have an MGM star treading the boards as the third spear carrier from the left. "We can allow you to play the lead or nothing." Ava told Peck and the playhouse thanks but no thanks.

Another watershed moment: Ava bought her first house. She had become sick of apartment living and the noise and the traffic and the sense of impermanence. For many months she went looking at properties, finally settling on a place high on a hill above Nichols Canyon, a modest pink house surrounded by a picket fence. She spent every weekend for months putting it in shape, shopping for fabrics, furnishing one room at a time. She spent all day at a gallery just to find the right images she wanted to hang in her bedroom, choosing a series of Degas prints of dancing girls. To proudly display the hard-won collection of books—many of them actually read—she had amassed since receiving that first syllabus from Artie, she filled the walls of the den with a set of huge antique walnut bookcases, now at last a proper resting place for *Buddenbrooks* and *Babbitt*.

She took particular interest in the yard and garden. She was still a farm girl, no matter what they said of her, still her father's girl. Whatever anyone said about her acting, she knew how to plant and grow, how to weed and prune and dig. The soil proved difficult, as hard to prepare as that damned red clay back home. She and Bappie and her maid and some reluctant volunteers struggled to bring it to life. Visitors said, "Get a landscaper, for God's sake! You're a movie star!"

She filled the sandy hillside that ran below the backyard with purple and yellow ice plant. She had yellow roses run all around the picket fence. A trellis was put up at one side of the house and against it petunias and giant honeysuckle. Nearby she created a drying yard. On the first day they did a wash and put the yard to use, she stood outside and looked at the sheets and towels and blue jeans hanging on the line, she watched the laundry whipping in the breeze, and it looked like a scene from home, long ago, bringing memories of Brogden and the Teacherage and her mother.

Ava had been hiring part-time and live-in maids for years. For a while the job had been held by an efficient young black woman from the Midwest, and when she had suddenly needed to return home for an indefinite period she recommended her younger sister to take her place. Mearene Jordan was a slim, sweet-faced African American with a pleasant manner, a good sense of humor, and a sympathetic ear Ava responded to at once. Soon Mearene—Ava dubbed her "Reenie"—became more than a servant, in time a pal, a sounding board, a drinking buddy, and a member of the family as much as Bappie. Reenie would remain in Ava's employ, off and on, for close to thirty years and be her trusted friend forever, a bumpy ride at times, full of fights, feuds, and separations, but one that lasted till the end. "As good a friend as I've ever had," said Ava. Even before the friendship, Reenie would realize that Ava was no ordinary employer, no average white lady. The prejudiced attitudes that were as common as air in those days never entered Ava's head for a minute. "You were either nice or you were not nice," Reenie would say. "Ava was not color conscious at all."

Racial divides were genuinely absurd to her. She expressed her lack of concern for such things in what was then disarming if not outright daring behavior. George Jacobs, Frank Sinatra's African-American valet in the 1950s and a friend to Ava, recalled: "The most down-to-earth movie star you could ever imagine. She always told me she was part black, that 'poor white trash' always had some black blood in them."* Ava came to have a number of friends among the black showbiz community in Hollywood,

---

*Quotes like that and Ava Gardner's color-blind friendships and roles like the half-black Julie in *Show Boat,* have no doubt fueled continuing suppositions about her ethnic background. In recent times, she has been claimed (along with Elvis Presley and a few other attractive celebrities) as a member of the mysterious mixed-race tribe known as the Melungeons, a Southern-states ethnic group composed of African, American-Indian, and Mediterranean bloodlines. The author is aware of no genealogical evidence for these claims.

including Dorothy Dandridge, Herb Jeffries, Lena Horne, and musician and vocal coach Phil Moore. These were not relationships with an asterisk attached, guilt-ridden or condescending, but simple, real friendships. She went to their houses and they to hers, they socialized, argued, got drunk. With her black friends she would be seen at the bebop clubs in the ghetto neighborhood of Central Avenue, her regular appearances incurring the wrath of the LA Vice Department, made nervous by too much race mixing, especially any involving famous, beautiful white women.

Lena Horne, who lived not far from Ava's Nichols Canyon house, would come to call Ava her younger sister, her spiritual kin. "She didn't feel she was born to rule," Lena wrote. "She felt that life was crappy and that a lot of people got mistreated for weird reasons and she liked to see people like each other." They shared a similar taste in men, said Lena. "Musicians mostly, black and white. . . . We were both regretful that frequently the finest lovers were not the ones you really *loved*." The two would sit together high above the canyon for long hours discussing men and women and love and the ironies and inequities of it all.

The sorry state of racial relations in America and his call for strong civil rights legislation were among the things that drew Ava to the 1948 presidential candidacy of Henry Wallace, FDR's onetime vice president, now running a third-party campaign against Harry Truman, the man who had taken his job and become president on Roosevelt's death. Ava's first visit back home in two years coincided with Wallace's tumultous campaign swing through the South. As he moved from state to state giving speeches, demanding integrated audiences wherever he spoke, proponents of the Jim Crow status quo greeted him with catcalls, tomatoes, violence. A young campaign worker was stabbed in the chest. When Wallace came to Raleigh, North Carolina, Ava agreed to join the candidate on the dais at a luncheon at the Sir Walter Hotel. Wallace spoke passionately of the struggle at hand against prejudice and intolerance in the South. "I know we cannot legislate love," said the Progressive Party candidate, "but we most certainly can and will legislate against hate."

Ava chatted with Wallace afterward, promising to help his campaign in any way she could. "He is a fine man," she told reporters. Some found Wallace to be a naive idealist and a Stalinist appeaser, including Louis B.

Mayer, who summoned Ava to his office and advised her to stay away
from such "radical" engagements. "I warned Katharine Hepburn as I'm
warning you, and she wouldn't listen to me and look at her, she's destroyed her career!"

What in fact concerned Mayer and the men on the third floor far more
than Ava's progressive politics was her radical social life. The gossip filtered through to Mayer like so many dispatches from a war zone. She
drank too much, she used foul language in public, knew too many men.
There were rumors, stories told—raucous behavior, a prurient interest in
sex—taking off her clothes for that bearded artist at Universal, and the
time, at a barbecue at William Holden's house, Ronald Reagan had come
upon Ava, the black model Maddy Comfort, and artist Paul Clemens all
splashing around together, all three stark naked; Reagan had nearly fallen
into the pool himself he was so startled—stories like the one of her night
in San Francisco on a publicity appearance for *The Hucksters*, a drunken
night on the town when Ava had coaxed an old hack journalist to take her
to see the town's most notorious brothel and she'd mingled with the
whores, looked through two-way mirrors, and god knew what-all had
gone on. Stories, rumors of aggressive seductions, group sex parties, an
interracial romance—with another woman. With Ava, Metro fretted,
there was at any moment the potential for a career-destroying scandal—
now, Mayer and his boys moaned, after all the time and money they had
invested in making her a star, all the money that was to be made, what a
painful irony it was.

But what could you do? She was defiant, this girl they had nurtured
since she had come out of the woods seven years ago. Threats fell on deaf
ears with Ava. She would threaten right back—say she was thinking of
leaving the business, quitting to get an education, going back to North
Carolina, crazy things. All they could do was keep a close watch and try
to keep her from destroying their valuable property. What a business we
are in, they would grumble—where the merchandise went off on its own
at night and might not come back in one piece in the morning.

One evening the studio had set her up on an important interview with
some reporters from *Time*. Visiting from the New York office, Henry
Grunwald (the magazine's future managing editor), along with the head
of the LA bureau, sat quizzing the star over dinner at an Italian restaurant.
As Grunwald recalled the scene, Metro publicist George Nichols had

planted himself firmly between the reporters and the star to referee the interview and to make sure Ava behaved, which in no time at all she had refused to do. Grunwald found her altogether "fantastic." Yes, she told him, she certainly did have a reputation as a sexpot, and yes, it was pretty fucking well deserved. Eyeing a young member of the waitstaff standing nearby, she said, "People think I am the type who would take the busboy out back. And"—the young man trembled as she looked him over—"I just might."

"Fantastic," breathed Grunwald.

Nichols tried desperately to change the subject, to which efforts Ava responded with hostility. In another moment, fed up with the flack's interruptions, she excused herself to go to the ladies room. Grunwald sensed she was ditching them and gave pursuit, catching up with her in the parking lot. Without saying a word Ava let him into the car and sped off. "She was the most reckless driver I have ever known," he would write. "After a hair-raising ride we arrived at her home and proceeded to attack a bottle of Courvoisier. She had just kicked off her shoes and started dancing on the coffee table when Nichols arrived, panting and fuming."

In the autumn of 1949 Metro had loaned her out once more, this time to RKO, the studio now owned and run by her old friend Howard Hughes. Hughes had yet to set foot on the lot, though he was in every other way a hands-on mogul, screening tests and dailies of every production, involved in scripting, casting, and editing, as well as directing the wiretapping of dressing rooms and demanding oaths of loyalty to the United States and signed denials of Communist affiliations from his employees.

My Forbidden Past—originally titled *Carriage Trade*—was an accursed project long before Ava Gardner arrived at the studio to begin filming— and indeed it remained an albatross of a production long after she was gone. Hughes had alienated the producer, Polan Banks, and fired the originally scheduled star, Ann Sheridan (who successfully sued him for damages). Set in 1890s New Orleans, *My Forbidden Past* was a plot-heavy, convoluted melodrama about a vindictive heiress seeking revenge on her former flame, and nearly sending him to the gallows for a murder he did not commit before her final, self-sacrificing change of heart. It was a strong part for Ava, a passionate, self-absorbed villainess of the sort that had made Bette Davis's reputation a decade before, and she performed it well. But the film, as released, defied enjoyment; it was slow and unlikable and lifeless. There was something rough, unfinished about it all, the blame for this probably lying with Hughes, who personally fussed over the film, reediting and trimming it month after month, to what end no one could fathom. It would not be released for nearly two years after principal photography had concluded, and after its brief run in the theaters was written off as a seven-hundred-thousand-dollar loss to the stockholders.

Ava's costar was RKO's broad-shouldered, hipster workhorse, Robert Mitchum. It took little time on the set for these two to find common cause. They were birds of a feather in many ways. Ava felt a strong surge of attraction for the insolent, amusing, smoldering actor. She flirted and teased him outrageously in their romantic scenes, bringing Mitchum to the very edge of losing his cool, a thing theretofore impossible to imagine. Ava took to hanging out in his dressing room because hers was "way over there on the other side of the lot" or something; she'd sit around with Mitchum and some of his cronies, Ava in her high-necked wasp-waisted 1890s costume and barefoot, swapping stories and swigging cocktails. Ava asked him for a lift home one night, and they stopped somewhere for a drink. It might have been a few drinks. In Ava's mostly decorous, often whitewashed memoir, she wrote regarding Mitchum: "Let me make a frank admission: if I *could* have gotten him into bed, I *would* have." The line (italics her own) may be read as pointedly ambiguous. Mitchum, in his comments to pals regarding Ava, left less room for interpretation: She *could* get him into bed, and she *did*. Mitchum would tell people for years to come that Ava was the most beautiful and exciting woman he had ever known.

"That was when I first met Ava, when she was going around with Bob," recalled Herb Jeffries, the tall, handsome singer (formerly of the Duke Ellington Band) and actor in movies ("the Bronze Buckaroo," the first black cowboy star). "I was working in a club called El Morocco. And he was doing a picture with her, and he brought her in to hear me sing. Several times they came in to see me. They were having a fling, yeah, yeah. Robert was a great club carouser, and I think the both of them were redecorating some of the clubs on Sunset Boulevard. They were having a lot of fun. I'd go over to the table with them and have a drink. And Ava and I got along very well, we became friends. She came to see me sing by herself as well. She was always very warm, very friendly, like somebody that wasn't even in the business. No big ego on her at all. She was far above that. And Bob was the greatest guy. Yeah, they were having some fun."

They would slip out the RKO gate each evening when filming for the day was concluded, headed off on a long nocturnal adventure among the bars and jazz clubs and after-hours hangouts of Los Angeles. Ava thought she knew the town's nightspots pretty well, but Mitchum would introduce her to places, whole neighborhoods, she had never known existed, a hep underground ten strata deep, filled with amiably unsavory characters, each of whom seemed to be Bob's best friend. Mitchum was only a few months out of prison, where he had served time on a conspiracy-to-possess-marijuana charge—caught by the cops in a Hollywood Hills bungalow with some reefer and a pair of brassy blond starlets. Mitchum had managed to survive a scandal that might have ended almost anyone else's career. Nonetheless, and despite still being on probation, he was far from on his best behavior. He was still smoking dope, some nights as frequently and openly as tobacco. Ava had little to no interest in drugs, had once snorted some cocaine off the fingertips of Errol Flynn (he'd sworn it would help her get to an early morning hairdressing call in tiptop form), and had smoked a little grass during her marriage to Artie, and neither experience had impressed her. Bob, a proselytizer for pot, thought she had perhaps gotten some inferior product and suggested she give it another try, offered a joint from his shirt pocket, and lit her up. Mitchum had the pedigree of all his weed: This, he explained, was from the crop of a one-eyed Dutch farmer on one of the lesser Banda Islands in the South China Sea. Ava smoked away, and later that night, after a disconcerting period of what felt like uncontrollable levitation, she swore off grass for good.

"I think," she would write years later, "every girl who ever worked with Bob fell in love with him, and I was no exception."

Love or lust or infatuation, for a moment in time it seemed real, like it was going somewhere.

But there was a problem. Mitchum was married to his childhood sweet-heart. It was a far-from-perfect marriage and Mitchum had strayed before, but his wife, Dorothy, had a hold on him one way or another; she was his home port, and he always sooner or later went back, a pattern Ava was un-aware of at the moment. It was a hot affair, and Ava thought Mitchum as smitten with her as she was with him. She urged him to leave his wife so they could be together, at which point Robert suggested that Dorothy would probably not like the idea. "Let me talk to her," said Ava, and ac-cording to Mitchum she had actually called Mrs. Mitchum on the phone to discuss what they were going to do about the situation. Ava had asked Dorothy if she hadn't had him long enough and if it wasn't time to give another gal a chance? Dorothy, in Mitchum's wry recounting, answered, "No," to both questions and hung up the phone. "One of the most under-standing wives I've ever met," wrote Ava, cagily, in her autobiography.

Mitchum drifted away with the end of filming.

It was always the same damn thing, somebody wanted too much and somebody not enough. You hurt or you got hurt, and you could never trust love to do the right thing. Love was a trick, a double cross. She was making an early resolution, swearing off love for the new year.

Torchy Ava Gardner Croons "Where's the Right Man?" Tune
By Hedda Hopper

Ava Gardner, the torchiest thing we have in Hollywood today, admits she's "man-hungry." Don't get her wrong . . . she thoroughly likes her job as a four-figure working girl on the Metro-Goldwyn-Mayer soundstages. But she's had the nightclubs and the glamour romeos and the parties . . . and she'd trade it all any day for a man who would give her a home, a family, and all the other things in the good, old-fashioned American concept of what's really worthwhile.

"There is just one thing missing," she says, "that would make the whole picture perfect for me."

We know what she means. But stop pushing, fellows, She swears she'll know him when she sees him. No. 3 is her lucky number, and No. 3's coming up.

PART TWO

FIVE

Frankie Goes to Hollywood

He was born, as the story goes, too big for this world: nearly fourteen pounds, a traumatic breech birth, forceps tearing open the baby's face and neck, left for dead by the distracted doctor. His grandmother refused the physician's pronouncement and rushed the boy to the kitchen sink, a torrent of cold December water shocking him back to life.

He was from Hoboken, a square mile of working-class Jersey town across the river from Manhattan, his people Italian immigrants and new Americans: Marty Sinatra from Sicily at the country's southern tip, mother Dolly from Genoa in the north. The father was inarticulate, introverted; a tattooed, short-money pug and laborer who could not read or write. Dolly was smart, brash, strong-willed, a candy dipper, a midwife, a wheeler-dealer in local politics. Dolly could have no more children after that first, damaging birth, so the boy, Francis Albert, grew up an only child in a neighborhood of big families. He was an isolated, self-involved kid, frail, sometimes the victim of local toughs and gang violence. But he had a gift of music in his throat and the imagination to know what he might do with it. It took some time, a slow meandering course, via small club bookings and radio remotes, with at last a big break in 1939 at the age of twenty-four as vocalist with trumpeter Harry James's struggling new band, and then eight months later a place at the summit of the big-band world, singing for Tommy Dorsey's all-star outfit.

Vocalists were a minor element in the impact of a swing band in that era, but the captivating qualities of Sinatra's voice and lyric phrasing brought him plenty of individual attention. His innovative, self-created manner of singing took the intimate crooning of Bing Crosby and the more sensuous stylings of Billie Holiday and wove them through a lyrical musicality likened to classic Italian bel canto. Inevitably he would leave Dorsey for a solo career, quickly achieving a level of popularity and acclaim that put him among the handful of most successful performers in the world. He was at first famously the idol swooned over by young females of the war years, disdained by males, some resenting his escape from military service (reportedly for the punctured eardrum sustained during that natal trauma—though other factors may have been considered, including a diagnosed psychoneurosis, and the fact that he was the married father of a small child). The resentments mostly faded, worn down by his brilliance and omnipresence, and the sound of Frank Sinatra's voice— "the Voice," as it was known—became the sound of the age, the emotional identity of the war years felt in the yearning, almost desperate romanticism of Sinatra's dreamy ballads with their lush, enveloping Alex Stordahl arrangements.

Sinatra had married in 1939, a raven-haired Italian American Jersey girl named Nancy Barbato. She was a homebody, devoted and maternal, not glamorous but with a certain plainspoken beauty, a neighborhood girl with the earthy dark looks that evoked the old country. He was no Greek god, average-looking at first glance except for the strikingly blue eyes, another face from the neighborhood, scrawny in physique, with the scars of his brutal birth evident on his face and neck; but he glowed with the fury of his talent and charisma, and in success he presented himself in dazzling array—hand-tailored and avant-mode wardrobe, manicures and onyx pinky rings that guaranteed he was never going to be mistaken for an average mook from Monroe Street in Hoboken. Nancy bore with him three children, in the second, the sixth, and the ninth years of their marriage: two girls and a boy. She was a great mother and a loving, loyal wife. He was a devoted dad and errant husband, an egotist and compulsive womanizer who denied himself few if any of the pleasures his fame and power made possible.

In 1944 the Sinatras relocated from their New Jersey home to California, and Frank signed on at Metro-Goldwyn-Mayer. He starred with Gene Kelly in the hit musical *Anchors Aweigh*, directed by George Sidney, Sinatra playing what would be his typical role as a shy, small-town boy who had no experience with girls. Once he had become settled in Hollywood, with its increased, constant temptations, his philandering increased, and he seemed to look upon his marriage as little more than a sentimental formality, or so some said. He carried on affairs all but openly with various available women, including Marilyn Maxwell, Marlene Dietrich, and in 1946 Lana Turner, with Turner believing for a time that he was leaving his wife to marry her. He maintained separate residences or a presence in shared bachelor pads apart from the family home where Nancy raised the kids. He needed places to bring women, places where he and hedonistic pals like songwriter Jimmy van Heusen could host raucous gatherings often attended by contingents of prostitutes. Nonetheless, however tattered, the marriage remained a fact, and the family continued to grow: the third child, Christina, would be born in June 1948.

In 1948, Frank Sinatra was, as he had been for many years, a prominent and important star of films, radio, recordings, and concerts, with a growing international following now that the end of war had returned American pop culture to the world market. Few others in show business could claim such a major and multifaceted success. Nevertheless, a decline in Sinatra's fortunes was at hand. The bobby-soxers had stopped their screaming, and a new generation looked for other, younger singing idols. Popular music itself was shifting away from the romantic balladry and lush orchestrations of the war years, veering toward the nascent sound of folk and rock and roll, styles that to Frank Sinatra would forever be anathema. At MGM he had found little success away from his roles as Gene Kelly's sidekick. His record sales were not what they had been, and for the first time since his ascent to stardom the critical and popular polls of favorite vocalists no longer ranked him the best of all. Brawls with columnists and newspaper exposés that claimed to tie him to various organized crime figures or to Communist political fronts further chipped at his luster. As the 1940s drew to their end, a difficult and dramatic period in Frank Sinatra's life was about to begin, a period of great professional losses and personal crises, of ecstasies and despair, of self-destruction and at last spectacular regeneration. He was about to fall in love with Ava Gardner.

They had actually met many times through the years, even been out on a date once. Skitch Henderson, the musician and bandleader, working as a rehearsal pianist at Metro just before the war, believed he had introduced Ava to Frank for the first time ever, soon after she had arrived at the studio; it was following a concert, Frank was still with the Dorsey band, and he had come over to say hi. "It was just, Frank this is Ava, Ava this is Frank, you know, but I think that was the first they set eyes on each other." They had later passed each other in the corridors of nightclubs, at the studio, at charity events like the celebrity baseball game in which she had been a cheerleader for his team, the Swooners—they had posed together for photographers, Ava with her arm around him. Once at the Mocambo, married to Mickey Rooney, she had been introduced by Mickey, and Sinatra had been jokingly flirtatious: "Why didn't I meet you first?" She had even once been to his house, making a brief appearance with Peter Lawford at the Sinatras' New Year's Eve party at Toluca Lake.

For a time they had been sort of neighbors, Ava in a small apartment house on Sunset Boulevard and Sinatra camped out in a bachelor pad in a high-rise building next door. One evening they had run into each other on the street, and he had talked her into going to dinner. Over food and drink she found herself attracted to his bright blue eyes and "incredible grin." He was pleased with himself, pleased with her, and his enthusiasm proved sufficiently winning to get her up to a different nearby apartment—she wasn't sure whose—and into a heated make-out session. Clearly he had wanted to ease her from the couch to the bedroom, but Ava knew about his marriage, his new child, felt a surge of conscience and pulled away. Enough with married men, she told herself, and not long afterward she had moved on to another neighborhood and saw no more of Frank Sinatra. For a while.

Autumn 1949. With Bappie in tow, Ava had gone to Palm Springs for a couple of weeks of rest and recreation in the desert air and sun. One night she went out to a large party at the home of producer Darryl F. Zanuck. Frank was there. He was grinning like an excited young boy at their reunion. They talked and laughed. At some point, the flirting starting to get under her skin, Ava broke off and shook her head at him.

"That all sounds swell, Frank—but you're *still married*."

"No, doll," he told her. "It's over. It is done."

They had both been drinking for hours and were looped and giddy when they left the party, announcing that Frank was going to drive her home. They slipped away with a fresh bottle of something from Zanuck's bar and got into Sinatra's Cadillac Brougham convertible. Frank didn't know where Ava was staying and didn't ask. They drove into the night, roaring out of town, headed into the desert flatlands. Frank pressed the accelerator to the floor, racing to nowhere with a crazed determination, Ava opening the bottle of booze and drinking it straight, passing it back and forth to Frank behind the wheel.

They reached the small outpost of Indio, surrounded by nothing but dirt and black sky, and Sinatra careened up over a street corner and squealed to a stop. He pulled Ava toward him, and for a while they kissed and squirmed and groped. As Ava pulled back to take another drink, Sinatra opened his glove compartment and took out two .38 Smith & Wessons, extended one pistol in a vaguely vertical direction, and fired it three times until a sharp plink sounded and one of the streetlights went out and glass tinkled to the dusty ground below. He tried for another and got it on the first shot.

Ava said, "Let me shoot something!" And she took the other gun and fired it at random into the sky, at the ground, into a hardware store window. Frank put the car in gear, screeched around back onto the street, and roared the car forward, steering with one hand, shooting at the streetlamps with the other. Ava turned around in the front seat and as the car accelerated she fired across the back of the car and let forth an ear-splitting rebel yell. They shot the .38s empty and then turned up a side street in a squeal of rubber, heading back for the main road. They had not yet regained the highway back to Palm Springs when they heard the siren and saw the flashing light of a police car. The car cut them off, and two officers approached with their own guns drawn.

"Christ," Sinatra mumbled, "what do these clowns want now?"

Ava lay on a bench in the police station and catnapped while Frank talked turkey with the police. The cop in charge was deferential to the two Hollywood stars, and agreed to let Frank phone his publicist in Los Angeles. As it is told, the publicist was awakened, talked to the policeman, and asked him to name a figure that would make the story go away and the policeman named the figure, and in a few hours, in a chartered plane, the publicist was in the desert with a suitcase full of cash. Ava was back in Palm Springs in the morning. Bappie was up and having breakfast, and Ava told her she had been out with Frank Sinatra and they had had a wonderful time.

In Los Angeles he came for her, a quiet date this time, with no guns drawn. They had dinner at a candlelit Italian restaurant in Hollywood. The evening was diametric to their Wild West night in the Springs. They were both sober. Frank was subdued and yet in a way no less intense than in his manic mood out on the desert. He talked to her with great feeling; he was earnest, romantic, and, she thought, honest. He did not try to evade the subject of his wife or family, but spoke of them with concern, loyalty, and love. The marriage, Frank told her, had been over for years, but it continued in name only for the sake of his kids. If Ava wondered why another child had been produced in the long-failed marriage only twelve or so months before, she did not pursue it. If she was feeling some awareness that he had probably turned on this sad-sweet intense charm with a hundred other women in a hundred other spaghetti joints, she did not pursue that either. There were the blue eyes to contend with, the voice, the hands holding hers beside the candlelight. She was in no mood to argue with his version of reality; it seemed to suit them both fine.

They drove to Ava's eagle's nest above Nichols Canyon, to the pink house, the yellow bedroom, and they made love for the first time. She would invest that night with an aura of magic, of myth. At the end of her life, constructing an autobiography, speaking memories into a portable tape recorder, by then as much a believer in the legend of their romance as any reader of *Modern Screen* magazine, she would recall those first intimate hours in epiphanic terms. "We became," she would record, "lovers forever—eternally. . . . I truly felt that no matter what happened we would always be in love."

She called him Francis. "He looks like Francis to me," she would say, the extent of her explanation, "and I know him better than anybody." They were much alike, in temperament, tastes, sympathies, neuroses. Each had been raised by a taciturn father and an outgoing mother, two children of the Great Depression, children of FDR, instinctive defenders of the underdog, resentful of authority. Both were wary of the better bred, and both at times fancied themselves victims of bigotry, whether cultural (Ava the "hillbilly") or ethnic ("I'd see a guy staring at me from the corner of the room," Sinatra would say, "and I knew what word was in his head. The word was 'guinea' "). Both felt discomfited by their lack of education (Sinatra was a high school dropout) and had become self-consciously self-improvers, diligent readers of good books and upscale journals, admirers of writers, composers, and intellectuals.

They were both independent-minded, hotheaded, selfish, possessive, suspicious—traits intensified by the alcohol of which they were equally fond; they were both generous, open, affectionate, sensitive, funny. Both were highly sensual people, with strong sexual drives. Ava would speak of Frank's ability to go on and on in bed, while Sinatra characterized her to friend Jimmy van Heusen as "out there" sexually, ready or eager to try anything. There were rumors—of modest provenance, but similar to gossip about some of Ava's later relationships—of a consensual brutality to their lovemaking.

They were both creatures of the night, proclaimed insomniacs. For both the night held the promise of elation as well as sadness—Sinatra famously described himself as "an 18-carat manic-depressive"—as the hours passed and the crowd all fell away and there was nothing left anywhere but sleep. Both often felt a painful sense of loneliness they would seek to deny in the brash public spectacle they so often made of their lives. "Ava gave the impression of being insecure, Frank of being supremely confident," said David Hanna, Ava's manager in the 1950s. "Actually, each had something of both qualities in their characters."

They were too much alike, perhaps, too much for comfort, for survival, for in the bond they forged there was a devastating insight, one into the other, like an X-ray into each one's heart and soul, as it would happen an insight dangerous and destructive in its exposure of weakness, vanity, lies, need.

Not long after the affair began in earnest, Ava ran into her friend Lana Turner. It was an encounter she had been avoiding. Lana had been crazy for Frank a couple of years before, spoken of herself as "engaged" to him despite his marital status, and she had back then confided to Ava many details about their passionate love life. Indeed, that first night Ava had gone to bed with Sinatra, she had been unavoidably reminded of the earlier affair and Lana's giddy rants about Frank's priapic endowment; she found out that Lana had not exaggerated those dimensions in the slightest (Sinatra naked, said pal Jackie Gleason, looked like a tuning fork). The Sinatra-Turner affair, though, had ended abruptly and terribly, with Lana rather brutally dumped.

"Darling," she said now, "I hear you've been seeing Frank. You haven't fallen for him, have you?"

"We're in love, baby," said Ava.

Lana gripped her by the forearm. "Don't let him hurt you, sweetie. He'll lead you on, he'll tell you whatever you want to hear, but you mustn't believe him."

"We're gone for each other," said Ava. "This is for keeps."

"He'll never leave that wife of his. I'm warning you."

"He's going to leave her if he wants to be with me. And he does."

"Have they separated, darling? I haven't read anything in the papers about it."

Nancy Sinatra remained defiantly devoted. She would not be moved by her husband's proclaimed love for another woman. She had seen it all before, lived through it, survived, and remained Mrs. Frank Sinatra. Frank's advisers, at the same time, warned him of the backlash that was sure to come if his philandering were to become public knowledge.

Ava, too, still had ties to past relationships. She had been seeing Howard Duff off and on for more than two years. They went out now one last time, and she told him it was finally over, there was someone else. Duff said, "I know, I know," repeated it over and over like a moan and could say nothing else and finished his drink and went away without ever looking at her again.

Howard Hughes, who did not need to be told anything about the developing relationship with Sinatra since his spies had apprised him of every bit of it, demanded Ava meet him for a late dinner, told her that he had some very important news for her that she could not afford to ignore.

"This man you've been seeing," Hughes said. "You have to stay away from him."

"Oh, please, Howard, is that what this is about?"

"There are things about this man, Ava," he persisted, "of which you have no idea. He has some very shady associates. I'm talking about criminal associations and things you are better off not knowing, but you've got to trust me, I know what the heck I'm talking about."

"We're in love, Howard."

"Listen to me, this character has got women all over town."

"Howard, you're one to talk!"

"I mean call girls, niggers. . . . I can show you evidence that—"

"You've said enough!"

"He's not good enough for you, Ava! You've got to listen to me—"

This time she got up and left the restaurant.

There was another guy who had been pursuing her then, a young, good-looking thug named Johnny Stompanato, a lieutenant of racket king Mickey Cohen. Stompanato had a thing for young movie actresses (like who didn't) and had been sniffing around Ava for weeks. Ava told Frank that she barely knew the guy, but when somebody tipped him that she and Johnny had been seen sitting together at the Cock and Bull in Hollywood, he called Mickey Cohen directly and asked to come over to discuss a thing—and right away. Cohen told him it was not a good idea to come over as he was under twenty-four-hour observation by the police just then, but Sinatra insisted.

"Lookit," Sinatra said, "I want you to do me this favor. I want you to tell your guy Stompanato to stop seeing Ava Gardner."

Cohen, under a lot of stress from trying to stay out of prison, couldn't believe Sinatra wanted to risk the cops looking him over for a case of "hot nuts." Cohen told him, "This is what ya call important? I don't mix in with no guys and their broads, Frank. Why don't ya go on home to Nancy where you belong?"

For a time, while Sinatra supposedly negotiated with his wife, they remained discreet, sticking to dimly lit restaurants, nights tucked away together at her house in the hills or various friends' homes or rented playpens. But neither had a lot of experience with a low profile, and before long they were drawn back to the bright light, to the action. In December, Ava followed Frank to New York, where he was to be a guest on a radio program. They were given a joint birthday party by Jack Entratter, who ran the Copacabana and was negotiating to bring Frank to the club for a long-running gig. In New York they did their best not to provide any revealing photos, but the press caught sight of them together at a Broadway opening. They were in fact sharing a bed in the Hampshire House suite of Columbia Records exec Manie Sachs, Frank's close associate at the label.

Now Ava was entering into Frank's professional world, mixing with the cronies and hangers-on as well as the more serious support group that had helped to make possible his spectacular career. There was, most important, George Evans, a devoted and cunning personal publicist who had orchestrated Sinatra's war-years climb to the pinnacle of showbiz success. Evans was the man who had famously seeded the Paramount Theater with bobby-soxers paid to scream and faint, causing by example a legendary riot of unhinged swooning in the theater and miles of subsequent press attention. Evans had been there at each new level of success, smoothing the path, helping to mold Sinatra's public image—modest, demure, family man, notwithstanding the erotic effect of his singing—and he and his team were the people who ran interference on Frank's many fuckups, picking up the pieces when the notoriously volatile and impulsive entertainer did something—again and again—to risk public disapproval and professional suicide, from drunken brawls to vicious feuds with reporters and columnists (he had notoriously given a beat down to one by the name of Lee Mortimer), from unsavory acquaintance with figures from the world of organized crime to sexual affairs. From the beginning, Sinatra's obsessive pursuit of women other than his wife had been Evans's number one concern, behavior that, if exposed, Evans believed would have a devastating effect on the man's public image as husband and father, the earnest milquetoast of those MGM musicals and humble host on the radio.

It did not take Ava long to realize the antagonism directed at her by Evans and some of the others who suckled at the Sinatra teat. There were awkward glances and whispered asides that provoked an incipient paranoia, which a few drinks always made worse. There was nothing she hated more than people talking behind her back, she would say. She had had the days when people had mocked her and put her down, and she was not about to take any of that shit anymore, and certainly not from Frank's flunkies. She saw Frank's fierce reaction to disrespect and she made it her own. When Evans on one occasion pointedly ignored her and asked Frank to excuse himself for a few private words, Ava abruptly grabbed her coat and stormed off, disappearing completely for days.

"What do you got to be like that for?" Frank would say when he had tracked her down.

"Why do you let that jerk tell you what to do? Is he in charge or are you in charge? Maybe I should go out with *him* if he's so fucking special."

"He does what's good for me . . . what I tell him to do."

"Didn't look that way to me, baby."

Frank would be caught short: What the fuck? No woman had ever behaved like that toward him. She could go from affection to fury in an instant, and when she wanted to get at him she knew at once the buttons to push. Sometimes he thought she could read his mind, get right inside his secret thoughts or fears like a witch. Ava seemed to intuit that Evans had been behind the boyish, shy little titmouse image Sinatra had long projected in the movies and on *Your Hit Parade*, and she needled him, made jokes about it. Frank would snarl back, "Oh, quit your bullshit." But having her put things like that into words would unnerve him. In no time at all George Evans, his loyal and incalculably valuable associate, became a demeaning presence, an obstacle in the way of Ava's respect. Evans, meanwhile, sensing that a feud was on, unmindfully charged up his rhetoric against her. He had seen the bimbos come before, and he had shooed them away before, and he believed he could do the same with this one, as if Ava were just another pliable, easygoing Marilyn Maxwell or one of the other gonetomorrow "broads." Ava was trouble, he told Frank, and there were too many other problems in his career just now to risk making a mess that Evans couldn't promise to be able to clean up; why didn't he get some sense and go back to Nancy and cool off for a while. Sinatra listened, he looked the publicist up and down; then he looked Ava Gardner up and down.

George Evans was history.

The problem with Nancy Sinatra proved less easy to resolve. Ava and Frank had begun to talk about marriage. Frank wanted it, Ava was willing, but what to do about Nancy? In January, at Ava's urging, Frank had made a dramatic show of removing all of his belongings from the family house on Carolwood Drive. Still, his wife insisted it was a temporary situation, and when Frank had gotten over his latest infatuation he would be back. Ava cursed her. "She's pathetic," she said. "Why would any woman want to hold a man who doesn't want her?"

With a mounting set of debts and tax liens added to his already extravagant spending habits, plus the waning of his popularity in other venues, Sinatra was now being forced to return to concert and club performing, something he had done rarely in the past several years, and then only with a few high-profile engagements. For the last week of January he was booked for a week as the inaugural act at the Shamrock Hotel, a new luxury lodging in Houston, Texas. The opening had to be postponed several days when Sinatra learned, en route to Texas, that George Evans, at forty-eight, had dropped dead of a coronary. Friends would recall Sinatra's grave concern that his recent harsh words and firing of his old associate had in some way contributed to the unexpected tragedy. Ava had heard about the death from one of Frank's inner circle, but Frank himself would not speak of Evans to her, ever. She decided on impulse to fly to Houston and surprise him at the Shamrock gig—to comfort him and perhaps to remind him that he had made the right decision in choosing her over his publicist.

She arrived late for his performance, the house lights down, but even in the dark she caught every eye and provoked a stir of excited whispers across the entire room. When he saw her Sinatra beamed as if he had been hit with a hot red spotlight. If the audience wondered about a possible relationship between the two stars, Sinatra did little to disconnect the dots, compulsively directing each song directly to Ava as if everyone else in the room had gone home.

Houston's mayor, Oscar Holcombe, hosted a dinner for Frank and guests at Vincent's Sorrento restaurant in town. Happy to get the publicity, the restaurant's owner, Tony Vallone, had okayed a photographer from the *Houston Post* to approach the mayor's table.

"Mind if I take a shot of you folks eating your spaghetti?" the photographer said, bringing the viewfinder to his eye.

Some of the guests were already lifting their heads and wineglasses and smiling for the camera as Sinatra said, "No pictures, with or without spaghetti."

Accounts differ: The photographer didn't move away fast enough and Sinatra growled, "Beat it, you bum," leaping out of his chair to chase him off, or the photographer snapped a flash shot anyway and Frank did the leap bit and grabbed for the camera. Ava screamed, "Frank, stop it!" then turned away in anger or embarrassment. Vallone moved in quickly to break it up and rushed the newspaper man out of harm's way, which was more than he could do for Frank Sinatra and Ava Gardner. An account of the incident appeared in newspapers across the country, including the *Los Angeles Times*.

As a result, Nancy Sinatra changed the locks on the house. The public humiliation of seeing her husband's affair all but confirmed for the whole country became too much. She sought a lawyer. For Mrs. Sinatra, too, the loss of George Evans had proved significant; in the past he had always been on hand to mollify her with a bullshit alibi for her husband's philandering, and now he was no longer there to tell her that Ava would go away or that a press release would straighten out the facts for her and the world, explain how Miss Gardner had in fact been in Houston merely to visit her dying aunt.

On Valentine's Day, 1950, Nancy announced her intentions, bared her feelings for public consumption: "My married life with Frank has become most unhappy and almost unbearable. We have therefore separated. I have requested my attorney to attempt to work out a property settlement, but I do not contemplate divorce proceedings in the foreseeable future."

Now, Ava would remember, the shit hit the fan.

Though both had been fully aware that the potential for scandal was hanging over their affair while Frank remained famously married with children, neither had any premonition of how big the negative reaction would become. A conflagration was about to engulf them. The antagonism came from many and diverse sources, various constituencies, agendas, and vendettas. There were all of the minimally sophisticated movie-magazine-reading citizens who had invested too much faith in the idealized image of Frankie as smiling, humble family man, as well as in the murkier persona of Ava as femme fatale. There was the heartland public that did not take tales of adultery at all lightly, those who shared the Sinatras' Roman Catholic background expressing particular offense (nuns at some Catholic schools supposedly asked the students to pray for Mrs. Sinatra); there were the wives from the same heartland stirred to outrage by Frank's and his jezebel's humiliation of Nancy. There was the press, the right-wing columnists who had seethed over Sinatra's "pinko" sympathies (Ava's similar politics had gone largely unnoticed), and all those other newsmen who despised Sinatra for his physical and verbal attacks on their brethren in the corps, only too happy to have a chance to strike back. And perhaps goading it all there was the climate of the times, an era of angry moralizing and witch hunts and blacklists: In the same period Ingrid Bergman's adulterous affair and the controversial politics of various film people had gotten them banned from working in Hollywood. Fearful, hypocritically pious, and vindictive impulses were everywhere. For Ava and Frank it was as though they had stepped into a fire, bad enough in itself, and it had brought forth an army of pyromaniacs all toting five-gallon cans of gasoline.

Both were flooded with correspondence from an outraged citizenry. Angry letters by the hundreds were also received by Metro, Columbia Records, radio stations, and every movie magazine and Hollywood columnist. One of the singer's fan clubs reportedly shipped a package addressed to "Frankie Not-So-Hot-Tra," enclosing a stack of his old records, broken. Many of the missives sent directly to Ava began with such informal salutations as "Dear Bitch." One reproving letter Sinatra received came from Willie Moretti, the syphilitic don of the New Jersey mob: "I am very much surprised what I have been reading in the newspapers between you and your darling wife." (It was probably the last time the two would correspond, since, a bit later, Moretti met his end in a hail of bullets at Joe's Elbow Room in Cliffside Park, New Jersey.)

Columnist Hedda Hopper's files filled with combustible letters from enraged readers.

"I don't know if I should condemn [Sinatra] or pity him. Any man who would put a wife of Nancy's calibre in the position of competing with a

The Love Goddess, born of the sea and the sky: Ava Gardner, 1947.

Ava, age eighteen, in her first moments before a motion picture camera, on a soundstage in Hell's Kitchen, New York, summer of 1941. *(Courtesy of Diana Altman)*

From her original screen test for MGM, the close-up that brought Ava Gardner to Hollywood. *(Courtesy of Diana Altman)*

Ava with her oldest sister, Beatrice, nicknamed "Bappie" (their brother, Jack Gardner, is seen in the photograph on the table), visiting North Carolina the year after their move to California. *(State Library Collection, Raleigh, North Carolina, courtesy* Raleigh News & Observer*)*

Starlet: in training as a movie actress, Ava spent her first years at MGM mainly in extra work—walk-ons and posing for photographs, images to promote her name and the studio—most of it sweetly sexy cheesecake work done in the portrait gallery or in salubrious locations like hotel swimming pools and the beach at Santa Monica.

Honeymooners Mr. and Mrs. Mickey Rooney visit the bride's family in North Carolina. Mollie Gardner, delighted by her irrepressible new son-in-law, offers a platter of her legendary Southern fried chicken. *(State Library Collection, Raleigh, North Carolina, courtesy* Raleigh News & Observer*)*

Nightclubbing, 1945, Ava and husband Number Two, Artie Shaw, brilliant, imperious superstar of the Big Band era. Shaw encouraged her intellectual development while trampling her self-esteem. *(Courtesy Associated Press)*

Howard Hughes, not long after his most spectacular airplane crash in the summer of 1946. Hughes and Ava had a complicated, tumultuous relationship lasting more than a dozen years. *(Courtesy Houston Library Research Center)*

The big break: the sensational stars of *The Killers*, Burt Lancaster, making his screen debut, and Ava Gardner, a virtual newcomer even after nearly six years in the movies. *(Courtesy Museum of Modern Art)*

Architects (with screenwriters John Huston and Anthony Veiller) of Ava Gardner's movie stardom, here on the set of *The Killers,* director Robert Siodmak (*left*) and producer Mark Hellinger. *(Mark Hellinger Collection, USC Cinema-Television Library)*

Eight-story billboard advertisement for the premiere New York run of *The Killers* in the summer of 1946. *(Mark Hellinger Collection, USC Cinema-Television Library)*

Opening week for *The Killers,* the Winter Garden box office and entrance with the larger-than-life cutout of Ava Gardner as Kitty Collins, femme fatale in black satin. *(Mark Hellinger Collection, USC Cinema-Television Library)*

Getting splashed on the set of *The Bribe*, Ava and Robert Taylor, discreet lovers. *(Courtesy Cinedoc)*

Ava Gardner and Robert Mitchum in *My Forbidden Past*, produced by Howard Hughes, shot in 1949, and not released for two years while Hughes played with the editing. Ava and Bob enjoyed each other's company, after work off on nocturnal adventures. "Yeah, they were having some fun." *(Courtesy Museum of Modern Art)*

Ava posing for the legendary Man Ray. The painting, intended for the film *Pandora and the Flying Dutchman*, was rejected, but a photograph of Ava by the artist was used. "She was," said Ray, "absolutely ravishing." *(Lewin Collection, USC Cinema-Television Library)*

Ava on the beach at Tossa de Mar, Spain, with the adoring Albert Lewin, writer-producer-director of *Pandora*. *(Lewin Collection, USC Cinema-Television Library)*

Mario Cabre, matador, actor, poet. *(Lewin Collection, USC Cinema-Television Library)*

Between takes on the Costa Brava, Ava as Pandora the temptress, James Mason, her Flying Dutchman, trying not to be tempted. *(Lewin Collection, USC Cinema-Television Library)*

A "Romance of the Century": Ava Gardner and
Frank Sinatra. Here, reunited after another angry
breakup, at the rally for presidential candidate
Adlai Stevenson at the Palladium in Los Angeles,
October 1952. *(Courtesy Associated Press)*

At the height of the "scandal," summer of 1951, Ava and Frank at the Riverside in Reno,
Nevada. Frank, fortunes declining, sports a new look with an Errol Flynn mustache.
(Courtesy Associated Press)

Hounded by the press: newspapers and magazines charted the Gardner-Sinatra affair and then marriage with daily updates and the most intimate revelations.

Ava would make three films with her girlhood idol, Clark Gable. Their best film together, *Mogambo* (1953), was a remake of Gable's earlier hit *Red Dust*, a movie Ava had seen with her mother more than two decades earlier. *(Courtesy Museum of Modern Art)*

Publicity poster for *Mogambo*. *(Author's collection)*

tramp of Ava's character—or should I say lack of it—is either a low-down skunk or is just so insane he should be locked up for his own good."

Pity was not considered an option in the case of Frank's home-wrecking lover:

"Ava is sure a snake in my book. . . ."

"She is probably getting ulcers and she should—hope they get perforated . . ."

"Ava has behaved as a call girl might—vulgar language but what else does her conduct look like. . . . She has had hundreds—do I exaggerate, boyfriends, and I think we can safely say she knows her way around men."

"You know there are millions and millions of women like me, wives and mothers who have had to make sacrifices for their husband and children, and when we see one of our own kind, Nancy Sinatra, receive such a deal because of a person like Ava it hurts us to the soul and makes us wish for the destruction of the cause. Maybe it will be very soon. Those hateful, malicious, plotting, scheming thoughts imprint themselves on the face and Ava is definitely showing it. She looks hard as nails."

"Though I don't want to wish Ava harm, I do wish she'd fall down and break her neck. . . ."

"Maneuvering hussy . . ."

"Why don't they mind their own fucking business," said Ava.

"You tell 'em, baby," said Frank.

Under the circumstances MGM was considerably relieved to know that their star would soon be leaving the country for several months to make a movie in England and Spain, a deal that had been arranged sometime before the scandal had broken. Ava was delighted, too, having for many years nurtured a dream of visiting Europe. Frank was not so delighted. He was stuck in New York. He asked her to tell the studio to forget it, forget Europe. She refused. His passion for her was burning white-hot. Hers for him, he often feared, was not as strong as that. He had to fight for her love every day—every hour it sometimes felt. He was not used to being without the upper hand. Ava was unpredictable, responsive only to her emotions, the feelings of now. Knowing she was going to be away for months on another continent, with Christ knew what distractions to come, left Sinatra in a state of chronic anxiety.

In mid-March Ava arrived in New York City to spend two weeks with Frank before she left the country. She knew how much he wanted her to be with him as he began a crucial, long-running engagement at the Copacabana, his first New York nightclub appearance in more than five years. She moved in with him at the Hampshire House. The press was poised. Immediately there were gossip items about the two stars "staying at the same hotel."

"The main reason I am in New York is because I am on my way to make a picture," Ava stated for the record. "Inasmuch as Frank is officially separated from his wife, I believe I have a right to be seen with him. However, since he is still officially married it would be in the worst possible taste to discuss any future plans. One thing I'm sure of is that Frank's plans to leave Nancy came into his life long before I ever did."

It was a tempestuous two weeks. Sinatra was a wreck, drinking and smoking too much, swacked on a variety of pills—ups, downs, outs—beset by the scandal, beset by what he perceived as an ever-invasive press, by his workload of daily performing and rehearsing, by the growing signs of a crumbling career. The Copa showcase—three shows a night—was turning out to be a mixed bag—reviewers squawked that his voice was not what it had been; audiences no longer screamed as in the old Paramount days, though many of them did make noise, chattering to one another while he sang. At the same time, his records were not selling, and his new fifteen-minute radio program, *Light Up Time*, had sunk in the ratings and was headed for extinction.

But what compelled more of his attention than anything else, sapped more of his juice, was a love affair that continually offered every bit as much pain as pleasure. They were crazily volatile together, bouncing from love to jealousy to rage to love again. They were always on the edge of something explosive. Studying each other with a hungry lust as if ready to race for the nearest bedroom one minute, then screaming and cursing at the top of their lungs, drinks knocked over, chairs knocked over, one or the other storming away. With Ava mad at him and out of his sight, Sinatra would take an emotional nosedive, frantic to make up with her, unable to think of anything else till they were together again. It was an exhausting experience for both of them, though more visibly, more extremely so for the stressed, strung-out Sinatra. He looked at times like a beaten boxer never let out of the ring.

Skitch Henderson was a frequent Sinatra collaborator and at this time was Frank's bandleader at the Copa and piano player on the New York radio show. "He was absolutely obsessed with Ava," he recalled fifty-four years later. "Absolutely crazy in love. It is a kind of legendary romance now, but I have to say the reality was even stronger. I don't like to say it because I loved Nancy, his first wife, and still do, but he was ready to do anything for Ava.

"She was like a Svengali to him. She was an enigma. A mysterious presence. You didn't quite know how she had done it to him, and I'm not sure I wanted to know. She was ruthless with him. And it used to affect his mood a great deal. It could be horrible to be with him then. Her acid tongue and her ability to just put you away. If ever I knew a tiger, or a panther . . . I'm trying to think of an animal that would describe her. . . . To be honest—I didn't let anyone on to this—but I did what I could to stay out of her way. I was scared to death of her."

One of the last nights before Ava flew away to Europe, she had been to the club as always, backstage in the dressing room with him giving support before he went on, then an enthusiastic audience member, loudly applauding. They were billing and cooing through a late supper. Then it came, the little thing to set off Frank's compulsiveness or Ava's emerald-eyed monster, ready to bite your hand off at the elbow in the blink of another woman's eye: a waitress it might have been this time, someone winking or whispering or something, and they were at it.

"You bastard!"

"Screw you!"

"You want her? Instead of me? To hell with you then!"

And Ava was gone into the New York night. Sinatra simmered for a moment, then charged out after her, but she had already disappeared. She had gone back to the suite on Central Park South, paced around restlessly, then remembered an old friend who was living in Manhattan just up the street, another night owl. She found his number in her book and called him. Artie. He and his new girlfriend were up, and Ava asked him if he'd be up a little while longer. Could she come over? Had to talk to somebody. And Artie said sure, she should come over for a nightcap.

She was sitting in the living room of Artie's apartment having a drink with her ex-husband and his girlfriend, Ruth—the couple in their nightclothes and bathrobes—when the doorbell rang. Artie got up, came back with Frank and Frank's song plugger/crony/bodyguard Hank Sanicola. Ava reckoned she had "accidentally" left her phone book open back at the hotel, to the page with Artie's number. Frank hated Shaw and seethed at the idea that Ava sometimes talked to him, sought his advice, that she might still hold some affection for the clarinet-playing bum.

"How about a drink, Frank?" said Shaw.

Sinatra ignored him, stared hard at Ava, began to berate her, the bulky song plugger hovering behind in a classic henchman's pose. Artie's girlfriend said something about Sinatra's tone and Sinatra said something back at her, something that made Shaw step up. He knew the sort of thing that got Frank's attention and told him he had a very-large-caliber pistol on hand.

"You talk like that to my woman," Shaw said, "I'll blow a nice big hole through your guts."

Sinatra stopped talking, made a highly dramatic volte-face and went out the door, Sanicola stumbling to catch up.

"Oh, shit," said Ava.

When she got back to the Hampshire House, Frank was there. Ava was tipsy, falling asleep, and told him to forget about it. They could continue fighting in the morning if he wanted. But Sinatra wanted one last round.

"If I don't mean anything more to you why don't we just call it quits. . . . I've got nothing to live for anyway. . . . You hear me?"

Sinatra went into his room. As Ava recalled it, the phone rang, and it was Frank calling from a few yards away in the bedroom.

"So long, baby, it's been fun."

And then a roaring explosion—maybe a second—sounded in the receiver and could be heard throughout the suite as well. Ava ran to the bedroom and saw the gun smoke and saw Frank stretched out on his stomach. She screamed his name and scrambled onto the bed. She saw that smoke was curling from within the mattress, and then Sinatra rolled on his side, clutching a revolver, his finger still on the trigger.

"Frank!"

He smiled grimly. "Hello."

"Goddamn you!"

For a moment she had thought he had done it, and when it turned out to be one of his practical jokes she felt relief instead of anger and grabbed him in her arms. Someone called the management about a gunshot and the management called the police and poor Hank Sanicola had to get out of bed quick and come upstairs and help hide the gun and the mattress with the bullet hole and the powder burns.

On March 25, 1950, Ava and Bappie departed New York for London. The newspapers had printed advance notice of her travel date, allowing a few dozen or so of the scandalized public to reach her with irate letters sent care of the Hampshire House, including many expressing the hope that her aircraft might crash en route. Whatever her feelings for Frank Sinatra—and, yes, she told herself, she did love the man despite plenty of cause for throwing in the towel—it was with a sense of great relief that she boarded the BOAC aircraft that evening, increasingly so as she felt the power of the Rolls-Royce engines surge through the cabin and the wheels snap up and America fade away. She was, yes, happily leaving Frank and Nancy and all those wonderful letter writers behind her, and after one last look out the window to make sure that none of them was clinging to the wing, she settled back in her seat and closed the past from her thoughts, turning them only to the adventure ahead, allowing her glass to be filled with champagne by a pretty English stewardess and enjoying the bubbles popping gently against her upper lip.

SIX

Torrid Was Your Blood

The 'Love Goddess' flew out of the skies to England yesterday," reported the *Daily Express*. "Green-eyed Ava Gardner, voted 'The World's Best Shape,' went straight to a room at London's Claridge's Hotel at 8 a.m., locked the door and went to sleep. The Shape was feeling out of shape."

The Daily Mirror informed the kingdom, "Ava Gardner, 5ft. 6ins. Hollywood 'Venus Girl' with hazel eyes, a dimpled chin, and a face and figure film producers pay £20,000 a year for, flew into London yesterday. Then she disappeared . . . locked herself in her bedroom at Claridge's, ordered that no calls be put through, and went to bed—in pyjamas because she doesn't like nighties in cold weather."

"At Claridge's," stated the *Daily Mail*, "all was tiptoe and shush."

Pandora and the Flying Dutchman was the creation of Albert Lewin, one of the more original and eccentric filmmakers in the history of the big studio system. For many years an MGM producer and executive, he defied every stereotype of the breed: a Harvard graduate, former professor, doctoral candidate at Columbia University (all but the dissertation when Metro found him), an unregenerate intellectual, expert on art and ancient history, patron of objectivist poets, surrealist painters, and Danish explorers, friend of Djuna Barnes, Max Ernst, and Man Ray. In 1942, Lewin left MGM to independently produce, write, and direct a version of Maugham's

The Moon and Sixpence, starring George Sanders as a supercilious Paul Gauguin figure finding inspiration among the palm trees and nymphs of Tahiti. Returning to the fold at Metro, Lewin wrote and directed *The Picture of Dorian Gray* from Wilde, filmed amid much complaint from the front office but completed without compromise, a remarkable adaptation, literate, precise, and haunting (with its memorable Technicolor insert of the Ivan Albright portrait of a decayed Dorian), and perhaps the oddest and least likely production to come from the Culver City lot since Tod Browning's *Freaks*.

After one more remarkably idiosyncratic independent production (*The Private Affairs of Bel Ami*, from Guy de Maupassant's novel), Lewin again came back to MGM and again defied Hollywood precedent in a dual relationship as production executive and sometime independent writer-director with the presumption of Metro distribution. *Pandora* was Lewin's first original screenplay, a story in which he had managed to include most of his consuming obsessions: myth, magic, beauty, sexual obsession, decadence, the nature of art, the cruelty of love. It was the tale of Pandora Reynolds, a beautiful American playgirl, resented and worshipped center of attention for a group of British expatriates living in the village of Esperanza on the Mediterranean coast of Spain in the 1930s. Bored and destructive, unable to feel love, she drives one man to his death and another to a terrible sacrifice, becomes on a whim engaged to David, a race-car driver, while leading on yet another man, Juan Montalvo, a violently jealous matador. Into the bay sails a yacht with a single occupant, the mysterious Hendrick van der Zee. Intrigued, Pandora swims out to the vessel, coming upon van der Zee as he is completing a painting of the mythical Pandora, the first mortal woman; the figure bears a striking, disturbing resemblance to the American Pandora, who impulsively destroys the work. Intrigued by the enigmatic Dutchman, the one man in Esperanza who seems not desperate for her affections, Pandora becomes infatuated with him, enraging Montalvo, who murders him in a jealous rage; but in a mysterious turn of events, van der Zee returns to life and causes Montalvo to meet his own death in the bullring. A resident archaeologist uncovers the bizarre truth that Hendrick is the immortal Flying Dutchman of age-old myth, condemned to wander the world forever for the murder of his bride—"blown back and forth between Death and Life, neither of the two willing to claim him"—until the time he can find a woman willing to die for the love of him. Pandora Reynolds becomes that woman, his redemption, and her own.

It was a script conceived, by Lewin's admission, "with a deliberately surrealist intention," loyal to the manifesto of André Breton in its calmly irrational storytelling, its blurring of the lines between the real and the fantastic, its bland acceptance of magic and myth, and its exaltation of fate and *l'amour fou*. Lewin knew that his Pandora, weighted with the burden of cross-references to the mythic first woman and ultimate femme fatale, had to be cast with an actress of appropriately legendary beauty and allure. His first thought for the role was the movies' own most mythic creation, Greta Garbo, but when this proved unrealistic (retired from the screen since 1942, she would never make another film), Lewin cast his eye about for another screen goddess and found her in Ava Gardner—the young woman who had so convincingly embodied Venus come to earth and seemed, according to the newspapers, to be leading a style of life not unlike the fatal woman of his screenplay. There was a description of the character in the script: "Complex, moody, restless with the discontent of a romantic soul which has not yet found the true object of her desires." Ava said, "It is almost me."

In Hollywood she posed for Lewin's buddy Man Ray for two works intended to be seen in the film, a painted portrait Lewin ultimately rejected, and a charming photograph meant to look like a Renaissance miniature. "She was," Man Ray would remember, "absolutely ravishing—no film, I thought, had ever done her justice. And as a model, no one in my experience with mannequins and professionals surpassed her."

In London, as Ava slept through the day, a crowd filtered in and out of the outer rooms of the suite: producers, dress fitters, studio representatives, a cinematographer, reporters, photographers. Hosting the group, until Bappie joined them after her briefer slumber, was Minna Wallis, by coincidence in town, delightedly sharing with the crowd titbits of information about her beautiful, adored young friend. The name, first of all, was pronounced "Ay-vah" not "Ah-vah" as many present had believed. As for Mr. Frank Sinatra, no, he was not to Minna Wallis's knowledge going to be Ay-vah's husband number three. And yes, she had indeed been visiting a psychiatrist. "To recover from an inferiority complex," Minna Wallis explained. "She wanted a new set of standards to judge people by. But she isn't going to one anymore. It was just a phase.

"Ava's intelligent, you know," said Minna, helpfully. "Surprising for a pretty girl, but she is."

Rested, the star appeared at a press conference in the Claridge's banquet room, and was beheld by the reporters of London as beautiful, adorable, and sly (perhaps even intelligent). "I agree that arriving stars from Hollywood are quoted as saying a lot of darned silly things," she told them, "but just think of the darned silly questions they're asked."

She met with Albert Lewin, a cheerful, white-haired, very short, and nearly deaf man (he wore an enormous hearing aid at all times) who was from the first day adoringly appreciative of his casting choice. She also conferred with the film's director of photography, Jack Cardiff, supreme master of light and lens, whose previous credits in Technicolor included his stunning work for Powell-Pressburger's *Black Narcissus* and *The Red Shoes* and Hitchcock's *Under Capricorn*.

"We met at her hotel," Jack Cardiff recalled, "and she was very nice and of course very beautiful, with a wonderful sexy voice and an extraordinary way of moving, like a cat . . . and almost the first thing she said to me was, 'Jack, you have to watch how you light me when I'm having my period.'

"It was rather disarming. But that was Ava, just very natural and frank about everything. I mean she said it just as you would say, 'Watch me when I have a bad cold.' I told her yes, I would try to watch out how I lit her on those days."

Between color tests and dress fittings there was time to explore London, and Ava reveled in her first encounter with the city she would one day make her home. The only disappointment came at mealtime, the holdover of wartime rationing and the contrast with California plenty painfully visible in portions that taunted a woman with Ava's vast appetite. At her first dinner she looked at the size of the steak she had been served and ordered the waiter to bring two more.

One weekend, with Bappie, she had her first look at Paris, Metro arranging for a suite at the George V and a chauffeured limousine. Wanting to see something of the "real Paris," they ditched their chauffeur outside the Tour d'Argent and wandered off on their own, ending the night drinking champagne in a glitzy lesbian nightclub. (The visit to the club was a naive accident, Ava would claim, disingenuously, perhaps, as she had a continuing curiosity about the sexual demimonde and through the years paid visits to gay bars, red-light zones, and brothels all over the world.)

On April 14 she departed Northolt Airport for Barcelona. A limousine took the two sisters north along the Costa Brava to Tossa de Mar, a small fishing village between sea and mountain, with whitewashed homes and walled enclosures little altered since the Middle Ages. Lewin had chosen it for its scenic beauty, historical associations and inspirational metaphysics well suited to his *Pandora*. The blue Mediterranean and the scalloped beach and the flower-bedecked houses and outdoor markets were perfectly production-designed for the Technicolor camera; there were numerous archaeological remnants of ancient Rome and others as old as the Pale-olithic period, evoking a world of myth and legend; and for more recent inspiration, Tossa had been frequented by Marc Chagall and other modern artists and was not far from Cadeques, birthplace of surrealist Salvador Dalí, aesthetic associations Albert Lewin found most compatible. For some of the exterior scenes, arrangements had been made to rent the large summer estate of Spanish business magnate Don Alberto Puig and, remarkably, the grounds contained visible Roman remains and archaeological fragments almost exactly like those Lewin had imagined in his script. To film the bullfighting scenes they would be allowed the use of the *plaza de toros* in nearby Gerona. From the Bertrand family of Barcelona they rented the 250-ton schooner *Orion* to play the role of the Flying Dutchman's yacht.

For Ava, Spain was immediately a place of enchantment. With the passion of the people, with the flaring dark romanticism of the culture, she made an instant, heartfelt, lasting connection. The fury of the flamenco, the blood sport, the wine and dance and dinners till midnight—all the clichés of the travel writers' lexicon—she experienced them all with an open and eager enthusiasm, and they had a life-altering result. "It was, I think, the first time there for all of us and it was very glamorous," said Angela Allen, *Pandora*'s script girl. "A sweet little fishing village—nowadays you wouldn't even recognize it, it's a big resort. But it was romantic and strange and a lot of wine flowing. You got into the swing of it, and I think Ava more than anyone. She got hooked on Spain and all that went with it, including the bullfights—and the bullfighters."

Ava, Lewin, and costar James Mason (who would arrive sometime after shooting began) each had their own villas in or around Tossa, with rented rooms or hotel accommodations for the rest of the cast and crew. For the first day or two there were elements of discord. One of the supporting actors, suffering from parochial anti-Americanism, stirred up resentment against the pampered Hollywood contingent (Mason, having abandoned the British film industry for California four years before, and contemplating U.S. citizenship, was in this period routinely damned in the British press as an honorary American). "There were some people who were such laughable snobs," recalled Jeanie Sims, the English production assistant. "So worried about someone getting too much money or something. Acting very spiteful, and, you know, we were all there and employed because Al Lewin had written this script. And Lewin was an absolutely lovely man. I loved him, adored him. And he adored his cast and crew. Anyway, this actor—I won't say his name, but he's dead now—tried to stir up things against the Americans, but he couldn't with Ava because she was just too delightful. Everybody liked her, everyone on the crew loved her. You couldn't not, because she had such a vibrant personality. She laughed all the time, she was quite jolly, and very good company. Everybody that I knew, then and later, who knew her, loved her."

"She was totally delightful," recalled Sheila Sim (Lady Attenborough), playing the character of Janet in the film. "So very friendly. I became very, very fond of her. So sweet to everybody. She was not standoffish in any way and was enormously generous."

Shooting began at seven in the morning and lasted until eight in the evening. Even with the long hours, the production quickly fell behind schedule. Lewin had called for numerous elaborate visual sequences and complicated, predetermined compositions utilizing various deep-focus and trompe l'oeil effects, some in homage to the surrealist masters. "He loved offbeat modern art and had many visual ideas and knew the idea behind everything he wanted," Jack Cardiff remembered, "and for both John Bryan, the art director, and myself it was fascinating to work with such an artistically minded person—much more so than most other producers or directors I worked with. But he was very specific about what he wanted, and it required all sorts of things to be built, a huge bell tower which was really something to construct and to shoot, and these giant heads of statues and so on." Without the controlled environment of a studio—or its hierarchy hurrying him along—Lewin followed an odd and painstaking course to fulfill his vision. A more conventional approach would have allowed revisions to certain types of sequences for location shooting or faked them in the studio, such as the lengthy scenes set at night out of doors on the broad Tossa beach. "It required," recalled Jack Cardiff, "that we shoot these night scenes day-for-night, with lights, in the Spanish sun, on this bright white beach. The glare was tremendous, and poor James Mason could not stand the reflected light in his eyes and Ava would be wearing sunglasses until we started a take, which was even worse because when she took them off she couldn't open her eyes at all or they would fill with tears, and they were supposed to be standing in moonlight only. I had to cover a large portion of the beach with black net, which was very difficult, and on one occasion, amazingly enough, we actually painted the beach, sprayed it with dark brown paint, brown and blue, and this took some of the glare off. It was just impossible. We ended up doing the close-ups in the studio."

"He would drive us mad," Angela Allen recalled. "He would ask for things technically and we had to keep saying, 'No, no, this won't work' or 'That won't work.'"

"As a director, well, I found him a little unnerving," said Sheila Sim. "He was always running off to do something with the technical side. Some things American were very strange to us. He wasn't terribly good at communicating."

James Mason, who had enjoyed his time in Hollywood getting to know the erudite Lewin, found him a less than inspiring collaborator on the Catalan coast. Siding with the sniping Nigel Patrick, Mason felt he had become a "cool führer," throwing his authority around. Regarding his direction of the film, Mason believed Lewin's deafness had a detrimental effect on many scenes, that he did not catch the actors' spoken errors and that his lack of hearing affected the pacing of scenes, made him oblivious to "the pulse of life."

"We used to be evil," said Angela Allen. "Everybody'd go quiet and whispering, and then he was pushing his hearing aid up because of course he couldn't hear a word. And then, you know, he'd get the hearing aid at full blast and then everyone would shout. The actors used to play that awful game on him."

Mason and the other performers' dissatisfaction may have been provoked in part by feelings of neglect, for it was evident that most of Albert Lewin's attention was being directed at his gorgeous Pandora.

"Of course," said Jack Cardiff, "Lewin thought Ava was a goddess. He thought she was the most beautiful woman in the world, and he used to just gaze and gaze at her. And we would shoot her, and he would say, 'I want to do another close-up. Closer.' And we would do that. And then he would say, 'Let's do another one. Different angle.' Then one more, '*Closer*.' And on and on like that. It became that all we were doing was close-ups of Ava Gardner's face. He couldn't stop himself. And the continuity girl, Angela Allen, had to make notes and coordinate what was being shot and she'd say to me, 'I don't know what he's shooting. Where is he going to cut in all these shots? There's nothing like it in the script.' But he was so enthralled with Ava, and he just adored doing all of these close-ups of her."

"As an actress she was rather nervous," Sheila Sim recalled. "She did not have great faith in her talent, actually. And I think she was a much better actress than she was given credit for, but I think she had a problem in that her beauty was so distracting to people you couldn't concentrate on her performance. I have never known anyone so beautiful. A totally beautiful, perfect figure and face, whatever she was doing, or whatever clothes she was wearing, totally, absolutely lovely. And she moved so beautifully, had an instinctive gracefulness, fascinating to watch. She was very talented in many ways."

"I remember one time we were shooting a scene of Ava by herself," said Jeanie Sims. "She was supposed to be lost in some deep thought about the man she was in love with. And she couldn't sort of get it right for Al. He was very gentle with her, but he was a bit frustrated or sad that he couldn't quite get what he wanted from her, some look of complete absorption in this love affair. Then Al finally went over and said to her, 'Ava, is there some one person in your life who you love or have loved more than anyone else on earth?' And she answered him so quietly I could not hear her. And he told her to think of that person and it was just the impetus she needed, and she got it perfect on the next shot. And afterward I was a bit curious, and I asked Al what she had said, who she had loved more than anyone, and Al said, 'The clarinet player—Artie Shaw.' And, you know, I thought how interesting because she was thinking of Shaw and in the newspapers there was all that talk about Ava and Frank Sinatra."

In New York City, Frank Sinatra's world was coming apart. In shattering succession he had separated from his wife and family, buried his chief strategist, George Evans, lost Manie Sachs, his closest ally at Columbia Records, and seen him replaced by Mitch Miller (far less sympathetic, in Sinatra's mind), he was about to be dismissed by his talent agency, and he had been shown the door at MGM, reportedly because of a rude joke at L. B. Mayer's expense, though many believe the studio had simply wanted him gone, at least in part because of the trouble he was causing for their more valuable investment, Ava Gardner. Forced against his own best judgment to take an eight-week, three-shows-a-night gig at the Copacabana, he had been further straining his throat and nerves with daily live radio broadcasts on the *Light Up Time* program, a series of live appearances at the Capitol Theater, and numerous recording sessions. His records were not selling, his press was largely derisive, he owed close to a million dollars to the government and to his record company (advances paid by Columbia unlikely to ever earn out). And the woman with whom he was crazy in love was in another country in a goddamned nowhere village that barely had a working telephone to let him hear her voice. In addition to an excessive ingestion of alcohol, he was becoming addicted to sleeping pills and other medications to relieve . . . everything. Standing tall against any and all calamities, there had always been one invincible factor on Sinatra's side, his overwhelming talent and artistry as a performer and recording artist, but now even these had begun to dissipate.

After the first weeks at the Copa his throat had begun to evidence growing distress, affecting as well his ability to make records with his usual brilliance and command.

"Listen, Sinatra had a marvelous voice," said Mitch Miller, recalling a period fifty-four years earlier. "But it was very fragile. There were certain guys like Gordon MacRae who could stay up all night and drink and sing the next day—he could sing underwater. But if Frank didn't get enough sleep or if he drank a lot the night before, it would show up. And Frank was a guy—call it ego or what you want—he liked to suffer out loud, to be dramatic. There were plenty of people, big entertainers, who had a wild life or had big problems, but they kept it quiet. Frank had to do his suffering in public, so everyone could see it. And this was a time he was having trouble with Ava, she was in Spain, and it showed in his work. He would come in to record, and he couldn't get through a number without his voice cracking. And finally what I did was I shut off his mike and I made music tracks and then brought him back by himself at one o'clock in the morning without anybody else around and we worked till he could get it. No one did that then, tracking was against the union rules. But no one could tell that's how we made those records because I knew how to do it—you brought up the rhythm section and so on—but that was what we had to do because he couldn't get it down the other way."

Ava was seemingly never far from Sinatra's thoughts or emotions. Every day he would send off a heartfelt cable and then telephone her in the early evening in New York, late night in Spain, and try again sometime after midnight, early morning in Tossa de Mar. But long-distance telecommunication in Catalonia was still erratic at best. Sometimes hours of transatlantic operator assistance were necessary only to be told again that the lines were down or that no one was answering. When at last he would reach her, the connection was often filled with static and her voice a maddeningly faint and broken echo. Conversations would end with his frantic declaration of love and anguished hope that he had correctly heard Ava declare the same.

"This love I feel for her, it's sapping me of everything I got," he cried to Hank Sanicola, as reported by Sinatra biographer J. Randy Taraborrelli. "I got no energy for anything. What is this spell she has me under?"

"That Ava broad is gonna be the death of you," said Sanicola in a tone weighted with sycophantic weltschmerz and linguine. "This woman has you so fucked up, you'll do anything in the world to be with her. Is the sex that good, Frank? Is it?"

On April 26, Sinatra appeared as usual for his Copa shows. "It was a wonderful room, a terrible house orchestra, and a hilarious, old-fashioned chorus line of three or four showgirls," remembered Skitch Henderson, Frank's bandleader for the engagement. "And Frank was a hit. Whatever else was going on, we were selling out. And most nights Frank was wonderful." On this night, however, his dinner show had not gone well, his voice cracking and scratching repeatedly. A doctor had been summoned and advised that he cancel the rest of the night and go home. But Sinatra had read a taunt in the newspaper that he was not up to completing his Copa gig, and he insisted on working. At two-thirty in the morning, as Skitch Henderson brought the music up, Frank stepped out on the stage and sang his first number, "I Have But One Heart."

At the song's end, as the audience applauded, Sinatra said, "That one was for you, Ava."

He began to sing again—"It All Depends on You"—and abruptly no further sound came out of his mouth. He felt what he thought was spittle bubbling at the side of his mouth, dabbed it with his handkerchief, and saw that it was blood.

"He just stopped," said Henderson. "I didn't know what had happened, I wasn't aware of it till afterward. I expected he would gather himself together in another moment. But nothing happened. He croaked something and walked off the stage, walked out of the club."

Sinatra was diagnosed with a submucosal throat hemorrhage. The remaining days of his Copacabana engagement were canceled along with all other scheduled performances.

"It happens to every singer at some time. It happens to opera singers all the time," said Skitch Henderson. "It wasn't as tumultous as it has been made out. But it became a great trauma for him, although I felt it was in part a manufactured trauma because of his mental state at the time."

Sinatra was advised to lie low, rest, not sing for two months. He communicated with people by writing his words down on a scratch pad. In New York and Miami he lay about, recuperating, seeing doctors, scribbling notes, and thinking of Ava Gardner.

While Sinatra suffered in America, in Spain, Ava pursued another, happier philosophy: out of sight, out of mind. After the long hours in the glare of the Spanish sun and of Al Lewin's camera examining her every pore, she was eager for fun at nightfall. There was not a great deal of nightlife in Tossa and neighboring villages, but what there was could be intense—taverns where the gypsies danced and played till dawn and the wine and brandy flowed as freely as the cold springs in the looming Cadiretes Massif. "There were parties, and the Spanish parties, of course, went all the way through the night," recalled Sheila Sim. "And we came when they invited us, for ten o'clock. And of course what they hadn't made clear was that it wouldn't be remotely starting till midnight. And Ava would be out all night, much to our fury, because when she'd arrive on the set, arrive for makeup, she looked so beautiful. It was really quite maddening for those of us who had to wear so much makeup to make us look reasonable in front of the camera. She didn't need anything." (Jack Cardiff, looking at the star perhaps more intently than others, would recall sometimes having to take special care with the lights on mornings when Ava's eyes did show their lack of sleep.)

"And Ava, of course, in those days," said Sheila Sim, "was young and undisciplined. A very, very wild spirit."

"She was an extraordinary creature," said John Hawkesworth, the young Englishman in charge of set dressing on the location. "A wonderful girl. I liked her very much. Stronger than any of us. Amazing. She would join us for dinner some nights at the café, and she could eat twice as much as anyone and drink three times as much. She would come out with her sister, whom she brought I think out of kindness, a much older and rather pathetic woman, with a look of alcoholism and rather going to fat. And they would drink, and then the sister would drop out and Ava would go on through the night enjoying herself."

Jeanie Sims: "Ava . . . how shall I say . . . was very romantic and she enjoyed boys and she enjoyed some of the girls, I think, too, but she certainly liked lots of boys. She liked to be smitten and liked to have people smitten with her. James Mason was not available because James was there with his wife, and I think Pamela was very careful to keep James to herself and you didn't see a lot of him. And it was inevitable, I suppose, that Ava would take an interest in Mario . . . the bullfighter. And he certainly took an interest in her."

"She fell for the bullfighter, yes," said Angela Allen. "He looked quite glamorous to her and they had a fling, I think that's the right way to describe it. And for him it was quite a great catch to be going out with a Hollywood star. He was a bit second rate."

For the role of Juan Montalvo, the murderous matador, Lewin had with inspiration cast a real-life bullfighter with acting experience, Mario Cabre, a movie-star handsome and charismatic *torero* of minor repute in the ring. Cabre would allow Lewin to shoot the bullfighting sequences much more freely without having to resort to fakery or cutaways to a stunt matador. Cabre was charming and well liked, though a bit of a figure of fun, a glutton for attention, an amateur poet, irrepressibly so, soon inspired by a new, emerald-eyed muse. "Mario," said Ava, "was handsome and macho as only a Latin knows how to be, but he was also brash, conceited, noisy, and totally convinced that he was the only man in the world for me."

Ava had at first been amused—but no more—by Cabre's infatuation with her until they had all gone to see him in the bullring. "Oh, she really loved it when she went to that first bullfight," John Hawkesworth recalled. "It just got into her blood right away, I think: the excitement and the color and the drama of the thing, she loved it."

"If you've ever been to a bullfight," said Jeanie Sims, "you know it's a rather dramatic atmosphere, the pageantry and the sound of the trumpeters. And, well, she saw Mario in his costume, his 'suit of lights,' and waving his cape and his sword, and I think she was very impressed. And to see him bravely standing up to this great bull—it gave her a different impression of him, I suppose."

Cabre, that day in the bullring, had thrown her his cap and had made the traditional dedication of the bull to her honor. And Ava, gripping the matador's cap in her hands, had watched with anguish and excitement the mounting drama of the *estocade*, and she had shown a great emotional (and some said erotic) release in the tragic last moments and the final deadly lunge of Cabre's sword that collapsed the huge animal at his feet.

Next thing anyone knew, Ava and Mario were what the columnists would call "an item"—dining together, seen holding hands, walking the old streets of the walled *enceinte* and along the beach under the Mediterranean moon. "After one of those romantic, star-filled, dance-filled, booze-filled Spanish nights," Ava would write, "I woke up to find myself in bed with Mario Cabre." Cabre's more metaphor-charged version of those events was captured in *numero uno* of his "Ava poems":

> The night was of one color
> Yet when she came the sky held a rainbow.
> For Ava was the dawn.

She would recall it as a one-night-only "single mistake," but others remembered a more lingering relationship. At first, recalled Jeanie Sims, all communication between the two was in sign language, since Cabre did not speak English (his lines in the film were memorized, it was said, parrot fashion). "Mario spoke to her in Spanish, and Ava spoke no language except American. Ava said to me, 'I'm enjoying my time with Mario, but neither of us can understand what we're saying.' I said, 'Is that important?' And Ava said, 'It is, rather, you know. I'd like to get to know him better. Know what he's saying to me.' And that's when I got dragged in as translator, because Mario did speak French and so did I, sort of fractured French, but I was understandable. So I was made to be there with them, and Mario would speak French to me while staring at her, and I would then translate it for Ava, and she would speak English and I would translate it to French for Mario. Luckily I was not feeling that well and became laid up for a couple of weeks with jaundice, so I didn't have to continue this translating job, and by the time I was back on my feet—the Spanish doctor prescribed a bottle of wine a day—they had been together so much that they could understand each other pretty well without my help."

"He was a nice man," said Jack Cardiff. "Didn't speak more than three words of English, but he was very genuinely in love with her, I think. And he wanted to show off a bit, and he had a private showing in the bullring for Ava and I was there, at just before dusk actually. He got this bull out and she was there watching him and he did the *mariposa*, the butterfly, where he holds the cape behind him and walks backwards, which is the most dangerous move—it's almost suicidal. But he was trying to show off. Ava was really terrified that he would be killed, and she was still upset about it after. And he did it very well. He was quite brave. But I don't think he realized what he was getting into with Ava and that she was too much of a handful for him. He would write poems in Spanish about her and read them, and she was very naughty because she would say things to him in English, knowing that he didn't understand, and some of the things she said could be pretty derisive."

The "Ava poems," which Cabre began to recite at full voice to anyone who would listen, were passionate, intimate, and in parts just a bit—*un poco*—indelicate. "*How torrid was your blood when you caressed me,*" began one stanza. "*And Plowed your fingernails under my skin. . . .*"

Cabre was particularly eager to share his feelings for the beautiful American with any and all available members of the press. "After working for a fortnight with Ava I know she is the woman I love with all my heart and soul," he declaimed to one gathering of journalists. "Many times have I been gored by *el toro*. But Ava, she has struck me deeper than any horn of the bull. *Here*—in my heart! Oh, my Ava, from your fingers caresses sprout. . . . Your lips give rapture."

Thanks to Mario's rapport with the Spanish reporters who passed through Tossa de Mar, word of the romance spread throughout the Iberian Peninsula and soon across the Atlantic to the United States. Photos of Ava and Cabre together appeared in one weekly under the caption, "This Is a Real Romance, Not Film." Ava was quoted: "My third love will be eternal," and her *numero tres* was understood to mean Mario Cabre.

On May 11, Frank Sinatra landed in Barcelona. They had talked about him coming over for a few days sometime or other. Sinatra had suddenly decided that now was the time.

A crowd of press representatives awaited him at Prat de Llobregat airfield. They found him looking "tired and forlorn," in a "grouchy mood." Was he there to visit Ava Gardner? asked one reporter.

"Yes."

"Is she your *novia*?" asked another. "Your sweetheart?"

"No comment."

They eagerly updated him on the latest details of Ava's friendship with the matador, Sinatra listening glumly, saying he had heard Cabre's name, knew nothing about him. He was holding a package wrapped in tissue paper, and someone asked if that was a present for Ava Gardner.

"What do you think, pal?"

"I think it's jewelry for Miss Gardner."

(Sinatra had brought two gifts from home: six bottles of Coca-Cola— she had bemoaned its unavailability in Tossa—and a ten-thousand-dollar emerald necklace, which would be impounded by the Spanish authorities and released to her only when she left the country.)

Sinatra said, "Why don't you people leave me alone?"

The reporters seemed reluctant to do that. Sinatra said he was in Spain for a rest, had a problem with his throat, and was under doctor's orders to talk as little as possible. A reporter asked if he had anything else to say.

"I think," said Sinatra, "Bing Crosby is the best singer in the world."

"Sinatra arrived suddenly and unexpectedly," recalled Jeanie Sims. "And there was a problem. Ava was not on the location where she was supposed to be. She and Mario had gone off on their own somewhere and couldn't be found and somebody came to me; the publicist, I think, said, 'What are we going to do?' He said, 'We can't let him go to the location because everyone told him Ava is there and she isn't.' So they sent me to intercept him and keep him from finding out she was with Mario. So I did. I met him and took him around to the various spots. And I'm quite sure he knew exactly what was going on, but he gave no indication. He was really nice to me, even when it got to the point of desperation and I was taking him to meet the electricians and the Spanish crew. We went to the bar and I even said, 'Why don't you sing us a song?' but he just laughed and said, 'No, I'm on holiday.' And the electricians who were there and not working started a poker game and they said, 'Why don't you join in?' And Sinatra said, 'Fine,' and he sat there and played poker until someone had managed to find Ava and get her away from Mario. And finally she showed up, saying, 'Oh, what a lovely surprise! Darling! *How great!*' "

They drove off in Frank's rented automobile. Ava was startled by his ravaged appearance. He had dropped what looked like twenty pounds, a considerable loss for an already skinny man. His face was drawn, haunted, showed not only the exhaustion of a long flight but every other strain he had experienced in the last five months.

"Francis, honey, you look like shit," Ava told him.

They drove out into the countryside, tried to get comfortable with each other again. Later they went to the Bier, a tiny tavern on the beach Ava liked, and they drank a powerful homemade aperitif, nibbling from an unending array of tapas the owner brought out from the tiny kitchen; they drank enough to get them both blotto and looking at each other with the old tenderness and heat.

But then Sinatra remembered the matter that had brought him to Spain in such a hurry.

"So what is with you and this fucking greaseball?"

"Who? You mean Mario?"

"Is that what you call him?"

"Nothing."

"It's in all the papers, sweetheart."

"Frank, you of all people know better than to believe what you read in those things. . . . We're making a movie together, that's all."

The *Pandora* people had anxiously gotten Mario away from them. John Hawkesworth, the set dresser, shared a room at the hotel with Cabre and saw the matador's reaction to Sinatra's arrival. "My bullfighter had no sense of humor whatever, and he was crazy for Ava, though I think it was completely one-sided. He was in a fury over Sinatra coming all the way from Hollywood to see her. And he said—we spoke French to each other—'When I see him . . . I am going to kill him.' He was very serious sounding. And the man had swords and knives all over the room. So I went to Al and I told him. I said, 'We better be careful, Al, because we could have a lot of trouble. This bullfighter is passionately in love with Ava, and he means business.' And Al said, 'You're right, it would not be good for one of our actors to murder Frank Sinatra.' And quickly Al had me get Mario away from there and take him to Gerona to start rehearsing for the bullfight scenes and not come back till Sinatra was gone."

A villa was found for Frank, for appearance's sake. The second day he came to the set where they were filming and restlessly watched Ava shoot a few setups. After that he stayed in his house during the day, and they met later for dinner.

Quarters were too close to completely avoid the reporters skulking about the village, and it seemed better to throw them a few half-truths than give them free reign to make up their own. "Ava is a wonderful girl," said Frank, sipping chilled champagne in the hotel that served as the production company's headquarters, a phonograph now playing some of his records to make him feel welcome. "I knew she would be homesick in a strange country, and I knew how I would feel if I were alone. Of course, I knew what people would say when I flew here. I am not a youth anymore. I expected this curiosity."

Later in the week it began to rain all over Catalonia, and filming was halted. It gave Frank and Ava more time to be together, and more time to get on each other's nerves. Jealousy hung over the reunion—Frank brooding about the rival who was being kept hidden away until he left. The hours of romance and fun—they ate, drank, made love, went out on a boat tuna fishing with one of the village fishermen—were regularly interrupted by sniping and shouting. They made up, fought, made out, fought. Finally, with Ava called back to work, Sinatra cut short his stay, kissed her good-bye, and, miserably, got in his car and drove back to Barcelona.

Mario Cabre, meanwhile, had been talking to the press again. "Who is Sinatra? When he is gone I will be back with Divine Ava. . . . Our love will survive, because she is the kind of woman you dream of, but, in her case when you wake up, the dream continues!"

Frank turned up in Paris a couple of days later, traveling with his composer/pilot/whorehound buddy Jimmy van Heusen. From a phone in the Club Lido on the Champs-Elysées, Sinatra took an overseas call from Broadway columnist Earl Wilson. Willing to set the record straight for the U.S. public, Sinatra told Wilson that the Spanish press had "bullied and bulldozed" him and tried to stir up trouble. "It's a lousy trick they pulled," he shouted into the phone. Wilson believed he could hear champagne bubbling in the background and interjected for his readers that the Club Lido had bare-breasted chorus girls although "the floor show is American-type and decent." Sinatra continued: "This bullfighter is nothing to her. Nothing! NOTHING! This girl is very upset because she's had nothing to do with this boy. The Spanish press has tried to make a hero out of this guy. It would be a feather in their cap if they could claim he had

Ava interested in him. As a matter of fact—and off the record—we're closer now than we've ever been! We've kept this [as] clean as anybody could just so nobody could hit below the belt. We were well chaperoned all the time, like a high school dance. ALL THE TIME!" Earl Wilson suggested that if Frank continued shouting he was going to hurt his voice again. "Here's something you can use," Sinatra told him. "Everybody's talking about Ava and me getting married—EVERYBODY—except Ava and me!"

Mario Cabre's shining hour, his very real bullfight to be filmed for the movie, was now at hand. The company was all driven out to the grand old *plaza de toros* at Gerona. The rain had stopped; it was a beautiful warm day. Saving money on extras (Lewin was already £25,000 over budget) they had simply put up ads for the bullfight and let everyone in for free. "My boss, John Bryan, the designer, gave me all sorts of extraordinary things to do on this production," said John Hawkesworth. "Things I was not qualified to do at all. And one of these was to arrange for the bullfight and to buy the bulls we would have there for Mario to fight. I had only joined the film industry in England three or four years before, and I had no experience with buying bulls in Spain, I assure you. I had to go to Barcelona to buy the bulls, and they arrived just in time for the filming. And it turned out I had bought the wrong sort of bull. They had these very huge horns and were much more dangerous for fighting, and they were all we had now and I felt very sorry for Mario because he was going to fight them anyway."

Further complicating matters, it was determined that the British censors would not allow any footage of the bullfight with the animal bearing the wounds from *la suerte de banderillas*, the second part of the *tercera*, when the short spears or darts are stabbed into the bull's backbone to sap his strength before the fight properly begins. It was suggested that the *banderillas* be stuck to the bull's back with suction cups, but this was rejected as being still possibly censorable not to mention insulting to the bull. They decided the best idea was to shoot an international version with the *banderillas* and another version with none. Cabre was asked if for the British market he wouldn't mind fighting the bull with all its titanic power intact, more dangerous by far, but the matador agreed, bravely conceding that the show must go on. Cabre seemed, as always, distracted by Ava. It was suggested that Mario take his time with the bull so that they would be sure to get enough coverage for the editing of the scene. Cabre, standing over his object of love in her front row seat in the plaza, explained that a bull ordinarily could not be fought for more than twenty-five minutes; longer than that and the animal becomes bored or sees through the game with the cape and charges directly at the matador and certainly kills him. But, for the sake of the film, Cabre would try to keep the bull going as long as he and the beast were both willing. He turned to Ava, sighed fatalistically, and smiled; someone translated his words to be: "Bulls hate to rehearse." Essentially, the bullfight for the film would be more dangerous than a "real" one would have been. Heading out into the ring, Cabre told John Hawkesworth, "Perhaps today I am going to die for Ava Gardner."

"We shot the bullfight exactly as it was happening," Hawkesworth recalled. "There was no planning or faking anything. He fought the bull right there in front of the public. And everything went well until the last bit, when the bull and the matador meet each other face to face. And the bull got too close and knocked him over. It turned around right away and charged him, it went right onto him with the horns down and I thought, 'Oh, no, that's the end of him! The bull's going to rip him to pieces!' And I thought, 'And I'll get the blame!' "

But the bull's big horns just grazed the Spaniard's skin, and his *cuadrilla*—his team of assistants— was upon the beast in a moment and the matador was whisked to safety. "*De nada*" said Cabre. He was more disturbed watching the filming of the scene in which he did not perform on camera but which showed his movie character Montalvo's death at the horns of the bull. This one moment of fakery was to be shot using a life-size rubber dummy created in Mario's likeness. The bull seemed to show great delight in gutting the Mario dummy. Cabre, taking the hint, said, "This could happen to me one day." They were about to conclude the filming when the bull suddenly turned to the camera crew filming on a wooden rostrum and charged them directly, crashing into the platform, convulsing it, and nearly toppling it over. The camera was still turning, and the operator (or someone) shouted: "What a damn good shot we got!"

At last it was time to return to London. Cast and crew gathered for a final seaside party, most eager to go home, but some, like Ava Gardner, only too eager to return again to Spain. Mario Cabre had written new poems to recite, mostly sad laments for his departing beloved.

They were to see each other again, for Mario would come to England to shoot the interior sequences but he sensed—correctly—that things would not be the same away from his native land. "She is a perfect angel," he moaned to any who would listen. "I am desperately in love." They kissed once more before she was driven off to the airport. Mario shouted to her in English, words learned from his American friend: "Good-bye, baby!"

Later, Ava would explain to the *Daily Mirror,* "The stories that Spanish bullfighter Mario Cabre has a mad crush on me are just a publicity gag to help our picture. It's a shame to involve the boy in this sort of story."

Elsewhere in the news, in New York City, Pepita Marco, a Spanish dancer in a Greenwich Village nightclub, declared to reporters that on account of stories about her fiancé and some Hollywood actress she had broken off her engagement to Mario Cabre and before witnesses had torn up his photograph and stamped on the fallen pieces. Asked about the raven-haired dancer, Cabre said, "It is not true we are engaged. A girl for marrying is one thing and a girl for amusement is something else. She is trying to get publicity!"

Shooting of the interior sequences at Shepperton Studios went on through the month of June. Ava took up residence in a Park Lane luxury flat, her upstairs neighbor her old friend George Raft, who was also in London making a picture. Reporters camped out at the entrance to the building, recording her various entrances and exits with all the professionalism and objectivity of aroused autograph seekers; one journalist, greeted by Ava on her arrival one evening, seemed all but sexually undone by the brief encounter ("Her perfume—a cloud of it, exotic, French—sent me into raptures!"). The newspapers squinted for a fresh romantic liaison and briefly linked her with a performer named Jack La Rouq, a violinist at a café called The Society (Ava: "Oh, yes, I know him, but never outside the club. And now it's romance! How typical!"). Leatrice Gilbert, Ava's old comrade from their early days at MGM, who had abandoned all that for marriage and motherhood, ran into her former fellow starlet in London at a party in the home of expatriate American actors Ben Lyons and Bebe Daniels. "Gregory Peck and his first wife were there and some others, and we were all playing canasta, and Ava came in and she looked marvelous. And she was very sweet and she remembered me. We talked and she came and watched us play cards. I watched her and thought of the girl I had known before. She was still very sweet, but I could see the changes; she was harder, she was drinking. The innocence, I think, was now gone."

At the end of the month Frank Sinatra arrived for a two-week engagement at the Palladium to begin on July 10, moving into a seventh-floor flat on Berkeley Square. Some of his old confidence had been restored by recent events: He had signed a contract with the CBS network for a weekly television series and separate radio program at a salary of a million dollars per annum, and this, his first concert appearance in Britain, was being promoted as a major event of the season. Sinatra rehearsed every day. In the evenings he and Ava went out, to dinners in the West End, one night to the countryside for a meal at Bray-on-Thames, and on to the cafés and nightclubs until late. Many nights they went out with some of Ava's new English friends from the *Pandora* company, such as Jack Cardiff and his wife, Julie.

Cardiff recalled, "Frank used to call Ava many times when we were in Spain. And I had told her how much I liked his singing and that my favorite record of his was 'I Fall in Love Too Easily,' and she'd obviously told him on the phone what I'd said and he sent over a copy of the record, signed by him—which I still have to this day. And in London we went out with them several nights. But it was just too much for me. Ava was a person who found it very difficult to relax. If we went to one nightclub, she would immediately say she wanted to leave and go somewhere else and then to another one and another one. It would go on like that right until the sun came up and breakfast time. It was too much for me, and I had to give it up." Everywhere they went somebody always tried to get Sinatra to get up and sing something, and he always refused, but there was one night Cardiff never forgot when Frank suddenly broke into song, directed at Ava, sotto voce, as the four of them sat at a table eating dinner. "It was," Cardiff recalled, "quite a unique experience to hear Sinatra singing without a mike, so close to us and so quietly."

The press pursued the couple at all times, as did a number of deter-mined members of Sinatra's British fan club, some of them appointed "spotters" who relayed info on their idol's movements and when he and Ava took off in a taxi would pursue them through the London streets on bicycles.

"My husband, Dick [Attenborough], and I saw them several times while they were in London," Sheila Sim recalled. "It was a terrific love af-fair, but it was very volatile. One night we were going out together, we were taking them to the theater. Dick recalls that we were seeing a new musical of Noël Coward [it was the opening-night performance of Cow-ard's *Ace of Clubs*]. We picked them up where they were staying and there was a crowd of thirty or forty people, I don't know, it seemed like a huge crowd outside waiting to see them. And Ava came whistling right out— she refused to stop for any of the autograph seekers, and she got right into the car. And then she looked around and Frank was still outside, and he had stopped and was signing autographs for everyone. And Ava became absolutely livid—she said they had just made a pact, apparently before they came out of the hotel, that they would not stop or sign anything. And he did the opposite! He stopped immediately. And when he finally joined us they had the most almighty row in the car. And so by the time we got to the Cambridge Theatre both of them were in a very bad mood.

"Ava and Frank were very edgy about the press and the photographers. They got very agitated about all that, Frank much more agitated than she was—Ava was much calmer; I don't think she cared a bit whether anyone took her picture or not. And we had planned to get to the theater early to try and forestall any sort of situation arising. But a photographer had come right down to the seats before the curtain went up. And he came in front of Frank and Ava and took a picture. Frank jumped up in a fury and went at him. And he grabbed the photographer bodily, and the two of them went rolling around and Frank just dragged him out of the theater! Threw him out! Very unexpected to have this happening at a Noël Cow-ard play, and a bit dismaying! But there you are. He was very agitated by such things. Otherwise he was a delightful character."

Headlined on a bill that included local variety favorites Max Wall, Maudie Edwards, and Wilson, Keppel & Betty, Sinatra's debut at the Lon-don Palladium was a great success. Due to the disruptions of the war, the British public had never been part of the original "swoon" era, and now a similar if more contained craze was finally upon them, giving Sinatra the sort of enthusiastic response he had not seen in a while. ("I watched mass hysteria," wrote the reporter for *Musical Express*. "He has his audience spellbound.") On opening night the London police held back a crowd of nearly a thousand excited fans, though at one point Sinatra was set upon by what were described as "two tall redheads" who had managed to break through the barriers and accost the singer, wrestling with him for possession of his trademark bow tie. The opening-night audience was studded with celebrities, including Ava, who would slip away before the encore to avoid press attention, and Noël Coward, who stayed to the end and did not beat up a single photographer.

After nearly four months Ava's *Pandora* adventure had concluded. It had been in many ways an epochal experience, opening for her new worlds of interest in the Old World, in Spain, in London, places she would come to know very well in years ahead. In gathering those experiences she had appeared to some as amusingly, charmingly naive, enjoying some of her first encounters with venerable cultural institutions with the wonder and enthusiasm of a little girl. Jack Cardiff would remember going with her for her first visit to the ballet at Covent Garden, Ava leaning forward enthralled by the performance of Margot Fonteyn in *Sleeping Beauty* and, childlike, chewing her bubble gum slowly or fast in rhythm with her changing degrees of rapture. It was understandable that she was often viewed with condescension by associates gifted with a more sophisticated background; few of them yet recognized the imagination and spirit that would one day enable her to make a place—a home and a vivid presence—in those worlds so different from the one in which she was born, on a dirt road in Grabtown.

The film she had made, *Pandora and the Flying Dutchman*, was a remarkable, original achievement, strikingly visual and boldly colored, deliriously romantic, daringly literary, mystic, baroque. Or: It was a folly, a catastrophe of pretentiousness and willful inexplicability. Take your pick. Some of the daily Anglo-American reviewers, confident of their own vast talents, poked fun at Lewin's assumption of scholarship and his supposed over-the-top aestheticism (among other memorable elements of Lewin's visual design were compositions that paid homage to works by de

214 • AVA GARDNER

Chirico, Delvaux, Dalí, and Man Ray). The film found its most sympathetic critical reception in Paris, headquarters of the surrealist movement from which *Pandora* took so much of its inspiration. There writers on film at *Cahiers du Cinema* and *Positif* and elsewhere applauded its ravishing visuals, dream logic, and provocative allusiveness and particularly savored the mythic presentation of its glorious female star. In a special issue of *Cahiers* devoted, in alphabetized entries, to the women of film, François Truffaut dedicated the letter *G* to Gardner as Pandora, rhapsodizing (in Susan Felleman's translation): "Ava Gardner's body is yet that of the first woman, who, along with her hair, undoes the ties of all fatalities . . . cinema, once again the magic lantern of our childhood, has borne us very far and very high on the wings of a dream." Critic Ado Kyrou declared that Ava now belonged in the exclusive pantheon with Lya Lys of Dalí and Buñuel's *L'Age d'Or* as the "greatest surrealist woman in the history of film."

Back in America, Ava and Frank had little time together before they were once again separated by their work. Ava was needed in Hollywood to begin preparations for the role of Julie in the new Arthur Freed Technicolor production of the musical *Show Boat*. Sinatra, meanwhile, tied to New York City for his new CBS television and radio shows, took a two-year lease on a Manhattan apartment. On September 28 the Superior Court in Santa Monica granted by default a decree of separate maintenance to Nancy Sinatra. She was awarded one-third of her husband's annual gross income up to $150,000 and 10 percent of everything above that. She was given the family residence in Holmby Hills, the 1950 Cadillac, and custody of the three children. Frank was allowed to keep his Palm Springs home, his '49 Caddy, whatever cash assets he had on hand, and his phonograph records. Ava cursed his wife as greedy. Frank wondered if he could come up with the monthly payments. Despite his enormous income, he was in debt, had constant huge operating expenses, an entourage that had to be cared for, and taxes to be paid. He had been fronted so much money by Columbia Records (supposedly to settle his tax bill) that he could expect virtually no royalties for the recordings he would make for years to come even if his record sales improved. He joked to a columnist that he expected he would end up running a filling station in New Jersey, a pointed reference, perhaps—that was exactly the fate of Ava's boyfriend, Burt Lancaster, in *The Killers*, just before her hired gunmen shot him to death.

And still Nancy would not talk about a divorce. It was the religion, Frank told Ava; she just couldn't go against the rule book. But Ava heard the whispered scuttlebutt from others: "She thinks she can wait you out, you two will blow over and she'll have him back one day. That's all she wants." To Ava it was an infuriating irony: There they were, wanting to do the right thing and get married, and there was this woman using her religion as an excuse to keep them "living in sin." Some who listened to her gripe about the situation suggested she simply give it up. Was it worth all this mess? they asked. The affair and the scandal had provoked the first serious rift in her relationship with Bappie, who disliked Sinatra and believed he was harming her career. "You hang on to him, Ave," Bappie told her, "and he's going to ruin you like he's ruined himself." The disagreement over Frank left the two sisters not talking to each other for months.

But how committed was she to this difficult man? Depending on the circumstances, Ava's feelings for Frank could still fluctuate greatly: from love and longing to ambivalence, resentment, contempt. Unlike Sinatra, whose obsessive love burned even hotter when they were apart, Ava, once she was on her own again in California, found it hard to stay focused exclusively on her missing guy. As in Spain, she was susceptible to sensual temptations (she had no doubt—and indeed would eventually have proof—that Frank was not faithful either, despite his seemingly far more intense dedication to the relationship). Indeed, back in California she seemed at times to behave as though quite unburdened of any emotional or physical commitment to Frank at all. Actor Robert Stack would tell of a provocative if unsatisfying encounter with Ava that autumn after her return from Spain. Stack had recently finished filming *The Bullfighter and the Lady* in Mexico for director Budd Boetticher and was sitting with a friend in a booth at the Naples Restaurant in Hollywood; he was recalling his experiences as a movie matador, using a table napkin to demonstrate a certain pass of the cape when fighting a bull. Ava, in the next booth, was drawn to the conversation at once. "How did it feel to face an animal that wants to kill you?" she asked him. One thing led to another, and Stack found himself at the pink house in the hills making martinis while Ava changed into something presumably more comfortable. They lay about talking and sipping cocktails. Ava's ardor seemed to increase with each of Stack's recollections of his dangerous time in the bullring.

Eventually, Ava, according to Stack, turned the conversation away from the *toros* and toward a consideration of what she referred to as "shared sex." She spoke amusedly of some new friends she had made, a young couple who liked to have sexual foursomes and, further, that perhaps this couple might be induced to come over for a drink later in the evening. As Stack would recall it, the prospect of remarkable erotic adventure ended abruptly with the actor feeling the effects of a case of sudden flu or food poisoning and rushing out of the house without apology. (Stack believed Ava's disappointment in him may have caused her to nix his casting opposite her in *The Sun Also Rises* six years later.)

Show Boat had been considered the great musical of the American theater since its Broadway debut on December 27, 1927, a groundbreaker in its introduction of serious and even tragic matters into the whimsical world of operetta. Based on a novel by Edna Ferber, it was a story of life and love aboard the Mississippi paddle-wheeler *Cotton Blossom*, with a legendary score by Jerome Kern and Oscar Hammerstein II, that included the songs "Can't Help Lovin' Dat Man," "Make Believe," and "Ol' Man River." Metro and Arthur Freed had been eager to make a new color version of the property since its New York revival in 1946. Freed conceived the remake as not only a dazzling entertainment in the tradition of his other great musicals but also a satisfying drama that dealt with themes of love and family, sacrifice, and racial prejudice. To write the screenplay he had hired John Lee Mahin (rather than any of the witty Broadway writers he usually employed for his films), a hard-nosed craftsman who, it was presumed, would not let the music numbers get in the way of the characters and story (one of Mahin's first scripts was for the film Ava and her mother had so enjoyed in 1932, *Red Dust*). As encouraged by Freed, Mahin was to increase the importance of the character of Julie—the part now assigned to Ava Gardner—the tragic-romantic chanteuse, a woman of mixed blood, passing for white, driven by love and a bigoted society into a life of drunken self-destruction. "Who do people most remember out of the earlier *Show Boat?*" Freed asked. "It is Helen Morgan, who played Julie. She acted the character that lives in the mind partly because she is a tragic figure." For a time the role in the remake was intended for Judy Garland, but by 1950 Judy was on her own destructive path and headed out the door at MGM. Dore Schary (taking creative control of the studio as Louis Mayer slid from grace in a power struggle with the New York office) had been pushing singer Dinah Shore for the part, an idea strongly resisted by the Freed unit. Although the other major roles were to be filled with tradi-tional musical-comedy talent—Howard Keel, Kathryn Grayson, and Marge and Gower Champion—Freed felt that in lieu of Garland as Julie they should cast someone associated with straight drama rather than mu-sicals. Although some questioned the decision, Ava Gardner was seen by the producer and others on his team as an exciting, attention-getting addi-tion to the film, an authentic Southern girl like Julie, with her own reputa-tion for extravagant romances and controversy.

And she could sing. Or could she? Nervous at the opportunity before her Ava gave many hours to rehearsing her solo songs, "Bill" and "Can't Help Lovin' Dat Man," in anticipation of an early November "prerecord" date (in movie musicals all the numbers were recorded in advance, the performers miming to an audio playback during filming). She asked for help from her friend Phil Moore, an African-American musician who had been a rehearsal pianist at MGM. Moore agreed to work with her on the songs in the evenings when she left the studio. But Moore would recall Ava as not always having her mind on her work. "Man, she was acting out everything. Short, short dresses. Being rather coarse and loud in her speech. . . . Sitting in unfeminine positions with dress up to here! And no drawers." The musician, charismatic and known as something of a ladies' man, was then living with Dorothy Dandridge, the beautiful black singer-actress, though they maintained two separate apartments in their house off Sunset Boulevard. Moore had a small rehearsal space in his apartment, with a microphone, so that when Ava came over they could approximate recording conditions. But when she arrived in the evening she told him it made her "too nervous" to sing to a mike and with all those lights on. Soon they were sitting together at the piano, with no illumination in the room except for a tiny pin light on the sheet music. One night Dorothy Dandridge arrived unexpectedly through the back door and found Moore and Ava together in the dark. "Needless to say," Moore told biographer Donald Bogle, "this didn't sit too well with Miss D." Ava no doubt ex-plained to Dorothy about the problem she had with her nerves.

For weeks she worked on the songs, with Freed's talented team, with Phil Moore, sang them again and again in the shower, made her own demo recordings, and had even overcome her usual nervousness about singing in public, doing a rendition of "Bill" before an audience of paraplegic veterans at a Long Beach hospital (the crowd demanded two encores). She was satisfied with the job she had done when the studio recording sessions were completed: Her voice—a "whiskey tenor," she called it—was spare, her singing tentative but heartfelt, with a dramatic power, conveying as much a characterization as a tune, wonderful. The Freed team sat around all through production and listened and listened again, arguing over the results. Some days it seemed acceptable, other days not. In the end the decision was made that Ava's throaty, modest vocals stood in too great contrast to the rich voices of Keel, Grayson, and others, and so a professional singer—Annette Warren—was brought into the studio to be the singing voice of Ava in the film; with the scenes already shot, Warren had to synchronize her singing to the lip movements of Ava, who was synching same to the playback of her original recordings (one of which had been more or less copied from the phrasing of a rendition by Lena Horne). Gone was the bluesy tone of Ava's singing, replaced by a conventional-sounding soprano (although due to concerns about false advertising, Ava's original renditions of the songs would end up being the ones used on the record of the sound track). When she learned of the switch Ava was hurt, and when she saw the finished footage she was insulted and embarrassed—she had been dubbed in movies before, but usually with a voice that was chosen to sound like hers, which Annette Warren's voice clearly did not. Monica Lewis, the voluptuous blond jazz singer who was then under contract at Metro and a new friend of Ava's, recalled, "Ava was very independent and she had her own way of seeking information. And I give her a lot of credit because she didn't come from, you know, Vassar, and she knew she didn't have a lot of education and so when she wanted to learn something or achieve something she really put her heart into it. And she thought she had done a good job with these songs. I had a record that was hot at the moment, and so she wanted my opinion. So she played the demo recordings she had made for me and she said, 'I can't sing like you can, I can't sing like some of them in the picture . . . but aren't these okay?' And I said, 'Yes, they are.' And they were. They worked perfectly with her speaking voice, and she was very musical, she was in tune, there was no sweat. And she was distraught. And I felt so bad for her because there was no real reason to have to use a professional singer. She thought it was just another example of how they put her down and it became one of a list of reasons she had for hating the studio and wanting to get away from them."

"I got to watch her when she was doing one of her musical scenes, singing to her own playback," recalled Marge Champion, the dancer-actress who played Ellie May Shipley in the film. "And it worked perfectly; everyone thought so when they watched her do it. She was this character, drunk and depressed, and sounded just like that character would, this sad romantic woman born on the levee. Today they never would have taken her voice off the film. Back then they were so concerned that everything had to be perfect."

For *Show Boat*, Ava was reunited with her first Hollywood director—George Sidney, the man who had coached her through a screen test on her arrival at Culver City. At the outset they shared a private joke: Back in 1941 his chief concern had been to get her to lose her "Deep South" accent; now, for the part of Julie, he was going to have to help her find it again. It had been a remarkable ten-year ride for both of them, from short subjects to B features to their standing in 1950 making MGM's most expensive film of the year. Sidney took great personal pride in his eye for talent when he thought of the raw, noncomprehending nonactress he had first met and had endorsed to the front office back in 1941 and the woman who was now giving him what he felt was an artful, nuanced performance and radiating with the star quality that was the rarest talent of all.

"She was just such a wonderful gal," recalled Howard Keel, the great baritone singer-star of Metro's fifties musicals. "A wonderful actress in that thing, my God, and her singing had a wonderful huskiness to it, she sounded very natural. She was really a great gal and we were great friends. We would get together at the end of the day, me and Ava and Katie [Grayson]. And I think we helped her a lot, just being together. Kathryn Grayson was a wonderful gal and a lot of fun, a lovely, lovely woman." ("Graycie," Ava once said of her friend and costar, "had the biggest boobs in Hollywood . . . with her they didn't need 3-D.") When they were finished filming in the evening the stars often got together in Ava's dressing room, where cocktails were served despite the studio edict against alcohol on the lot. "She didn't give a shit about what they said anyhow," Howard Keel remembered. "We'd sneak some in for the end of the day. Tequila.

Doesn't show on your breath as much. Listen, when Ava wanted to do something, she did it. She was a real wonderful, independent character, and no one was going to handle her."

"She was a straightforward, honest, terrific person," said Marge Champion. "People underestimated her all the time. She was not only one of the most beautiful women you ever laid eyes on but she was also smart about many things and had an instinctive knowledge of what was good for her—except when it came to men! She was one of those people who broke the rules all the time. Spontaneous. A real child of nature. She lived just below where we lived in the Hollywood Hills. We were above her, very close to the top of the canyon, and we had a swimming pool and she would just come up and go have a swim. And she always skinny-dipped. And one time she was out there and a boy came to make a delivery and couldn't find anybody in, and he was looking over the wall to get our attention at the pool. And I wondered what he would have thought if he'd known he was looking at Ava Gardner naked in the pool. But it didn't faze her. She was a straightforward person who did whatever she wanted."

Much of the filming was done on and around the studio-constructed *Cotton Blossom*, a 171-foot paddle-wheel river craft that was said to be the largest single combined prop and set ever used in a Holywood production. Made to move by a motor-driven length of steel cable, it lay on a track at the concrete bottom of MGM River, a three-quarter-mile stream that was now done up to look like assorted segments and ports of the Mississippi but had previously portrayed the rivers Thames, Amazon, and Yangtze. There had been discussions of substantial location shooting on the real Mississippi, but eventually George Sidney had settled for a brief jaunt with a small camera crew to grab some evocative footage at Vicksburg and Baton Rouge and other spots along the river. Despite the fact that all principal photography was done within the walls of the Culver City studio, the production was not without its unpredictabilities. A fire that broke out on the *Cotton Blossom* one night threatened to destroy the film's title char-acter. A more persistent danger came from a marmoset that was part of the showboat's menagerie. The monkey bit his trainer, attacked a prop man, nipped Kathy Grayson on the arm, and finally got his claws into Ava Gardner. She had been posing for some publicity stills, holding the animal on her arm, when George Sidney noticed on Ava's blouse a growing red stain around one breast. The monkey had dug his claw into her erect nipple and she was bleeding. Very carefully the beast was extracted from the flesh, and Ava was hurried to a nurse's attention.

In New York City, while Ava filmed, Frank appeared on his new CBS television series (the *Frank Sinatra Show*), broadcast each Saturday night at nine. The show caused little stir. The weekly television appearances, like the successful Palladium engagement in London, could not stop the air of failure that continued to attach to the performer's name. Sinatra was understandably miserable, seeing his career spinning downward and cripplingly in love with a woman whose affection for him seemed uncertain to last. He spent much of his time alone, a bundle of self-pity. The hangers-on were dismissed. What was the good of a king's entourage if you didn't feel like a king? He often left the television studio on his own, slumped and silent, wandering into the night. His favorite restaurant was Patsy's, a homey Italian place on Fifty-sixth Street off Broadway. In Patsy's, Frank was still a hero undiminished, and one night in late November—while Ava was in Hollywood filming her most prestigious assignment—he was having dinner, sitting by himself, as he had done for many nights past. As he was getting ready to leave he spoke to Pasquale Scognamillo, the owner, asking him what they would be serving for Thanksgiving dinner the next day. On the holiday most Americans spent at home with their families, Sinatra was planning to come by himself to Patsy's. Scognamillo told him something, then slipped away and removed the sign near the cash register that said, CLOSED FOR THANKSGIVING; when the singer had left (the *New York Times* reported), Scognamillo went around to his staff to invite them to come back the next day with their families for Thanksgiving dinner. He said, "I don't want Mr. Sinatra to eat alone."

They were reunited at Christmas. Frank brought with him from the East some more disquieting news. There was some new committee in Washington, a bunch of busybodies led by Senator Estes Kefauver, supposed to be investigating some sort of shadowy organization they were calling the Mafia. Frank explained it was some kind of bullshit anti-Italian jazz these bluenoses had been trying to put over for years—what the hell kind of name was Estes?—but some of Kefauver's investigators, probably egged on by someone like that creep Lee Mortimer, whom Frank had punched in the mouth a few years before—well, some of these investigators were looking him over now. They had some snapshot of him shaking hands with Lucky Luciano or something, and maybe they were going to haul him in to their committee and grill him like he was a criminal, smear him with guilt by association, ruin what was left of his career. He could see all his friends in the press having a good time putting him on the front page as a friend of killers and white slavers. Some of those guys they talked about, sure he knew them, Frank told her; they owned a lot of nightclubs where he worked. So why didn't they investigate every Dave and Dora who came in from the sticks to sit at a ringside table for his shows? They were doing business with those same guys. (Frank would find a well-connected lawyer to talk things out with the Kefauver people, and the investigator agreed to take Sinatra's testimony in a private session in a New York office, at three in the morning.)

For Christmas Frank gave Ava a puppy. It was a Pembroke Welsh corgi they named Rags. The puppy became her beloved baby and she became devoted to the breed, and from then until the day she died a pampered corgi or two would be a member of the family.

In April 1951, Metro had begun test screenings of *Show Boat*. There was some trepidation regarding the public's reaction to Ava Gardner in this expensive production. It was her first film made at the studio since all the bad publicity regarding the affair with Sinatra (the reaction to the aberrant *Pandora* was not considered indicative of anything box-office-wise). There were preview screenings in West Los Angeles, Pacific Palisades, and other neighborhood theaters. At each preview, the audiences were asked to note their reaction on little cards the studio supplied. Dore Schary and advisers peered at the responses, peered again, and smiled. Not only was there little or no evidence of negative attitude toward Ava Gardner, she was testing as far and away the strongest and most positive element in the film. At the Picwood Theater in West LA her performance was rated "excellent" on 248 of 312 report cards, nearly 50 percent higher than any of the other players, and rated much higher than the film itself.

At the Bay Theater in Palisades her numbers were even higher. Each subsequent screening brought similar results. Here and there a few viewers criticized Ava as overacting in her big scenes, some women respondents looked unfavorably at the scenes of Ava drunk, and one knowing fellow strongly protested the studio not using Judy Garland as planned, but the great majority were positive in the extreme:

"Ava Gardner stole the show."

"Gardner's great."

"Ava Gardner was wonderful."

"Ava was so lovely."

"Ava Gardner was marvelous. I've never cried so hard in a movie since *Johnny Belinda*."

"Ava Gardner was superb in the scene where she was drunk."

"Miss Gardner excels anything she has done in the past."

"Best scene Ava Gardner with no makeup."

"Congratulations to Miss Gardner she is learning to act."

"Let Ava sing her own songs!"

"Best scenes Ava singing."

"Best scene Ava Gardner telling Howard Keel about the baby."

"Dramatic scene of Ava Gardner on the riverboat. I have to admit she's better than I ever expected."

"Scenes like most everything Ava Gardner was in."

"Ava did better than Helen Morgan."

"Colored fellow who sang and Miss Gardner deserve extra mention."

"Where has Gardner been keeping that voice?"

"Ava Gardner is terrific."

"Ava Gardner is tops."

"Ava Gardner a sensation."

"Her ever-increasing box-office popularity"—wrote someone or other in a *Quick* magazine article titled "Ava Gardner: Too Much Spice?"— "makes her a hot potato the studio doesn't want to drop." A tide had turned. As the new year—1951—proceeded, observers of the zeitgeist, those observers with their own Hollywood column, speculated that the public had gradually begun to come around to Ava's side in her recent and controversial affair of the heart. It was thought that the publicity about

Nancy's sizable maintenance award and the very duration of the affair had begun to make people see things in a new light: Was the real story in fact that Nancy was the bitter woman standing in the way of what appeared to be Ava's true and lasting love? Especially when they were able to see the actress so sympathetically and romantically embodying the role of Julie Laverne, people could now believe—even some of those who had once written letters addressed to "Bitch" and "Jezebel"—that they had perhaps been wrong, jumped the gun, not seen the big picture of a woman who had fallen in love, whatever the consequences. Those who devoured gossip columns and movie magazine scoops were now in the fullness of time coming to the conclusion that they would after all be much more entertained in reading about glamorous, romantic Ava Gardner and her spirited affair with Frank Sinatra than about Frank and his now presumed clinging, stay-at-home wife. (It was, to be clear, interest in Ava first and foremost that drove the press and public attention in the affair; in this period the actress's image would be on more than three hundred magazine covers while Sinatra's would adorn not one.) Having stood her ground, toughed it out, and come out the winner, Ava's reaction to the change in perception was more or less as it had always been: They could all mind their own fucking business.

Pleased with the reaction to *Show Boat*, Dore Schary had happily granted Ava time off to be with Sinatra in New York. She arrived in Manhattan filled with a new confidence, already hearing great things about her work in the movie and with promises of a sizable increase in salary and bonuses for her next contract renewal that would bring in as much as a million dollars per year. Sinatra by contrast had no good news to share. His state of mind at her arrival is best summed up in the recorded performance he gave at Columbia Records' Thirtieth Street studio on March 27. On that day he recorded a new song written by Jack Wolf and Joel Herron. After the writers heard what Sinatra had done with it, how he had transformed the song by his interpretation, the two decided, rather unusually, to credit him as a co-composer. It was called "I'm a Fool to Want You," an operatic torch song sung to a femme-fatale love object of colossal, all-consuming destructiveness (one whose kiss, according to the lyrics, "the devil has known"). After performing the song—one take only—in a devastatingly dramatic fashion, like a passionate musical suicide note, Sinatra was said by some to have come away from the microphone in tears—mythmaking perhaps; "A bullshit story," says Mitch Miller—others claimed that he finished, then silently, abruptly, left the studio without looking back. Anyway, he wasn't smiling.

Ava went with Frank to see him do his live television show. It was disconcerting, amateurish. "Stagehands running in and out," she'd recall it. "You never knew what camera was on you. I got a nervous breakdown just watching." The whole thing seemed low rent: They had Frank telling bad jokes and doing sketches that sounded like leftovers from an old burlesque act. On April 25 Sinatra began a two-week engagement at the Paramount Theater, the scene of the Voice's midforties triumphs, when the girls had swooned in the aisles and the crowds on the street outside the theater had tied up traffic on Broadway. Appearing with him at the Paramount—and guesting at the same time on the television show— were Joe Bushkin and his orchestra. Bushkin went back with Frank to the Dorsey days and had written one of his first hit songs, "Oh, Look at Me Now" (and Frank had also introduced Bushkin's wartime ditty, "There'll Be a Hot Time in the Town of Berlin When the Yanks Go Marching In"). "This was a tough period for Frank," Joe Bushkin remembered. "He was not drawing. Some shows, like the supper show, the theater would be half empty. I remember Frank coming to the theater one morning and he said, 'You know, Joe, the only autographs I'm being asked for now are from process servers.' He was in a tough spot. He owed a lot of money, and he had to pay Nancy. And he'd say to me, 'I have no idea how the hell I'm gonna come up with the money I need to get semi-even with all this.' Well, he was making some good money but he was very good about spending it, you know. And this was a time he was really in love with Ava. But she could be rough on him. She was very independent, and she didn't tolerate any nonsense from a man that she was with, you know? And if there was something that he said, she would kind of blow up, you know? Like all of a sudden she's yelling, 'Who the fuck do you think you are?' That kinda thing. She was always the bandleader in that duo. That's a way of putting it: She was the bandleader."

It was not all bad news. Frank told Ava that Nancy had begun to crack, he believed that there might be something happening any day on the divorce front. And there was another hopeful development—a studio, Universal, had finally offered him a movie. It was called *Meet Danny Wilson*, and unlike that candy-box, kissing-bandit shit they had made him do at Metro, this was a part with some balls, a nightclub singer on the rise all mixed up with dames and mobsters. It was a part he could really sink his teeth into, he told her, identify with—matter of fact, the wiseguy screenwriter seemed to have had Frank's real life in mind when he was writing it, but he was going to let that pass for the moment. The deal was a one-shot flat-rate twenty-five grand, the picture to be shot in the summer back in Hollywood.

Before they returned to Los Angeles, Ava told Frank she wanted to meet his parents, still living across the river in Jersey. Even more, she wanted *him* to see his parents again—they had had a feud, Ava thought something to do with finances, and Frank had not spoken to them in nearly two years.

"No."

"What do you mean, no?"

"No."

"Why the fuck not?"

"Absolutely not."

"If we're gonna get married I need to meet your goddamn folks."

"Did you hear what I said? No!"

So Ava made the call to Hoboken, and Mrs. Sinatra invited them to dinner that same night. It turned out to be a good call indeed. Dolly Sinatra greeted her with a warm embrace, crying, "You've brought my son home to me!"

They sat and chatted in the humble, spotlessly clean, crucifix-laden Hoboken home, father Marty quiet and withdrawn as usual, Dolly holding court, dragging out albums of photos of baby Frank as grown-up Frank squirmed in comical discomfort. The two women—both soon relaxed enough to revert to their usual four-letter vocabularies—got along like gangbusters.

Before they left New York, Frank had one more recording session to do for Mitch Miller, on May 10. He had been appearing at the Paramount and on his television show with a young TV personality of the moment, a huge-bosomed blonde named Dagmar (Joe Bushkin: "Frank used to introduce her and say, 'Please nobody sit in the front row, if she takes a bow you'll get crushed.' "). Novelty records were doing well in the market, and Mitch or someone came up with a kooky thing he had Frank record with Dagmar and somebody imitating a horny canine. It was called "Mama Will Bark," and for Sinatra it would forever symbolize the nadir, the ground zero of his professional decline, the greatest singer in modern history reduced to competing for high notes with a fucking dog.

On May 29 Nancy's team of attorneys released a statement: Mrs. Sinatra was divorcing her husband and would file suit sometime in the next two weeks. To celebrate Ava and Frank returned to California, spent the Memorial Day weekend together at the swank Sand and Sea Beach Club. It was a perfect three days, spoiled only slightly at the very end as newsmen caught them exiting the club, Ava trapped as she waited for Frank to come out with the car.

Frank went back to New York to play a week at the Latin Quarter and do his final television show for the season. Ava began work on her new assignment, *Lone Star*, in which she was reteamed with her pal Clark Gable. A quasi-historical tale of the battle for the future of Texas, it would offer Gable as the cattle baron hero, Ava as the newspaper publisher heroine, and recent Oscar winner Broderick Crawford as the burly bad guy. Although expensively produced, the movie had an air of utter ordinariness to it—minus a few hundred extras and the star names it could have passed for another Republic B Western. Gable had largely outlived his usefulness at Metro and was near the end of his long term there; a black-and-white horse opera was considered the best the studio could do for the King at this moment in their relationship, but it was once again a case of two steps forward and two steps back for Ava, following up her magnetic turn in *Show Boat* with a part that could have been taken by any utility leading lady. Ava loved working with Clark again but hated the front office for sticking her into such a piece of crap. Direction was by the skilled Vincent Sherman, who could not argue with Ava's opinion of the project. "We both wondered how we had gotten stuck with making this thing," Vincent Sherman recalled. "It was a terrible picture, and she didn't really want to do it. But, you know, you need to get paid, and you're under contract so there wasn't much choice. She was a lovely gal, and I wish we could have made a better picture together because I thought she was just great."

A great deal of drinking went on. Without the Old Testament presence of Louis Mayer inflicting discipline anymore, people tended to bend the rules more openly. Gable and Ava were tippling, and Broderick Crawford was often in an alcoholic stupor while filming. Murray Garrett, a syndicated photographer who spent a day on the set taking pictures, recalled, "We were outside on the back lot and I was standing near the camera and Ava was sitting in a camp chair, and we were watching them shoot this big scene with all these extras and horses, and it was Gable confronting Crawford on horseback, and Crawford wants to take over the town, and Gable shouts some lines about they've got to protect the citizens or something. Gable says, 'What are we going to do about the people?' and Brod Crawford was out of it, just couldn't remember his line, didn't know what to say, and without breaking character he screams, 'Fuck the people!' And he rides away on his horse. I was standing near Ava and she just fell on her ass, screaming with laughter. Then everybody did. And Vince Sherman finally says, 'Oh, shit, let's break for lunch.' "

When they were back in California together for the summer, the couple divided their time between a rented house at the Palisades and Frank's place in Palm Springs. The heat had come off a bit in terms of the moralizing editorials and public outrage, but the press interest was as large as ever—now they were the reigning romantic couple of Hollywood, the two passionate stars whose love for each other was so great that they had risked career suicide. The press fed on them, said Ava, "like bees on a honeypot." Ignore it, friends advised, don't let it get to you. Not as easy as you think, Ava would tell them, "when you practically can't go to the bathroom without finding yourself on page one."

In August they decided to get away for what they thought would be a secret holiday in Mexico. But word of the trip leaked out, and the press of two nations went on high alert—there was suspicion that the couple might be going there for a quickie divorce and marriage. Reporters caught up with them at the Los Angeles airport. There was a squabble, angry words. Somebody said, "You shouldn't act that way, Frankie. The press made you what you are!"

Sinatra growled, "The press didn't make me, it was my singing! You miserable crumbs!"

Observers saw the couple holding hands on the flight, kissing and cooing most of the way to Mexico. Frank was attentive, adoring. On a stopover in El Paso he fought with the airline officials to let him enter the airport and buy some sandwiches: Ava didn't like the food they served on the plane. In Mexico City they took a pair of adjoining rooms at the Hotel del Prado and locked the doors, had all their meals sent up, and did not come out until they left the city for Acapulco.

In the Pacific resort they hired as guide and bodyguard Raul "Chupetas" Garcia, an Acapulco legend, the leader and champion of the Quebrada cliff divers. "Ava was so beautiful and so much fun," Garcia remembered, in Acapulco fifty-two years later. "I take them everywhere here. I take them swimming, to see everything. I take good care of Frank and Ava. They swim, they drink cocktails. They come to see me dive. They go with Teddy Stauffer and Hedy Lamarr at La Perla." Stauffer, the German bandleader-turned-gigolo-turned-beachcomber, now an Acapulco entrepreneur was married to onetime MGM star Lamarr, who had been on the train that had taken Ava to California in the summer of 1941. "Hedy was beautiful lady. And Ava was *more* beautiful lady! To see them both faces together—ah, *muy guapa*! Fantastic!

"Frank and Ava they are so much in love when they come here. But they have such problem with the Mexican photographers. They don't want to let them be happy. We go to the hotels, to nightclubs, they don't never want to let them be free. They bother them all the time."

The papers would report that in one encounter with an unruly shutterbug, Sinatra/Gardner's bodyguard threatened to execute the man with his revolver unless he handed over the film in his camera. Garcia, a half century later, could recall no such gunplay but, yes, it was *verdad* that there were times when one was reduced to physical violence in dealing with such persons. "I have to fight these bums. I hit one good. I guarantee you. He comes with the camera and I am with Sinatra and Ava, and this kid he takes pictures more times. He say to Sinatra, try to stop him, 'Come on, come on, what you want to do?' And so I grabbed him. Boom! That's it. Sinatra say he not want to come back to Acapulco, and I tell him I will talk to the president of Mexico and stop this problem with the photographers."

For their return to the States, Sinatra was determined not to fly back on a commercial flight so that they could avoid public scrutiny and the press. A Mexican acquaintance came to the rescue, wealthy sportsman Jorge Pasquel loaning them his private airplane, *El Fantasma*, a converted U.S. Air Force bomber. But then at the LA airport there was a delay finding the health inspector, and it took so long to get their mountain of luggage through customs that the press caught up with them anyway.

"We got a tip that they were landing at a remote part of the airport and in a Mexican military plane" recalled reporter and columnist James Bacon. "I got down there, and somebody from the *LA Times* and a cameraman from KTTV—there were about five or six of us. And we were all there when Frank and Ava ran over and got in the car. And Frank was mad right away, I guess, because it was a private flight, and he didn't expect anyone would find out about it. KTTV had a crippled cameraman who was shining the camera light into his face, Frank said. And Frank got the car going and stepped on the gas. And the wheels, I guess, were turned toward us before, you know—before he could straighten them out."

The black Cadillac careened off across the field and even onto the runway before turning noisily in the direction of the exit gate. Waiting there was another newspaper guy, a photographer named William Eccles. Eccles was poised to snap a picture as the car approached, but then Sinatra swerved directly at him, so Eccles said, the car bumper grazing the man's legs, Sinatra screaming out the open window, "Next time I'll kill you!"

It had been nearly three months since attorneys had announced Nancy Sinatra's intention to divorce her husband, and she had not filed suit. Ava began to believe that the woman had been playing with them and still had no intention of letting Frank go. Ava gave him an ultimatum: They had to get this settled right away or maybe they just needed to give it up for good, it wasn't meant to be. Frank pleaded with Nancy, then made a new plan. He was booked to work that summer at the Riverside in Reno and right after that the Desert Inn in Las Vegas. He would establish a six-week residence in Nevada, file for divorce himself, and hope for the best.

Ava came to stay with him at Lake Tahoe for the Labor Day weekend.

With Hank Sanicola and his wife, Paula, they shared a chalet at the Cal-Neva resort. Frank sported a new mustache, something he thought might offset the drawn, lined look of him with all the weight he had lost. Ava told him it looked terrible ("pimplike," writer Pete Hamill called it). They spent three long days and nights of booze, boating, gambling, more booze. It was the usual roller coaster, as the hours went on and the bottles got emptier, the tongues got looser, old grievances stirred up. Somehow the subject of Mario Cabre was introduced, and somehow Ava, after much badgering and assurances that it did not matter if she confessed, admitted to Frank that she *had* slept with the bullfighter. Sinatra did not take the revelation well after all. ("He never forgave me," said Ava. "Ever.") The arguing simmered and burned and never really stopped. At some point things took an ugly turn, certain words were spoken, Ava took furious exception, and next thing she was gone, roaring across the Nevada highlands to Los Angeles, sipping bourbon to keep off the chill. She had arrived home with the sun just coming up and the telephone ringing. It was Sanicola in Tahoe breathlessly telling her that Frank had been so upset he'd taken an overdose of phenobarbital, and they were all terrified. "Oh, God, Ava, you gotta come back right away, I don't know what's gonna happen!"

Exasperated and skeptical (remembering Frank's fake-out at the Hampshire House the year before) and yet frantic and knowing her man's increasingly unstable state of mind, Ava did the only thing she could do and headed for the airport. By midday she arrived back at the Cal-Neva and reached the chalet to find a roomful of agitated and exhausted people. It had turned out to be not so bad as they feared after all, said Sanicola. Frank hadn't taken quite enough pills to do any harm, didn't even need the doc's stomach pump.

"Our guy's okay."

She went into the bedroom and found him the best-rested person in the chalet.

And so it went.

She stayed with him for his entire engagement in Las Vegas. It was his first time working in the town that he would in the years ahead help make a world capital of entertainment, the place that would make him its holy, eternal father. For now it was enough to get a paycheck and humbly sing his songs to the crowd of distracted dice players and shit-kicking cowboys. Ava was pleased to be there, sitting in the audience every night in the Painted Desert Room and cheering him on, filled with pride in his talent, with love for the man.

But nothing could stop their endless squabbling. Friends, visitors, would be with them in the evening, woefully expectant, knowing the blowup would inevitably come, just not knowing when or what would set it off this time. Axel Stordahl, Frank's arranger and bandleader, remembered sitting at a table at the Desert Inn that September with Frank and Ava and Stordahl's wife, singer June Hutton. "Ava was chatting away happily. And then suddenly she went moody. She said, 'Let's get out of this trap.' She thought Frank was looking at a girl in the audience a little longer than necessary. They ended up throwing books and lamps at each other after the show, and Frank walked out in the middle of the night."

There was nothing apparently too trivial to stir up their jealousy and resentments. Singer Rosemary Clooney was working up the Strip at the Thunderbird during Frank's Desert Inn engagement and recalled how Ava would drop by for part of her show. ("She was fresh and funny, so beautiful it hurt your eyes to look at her.") Clooney sang Gershwin's "They Can't Take That Away from Me," which Ava told her was a song she loved. "Every time I get a chance, I'm going to come down here and listen to you sing it, even though the old man doesn't like it much."

Clooney couldn't understand what Sinatra had against the Gershwin classic, till she recalled that Artie Shaw had once had a big hit with it. "Although she'd been divorced for several years, Frank was still gripped by jealousy."

"I'm possessive and jealous and so is Frank," Ava would say. "He has a temper that bursts into flames while mine burns inside for hours." And vice versa, she might have added, ad infinitum.

Nancy Sinatra fought the Nevada divorce. But it was an empty, defeated gesture—in the end it became only about money, not about holding on to something she now realized no longer existed. When certain new or promised payments were made, the split was settled, done.

Two days after the divorce became final on October 30, Ava and Frank took the train from Penn Station in New York to Philadelphia.

Manie Sachs, Frank's abiding friend and guru, formerly of Columbia Records, hailed from Philadephia and had offered to host the wedding in a friend's suburban mansion. At City Hall they filled out a marriage application in the chambers of Judge Charles Klein, handed over blood-test certificates and copies of their divorce papers. The plan was to get married five days later, plenty of time, as it turned out, for arguments, screaming, threats, jealous outbursts, disappearances, and calling off the whole thing, twice.

The worst of these threats to the happy event occurred the night before they were to leave for Pennsylvania. Amid the crowd of wedding guests gathering in the Hampshire House suite, a bellhop arrived with a letter for Ava. It contained a lurid confession from a woman who identified herself as Frank's mistress, a position she claimed to retain to the present moment. Determined not to have her story misinterpreted or dismissed as phony, the woman detailed physical characteristics and particular, unusual sexual proclivities of Sinatra's that could not have been learned about him in the pages of *Modern Screen*. There were dates and locations of their liaisons. . . . Ava knew it had to be true (and never changed her mind, but later she would conclude that Howard Hughes was involved in all this, arranging for Frank's bimbo to tell her tale at just that moment). Reeling and afraid she was going to vomit, she told Bappie to announce that the wedding was off, and rushed away, locking herself in her bedroom. The hubbub in the outer room turned into chaos. In shifts people came in to reason with her, none except Bappie aware of the reason for the latest crisis. In the end, as she did again and again—as Sinatra did too—she put the hurt aside, accepted a fresh new scar on their relationship, and went ahead and fulfilled what was clearly meant to be her and Frank's destiny.

On November 7, 1951, on a rainy midweek morning, they came out of the Hampshire House, got into a chauffeured black Cadillac limousine, and headed for Pennsylvania. A caterer had leaked the original location for the wedding and so a last-minute switch had been made to the Germantown home of Manie Sachs's dress-manufacturer brother, Lester. Somebody leaked this news, too. When the limo pulled up to the Sachs house a cluster of newsmen and photographers was already waiting.

"How did you creeps know where we were?" Sinatra growled as Ava rushed inside. "I don't want no circus. I swear, I'll knock any guy on his can who tries to get in."

Later somebody in the crowd sent a note inside, a formal request for a picture. Sinatra came storming out.

"Who sent this? Who sent this? Who? You? You? You're not getting any pictures, understand? You'll get shots from our photographer when he gets around to it."

"I'd like to take my own picture," said one man with a camera.

"I'll betcha fifty dollars you don't," said Sinatra. "And another fifty dollars that if you even point your camera at me, I'll knock you on your ear."

Exit, slammed door, back to the happy occasion.

She wore a gown by Howard Greer, mauve-toned marquisette with a strapless top of pink taffeta. Twenty guests were there, Bappie as Ava's only family in attendance (just as she had been at her sister's previous two weddings), Axel Stordahl as best man, his wife, June, the matron of honor, Manie Sachs giving the bride away, escorting her downstairs as arranger Dick Jones banged out The Wedding March on an untuned piano. Judge Joseph Sloane presided over the brief ceremony. Frank and Ava kissed. Sinatra happily reached out to shake the judge's hand, saying, "Well, we finally made it." Ava rushed over to where Dolly Sinatra was standing and hugged her new mother-in-law. Dolly burst into tears.

The guests gathered around the couple and toasted them with champagne. Ava took a knife to the seven-tiered white-frosted wedding cake and messily fed a slice to her husband.

Outside in the rain, in their rumpled overcoats and wet hats, the crowd of reporters and photographers stood in glum witness to the unseen activities within the house, like a Greek chorus occasionally erupting with commentary:

"Hey, Frankie, come back out . . ."

"Pucker up, Frankie, I want to punch your fucking kisser!"

Shortly after the ceremony, Ava changed from her wedding gown to a brown Christian Dior travel suit and joined Frank at the back door. They came out of the house, got into a green convertible, and drove off. Several cars followed them to the airport where the newlyweds went directly on board a chartered twin-engined Beechcraft plane and flew away. Some hours later the couple were seen at Miami International Airport, racing across the terminal to a waiting convertible.

A ramp attendant who saw them said they were running just as fast as they could.

SEVEN

Tempt Me to Madness

There is one extant press photo of the couple on their honeymoon that does not show them running, snarling, cringing, cowering. Of course it was taken from a distance, and from the rear. They are walking together on an empty stretch of Miami Beach, both barefoot on the sand but otherwise still dressed in their heavy northern clothing. Ava wears her husband's jacket on her shoulders; in November in Miami the saline breeze off the Atlantic Ocean can turn very cold. They do not appear to be talking to each other in the picture, only holding hands as they walk back to their beachside hotel. It is early morning and they are alone, except for the stalking photographer.

The private plane from Philadelphia had been an extravagance, Ava thought, but Frank had insisted; the only way to get away from those bastard reporters, he had told her. Reporters or not, Frank was a private-plane sort of guy, and it was not the day to challenge his sense of himself; but later it irked when she found out he had had the bill for the airplane sent to Morgan Maree (her financial manager in LA). Manie Sachs had cornered her before they ran from the house in Philadelphia that night; he'd said to her: "Take good care of him, Ava. It won't be easy, but you've got to help him get back his confidence." It *wasn't* easy, or cheap— Frank's finances were in such disarray that she would end up paying for the entire honeymoon.

They had arrived in Miami in the wee hours of the morning and been driven to the small oceanfront hotel they had chosen to avoid attention.

They didn't have a lot of time to themselves before word leaked of their whereabouts. "Privacy was impossible," Ava would recall. On the second morning Sinatra had supposedly flung open the curtains and a flashbulb had instantly gone off in his face.

They flew on to Havana, Cuba, taking a third-floor suite at the regal Hotel Nacional, and for two days they romped in Fulgencio Batista's corrupt playground. And for forty-eight hours, magically, they had an uninterrupted good time. Ava loved the dirty, humid, decadent city—the hot breath of sin and sex everywhere. On the last night they had come back to the Nacional after many Cuba libres—they had been to the voodoo show at the Tropicana, then wandered the dark, hooker-laden streets of La Playita—and Ava, in a state of drunken bliss, had hung over the balcony so far she looked as if she was going to slide off into space but then came back inside, taking Frank in her arms and to the bed, convinced she had never been so happy or so much in love.

But once they returned home the old pressures and conflicts began anew. The course of Sinatra's career seemed unchanged, still in a downward spiral. The film he had made at Universal, *Meet Danny Wilson*, containing perhaps his best acting work to date as well as much great singing, was released in February, received poor reviews, and quickly disappeared. No other film work was offered. His CBS television show, in its second season, was doing worse than ever in the ratings. The network had now placed him opposite the very popular Milton Berle on NBC. The comedian mocked his rival on the air: Introducing some new girl singer, Berle said, "My next guest has never been seen on television before—last week she did the *Frank Sinatra Show*."

CBS canceled the program on April 1.

In June, Columbia Records decided not to continue its ten-year-old relationship with Sinatra. Within days his talent agency, MCA, would make the same decision.

If marriage had stopped most of the public hectoring, hate mail, and church sermons condemning them to hell for adultery, they still got their share of bad press. Sinatra was a hated figure to many columnists (many never forgave his reportedly unfair physical attack on the admittedly loathsome Lee Mortimer) and to editorialists and political writers of the rabid right. And now, as Frank's bride, Ava was welcomed as their new object of scorn. When the Sinatras went to London for Frank to appear at a charity benefit sponsored by the Duke of Edinburgh, an editorial in the *Richmond Times Dispatch* was headlined: "Goodbye Frankie and Ava, and Don't Come Back." Columnist Westbrook Pegler published a screed chiding the royal family for associating with the "badly discredited" couple (the same column also referred to the Duke as "dumb" and members of the Roosevelt and Truman administrations as "vermin").

A festering problem for the newlyweds was the fact that their work continually kept them thousands of miles apart. Stuck in New York under nerve-racking circumstances until the end of April, Sinatra wanted Ava there with him. The fact that she had a career and her own contract to uphold seemed irrelevant to him. Never very comfortable with making allowances for anybody but himself, Sinatra, now that they were actually married, felt more secure in his "traditional" demands on his wife. But Ava sympathized. She told him she didn't want to go to Hollywood, would rather be there with him in New York, and in fact she had several times already turned down roles and requested a variety of allowances from the studio in order to accommodate Frank's schedule. Frank would be appeased by these efforts, though seldom thankful, or eager to reciprocate, and as soon as she had to return to her own professional responsibilities he went back to complaining.

Metro had arranged for her to be loaned to Twentieth Century–Fox for a film of Hemingway's "The Snows of Kilimanjaro," a last-minute deal when another actress had been found inadequate. "Snows" was a short story like "The Killers," but much longer and far more elaborate in content than the gangster vignette. Still, screenwriter Casey Robinson and producer Darryl Zanuck saw fit to plunder bits and pieces of several other Hemingway stories to round out the tale of a celebrated, macho American author, to be played by Gregory Peck, dying on the African veldt in the shadow of the snowcapped mountain of the title and feverishly recalling his life and love affairs on three continents (Susan Hayward, Hildegarde Neff, and Helene Stanley were to play the other women in the hero's recollections). In the story Hemingway's protagonist at last expires from his infection, but the Hollywood variant would get to live on in the arms of a hot redhead, at least past the fade-out and end title. Ava Gardner was cast to play—as one of the series of newspaper ads for the film had it—

"Cynthia, from Montparnasse, a model with green-gray eyes and legs like a colt, who lit a fire in Harry Street that could only be quenched by . . . *The Snows of Kilimanjaro*." Largely borrowed from the Lady Brett character in *The Sun Also Rises*, Cynthia is a dazzling, uninhibited playgirl in Paris (a nude model for aspiring expressionists) and Harry's muse; he devotes much of his first novel to capturing her in prose, representative selections glimpsed in typescript: " 'You're everything,' I thought. 'Everything. On Wheels!' " (Hemingway must have gone looking for Casey Robinson with a hunting rifle when he saw this writing sample come on the screen.) Cynthia and Harry live together, not always happily, travel to Africa (where Robinson takes stuff from "The Short Happy Life of Francis Macomber," a Hemingway story Gregory Peck had already filmed five years earlier); then to Spain, where Cynthia runs away with a flamenco dancer; then turns up helping fight the Spanish civil war (reunited with ambulance driver Harry, as the screenwriter now grabs some scenes from *A Farewell to Arms* to round off his ruthless borrowings). The writer and producer were both Hemingway idolators ("If I could have been anybody else I'd like to have been Hemingway," Zanuck once said), and were intent on making this the ultimate adaptation of the man's work and of his life, too. But the final result was a sometimes risibly self-serious affair, further marred by a production that reduced the various exciting locales of the story to a series of phony back-lot and soundstage sets and some fuzzy stock footage.

Ava had been impressed by the role of Cynthia, and saw that it contained many parallels with her own life and personality. "Cynthia," she would write, "was probably the first [part] I understood and felt comfortable with, the first role I truly wanted to play." Ironically, then, she had to give the producers an ultimatum regarding her participation: Under Frank's ranting instructions, she could give them only and exactly ten days to shoot all her scenes before she had to return to him in New York, take it or leave it. Not happily, the studio rearranged shooting schedules and cut corners in order to cram all of her scenes into the allotted time. Still, it would be a fine performance she gave in those ten days, perfectly capturing Cynthia's mercurial, romantic nature (and, she said, with no help from the traffic directing of veteran Henry King). The film reunited her with the sympathetic Peck, who made much over her work, what he saw as her growth as an actress since the time of *The Great Sinner*. Peck was not always in a pleasant mood; his marriage was beginning to crumble, and there were rumors of outside interests but none involving his costar, who regarded him as a warm friend and brother.

The rush to get all of Ava's footage in the can may have contributed to an injury Peck suffered during their last scene together: Ava trapped under a vehicle on a Spanish battlefield and Peck frantically attempting to drag her body free. Peck miscalculated his position when he pulled Ava out and ripped a ligament in his leg, causing much pain and a halt in shooting. Despite their best efforts to make Ava's deadline, they fell behind and there remained a few last shots to be filmed. She was asked if she would mind extending her services to the picture for another twenty-four hours. Ava agreed at once, but when she told Frank of the brief delay he went into a tirade. She hung up on him, furious: All she and an entire production crew had done to accommodate him had been acknowledged with selfish, childish belligerence.

In late March she was back in New York for Frank's return engagement at the Paramount Theater. The sales were weaker than the year before. Some were referring to the appearance as a disaster. Frank's most sympathetic observer among the Broadway columnists, Earl Wilson, volunteered to try and drum up some excitement for the show—plugging it in the column—and arranging for visiting celebrities to come to the theater (which would be the excuse for another plug). One night Wilson and a Columbia Records publicist got singer Johnnie Ray to the Paramount, and between shows Ray, with a couple of friends, was taken backstage to see Sinatra. Young Ray was one of Columbia's hot new stars, the sensation of the moment with his hit recording of "Cry," a melodramatically rendered torch song. An eccentric, partially deaf, slightly effeminate bisexual who performed with flamboyant intensity, Ray's appeal had a somewhat freakish cast. To Sinatra, Ray was a prime representative of Mitch Miller's growing carnival of sideshow acts, gimmicks, and novelty numbers: the mincing Ray, Frankie ("Mule Train") Laine with his lousy bullwhip, Rosie ("Hey Mambo") Clooney and what he considered her insulting ethnic accents. To Sinatra the fact that the public was eating up such shit and ignoring his own artful recordings made it of course all the more infuriating.

Nevertheless he was perfectly gracious backstage in his dressing room, hosting Johnnie and his friends and introducing each of them to his wife. Ava had heard Ray's hit record—you could not avoid the thing that year—and was intrigued to meet the tousle-haired, lanky, quirky young man who had sung it. The group chatted for a bit until Sinatra was called out of the room to deal with something or other, at which moment Ava shifted up from her chair and settled herself on Johnnie Ray's lap and began touching and "petting" him. Ray's friends, recalling the scene for the singer's biographer, described a distinctly uncomfortable situation, much more so when Sinatra returned in midpet. Here was a scene he found wrong in so many ways: His wife wriggling on another man's lap, and the man—if that was what you called him—a member of Mitch Miller's despised freak show. Sinatra stood silent among the group for a moment, then grabbed Ava by the arm, jerked her from Johnnie Ray's lap and rushed her out of his dressing room without a word, leaving the guests to exit at their leisure.

Late in April, Frank was booked to do a series of concerts in the Hawaiian Islands. He told Ava it would be great if they took advantage of the visit and added on a week or so of vacation. MGM told Ava it would be great if she reported to work for her next assignment, a romantic drama called *Sombrero* to be shot on location in Mexico. Frank was in no mood to be contradicted, and *Sombrero* looked like a dog, so Ava sent the studio her regrets. A message was quickly relayed from the office of Eddie Mannix that Miss Gardner was expressly forbidden to go to Hawaii without the permission of her employers. On April 22, Mannix was informed that Ava had left that morning for Honolulu. The studio sent Yvonne De Carlo to Mexico to make *Sombrero* and put Ava Gardner on suspension, with all further salary payments to the actress to be withheld.

One rainy day in Hawaii, Frank Sinatra performed before a few hundred customers in a tent at the Kauai County Fair, water leaking through the canvas, dripping down on his immaculate tuxedo. Sinatra chatted with a sympathetic local reporter, speaking words more of hope than reality: "Tonight marks the first night on the way back. I can feel it in every bone."

To Ava he spoke more honestly. A newsman recorded the private conversation. "I'm washed up. I oughta just face it. The public is finished with me."

"No one with your talent is ever washed up," she told him. "This is just a bad time. Here, rub my ass. It'll give you good luck."

And he rubbed it.

Ava's devotion to her man was playing havoc with her own career. With her growing power as both a star and an actress, it was a time when she should have been working carefully with the studio to choose strong roles, develop significant projects, forge alliances with stimulating collaborators. Instead she was becoming increasingly disengaged, dropping out of planned productions (the most intriguing of these *Sister Carrie* opposite Laurence Olivier) and negotiating for assignments that could be scheduled around her husband's nightclub performances in Chicago and Atlantic City. Just as the powers at Metro might have been most inclined to give her the attention and respect they had withheld for a decade, she was doing her best to antagonize them. At a moment in time when there were few motion picture stars commanding more attention than Ava Gardner, she was effectively unemployed and without income.

Ava's agent went in to squabble with the studio. Her contract was due to expire soon. Metro understood that however badly she had behaved, there was still a lot of money to be made from a continued alliance with the star. A treaty was negotiated: first, the suspension would be ended immediately and withheld payments restored, in return for which Ava would be available almost immediately and without complaint for her next assignment of the studio's choosing; the seven-year, multifilm contract provided for payments of from $90,000 to $130,000 per picture. The most disconcerting part of the negotiations, as the executives saw it, was Ava's attempt once again to make the studio suffer for her spouse's dwindling fortunes, now with her insistence on what they came to call "the Sinatra Clause." As Frank was getting no offers of movie work at all, Ava— presumably with Sinatra's blessing and perhaps his urging—demanded that MGM formally include an agreement to produce a film that would star her with her husband. She and Frank even had a project in mind, a film from a Broadway musical called *St. Louis Woman,* and Ava had them mention that in the clause as well. In the end, the studio would make this offer so vague and nonbinding as to be meaningless. Still, it was something she could show Frank all down in rich legalese, let him know she was on his side.

With the suspension lifted, Metro immediately assigned her to another film, one of no promise and a role that was clearly without challenge or prestige. From a poor script by the talented Frank Fenton, *Ride, Vaquero!* was superior to *Lone Star* only in its lush Technicolor exterior photography. A range-war Western in which good bad guy Robert Taylor and bad bad guy Anthony Quinn oppose nice-guy settler Howard Keel and his emerald-eyed wife, the film was partially shot on location at Kenab, Utah. "It was really the asshole of creation," recalled Howard Keel. "Beautiful territory, but we were out there for about, oh, Christ, a month, and there was nothing there and nothing to do there. Nothing." Ava passed the time drinking with the stuntmen and hating director John Farrow, a man she found to be a mean and lecherous character, cruel in equal measure to the horses and to the whores he flew in from Los Angeles.

California, that late spring and summer of 1952, was going to be about normal: about love, happiness, domesticity, laying the foundation for a future together. It was a time for Ava and Frank to stop rushing around the country and to settle down, show the world—and they were more than a little interested in getting some incontrovertible proof for themselves— that they could live in peace, in one place, show that it had all been the right thing after all, worth all the commotion and the craziness of the past two years.

Frank worked to restore his stature with his children. One day he had been out spending time with Nancy junior and then, impulsively, he decided to bring his twelve-year-old daughter home to meet her stepmother. Ava greeted the girl with apprehension, imagining the demonic profile she must have had in the household of Frank's first wife, but little Nancy proved to be more awed than resentful. "What I saw knocked my little socks off," she would write in a 1985 memoir. "I could imagine a bit of what my father felt. And he was swept away. . . . My heart melted just looking at her. I was only a kid. I didn't know about beauty—that awesome kind of beauty . . . she was just the most beautiful creature I had ever seen in my life. I couldn't stop staring at her." Nancy would come to stay with them for some weekends in Los Angeles and in Palm Springs. Even as she became more familiar with her father's new wife, the woman remained to her a mysterious, unreal presence, "a goddess." Ava did her best to be friendly and fun (she bestowed on the girl her first lipstick, neon orange Tangee Natural that magically adjusted to the pigmentation of your lips). Nevertheless, the mood underlying these visits was anxious and sad, and Ava knew it.

Frank and Ava told friends they wanted children of their own. Ava had said it to a hundred reporters through the years: To have a family, three, four, six kids, that was her real destiny, not movie stardom. It might have been that she had voiced these sentiments in part to hear herself say them, to read them in black-and-white, for her actions regarding the prospect of childbirth had always been more ambivalent, confused, and fearful, and events in the months ahead would prove that these mixed feelings had by no means gone away.

Ava did become pregnant. That much is clear. However, the details of the matter of the pregnancy—or pregnancies—and the circumstances by which she did not give birth to a child, remain in some dispute. As she recalled it in her memoir, Ava had discovered she was pregnant in late autumn of 1952 while on location in Africa for the movie *Mogambo*. The future of her marriage was by then not at all secure, and she no longer felt confident in her ability to offer a child the proper attention and a stable home life; while Frank was back in America, and without consulting him, Ava had the pregnancy medically aborted. Her book would go on to explain how, very soon afterward, she discovered she was pregnant again, that Sinatra knew about it but was unable to prevent her from having a second abortion. Some who knew Ava and/or Frank have questioned this claim of a second pregnancy and termination during the time of the *Mogambo* filming, suggesting that Ava had gotten confused while recording her autobiography. (It has been speculated that the book's erratic creation, containing Ava's sometimes blurred memories and posthumous editing and rewriting by hired hands, may have introduced some conflated material along the way to publication.) Sinatra himself was said to have read Ava's book and privately disputed the story of the second pregnancy. But others on the scene at the time confirm Ava's version of events, with one proviso: that the father was thought to be not Ava's husband but one of the members of the company on the African locations.

The possibility of one other pregnancy, not considered elsewhere, comes from actor Roddy McDowall, who had known Ava from the forties at MGM and in 1969 would star her in his only film as a director, *Tam Lin*. According to McDowall, as told to producer and film historian David Stenn, Ava revealed to him that during that same first year of marriage she had unknowingly been with child and suffered a miscarriage after a fall during a drunken brawl with her husband. McDowall, who was clearly more sympathetic to Ava's cause, put the blame for the tragedy on Sinatra. "Roddy didn't gossip in that way at all," said Stenn. "This was the only thing he ever told me like that about anybody. Roddy loved Ava, and I think he was very angry that this had ever happened to her." There is no other evidence of such an incident, but in this same time period Ava was reported to have had a medical emergency, and was rushed to Cedars of Lebanon Hospital in the predawn hours of May 24, a week when Sinatra was performing locally at the Cocoanut Grove. The exact nature of the emergency was never revealed, but the doctor summoned to treat her was Dr. Leon Krohn, a gynecologist and longtime friend and associate of Ava's husband.

No, they did not turn out to be very good at normal.

As the summer went on, the old combustibility had returned in full measure. However much they may have loved each other, the relationship was still mostly sustained by two elements: lust and anger. "We never fought in bed," Ava would tell friends. "The fight would start on the way to the bidet." The "love nest" in the Pacific Palisades became the neighborhood tinderbox, ever ready to explode with the newlyweds' raging disagreements. It was the same old crazy, exhausting act, jealousies, resentments, taunts, anything, nothing. They were the Battling Sinatras, a public amusement or an outrage, depending on how close you were sitting to the screamed obscenities and the flying ashtrays.

This sort of thing, all the time: One night Ava had gone out to dinner with Lana Turner and another actress friend. They were at Frascati's in Beverly Hills, one of Ava's favorites. Halfway through a pleasant meal, Frank had charged into the restaurant, red-faced with booze. He lurched up to the table with the three screen beauties and began berating his wife, some earlier, unfinished argument he now picked up in media res. Ava simply ignored him and continued chatting. The other two took their cue from Ava and similarly pretended that Frank wasn't there. Sinatra looked over the three women and started screaming at them (the scene recalled by restaurateur Kurt Niklas).

"Lesbians! You're a bunch of goddamned lesbians! All of you! Lesbians! Lesbians! Lesbians!"

The women did their best to act as if there was nothing wrong and that no one was standing there calling them lesbians. The rest of Frascati's stared in open-mouthed shock. Frank then turned and stormed out of the restaurant, screaming behind him all the way: "Lesbians! Lesbians! Lesbians!"

That summer Howard Hughes made one of his periodic forays into Ava's life. Frank learned of phone conversations the pair were having and became enraged. In the peculiar way they both had of fanning the flames of an argument until there was a proper, all-consuming conflagration, Ava let it be known that Hughes had in the past supplied her with proof of Frank's philandering, and even turned a suspicion into fact, crediting Howard with arranging for her to receive that pornographic pre-wedding-day letter from her fiancé's mistress. It was too much. Frank told her he had had enough of fucking Howard Hughes and he was going to settle the fucker's hash once and for all. Grabbing a bottle of Jack and a revolver he stormed off to find the billionaire and presumably shoot him dead. Sinatra drove around Los Angeles for much of the night, rushing in and out of various Hughes haunts with his .38 under his jacket, drunkenly ready and eager to bring down that Texas *cazzone* and his Mormon bodyguards in a blazing gunfight.

Hughes, alas, was out of town.

By autumn the papers began to report on a marriage in trouble. Syndicated columnist Earl Wilson wrote, "Eleven months after their wedding, Frank Sinatra and Ava are desperately trying to avert a crack up." In September they had been in New York while Frank performed across the river at Bill Miller's Riviera in Fort Lee. One night Marilyn Maxwell had been in the audience, and Ava thought Frank had been singing a song to her. That was it: She threw a cursing fit and left the club before he was off the stage. She went back to their hotel, packed, put her wedding ring in an envelope addressed to her husband, and left for Hollywood. "It's anything that might happen between a man and a wife," Sinatra said to the *Los Angeles Times*. "Just a mild rift." But that same day, to the trusted Earl Wilson, Frank spoke less optimistically: "I am nuts about her and I don't think it's dead but it's certainly all up in the air." They did not speak to each other at all for several weeks. Frank lost the returned wedding ring in the meanwhile and had to have a duplicate made to bring back to California. She reluctantly accepted it. There was a reconciliation then, in mid-October. They went ahead with arrangements for Frank to accompany her to East Africa in November, when she would begin location work on a new film. But the truce was barely a couple of days old when they had one of their biggest fights to date, one that involved a brawl, two love goddesses, police, rumors of sex orgies, and the inappropriate use of a douche bag.

On Saturday the eighteenth they had gone out to eat, an argument had broken out, and they returned to the Palisades house, both drunk and angry. Ava was giving him the silent treatment and disappeared to take a bath. Sinatra had a few thoughts not yet expressed and burst in on her. Ava screamed for him to get the hell out, and Frank at last said, "Okay, baby, I'll get out. You can find me in Palm Springs. I'll be there fucking Lana Turner!" She heard doors slamming and the car screeching out the driveway, and she screamed and punched the bathwater. She lay there in the tub in a simmering, inebriated rage, pondering her husband's exit line until it had become in her mind a vivid actuality. Frank had, in fact, already offered Lana use of the house at the Springs for a weekend getaway. Lana was a good friend of Ava's, but she knew what a thing Lana and Frank once had and . . . who the hell knew what to think? An hour later she had picked up a reluctant Bappie at her apartment and the two of them were speeding east into the desert.

At Frank's house (a modernist structure on Alejo a minute from the center of town) they found Lana and her business manager, Ben Cole, settled in and relaxing by the swimming pool. But no Frank. Ava gave Lana a variant account of events; Lana offered to leave, and Ava told her no, there was room for everybody. Ava and Bappie joined them for a swim, and then they all went into the kitchen to fix a meal. They were about to sit down to eat when the back door burst open and Frank charged in. Lana would recall Frank's red face and "blazing eyes."

"I bet you two broads have really been cutting me up," Sinatra said. Then he pointed at Ava and said, "You! Get in the bedroom. I want to talk to you."

Ava shrugged, went into the bedroom. Lana and Ben Cole stood around until they heard the screamed epithets and the sound of furniture being thrown against the walls, and they decided to make a hasty exit. Ava recalled Lana and Cole and Bappie all still there and Frank coming out and ordering everyone to "get the hell out of my house!"

Ava said, "Fine! But I'm taking everything that belongs to me!"

As Ava's friend Esther Williams recalled hearing the story, Sinatra "found an article hanging in the bathroom and he filled it with water and went out to the porch where Ava was saying good night to Lana and he threw water from that . . . that article of usefulness known as a douche bag. He threw the water on both Lana and Ava standing there."

Ava ran back inside and began tearing paintings off the walls, books and records from the shelves, flinging them all over the floor, and Sinatra raging just behind her, scooping up the items and tossing them out through the open front door. Neighbors called the police. The squad cars came roaring up the driveway, red lights flashing, radios squawking, and several officers rushed up to the house as Sinatra was trying to evict his wife bodily and Ava was clinging to the doorway with both hands. The police chief arrived, an acquaintance of Sinatra's, and he managed to separate the couple although they continued cursing at each other and throwing things. Lana Turner and Ben Cole, who had gone off and rented a bungalow at a nearby resort, returned to see if the situation had improved and to get Lana's clothes. Lana and Ben told Bappie and Ava to come stay with them for the night. "Bappie and I went off with the cops," said Ava, "leaving Mr. Sinatra to be king of the roost."

By Monday the incident was the hottest piece of gossip in Hollywood, although much embellished with rumor and lurid fantasy. One lubricious story retold for decades was that Frank had walked in on Lana and Ava in bed together. "There was even a version," Lana Turner would recall, "that Ava and I had gotten mad at Frank, picked up a strange man and shared him between us—and Frank had walked in on that scene. The simple fact is that Ava, Ben and I were about to eat chicken in the kitchen when Frank appeared. . . .

"Their marriage," said Lana, "was a dreadful fiasco."

They did not see or speak to each other for nearly two weeks. Finally politics brought them back together. They were both loyal supporters of Adlai Stevenson, the Democratic nominee battling Dwight Eisenhower in the upcoming presidential election. Ava had earlier promised to appear and introduce her husband at a huge rally for the candidate at the Palladium. "I didn't intend to let my personal problems with Frank spoil any part of Mr. Stevenson's night," she would say later. "So, despite the Palm Springs incident, I showed up as scheduled for the rally. I stood in the wings and—as always happened when I saw Frank—my heart melted and the battle was forgotten." There had been a script prepared for her to read, but Ava tossed it aside before she walked up to the microphone. "I introduced him to the audience as a wonderful man and a great guy. I think Frank was as surprised at the introduction as I was."

Murray Garrett, the syndicated photographer, was part of the press contingent covering the rally from backstage at the theatre. "She'd introduced Frank and he goes on stage and kisses her and they start playing 'Birth of the Blues.' Ava comes backstage now and every photographer and reporter there just gathered around her and started firing questions. And she wasn't really paying any attention, she was just looking toward the stage where Frank was singing, smiling to herself. And this one idiot guy, from Chicago, I think, he says to her, 'Hey, Ava, Sinatra's career is over, he can't sing anymore. . . . What do you see in this guy? He's just a hundred-and-nineteen-pound has been.' And Ava says, very demurely, no venom, just very cool, in the most perfect ladylike diction, 'Well, I'll tell you—nineteen pounds is cock.'

"I mean, you got to remember, this was 1952. Nobody talked like that. And the guy that asked the question just stood there frozen, like somebody had hit him. And then people started laughing, and Ava just smiled and went back to looking at Frank out on the stage."

"The reconciliation of Frankie Sinatra and Ava Gardner is on the up-and-up," said the *Los Angeles Daily News* on October 30. "Whatever that means. But, say the gossipers and keyhole detectives, the pair have patched up their crazy-quilt marriage, and the Thin Man will escort his Ava to Africa, where she is to emote in an adventurous epic."

Under Dore Schary, Metro had begun a policy of remaking some of their old hits and each year the studio's slate of new productions was to be filled with titles or properties from out of the past—*Scaramouche*, *The Prisoner of Zenda*, *The Merry Widow*, *Rose Marie*, *The Student Prince*, *The Painted Veil*, *The Women*. Now it was decided to make a fresh version of one of their biggest hits from the Pre-Code 1930s, the rollicking, sultry comedy-drama *Red Dust*, with the screenwriter of the earlier film, John Lee Mahin, given the job of revising his own work (derived from a play by Wilson Collison). With thoughts of the recent success of *King Solomon's Mines*, excitingly filmed on location in Africa, the *Red Dust* remake would be taken out of its Southeast Asian rubber plantation setting and placed in the Technicolor-friendly safari country of Kenya and Tanganyika, leaving plenty of room for scenic diversions and the intrusion of big game. In Mahin's revision—*Mogambo* it would be called, Swahili for "passion" said the linguists in the publicity department—hunter-trapper Vic Marswell crosses paths with the stranded Eloise "Honey Bear" Kelly, an ebullient wandering playgirl. The two have a lighthearted romance, until the arrival of Donald and Linda Nordley, a guileless English couple on a scientific mission. Vic and Linda fall into a passionate affair, to Kelly's dismay. The affair ends terribly, and by the fade-out Vic has come to realize that the overlooked Kelly is the woman for him. Woven into the melodrama were scenes with dangerous wild animals, cute baby animals, tribal ceremonies, and native attacks. At the outset the part of the big-game-hunter hero had been seen as a natural for *King Solomon's Mines* star Stewart Granger (who claimed the idea for a *Red Dust* remake in Africa was his own), but in the end the part went to Clark Gable, the man who had played the studly protagonist in the steamy original twenty years earlier (it was a real tribute to Gable's eternal appeal and vigor; none of the original stars of the other films to be remade were even remotely considered for another go). Ava, in her third pairing with Gable, would play the part of the sweet good-time girl endearingly and erotically portrayed by Jean Harlow in 1932, the studio casting the woman some saw as a throwback to the late Harlow's brand of earthiness, sexiness, and humor. Portraying the Nordleys would be Donald Sinden (now Sir Donald), a rising star from the British stage with one previous film credit, and Grace Kelly, the patrician Philadelphia blond with two films under her belt, a year away from her major stardom. Producing the film was Metro veteran Sam Zimbalist, and hired to direct was one of the most highly regarded creative figures in Hollywood, John Ford.

Ava was too much an old Hollywood hand now to spend time wondering at the irony of costarring with Clark Gable in a remake of the film— starring Clark Gable—that had been such a hit with her and her mother two decades before. But it deserved at least a moment's reflection as evidence of the distance traveled in those twenty years, remarkable link between the little Piedmont girl staring up at the big black-and-white images of Gable inside the Howell Theater in Smithfield and the worldly woman—Clark's costar—who in early November, 1952, stepped aboard a Stratocruiser en route to Nairobi.

Frank had decided to come with her—he had nothing better to do, and Ava was going to be out of the country for many months. But he was sensitive to the way some people saw it, the has-been in attendance on his more successful spouse. When a reporter asked if they were going to find a role for Frank in *Mogambo* he snapped sarcastically, "Yeah, I'm going to play a native, in blackface." Ava, trying to help, had made things sound worse: Someone asked her what Frank would be doing while she made the movie, and she said, "Oh, he'll do his act in some African nightclubs." Somebody cracked, "Who's opening for him, Tarzan?"

In Cairo the airplane stopped for refueling, Ava and Frank tucked into their sleeping compartment. A photographer came aboard, located the couple, and attempted to take a picture. Sinatra lashed out, the photographer ran, and Sinatra gave chase, charging onto the Egyptian runway in his pajamas.

The principal cast members were gathered together at the New Stanley Hotel in Nairobi a few days before filming. "They had us all down there early to get used to the climate and the water and to get a bit of a suntan," recalled Sir Donald Sinden. "For the first couple of evenings I had dinner with Clark Gable and Grace Kelly, and on the second evening we were in the dining room and I said to Clark Gable, 'I wonder when Ava Gardner will arrive?' And Gable said, 'She's here. She won't come down. She has all her meals sent up to her room.' And I said, 'Well, that's very antisocial. English actors don't behave like that. I've a good mind to go up and bring her down.' He said, 'You wouldn't.' I said, 'I jolly well will.' And off I went to her room, knocked on the door, no answer, knocked again, and then a voice said, 'Who is it?' It was a bit difficult introducing yourself through a closed door, but I said, 'My name is Donald Sinden.' She said, 'Who? What?' I said, 'I've come to take you down to dinner.' And there was a pause and then the door was kicked open and there was Ava standing with her back to the light, which was a most impressive sight because she was wearing a quite diaphanous dressing gown that outlined her complete figure. And she looked at me from head to toe and she said, 'You've come to take me down to dinner?' I said yes. There was a pause, then she said, 'Okay, then. I need to take a bath first.' And she went into the bathroom, leaving the door open. Which is pretty frightening for a young chap, you know. Somebody less of a gentleman would have looked, but I didn't. She said, 'Help yourself to a drink,' which I did. I heard this splashing of the water and everything in the bathroom. She then came out with the same dressing gown on and started floating around the room looking for something and she picked up a small tin of Nivea cream and then flung it aside, saying, 'Godammit, I thought that was my Dutch cap [diaphragm].' So this was my exotic first encounter with the most beautiful woman in the world. She was totally uninhibited.

"Eventually we came downstairs to the dining room, and everyone looked up and I must say they were mightily impressed with me. And here she had been not wanting to deal with other people—forgive me, the Americans do it far more than the English do—being conscious of her own publicity, her own importance. But from then she and I got on like a house afire. And she was a delight. But she did have some habits—one of the things I dislike in life is somebody helping themself to your food. And while we were eating Ava suddenly darted her fork across the table and took something off my plate. I said, 'Please don't do that.' She said, 'What's the matter, honey?' I said, 'I do dislike people mucking around with other people's food.' And she laughed. But we got on extraordinarily well.

"They wanted us all to get ourselves a bit tanned before we went off to film, and so every day all of us went up to the roof of the hotel where there was a swimming pool, Clark and Grace and Ava and myself, and we all sat around and sunbathed and got to know each other. Ava and Clark had worked together before and they were good friends. She said something rather funny that I thought summed him up more than any other remark I've heard. She said, 'Clark is the sort of guy that if you say, "Hiya Clark, how are you?" he's stuck for an answer.' But she was very fond of him."

To make a large-scale MGM Technicolor production in the wilds of Kenya, Tanganyika, and Uganda required an enormous operation, a company of nearly six hundred, from cast and crew to drivers, bearers, pilots, guards, guides, hunters, chefs, servants, nurses, tribal extras (gathered from the local Turkana and Samburu as well as imported members of the particularly fierce-looking Makonde of Portuguese East Africa and some of the expert canoe paddlers of the Congo's Wagenia tribe), and a witch doctor. "We went right into the wilds, nothing there but jungle and animals," recalled Roy Parkinson, the film's production manager. "We would clear out an airstrip in the bush, then fly the units out there and set up a camp. A small airplane flew the rushes back every other day to Nairobi and then they were put on another plane and flown back to London for processing. It would be days before we knew what anything we shot looked like."

In charge of securing locations, managing the location camps and keeping an eye on big game was Frank Maurice "Bunny" Allen, a legendarily fearless, craggily handsome "white hunter" very much in the Stewart Granger mold. At each location in the African interior a virtual city of as many as three hundred tents was erected. The initial camp was set up on the crocodile-infested Kagera River along the Tanganyika-Uganda border 150 miles from the shores of Lake Victoria, then a second at the northern frontier, overlooking Uaso Nyiro River near the Ethiopian border. Conditions in the bush were varyingly primitive—water for showers had to be drawn from the river, heated over an open fire, and then loaded into a small tank—and luxurious, with a replenished supply of delicacies and French wines flown in from Europe. Also gin, vodka, and scotch. "At the Kagera Camp," Bunny Allen recalled, "they drank enough to drown the Titanic."

Filming began in an unpleasant atmosphere. John Ford was a genius of moviemaking, pure and simple, but he was also a crabbed, calculatingly cruel man who frequently took a miserable pleasure in humiliating people who had the misfortune to be trying to make a movie for him. This worked well with the powerless and the sycophantic and those members of Ford's professional "family" who loved him despite everything, but on *Mogambo* Ford's intimidation tactics proved largely futile. Gable was a dignified man who worked in a spirit of comradely professionalism, and when Ford tried to belittle the star, Gable made it clear Ford would be sending back no more footage of him to MGM until the director's behavior improved. Ford turned the same charm on Ava Gardner, telling her that he had wanted Maureen O'Hara for her part, and deriding her when she spoke too flippantly after a botched take ("That was a real fuckup!" quoth Gardner). Ava told him he could take the dirty handkerchief he liked to chew on while working and shove it up his ass. Ford reassessed his position on this MGM production with two MGM stars, adjusted his attitude, and was soon making nice. A couple of days later he told Ava, "You're damn good." From then on they were buddies (Ava: "The meanest man on earth. Thoroughly evil. Adored him!") and worked together beautifully. Ford's magic helped Ava to create a characterization that glowed with life. To many who knew her, the performance in *Mogambo* would be the one that best captured the Ava they knew, the fun, the charm, the humor, even the flashes of temper and self-doubt.

Whatever his character flaws, Ford's talent was enormous, and few were not awed by his directorial inventiveness and amazing skill at composition and staging (this despite damaged eyes "giving him hell" and working often in the midst of bouts with amoebic dysentery that had him running to squat painfully on makeshift wooden toilets for hours per day). Donald Sinden, who suffered his own battles with Ford ("He blamed me personally for all the problems of Ireland from the time of William of Orange") recalled, "He had an incredible eye. I had to take my hat off to him. I went out scouting locations with him a couple of times. We'd be out in the wilds and he would say, 'Stop the Jeep.' And he'd stand in the middle of nowhere, turn this way and that, hold out his fingers as a frame for the shot, and say, 'Put the camera here.' And it would be perfect. If you had spent three weeks looking you couldn't have found a better shot.

"He could make a wonderful scene from nothing. I remember watching him and Ava do a delightful scene; a total improvisation. We discovered this farm with an elephant compound, no one on the film had known it existed. Ford saw it and said, 'We've got to get this in the picture.' And Ava said to Ford, 'What do you want me to do?' He said, 'Just go in and play with the elephant, give it some food.' It was in a corral. So Ava, who was playing very much of an urban character let loose in the country, shall we say, goes in with the food. No one else in there, they stuck the camera through a hole in the fence. And the elephant began following Ava around. It was really very charming, and Ava was wonderful, improvising with this animal, very natural. Ava didn't know how long the shot was meant to go on, and she finally looked up at Ford as if to ask, 'Is anybody going to say *Cut*?' And at that moment the elephant could take no more and butted her, and she fell into a muddy pool. Immediately people on the crew started to go to help her, and Ford said, 'Get back, get back! Leave her alone! Keep filming!' And he wouldn't allow anyone to go in, and poor Ava was struggling in the mud. But the whole scene was quite brilliant. And it went right into the movie."

While Ava was off all day creating what would be an acclaimed Oscar-nominated performance, Frank Sinatra stayed behind in the camp and suffered. He was not a tent-and-river-water kind of guy, and the inconveniences of the bush on top of his career anxieties and the idleness of being in the middle of nowhere with nothing to do, put him in a tense, unhappy frame of mind, which, in the evening, with the addition of chilled gin, often brought out the same in his wife. "All was not well with them," said Bunny Allen. "And as a result Ava was very testy at this time." The Sinatras battled—and did everything else—with their usual lack of self-consciousness. The open conditions of the safari camp made the dramatic ups and downs of their relationship sometimes uncomfortably apparent to their neighbors.

"Frank and Ava shared a tent three away from mine," Donald Sinden recalled. "And I needn't tell you the tents were not very thick. One night we'd all had dinner together like jolly chaps, and then we all retired to our tents. A little later a great row broke out. Frank and Ava. And you should have heard the language and the screams and shouts. What it was all about I don't know. Cursing and screaming like wild creatures. I had not even gotten into bed yet, and so I put my head out of my tent to see what the devil was going on. And I see Clark Gable and Grace Kelly are also sticking their heads out at the same time! And there were things being thrown from Ava's tent, pots and things, flying out of the tent; they were throwing them at each other! Then, suddenly, silence.

"The argument was over, and the next thing you heard they were in bed and the bed was creaking. And you've never heard a bed creaking so loud!"

Then Frank went away. A call had come for him: an audition with Columbia Pictures. It was the opportunity he had been desperately seeking for months, ever since seeing a news item about Harry Cohn at Columbia making a film of *From Here to Eternity*, James Jones' acclaimed bestseller about the peacetime Army in Hawaii on the eve of World War II. There was a character in the story named Maggio, a frail but feisty, impudent, tragic Italian American sidekick to the book's protagonist, Robert E. Lee Prewitt. Sinatra seized upon the idea of playing Maggio, a part he thought could be a comeback and breakthrough for him in the movies, a perfect part for him—he knew Maggio, he said, he *was* Maggio, it was a part he was born to play. Nearly everyone up to and including Harry Cohn was uninspired by Sinatra's idea, even at the bargain rate Sinatra was offering for his services. Sinatra didn't give up. In the fall he had recruited Ava to pitch for him and finally, through her painter friend Paul Clemens—then living in a bungalow on the Cohn estate—she had been asked to a dinner party the Cohns were throwing.* During the meal Ava made her pitch for giving Frank the role of Maggio, and Harry's wife, Joan, got on her side. Cohn still said he wasn't interested, but in the meantime his preferred choice for the part, Eli Wallach, had become unavailable. In November,

*About her upcoming project, Harry Cohn offered this bit of movie mogul wisdom: "*Mogambo?* That's a lousy title. *Mogambo Starring Clark Gable and Ava Gardner*—that's a fucking *great* title!"

Cohn sent word that he was at least willing to consider Sinatra if he wanted to come back to California and do a screen test, but he would have to pay for his own transportation (Ava would end up fronting him the money for the flights).

Frank took the production plane to Nairobi and headed for Hollywood. "The immediate change in Ava was quite amazing," recalled Bunny Allen. She now became "a sweet, beautiful and most adorable girl."

As it has been told—especially by Bunny Allen himself—Ava and the great white hunter became very friendly after Sinatra's departure. Eva Monley was a production coordinator on the film ("I was a kind of Junior Keep-it-all-together"), a Brit raised in East Africa who spoke Swahili and had known Allen before *Mogambo*. "Bunny was a great friend of mine, absolutely; we had a lot of love. He ran a wonderful camp, he really did. And if you were a female you had to have an affair with him. I was in the queue with everybody else. Ava and Bunny? They had a very little thing together. He was not her type of man, I think. He was always busy with other women, and that was not to her liking. A one-night encounter. Give him two nights. He bragged about it for years. He had a wife at the time in camp as well, so it was all a bit complicated for him." (Another person who was on the location "strongly disagreed" that there could have been anything between Ava and Bunny Allen, explaining as proof, "He was already having an affair with two other people!")

Ava got Bunny to take her on a mini-safari in the bush. She urged him to take her where she could see some wild animals from close-up. At one point, moving through tall grass, Allen realized he had walked them straight into a large herd of elephants. "A complete surround of cow elephants, gently cropping the bushes very close to us." Ava was thrilled. Bunny less so: "I knew what could have happened." Suddenly, so close it seemed right at her feet, Ava heard a loud "sploshing" sound and jumped against Allen in fright. The hunter whispered in her ear, "It's all right. Elephant's just gone to the bathroom." Ava looked up at him and burst out laughing, which sent the herd trampling in the opposite direction.

If Bunny Allen became too preoccupied to keep her company, there were others in the company to take his place.

"Ava couldn't be alone," said Eva Monley. "That was the big thing with her. Something to do with her childhood or something, but she didn't like to be alone. That was, I think, why she had so many affairs. She'd bring someone back to her tent, say, 'Hey, come on, have a drink with me, I'm bored all by myself,' and she'd bring back a prop man or whoever. She liked to have lots of men around her. She just enjoyed them. She got rid of one, and she'd go find another one. She had a great time with Frank and then he was gone, and she found a prop man and he was rather good. I only know because I was in charge of the tents and I'd come by and she'd say, 'Monley, come over here, I've got to tell you something! I was with this man . . .' It was crazy, the whole thing. But she enjoyed herself. She just lived life from day to day."

As had happened during the filming of *Pandora*, there was a curious, Pirandellian crossover between movie and reality. The company seemed to be living out chunks of their script: the leading lady fiddling with a big-game hunter, and Clark Gable and Grace Kelly falling for each other just as their characters did in the movie; there was lust, cuckoldry, angry natives (Mau-Mau bandits slaughtering the whites on a nearby farm one night), and dangerous beasts (two lions invading the camp on several mornings and looting the kitchen, and an attack by three rhinos nearly killing the cameraman). Ava Gardner was free-spirited "Honey Bear" to the life but a lustier version MGM wouldn't dare to put on-screen. Producer Sam Zimbalist, delighted with Ava's performance, at the same time and with nervous apprehension took note of her antic behavior at the camp: The affairs with members of the crew, the drunkenness and fighting, the exhibitionism in front of the boys who prepared her bath; one night, Zimbalist would recount, Ava and Grace Kelly had been strolling among the African extras and Ava said, "Gracie, have you ever seen a black cock?" and then lifted a tribesman's loincloth to show her one. ("Frank's is bigger," she supposedly sighed.)

"Ava," said Eva Monley, "walked the way she wanted to walk and she talked the way she wanted to talk, if you see what I mean. She was very special and had her own energy."

It was at Kagera, in November, that Ava discovered she was pregnant. She determined to end the pregnancy immediately before Frank returned to Africa and tried to stop her. With the help of MGM problem solvers it was arranged for her to fly to England and have an abortion performed at a private clinic in London. Considering the event in the late 1980s, preparing her life story for eventual publication and public scrutiny, in conditions of illness and nostalgia, she would remember the discovery and the decision to abort the baby as deeply reasoned, sadly inevitable: "I felt that unless you were prepared to devote practically all your time to your child in its early years it was unfair to the baby. If a child is unwanted . . . it is handicapped from the time it is born." Some who were there at the time recalled other factors influencing Ava's decision, possibly unwelcome memories deliberately unremembered at the end of her life. Robert Surtees, *Mogambo*'s director of photography in Africa, told Charles Higham in 1974 that his wife had accompanied Ava to London and had been at her side at all times through the operation, the recovery, and then the return to Kagera. After it was all over, Surtees said, Ava told his wife: "I hated Frankie so much. I wanted that baby to go unborn."

The studio put out a press release to explain their star's sudden visit to London and what they called her "tropical infection." The major newspapers and news syndicates printed the story without question. "Ava Gardner Stricken on Set in Africa," headlined the AP article printed in the *Los Angeles Times*: "Doctors pumped powerful shots of antibiotics into Actress Ava Gardner tonight. . . . The Hollywood beauty who made the mistake of drinking the local water in Kenya's native country lay in pain with stomach troubles. But her doctors said it is not serious and promised to have her back on her feet again in a couple of days." Ava, recovering in the Savoy Hotel in London, told a version of the same story to Frank when he called from California. He did not learn the truth until they were reunited at the *Mogambo* location in December.

The screen test for the role of Maggio had gone well. Cohn would not make a decision right away, but Sinatra felt in his bones he had nailed it, and others who had been on the set agreed with him. But with no immediate word from Columbia, the enthusiasm started to fade. There had been other times in the past couple of years he had thought he was turning things around, and something had always gone wrong. Packed to go back to Africa in time for Christmas and Ava's birthday, he made a visit to Ruser's, a jewelry store in Beverly Hills he had frequented in the past, looking to pick up a present for his wife. Billy Ruser, the owner, said he would show him something he thought Ava would love, a gorgeous pair of emerald earrings.

"Yeah, that she would like," Frank said when they were brought out. "How much?"

"Twenty-two thousand," said Ruser.

Sinatra leaned back from the counter and looked away, stricken.

"Frank, give the earrings to Ava," the jeweler said.

"Billy, I can't afford these."

Ruser said, "Don't worry about it. You pay me when you have it."

Whether he had known of the pregnancy earlier or not, it was in December, in the African wilds, that he learned of the abortion. The few who would ever claim to have heard Sinatra speak of the matter would recall him as stricken, devastated. It was a crushing revelation in many ways, the tragedy of a lost child to endure, the blow to his masculine pride and sense of control, and perhaps worst of all to a man still painfully in love, the lingering implication of her action—a terrible signal that all that talk of family and future was no longer a reality to his wife, that part of her might have already left him behind. "He never got over it, he never discussed it," said Hank Sanicola. "The only thing he ever said to me about it was, 'I shoulda beaten her fuckin' brains out for what she did to me and the baby, but I loved her too much.'"

The *Mogambo* company's stay at the Kagera River camp was to conclude just before Christmas. It had been quite an adventure: thrilling, tedious, exhausting. There had been danger: many close calls, the truck in which Ava and Gable were riding attacked by a rhino, and another time an angry mama hippopotamus nearly capsizing the canoe in which the actress was sitting, the strenuous, increased strokes of the Congolese rowers saving the day by mere seconds. And there had been death: a twenty-six-year-old production assistant from England and two Africans killed when their Land Rover went off the side of a mountain road. And romance. "Three or four marriages sprang out of seeds sown during the safari," Bunny Allen would recall. "And affairs—crikey, one runs out of fingers! And some of the affairs were too short to be noticed—all hot and scorching one night and cold as charity in the morning!"

Metro bankrolled a grand-scale Christmas party in the wild. A chartered cargo plane brought in a vast supply of goodies: two hundred fresh turkeys, crates of champagne. A twisted baobob was covered with painted lightbulbs. A dance floor was laid out on the dirt. Frank Sinatra sang. John Ford recited "The Night Before Christmas." A chorus of fifty Congolese sang carols in French. "These handsome oarsmen with minimal clothes and these great voices, holding their oars on their shoulders," Eva Monley recalled. "It was an amazing scene. I remember Ava completely taken aback. The whole place was deadly silent except for the Christmas songs soaring into the night. Then came the cakes and the champagne. People began dancing on the tables. Africa does that to you."

Late in January 1953 the *Mogambo* company departed from Nairobi. After a brief time off they would begin shooting interior sequences at Elstree Studios in England. Frank had returned to the States for a singing engagement at the Boston Latin Quarter. Ava decided she wanted to make a stopover in Rome en route to London and persuaded Grace Kelly and Robert Surtees to come along. When they had first met, Grace had been taken aback by Ava's wild behavior and after witnessing her brawls with Sinatra, she had reported to a friend, "Ava is such a mess it's unbelievable." But her opinion would change considerably during their weeks in the African bush, as Grace came to appreciate Ava's unrestrained style and began to loosen her own very restrained facade, falling into an intense love affair with Clark Gable and becoming more familiar with the allure of alcoholic refreshment (though after a few drinks she usually ended up turning pink and running into the bushes to vomit). By the time they reached Rome together, Grace was an adoring friend and tentative emulator. On their night out Ava demanded they visit some Roman whorehouses, Grace seconded the idea, and Surtees, who had spent a year in the city filming *Quo Vadis*, reckoned he knew enough of such places to play tour guide. They went from brothel to brothel, chatting with the girls, buying drinks for the house. By the end of the tour the demure Grace Kelly had even found a boyfriend at one place and had dragged him into the backseat of the taxi for some heavy necking as they drove back to the Hotel Excelsior and called it a night.

In the 1950s, Hollywood was increasingly finding it advantageous to produce films in other countries, where profits frozen by local tax laws could be accessed, where the costs were generally much cheaper and craft-guild rules could be circumvented, and where new and scenic locations were available to the color camera and—as of '53—wide-screen lens. In addition, a loophole in the American tax code of the period allowed a hefty income exclusion to anyone residing outside the United States for eighteen months, for film people a lucrative advantage to making a movie or two overseas. To that end, and eager to see more of the world anyway, Ava had followed the advice of her financial team at Morgan Maree in Los Angeles and arranged with Metro for back-to-back assignments overseas. Following *Mogambo* Ava would be playing Guinevere in *Knights of the Round Table*, filming in the studio outside London and on locations in the English countryside and in Ireland.

With three weeks off at the conclusion of *Mogambo* and unable to return to America, she happily went on holiday to Spain, seeing her friend and Madrid resident Doreen Grant and her film executive husband, accompanying them and some new acquaintances to the *feria* in Seville. At a party she would meet a young man, a matador—indeed the most famous matador in Spain, Luis Miguel Dominguín. A charming man, she thought, very handsome and very sexy, with a relaxed, cool style (so different from the pompous and vain Mario Cabre, her previous point of reference for bullfighters). They had done some *innocent* flirting. He spoke no English, and after all she was a married lady and he'd had a beautiful girlfriend with him at the time.

Ava came away more enchanted with Spain than ever.

Sinatra had stayed in touch with phone calls and letters. While working in Boston he received the news he had been praying for: Harry Cohn had decided to give him the role of Maggio in *From Here to Eternity*, adding him to a cast that would include Montgomery Clift, Burt Lancaster, Deborah Kerr, Donna Reed, and Ernest Borgnine. Ava told him how happy she was, that this would do much to turn his bad luck around, just as he was saying. Then to herself she wondered how he could pin so much hope on one lousy part. Good pictures were a fluke, not a sure thing. Perhaps the loudmouth Harry Cohn would screw it all up. Just because people liked a book, there was no guarantee they were going to like the movie. Hadn't she done a picture based on some goddamned classic by Dostoyevsky? You couldn't drag anybody to see that dog.

Knights of the Round Table costarred Robert Taylor as Lancelot and Mel Ferrer as King Arthur. Producer Pandro Berman and director Richard Thorpe had reteamed after their surprisingly successful adaptation of another tale of knighthood in flower, *Ivanhoe*. Thorpe was an old Metro veteran, with some good pictures in his past (notably the MGM *Tarzans* with Johnny Weissmuller), but he was mainly prized by people like Pan Berman for his ability to get usable film in the can faster than anybody. Ava, whose part was something of an afterthought amid all the clanking armor and swordplay, quickly realized that the film would not be so good ("It stinks," she told one English reporter without hesitation when asked for a review of the work-in-progress) and resigned herself to clocking in and out and collecting her paycheck. There was so much location work for which she was not needed that the studio agreed to give her some time off early in the production so she could join Frank in May for his first extensive concert tour of Europe.

There had been exciting developments in Frank Sinatra's career since he and Ava had parted company in the winter. *From Here to Eternity* was in the can and he was very pleased with his performance. He had found new representation at the William Morris Agency, and his agents had at last obtained for him a recording contract (though one with a minimal union-scale advance) with Capitol Records in Hollywood. In April, when he went into the studio to record, he was paired for the first time with arranger-conductor Nelson Riddle, whose complex, heartbeat-pulsed, irresistible arrangements would immeasurably help Sinatra find what became his new style and new sound—swaggering, sexy, brassy, ultra-rhythmic.

The results of these developments were still uncertain at the time Frank returned to Europe in the spring, his professional future in abeyance, but hope seemed now definitely on the horizon. It became a happy reunion in London, Ava delighted to see her "old man" recharged and affectionate, the funk and anger of the winter in Africa—memories of her terminated pregnancy—apparently faded away. Frank's absences tended to make

Ava's heart less fond—it was just her nature—but when she saw him now in the flesh, at the airport, she immediately melted. The tour was going to be a "second honeymoon," work combined with much pleasure. They expected good things from Frank's Continental dates. The audiences had been so enthusiastic at his debut in London two years ago that he and Ava could only ponder with excitement how *paisan* Sinatra would be received in Naples and Milan.

Not well, as it happened. In Naples the audience showed more interest in seeing Ava in her seat than listening to the singer on the stage. A spotlight found her, the crowd chanted her name, drowning out the music. There was a near-riot. Ava was rushed out of the theater, Frank put down his microphone and walked off until order was restored. In other cities in Italy, Sweden, and Denmark, newspapers heralded his arrival with stories of a failing career. Everywhere he performed to half-empty theaters. There would be fights with photographers, blowups with airline personnel, editorials headlined: SINATRA GO HOME. They returned to England under a cloud. The second honeymoon was over.

The plan had been for Sinatra to stay with Ava at her Regent's Park flat in London until she had completed her work on *Knights of the Round Table*. But Frank found the return to his secondary role intolerable. The European tour had, anyway, left him bruised, embarrassed. He wanted done with the whole continent. He complained of the plumbing, the rain, the food. They fought—at home, in nightclubs, in taxis. Finally, a month early, he said he was leaving; he had some shows to rehearse and Columbia would be wanting him to publicize *From Here to Eternity*, which was set to have its premiere in mid-August.

"Where's Frankie?" people asked her.

"Oh, he didn't like the bathrooms," she would say. "Me, I don't mind European plumbing so much."

For the next month in London she lived quietly. No scandals, no brawls. She started going to bed early. She even gave up alcohol for a while. "I'm on a health kick. Grapefruit juice is all." When she went out it was to plays and to concerts. Many nights she stayed home and cooked for herself, sometimes for a few friends, giving a number of English people their first taste of authentic Southern fried chicken, her mother's recipe.

She roamed the city alone, not bothered, unphotographed—was it really as easy as that? When you stopped running away from them they stopped chasing you? With Frank it always seemed a life-and-death struggle. Compared to moving around in public with her husband, she felt blissfully invisible. She went to prim little shops and to flea markets and ate sandwiches in the park. One day she strolled over to Rillington Street to see the house where they had recently discovered the serial killer John Christie's victims; she stood gawking through the iron fence with a chatty East Ender who explained where each body had been found and in what state of decomposition, then blithely asked for an autograph.

In August Frank's movie opened, and it was a sensation. He called her, "I'm back, baby. I'm back!" His records were starting to sell again, the critics returned to his corner, praising the new bright sound and the voice, different now, older but freer, sharp as a razor on the rhythm numbers, with a wounded soulfulness on the ballads. ("It's like a cello," said Nelson Riddle of Frank's new vocal instrument. "Ava taught him the hard way.") He wanted her to come home, he told her on the phone, in letters and cables, to share it with him; he needed her, when the hell was she coming back? Did she still love him or didn't she? He would call every day, pleading one time, angry and slamming the phone down the next.

So she went. It meant losing her tax break. Clark Gable told her, "It's going to cost you a hundred fifty thousand bucks the moment you put your foot down in New York."

There would be other conversations with Frank in the days before she departed London. At times he was insufferably full of himself about his regained success. She could grant him his pleasure in this "comeback," he had pined for it for so long. But much of it took the form of harsh teasing and taunts, how the women were throwing themselves at him, how he was thinking that instead of making *St. Louis Woman* with Ava he might instead make a musical with the "new" big thing in Hollywood, the sexy Marilyn Monroe.

Ava made a last-minute decision to return to America by way of Spain, fitting in another visit to Madrid, taking a few days to see some of her new friends and acquaintances in that city of which she had grown so fond. And once again she ran into the charming and handsome Luis Miguel

Dominguín. He had even picked up a few lines of English since their last meeting.

She arrived at Idlewild Airport on September 7. Frank was not there to meet her. After the long flight she was tired, hungover, now furious. A reporter caught up with her. Would she be seeing her husband later? "Not today. I have no definite plans. I don't want to discuss it."

When he did catch up with her—he was commuting between the Waldorf and the 500 Club in Atlantic City—she refused to talk to him. He hadn't known she was coming, he said, pleading his case via Hedda Hopper. "I don't understand it. We'd had no trouble. I can't make a statement because I don't know what she is planning. It's a crying shame, because everything was going so well with us."

She holed up at the Hampshire House and nursed her grudge. Frank phoned, left frantic messages, then abusive ones. She had them not put through any more of his calls. They had been playing these games for nearly four years. They were reflexive by now, almost empty of reason or goal. Dolly Sinatra came over from New Jersey. "Frankie is so upset," she told Ava. "It's drivin' him nuts you two not speakin'." Frank was drinking too much, the mother-in-law told her, he was back on the sleeping pills. "You know you two kids love each other so quit all this fuckin' shit for God's sake!" Dolly played matchmaker, brought them to her new place in Weehawken for a big dinner, Frank coming up the road from Bill Miller's club between shows, not knowing who would be there. Frank speechless. "Hello, Francis." And so they kissed and made up. She had to come along back with him for his last show, and he sang to Ava as if there were no one else in the room. "Everything was forgotten," she would say, "except pride and love for my old man."

"The Voice unleashed a torrent of sound at the sultry Ava," said the reviewer in the *New York Journal-American*. "Emotion poured from him like molten lava."

"Honey, Frankie and I are both high-strung people," she told columnist Sidney Skolsky. "We explode fast, maybe faster than most married couples. But it's great fun making up."

The explosions continued. One night he had promised to be back to the hotel by 2:00 A.M. and then wandered in at dawn. Another night at the club in Jersey she went missing, her reserved table empty, destroying his concentration, ruining the show. It was the same old thing, of course, but somehow not the same—worse, because attrition was at work, the wounds no longer healing properly between battles. There was love, still, but it had become all tangled up with resentment and exasperation and boredom. Ava complained to some of her friends that Frank's rising fortunes, his career turning around now after *From Here to Eternity*, made him more arrogant than ever. (And Sinatra might have agreed—his time had come again, why not rub it in people's faces, take some payback; why did she have to break his balls like it was six months ago, like he was still a loser?) Making up was not as much fun as it had once been. She complained to some others that Frank no longer satisfied her in bed. She could not have an orgasm with him anymore, she confided to close friends. She even voiced this intimate complaint to her ex-husband. "When we were, you know, doing it," she asked Artie Shaw, "was it good?" Shaw said, "If everything else had been anywhere near as good, we'd have been together forever and I'd never have let you out of my sight."

At the age of eighty-nine, recalling the encounter in an interview with Kristine McKenna and perhaps finding some payback of his own, Shaw said, "She gave a sigh of relief. I asked why. She said, 'With him it's impossible.' I said I thought he was a big stud. She said, 'No, it's like being in bed with a woman.'"

On October 2 they went to the premiere of *Mogambo* at Radio City Music Hall. The reviews for the film were filled with praise for Ava's warm, funny, lovable portrayal of "Honey Bear Kelly," a performance that would gain her an Oscar nomination for best actress of the year. A reporter got her to the phone the morning after the picture's opening and read her a sampling of the critical reaction. "Don't believe a word of it," she told him. "I don't."

From New York she and Frank returned together to California, drove out to Palm Springs. They were going to lie low until Frank's opening at the Sands in Las Vegas. Then the evening he was to fly to Nevada to begin rehearsals they drove to LA for a quiet dinner before she took him to the airport. Everything had been fine, but some friend of Frank's had seen them and come over, and Frank and the friend had yakked it up for an hour. It was her last hour with him, and now there was no time left but to rush to the airport. Ava blew up. Frank shouted back; he stood up, he walked out of the restaurant without another word, and he took a taxi to the airport.

The plan had been for her to follow him out to Las Vegas for his opening night. Frank didn't call, and she didn't go. "Why would she do a thing like that to me?" Sinatra whined to Louella Parsons. "I've been at her beck and call. No matter where she's been, I've flown to her regardless of the fact that I also had some important engagements. . . . She doesn't understand that I've got a career to worry about, too.

"No, Ava's wrong this time. I've been wrong other times, but this time it's all her fault. She'll have to call me. . . .

"She doesn't love me anymore or she wouldn't do this. . . . I can't eat, I can't sleep, I love her."

Out in Las Vegas it became like a nightly birthday party for Frank Sinatra, a king restored to his throne, the treasure houses of the pleasure palace flung open to him once more. He was damned if he was going to let his wife ruin this triumphal occasion or feel guilty for enjoying the spoils of victory. Some say Ava heard word of Frank fiddling with some of the Copa Room's statuesque showgirls, that she had gotten a call through to him in his room at the hotel one night and she had heard a woman whispering to him in the background. Or was it as Ava would remember it in later days, Frank calling her from Vegas himself, showing off, telling her, yes, right now he was in bed with another woman, telling her that if he was going to be constantly accused of infidelity when he was innocent then he might as well enjoy the benefits of being guilty. And then as she remembered it, she had put down the telephone and she knew that something had happened then, a crossroads, a point of no return reached, and that the marriage was over.

Sydney Guilaroff, MGM's chief hair stylist, a friend and something of a fairy godfather to Ava since her earliest days at the studio, remembered her showing up at his house, unannounced, late in the night, lurching out of her car, and standing in the driveway in tears. He ran out and found her anguished and frantic and crying, "almost to the point of a nervous breakdown." She refused to come inside with him, and Guilaroff stood with her near her car and held her as she sobbed.

Guilaroff said, "Come in, for god's sake, let's sit and talk."

She refused. After some time she urged him to go inside and leave her alone.

Reluctantly he went back into the house, but he couldn't go to bed with Ava out there, so upset, and he sat in his front room in the dark and looked out at her through the window. "For hours I watched her pace up and down in my garden, bathed in moonlight, lost in grief. Eventually she just trudged off into the night."

Ava escaped to Palm Springs—not to Frank's place, but renting a house for herself on the road to the airport—and remained there, sober, she said, suffering, pondering her decision.

"Everything will be straightened out," Sinatra told Hedda Hopper. "It's just a misunderstanding."

That was all it was. She was going to forgive him. He would get her something nice, tell her how crazy he was for her. And they would be off to the races again.

On October 29 Howard Strickling at MGM issued a press release: "Ava Gardner and Frank Sinatra stated today that having reluctantly exhausted every effort to reconcile their differences, they could find no mutual basis on which to continue their marriage. Both expressed deep regret and great respect for each other. Their separation is final and Miss Gardner will seek a divorce."

Ava went to see Ben Thau at Culver City and told him, "Get me out of the country!" She wanted to get away from Frank, from Hollywood, the stalking local press, all of it. She had an idea about a publicity tour: Send her around the world to publicize *Mogambo*. Thau got back to her with another idea. There was a project Joseph Mankiewicz was producing in Rome in the next month, *The Barefoot Contessa*, it was called. Mankiewicz, it seemed, had been after them for Ava for a while but the studio had not been interested. Mankiewicz had yelled at Nick Schenck in the New York office, called him an idiot for the way he had screwed with the aspect ratio of *Julius Caesar*, the studio's last association with the writer-director. Ava pleaded with them to get to Mankiewicz and get her that part. Thau wondered whether somebody had already signed for it—they knew Jennifer Jones had been interested and Yvonne De Carlo, and some Italian actress he'd never heard of. And even if it was still available, it was certain that Nick Schenck would veto it or ask an impossible amount of money from Mankiewicz as an act of revenge. Well, the best he could do was to go ahead and make some inquiries, and in the meanwhile, Ben Thau said, he could get her a copy of the script and see what she thought. Ava said she thought the picture was shooting in Rome, and the character was barefoot, and go make the deal.

In the end she made a direct plea in the form of a telegram to old man Schenck himself:

I AM DESPERATELY ANXIOUS TO DO THIS PICTURE . . . YOU MUST KNOW MY TERRI-BLE DISAPPOINTMENT AT NOT BEING ABLE TO ACCUMULATE SOME MONEY AND SE-CURITY WHICH I HAD CONTEMPLATED WHEN I MADE MY NEW CONTRACT WITH METRO [this in reference to the huge loss she had sustained when returning to America too soon to appreciate a tax benefit] AND I THINK THE LEAST THAT THE COMPANY CAN DO IS TO GIVE ME SOME MEASURE OF HAPPINESS IN DOING THE KIND OF PART I WANT TO DO AT THIS TIME AS I COULD LEAVE FOR EUROPE IMME-DIATELY.

Metro made the deal. She would fly to Italy in the last week of November. Almost at once she began to think of the trip as not another four- or six-month sojourn to make a movie, but as the first leg of a permanent escape. Even after twelve years of living in Los Angeles she felt few if any ties to the place, had less than a handful of close friends, and no roots that could not be settled with a phone call to a realtor. . . . About Hollywood she had almost entirely negative feelings. Yes, she wanted to put the entire shallow, prying, perverse place behind her. Europe appeared to her as adventure, a fresh start, a future without the baggage of the past. She dreamed particularly of Spain, with all its from-the-blood passion and authenticity looming before her as the antithesis of Hollywood phoniness.

Her dream Spain overlooked the fears and treachery of a land under the yoke of the Franco fascists, but it was very real in her imagination.

As the days passed after Ava's publicist at MGM announced the end of their marriage, Frank Sinatra had gradually and painfully begun to understand that this was not after all like the feuds and separations of the past. The confidence that had fueled his taunting assault from Las Vegas went away. He took stock, humbled himself, called with protestations, apologies. Ava made herself unavailable, or talked to him briefly, bluntly. She had been angry, stubborn, cruel even, many times in the past, but now, he found, there was a cold intractability that had never been there before. A fear of actually losing her began to invade him like a terrible spreading fever.

"Frank was torching for Ava . . . heavy . . . heavy," remembered Milton Ebbins, Peter Lawford's manager and an adjunct member of the Rat Pack–to be. "And Ava, she wasn't pining for anybody. She was putting him behind her, and that was that. She was out and laughing.

"Peter Lawford and I were having lunch at Frascati's in Beverly Hills. Ava was finishing up some business with her financial adviser, and her sister was with her as well. Peter knew her quite well for many years and went to say hello. Ava said, 'Peter, when you're done why don't you come join us for a drink at the Luau?' That was a Chinese restaurant up the street on Rodeo. And Peter was not going to go—because of Sinatra. But I was a big fan of Ava's as was everybody else, and I wanted to go and meet her. It was my idea to go to the Luau; Peter went because I asked him to. So we went, and I met Ava and her sister. And Ava was terrific. A wonderful gal. Extremely attractive, funny, very amusing. She was drinking, but she wasn't drunk. Ava and Peter had known each other for a long time, and it seemed that they might have gone out. Peter never went into detail about their past, but he had been with Lana Turner, and this one and that, he had made the rounds. And some didn't like him: He had had a thing with this one star and afterward she hated his guts and wouldn't even say hello to him.

"Anyway, that was it. I thought it would be nice to have a drink with Ava Gardner. We were only there a few minutes. But it was in Hedda Hopper's column the next day, something about Peter and Ava having a drink together. And then I got a call from Peter. Peter was hysterical. Frank had called him. He said, 'Frank said I'm a dead man! He said he was sending somebody to break my legs for being with Ava! What am I going to do?' So I had to try and find Sinatra before this got out of hand. And I tracked him down to New York, he was staying at Jimmy van Heusen's place. Van Heusen was a very kind, loyal friend. But van Heusen was like, 'Yeah, he's here! Jesus Christ, and he's driving me crazy!' All about Ava. And eventually they got Frank onto the phone. And he started threatening me. He was furious, furious with Peter. His legs were going to be broken for seeing Ava. I said, 'Frank, Frank, listen to me, it wasn't Peter. *I* wanted to see Ava!' He said, 'What?!' I said, 'Listen, it was my idea to go to the Luau, I just wanted to meet Ava is all.' I told him the whole story just as I've told it now. And it took some time to calm him down. I think he believed me. Well, he never said anything more. He never says that he's sorry. And when he got a hate on, forget it. He didn't talk to Peter for years."

He was a stricken, desperate man, sleepless, inconsolable. In van Heusen's Fifty-seventh Street apartment he would sit up all night drinking, marathon sessions with a commanded audience of friends and flunkies to hear his tale of woe, until each had made his escape or passed out from exhaustion. He couldn't rid himself of her for a minute. She went round and round in his head till he thought it would explode. The siren in that Billy Strayhorn thing she loved so much. Now it was his fucking theme song. You came along . . . to tempt me to madness. He would sit, staring at her photograph, then in an angry outburst tear it to shreds, then crawl around on the floor putting the pieces together . . . so the legend says, he had reconstructed one prized now-shredded picture except for a single missing piece, and when a passing delivery boy discovered it, Sinatra gratefully took the gold watch from his wrist and gave it to him.

Los Angeles Daily News, Nov. 23, 1953
AVA GARDNER ITALY BOUND SANS FRANKIE
Smokey-eyed actress Ava Gardner was packing for Rome, and one of the things she did not slip into her suitcase was down-to-118 pound Frank Sinatra.

On the night of November 18, he had found himself alone in the apartment in New York City, van Heusen out, the flunkies all dispersed. Lonely, full of booze and pills and despair, strolling about the halls in his pajamas, he had wandered into the kitchen and taken a knife and he had run the blade across each of his thin wrists. Van Heusen came home and found him dazed and his arms and white pajamas wet and red.

"Jimmy," he said, "I can't stop the bleeding."

PART THREE

EIGHT

Spanish for Cinderella

She arrived from New York at Rome's Ciampino Airport, met by a pulsing mob of international photographers and reporters, and when at last she emerged into sight through the gangway—after every other passenger had disembarked before her and the mob had grown crazed with anticipation—the whoosh and flare of a hundred flash cameras going off was like a sudden burst of thunder and lightning. David Hanna, newly appointed head of publicity for Joseph Mankiewicz's production company, Figaro, Inc., whose fortunes were to be tied to Ava Gardner for the next six years, would remember that first glimpse of the actress as she stepped onto the metal stairway after a very long flight from New York and confronted the Roman clamor: serene, self-possessed, "a devastating picture of simplicity, directness and charm." With the help of some burly private security guards, Hanna and Mankiewicz ushered her through customs, outside to a waiting Cadillac, and on to a suite at the Grand Hotel.

At the hotel she had a brief chat with Mankiewicz, the worldly Hollywood veteran who had written and directed the Oscar-winning hits *A Letter to Three Wives* and *All About Eve*. Stretched out on a divan in her flower-filled suite, barefoot, sipping champagne, Ava blandly told Mankiewicz she had not yet read his script. She had wanted to go to Rome, she said, and his title had "spoken" to her. She raised her legs in the air and wiggled her naked toes, telling the writer-director she'd be willing to do the whole picture without shoes. Mankiewicz chuckled, said there were a few scenes where footwear would be required. Dinner that night at Alfredo's with Dave Hanna and United Artists exec Arthur Krim (UA co-producing with two Italian financiers), Alfredo himself coming out to prepare his famous fettucine for the Hollywood star, Hanna watching in awe as she tucked into the big bowl of pasta and much more to come. "I never diet," she told him. "And I never exercise, unless I'm running to get to my next meal."

The next morning she began looking at apartments, settling on a dark, rambling first-floor flat in an ancient house on the noisy Corso d'Italia. For several days she lost herself in the unlikely pleasures of house-cleaning, commanding a battery of young female assistants, scrubbing and redecorating and removing cobwebs half as old as Rome. Then each morning she went for fittings with *Contessa*'s appointed dressmakers, the Sorelle Fontana on the Via Veneto. The House of Fontana made startlingly beautiful and sexy clothes, particularly formal wear that utilized luscious fabrics and intricate work ("they had embroiderers and beaders," according to *Vogue*, "whose skills rivaled those of medieval nuns"). The connection with the brilliant couturiers—sisters Giovanna, Micol, and Zoe—would result not only in the gorgeous costumes Ava would wear in the film but in a momentous cultural collaboration. The Fontanas and their sumptuous, artful, and sensuous designs would become the beacons of a new era in haute couture, crucial in the taking of the fashion spotlight from France to Italy in the 1950s, and Ava Gardner would be their avatar—as customer, booster, and good friend of the sisters—their most glamorous representative.

In the afternoons she posed for sculptor Assen Peikov, an affable, mustachioed Bulgarian creating the film's marble statue of the countess, larger than life and more goddesslike than her Venus. She posed in a slip in Peikov's drafty studio (conditions at the film studio and her new apartment were likewise cold and damp that Roman winter, and she would end up with competing flus in time for the holidays). "She is," the sculptor announced, "a little square in the shoulders." Following its impressive appearance in *The Barefoot Contessa*, the statue would be purchased by Frank Sinatra and end up for many years in the backyard of his California home.

At last she read Mankiewicz's script. It was a sophisticated work, set amid the worlds of filmmaking, café society, and the European upper crust. It told the story of Maria Vargas, a beautiful young Spanish dancer, her rise from a Madrid nightclub to global movie stardom, and a perverse, unstable marriage to a wealthy Italian nobleman, and finally her tragic fall. As with Mankiewicz's screenplay for *All About Eve*, *The Barefoot Contessa* advanced in flashback with a framing device and a series of narrative perspectives, though unlike *Eve*, with its cynical but lively comedy, this was a glum and tragic story that began where it ended with the title character's funeral (Eve would suffer a professional stabbing in the back, the contessa would be shot to death). Though it contained Mankiewicz's signature witty dialogue and cultural insights, the script was a tad bombastic, laden with symbology—for instance, bare feet representing authenticity and, somehow or other, a healthy sexual appetite; impotence, a decadent society. It was in large part a "scenario à clef," full of disguised versions of real-life figures, a rich Latin American playboy à la the notorious Baby Pignatari, a Texas tycoon who makes movies and collects beautiful women in the manner of Howard Hughes, the Texan's shifty fixer who might have been Hughes's own right hand, Johnny Meyer, and a wise, witty, rueful movie director and writer who was clearly Mankiewicz's alter ego and mouthpiece. The character of Maria Vargas, the doomed star out of the slums, was suspected of being based on a number of Hollywood actresses whose lives followed a similar trajectory. They included Linda Darnell (the married Mank's sometime girlfriend, who claimed he wrote it with her in mind, and with her in bed with him while he wrote it), the obscure Anne Chevalier, star of F. W. Murnau's *Tabu*, and Mankiewicz's own stated inspiration, Margarita Cansino, better known as Rita Hayworth, a Hispanic former nightclub dancer turned love goddess whose troubled life included a marriage to the playboy Prince Aly Khan. Whoever else he may have been thinking about as he wrote the role of Maria, Ava Gardner was Mankiewicz's first and only stated choice for the film and he paid plenty to get her (the cost was two hundred thousand dollars, a rare sum at the time—Nick Schenck's revenge—less than half going to the actress). It did appear to be inspired casting: In addition to bringing to the part her looks and mythic star status appropriate to playing a beautiful mythic movie star, there were numerous parallels between Ava Gardner and the invented contessa—her humble beginnings, her independence, her tempestuous affairs, her long-running friendship with Howard Hughes, not to mention the shared fondness for bare feet. Maria Vargas's life is linked to the Cinderella story; once upon a time Ava Gardner had been referred to in the columns as "the Cinderella of Hollywood." "Hell, Joe," she told Mankiewicz, "I'm not an actress, but I think I understand this girl. She's a lot like me."

Mankiewicz's preference for Gardner might also have been influenced by the actress's performance as a similarly willful and doomed beauty in *Pandora and the Flying Dutchman* three years before. There were other reflections of Al Lewin's film: Besides Ava, Marius Goring would appear in both films, and the director had tried hard to land James Mason for the part of the Italian count, but the actor, in search of greater status in Hollywood, felt that the role of an impotent murderer would not help his quest (Rossano Brazzi was cast instead). Also common to both films was cinematographer Jack Cardiff, providing *Contessa* with extraordinarily rich, darkly glowing Technicolor images as he had done for *Pandora*.

With a good deal of her prep work finished, Ava was taking time off for Christmas, with plans to spend the holiday week (and her birthday) in Spain. She was finalizing the arrangements for her stay in Madrid when she received a call from Frank.

Back in November, on a very lonely and confused night in New York City, he had been rushed to Mt. Sinai Hospital with his wrists slashed. For public consumption it was announced that Mr. Sinatra was being treated for nervous exhaustion (and that he had simultaneously suffered a domestic accident with a broken glass). After three days the singer checked himself out of the hospital and took a plane to Los Angeles. He drove up to the house above Nichols Canyon. He had come to plead with her, to ask her to give their marriage another try. Ava had feared it turning into a terrible scene of some sort, pitiful or violent. But there had been no fight and little emotion left in him that afternoon—she suspected he was on a great deal of medication—and so it became only a rather quiet and empty reunion with much left unsaid. He had wished her bon voyage and offered his hope that they could be together at Christmastime.

Now he was coming to see her.

"I won't be in Rome. I'm going to Madrid."

"Then Madrid. Baby, I'll go to the North Pole. I want us to be together."

Ava had other plans in mind for this trip, and they did not include Frank. But she didn't have the heart to tell him not to come. The love she had felt for him in the past was still there within her, covered over now like a bandaged wound, not yet healed underneath and perhaps still easily reopened. She decided she would simply have to go on, let things happen as they might, though she didn't expect it would be pretty.

She left Rome on her thirty-first birthday. In Madrid she was met by her American friends Frank and Doreen Grant and brought to stay at their villa. Through the Grants she came to know others among Madrid's elite expatriate circle, including most significantly the Sicres—Ricardo and Betty—who were to become her close, beloved pals and advisers in Spain. It was at a party in the Sicre house in Madrid that Ava had been introduced to Luis Miguel Dominguín.

Hemingway had once described Dominguín as a mixture of Hamlet and Don Juan. He was, after Generalissimo Franco, the most famous citizen of Spain, and, unlike the general, almost universally admired. Born Luis Miguel Gonzalez Lucas to a bullfighting dynasty (Dominguín was his father's "ring name," which he assumed as his own), he was a prodigy of the *corrida*, at twelve having killed his first bull, by seventeen risen to the elite rank of matador whose carefully nurtured opponents were the most powerful and deadliest fighting beasts on earth. With the death of Manolete in 1947—a tragedy to which he had been an eyewitness—his standing began a rapid rise until in the early 1950s he was widely considered Manolete's successor as the greatest of all living matadors, and some said better than that—the greatest of the century, living or dead. In the ring, wrote Hemingway, "He was proud without being arrogant, tranquil, at ease at all times, and in full control of everything that went on. It was a pleasure to see him direct the fight and to watch his intelligence at work. He had the complete and respectful concentration on his work which marks all great artists."

His technique dazzled everyone, from the jaded and nitpicking aficionados who placed him among the immortals of an ancient tradition to the women of all ages for whom the gleamingly handsome young man was an idol and sex symbol of movie star proportions. He was that rare thing, a star who seemed fully worthy of stardom—graceful, fearless, funny, well-mannered, and smart. His elegance, style, and good looks, in fact, shone above and beyond his celebrity status. Ava Gardner had never heard of him when they first met, but she *had* been entranced. But of course, when she did learn that the rakishly good-looking Spaniard was also the greatest of all *toreros* and the hero of his nation it did not make him any less attractive.

Dominguín's appreciation of the opposite sex and his many romances were well known. At the time of his introduction to Ava Gardner he was in the company of his latest love, a spectacular-looking young woman of Portuguese-Thai descent named Noelle. Ava had bumped into them in the lobby of the Hotel Alfonso XIII during the *feria* in Seville. Luis Miguel had grinned, kissed her hand and introduced her to his young girlfriend (Dominguín was four years Ava's junior; the girl appeared perhaps five years younger than that).

"What a charming creature," said Ava. (The Spanish press would detail this delicate encounter.)

They went out together that evening—Luis Miguel and Noelle and Ava—and as the evening proceeded Dominguín's girlfriend began to suspect that this woman from Hollywood—a married woman no less—was after her man. "I noticed the way she lifted her glass to him, danced with him and let her fingers glide over his back," she would recall. "Later in the car, she pretended that there wasn't enough room and sat down smack on Miguelo's lap. I then knew that this cat was bent on destroying my happiness."

Indeed. The Eurasian beauty was gone from Dominguín's life by December, and by Christmas week Ava Gardner was a part of it. He was now officially, if rather mysteriously, retired. A bull's horn had only lately gone through a muscle in his leg. One week after the goring he was back, but the wounded limb could not hold him upright, and he had been forced to withdraw from the fight. Doctors advised that there was a good possibility of his suddenly toppling over in the ring if the muscle did not mend properly. In the prideful world of the *matadores de toros* it was easier to retire on a whim—to arrogantly claim you were bored with the poor selection of bulls that year or had other interests—than due to injury or doctor's orders, and so Dominguín let it be known that he had abandoned the bullring just because he felt like it to chase the young ladies and to spend his money. He divided his time now among his ranch, his business concerns, and his social affairs. Ava met with him almost instantly upon her return to Madrid and found him as good-looking, charming, and humorous as she remembered, perhaps even more so now without the threat of death hanging over him each Sunday. They still had no language in common, a few scattered phrases and hand gestures, but Ava made it easy for him to understand what she wanted. Her physical desire for the man was intense—she had been thinking about him, truth to tell, from the moment they met, and that was reason enough not to delay the romance any longer (she had been without a sexual partner for months). She was also not a little distressed over Frank's pursuit, could not trust her resolve in the face of his determination, and so felt a pressing need to affirm a new romantic alliance right then, before anyone could do anything to stop it. All but running to get there, she went with Luis Miguel to the Hotel Wellington near the Retiro Park, and in the room Dominguín rented they made love, just hours before Sinatra's arrival in town.

It was, as she had expected, an unpleasant reunion with Frank. For all the love he declared that he felt for her, it was now mostly disguised by a seething anger and righteous indignation that seemed at times ready to boil over into violence. "Love" could only very loosely be the proper word to describe the traumatizing obsession he felt for her. She was like a drug that no longer provided pleasure in its use but that his body, addicted, went on craving for survival.

She did little to disguise the fact that she was seeing another man, but stopped short of an outright admission. Who knew what he might try to do in his state of mind if she pushed him too far? They argued, seethed. At last an inadvertent truce was called when both of them were felled by viruses.

On the twenty-ninth Ava returned to Rome, with Frank glumly clinging to her arm, like a cop transporting a prisoner. In the customs hall he lunged at a photographer. Ava groaned and raised her arm to block him.

"Please, Frank, stop it!"

It had been planned that they would host a New Year's party at Ava's apartment, a publicity event, really, since they knew almost none of the guests. They spent the three days after that holed up in the apartment, foiling the band of photographers who clustered outside the front door at all times. Inside the house were harsh words, pleas, reminiscences, silence. When Ava next emerged from the house Sinatra was already gone, sneaked out a back entrance and off to America, due in Hollywood to begin work on a movie with Marilyn Monroe (it would be canceled). Until the moment Frank departed he—and he alone—had remained adamant: The two of them were not over.

At once she sent a message to Luis Miguel inviting him to Rome. Within days they were living together on the Corso d'Italia.

The rest of *The Barefoot Contessa* cast—including Humphrey Bogart, Edmond O'Brien, Warren Stevens, Mari Aldon, Rossano Brazzi, and Valentina Cortese—assembled in the first week of January, with filming scheduled to begin on the eleventh. Bogart, to play world-weary writer-director Harry Dawes, arrived on January 4 in the company of his wig maker/mistress Verita Thompson and was installed at the Excelsior Hotel, his lodging of choice largely on account of its renowned bartender and easy access to the ham and eggs and other American fare at George's restaurant across the street. One of the preeminent stars of the last ten years and more, recent winner of the Oscar for his endearing comic turn in *The African Queen*, Bogart was contracted to receive top billing in *Contessa*'s credits but he was getting only half the salary being paid to Ava Gardner—and about one-tenth the publicity. He was one of the few Hollywood legends Ava had never met and she looked forward to working with him in his role as the contessa's trusted adviser and friend. Alas, from the start Ava and Bogie proved to be incompatible personalities. Bogart was a needler, enjoyed finding and poking a person's raw nerve ("I like a little agitation now and then," he told Dave Hanna, "keeps things lively"), and he was a fan and friend of Sinatra's besides. On the morning of the first day of shooting, Bogie came by his costar's dressing room to say hello. Stuffed into the tiny room were Ava, a makeup man, Ava's Italian secretary/translator (supposedly a princess of the long-deposed royal family), Luis Miguel, and Bappie (who had recently arrived from California with an emergency replenishment of Ava's Larder: Hershey chocolate bars, chewing gum, marshmallows, popcorn, and Jack Daniel's whiskey). Bogart remarked that it looked like the circus was in town, and when introduced to Dominguín, he made a crack regarding men who wore "capes and little ballerina slippers." Ava laughed it off, but it was to be the beginning of a rocky relationship. Their rapport did not improve on the set.

Ava's "stage fright" was still in place, and she found her confidence shriveling when confronted with Bogart's chronic irritability and what she perceived as his deliberate disruptions of her concentration with his complaints. Shooting one of their first scenes together, Bogie turned away from her during a take and shouted, "Hey, Mankiewicz, can you tell this dame to speak up? I can't hear a goddamn word she says!" To others he grumbled, "She's giving me nothing to work with." When not complaining, the sad fact was that Bogart ruined countless otherwise good takes with his racking coughs—warning heralds of the cancer that would kill him three years later ("Many takes," Edmond O'Brien told Mankiewicz's biographer Kenneth Geist, "were printed simply for the lines Mankiewicz could get between the coughs").

Ultimately more damaging to Ava's confidence was an inability to make any creative connection with her director. As she saw it, not only did Mankiewicz fail to defend her from Bogart's antagonism, but he gave her insufficient help in shaping her performance. Her technique as it had haphazardly evolved through the years was an instinctive naturalism, making her character believable by going through the action of the scene and reacting to the other actors with the conviction that it was real life. But Mankiewicz's scenes seemed to thwart this approach—it struck Ava that much of his Maria was all poses and speechifying. Too often there was nothing to act, only talk and more talk. She needed more support to bring Maria Vargas to life, and the director would only realize it too late. To Kenneth Geist he considered with regret this failing: "It was almost unforgivably stupid of me not to recognize how really nervous and sensitive she was. She was aware that this was a tremendously difficult part and she was terribly insecure about her ability to do it. I think I failed her, in one respect, because I didn't give her enough security." A passing, meaningless wisecrack by Mankiewicz when he happened to catch her perched on a sofa on the set, apparently daydreaming ("You're the sittingest actress I ever saw") served as a last straw, and Ava petulantly withdrew her trust in him for the duration. The gulf that existed between them was a blow to Mankiewicz's confidence as well, for he saw himself as particularly adept at directing women, at understanding their nature, their psychological needs as artists (and apparently their physical needs too: Bristling at a comparison to George Cukor, famously a "women's director," Mankiewicz snapped, "George only befriended female stars. I fucked them").

Regardless of personality clashes or questions of ability, giving life to Maria Vargas as written was inherently problematic. Mankiewicz had a blind spot regarding his characters' logorrhea, and Maria carried a further burden of unbelievability in that her ruminations, in English, were those of a supposedly uneducated *madrileña* slum girl. In the end it was a part that would have likely given trouble to any actress of whatever talent and with or without carnal knowledge of Joe Mankiewicz.

Despite the burden of Bogart and her mistrust of Mankiewicz, there was still much about the production for Ava to enjoy. She had never been more glamorously, stylishly presented in a film, thanks to the series of dazzling costumes—virtually an entire season's worth of couture—created for her by the Fontanas; and thanks to the magical lighting schemes of Jack Cardiff, his Technicolor palette capturing her glowing beauty with subtle perfection. She felt particularly excited and pleasingly challenged by *Contessa*'s dancing sequence, her first on film. Another case of life and art intersecting, she had, since *Pandora*, a growing enchantment with the rhythms and passions of flamenco. For three weeks she threw herself into dance rehearsals, and the sequence—filmed in the Tivoli olive groves outside Rome, Ava moving with flair and intensity, daringly erotic in a tight (and in some shots nearly transparent) sweater—would become one of her career favorites.

Filming continued until April, with two weeks away from Cinecittà on locations at San Remo and Portofino, Ava hauling her entourage (it had expanded now to include Dave Hanna; a driver, Mario; the visiting Doreen Grant; and two or three others whose exact duties or origins were never quite established) to both places. With Sinatra banished, her new boyfriend in hand and the damp winter weather gone, Ava seemed renewed, charged with energy and joy of living. During the stay in San Remo, even after a long day's work, she would slither into one of her Fontana gowns and with Dominguín and perhaps some others head off in the car for Monte Carlo and a night's play at the casino. She slept, slowed down, only when absolutely required.

Toward the middle of production Lauren Bacall—Mrs. Humphrey Bogart—arrived for a visit with her husband. She came bearing a gift for Ava. It was a white coconut cake of the sort Ava traditionally had on her birthday, and it was a gift from Frank. "Betty [Bacall] got a little miffed about that cake," Verita Thompson would recall. "She had felt responsible for her charge and had hand-carried it by taxi and limousine and several thousand miles across the Atlantic by plane to ensure its arrival in one piece. And when she finally presented it to Ava, Ava thanked her but pushed it aside and didn't even open the box. The action was so uncharacteristic." Everyone pondered Ava's reaction to the cake, and in spite of all the more provocative evidence she had made available to them for weeks—she had been shacked up with a bullfighter, for starters—it was the dismissal of Sinatra's sentimental gift, the baked, frosted offering sitting forlornly in its unopened box, that became proof to them all that the romance between Frank and Ava was now indisputably over.

Filming concluded in April. Luis Miguel and much of the entourage had gone home. Eager to be back in Madrid with Luis, Ava hurried through her final obligations, completing the dialogue dubbing in a matter of a few hours and then a still session, shot late at night in a small photo studio at Cinecittà. To Hanna the night was a revelation—she seemed more creative, more inspired there with the still camera than she had been on the film set. She confidently took charge of the session, arranged the proper mood enhancements (a portable bar and a record player and records), chose her own costumes and props. Hanna: "She even whipped off her slip to show her figure to better advantage in one form-fitting gown and slyly put Vaseline in the crease of her bosoms to highlight them. The evening was a tour de force and I could see that Ava was really at home in front of the still camera, that her affinity for it seemed to have been born in her."

She extended her modeling career with a playful surprise for the Fontana sisters. At an afternoon fashion show for the house, Ava turned up unannounced on the runway in one of the outfits designed for her movie, strutting and flouncing in imitation of the other models, as the audience of wealthy patrons watched in astonishment. A newspaper reported that she "cavorted hoydenishly backstage before and after the show."

Now, returned to Madrid, she could devote herself to the new romance without distraction. She took a two-room suite at the Castellana Hilton and for a week she and Domínguín were seldom out of it—seldom out of the bed, to be exact. Feelings, responses that had shut down inside her in the declining days with Sinatra were now reignited. Night and day they crawled over each other like two happy, concupiscent kittens. "If I was part of Luis Miguel's convalescence," she would write, "he was part of mine after the goring Frank and I had given each other."

They liked each other, and it was such a relief. It didn't have to be love, did it? Not that goddamn word that made everything crazy and out of control. They laughed, they drank, they fucked, they had a wonderful time. "I was his girlfriend, he was my guy; it was as simple as that."

Gentle, boyishly playful, with a wicked sense of humor and a penchant for practical jokes (he was particularly amused by getting Bappie innocently to say to local people certain Spanish phrases that turned out to be wildly obscene), it was difficult to picture him in the grim, life-and-death atmosphere of the *corrida*. And yet the evidence of his deadly work was there in the flesh: When she first saw him undressed, in the light, she had caught her breath—his legs, his inner thighs, his buttocks were full of deep gouges, missing pieces, and thick red-brown scar tissue, all souvenirs of the brave bulls. Some of the scars looked like the most ragged of repair jobs (emergency surgery was performed in the bowels of the bullring, and the doctors, the matador joked, were veterinarians). In time she would hear the history behind many of those wounds, stories that—even told with Luis Miguel's usual modest understatement, and in broken English besides—could make you faint with horror. The worst story was one Domínguín himself hated to recall, for the memory often took away his desire for sex for at least twenty-four hours. It was the first time, he explained, that a bull had gored him in the balls. The great angry beast had put the horn right through his *cojones* and lifted him till his feet left the ground. His *cuadrilla* had run in and managed to carry him away, and he'd been rushed to the bare-walled, bloodstained dispensary, convulsed with pain. The doctors readied the ether to knock him out before the surgery but Domínguín had refused an anesthetic. He had seen it as a test of will, to stand up to the fear he was feeling and to conquer it or to surrender to it and be ruined, for fear of any kind, the matador believed, ruined you for the arena. The doctors had told him he was insane and then they had given him three handkerchiefs to bite into for the pain and they had poured an entire bottle of iodine over his balls and his scrotum, which was completely torn open and spread out on the operating table. By the end of the operation Dominguín had chewed through the three handkerchiefs and had loosened some teeth in the process. Two days later, in Toledo, he was back in the ring.

One night in Madrid, in that spring of 1954, Ava had been sleeping in her bed at the Hilton, Luis Miguel cuddled up close behind her, when suddenly she awoke in agony. Dominguín called for help, and she was rushed to the nearest hospital. The pain—an excruciating tearing, biting sensation in her stomach and lower back—was the worst she had ever known. Doctors diagnosed kidney stones, formations of jagged calcium crystals in the urinary tract. The stones would take from a few days to a week to pass from her system—unless they didn't. Ava, not following her bullfighter's stoic regimen in times of discomfort, screamed for painkillers.

She lay there suffering in her hospital bed, intermittently howling curses that even without translation made the Spanish nuns who served as nurses turn crimson. Dominguín became her devoted attendant. He remained with her around the clock, napping on the floor on a small pallet the nuns brought for him. He fretted over her, sang softly in her ear. He had the room filled with fresh flowers. One night she awoke and found him kneeling beside her bed as in prayer, in the dark, staring at her with wide, moist eyes. She saw his distraught, devotional expression, the unmistakable look of love, and she could only think, Goddammit, I've done it again.

One day Dominguín disappeared, for a while, and when he returned Ernest Hemingway was with him. Ava recognized the visitor at once, the burly, bearded literary icon, the only writer in the world with the public profile of a movie star. She greeted him with enthusiasm. Quite aside from the fact that she had acted in two adaptations of his work, she had also read him from cover to cover—Artie had ordered it in the beginning, yes, but she had gone back to him of her own volition, and *A Farewell to Arms* was possibly her favorite book. She'd even tried to interest her studio in remaking it.

Writer A. E. Hotchner, Hemingway's buddy and part of his entourage in town for the Feria de San Isidro bullfights, had come along to visit Ava in the hospital. "She was being very crabby on the phone when we got there," he remembered, "talking to Hollywood, cursing up a storm. There was some picture they wanted her to do, and she was not interested and telling them what they could do with it. She's screaming all these four-letter words into the phone while the nuns are all around plumping up her pillows. I must say, as everyone already has, she was gorgeous. And to listen to her talk, she was funny and very irreverent."

Ava hung up the phone and beamed at Hemingway, beckoning him to sit with her on the bed. "Ernest!"

Ava thanked him profusely for coming and informed all present that she had been in two movies based on Hemingway stories, and one of them had made her a star.

"*The Killers* was okay," Hemingway said. "But the only good things in *Snows of Kilimanjaro* were you and the dead cat."

They talked about Hollywood, and Ava said living there had driven her to an analyst's couch. Hemingway said he was afraid of such things.

"You've never been to a shrink?" Ava said.

Hemingway told her, "My analyst is my Corona Portable Number Three." His typewriter.

Dominguín arranged an outing to coincide with Ava's release from the hospital (the doctors had warned her that two more stones remained to be passed), a trip to the bull-breeding ranch of his friend Antonio Perez. There would be a *tienta*, a testing of the young *toros*. They drove out to the countryside in two cars, Hemingway and his wife, Mary, Hotchner and one other traveling companion in one car, and in the other Dominguín, his driver, Ava, and Peter Viertel, the screenwriter and novelist (*White Hunter, Black Heart*, the classic fictional examination of John Huston) and a friend of Hemingway's for some years. Viertel had met Ava in California in the midforties, when she was married to Shaw, had swum with her in the pool at the Tudor-style mansion.

Arriving at the Perez ranch, everyone proceeded to the *plazita*, a miniature bullring, and Ava stood with Hemingway and some others at the *barrera*, where they could see the bulls coming into the ring. Hemingway explained the proceedings, how they would test the young animals with a kind of practice fighting to gauge their potential ferocity and courage, and how the breeders would take notes and decide which of the young stock were meant for the *corrida* and which were not. Between bulls there was small talk, Hemingway eager to hear juicy gossip about this or that Hollywood actress, and the two traded African adventure stories (Hemingway had not long ago been in a plane crash in the jungle coming back from a safari, and initially newspapers around the world had declared him dead). Hemingway by now called her "Daughter," which struck Ava with a particular warmth as it had been the way she was always addressed by her father. She in turn began calling him—as most of the others in his party did—"Papa." They got along very well. Mary Hemingway, after an initial suspiciousness (ordinarily, according to Hotchner, "Mary hated any woman that was acceptable to Ernest . . . just a ball of jealousy"), took a liking to Ava as well.

At the *tienta* Ava was seeing Dominguín in the ring for the first time, though it was a miniature version of the great plazas where he shone before thousands of cheering spectators. There was to be no killing, but he worked the *muleta* with several animals, and his skill and artistry were evident even under the reduced circumstances. After one graceful performance, Hotchner recalled in his memoir of the writer, Hemingway told Ava, "You see what Luis Miguel did to that cow? He made it into something. He convinced it . . . made a star out of it. That cow went out of here proud as hell."

Ava sighed. "He's a lovely man, isn't he?"

Then Dominguín came to take her into the ring with him. Ava squealed, held back. "She was very reluctant," said Hotchner. "But he coaxed her. He took her into the ring and had her hold the cape and make some passes at the animal. She was frightened, but Dominguín knew what he was doing, and by the end she was really enjoying herself."

"They made a handsome couple," Peter Viertel would write, "the young movie queen and her bullfighter. Yet I had the suspicion that they were acting out a storybook romance that was expected of them as mythical figures, an expectation that was certain to complicate their relationship in the long run."

———

Hemingway was staying on in Madrid to the end of the *feria*. Ava was leaving town, going back to America to get her divorce from Frank, and so she went to see the writer once more and say good-bye. Papa invited her to come visit him at his home in Cuba, then asked a special favor: a gift of one of her expelled kidney stones, as a good-luck charm. Ava, rolling her eyes (or so one might hope), said she would see what she could do.*

On May 24 Ava and Luis Miguel attended the *festiva brava*, sitting in Miguel's regular front-row seats. Chenel, considered by some as Spain's top matador on Dominguín's retirement, was gored by a bull that day, a horn catching him in the leg, throwing him high in the air, and dropping him down on the hard ground with his thigh ripped open for six inches. From the front row, on the costlier *sombra*, or shaded side of the arena out of the glare of the afternoon sun, you could see in sharp focus where the bull had ripped the flesh, and you could see the blood rippling down on his leg and dark stains on the sand beneath him.

Later Ava and Dominguín went back to the Castellana Hilton and they made love and in the morning she kissed him good-bye and flew to America.

It was going to be her last visit to Hollywood, she told everyone. She was going to straighten things out with the studio, sign on the dotted line to end her marriage, and then she was going back to Europe for good.

Metro was again displeased with Ava Gardner. A film had been planned for her, *Love Me or Leave Me*, the life story of the Roaring Twenties chanteuse Ruth Etting. Ava told them she would not be doing it. Whatever the project's merits, she could not see beyond the fact that they intended to have someone else's voice coming out of her mouth when she sang—still angry after what she saw as her humiliation over the songs in *Show Boat*, she wanted nothing more to do with any phony MGM musicals. ("I stand there mouthing words like a goddamn goldfish," she'd squawked at them from Spain, "while you're piping in some goddamn dubbed voice!") She had told them at the time that even if she had wanted

---

*Hemingway did receive the odd amulet, and carried it with him for some years.

to go back to Los Angeles and do the Ruth Etting story, she was in a god-damn hospital with goddamn painful kidney stones. They still threatened her with suspension. Dave Hanna had told her that people in Hollywood thought she was faking her illness to keep from working. Now she was carrying with her from Madrid a copy of the hospital X-ray of her insides with the stones visible. She was going to give the X-ray to Dore Schary; maybe he'd like to release it to Hedda Hopper or to one of the newspapers for their Sunday supplements.

After her acrimonious meeting with Metro she was preparing to leave LA for Nevada to take up the necessary six weeks' residence for an expedient divorce, when who should pop up before her but Howard Hughes, like a genie out of a bottle she thought she had long ago thrown back into the ocean. Hughes, as usual, knew everything that was happening, had happened, without her having to say a word. He looked like the cat who'd made a good dinner of the canary, barely containing his pleasure in the knowledge that the marriage to the hated Sinatra was in its final weeks.

"I understand you're headed out to Lake Tahoe," Hughes said with a thin-lipped smile.

She had decided against going to Las Vegas (where she had long ago effected her severance from Mickey Rooney) when she learned the extraordinary news that all three of her husbands, exes and present, were currently playing in the small desert town, making it just a little too crowded even for a woman with a penchant for dramatic encounters.

Hughes said, "You let me take care of everything. I own or lease half the houses on that lake anyway."

Hughes explained that he was very busy with some delicate business matters at the moment—among the items on his plate was a dangerous feud with the secretary of defense over aircraft contracts, a risky scheme to buy RKO Pictures outright from its nosy stockholders, the establishment of a multi-million-dollar hospital charity/tax dodge, and the overseeing of the invention of a new three-dimensional camera that would best exploit the well-known chest of actress Jane Russell. But, Hughes told Ava, he hoped to have time to visit her out at Tahoe very soon. Hughes said they had a lot of catching up to do now that she was going to be a free woman again.

This all happened just a few weeks after Hughes had planned to marry Kathryn Grayson—Ava's bosomy buddy from *Show Boat*—until

Grayson experienced a premonition of tragedy and called it off at the last minute (as it happened, her young nephew would have a fatal accident at exactly the hour planned for the wedding). Not that Howard was as free of female entanglements as he hoped to be to renew his romantic pursuit of Ava. There was sexy ingenue Terry Moore, who claimed to have married Hughes in a shipboard ceremony, and he had stashed about two dozen starlets around LA waiting for a promised big break in movies. And as Hughes was preparing the vacation home for Ava's comfortable stay on the shore of Lake Tahoe near Zephyr Cove, while she waited for her divorce, he was simultaneously getting his longtime, on-again-off-again girlfriend Jean Peters ensconced in another lakeside house up the road. Peters, the beautiful star of *Pickup on South Street* and *Three Coins in the Fountain,* had recently impulsively fallen in love and gotten married to someone, and now, thirty-some days later, Hughes was helping her to get a divorce, too (as it is said, to get a job done send the busy man).

Knowing she would probably regret it eventually, Ava agreed to let Howard take care of her lodgings and sundries in Nevada, and in the second week of June she and her maid, Reenie, drove out to Lake Tahoe and settled into the luxurious cottage provided for the necessary six-week stay.

Hughes being Hughes, he immediately assigned someone to keep Ava under twenty-four-hour surveillance. This job went to a new associate, Robert Maheu, chief exec of his own exclusive investigative agency with important connections in the capital and especially at the CIA. It was absurd to hire a high-priced Washington-based operative of Maheu's stature to do work normally handled by a cheap hotel dick, but Maheu savored his new relationship with the eccentric Hughes and so took the job and then subcontracted it to a local private eye in Nevada. The house on Lake Tahoe had already been wired with microphones before Ava's arrival, so it only remained for the Zephyr Cove detective to set up shop in the woods near the house, keep tabs on the actress's visitors, and follow her when she went away. He would sit there behind some bushes, occasionally taking a look through his binoculars at Ava Gardner sunbathing or drinking on the patio, then take a bite of one of the sardine sandwiches his wife had packed for him, once in a while having to get up and head for his car and follow the movie actress into town or over to the Cal-Neva casino.

By that summer of 1954, the world had become Frank Sinatra's oyster once more. In March he had run up onto the stage of the Pantages Theater and accepted the gold statue for Best Supporting Actor in *From Here to Eternity*. He could pick and choose now from among dozens of offered film projects. He was again a popular recording artist and the darling of the music critics. The money thrown at him, by movie studios, television networks, Vegas casinos and theaters and nightclubs around the world, amounted to an incalculable fortune, millions many times over. Women—from chorus girls to the socially registered—threw themselves at him wherever he went. About the only thing in the world he could not have was Ava Gardner.

He had found out about the bullfighter, thrown a tantrum when she'd told him, torn a room to pieces. And then he had come back from Europe, knowing it was all over, wanting to move on. "What else can I do?" he said to Jimmy van Heusen. "This broad is gonna kill me. Who the fuck does she think she is? I swear to you, no woman will ever do this to me again." But it was easier said than done. He couldn't get past her. Either he had to have her back, to love her, to have her loving him again. Or it was anger and resentment, needing to get even with her, to make her suffer as he had suffered, to find a way to show her he was the one who decided when things were *done*.

"One night we went to Frank's for a dinner party," recalled Betty Comden, the lyricist and the co-screenwriter of *On the Town* and *Singin' in the Rain*. "And we saw that one of the rooms was filled with pictures of Ava, and around the pictures were lit candles. It was like the altar of a little church."

On the other hand: Irving "Swifty" Lazar, the dapper, diminutive Hollywood-based literary agent, was Frank's neighbor at his new digs, an apartment house on Wilshire Boulevard in Westwood. Lazar had come home very late one night and saw that Sinatra's door was open and the lights on. Wondering if there was a problem, he stuck his head through the doorway and saw Sinatra by himself, evidently very drunk, slumped in an armchair, holding a gun. Cautiously Lazar stepped inside and as he did he saw that Sinatra was aiming his gun—an air gun, it turned out to be—at three large portrait images of Ava he had propped up on the floor. The three faces of Ava were full of pellet holes where Sinatra had been shooting at them—all night long, as it appeared.

One day Sinatra showed up at the house where Ava was staying on

Lake Tahoe. As Robert Maheu would recall the story, the detective staking out the place had looked through his binoculars, and there was Sinatra entering the house. The detective had been particularly instructed to keep an eye out for this man and so he watched with diligence now as Sinatra went inside with Gardner, catching glimpses of them moving about within the house. Sinatra, Maheu figured, was trying to persuade Ava to drop the divorce business and to get back together with him. "He was successful enough," Maheu wrote, "to persuade her to go on a romantic little boat ride with him on the lake." Under the circumstances, as Maheu saw it, the practical thing for the private dick to do was to stay by the shoreline out of sight and wait for them to return with the rented boat. "Instead . . . my man impulsively rented one himself and went out after them!"

Sinatra quickly realized that they were being pursued on the lake and, according to Maheu, "went nuts." There was a nautical chase, and the detective was barely able to get back to shore and disappear ahead of the angry, pursuing crooner. Sinatra departed Tahoe soon after. Ava had not changed her mind.

As the weeks rolled by, boredom set in. Longing for some attention and affection, Ava put through a call to her Madrid friend Betty Wallers, with instructions to tell Miguel to come to America at once and keep her company. Days later, on July 7, Dominguín arrived from Spain.

The couple had a lusty reunion. For a week they sunbathed, swam, went fishing, went to bed. At the casino Luis Miguel held her hand as she played roulette. Columnist Earl Wilson and his wife, visiting from New York, paid a brief visit.

Ava introduced them to the great matador and then sent him to refill her drink. "He's trying to learn English," she said. "Miguel, get a piece of ice. A piece of *ice*—that's not the same as a piece of *ass*."

One night she and Dominguín had been out to the casino, Ava had been drinking too much, and a fight broke out. It wasn't that they had never fought before. Ava had lost her temper many times about something or other, and she had screamed and stamped her feet, but Miguel had usually been unimpressed or else amused by her theatrics, smiling at her while she ranted, not understanding or not trying to understand, and usually just waiting for an opportune moment to slip his hand around her rear end. On one occasion witnessed by Jack Cardiff, when he and his wife were visiting the couple at Domínguín's hacienda outside Madrid, Ava had lost her temper and wouldn't shut up. The matador had finally gone over to her, swept her up in his arms, and thrown her fully dressed into the swimming pool.

On the night of the big argument at Lake Tahoe, Ava had turned her back on him, stormed off to her bedroom, and slammed the door. Obviously apprised of everything that went on in the house (aside from planted microphones, Ava suspected the servants were Howard Hughes's paid informants), Hughes's man Johnny Meyer showed up as if on cue, lending Luis Miguel a shoulder to cry on. Meyer carefully pricked the easygoing Domínguín where he was vulnerable—his pride and his native machismo—urging the bullfighter to teach Ava a lesson, make her know he didn't stand for such behavior from a female; take it from Johnny, it was the only way to deal with an American woman. Soon Meyer had hustled Domínguín out of the house and off to the airport, where an aircraft was already waiting to fly him away.

A reporter caught up with him in Los Angeles. Were he and Ava Gardner intending to marry? "No marriage to Ava," Domínguín said. "I am too infirm." (Writer Peter Viertel had agreed to let Domínguín stay with him in Los Angeles and asked his friend Kathy Parrish, wife of director Robert Parrish, to meet the bullfighter at the airport. She had met him once before, in Madrid. "He was wearing his 'suit of lights' then," she recalled, "and looked so romantic, like the ultimate hero. When I picked him up after he'd left Ava he looked miserable and as romantic as a dentist.")

With the competition seemingly eliminated and before she had a chance to import God knew what other men she had lined up, Howard Hughes returned to plead his case. One evening they went out on the lake, floating about under a midsummer moon. Howard presented her with a gift, a fabulously expensive sapphire-and-diamond ring. Then, as she was languidly modeling the ring under the moonlight, Howard proposed.

"Come on, how about it? You've been married three times already, don't you think it's my turn?"

298 · AVA GARDNER

"Your turn?" Ava said, emitting one of her earsplitting cackles. "Howard . . . honey . . . you crack me up. You make it sound like I'm a pony ride at the county fair."

Hughes waved an arm. "Don't make fun of me! I've been waiting over ten years for you to come to your senses. Just think of the life you could have with me. I'll supply you with every luxury imaginable. Why don't you be sensible and let us settle this thing. Eventually you could learn to love me if you gave it half a chance."

Her six weeks' residence in Nevada completed, Ava could apply for her divorce. Newsmen had staked out the courthouse on the day she was scheduled to testify. She didn't show. With the advice of her lawyer and accountants she had decided to ask Frank for repayment of the money she had loaned him through their time together. She was not asking for alimony, property settlement, nothing. But she felt it was only right for him to repay some of the extravagances he had grandiosely insisted upon and for which she had picked up the tab (there was also the time she had come back from Europe on his account, incurring a huge tax burden as a result). Many times he had told her he would pay her back when he could, so why not make good before they went their separate ways? He was becoming wealthy beyond belief; with his new contracts and movie deals and his piece of a Vegas casino, he could certainly afford to set things straight with her.

But Frank reacted to the suggestion with hostility. That was what it was all about now, baby, money?

She couldn't believe he'd say such a thing. It was Frank who had to have money for the power it bought him to make people jump, to pay his way out of problems, to make his waiters and flunkies worship him for those hundred-dollar tips. She had never gone after any of her husbands for money the way other wives had done, despite the urging of her attorneys. If she was interested in money, she fumed, she would have married Howard Hughes any of the fifty times he proposed: Howard who could buy and sell Frank ten times over in a morning and forget about it by the afternoon.

Working herself into quite a state over Frank's refusal to make restitution, she simply abandoned the divorce proceedings until things could be settled. Perhaps she might come back and seek a piece of his income after all, the way Nancy had done; that might be quite an annuity in the years ahead. Instead of going to court she abruptly agreed to accompany Howard on a business trip to Florida. In the space of two hours, Ava and Reenie packed, left the Tahoe divorce cottage for the airport, and were headed for Miami. Then Jean Peters, on a separate flight, did the same. And then Jean Peters's former husband followed *her* to Miami (but that is another story for another time).

Howard installed Ava and Reenie at a rented villa in a tony residential neighborhood north of Miami Beach. The two women occupied the two bedroom suites, and when Howard finally arrived to stay with them a couple of days later, he was left with the only remaining sleeping quarters, a small bedroom near the kitchen intended for a maid. The two ladies giggled over the tall tycoon crammed into the servant's quarters, but they both agreed that he was very sweet to accept the situation without complaint. For two weeks Ava and Reenie did nothing more strenuous than the backstroke in the villa's kidney-shaped pool. Howard would visit for a day or two, then disappear. Gradually, predictably, Ava grew bored, Howard grew tedious. He was once again becoming strenuous in his desire to take what Ava had no interest in giving. All the old tensions returned to the relationship, Howard poking around at her, seeing if there wasn't some way his wealth could find a route to her heart, and Ava resenting the very idea that she might put a price on her seduction or her love. One night Reenie had been strolling the grounds when she struck up a conversation with one of the armed plainclothes guards assigned by Hughes to watch over the property and its guests. The talkative guard confided, one hired hand to another, that Mr. Hughes had on the premises some famous zillion-dollar Romanoff necklace that he was going to give to his girlfriend the second she went to bed with him, and so, said the guard, a word to the wise: If the dame in there liked expensive jewelry, she might want to make up her mind and hop under the sheets with the guy before he sent the necklace back to the shop. Whether Ava was really outraged by the idea of Howard sharing such intimate plans for her with the security man, or whether she was simply following the ritualistic next step in a psychological game she and Hughes had been playing with each other for more than a decade is difficult to say. She heard the story, let out a growl, and told Reenie to pack them up, they were leaving *at once*—for Havana.

Registered at the Nacional under the name Miss Grey, she languished now under the Cuban sun, drank daiquiris in the Floridita, went nightclubbing and gambling with an assortment of new acquaintances. She spent many afternoons and evenings at the Finca Vigía, Hemingway's hacienda near San Francisco de Paulo. Her nude swims in Papa's pool became local legend, observed—to judge from all those who would claim through the years to have been eyewitnesses—not only by Papa but by half the men on the island. When David Hanna tracked her down via telephone from Los Angeles to discuss plans for the New York premiere of *The Barefoot Contessa,* she was restless again, ready for new worlds to conquer. Ava offered an idea that Metro had previously rejected for another film: a *Barefoot* promotional tour of South America. She had an itch to visit Rio de Janeiro and a couple of other spots down there and liked the idea of someone else picking up the tab. Lacking MGM's heavy-footed officialism, United Artists responded to the actress's offer at once and with enthusiasm. As Ava wanted to leave as soon as possible, and the company wanted her in New York for the September premiere, Hanna hurriedly contacted the UA reps in Brazil, Argentina, Chile, Peru, and Venezuela to make arrangements, alert the press, and so on. There was an immediate problem with Brazil: It seemed that the country's leader had shot himself to death—at least that was the official story—and the country was under martial law, revolution reported as imminent. Hanna advised his star of the situation but she was unimpressed, said she was not going to go to South America and not get to visit Rio. After all, the revolution wasn't even a certainty.

The tour became a high-water mark, flash point evidence of Ava Gardner as international phenomenon. At city after city her arrival was met with huge crowds, great waves of Chileans, Argentines, Uruguayans, so frantic and ecstatic swarming over each airport along the route that they might have been there to greet a messiah. Ava had known from the amount of fan mail and from her box office success in South American countries that she had a particularly strong following there—"They like me because I look Spanish," she told Hanna. But she was not prepared for the size of the crowds and their emotionality. People lined the routes from the various airports, cheering and tossing flowers. Even the controlled environment of the press receptions held within stately hotel ballrooms often verged on the riotous, fistfights breaking out among reporters vying for a closer glimpse of the beautiful star. At Lima, when Ava's late arrival coincided with the landing of the president of Peru it was said that even the official military band come to play for the president's return abandoned the post to join those awaiting the visitor from Hollywood.

In Rio the crowd at last became uncontrollable, dangerous. Long before the plane even touched down, the police had been overwhelmed, the mob breaking past the fences and barriers to swarm the runway. The passengers on board glimpsed the frightening, extraordinary sight of the landing strip itself lined with people. A landing was somehow made and the aircraft taxied to the stopping point at the terminal. But the runway crew were barely able to place the ramp in position before the crowd moved up. That the screaming mob of men, women, and children did not actually charge up the steps and rush inside the airplane was, under the circumstances, inexplicable. The police at last broke through to the ramp and forced an opening—really a gauntlet—through which the passengers were forced to run. Ava and Dave Hanna waited for the arrival of someone with a plan for the star's escape, but no one came. Ava grew impatient and decided to brave it out. "They'll let a woman through," she said. Hanna felt queasy, glancing down at the unruly crowd, imagining them fresh from overthrowing the government, seeing the narrow passage the police made already swallowed up and thinking of the strong possibility of his charge being literally torn to bits. Just before the actress attempted to go out, the pilot came and whisked her out through the opposite side of the plane, where another portable stairway had been brought up.

Somehow they managed to get her a running start across the field before the mob caught on. She was hurried into a building at one end of the airport where reporters and photographers had been corralled and literally locked up to await a scheduled press conference. The conditions were barely less chaotic than those out on the field. This mob inside, reporters and film crews and assorted interlopers with no connection to the press, now tightened around Ava Gardner in a squirming circle. Cameras blindingly flashed directly in faces, and the blazing-hot lights of a television crew fell against the back of a man's neck, burning hair and flesh. Ava fared badly, helplessly pushed along by the swarm on every side, men thrusting themselves against her from the front and from behind, grabbing, fingers reaching out from between other bodies to pinch and probe her.

Airport personnel at last appeared to effect some belated rescue. Hobbling with a broken heel, she was ushered down a corridor, out to the street, into a taxi. When the taxi driver failed to get the car moving—with the mob approaching fast—Ava took off her damaged shoe and hit him on the head.

The fun didn't end there. The UA rep had booked them into a second-rate hotel—a kickback was suspected—and when Ava demanded her bags be taken downstairs and sent over to the more appropriately luxurious Copacabana Palace, there occurred a brief predawn tussle with the manager of the shoddy place, shouting, drinks thrown in faces and the manager, fearful of the terrible publicity the rejection of his hotel would cause him, preemptively called every newspaper in town to report that Hollywood star Ava Gardner had destroyed her beautiful room during a drunken orgy and had been evicted. The story ran in all the local papers the next day and the day after that had been picked up worldwide. "A warm Latin welcome dropped to subfreezing," reported UP. "Miss Gardner, her 16 suitcases and her retinue were out in the cold. They left the hotel at the request of the management, which submitted a bill for liquor, a broken table, splintered glasses, smashed pictures and water stains on a wall."

Ava, furious, decided to leave Rio the following evening, three days ahead of schedule. She remained in her suite at the Palace all day and into the night, cursing Brazil and ordering room service. Then, long after midnight, she called David Hanna in his room, said that she had come thousands of miles to see Rio, and she was damn well going to go take a look at the place. The publicist climbed out of bed and got dressed, fearful of not going with her—and fearful of going with her too. A driver took them along the shoreline of broad moonlit beaches and up into the hills, past shantytowns flickeringly lit by open bonfires. At dawn they found a marketplace just stirring to life, and they bought baskets of fresh fruit from the first vendors. They were returning to the hotel, again driving alongside the broad sandy beaches, now lit up red and gold with the rising sun. Ava wanted to go down to the ocean. There was not another soul on the beach and she stood there in the dawning sunlight for a couple of minutes, star-

ing down at the water rolling in and across her bare feet. Dave Hanna sat
in the car, watching her through the window, sleepily bemused by the jux-
taposition of the gentle image before him, the woman all alone on Copacabana Beach, and the hellish scene at the airport the day before.

Flying back to the States, they saw that the story of Ava's drunken,
furniture-breaking hotel orgy was still being reported in the American
press. Several items mentioned Dave Hanna by name, reporting that Ava
Gardner had thrown a glass of booze in his face. He had even received a
cablegram from an associate decrying his ordeal and urging him to refuse
to work for such a person. Hanna had found it amusing—the number of
wrong assumptions in one brief missive. Ava, not so amused, seized on
the fact that no one had cabled her a similar message of support. "Not
Beatrice, not my agent—no one—not one damned soul. And you know
why? Because they believe it."

In New York, Dominguín was waiting for her. Lonely and upset, she
had put a call through to him from Rio; he'd agreed to meet her in Manhattan. They were happily reunited in a suite at the Drake Hotel, and for
two days no one saw them but the room-service waiters. But for all their
continued physical compatibility, things had changed. Dominguín had
changed: He had come to the conclusion that their informal, live-for-
today relationship was an untenable one. He loved her, he wanted to
marry her, to have children with her. He proposed; an ultimatum.

Ava said she was not ready to get married again, and she did not know
when she would be ready. Dominguín said he was sorry to hear that and
returned to Spain. Before the year concluded he would marry a beautiful
dark-haired movie actress from Italy named Lucia Bose; some called her
Italy's answer to Ava Gardner.

A few days before the *Barefoot* premiere, Ava got a call from Sammy
Davis, Jr. The African-American entertainer, a rising name on the nightclub circuit in the midfifties, had long been a solicitous friend and stalwart
supporter of Sinatra's and had cultivated a friendship with Ava as well,
sending her gifts and well-wishing telegrams from the time she and Frank
had started going together. Performing at the Apollo Theater uptown,

Sammy was going to be named an honorary mayor of Harlem and was hoping to have some famous friends in attendance for the occasion. Ava agreed to be there. She stood on the Apollo stage with a group of black performers and local civic leaders and politicians; she was introduced, met with uproarious cheers from the audience, stepped to the microphone, and hailed Sammy as a great performer.

Davis, believing that a good way to repay one favor was to ask another, called Ava the next day with a new request: A leading "Negro" magazine was offering to put him on the cover of their December issue posed as Santa Claus if he could get a celebrity friend to be in the picture with him, someone to sort of sit there and pretend to tell Santa what they wanted for Christmas. It would simply be a gas, Sammy said, if Ava was willing to be that friend. The request was a passive-aggressive act on Davis's part—he had to be all too aware that a white female, certainly a celebrated white female love goddess, did not readily pose for photos perched on the knee of a black Santa Claus without the potentiality of dramatic repercussions, not in the United States in the autumn of 1954. Had one of Ava's PR tacticians heard the suggestion, he would have ruled it out at once, but MGM was still giving her the cold shoulder and providing no advice at the moment, and David Hanna was just then confined to his apartment with a lingering amoebic souvenir of South America. Ava—indifferent or oblivious or defiant of racist conformity—told Sammy she would do it. The next day a photographer and crew arrived at the Drake Hotel along with a magazine editor, then Sam, his press agent, and assorted hangers-on. The crew draped red backdrop everywhere, Davis climbed into his Santa suit, and the pictures were taken. Later everyone sat around the suite to enjoy a cocktail or two. The photographer took up his camera and caught a few shots of the party—casual, candid stuff to include in the magazine, why not—of Ava and Sammy chatting and laughing together, drinks in hand, Ava with her bare foot up on the armrest by Sammy's leg, and one of Sammy leaning over Ava in her chair, and another with the two of them smiling for the camera, Sammy crouched around behind with his arm around her shoulder and Ava holding his hand.

As it happened the publication of the pictures in *Our World* went virtually unnoticed, even with an accompanying article (actually an adapted interview) under Ava Gardner's byline, provocatively titled "Sammy Sends Me." The trouble came with the republication of some of those photos in a different context and in a popular—and infernal—publication called *Confidential*.

It was Howard Hughes—of course—who was the first to learn of the planned scandal story (his informers spied on the informers). "They are about to do a devastating thing on you in *Confidential*," he told her sadly, "about you and your black lover, Sammy Davis." (He assumed it to be true, another of her blows to his heart.)

The piece was titled "What Makes Ava Run for Sammy Davis, Jr.?" (an unwelcome play on the title of Budd Schulberg's famous novel), and contained the Drake Hotel pictures now with insinuating captions, plus a chronicle of implied erotic encounters between Ava and Davis and Ava and assorted other "colored" crooners and musicians, including Herb Jeffries, Dizzy Gillespie, and Cuban mambo king Perez Prado. ("Dark-skinned gents," wrote *Confidential*'s pseudonymous "Horton Streete," "have been proving their powerful fascination for Ava for years.") The piece cynically churned together a few facts, some lurid conjecture, and the unquestioned evidence of Ava Gardner's acquaintance with Davis and a number of jazz musicians. "Everyone saw that thing in *Confidential*," recalled Herb Jeffries a half century later. "They tried to link me to her romantically. But as God in heaven is my witness I didn't know her that way. She was a fan and came to see me in the clubs where I worked. It was very flattering to one's ego, but I have to tell the truth. She's dead now, and it would be nice for me to go ahead and lie, because everyone seems to have believed it. But it's not so. I've had enough interesting and strange things happen in my life not to have to lie about anything."

However much of Mr. Streete's work was fantasy, the impact of the article was real and for a moment in time held the potential for a career-rocking scandal. *Confidential*, with its fresh formula for showbiz gossip as pornography, had not yet been around long enough to have its credibility dismissed out of hand (or its liability tested in court), and the mere existence of the published photos of Ava and Sammy casually holding hands and Davis with his arm around her were a sufficient call to arms for some in the feverishly racialist regions of America. MGM received letters by the thousands complaining of their star's behavior. "People all over the country said they would never see one of her pictures again," a Metro exec told journalist Joe Hyams. "The things they called her were disgraceful." A telegram from the mayor of Shreveport, Louisiana, informed the studio of a plan to ban all future Ava Gardner movies from that city, and in Smithfield, North Carolina, it was reported, the chamber of commerce had forthwith removed the motto BIRTHPLACE OF AVA GARDNER from their promotional literature. "Even my own family criticized me," said Ava. "And there wasn't any use in telling them how it happened. They wouldn't understand. Hell, they wouldn't even believe it."

Metro fretted over the consequences for weeks. The studio attorneys were prepared to launch a lawsuit against *Confidential*, but Howard Strickling, head of publicity and Ava's longtime ally at the studio, told them to forget it. The magazine was a rag published in a sewer, said Strickling, and no matter what happened they would never pay off and would try to drag the case on for years. The lawsuit would merely bring the story unending publicity all over the world. "The best thing to do," said the master of ballyhoo, "is ignore it completely."

The "scandal" blew away—with Ava soon gone from America and nothing more to add to the story, perhaps people had difficulty remaining incensed. Within certain inner circles of showbiz, however, the story did stay in play for a while longer. Sammy Davis had made voluble public statements regarding the inaccuracy of the *Confidential* innuendo, and was said to have given Frank Sinatra several heartfelt assurances regarding same. But still, there was talk. People heard things. Sam was legendarily a Sinatra acolyte, an idolatrous mimic—dressed like Frank, sang like Frank, moved and smoked and drank like Frank. It was known to some that Davis also developed a curious, persistent habit of pursuing former female acquaintances of Frank's, taking ex-Sinatra girlfriends to bed in a kind of ultimate, intimate mimicry of his idol's life. Pursuing Ava Gardner behind Sinatra's back would have taken this game of second-hand seduction into more dangerous territory, but some believed Davis was capable of it (it was said, for example, that he continued an affair with Kim Novak even after his life had been threatened by gangsters if he did not give her up). Arthur Silber, Jr. was Davis's personal assistant, bodyguard, and friend from the 1940s to the 1990s, and lived at Davis's house in Los Angeles in the fifties. "I used to drive Sammy to wherever he was going and then pick him up at an appointed time," Silber recalled. "On two nights I dropped him off at Ava's house in Los Angeles and left him there and he got home by his own means, which was unusual. These were not dinner parties but more in the way of a rendezvous. That was how it looked to me, that was my feeling, knowing Sammy's habits as I did. It was not something that he was ever going to say much about because of Sinatra, but I had a pretty good idea what was going on."

United Artists promoted the release of *The Barefoot Contessa* as a major cultural event. The publicity campaign had already stirred up great interest, with the memorable posters and advertisements with their sketched rendering of an ecstatic Ava and the printed declaration: "The World's Most Beautiful Animal." It was the delirious worldwide hype more than the film itself that confirmed the movie star's divine ascension. For a moment in time, however brief, no other performer held such a grip on the planet's imagination.

Just before *Barefoot* was ready for release, Howard Hughes threatened UA with a legal injunction to stop the film's exhibition. Hughes had his lawyer suggest that the Hughes-like Kirk Edwards character "cut too close to the bone" and would be legally actionable as written (the original script included references to the character's Texas background, to the source of his wealth, to his going into the movie business to meet girls, his various hideaways and more, and a scene of Maria beating up the tycoon that was remarkably like Ava's actual battle with Hughes in the forties). Editor William Hornbeck was forced to fly to the lab in London to make thirteenth-hour cuts and changes to the sound track (for example, Edwards turned into a Wall Streeter instead of a Texan); Hughes revealed no personal anger, only the need to protect his professional reputation, and actually arranged Hornbeck's transportation. It is difficult to say whether or not the cuts did any harm to Warren Stevens's monotonous performance as Edwards.

At the world premiere in New York, Ava arrived looking glorious in a Fontana creation, publicist David Hanna serving as utilitarian escort (the world's most beautiful animal unable to find a date!). The premiere screening would be her first view of the film; in Rome she had seen only scattered rushes and those edited scenes she had viewed for the purpose of postdubbing some dialogue. The film played well at the beginning, the audience responding favorably to the dramatic opening and the witty lines, to the glorious painterly style of cinematographer Cardiff, eventually to the arrival of the star in all her sumptuous beauty. Long dialogue exchanges and monologues, some more like spoken essays, began to lessen the film's initial spell. Shortly after the midway point, Ava nudged Hanna to get her out.

They stopped by Hanna's apartment for a drink before heading to the postpremiere party. The publicist waited for some amplification of the star's reaction to the film or her performance, some show of anger or fear or disappointment to which he would offer the expected calming respónse. Instead she said nothing about it. The film seemed already gone from her mind, the possible critical response, the response of future ticket buyers, recriminations for the months of work that had been given to the project, the need most stars had for comforting and reassurances at such moments, were of no apparent interest to her.

The film, as suspected by many who attended the premiere, did not become the road show sensation as planned. Mankiewicz's Shavian dissection of the worlds of moviemaking and high society was judged too talky and dull by the carriage trade, and too rich for the blood—and too talky—by the common man. It was either too sophisticated or not sophisticated enough. The handling of the decisive matter of the count's sexual impotence, which sets in place the events that lead to Maria's murder, was reported to have provoked derisive laughter at some screenings, while at others the audiences were simply unable to grasp what was going on (screenwriter Walter Bernstein recalled seeing the movie in Boston in a theater full of sailors on leave, all of them restively baffled by Rossano Brazzi's predicament until one cried out, "He's got no dick! He's got no dick!").

It was, to be sure, a flawed and decidedly verbose film, but one that contained much that was impossible to forget. Visually, the film was a remarkable, glowing object of beauty. There was the melancholy beauty of the opening in the rainy Rapallo cemetery, the camera craning above the hillocks of black umbrellas, Bogart/Harry Dawes's ruefully funny voice-over (a line timed to reflect the 3-D craze: "I go way back—back to when the movies had two dimensions and one dimension—and sometimes no dimension at all."); Ava's passionate dance by the gypsy encampment; and the final glimpse of the contessa in death, a dark, exquisite image worthy of Vermeer, with Bogart again, removing the shoes of his beautiful friend and woefully unable to remember the Spanish word for Cinderella.

Breathtaking to behold, Ava had never looked more beautiful—or more like a star (as Oscar Muldoon, the publicist, says of Maria Vargas—whether she was "born with it or got it from a public drinking cup, *she had it*."). Ava Gardner's physical presence, her visual impact on the screen, was stunning. Her performance, however, appeared inhibited, remote, evidencing her difficulties with the role and the lack of rapport with Mankiewicz; though, to be optimistic, the ultimate enigmatic quality of Ava's Maria could be judged as at least partly intrinsic to Mankiewicz's conception, his contessa a case study observed, reflected upon, not an intimate portrait.

As with *Pandora*, the film found its most fervent admirers among the cinephiles of France. "Brilliant, intelligent, and elegant," wrote François Truffaut. "One of the most beautiful portraits of woman ever filmed, in the person of Ava Gardner, Hollywood's most exquisitely beautiful actress." *The Barefoot Contessa* was equally adored by Jean-Luc Godard; Mankiewicz's film, with its erudite dialogue, philosophical discourse, its glamorous Italian setting, and aestheticized visuals, would be the template for Godard's 1963 masterpiece, *Le Mépris* (Contempt).

The day after the premiere, Ava appeared at the Capitol Theater to sign autographs for the film's first patrons. Hundreds of men and women streamed up Broadway to the Capitol foyer, and though there was the occasional anxious scuffle as the people caught their first sight of the movie star, it remained a civil gathering. Ava looked over the orderly crowd, turned to her publicist and winked. "It was more fun in Rio," she said.

United Artists, now aware that their film needed all the extra help it could get, endorsed sending Ava on a second international tour, this one to touch down in Tokyo, Hong Kong, Singapore, Rome, Stockholm, and Berlin, culminating in London for *Contessa*'s British premiere. There was no repeat of the apocalyptic conditions in South America. After a first, frivolous bad impression of Tokyo from the air ("Hell! It looks like North Carolina," she told Hanna. "I hate this place already!"), she came to much enjoy the brisk modern city and the civilized fans who bowed and offered little slips of paper with adoring, handwritten poems. She appeared onstage in Tokyo and enchanted the audience with her endorsement of the local custom of removing one's shoes when entering a home—at which point she happily removed her own and continued the appearance barefoot. In Japan (and later in Germany) she arranged to make appearances at a U.S. military base and hospital, putting on a little show "for the boys," singing her two songs from *Show Boat* plus a rendition of "One for My Baby," a thing her "old man" had recorded back in the forties. In Hong Kong she charmed the gathered crowd by appearing in a traditional Chinese dress, a custom-made silk number with a slit up one leg. At her hotel she ran into another Hollywood American, Bill Boyd, the great Hopalong Cassidy, and at dinner Boyd presented Ava with the tin button and documentation to make her an official member of Hoppy's International Fan Club.

She arrived in London in January, having logged 49,639 miles in the air. Reporters gathered around for the usual inquest.

At thirty-two," Ava told them, "I'm the second oldest actress at MGM. At the studio they call me 'Mother Gardner.' "

"Create? I don't create anything. I leave that to the scriptwriter and the director. I'm not an actress. I have no theories about the job. I just do what it tells me to do in the script. I read it through and usually it is a terrible chore, the same old clichés over and over again."

"I make films for the money."

"I owe my success to luck."

"My mother and father had the happiness I hope to find for myself someday."

"I still believe that the most important thing in life is to be loved."

Released by United Artists into the custody of MGM once more, she was immediately to begin work on a new film, *Bhowani Junction*, playing the Anglo-Indian heroine of John Masters's best-selling novel. Set in the turbulent period prior to Indian independence from Britain, in a North Indian hub full of religious and political tensions and violent rival insurgencies, the story centered around the conflicting allegiances—cultural, national, and personal—of returning Women's Army Corps soldier Miss Victoria

Jones, daughter of an Anglo father and Indian mother. Jones's tripartite identity crisis is explored in romances with men from each of her three worlds, first with a boorish Anglo-Indian, next with a militant Sikh, and finally with an imperious British colonel. The novel was considered by some, mainly Indian intellectuals and politicians, as controversial—racist, imperialist, and/or insulting. The negative response among Indians seemed largely centered around the "airing dirty laundry" aspect of the delicate mixed-race issue and on the fact that the fictional half-Indian Miss Jones had a very active sex life. Others felt that, despite his own service to the Raj, Masters was in fact understanding of all sides in his story and clearly sympathetic to the plight of the Anglo-Indians, and to his heroine, who narrates much of the novel. *Bhowani*'s ingredients—a strong female protagonist, dramatic historical backdrop, scenes of sex, riot, a train wreck, an attempted rape and an attempted assassination—offered the possibility of a subcontinental *Gone With the Wind*, and Metro was providing the budget for an epic production. It was certainly strong, exciting material, and the character of Victoria Jones one of the most complex and nuanced of Ava's career.

The director assigned was George Cukor (whose distinguished filmography included *Dinner at Eight, David Copperfield, Camille, Philadelphia Story,* and *Adam's Rib*), coming to the project direct from his masterful work on the remake of *A Star Is Born* with Judy Garland. That project had in effect sponsored the reinvention of Cukor as an exciting visual stylist, working for the first time in color and wide screen and with the contributions of the famed photographer George Hoyningen-Huene as color consultant. *Bhowani*, too, would benefit from Hoyningen-Huene (and brilliant cinematographer Freddie Young) and from Cukor's new visual adventurism as well as from the decision to make the film on authentic locations. Reasonably authentic, anyway: The original plan to shoot in India was thwarted by a prickly new government determined to have a say in the film's controversial content; Metro made a deal with a cooperative Pakistan instead, and it was arranged that the film would be shot in the ancient Punjabi capital city of Lahore.

Playing the men in Victoria Jones's life were Stewart Granger, Metro's swashbuckler du jour, as the cruel-to-be-kind British colonel Rodney Savage; Bill Travers (an actor from whom the studio was expecting great things, although Cukor was not, and openly disdained the casting choice) as the priggish but ultimately redeemed Anglo-Indian, Patrick; and a young stage actor, Francis Matthews, picked by Cukor to play Ranjit, the sexy Sikh (Cukor claiming to have tested a number of Indian actors for the part, all of them striking him as like "Armenian opera singers").

Renowned for his rapport with actresses, Cukor had directed to great effect most of the Metro movie queens of the last twenty-five years, from Garbo to Lana Turner ("Every bitch on the lot except Lassie," as he put it to Ava), and he was very much looking forward to this first collaboration with the studio's current grand dame. She began the relationship with her back up, as she had hoped for a bit of time off after her draining round-the-world tour, and Cukor had been abrupt in telling her to report for "character-building" preproduction chores. Starting in the first week of January, while berthed at the Savoy in London, Ava met with a speech coach for help in creating a believable rendition of Victoria Jones's British Indian accent; and on several occasions she was taken to a military base out of town to spend time with a Women's Army Corps unit, kitted out in her uniform for the film and following a few genuine WACs on their assignments.

In February members of the production began making their way to Pakistan. There would be in total over one hundred British and American personnel sent to the distant location. Ava had arranged to fly out with Stewart Granger, and took a brief sightseeing stopover with him in Copenhagen. Ava remembered Granger (known to friends as "Jimmy") as "great fun . . . talkative, assertive and a nice guy under it all" (the "under it all" likely a reference to what some considered Stewart Granger's sometimes overbearing surface). Although in Hollywood Ava had been socially friendly with both Granger and his actress wife, Jean Simmons, he would claim that she had blithely attempted to seduce him early in their *Bhowani* sojourn, floating into his hotel room, diaphanously clad, for a late-night heart-to-heart, a temptation Granger said he had abruptly curtailed out of a sense of spousal rectitude.

Ava: "Don't you find me attractive?"

Granger: "You're probably the most attractive woman in the world, but I'm married."

Ava: "Oh, fuck Jean."

Granger: "I'd love to, darling, but she's not here."

Ava remembered the situation a bit differently in her memoir, recording that Granger had acted silly and jumped the gun in his fear of her seductive powers ("Honey," she said she told him, "you've been reading the wrong press clips").

In Lahore the *Bhowani* company was billeted at the venerable Faletti's Hotel on the edge of the commercial district, the city's finest lodging, offering all the modern conveniences of the year 1880. Lahore was an ancient city, containing magnificent palaces and mosques and elaborate gardens and an array of fascinating architectural works in the style known as "Mughal Gothic"; it was also a city beset by hectic overcrowding and squalor. "There were terribly poor people, and the sights you saw were detailed suffering, terribly upsetting," actor Francis Matthews recalled. "To those who were used to London or Beverly Hills it was a damned hard town to live in," remembered Eva Monley, a veteran of the *Mogambo* shoot, who had left her native Kenya to become a part of the Anglo-American film world for the next fifty years. "People didn't like the climate or the dirt. It was a hard case if you didn't know that kind of habit, a lot of people came down ill. We had a very difficult time with the food. Cukor simply refused to eat it, and I couldn't eat much of it either, so we were always sitting together for meals of boiled eggs and not much else."

Ava was given the hotel's grandest two-room suite, room 55—forever after to be known as the "Ava Gardner Suite"—with veranda, multiple overhead fans, bathtub, and private refrigerator (which she would stock with foodstuffs air-shipped from California). But even this luxury failed to bring much comfort. The climate was hellishly humid, and when the electricity failed on many evenings, the fans went from listless to motionless and the temperature would rise another twenty degrees, making sleep impossible—that plus the all-night howling of what the room servant assured her were rabid prowling dogs. Other creatures made their presence known as well. One afternoon a buffet luncheon was held in the hotel gardens with Ava, Granger, Cukor, and many local dignitaries in attendance: No sooner had the great platters been laid out than a black cloud swept over the lawn and descended on the buffet table, squawking carrion crows, sending the guests running in a panic as the birds helped themselves to the feast and even plucked food from people's hands. One night Ava emerged from the bathtub after a long soak and was attacked by a large bat. The flapping, echolocating animal, determined to make a new home in the actress's chestnut hair, chased her from the bathroom and outdoors onto the open veranda. As the maid raced after her to cover Ava's naked body with a towel, a hotel employee responded to her screams and attacked the flying intruder with a tennis racket ("I think that was all a plan of hers," Eva Monley joked, "just to run around with no clothes on").

Conditions away from Faletti's were not as comfortable. "Outside it was teeming," Ava would recall. "Flies, smells, carts, horses, and masses of humanity." As it did many others in the company, the damp, unrelenting heat left Ava continually sweating and exhausted while she worked, and she was often working while just recovered from or just about to fall prey to a bout of fever or dysentery. Sometimes the level of physical discomfort was caught on camera. Once, for a shot filmed in town, in which she was to rush out around a corner from off-camera, she had unknowingly backed into some open sewage, and when she reappeared in camera range she came forth vomiting.

Few in the cast or crew did not become ill, often causing delays or awkward changes in the shooting schedule. At one point the entire company of British stuntmen was confined to sickbed. Stewart Granger's assistant/bodyguard Bob Porter contracted meningitis and nearly died ("rescued" from a local hospital, he was nursed back to health by Ava and others at the hotel). Francis Matthews, who managed to evade the plague of intestinal and other ailments, fell unconscious from heat exhaustion. Director Cukor was often under the weather, but refused to take any time off, keeping himself going with a variety of pills that put him to sleep, woke him up, and fortified him against pain ("Cukor had so many medicines with him," remembered Matthews, "that some of the locals thought he was a doctor").

Many exterior shots called for huge crowd scenes, their coordination at times slowing the work to a crawl, which was no fault of Cukor, who directed the hundreds of extras with the precision of a skilled troop commander, waving a few pages of rolled-up script like a field marshal's swagger stick.

Several sequences in the film took place in and around the clamorous railway depot, and crowds of more than a thousand were required to fill out the background. The extras were recruited and given chits for the next morning's shoot in the evening when filming had concluded for the day. Each evening there was an endless queue of Lahoris eager for the work—

the modest day's pay was for them the equal of an average weekly salary. Some nights there were fights and riots, and the police had to be called in to restore order—to some in the *Bhowani* company it looked so familiar from the script that the rioters might have been rehearsing.

The oppressive atmosphere encouraged frayed tempers. Stewart Granger maintained a running feud with Cukor (who was known to have wanted Trevor Howard for the part of Colonel Savage), disparaging him personally ("Granger," as one member of the production put it, "did not want to work with a man who was going to give him 'infections' ") and professionally as the wrong man for the job. "Here he is, a little homosexual Jew from Brooklyn," Granger recalled to the director's biographer, "and I'm playing an English colonel, and my father was a colonel in the Indian Army, and I was in the English Army, and he's telling me how to say the lines."

Granger, perhaps lost in familial memories, at times behaved as if unaware that the days of the Raj had passed, that the Pakistanis were no longer colonial suppliants. One incident, which might easily have come directly from the film they were making, involved a spat over attentions paid to Ava Gardner by a young Anglo-Pakistani officer. Shah Rafi Alam, the son of the inspector general of West Punjab and a dashing star of the Lahore Polo Club, was enjoying a new acquaintance with the visiting American movie actress, to the evident displeasure of her costar. When at one point Ava somehow found herself sitting in Alam's lap, Stewart Granger had had enough and a brawl ensued. The two scuffled and swung at each other, and the Pakistani officer was said to have landed a solid blow to Granger's nose before onlookers rushed in and pulled them apart.

Part of Granger's complaint about Cukor was that the director had lost sight of the Masters novel, sending the film off in too many directions, many of them emphasizing Victoria and not the colonel. It was true that Cukor had begun filming, against his usual procedure, with a script in disarray. Unhappy with the first version Metro had provided (written by Robert Ardrey), he had gotten Sonya Levien and Ivan Moffat to start from scratch but too late—the screenwriters were still working on many scenes as Cukor had to leave them behind and start off across the globe looking at locations, and after that the filming had to begin. The situation left the director to discover the nuance, the deeper meaning, or the truth of certain scenes through instinct and improvisation with his actors, rather than through the usual long conferences talking things out with the writers. Considering Cukor's traditional empathy for actresses—and his ongoing feud with Granger—it was not surprising that he focused so much attention on the performance and presentation of Ava Gardner. He began working with her, he began filming her, he began considering the results as captured on celluloid. He became fascinated by her. It might be asked if he had ever met an actress who did not fascinate him? (Yes. Lana Turner.) But Ava offered Cukor more than he had expected: extraordinary beauty, of course, and intelligence, and what he saw as a quality of fatalism, of desperation, and a magic on film that he likened to what he had seen long ago in Garbo. Why the hell had no one done anything about this before? Cukor wanted to know. The girl could do marvelous things—she could do marvelous things without doing anything at all, just a turn of her lips, the set of her eyes. He came up with shots just to see how she would look, how she would respond. In scenes like those during Victoria Jones's immersion in Indian culture, scenes with the actress clad in colorful silk saris, Cukor was so enraptured by the look of her that—like Albert Lewin and others before—it was difficult for him to stop shooting, always the urge for one more angle, one more close-up, and then another. As they worked together, the sensuality Cukor saw in his star emboldened him to expand the film's love scenes, almost compulsively adding elements of daring eroticism that he had to know would not escape the censor's scissors. They improvised a passionate sequence with Ava and Bill Travers that Cukor likened to a later, groundbreaking moment in Louis Malle's *Les Amants*: Ava's face in close-up, reacting to what is implied to be Travers in an act of cunnilingus. "Marvelous erotic scenes," Cukor would recall. "All cut by the censors."

"He was very concerned with her," said Francis Matthews. "He was extremely helpful; he would take her aside for long sessions of talk about the scene. He was sure this was going to be an Oscar-winning performance for her. He would talk to her quietly for a very long time and try and inspire her. And when he was done he would turn to give me direction, which usually amounted to him yelling, 'Try and get it right!' "

Matthews, the handsome young British actor Cukor had cast to play Victoria's Sikh lover Ranjit Kasel, was flown out to Pakistan with Lionel Jeffries (playing the villainous Lieutenant McDaniel) several weeks after location filming had begun. He recalled: "When Lionel and I got there Cukor asked us to have dinner with him in his suite. He and Hoyningen-Huene, the color consultant, were an item, and they shared a large suite at the hotel. Cukor did not turn out to be a particularly nice man to me. I have my suspicions why: At the time I was a pretty good-looking man and he was rather predatory. So there was some tension, which was not my fault, you see.

"When we left George's that first night, Lionel and myself, we were coming along the arched corridor below, it was an open terrace, and we walked right into Ava Gardner. She gave us a big greeting. 'Hiya boys! I'm Ava!' And she was just a vision. And she said, 'I'm really glad to see you guys. It's gotten pretty dull around here.' And she talked and joked with us, and she was terribly funny and she was absolutely adorable.

"I didn't see her again right away because George Cukor sent me off to Amritsar, the holy city of the Sikhs, to do some studying of the religion, to help me understand the character. He wanted everything in the film to feel authentic. So off I went to meet with the gurus, and I was allowed inside the temple and I observed the ceremonies. And Cukor also had me working with an Indian adviser to help me with an accent, and I went through the script with him phonetically so I would sound like an Indian, and I learned from him how to speak with a very strong Indian accent. Which it turned out George wouldn't let me do at all. The first time I opened my mouth for a scene he screamed at me, 'What's with that god-damned chinky Chinese accent!'

"So I had been away, and I'd returned from Amritsar. I hadn't started acting yet. I was in my room, it was late in the evening, almost midnight, and I got a phone call. It was Ava. She said, 'I'm sorry, did I disturb you? I know it's late but I can't sleep, and it's so damn hot. How do you feel about going out into the town with me? I'm not shooting tomorrow, and I've been stuck in my room and I want to go out!'

"So, of course, I said, 'Yes, Ava. All right. I'm not shooting tomorrow either. I'll call a cab.' She said, 'No, I want to go out and find a tonga.' Which was a covered horse-drawn carriage. One of the studio publicity men caught up with us. He said, 'Listen here. Ava's told me that she's going into the town with you.' He was very concerned. I was very green and young and didn't know there were any rules about such things. But I learned. She was considered rather like royalty. They watched over her and were afraid of her mingling with ordinary people. It was just like in the film *Roman Holiday*. And the publicity man said, 'She wants to do this, and we don't think this is a good idea. You'd better take good care of her.'

"We went anyway. We were gone for hours, explored all over the city. At about one or two o'clock in the morning Ava said she wanted to see one of the houses with the 'dancing girls.' That was a euphemism. They were really brothels.

"We headed deep into the old native quarters, very murky. And a guy stopped us. He said, 'I know who is this lady. She should not be here. This is very dangerous.' We told him what we were doing, and he climbed into the tonga with us, saying, 'I will take you where you want to go. But you must let me protect you. It is very bad here.' And he took us to a place. A very simple place with a couple of musicians playing sitar and about five girls, and Ava and I sat on the floor cross-legged. And the man in charge had the girls dance for us. And the musicians must have played the only Western tune they knew, to please us. Ava said, 'Goddammit, that's 'The Isle of Capri.' Can't you play something else?' And so then they played the same song, but much faster.

"We had a glorious time together. And then a couple of nights later she asked me to accompany her to the movie premiere in the town: It was the premiere of *The Barefoot Contessa*. And we went to the premiere, and we were photographed for the newspapers. Right after that we started working together. She was very kind to me and very protective when Cukor started screaming at me all the time. He screamed at me for six months. And Ava kept telling me I shouldn't put up with his rudeness. She said, 'Just walk off the set.' Particularly when we got back to England and he was very nasty. She'd say, 'Walk off until he apologizes. What's he going to do, recast? Go back to Asia and reshoot for months?'

"We became good friends. We'd run our lines together. And we began eating together in her suite—she couldn't eat the local stuff, and she had things like T-bone steaks and American fries flown in every week. And we talked about everything under the sun. She was amazingly well read. Erudite. She was particularly well read about England. She loved English people. And Englishmen! She said they were polite and kind. And she was in a period when she loathed Hollywood. And she hated the press because they had pretty well torn her and Frank to pieces—not that they hadn't torn themselves to pieces, you know. It was a time when she had divorced Sinatra, or what she had told me was she was divorced but she had not yet picked up the papers. She was the nicest person to be with, very down-to-earth about everything. And she was just adorable. She was free, she wasn't married, and neither was I. It became a wonderful relationship."

The company returned to England in April.* Everyone felt as if they had been filming for a year, but there was still half a movie to be made, with exterior sequences—including the train wreck—to be shot in the English countryside, and nearly all the interiors as well as some soundstage exteriors left to be done in the MGM studios at Elstree. A terrible drama, a near tragedy, and much unexpected extra work was caused when Joseph Tomalty, the lovable and talented Irish comic actor who was playing Victoria's railwayman father and had filmed many scenes with Ava in Pakistan, was the victim of a serious auto accident. He just escaped death and remained disabled for several years. It meant replacing him (with Edward Chapman) and reshooting most of his dialogue scenes, and simply discarding several of them (the original actor can still be glimpsed in some of the long shots taken in Lahore). It was one of many blows to the finished film, as Tomalty and Ava had reportedly had a great deal of warm chemistry on camera as father and daughter, something that was not duplicated in the abruptly staged version with Chapman.

The most dramatic scene in the film had been saved for the English studio: the attempted rape of Victoria Jones and her killing of the assailant, the British officer McDaniel. Staged for maximum discomfort in an ugly, slimy reproduction of the railway yard, it involved McDaniel in a vicious attack, tearing at Victoria Jones's clothes, her hair, dragging her through the muck, a horrifying, violent degradation until Jones manages to grab a piece of iron railing and land a mortal blow to the lieutenant's skull. The sequence was brilliantly designed and photographed, blending the location footage with the soundstage set into a vision of muddy hell. As filmed

---

*According to local legend, on the film company's departure from Pakistan a Lahori gentleman with the wherewithal purchased from someone at Faletti's Hotel the pillow on which Ava Gardner slept during her stay at the hotel; fifty years later the pillow was said to remain a prized possession of this unnamed man.

it was a bold, almost transgressive scene for a Hollywood production of the mid-1950s, powerful and painful. Ava Gardner, throwing herself into it body and soul, performed with an abandon and intensity she had never before attempted. The scene became for her a kind of breakthrough, a revelation to herself of the possibilities she possessed as an actress, though one achieved at great emotional cost. Anticipation of having to perform the scene had given her an extreme anxiety attack, and she felt worse during and after the performance. When it was over she was trembling and shaking, Ava would recall, and she left the set without speaking to anyone, ran inside her trailer, and swallowed a great deal of whiskey. "At that moment I felt sick with fright," she remembered, "as if I'd been literally fighting for my life." When Cukor came to comfort her she demanded he bring Lionel Jeffries to see her at once. "Now! Because unless I see him and give him a big hug, I'll never speak to him as long as I live." Jeffries, of course, came over for his hug, and Ava eventually calmed down. She had never performed anything that so deeply affected her, and never would again.

Ava's close friendship with Francis Matthews continued in England. "Cukor didn't like it much. He eventually separated us. He said, 'I'm sending her away. You're distracting her. She's too fond of you. It's not good.'

"I was young, and I didn't know really whether it was love or if it was infatuation with a big star. I suppose that might have been part of it. With me she was just like a young girl. We used to laugh; we had great fun together. I played cricket all the time, I was with the Stage Cricket Club and I was always going off to play. 'What the hell, are you going to play cricket again?' she'd say. And one day she had me take her to Lord's. She said, 'I want to see what this goddamned game is about.' And we conned our way into the members' stand because it was Ava Gardner. And she couldn't stand the game. She'd say, 'This guy has hit the ball three times, why doesn't he run?' I would explain, and she'd say, 'I can't imagine why you want to play this stupid game!' But then she'd say to me, 'I want to marry you and have a lot of little cricketers.'

"We had some funny times then . . ."

Cukor completed *Bhowani Junction* by early summer. His first cut of the film ran just over two and a half hours. It was, according to some of the handful who saw this version, an exceptional film in all ways, of true epic dimension, capturing the color and sound and fury of India, and at its center a magnificent performance by Ava Gardner that was powerful, sensitive, and erotic. Within hours of the director delivering his version of the film, the knives of the second-guessers were out and flashing. From producer Pandro Berman and various voices in Hollywood there were immediate calls for cuts, changes, rewrites, and reshoots. Eventually they would demand a major reconstruction of the film's plot and its theme. Having invested millions and months in a story whose entire premise revolved around the problems of love, race, and ethnicity, the studio now concluded that this premise would be the movie's undoing in the marketplace. It was belatedly determined that audiences did not want to see Ava Gardner kissing the Anglo-Indian character played by Bill Travers or the good-looking Sikh played by Francis Matthews. It did not matter that all the lovers on the screen were either British or American in various shades of Max Factor. "The last twenty minutes of my role disappeared," recalled Francis Matthews. "The people at the sneak previews in England and America said, 'Why is she kissing an Indian?' My loves scenes with Ava were cut right out." Instead of the ending Cukor had shot, from Masters's book, with Bill Travers's character, Patrick, ending up with Victoria Jones (Masters's endorsement of the Anglo-Indians as worthy citizens of an independent India), there was a new ending in which Patrick is killed (the climax of the film in the railway tunnel filmed again, this time in an abandoned London Underground station). To cover all the missing pieces and gaps in the narrative and to put more focus on the story's one European love interest, a voice-over was recorded by Stewart Granger so that Col. Savage became the film's narrator, telling the story—often redundantly—in flashback. The released cut of the film ran 110 minutes, 40 minutes—and several subplots—short of Cukor's version.

Francis Matthews, who came in long after filming ended to dub some lines for the new cut of the film, recalled a very distraught George Cukor fighting the studio's changes. "This is the gospel truth: Cukor was in tears in the dubbing room. He said, 'Get Pandro Berman here. I'm not going to do this; this is ruining my movie. We did this right the first time, why are we changing it?' And he wouldn't do anything until Pandro was there, and they had this terrible row and George burst into tears. He said, 'Listen, I made a good movie here. You are crucifying this movie and turning it into a goddamn Hollywood love story, and it's going to be crap.' It was quite an experience witnessing this. I had my problems with George, but I realized then how deeply concerned he was about his work and how much he had put into it. And he was dead right. He had made an incredible film. There were scenes in it that were overwhelming, beautiful, and they took them out. It was such a good film, and it became a good film struggling to get out, struggling to get out.''

George Cukor's admiration for Ava's performance and his fascination with her as a star remained undiminished. They stayed friends, and for many years Cukor tried to find viable projects for a creative reunion. While he was still finishing up with *Bhowani Junction* in London, he entertained an idea for filming a new version of *Carmen* outlined by critic and cultural gadfly Kenneth Tynan, and Cukor at once felt it would be a perfect vehicle for Ava. In late May he brought Tynan with him to a lunch with the actress. No film ever came of the meeting, although Ava found the stuttering, wickedly witty Tynan amusing company and brought him into her circle of London friends. Tynan would recall with a mixture of enthusiasm and horror a night spent out and about with the movie star, "six enthusiastic flamenco singers and several bottles of vodka." Miss Gardner, he wrote to critic Cyril Connolly (by way of apology for broken engagement due to night with Gardner, hangover, and so on), "is . . . not easily discouraged when she gets the smell of riot in her nostrils, and I allowed myself to be swept in an open car across London with her entourage, which was joined at odd times by a policeman and a rich swimmer named Esther Williams, on whose presence Miss Gardner insisted, saying that a party wasn't a party without a drunken bitch lying in a pool of tears."

Ava's obligations to *Bhowani Junction* concluded in July. She was returning to Spain, permanently now, she had decided, with plans to buy a house. A few possessions she prized—a piano, her silver and linens—were being shipped from Los Angeles. "I want a place just outside Madrid," she told people. "If I don't find the right place I'll build something. My new contract says I make two films a year. Some of them may be a piece of cheese, I don't have the right to approve scripts in advance, and if some of them are made in Hollywood I'll go there, but home will be Spain."

For Ava and Francis Matthews there were a few last nights on the town together. "We went to dinner, and we went round to the nightclubs getting stoned, as was her pleasure. We went out with her English friends, who were from every sort of background. She could go all night, you know. She was a wild country girl and liked to let her hair down and fling off her shoes and have a good time."

They would go on till every club had closed down for the night, and she would lead them off to Covent Garden, behind the opera house, where the vegetable markets would be open all night. And she would get everyone drinks and she would chat with the vegetable porters who were working (and who all seemed to know her) and she would dance the flamenco, there in Covent Garden with the sun about to come up.

"I was wild about her. I really was. We were neither of us responsible to anybody else for our lives, so it wasn't wrong or anything, but I was a strong cradle Catholic and took these things very seriously. It's very difficult to describe what I was like then, very naive. And Ava was trying not to take things so seriously. She had been hurt by men, I think. She had been with these guys who had not been so nice to her, and I don't think they knew how lucky they were, actually. And Ava used to say to me, 'Bloody Frankie was a confused Catholic as well, with his wife and all, confused about his religion and everything.' She'd say, 'I keep picking Catholics.' She gave me a photograph of herself and on the photo this is what she wrote:

'To Francis, my favorite Sikh
I send all my love at least once a week
though unnaturally meek as a good Catho-lic
be careful my boy 'cause I'm taking a peek.'

"Then she was gone, off to Spain. She wrote to me a couple of times. The last time I saw her was the year after we finished *Bhowani*. They were starting a film [*The Little Hut*] and I think Mark Robson was the director, and they needed to do a reading with David Niven and Ava and Stewart Granger, but Granger was not available, he was working in Hollywood. And someone rang round and asked if I would do a reading with Ava and Niven. So I agreed to do it. Most actors who'd just had a starring role would have refused, but I did it because I wanted to see Ava again. And it was a lovely meeting. I didn't see her after that. She lived near me many years later. But I never saw her again. She had moved on. It was something she did, have a close friend on a movie and then she'd go on with her life. She was very practical in that way."

NINE

Sun and Shadow

Two o'clock in the morning, a gray Cadillac convertible races over La Coruna highway north of Madrid, the driver a woman whose auburn-red hair flies in the dry, warm wind. Next to her sits a beautiful young Spaniard with broad shoulders and narrow hips. . . . Through the barbed-wire gate the woman drives into the garage and disappears with her companion. A record player intones melancholic flamenco songs. Later, a door opens and two nude figures come out and jump into the pool for a swim in the starlit night.

—"Ava Gardner: The Bullfighters' Delight"

She's running away from things and she's searching for things—heaven knows what.

—British newspaper item

She has become The Barefoot Contessa.

—British newspaper item

In December 1955, they moved into the new home at La Moraleja: Ava, Beatrice, Reenie, and Rags. The ranch-style villa was set on two acres of plush lawn amid scattered pines and weeping willows with tan hillside as distant backdrop. It had the advantages of space, comfort, and privacy and yet was only an eighteen-minute drive from the center of Madrid (nine if Ava was driving).

There were four bedrooms, three baths, two sitting rooms, a parlor, several large, raised fireplaces, a patio, and a swimming pool (said to be the largest private pool in the country). The purchase price had been fifty thousand dollars and she had spent another twenty-five thousand dollars on alterations, including wall-to-wall carpeting and mirrors for her bedroom walls and for the ceiling above her bed. For furnishings she roamed the region for weeks, selecting items in exclusive antiques shops, and in rustic flea markets. There were Louis XV tables and dressers under old hanging coach lights bought for a few coins. When they arrived from Los Angeles, her music filled one wall from floor to ceiling, overlooking the new state-of-the-art hi-fi system; to the thousands of jazz and pop records were added a growing selection of locally purchased flamenco recordings (dancing to that dark, dramatic sound had become her new obsession).

The developers had nicknamed the place *La Bruja*—the Witch—after the rooftop weathervane with its broomstick-riding iron crone. Ava approved: Frank had called her that many times, in anger and with affection, for the way she could read his mind and the many times she had predicted things and they had come to be so.

Buying a home at the same time and just down the road, were Ava's acquaintances of the past two years, Ricardo and Betty Sicre. For the long Iberian adventure ahead, the Sicres would become the closest of her new friends, at times her protectors, her counselors, and with their children her surrogate family in Spain. They were smart, dashing, wealthy, and well-connected to Spanish society and to the expatriate community. Ricardo was a Catalan who had fought in the Spanish civil war, became an American citizen, and served in World War II as an OSS espionage agent. Betty Lussier had been an air transport pilot in the war, then switched to spying, first as one of the handful of American agents working with the top-secret British unit decoding the German Enigma machine (her godfather was superspy Sir William Stephenson, better known by his code name, Intrepid), then as an agent in the field, a member of X-2 branch, tracking down German agents in Italy and France. The two spies met while interrogating Nazis, fell in love, married, and after the peace settled in Spain where Ricardo established a highly successful import-export business.

"Ricardo met her first," Betty Sicre remembered. "I was away in Morocco. He said, 'I've just met this wonderful girl.' He liked her very much, and the way he talked about her, as a nice country girl from North Carolina, I don't think he even knew how famous she was. And we met, and we liked each other immediately. She was a bit of a lost soul then, separated from Frank, and not quite sure what she wanted to do with herself. She only knew that she wanted to be away from Hollywood. She had a lot of memories she wanted to leave behind. She felt that she had never fitted in there. The way she spoke of it, she had come there with so little experience and had been dropped among these very sophisticated people. She was so young and she had gotten thrown into that fast life, a very debauched scene from the way she described it, people involved in drugs and sex things. That was why she started drinking, to try and cope. A lot of troubled people she had known in Hollywood. She spoke of Robert Walker, who had destroyed himself; it bothered her. And all the trauma with Frank. She wanted a fresh start. She was very shy—people find it hard to believe—and she did not like the constant social pressures and the constant prying of the press. In Spain she thought she could get away from all of that.

"We were all looking for a place and Ava said, 'Let's see if we can find something together.' And La Moraleja was just beginning to be developed. There were maybe eleven houses there—now there are thousands. So we found these two houses being finished and we told Ava to take her choice, and she took the one nearest the entrance gate and we took the one two houses further on. So, there we were, neighbors; and we became very close for many years and she was around while we raised our family and she was the godmother to my son; she had the kids stay with her on occasion and they cooked supper together and she'd put them to bed. She was great with kids. So she was a part of our lives and we became part of hers. . . . I took care of her fan mail for years. There was an enormous amount, and people just poured their hearts out to her. Now and then there was a letter that I'd say, 'Ava, you really have to answer this one.' But she was really not interested in it, and the most she would do was sign the pictures for people who asked for one . . . and, oh, she'd give me scripts they would send her to do and say, 'Read this, tell me if you think I should do it.' Otherwise she would send them all back. She had by then cut herself off from the studio people and advisers who might have helped with this sort of thing. She was really on her own.

"She didn't really much want to work. My husband thought she was a very lazy person, and I guess that was right. She liked to sleep late, and she was very lax about exercise. But she had positively the most beautiful body you could ever imagine. And she wasn't like some other beautiful stars who spend two hours getting ready before anyone can see them. She got up in the morning and she never even looked at her face, never looked in a mirror. She just popped out of bed and ran a hand through her hair. She wasn't a vain person at all.

"She wasn't big on many activities. She swam well and was a pretty good tennis player and she played some golf. But she slept so late the day was pretty much over by the time she got out. She was a night person. She liked to go out all night, and she really liked the life in Madrid because it started so late and went on so long."

There was a large, growing expatriate scene in Madrid, and Ava quickly became its glamorous centerpiece. "It was a wonderful, fun time in Spain in the fifties," recalled Imogen Wheeler, a resident for much of the decade. "It was rather like you read about Paris or the Riviera in the twenties. You met lots of interesting English-speaking people, film people and artists and writers as well as the usual business people and diplomats. But it wasn't one of those expat groups where they avoided the local life or tried to re-create things as they were at home. Everyone was very much part of the Spanish scene, lived a Spanish life.

"I met Ava through the Grants, Frank and Doreen. They had a wonderful villa on the edge of Madrid, and we used to all go out there on Fridays, party all weekend, come in for the bullfights on Sunday. We ate wonderful meals and drank and danced all night. I couldn't believe it when I saw her the first time. She had this face that was so beautiful, this extraordinary pale skin, like marble. I had loved seeing her in the films, but it was nothing like seeing her up close. The films gave you no idea that she was so exquisite!

"I knew them both. Bappie came to live with her. And I found them such completely different people. Ava was this extraordinary-looking, moody, complicated character. And Bappie was just this simple, fun-loving person, always joking, with this bright blond dyed hair and this blue mink stole she wore everywhere. She was going along for the ride, you know, and having fun. Very simple reaction to everything, the way she looked at life. She used to take things, I remember—yes, she would see something on the table at a restaurant or a dinner party, like the terra-cotta wine stands on the table or something like that, and she would just swipe them off the table and hide them under her stole. She'd just think, Ooh, that's nice. I think I'll take that with me. We'd all look at each other and not know what to say, and Bappie just went on like nobody had noticed."

Ava's arrival to stay, her many warm remarks about Spain, were met with affection and respect by the Spanish people. "Which couldn't have been easy," she would say. "After all, I represented everything they disapproved of: I was a woman, living alone, divorced, a non-Catholic, and an actress." Indeed the time was to come, as the reports of Ava's antic private life accumulated through the years, that the local attitude toward their most famous foreign resident would turn increasingly ambivalent. For now, anyway, good feeling reigned all around. She was adored, and politely. In Spain she could be a star but without all the pushing and shoving. "She could go most places without any problem at all," said Betty Sicre. "She would go to the bullfights with Bappie or a friend, just the two of them, and it was no problem. They left her alone." Ava liked to ascribe the respectful reaction of press and public to the national character, though in truth she was benefiting as much from Franco's stern fascist rule. For instance, the idea of reporters and photographers staking out a person's home as they did in Hollywood was unthinkable—everyone would be carted off to jail. ("She was very liberal politically," Betty Sicre recalled. "And she was very interested in what was going on in the U.S. elections, but she didn't get involved in Spanish politics. She never spoke Franco's name once that I can remember.")

In those first months Ava was full of a determination to fit in, to become something more than a tourist in her new country of residence. At home she took Spanish lessons from an elderly local teacher. The study would go well for a brief while, but eventually Ava would feel the need to offer teacher and student a reward for their diligence—*dos* martinis, or perhaps a pitcher of them since Reenie made them so well, and the lesson would be over for the day. Her spoken Spanish would never get much beyond the rudimentary.

She eagerly explored other parts of the country, often on road trips with Bappie or Reenie, heading out in the car to visit the fascinating old cities of Seville and Barcelona, driving through primitive whitewashed villages in the southern plains, mingling with Gypsy enclaves in Grenada. Her fascination with the flamenco grew. No less obsessive than the aficionados of the *corrida* who traveled the country to see every important fight, she haunted the flamenco clubs wherever she went, a patron of assorted Gypsy bands, drinking wine and brandy and gin and dancing the paso doble with them into the night. When there was no place to continue, she gathered them up, brought them home, and continued until dawn. "She became very taken with the Gypsy scene," recalled Imogen Wheeler. "It was not touristy like it is today, but very authentic and gritty, and you could have these fantastic nights. There were streets in Madrid, narrow old streets lined with bars on both sides, and you went in and out from one to the next through the night, filling your wineglass at each one, all of them with flamenco singers and musicians playing for tips or for free drinks. Or in Grenada, these caves where an entire family of Gypsies would be playing and dancing, from children to grandparents. When it would be very late at night and people were starting to leave, Ava would invite them to her place, and for some wine or some *pesetas* they would come and play and dance until morning."

Early in March Ava went off to spend a week on the island of Majorca with the renowned British poet, scholar, and novelist (*I, Claudius*, among others) Robert Graves. She had met the loftily—and impishly—brilliant Graves sometime before at a party at the Sicres', had been unaware of his name or work, and had thought him to be a vacationing scientist. It was the awkward start to a relationship Ava would eventually describe as "one of the most gratifying of my life." Said Betty Sicre, "Graves and my husband had met in a pub in England before the war and became fast friends. We used to visit him, and he came to stay with us. One time Ava was moping around Madrid, complaining that she had nothing to do, and I said, 'Why don't you go and visit Robert Graves?' She was interested in poetry and writers, and she thought that was something to do. And so we sent her off to go see Robert."

The Graves family came to meet her at the Palma airport, Ava arriving in a typical swirl of chaos, pursued across the San Bonet tarmac by two amorous Spanish wolves who had forced her, she said, to lock herself in the ladies' room for much of the flight from Madrid. "I was about twelve, and I was feeling great excitement at the chance to meet her," remembered

Lucia Graves, the writer's daughter. "I was then a student at the convent school right next to the airport, and I had to tell the nuns that an aunt of mine was arriving because they would never have let me go to meet Ava Gardner, a film star!

"First of all I couldn't believe how beautiful she was when she came down the steps off the plane. Just exquisite. And then I didn't believe how very normal and nice and straightforward she was. I remember telling her how I thought she was such a wonderful actress, and she said, 'Do you really think so?' She seemed genuinely surprised. She acted nothing like I imagined. She talked and laughed like any normal person! She was funny and very affectionate. She was just great."

Robert Graves, who had written of goddesses and temptresses as Ava had played the same on screen, had agreed to the Sicres' request that he take her under his wing with an eye to the possibilities of a professional liaison. "The glamour of Hollywood had always excited my father," said Lucia Graves. "He always had this Hollywood dream, trying to get these scripts going. So I'm sure he was tickled that this famous film star showed so much interest in him and wanted to read his poems. He enjoyed it. But then she was such a lovely person that he came to have a great affection for her—as we all did. And he admired her enormously for the way she fought against being tied down by Hollywood and trying to stick to her own ideas, her own way of living."

Ava arrived with a list she had drawn up of resolutions for Robert and his family to help implement: She must rest, swim in the sea, study Spanish grammar, and learn about poetry. As it turned out, there would be no time for studying Spanish, and Ava allowed no one to rest during the five-day visit. One cold winter morning on Camp de Mar beach, she did get to plunge into the freezing Mediterranean, to the silent awe of a crowd of gawkers. As for the poetry: She confessed to Graves that she seldom understood the things she had read. Robert reassured her, "You aren't supposed to understand it. You're supposed to enjoy it." Further, he told her, there was "little worth reading and much that was wrongly supposed to be worth reading." He gave her, though, one of his own ("Not to Sleep"), written sometime before he met her, but it seemed to fit the person he was coming to know, "pledged to love through all disaster."

A large party was given at the Graves home. In those days in Franco's Spain, you had to advise the Guardia Civil of your intention of having a gathering in your house, and a couple of guards would be sent along to see there was no trouble. "There was music and dancing, and Ava decided she wanted to dance with one of the Guardia Civil," Lucia Graves remembered. "And he refused. He said he was sorry, but he was on duty and could not dance. And she was rather surprised. She couldn't believe this young man was saying no to dancing with Ava Gardner! Everyone laughed about it and pulled his leg a bit, and the poor boy apologized and said he was only doing his duty, and Ava forgave him."

Ava had to see the nightlife of Palma, of course, and night after night dragged her hosts from one bar and *tablao* to another. It was exhausting entertaining her, and Beryl and Robert were soon taking turns staying up all night with their guest so one or the other could get to bed. Nevertheless, for Robert the five days proved "a most fantastic experience," and a warm friendship was founded. Robert and his wife had completed a film treatment, a bullfighting story called "El Embrujo de Sevilla," and Ava had taken a copy away with enthusiasm, declaring that she would get MGM to produce it. The studio rejected the idea abruptly, but Ava would continue to promote other potential projects for them, including a collaboration with Albert Lewin as director and a version of *I, Claudius* to be made in Rome with Ava in the role of the wicked Messalina.

Ava and the Graves family would visit each other many times in the years ahead, and with Robert she would carry on a long and heartfelt correspondence. He would send her poems with handwritten dedications, and she would write to him, sometimes with superficial highlights of recent events and passed-along greetings, other times as if to a spiritual adviser, seeking meaning and understanding in what often seemed her inchoate life. "It was a love-conspiracy between us," she would record, though explaining that there was never a thought of a physical relationship with the white-haired family man thirty years her senior. "Being with him and his wonderful wife, Beryl, and the kids gave me a kind of pleasure and satisfaction nothing else in my life could approach."

In mid-April 1956, she had gone to Monaco to attend the wedding of Grace Kelly to Prince Rainier Grimaldi, joining such luminaries as Egypt's ex-king Farouk, Gloria Swanson, the Duchess of Westminster, Somerset Maugham, Aristotle Onassis, and the Aga Khan. Ava had greater claim to an invitation than most—the whole thing had been set in motion at her flat in London where she had introduced Grace to gadabout journalist Rupert Allan, who had then dragged Grace to the Cannes Film Festival, where a photo opportunity with the prince turned into an engagement. Rainier, head of the oldest continuously ruling family in Europe, had been advised to take a high-profile American for his bride and reap the rewards of good PR and U.S. investment in his postage-stamp-size principality (as Dore Schary had rudely pointed out to the prince during a lunch in his honor at Metro, all of Monaco was smaller than the studio's back lot). The wedding had therefore been planned with maximum worldwide attention in mind, with its starry international guest list, and more press coverage than the invasion of Normandy on D-Day. The entire ceremony was filmed in 35mm and color under contract to Metro-Goldwyn-Mayer, with klieg lights everywhere for the sake of the big cameras, causing many guests to squint and don their sunglasses. From all the imported technicians, hairdressers, and publicists, it looked to Ava as though half of Culver City was in Monte Carlo. It was a goddamned MGM movie. She wondered if someone wouldn't call for a couple of retakes after the bride and groom had said their "I do's."

She had felt, beneath genuine happiness for her friend Gracie, a certain uncomfortable envy. The young woman, only twenty-six now, had charted the course of her life so smoothly, had come to Hollywood, conquered it in a year or two, grown tired of it, and quickly found a spectacular plan of escape. And Ava had seen at the wedding Grace's father giving her away, and imagining the love and support the girl must have received from him, she had fallen into a funk thinking of her own long-gone father and how much she could have used such a person in her life to lean on. The grass was always greener. She was unaware of the actual, more difficult relationship between Grace and her father, and not much more aware of the things that had made Kelly eager to jump ship in Hollywood: the whispered word-of-mouth campaigns against her, Hedda and Louella calling her a home wrecker for her affairs with some of her venerable costars.

At the wedding there was one missing celebrity from the guest list: Frank Sinatra. His seat for the ceremony, two away from Ava's (Rupert Allan between them for safety sake) would remain empty. He had come as far as London and then stopped. At the last minute the prospect of being so close to the woman who could do such damage to his ever-roiling psyche became too much for him. He returned home, letting it be known that he had not wanted to spoil Miss Kelly's day by causing unwanted commotion from the press.

But a reunion *was* at hand. Later that spring Sinatra was bound for Spain on a sixteen-week sojourn to star with Cary Grant and Sophia Loren in a film for Stanley Kramer, *The Pride and the Passion.*

Hedda Hopper had quizzed him just before his polar flight from Los Angeles.

"I'm looking forward to many exciting things," said Sinatra.

"Such as meeting Ava?" said Hopper.

"If I do meet Ava it will be in some public place. It will be a casual matter—hello, how are you, goodbye."

"No chance of a reconciliation?"

"There would have to be a complete change. . . . But complete. I don't think that could happen."

Shooting for the Kramer film was to be done mostly in Escorial and the countryside beyond, but Sinatra, no fan of location discomforts, had insisted on commuting from Madrid, where he was headquartered at the Castellana Hilton. To keep him company, Frank had brought along a new girlfriend, a pretty starlet named Peggy Connolly. But it became clear to everyone that his thoughts—however unspoken, and God forbid anyone else try to speak of such things in his presence—often turned to the missing, chestnut-haired woman who resided just outside the city. They had not lived in such close proximity for this long in nearly two years. But tempting as it was—grueling as it was—Sinatra stood his ground. In the end it was Ava who made the call, treating it as lightly as she might a ring-up to an uncle passing through from back home, though perhaps a bit less respectfully.

"You fuckin' idiot," she said. "You don't let me know you're in town? I have to read it in the papers?"

They chatted. Then they chatted again. Somebody said Peggy Connolly didn't think much of that, so Frank said for somebody to pack Peggy Connolly's stuff and take her the fuck to the airport.

They agreed to go out to dinner one night with some other people and then sat whispering to each other all through the meal as if no one else were there. After dinner they parted respectfully. Later in the night Frank had returned to his suite, and as assorted cronies and guests lay about having a nightcap, Frank got her on the phone. They were talking and then Frank began singing softly to her through the phone, one tune after another, a regular concert in sotto voce. Twenty minutes later guests saw Ava Gardner come through the door of the suite, and then she and Frank disappeared. Ava was wearing a mink coat and a negligee.

It was a one-night stand, not a reconciliation. But it was proof, just as Frank had said: They weren't over. Betty Sicre: "She realized that she was really still tied up with Sinatra emotionally. And I think that never changed. He was on her mind in some way just about every day of her life. She was hung up on him. She really loved him but they both had a temperament that blew up when they were together. You know, jealous when there was no need to be, and all of that. . . . Now and then they caught up with each other and considered starting again. At one point Frank wanted it very much. He would never have lived in Europe, but it was one of those times when they thought it might happen for them again and he offered to settle in New York with her. They planned for it. They would live in the East. They were going to have an apartment in the city and a place out on Long Island, on the sea. But it was wishful thinking. They couldn't make a life. And after a time Frank, I think, finally gave up on the idea and so did she. It was just a dream they sometimes shared together."

In the meantime. She already had a new love interest. Walter Chiari had been obsessed with her from the moment they had first met in Rome more than two years earlier, during the filming of *The Barefoot Contessa*. A ruggedly handsome Milanese two years younger than Ava, Chiari was a film and stage star in Italy, little known elsewhere in the world. The son of a policeman and a schoolteacher, Chiari had started as a vaudeville comedian and mimic and quickly rose to local stardom. He made movie comedies, many of them with another Italian favorite, the homely comic actor Toto. Press releases referred to Chiari as "the Danny Kaye of Italy." Ava had gone to see him perform. In his act he did a much-talked-about imitation of Frank Sinatra; Ava, in the audience, had reportedly "roared with laughter." He had come to see her at Cinecittà; he came again, joined her entourage for drinks and supper, and for a week or two he made a little space for himself on the periphery of her life, ready but not quite able to take things further when Domínguin arrived on the scene. (Chiari's girl-friend at the time and for the previous four years was actress Lucia Bose, who subsequently met and married Luis Miguel after Ava had turned down his proposal; the celebrity life in Europe was every bit as incestuous as it was in Hollywood.)

She had gone away to Spain and beyond after that, but Chiari had never stopped thinking about her. When she did return to Rome for some shop-ping he went to her, poured on the charm, took her out on the town. At last, after still more waiting and sniffing for his chance, Chiari found the stars in alignment. By the summer of 1956 they had begun an affair; they were working together on a movie and Chiari had moved in with her at her rented apartment on the Corso d'Italia. In Rome he took no chance that she would slip out of his grasp again. He stayed so close to her at all times that he learned to speak English just from watching her lips move. Ava found him amusing, good-looking, smart, and sexy. Some said he re-sembled Sinatra, though Chiari was taller and brawnier and didn't take himself nearly as seriously.

Bhowani Junction opened that spring. Box-office returns were very good at first, then quickly declined. Critical notices were mixed but often very pos-itive, especially for the film's star. Despite all the cutting and tampering, the quality of Ava's performance remained much in evidence. A keen if condescending admirer of the actress for many years, Leonard Mosley in the *Daily Express*, wrote: "She moves for all times out of the slapandtickle class of pinup stars. . . . Ava Gardner's lovely face, skillfully given just the right touch of chi-chi plumpness, did not for once touch me as much as the quality in her voice and the look in her eyes—a look which not only made her into an actress, but showed that now she had grown up in other ways. . . . Will she go on allowing her studio to put her in any old part? Or will she use the intelligence and ability she has now obviously acquired and pick her roles according to the acting opportunities they offer?"

For many months after *Bhowani Junction* had concluded filming, she had turned down every picture she had been offered, whether from Metro, from Bert Allenberg, her new agent at William Morris, from various European producers. She read some of the novels or the scripts they would send, gave some to friends in the film world like George Cukor or to her neighbors the Sicres, asking for advice, and others simply never got read, got left on an airplane or in a hotel room or fell into the swimming pool. No doubt there were some she would have been smart to accept, but many of the known offers were wisely rejected. Warner Bros. had wanted to reteam her with Clark Gable for a paltry Civil War drama called *A Band of Angels*, like *Show Boat* and *Bhowani* a story revolving around a female of "mixed blood," what Hollywood had evidently come to see as one of her specialties. Cukor read it. He told her: *"You'd be awful good in it . . . you jes talk lak you done in Grabtown and it's be perfect."* Cukor himself tried to find projects for them to do together. For two years he worked in vain to get Metro to back a new production of *Her Cardboard Lover*, a warhorse of a romantic comedy he had previously directed to no great acclaim in 1942, Norma Shearer's cinema swan song.

At last the next film was decided for her. Metro cast her as the horny heroine of *The Little Hut*, a French sex farce by André Roussin that had been translated into a West End hit by Nancy Mitford. She had reservations about what appeared to be very thin, silly material, but to let any more time go by without working meant extending her studio contract even farther into the future ("If I took another suspension they'd keep me at Metro for the rest of my life"). The film starred her with Stewart Granger and David Niven, and the director was Mark Robson. Most of the movie would be filmed on a single interior set at Cinecittà, with a few exterior sequences shot in London, and a second unit sent off to photograph some tropical scenery in Jamaica. Ava played Lady Susan Ashlow, Granger her inattentive husband, and Niven their ardent, treacherous best friend. The story largely revolved around the trio's becoming shipwrecked on a deserted Pacific island and a struggle by the men to win the sexual favors of the island's only female. Eventually they are joined by a bullying cannibal (actually a ship's steward in disguise, and played by Walter Chiari), adding a third would-be partner for Lady Susan's ménage. In the French stage original, the woman actually does go to bed with each of her male admirers, but this was considered too saucy for English-speaking cinemagoers of 1956 and so—like Billy Wilder's *The Seven Year Itch*—the plot was sanitized for the screen, and *The Little Hut* became a sex farce without anyone having any sex.

No one in the cast seemed to be working in devotion to the art of film. Granger, like Ava, glumly accepted his role to avoid suspension and also, he claimed, because his pregnant wife had wanted him out of the house, while Niven, not yet reaping the rewards of the successful *Around the World in 80 Days*, signed on with his usual amiable hack's lack of concern for the finished product (his philosophy, as expressed to Granger: "Well, it may be shit and not very good shit, but we have to go through it, so let's just be cheerful about it"). In Rome a press conference was held to promote the start of filming. As one of the "big stars," Granger had expected to share with Ava most of the press attention. "Suddenly," he told writer Sheridan Morley, "we're all shoved out of the way as the press stampede to photograph Ava's little Italian, who turns out to be a huge star locally. So that makes us laugh a lot." Later, Granger and Niven would find Ava and her "little Italian" most annoying: At lunchtime the couple would disappear together and not be seen for hours; everyone would end up sitting around doing nothing, waiting for their tryst to conclude.

Without a director or a project she respected, Ava now had begun to relax the professional discipline that had served her well for most of her fifteen years in the movie business. For all the anger and arguing that might have gone on with the front office in all that time, she had very seldom been the cause of any difficulty once the cameras rolled. There were two primary rules you learned at the Metro academy: Be on time, be prepared. Ava had lived by them. Other stars could be late, not know their lines, refuse to come to the set when called, refuse to continue a scene until their lines had been rewritten, throw tantrums, have directors fired. Ava had always resisted that sort of diva behavior.

However, her allegiance to the old ways was fading. The business itself, the studio system to which she had directed her professionalism, was not the same. Back in Hollywood, the great infrastructure of places like MGM was crumbling. Government edicts had stripped the studios of their exhibition arm. Audiences were defecting to television. At Culver City,

Mayer was gone. Now Schary, too, was gone. Even Clark Gable was gone. The feudal ways of the past could no longer be afforded. There would be no more contract players by the hundreds as before, no more Ava Gardners on the studio payroll while they took five, six years to teach her the business.

Without the old iron grip of the studios, the balance of power was shifting. Stars and powerful directors and producers had begun to set up shop independent of or in equal partnership with the studios. Ava saw in the very fact that Metro had met her demand to live and work in Europe, even though she was still bound to them by long-term contract, proof enough that the studio's iron fist had rusted. And yet in that sense of her potential power was also frustration: She was still under contract, and earning a fraction—perhaps one-third—of her market value. For all the changes in the business, she was essentially working under the same circumstances as in her first year of stardom. It had irked her in the 1940s when Metro had loaned her out to their great profit, and it irked her even more now when other stars of no greater popularity were reaping huge returns in payment and percentages. There was no single, sudden decision she made to become "difficult," only a chronic resentment nurtured for many years, now more and more finding a release. On *The Little Hut*, cables would fire back and forth across the Atlantic regarding her extravagant demands and unbelievable expenditures—personal hairdressers ordered in from two continents and three countries, whopping bills for liquor and entertainment and more. The studio's representative in Rome cabled Culver City: MAY BE POINT WHERE YOU DECIDE WHETHER AVA RUNS THIS PICTURE OR COMPANY DOES. But there was no one at the studio to decide.

The Little Hut, on release, was rather harshly judged, almost universally disdained, not least by all of its participants. Surely some patrons felt they had gotten their money's worth: Ava looked ravishing in a role that required her to wear no more than a black teddy for most of the running time.*

---

*In a contest promoting the release of *The Little Hut*, MGM gave the winner an entire, sizable Fijian island, renamed Ava Ava in honor of the film's star. It was later learned that *ava ava* was in fact a Polynesian name for a potent, homemade form of alcoholic refreshment.

Ava's romance with Chiari flourished through that summer and fall. He showed her Rome, took her around the Italian countryside. As she had done with Frank, she followed Walter on tour with his revue, sitting in the theaters in Turin and Milan and applauding louder than anyone. As with Frank, the couple had explosive arguments. And, as with her other guy, after the fighting there would be a very passionate time making up. By December there were reports of an imminent wedding. Ava denied it. For one thing, she was still married. In fact, she was more married than she had been for a while: Her Nevada residency had elapsed. She would now have to go back to the state for another six weeks or get her divorce somewhere else.

"I have asked her to marry me many times," said Chiari. "All over Europe. Everywhere. And she always answers, 'Who knows?'"

For nearly three years they saw each other, one way or another, off and on, up and down. After the first year the passion and fun had mostly gone from the relationship, but it dragged on for two more, unevenly sustained by Walter's dedication and Ava's lazy inability to cut him off, though she did try. As Chiari hung on, his appeal, then his dignity, faded in her eyes. She began almost to look for reasons to dislike him, to be mean to him. His international profile had risen in the time of their affair, and sometimes, when she was ill disposed, Ava would complain that he was using her to become more famous, to become known in Hollywood. "I was obsessed with her," Chiari told Charles Higham in 1967. "She was the most beautiful woman I had ever known. Yet somehow when we were together I often felt I was alone, that she had withdrawn from me in some mysterious and unsettling way."

"I think she just lost interest in him after a while," said Betty Sicre. "I don't know why it went on so long. There were things she found out about him that she didn't like. She said he was a cocaine fan and that caused tension between them. She was very anti–all drugs."

"Walter was *nice*," said Ava, summing up the relationship in her memoir. "The distance that separates liking from love is as wide as the Pacific."

There were other men in and out of her life during those years. As to exactly how many, Ava herself, to friends like Betty Sicre, toted a very modest sum, her busy love life a great exaggeration, she would say, while to the scandal press of the time the figure was for all practical purposes innumerable: a passing parade of men, many younger, from matadors to elevator *operadores*.

An unusual and largely unreported friendship in this period was with Dr. Archie McIndoe, a legendary plastic surgeon she had first met shortly after crashing her Mercedes-Benz en route to the Madrid airport. She had crashed other cars, too, a Cadillac, a Facel-Vega Frank Sinatra had given her for a present. One automobile she had driven straight into the sea at Biarritz and she had been forced to get out of the car and watch it float off and disappear. "She drove too fast," said Betty Sicre. "Always. And she was a terrible driver. She just got behind the wheel and started speeding, and I don't think she ever paid much attention to what she was doing."

In the Mercedes crash she had gone off the road, spun over twice, and landed upside down in a sea of broken glass. A huge bruise on her leg brought her to McIndoe's Harley Street clinic in London. The New Zealand–born surgeon was a legendary figure for his work on soldiers burned in combat during World War II. A charismatic and inspiring personality, Ava took to him as a friend, but perhaps more than that, according to Betty Sicre. "They were dating, she said. She was very fond of him." McIndoe was married.

Ava would spend time with the doctor at the Royal Air Force Hospital in East Grinstead, visiting with the pilots there, men who had suffered horrible scarring injuries, some surviving with only the vestiges of a face. She would visit with them, chat, hold their hands. It was difficult and depressing, but Archie forced her to find the strength and to see the need for doing it, and she loved him for it.

The Sun Also Rises, Ernest Hemingway's novel of disillusioned and dissolute expatriates in Paris and Spain, was considered one of the significant works of the twentieth century, both as a stylistic triumph and as the literary encapsulation of the so-called Lost Generation of the 1920s, those who had come out of the horrors of World War I stripped of ideals and hope. A number of attempts had been made through the years to adapt the book for the movies and the property had changed hands several times. In the forties, Howard Hawks bought the screen rights and put writer Samuel

Fuller to work on a script, but this adaptation, like all others, was thwarted by the restrictions of the Production Code. Hemingway's novel was full of censorable material, prostitutes, bad language, "amoral" attitudes, promiscuity, not to mention a protagonist—the book's narrator, Jake Barnes—sexually incapacitated by a terrible war wound. By the mid-1950s, though, restrictions had begun to loosen, and adult themes and more provocative material were slowly beginning to find their way into the English-speaking cinema. It was, in fact, Joseph Mankiewicz's borrowing of the Hemingway hero's genital wound for *The Barefoot Contessa* that pricked, so to speak, Darryl Zanuck's renewed interest in the Hemingway property. Perhaps, he thought, the time was right to do *The Sun Also Rises* justice at last. (It wasn't.)

The catalyst for much of the novel's action was the central female character, Lady Brett Ashley, a dazzling, passionate, troubled, troublemaking young English playgirl. Cynical and promiscuous on the surface, hopping in and out of frivolous, destructive sexual affairs, in Lady Brett's heart is a tragic frustration—the only man she loves, Jake, cannot share a physical relationship with her. As a role for the screen, Brett had glamorous style and sexuality and several interesting twists of character. Zanuck felt the part deserved a big name to play her, and several important stars were closely considered for the job, among them Jennifer Jones (her husband David Selznick all but begged Zanuck to take her), Audrey Hepburn (who declared in the end that she did not want to play a nymphomaniac), and Marilyn Monroe (Zanuck quickly shouted out of this unfathomable notion).

The project's appointed screenwriter, Peter Viertel, was the first to mention Ava Gardner in regard to the part, and the idea was quickly endorsed by Darryl. Once considered, it seemed inevitable: Aside from the fact that she had not yet been widowed by an English lord, there was very little else about the actress that did not seem custom designed to embody Hemingway's creation, including but not limited to her physical allure, her capricious love life, her often desperate joie de vivre, and her intimate knowledge of bullfighters. Ava agreed. She enjoyed one of Hemingway's observations of Brett: as charming when she is drunk as when she is sober. It was the sort of thing one liked to believe was so. "I always," said Ava, "felt close to Papa's women."

A draft of the screenplay soon arrived at her door in Madrid. Looking the script over, her initial enthusiasm turned to uncertainty. When she heard that Hemingway was back in Spain, vacationing at the Hotel Felipe II in the mountain resort of Escorial, she packed the screenplay and went up to see him. His reaction to the news that she had been offered the role of Lady Brett, Ava sensed, was not unalloyed pleasure.

"I guess you'll do," he told her. "You've got some vestiges of class."

Ava left her script for Papa to read. When she returned for his assessment, Hemingway was well along in one of his "black dog" moods, drunk and standing on a chair screaming about the debased and distorted adaptation of his work. The screen rights to *The Sun Also Rises* had long ago been given over to his first wife, Hadley, as part of a divorce settlement (and she in turn had been all but swindled out of them by the original buyers), so Hemingway had no financial stake in the new production, nor any great hope for it, only the bitter foretaste of another Hollywood violation.

Arriving hot on their trail was screenwriter Peter Viertel, who found Ava shaken by Hemingway's assessment and ready to walk away from the project. In the presence of his friend Peter, Hemingway modified his antagonism, though some of the script's lapses—like an unfortunate flashback sequence to explain Jake's wound, in which Lady Brett is surprisingly interjected as his hospital nurse—continued to enrage the great writer. Viertel eventually convinced Ava that they hoped to make a good film and that her role was a special one and that she might regret it if she turned it down.

Alas, as Papa had suspected, the production was fatally compromised before the first frame of film had even passed through the camera. Though Viertel would fight to preserve the author's tone and meaning, studio dictates subverted him all the way, glaringly so in the revised ending, which turned the haunted stoicism of Hemingway's last lines in the book into the movie's empty note of hope (Brett: "Darling, there must be an answer somewhere." Jake: "I'm sure there is"). Among many errors in judgment, Zanuck would cast several of *The Sun's* key roles with veteran, middle-aged actors: Tyrone Power (as Jake), Errol Flynn, Eddie Albert—hardly the jaded youths and recent soldiers of Hemingway's book. And to direct a film that might have benefited from the neurotic discernment of a Nicholas Ray or the Hemingwayesque perspective of a John Huston,

Zanuck accepted the eternal Fox house director, Henry King, whose moribund style had seemed old-fashioned in 1925. And Zanuck, instead of insisting on shooting the film at the story's specified European locales (Paris and northern Spain), which at the least would have offered the hope of visual authenticity, followed studio dictates and budget concerns and based the production in Mexico (there would be a brief stop in Paris for a few exterior street shots, but the Parisian interiors were all to be filmed in Mexico City). The colonial town of Morelia was chosen to try and pass it-self off as Pamplona, and the resident mestizos and Tarascan Indians would play the beret-wearing revelers of Basque Spain (when the assistant directors attempted to hire only the lighter-skinned locals as extras the company was predictably picketed with accusations of racism).*

Ava arrived in Mexico to begin filming in the spring of 1957, taken by car from the capital city to Morelia, four hours away. Seven years earlier she had gone on her first foreign sojourn eager to enjoy the adventure, alive to each new experience. Now she traveled to a distant location with all the enthusiasm of a commuter headed for the job on a Monday morning, with the return trip three months away. In Morelia, while everyone else, even Zanuck, sociably took up residence in a tumbledown motor court run by an American couple, Ava demanded private lodgings, and a house was found for her a couple of miles outside town. It was rote behavior by this time, a perquisite of status that you didn't not demand, even though she often felt lonely separated from the rest of the company.

There were some old acquaintances among her fellow cast members gathered in Morelia. Back in the forties she had gone out a time or two with both Ty Power and Errol Flynn. Then they had been two of the most beautiful men she had ever seen, Power dreamily romantic looking, Flynn the rugged, exuberant swashbuckler in life as in films. Now both appeared aged far beyond their years, Flynn especially, a spectacular wreck from dissipation, bleary and red faced. He was still delightful company, but it hurt her to see what he had done to himself. Both men would be dead in

---

*A second unit was dispatched to Pamplona, to shoot the July *feria*, the daily bullfights, and espe-cially the *encierro*, the traditional and frenzied running of the bulls that Hemingway's novel had made world famous, but none of the film's stars were present.

less than two years. Flynn was a tax exile now, living from paycheck to paycheck in Europe and on the island of Jamaica. Power had left Hollywood after two decades of stardom, telling confidantes his life "was empty, almost purposeless." And Darryl Zanuck, too, the last and youngest of the moguls and some thought the greatest, had abandoned his empire and his family to wander about Europe with a series of young mistresses. Fame, fortune, and the rest had left them all variously unhappy, unhealthy, and/or broke. Together, with Ava, they were a curious, ironic reflection of the young drifters in the movie they had come to make, a veritable Lost Generation of Hollywood exiles.

It was in Mexico that Ava first began to worry about her looks. There had barely been a day that had gone by as far back as she could remember that someone had not said or shown by their reaction that she was stunning to behold. That had not changed. But still, the clock never stopped its damned ticking. She had begun to see the signs of aging, the little lines, the bigger lines, the inability to snap back into shape quite so fast after a night or a weekend of good times. Observers would recall her on the set, "constantly, anxiously peering into a mirror." There was whispered talk at the rushes about the circles under her eyes, and an occasional puffiness. One morning she was having her face made up and someone said without further comment that tequila of all drinks was the hardest on the skin.

She gradually began to fear the presence of photographers. The girl they used to say photographed perfectly from every angle had now too often seen what an unfortunate candid pose could reveal. Roaming press photographers taking candid shots made her particularly nervous. She began to ask—demand—that they be barred from the set while she was working. Even when they promised you they would not print anything without your approval, and even when they did show you the proofs and you X-d out the bad shot, they double-crossed you and the bad pictures appeared anyway. It was easier just to refuse altogether. In Mexico a squadron of local press had descended one day, and the studio rep had pleaded with her to pose for a few shots for the sake of diplomacy and she had refused and stormed off the set. The Mexican papers printed the story, with editorial insults: What was the matter, they asked, was she getting too ugly? Was she afraid she would no longer attract any bullfighters?

She was thirty-four years old. By Hollywood standards of attrition it was the beginning of the end. Garbo had retired from the screen forever at thirty-six (the same age at which Marilyn Monroe would die). Rita Hayworth, at thirty-eight, had a few leading roles still ahead, but her time as a star was essentially over. Lana Turner, thirty-seven years old, had begun a new phase in her screen career playing the mothers of teenage kids. Thirty-four was not a good year for love goddesses.

Feeling lonely, but shy of the social cliques formed in town, Ava singled out Peter Viertel for friendship and one day invited him to her place for dinner. On his arrival Ava had martinis made, but Viertel asked for a Coca-Cola instead.

She told him, "I don't trust any man who doesn't drink."

Viertel switched to martinis. The writer, trying to have some positive influence on the disappointing direction of the movie, hoped to confer with Ava about her approach to the role of Lady Brett. Ava wasn't interested. Over more martinis, and then bottles of wine at dinner, she talked instead, and at length, of her life, the men who had done her wrong, the various burdens of fame, and the iniquities of the movie business. "It seemed strange to me," Viertel would write, "that the industry that had provided her with a status she must once have desired was finally accountable for her discontent."

It became very late, and Viertel was preparing to return to town when Ava asked that he stay the night. Determining that there was no sexual motive to her request, only "an almost panicky loneliness," he reluctantly agreed, expecting to be put up in the guest room. Ava, though, insisted he sleep with her in one of the double beds in her bedroom. "I told her that life had not equipped me physiologically for the role of teddy bear, a remark she ignored."

He lay uncomfortably a few feet from her until dawn, then he got up and walked the two miles back to town (running straight into a leering Errol Flynn). Ava appeared happier than usual on the set in the morning (Flynn no doubt leering once again). In the evening she requested that Viertel repeat the sleeping arrangements of the night before. An awkward, intimate but not-quite-romantic friendship had begun, and for the remainder of their time in Morelia, the writer ambivalantly accepted his role as

Ava's platonic bedmate, a relationship, it occurred to him, that had some resemblance to the one between Ava's film character and the impotent Jake Barnes (once again her art and life becoming oddly interchangeable). Viertel, a good-looking heterosexual who did not have Barnes's physiological problem, would remember being tempted and provocatively teased by his close proximity to the beautiful star—"Maybe I will let you make love to me," she told him once, while they were dancing, "to loosen you up"—but remained, somehow, Ava's roommate and not her lover.

Viertel, from his often close-up vantage point, observed as others had before him, a woman of mercurial temperament and wildly varying personality, charming and adorable at one moment, coarse and impossible the next. Alcohol, he saw, was the most obvious catalyst for her plunges into darker moods. With a few drinks she could travel the full trajectory from pleasantly high to violently unpredictable that would take others all night to achieve. Viertel took note of her tangled feelings toward the opposite sex, her many resentments and disappointments in love, as well as her impulse toward cruelty in her relationship with Walter Chiari—arrived finally from Rome—whom she would taunt with intimations of her infidelity, at one point conspiring to have him catch her in her room, wearing only her underwear, with Viertel quite obviously hiding from him in the bathroom, another uncomfortable scene into which she had drawn the writer, one he would recall as resembling something out of a Feydeau farce.

Filming dragged on into June, by which time no one involved held much expectation that a very good film was being made. Chiari arrived in Mexico, then Bappie. Ava abruptly declared that she was on the wagon, but after a week or so abruptly jumped off of it. At a restaurant one night, she behaved very badly, nearly causing a riot among the Mexican men at a nearby table, then excused herself to go to the ladies' room and never came back. A Mexican playboy she met at a tango palace agreed to take her on a tour of the real Mexico, as requested, to the bars and brothels. The playboy (later a hotel keeper on the Lebanese coast) and Ava drank much tequila and ended the night together in bed. He had roamed her glorious body, he would claim to reporters, telling her he was searching for a spot that had never been kissed . . . "And I got to the soles of her feet and I said, '*I found it!*' "

In May, in Mexico City, Ava went to the Department of Foreign Relations and registered a complaint for divorce. She offered as grounds under Mexican law her husband's unjustified abandonment of their home for more than six months (in fact, they had been separated for more than three years). In June the suit was filed, the spouse was notified of the impending action and agreed without complaint, and on July 5, in the Thirteenth Civil Court in Mexico City, Judge Agustin Espinosa de la Peni granted Ava Gardner a final divorce decree from Frank Sinatra.

In June, wending her way back to Europe, Ava made a visit to North Carolina, Walter Chiari in tow. The volatile, uninhibited couple provided an entertaining, exotic spectacle for the Smithfield relatives. After one great row at the house of her brother, Jack, Ava demanded that Chiari be thrown out and taken to the airport at once. As recounted by Doris Cannon, Jack dutifully packed up the visitor, escorted him to the car, and drove him to the Raleigh-Durham airport. By the time Ava's brother had gotten back home he found Chiari's bag sitting inside the doorway. The Italian had gotten a taxi at the airport, urged the driver to drive as they did in Rome, and beaten Jack back to Smithfield by some minutes. He and Ava had already resumed their argument where they had left off.

In October, back in Spain, she had gone with Walter and Bappie to visit the Andalusian bull ranch of Angelo Peralta, a wealthy breeder she had met through Ernest Hemingway. That day a large, excited crowd had gathered to watch the testing of the bulls in the *plaʒita* ring, and many had taken note of the presence of the famous *madrileña* from Hollywood, swarming around her with cheers of *"Viva Ava!"* And as the festivities continued, someone had come forward to suggest that the prestigious visitor enter the ring herself and take a turn on horseback with the *banderillas*, the barbed darts thrust into the bull's neck or back to lessen his ferocity. There had been some talk about a script, Ava to play a famous *rejoneador*, a bull-fighter on horseback, perhaps the offer was all tied up with that, a bit of a publicity stunt.

It was an absurd idea. For starters, she had little experience on horseback. And then there was this: It was a good way to be killed. And yet the absurdity and the mortal danger seemed to escape her, with an enthusiasm fueled by a considerable intake of absinthe and Spanish cognac mixed in a notorious combination known as a *solysombra* (sun and shadow), Bappie had gone off somewhere, and Walter Chiari seemed unaware of the risk. Suddenly it was happening. She was lifted onto the saddle of a restless black stallion, the reins placed in one hand and the two decorated *banderillas* in the other. And suddenly she was prancing into the sunlight at the center of the tiny bullring, and the crowd screamed in a deafening roar. Drunk and uncertain of what she was doing, she clung to the reins as the horse circled the arena floor at a gallop. And now horse and movie star were joined by the bull, a great snorting young animal bred only for terror, killing, and violent death. The creature charged them and grazed by, crashing into the wooden barrier behind. The bull swerved and charged again. As Ava leaned forward with the *banderilla* her horse reared up high and twisted back, escaping the charging horns. She was thrown from the saddle and sent to the ground with the speed of a whiplash, landing with a great thump in the dirt, the ground hitting the right side of her face with the force of a wooden bat swung straight at the cheekbone. Unable to move for several moments, she lay in great peril of being gored by the bull or stomped by the frightened horse before she could be rescued, lifted up and rushed away and out of the ring.

At first it had seemed like only a bruise and a close call. Brushed off, given a restorative drink, she was soon back on her feet. The *solysombras* had proved to be an efficient anesthetic for the pain. In a little while, though, she began to feel the throbbing ache and when she looked in a mirror she saw a terrible purple bruise. In another day her cheek showed a plump swelling atop the cheekbone, and it was nearly the size of her fist.

With increasing concern about the damage done to her face, she arranged to see Archie McIndoe in England, flying out, her features hidden by dark glasses and a scarf. After an examination, the plastic surgeon explained that of the limited number of medical remedies for a muscular trauma of that type, all held the possibility of leaving her face permanently disfigured. The safest bet, McIndoe told her, was to do nothing and hope that it would heal itself.

———

Time went on and the lump decreased, but it did not disappear. After several months there remained a solid bump the size of a walnut. Frank came to visit her in Madrid that year. He got his first look at the injury. "Honey," he said, "you ain't gonna make any films looking like that."

Frank recommended a highly regarded plastic surgeon he knew in New York. This doctor suggested she agree to one of the remedies—chemical injections—that McIndoe had warned her against. She could not decide what to do, and the injury got no better.

The press had begun to sniff around at her problem. Louella Parsons wrote, "There has been so much talk about Ava Gardner's beautiful face being badly scarred after her accident in a bullring in Spain. . . . As I exclusively reported, Ava came to America to consult one of the top plastic men, who advised an operation. Then she made two visits to a London specialist. Those who saw her say that her face was in a pitiful condition. . . . But time takes care of everything, and she'll be able to cover any disfiguration with makeup."

The problem weighed on her, depressed her. She would look at herself, and her face looked terrible. When would it go away? Would it ever go away? She feared getting the injections, and she feared not getting them. In public she ran in real fear now that someone would take her photograph. Friends tried to be reassuring, told her they could hardly see it anymore. But she could see it and feel it, hard and implacable, as she moved her finger back and forth on her cheek. She would look into the mirror and raise and lower her cheekbones and watch the results in her reflection, dismayed. She would close her eyes and wish it away, wish away that day in the *plaçita* and the horse and the goddamned *solysombras*, and open her eyes and it was there, still there and worse than ever, she would think. After a while she was touching it all the time, going back and back to look in the mirror; she could think of nothing else. It frightened her and saddened her. It was gone, the beauty, the perfection that she had never thought about before but that had always been there and had given her everything. Gone.

TEN

Vita, Dolce Vita

She began the last film of her MGM contract—the end of a seventeen-year relationship—in a state of anxiety and fear. She wanted only to be left alone, to keep out of sight while her face healed, to hide out at La Bruja and let time (as Sir Archibald recommended) take care of what she had recklessly done to herself. But her employers were waiting: *The Naked Maja,* an Italian production into which Metro had invested her in return for partial ownership and international distribution rights, was scheduled to begin shooting after the first of the year, and she saw no way of avoiding it. Terrified of going before the camera with her features still distorted, she was as much afraid of asking the producers for a postponement or to relieve her of the assignment altogether. To do so at such a time, she was certain, would be to confirm the speculation and fuel new gossip about her injury, to provide the scandal press with all the facts they needed and the rest they could think up on their own. Pictures taken of her fall had appeared in one magazine after another around the world (she had half-convinced herself that she had been set up that day at the *plaẓita* just to provide someone a lucrative photo opportunity; it gave her someone else besides herself to blame for the debacle). She imagined the press stalking her for a close-up, imagined the headlines: MIDNIGHT FOR THE HOLLYWOOD CINDERELLA. And if the public believed it, if they believed they were no longer going to get the perfection they were paying for—and if there was truth behind the juicy headlines, all the worse—then, she was certain, it meant the end of her as a star. For what else did she have to offer? Her skill as an actress? She would never believe it. They went to Katharine Hepburn or Bette Davis if they wanted a great performance, not to Ava Gardner. And to lose her value as a star meant to lose the opportunities ahead—the game plan she had been nurturing expectantly— to make real money and retire from the movies in a few years and on her own terms, to get out for good and not look back. No, she would have to take her chances, be available for the new film as scheduled, and hope that makeup and therapy and a good cinematographer would get her past this crisis without it ending up destroying her.

For months she remained in seclusion at La Moraleja. She had kept herself out of the sunlight. She had slept only on her back. She had put no makeup or creams on her face. She received facial massages from a woman therapist from Switzerland and administered a daily steam treatment from a machine called a *Gesicht Sauna* that David Hanna had obtained for her in Munich. Each morning—and each afternoon and evening and many times in between—she would go to the mirror to inspect the injury on her cheek, hoping to see evidence of an improvement, and each time she would look and then lurch away in despair. Bappie and Betty Sicre and others would tell her that from most angles it was hardly visible anymore, but she refused to believe them. It was not simply the hardened bruise itself but what she saw as an alteration to the contour of her entire face. The side of her face drooped, she thought, and the best side, too.

In January, reluctant, despondent, she left Madrid for Rome, via France. Hoping to avoid the photographers who now—with the ever-increasing celebrity traffic to and from the Eternal City—staked out the airport around the clock, she flew with Bappie to Nice, where she had arranged to be met by her Italian chauffeur, Mario, a devoted occasional employee since the days of *The Barefoot Contessa*. In Mario's Cadillac they drove across the French border and on south to Rome, arriving without public notice. With her usual flat on the Corso d'Italia occupied, she took up residence in a spacious penthouse apartment at 9 Piazza di Spagna.

The Naked Maja concerned the legendary—that is to say, not altogether confirmed by historical fact—dramatic relationship between the eighteenth-century Spanish court painter of genius, Francisco Goya, and the voluptuary Duchess of Alba, his reputed nude model for the notorious painting of the title. The film story had originated with Albert Lewin, who had spent the eight years since *Pandora* trying to find another project that would bring him back together with his adored muse. *The Naked Maja* made use of Lewin's knowledge of history and his obsession with painters and painting while providing a potentially strong, glamorous, and erotic central role for Ava Gardner in a production that was expected to be conveniently based in her own backyard. A deal was made with a rising Italian production company named Titanus. Once Gardner was contracted, however, Titanus went to work separating Lewin from his own project, and after some acrimony the writer-director was excised for a payment of one hundred thousand dollars. A new screenplay was begun from scratch by Italian hired hands. The company then encountered problems from the Spanish government, influenced by the still-powerful remnants of the Alba family, who did not approve of the film's subject (the clan traditionally denied that their ancestor had been the immodest model for the *Maja*). Instead of the palaces, cathedrals, and byways of Spain, the film would be made on soundstages and back lots in Rome, and the footage of the actual Goya paintings to be seen under the credits and elsewhere in the film would have to be shot at the museums in Madrid and Toledo by a minimal second unit under the guise of making a cultural documentary. So: no Lewin, the project's intellectual and aesthetic force, no authentic locations, and only limited access to the original art. Once again, Ava was starring in a film that had been seriously compromised before the first frame was ever exposed.

On Ava's arrival in Rome, Titanus then made what would prove to be the practical mistake of sending her their completely rewritten screenplay for approval. She did not approve. Not only did she genuinely feel that the new script—written in Italian and given a quick English translation—was terrible, she was only too eager to be presented with cause for delaying production and allowing more time for her face to heal. The producers accepted her verdict on the screenplay, and filming was postponed while the script went through another overhaul, and another, and one more after that, the script passing through various hands, Italian and American (including Norman Corwin, who had successfully scripted another painter's story, *Lust for Life*), with additions and edits from everyone including Ava, David Hanna (now signed on officially as the actress's "sidekick, personal manager, stooge"), and perhaps even Bappie taking a shot at improving the unwieldy dialogue and ponderous arrangement of scenes.

The script problems would turn out to be just one ingredient in a confused preproduction period, Titanus clearly not yet prepared for a motion picture of this scale and expense. Filming would not begin until May, five months after the original starting date.

Though relieved of the traumatizing prospect of going before the camera right away, she continued to suffer from various uncertainties and suspicions. The injury to her face established her emotional mood, a lingering sense of anger and hopelessness. She would peer into the mirror or stroke the bump with her fingertips, then scream in frustration, "What a goddamn fool I was!"

Dave Hanna began to sense that the fall, though real and damaging, had become for her something more, a dramatic punctuation—in the life of a woman whose natural life cycles seemed always to be achieved with great drama—an exclamation point for the end of her years of youth and beauty.

She was changing. Fears and character flaws that were once incipient or occasional now dominated her behavior. She was suspicious, her temper was even quicker to flare. Her paranoia regarding strangers and especially anyone in possession of a camera had reached a level of volatility that outstripped even that of her ex-husband.

Frank. She thought of him so much of the time now. She saw him, increasingly, in dreamy terms, her knight in shining armor. His years of failure and pathos were far in the past, and he had become more than ever before a figure of power and confidence. She took pride and solace in knowing that his affection for her remained strong and that she could turn to him if the need arose. One day she heard from him, he was coming to Europe. Would she like him to pay her a visit in Italy? Please come, she told him. But then, not too long before he was due in Rome, she began to see pictures and items in the papers about Frank in London with a new friend, the socially prominent, beautiful, American-born Lady Adele Beatty. Ava awoke from her dream at once. Frank called on arrival. She refused to talk to him. He called, sent messages, she remained out of his reach. One sleepless early morning she left the Piazza di Spagna flat to take Rags for his walk. She veered to a new route, and the corgi looked up at her with curiosity. They walked up to the Hassler Hotel, went to the front desk, and Ava had someone take her to Sinatra's suite.

"Where the hell you been, baby?" said Frank uneasily. "I've been calling for two days."

Rags recognized him right away, Ava dropped the leash and the dog jumped into Frank's arms. Frank lifted him and petted him along the flanks as he used to do years ago, and Rags let out a satisfied yelp. Then she took the dog back and she reached out to Frank and put in his hand the wedding ring he had given her long ago.

"Give that to your English lady," she said and turned and went out the door.

On the street outside the Hassler she started crying.

She returned to the piazza apartment miserable. "I shouldn't have . . . "I'm so sorry now." She said, "Rags was so happy to see him."

Sinatra, with the ring she had given him still gripped in his hand, had called for a car to take him to the airport; he was gone from Rome three hours later.

Late at night, sleepless in the big apartment above the Spanish Steps, she would often play his records, the volume on high, oblivious to the neighbors, as she lay in bed or sat outside on the terrace in the dark with a drink and a cigarette. Down below, three or four in the morning, people drifting home across the otherwise silent piazza would hear the distant, unexpected voice of the American singer echoing in the empty urban canyon.

Filming, at last, began. After many attempts to find a major star to play the part of Goya—Kirk Douglas, Gregory Peck, Laurence Olivier, and others had been approached—the role was given to a young New York stage actor, Tony Franciosa, a star from his acclaimed Broadway turns in *A Hatful of Rain* and *Orpheus Descending*. To direct, Titanus hired Hollywood studio veteran Henry Koster, whose credits included a previous and highly successful "costume picture" and the first release in Cinemascope, *The Robe*. All the remaining cast and crew were Italian, with the exception of Mickey Knox, another New Yorker and briefly a movie actor in Hollywood, a victim of the blacklist exiled in Europe, now working mostly behind the scenes as a translator and dialogue coach for coproductions like *The Naked Maja*. The cinematographer—whose work was a great concern to Ava—was a brilliant new talent, Giuseppe Rotunno, just beginning what would be a magnificent career. Rotunno's careful lighting and framing of the film's female star minimized the traces of her injury—revealed as at most a small dimple on her cheek—and in doing so eased her anxiety before the camera. She got along equally well with the rest of the Italian crew, a relaxed, happy-go-lucky lot whose slow start, long lunches, and late hours suited her fine. Filming was in the Italian style, without direct sound recording (dialogue to be postsynchronized). Many of the actors she performed with either spoke no English or had accents too thick to be understood. Sometimes the other actors did not speak their lines on camera but simply mouthed gibberish or counted numbers; you didn't so much interact with the other players as watch and wait for their lips to stop moving.

Filming went on through the summer, under ever-more-uncomfortable conditions. Because of the delayed start, they were forced to work in the humid midyear Roman heat, under hot lights, in a studio without air-conditioning. Ava's sumptuous regal costumes weighed on her like so many wool blankets in the high temperatures (in a letter to George Cukor she wished that she could do the picture as the title said: naked). For a while, at Ava's strong suggestion, they tried working only at night, a schedule she had always dreamed of imposing on a production, but the studio was even hotter at night after baking in the sun all day long. Koster's direction was static and uninspired, and the script was disjointed, rewritten day by day, with new scenes and dialogue delivered on loose scraps of paper. The heat, the disorganization, the scraps of paper—it became just a bad job that had to be done and no end in sight. For Ava the only enjoyment in the work came with the chance to perform another Spanish dance on film, the days of rehearsal with a charming Spanish dance instructor and then the ultimate staging and shooting of the scene. When that was finished she went back to her interrupted states of boredom and heat prostration.

For a time she was without a romantic interest. Walter Chiari, ironically, was then making a movie in Madrid. He returned to Rome for a weekend visit, they argued without pause, and she had sent him away at the end with orders not to bother her again until called for. Then came the encounter with Frank at the Hassler, after which the two had no further contact for months. As *The Naked Maja* began filming she set her gaze on her costar, Tony Franciosa—like her last husband an intense, at times high-strung Italian-American. But she seemed unable to catch his attention. He was married—tempestuously—to actress Shelley Winters. And he was preoccupied in feuding with Henry Koster (Franciosa was filled with the new methods of internalized acting and liked to work his way through each scene, find the psychological mood, the physical movements, and so on, while Koster belonged to the old-Hollywood shut-up-hit-your-mark-say-your-lines-and-lunch-everybody school of directing). When nothing happened between them, the notion slipped from Ava's thoughts; it was too hot to make a greater effort at seduction.

With Mickey Knox, the other young American actor on the production, Ava developed a pleasant rapport. In the tedious hours between setups the two would often sit together, chatting or running lines or playing a word game called Jotto. "She was terrific," Knox would remember. "Vivacious, alive, full of fun. And beautiful. More beautiful than on the screen. She had the scar from the fall, but it was nothing. It was very attractive, actually. Kind of sexy. She was great. She loved to laugh. And she was no dummy. She was a very intelligent woman. Back when I came to Hollywood I was making a picture with Mickey Rooney. We were playing boxers in this thing, and we were working out for our fight. I remember I asked him about Ava because I knew he'd been married to her. And Rooney said, *'Ahh, she was a fucking Red, for crissake!'* Ha! But at the time I was thinking, Well, that tells me something, that she was interested in the world around her. And she was. She was intelligent, congenial, amusing, aware. I liked her very much. I used to call her 'Avala'—a Jewish play on her name. And she responded to that. She said, 'The only other person that called me that was Artie.' Artie Shaw. So we got along, we became friends, she was great.

"At the same time it was difficult to be in her company. If you've ever been in the presence of certain extraordinary women, you'll know what I mean. I've experienced it a couple of times in my life. Facing beauty of that kind. It's not a completely pleasant experience. She gave you this ache in your gut because she was so appealing. And because she was not yours, you know? You felt a kind of vertigo being near her. She was so desirable you felt a little sick from it. Oh my God, she was extraordinary."

One day the friendship took a brief abrupt turn. At the studio after they had been shooting for some weeks, Knox found Ava in rehearsal for her dance, just the actress alone, working with the recorded music. He took a seat nearby and watched the choreographed routine, watched her beautiful, graceful movements repeated again and again. "I was amazed at how much talent she had as a dancer. I don't know how seriously she took acting, although she did her job as an actress very well, but when she did the rehearsals for the dance in the picture—boy, she gave it her all, she was serious about that. I was enchanted watching her."

At the finish of the rehearsal Ava came over to where Knox was sitting and dropped into a chair. "She sprawled in the chair next to me, and she stretched her legs. She said, 'Oh, my feet are killing me . . .' I said, 'Let me massage your feet.' And she looked at me and she said, 'Oh, that's great . . .' And I thought, Okay! Listen, I don't know if I was thinking beyond that; I guess in the back of my mind I was. But I knew from past experience, if you were ever going to find a time when you had an opening, massaging a woman's feet was the time." Knox got on his knees, took the actress's feet in his hands, and began squeezing and rubbing them to what he recalled as sounds of increasing pleasure. "She then suggested we continue the massage in her dressing room," Mickey Knox would remember. "So up we went."

The intimacy was brief. Exactly one day later, a new, close relationship suddenly developed between Ava and Tony Franciosa. Knox believed it was a case of *"droit de seigneur,"* movie-star version, Franciosa compelled to exert his hierarchical rights over a lesser member of the production. "It was the next day. Up until then he hadn't been interested in her. But the next day he made his move. I don't know how, but he knew something was up and he made a move. And that cut me out immediately."

Whatever the spark of motivation, an affair between the screen Goya and his Duchess now began. After the months of seclusion, the months of hard work, Ava, with a new love interest for inspiration, energetically revived her dormant social life. Into the hot Roman night she went in pursuit of fun and excitement, Franciosa in tow, he would recall, "like a kid in a chocolate factory." The movie became an afterthought for them both, a brief interruption in a lusty regime, Franciosa's months of serious research into the character of Goya tossed over in the heap with Al Lewin's script, of no interest to him now as he enjoyed the sexual attentions of "the most glamorous woman in the world." The bottles of champagne would start popping open by four in the afternoon, and the festivities would go on into the night, into the morning, from café to bar to nightclub to bed to studio. "She never slept," Franciosa would recall to writer Rex Reed, "and I never saw a woman drink so much and still look beautiful in front of a camera."

Once it became known that Ava Gardner was out on the town with her married costar, the press came running like hyenas at the scent of fresh meat. Rome in the summer of 1958 had become a kind of battlefield between the growing ranks of international stars and succulent starlets come to work in the city and the equally expanding army of photographers who stalked them. Itinerant press photographers covered the celebrity beat in many big cities, but nowhere in the world was there anything to compare with the joyfully ruthless camera-wielding hordes who roamed the streets of Rome, a subculture that would one day achieve iconic status in a motion picture by Fellini. The freelance photographers of Rome were, most of them, tough young men from the working class who had grown up on the streets in the chaos and desperation of the war years. As children many had been *scattini*, itinerant street photographers one step up from beggars, making a few *lire* by snapping pictures of sightseeing GI conquerors and foreign tourists. By the early 1950s these street kids had evolved into a rowdy corps of photojournalists, haunting the city in search of exploitable pictures to feed the tabloids, primarily images of criminal or accidental violence and of Roman politicians behaving badly, like the headline-making shots of the Communist Party leader escorting his wife to and from an orgy at a Via Corridoni whorehouse.

By the middle of the decade the photographers had turned to new prey, the movies' celebrated faces from America and Europe descending on Rome in such numbers that for a period of time the city was known as Hollywood on the Tiber. It was easy enough to find and photograph these famous faces, for every celebrity in town inevitably gravitated to the broad boulevard named the Via Veneto, and particularly to the three blocks of it between the Aurelian Wall and the U.S. embassy, a stretch composed almost entirely of hotels, clubs, and cafés (establishments including l'hotel Ambasciatori, the Café de Paris, the Bar Rosati, the Golden

Gate, Doney, Bricktop, Café Strega, Grand Hotel Flora, and the popular all-night pharmacy l'Alka Seltzer). There, on any given evening from the cocktail hour until sometime near sunup, at the outdoor tables that crowded the sidewalks, sipping espresso or Campari or scotch amid the potted azaleas and under the bright-lit signage, and with the buzz of traffic as sound track, one could reliably count on finding a sampling of movie stars—rising, falling, or eternal—from Gary Cooper to Mickey Hargitay. So plentiful were the opportunities to photograph these notables in their Via Veneto repose, that the average shot of a star pleasantly enjoying his or her aperitif of a Roman evening became a glut on the market, its value eventually so reduced that it became hardly worth the effort of releasing the shutter. To make a good sale by then—the chance to earn not a thousand *lire* but a hundred thousand—a photographer had to have captured something out of the ordinary, something newsworthy, violence or intemperance or lust, a side of the stars the public had not seen before. Photographers went in pursuit of celebrities as they had once pursued dissolute politicians, in the hope of catching them with their pants down, figuratively or literally, however the night might go. Fueled by their need to make a living, to eat, plus undenied feelings of class resentment ("We had nothing," said a veteran of the time, "and they, the rich who were living *la dolce vita*, had everything, beautiful women, cars, money"), the photographers' hunt for salable pictures became spirited, then aggressive, and finally, at times, violent. On nights when the stars failed to provide sufficient scandalous behavior, photographers stepped forth and provoked it, taunting and challenging this or that celebrity into a temper tantrum, a grab for the offending camera, an absurd chase through the street, a wrestling match or a punch-out, with luck all of it caught on film by the photographer's nearby partner—and sold the next morning to the highest bidder. One participant in these tumultuous encounters described the nightly scene around the Via Veneto and other celebrity haunts as a "theater of war."

For the roving photographers of Rome, Ava Gardner remained a most desirable subject, whether, for instance, snapped publicly brawling with local favorite Walter Chiari, or provocatively on her own, as when she was caught on film at the studio with wet, stringy hair and wearing little more than a bath towel (the photographer had sneaked into Cinecittà and hidden in a cardboard box for several hours before obtaining his memo-

Ava and Frank return to Rome at the end of a brief, unhappy Christmas reunion, December 1953. The marriage is over. On Ava's left is publicist David Hanna, soon to be Ava's personal manager. *(Courtesy Associated Press)*

Ava wearing a velvet bathing suit as Maria Vargas in *The Barefoot Contessa* (1954), written, produced, and directed by Joseph L. Mankiewicz. *(Courtesy Associated Press)*

BIG LIE ABOUT FILTER CIGARETTES

Confidential

TELLS THE FACTS AN[...]ES THE NAMES   Mar. 25c

WHAT MAKES AVA GARDNER RUN FOR SAMMY DAVIS JR.!

VIC DAMONE:
EX-SWEETIE SAYS
HE'S A POPPA!

America's Number 1 Shame: **TEEN-AGE DRUNKS**

SEE PAGE

WHISPER

NOV.
25¢

Life and Debt of the Big-mouth who said:
'I Killed No Man That
Didn't Need Killing'

[Mickey Cohen]

Burt Lancaster's
Mysterious
Miss-adventure
in Paris

Women Who Regretted Loving
GOOD-TIME CHARLIE

Charlie Chaplin

A MILLIONAIRE'S
STRANGE LOVE
for
AVA GARDNER
SEE PAGE 16

The 1950s was the heyday of the scandal magazines, and their perpetual cover girl was Ava Gardner, whose uninhibited lifestyle was heaven-sent to publications like *Confidential*, *Whisper*, and *Hush-Hush*. *(Author's collection)*

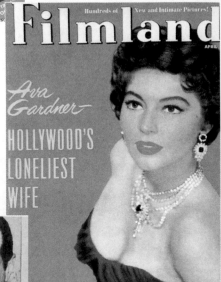

Hundreds of New and Intimate Pictures!

Filmland

APRIL

Ava Gardner

HOLLYWOOD'S
LONELIEST
WIFE

Midnight

VOL 18 — NO. 39   APRIL 10, 1972   F   30¢

Now It Can Be Told:
The Strange
Affair Between
Howard Hughes
& Ava Gardner

At a *tienta* in El Escorial, Spain, spring 1954, Ernest Hemingway demonstrates the proper use of the *muleta* to the world's greatest bullfighter, Luis Miguel Dominguín. Ava Gardner, the matador's girlfriend, looks on. *(Courtesy A. E. Hotchner)*

A press conference in Singapore, during the world tour to publicize *The Barefoot Contessa*, autumn 1954. *(Courtesy Associated Press)*

Ava Gardner as the Anglo-Indian Victoria Jones, with Stewart Granger, in *Bhowani Junction* (1956), directed by George Cukor. *(Courtesy Museum of Modern Art)*

The Little Hut (1957), starring Ava, Stewart Granger, and David Niven, filmed in Rome at Cinecittà studios, featured the small, amusing role of a *faux* cannibal for Ava's current lover, Walter Chiari, "the Italian Danny Kaye." *(Courtesy New York Public Library)*

In Spain, under the tutelage of Dominguín, Hemingway, and others, Ava became an *afi-cionada*, a devoted follower of the bullfight. As a guest at the festive testing of the young bulls in the small rings of wealthy ranchers, she could sometimes be tempted to make a few passes of the cape with one of the deadly animals. *(Courtesy Associated Press)*

Poster for *The Naked Maja* (1959)
(Author's Collection)

Ava as the Duchess of Alba in *The Naked Maja*, filmed in Rome. *(Courtesy Museum of Modern Art)*

Ava undergoing torture as the Spanish prostitute in *The Angel Wore Red* (1960), costarring
Dirk Bogarde. *(Courtesy Museum of Modern Art)*

Ava as Maxine Faulk, Mismaloya hotel keeper
in the John Huston–directed *The Night of
the Iguana* (1964), from the play by
Tennessee Williams, with Richard Burton as
the Reverend Shannon and Fidelmar Duran
and Roberto Leyva as the "beach boys" Pepe
and Pedro. *(Courtesy New York Public Library)*

In the mid-1960s Ava moved to England. Here
seen on a London street in 1969, with her
beloved corgi, Cara. *(Courtesy Associated Press)*

Ava as the legendary beauty Lily Langtry in Huston's *The Life and Times of Judge Roy Bean* (1972). Here, in her single scene in the film, Ava as Miss Langtry is greeted by the stationmaster, played by Huston crony and practical joker Billy Pearson. *(Courtesy British Film Institute)*

Ava with her much-younger love interest, Ian MacShane, in the odd fantasy film *Tam Lin* (1970), directed by Roddy McDowall. *(Courtesy Museum of Modern Art)*

Ava's London flat at Ennismore Gardens, her final home. *(Courtesy HS Photos)*

Ava as Mabel Dodge, D. H. Lawrence's wealthy American patroness, in *Priest of Love* (1981), with Janet Suzman as Frieda von Richthofen and Ian McKellen as Lawrence. *(Courtesy Associated Press)*

During the shooting of *The Sentinel* (1977) in New York City, Ava with Mearene "Reenie" Jordan, her longtime maid and companion. *(Courtesy Associated Press)*

Ava Gardner in 1985, in her final work as an actress, a guest appearance in a television pilot called *Maggie*. *(Courtesy Cinedoc)*

rable shot). Instant sales. Now, in a fresh, illicit liaison with Franciosa, she had placed the picture takers on full alert. Night after night they dogged the couple's trail, staked out each club and restaurant they entered, gave chase through the empty, predawn streets, Ava and Tony in a Thunderbird convertible or newly purchased Facel-Vega, the photographers swarming behind them on buzzing Lambrettas, gunning engines and screeching around ancient corners while the rest of the city was trying to sleep.

One night that summer, the night of August 15, the Feast of the Assumption, would come to be seen as the quintessence of this glamorous and absurd time in Rome. It was another long, humid night like all the rest that summer, but emblematic and influential—as some would have it, the night *La Dolce Vita* was born. Around two o'clock in the morning, a gang of photographers had spotted Farouk, the obese exiled King of Egypt, sitting at the Café de Paris with his fiancée and some other people. The photographers—five of them—decided to get some pictures and came charging at the group (in those days the need for a photoflash and the absence of telephoto lenses meant photographers were required to be very close to their subjects for a good picture), which the king and his bodyguards mistook for an assassination attempt. Farouk put the closest photographer into a headlock and wrestled him to the ground while the bodyguards battled with the others. Bodies crashed around, knocking over the café's metal tables and chairs, drinks spilling in the air. The police were summoned, but by the time they arrived, the photographers had run away, having received a tip that Ava Gardner and Tony Franciosa were arriving at Bricktop, the nightclub on the opposite side of the Via Veneto. The photographers charged again, Ava screamed as a bright Bruin flash went off directly in her face and Franciosa, enraged, lunged at the man. A fight ensued, and the photographer got much the worst of it. But Franciosa, unlike King Farouk, had no bodyguards, and so the other photographers were able to rush at him and drag their comrade away to safety. Ava, agitated by the violence, refused to leave the nightclub until the photographers had gone, but they waited her out, and when she exited the club at four-twenty that morning, many were still waiting for her and chased her home.

To those involved it was all just another night in Rome, nothing worth making a fuss about. But someone decided to write up the story for one of the daily newspapers, the story of the movie stars, the fat king and his girl-friend, the photographers and the all-night battle, titled it PHOTOGRAPHER ATTACKED BY FAROUK AND FRANCIOSA. The tale was then retold (now under the title THAT TERRIBLE NIGHT ON VIA VENETO) in the national weekly *L'espresso*. The piece caught the attention of filmmaker Federico Fellini, who had been trying to develop a scenario about Rome's decadent café society. Fellini went on to meet with the leader of the photographers in the fracas, a man named Tazio Secchiaroli. Tazio would supply Fellini with numerous stories from his hectic life as a freelance shooter, including many close encounters with Ava Gardner (it was Secchiaroli who had waited in that cardboard box for the shot of Ava in a towel), and from some of these stories Fellini and his collaborators would develop the screenplay for what became his epochal film, *La Dolce Vita* (The Sweet Life).*

Ava Gardner would become the prototype for *La Dolce Vita*'s visiting Hollywood star, played in the film by Anita Ekberg (herself not an un-known prey of the Italian photographers), a ravishing, wild, sometimes barefoot screen goddess whose desperate search for excitement goes on deep into the night. Ava's influence was felt throughout the film's first hour, even informing Ekberg's wardrobe, the provocative adaptation of an Italian clergyman's garb that was a replica of a controversial outfit originally created for Ava by the Fontana sisters; the outfit had caused so much negative comment in Italy for its supposed disrespect to the church that the sisters requested she allow them to take it back. Fellini's film, re-leased in 1960, was the cause of considerable analysis and punditry in me-dia and cultural circles. There was grave concern about the depiction of modern life as nothing more than joyless hedonism and spiritual empti-ness; to Ava Gardner the first half of *La Dolce Vita* must have looked like home movies.

---

*For the film, Fellini gave one of his photographer characters a name that would become the uni-versal term for anyone who practiced freelance celebrity photojournalism in the Roman mold: *Paparazzo*; Fellini sometimes said he had taken the name from the character of a hotelier in British writer George Gissing's 1909 book *By the Ionian Sea*, enjoying its appropriately pejora-tive sound, but Tazio Secchiaroli claimed it had been the actual nickname of a photographer friend of his.

Her romance with Tony Franciosa continued its passionate course until the arrival one day of Franciosa's wife, the volcanic presence known as Shelley Winters. Franciosa feared Winters's wrath, but he seemed incapable of disentangling himself from his alluring costar. And now the paparazzi pictures of the two had begun to surface in the press. Mickey Knox, having accepted Franciosa's *"droit"* philosophically, advised him of the potential disaster ahead. "The paparazzi were all around, and he was very volatile. I told him, 'You must be fucking crazy! Shelley's coming, and you're out there getting photographed!' But he was caught up in this thing. Then he wouldn't tell Ava Shelley was coming. I told him, 'You've got to tell Ava that Shelley is coming, don't surprise her.' He said, 'Yeah, yeah, you're right.' But he never did. He could punch a fucking paparazzo, but with these two women he didn't know what to do! I knew Shelley from the time she was an extra; I didn't want to be any part of this. And I was with Ava when Shelley arrived. I was playing Jotto with her. And all of a sudden Shelley pranced on the set, and she screams out, *'Ava!'* And the look on Ava's face was unbelievable. Tony hadn't said a word about his wife coming to town."

According to Winters (in her memoir) she had arrived in Rome to find her husband a physical and emotional wreck, shriveled, sick, frightened. What in the hell had he been up to? The studio driver told her that Franciosa had not slept in three days and not eaten in no one knew how long. "Whatever was happening on this film," Shelley mused, "whatever its name, was killing him."

Soon she learned its name.

In Shelley Winters's account, her husband admitted his wrongdoing—it may have been difficult to cover up at that point, with the evidence being displayed in newspapers and magazines around the world—and begged for forgiveness. *"Shell,"* he told her, "you left me alone for six months . . . *I'm not a very strong person."*

With some days off before two weeks of location shooting in Naples, Winters ordered her husband to go with her to the isle of Capri for a rest cure, taking a moment to confront Ava Gardner, whom Shelley would recall as being ready and eager to accompany the couple on their getaway.

"I got very quiet and said, 'Ava, I grew up in Brooklyn with Murder Incorporated as my playmates. . . . I went to junior high school with these men. Ava, I swear, if you so much as set a foot on Capri while my husband is recuperating, I'll put a contract out on you."

The affair was over.

But not quite. Shortly after the conclusion of filming in Italy, they all found themselves in London, all at the Savoy Hotel; Shelley and Tony in one suite and Ava in one on the floor below. Ava had called him, needed to see him again, she had said. "So I went down," Franciosa would recall, "and emerged days later."

The way it had finally ended, the end of the whole exhausting, crazy affair, Franciosa would remember as the weirdest part of all. One night they had been together in London, and Ava had told him she was pregnant and he was the father.

He didn't believe her. "And in fact it wasn't true," he told Rex Reed. "She wasn't pregnant. I was dumbfounded. At that moment the situation didn't seem romantic anymore. The fact that it wasn't true seemed very out of character for Ava.

"She never spoke to me again."

With the completion of *The Naked Maja*, Ava's life as a studio contract player ended. For the first time since she was eighteen years old, seventeen years ago, she was no longer in the employ of Metro-Goldwyn-Mayer. The separation caused no nostalgia on the actress's part, only relief (fears for the future were something else again). One could talk all one wanted about tradition and ties that bind, but as far as she was concerned the contract had been a license to steal. For *The Naked Maja*, Ava had received ninety thousand dollars from her studio. The going rate for a star of her rank was five times that amount and more. With a proper payout, she hoped, the business—the ordeal—of making movies, could be over within another few years, a few major vehicles to take her out in some sort of style and to leave her rich for life.

For consideration as her next film, her first as an independent contractor, David Hanna had relayed an offer from producer-director Stanley Kramer for her to star with Gregory Peck in the screen version of Nevil Shute's novel *On the Beach*, slated to begin filming in Australia in January. Apprised of the offer, Ava's representatives in Hollywood had urged her not to do this story of the poignant last days of the last people on earth following an apocalyptic nuclear war. Too depressing, the William Morris Agency told her, not the right part and a likely box-office flop. But she had been impressed by the screenplay, and she had been deeply touched by the character of the woman, Moira, a weary romantic who had seen too much of love but now enjoyed one last bittersweet—literally doomed— romance. David Hanna encouraged her to accept the offer, saying that Stanley Kramer was a class act, that the film would be treated with respect, and that it was a distinguished way to begin her freelance career, perhaps even the sort of thing that got one an Oscar. Ava said she wanted a half million dollars. Kramer countered with four hundred thousand and perks. He came to see her in Rome. She agreed to meet with him only on a night out, and with a raucous group she had gathered they went club hopping. She refused to talk business, refused to talk to Kramer very much at all, becoming preoccupied with some flamenco dancers and then at last disappearing into the night. It was an eccentric performance, and Kramer had been plainly distressed. He told Hanna that maybe after all Ingrid Bergman would be a better choice for the part. Hanna had had to give him a spiel, how she was shy—people didn't realize how shy she was—and did Kramer hear how she had cried when she read the script? Kramer nursed his second thoughts. Hanna was irked, knew he should have been used to her unpredictability, the unfathomable turns of behavior, but he still couldn't believe that after all her heartfelt ruminations about the future this was how she had chosen to begin her career as her own boss, muddying the first important, lucrative deal on a whim. And then Ava had come out of nowhere to meet with Kramer just a few hours before he left for the airport, and she had given a charming, charismatic performance; everything got settled, Kramer was starry-eyed, and she sent him off to Hollywood with a big kiss. Dave Hanna went to the bar at the Excelsior— the Snake Pit it was called by Americans—and had a stiff drink.

The hardened bruise on her face had gotten harder and she had flown to London for a weekend to let Sir Archibald McIndoe have another look. The doctor now told her that the accumulation of dead tissue below the surface had become attached to the cheekbone, and that to release this hardened buildup would require a small operation. An appointment was made. The idea of having her face sliced into by a surgeon's knife—even one in the skilled hands of Sir Archie—filled her with dread. The accident had already shown her the fragility, the impermanence of her appearance. A few days before the scheduled operation she canceled it. McIndoe called her some weeks later, asking her as a personal favor to make an appearance at his charity bazaar in East Grinstead, an annual event to benefit the hospital nurses' pension fund. She was not at all eager for a public display of that sort but couldn't bring herself to refuse him. They spoke several times in the days leading up to the bazaar, and McIndoe brought up the subject of her cheek, and eventually, subject to McIndoe's powers of persuasion, she had again agreed to have him perform the operation, scheduling it for the end of her brief appearance at the charity bazaar. The benefit would serve as a cover, no one would have to know about the other business at all. David Hanna had accompanied her to England and to the bazaar. There were photographers and reporters, a public appearance to be made, and the surgery—all the ingredients, he assumed, to cause his employer flamboyant distress, and he had steeled himself for the first awkward, temperamental, or irrational scene of many ahead. But the opposite had occurred, she had gone through it all like a charm, strong and upbeat, no problems at all. Her unpredictability, Hanna realized, was the only thing you could rely on; otherwise you lost as much sleep worrying about what she didn't do as what she did.

With a tiny incision behind the ear, allowing access to the bone, the doctor quickly removed the dead tissue, closed the opening, and was done. It was only when she had been wheeled into the recovery room with her face covered in bandages that Ava finally released her stifled fears, crying and sobbing uncontrollably. She asked Dave Hanna if he thought Sir Archie had really performed the operation on her face or if without telling her he had given the job to someone else, to some underling. Hanna was taken aback to realize that she wasn't joking.

Her face would heal as well as expected. A faint concave line on her cheek would remain as permanent evidence of a foolish afternoon.

Written in the Cold War atmosphere of A-bomb brinksmanship, Nevil Shute's *On the Beach*, adapted for film by veteran screenwriter John Paxton, posited a post-nuclear-holocaust world in which the end of humanity is at hand, the only survivors of the catastrophic conflict—the inhabitants of Australia and the crew of a single U.S. submarine—awaiting their inevitable, imminent end from the nearing clouds of radiation. The intertwined story lines followed the last chapter in the lives of assorted characters coping with their grim fate: a local naval officer and his young wife (to be played by Anthony Perkins and Donna Anderson); a scientist who had helped to create the weapons that were now to destroy him (Fred Astaire, in his first nonmusical role); the American sub commander, Dwight Towers, who has lost his family in the war (Gregory Peck) and Moira, the boozy, bittersweet woman who falls in love with him. For Stanley Kramer, a high-minded, politically liberal filmmaker with a tendency to preach (*The Defiant Ones*, *Judgment at Nuremberg*, and *Guess Who's Coming to Dinner?* among the other films on his résumé), *On the Beach* had an antiwar-anti-nuclear-proliferation message he felt born to tell.

Kramer had determined to shoot the film wherever possible at the Australian localities of each scene in Nevil Shute's book, including Frankston, Canadian Bay, the Phillip Island raceway, and all over the city of Melbourne. Although there had been a film industry in Australia for decades, large-scale studio space was limited, and Kramer decided to build his own from scratch, taking over the seventy-acre Royal Showgrounds, most often the site of agricultural fairs, transforming halls that had previously been used for judging sheep and cattle into soundstages, production departments, and dressing rooms. While the U.S. military had rejected all requests to aid Kramer with what they considered his gloomy, no-fun take on all-out nuclear war*, the Australian government, pleased to have their country's shores opened to international filmmaking, made available to the producer all that he needed including the use of their top-of-the-line submarine HMAS Andrew. Kramer's preparations and negotiations had gone on for months before actual filming began and there had been so much attention in the press that by the time his stars had arrived from Hollywood and elsewhere, there were few in all Austral-Oceania who were not aware of the cast list and planned locations and much else about *On the Beach*, the movie.

---

*According to Kramer, the Pentagon's Strangelovian spokesman told him: "Your story says an atomic war would wipe out the world, and that isn't so. Only about five hundred million people would be killed."

On New Year's Day 1959, Ava (with Bappie and Dave Hanna) departed from San Francisco for Australia (delaying her arrival by several days with a sudden, impulsive stopover in Hawaii: She simply decided to get off the plane in Honolulu and go swimming). A great crowd of press, fans, and gawkers came to the airport in Sydney to greet her arrival, and then another when she reached Melbourne, where production was headquartered. She had been gracious and appreciative of the initial welcome, the inescapable friendliness of the Australian people, but the crowds and the press kept coming at the same frenzied level the next day and the next, swarming around her rooms in an adjunct building on the grounds of the St. James Hotel in Yarra. *On the Beach* was the first large-scale, star-studded production to be made in Australia; the enthusiasm and curiosity were huge. Batteries of reporters and photographers had been assigned to the subject, charged with bringing back a daily supply of anecdotes, interviews, and pictures to meet the public's demand. Peck, Astaire, and Perkins came in for their share of scrutiny, but nothing to compare with the interest focused on Ava Gardner.

"She could not go anywhere without being bugged by people," recalled Tony Trabert, the American tennis star who had met Ava on the flight to Australia. "We got off in Sydney and she went on to Melbourne, and eventually we went down there to play a tournament and we invited Ava and her sister to come to the tournament and they did. A bunch of us went out to dinner with her afterward. She was a lovely, lovely person, and she was warm to everyone. But it was tough for her to be out like that. They wouldn't leave her alone. If you went to a restaurant, whatever you did. She couldn't just enjoy an evening. They would hide behind trees and drive by in a car and take pictures. They just haunted her. It was pretty tough for her to move around like a normal person. She could never have any peace. It made her reclusive. Most of the time there I think she stayed pretty much to herself."

For Ava and Australia's legendarily brash news gatherers, Melbourne became another Rome, another theater of war. They countered her reclusiveness and perceived disdain with printed back talk and gossip. She was chastised for her arrogant, finicky ways (one headline read, DON'T BE SNOOTY AVA!), for her refusal to do a Red Cross charity advertisement (as her costars had done), for arriving an hour late to work (actually, due to a schedule change), and for demanding that the wallpaper in her rooms be redone. They speculated about an affair between Ava and the married Tony Trabert. One piece of reportage threatened to turn the entire host city against her. Melbourne in those days self-consciously bore the reputation for a lack of cosmopolitan excitement, and so it was touching an open sore when she was quoted as saying, "*On the Beach* is a story about the end of the world, and Melbourne sure is the right place to film it." The quote was soon picked up and reprinted everywhere, some who read it reacting with amusement (especially if they didn't live in Melbourne), but quite a few concluding that Ava Gardner was a boorish, ungrateful guest. In fact, the offending quote had been made up by *Sydney Morning Herald* reporter Neil Jillett. Jillett had been assigned to get an interview with Gardner, but this proved impossible, and the only fresh news he had uncovered was the number of bottles of scotch the actress had ordered delivered to her flat. Dispatching his copy, he added the Melbourne quote, he would explain later, intending it as a joke, but somewhere en route to a morning edition the context got lost. "I wanted to do a correction," Jillett recalled, "but the editor didn't care. The line got picked up everywhere, and Ava had to answer for it, I'm afraid. I've researched it and found that it is the second-most-cited quote about Melbourne of all time, always with Ava having said it. And so I have had to live with the fact that in over forty years as a writer, my one famous line has been ascribed to someone else."

Trying to slow the negative publicity, Stanley Kramer pleaded with Ava to attend a brief press conference. "She was utterly unable to cope," Kramer would recall. "She was terrified. She began to shake as soon as they started asking personal questions. . . . The Melbourne press really gave her a bad time; asked questions about her tax situation, whether Frank Sinatra was coming to see her, how often he phoned her. . . . She was too frightened to be equal to them. . . . She refused to let them take any photographs, even if they agreed to throw away the pictures she didn't like. The press of course resented her. So they always printed the worst pictures of her they could get."

Through the months of filming, Kramer had found Ava to be a person of great fascination and great contradiction, appealing and impossible, funny and self-pitying, arrogant and painfully unsure of herself, often all in the same day. She was prone to what he called "flamenco moods," swinging transitions from happiness to depression, a condition he feared would take a great toll on her nervous system. As an actress, though, she was all he had hoped for and more. She was impressively professional, diligent, skilled (able, in one emotional scene, to cry on cue for seven takes in a row) and creatively engaged, adding detail and tone to the role of Moira, even wardrobe suggestions (some of them supplied from her own things). "She's avid to grasp every nuance of her next scene," Kramer would write of her. "Her projection really is extraordinary. Swiftly she can go from softness to pathos to violence." Those parts of her screen character that seemed to intersect with elements of her own life— Moira a sarcastic but vulnerable romantic, unlucky at love, turning to booze and one-night stands for momentary comfort—Kramer didn't dare to acknowledge in his directions, but it was clear that the actress was exploring the part from heart and soul, bringing to it emotional depth and intimate understanding. Due mainly to Ava's open and sensitive performance, the love affair between Moira and Dwight became on film one of the most tender and real in any Hollywood production of that era. Too tender and real, perhaps, for the sensitivities of author Nevil Shute, who argued strongly against Kramer's decision to let the couple have a sexual relationship, whereas the character of the commander in the novel pointedly abstained in deference to the memory of his dead wife. Kramer believed that Shute's attitude was too severe and puritanical, and that to follow the novelist's version in the matter was to deny the genuine love his two characters felt for each other and would trivialize the only affirmative subplot in the story. Shute became so enraged with Kramer's refusal to keep his characters unsullied that he turned against the production altogether; it has been suggested that Shute's lingering bitterness about the film may even have contributed to his sudden death the following year.

The weeks crawled by, full of hard work, heat—temperatures well over a hundred in that Australian January—countryside locations infested with fat, biting flies, and the pesky, ever-buzzing intrusions of gawkers and reporters. Melbourne was—if not the end of the world—a city of very quiet charms. There was little for a film star to do after a day's work other than try to avoid being photographed. The town in those days followed a conservative regimen, and liquor was not allowed to be sold after six in the evening (this savage law didn't change until 1966). Ava had in any case put herself on the wagon for a while, a temporary "health kick" to reduce her weight and the puffiness of her face she had noticed in the first rushes. The absence of alcohol made the nights pass even more slowly and uneventfully. There were occasional parties at the rented mansion of Gregory Peck and his new wife, Véronique, complete with meals prepared by an imported French chef, but Ava felt subdued, constrained in the company of her fellow stars, and while the others made small talk or played cards after dinner, she would slip away to the hallway by herself and sip a cup of tea or just sneak home (without the aid of liquor in such gatherings, she could be as shy and self-conscious as she had been at her first Hollywood parties eighteen years earlier). She felt stifled, lonely. Where was *her* redemptive romance like Moira's with her submarine commander? One evening she and Tony Perkins ended up together, and she found herself making a strong play for the young, sensitive actor. It was awkwardly rebuffed. Perkins's romantic interest was not in the opposite sex.

"I would overhear conversations when she and her sister were chatting," remembered Alan Harkness, the film's assistant editor. "And I understood that she was very bored. She didn't mix with many people, didn't have many people to talk to. Everyone tended to stay away from her, she seemed so unapproachable. They were a bit afraid of her. But I felt that a lot of the time that if anybody had just walked up to her and said 'Hi' and talked to her like a normal person, he would have been really welcomed, or if a young bloke had come up in a sports car and just said, 'You want to take a trip down the coast?' she would have jumped at it. People just stayed out of her way, and I think she really wished she could have gotten to know people.

"There was a wrap party on the stage, with music and dancing, everyone was there. And Ava was by herself, and for a while not a single person was asking her to dance. She was sitting there, bored. You wouldn't believe it. Here was Ava Gardner by herself, and no one would dance with her. And I finally went over to her. I thought, Gosh, I'm not going to let this opportunity go, I'll regret it. . . . So I went over and asked her to dance. And she was great. And the ice was broken, and others came up to dance with her then. But most times people I think tried to keep out of her way."

On impulse one night she called Walter Chiari in Italy and told him to come to Australia at once. She missed him, she needed him. Chiari said of course, he would be there in a matter of days. But by the time he arrived it was too late. The lovelorn mood in which Ava had longed to resume their feisty romance had dissipated. Chiari, desiring a reason for flying halfway around the world other than to be yelled at or ignored, made contact with an Australian promoter who booked him for a performance at the local stadium. It struck Ava as the latest example of what she saw as Walter's trading on their relationship for his own gain, the promoters interested in him only, she thought, as "Ava Gardner's boyfriend." Ava's attitude was, in any case, really just more evidence of her boredom with the man, another attempt to drive him off, and this one had the earmarks of success.

Wanting to get away from Walter and eager to be somewhere livelier than Melbourne, someplace that served booze past sundown—at Chiari's arrival she had gone off the wagon—Ava ordered David Hanna to arrange for them a weekend jaunt to Sydney. In that jumping city she tried to make up for weeks of lost time in forty-eight hours or so. The press caught her scent, and a string of reporters and photographers trailed along in the shadows as she wandered from dive to dive in Sydney's raffish, neon-lit King's Cross. The visit properly climaxed with an unpleasant scene that made all the newspapers, a run-in with a newspaperman of course, this after midnight in a club called the Corinthian Room, where she arrived with Hanna and Bappie and one or two others met along the way, taking a table near the music and ordering a drink (not her first).

"I was working for the *Sydney Sun* at that time," recalled journalist Steve Dunleavy forty-four years later in New York City, "and she was shooting *On the Beach* in Melbourne, and now she was in town and she was news. I caught up with her—it was about one or two in the morning—at a club owned by Joe Taylor, the Corinthian. There was a very-well-known singer appearing there by the name of Norm Erskine, and I knew him pretty well. I went to Norm and he told me, he said, 'I wouldn't go near her, man, she's in a foul mood—you go near her and she'll hit you with a champagne bottle . . .' I stayed anyway.

"I made my way over to the table. There were about four people with her, no other names there, just some hangers-on. They were all drunk.

"She had a PR guy, Dave Hanna. Nice guy. A hell of a nice guy. I came up to him and I said, 'Look, we want a picture of Ava,' and all that. I said, 'If you want to get the bottles off the table first'—it was common with celebrities to want to remove the evidence of alcohol for a picture—I said, 'that would be fine.' Anyway, he was very nice about it, but then Ava looks around at me and says, *'Who the fuck are you?'*

"I turned to her and I said, 'I'm terribly sorry to bother you, Miss Gardner, my name is Steve Dunleavy and I'm a reporter with the *Sydney Sun*, and we would like to have a picture of you . . .

"She started shouting four-letter words at me. And then she reached into the bucket for the champagne bottle, just as Norm Erskine had predicted! They must have taken it away. But she had a full glass of champagne in her hand and she threw that at me, the glass and all. She just drenched me with it. I remember I had on a very light tan suit. And of course my lead the next day was: 'Last night I shared a glass of champagne with actress Ava Gardner: she sipped it and I wore it.'

"And that's pretty much what happened. But the thing I remember about that night, although she was drunk—and I'd heard all the stories about her, the absolute marathon drinking she did—and she's cursing at me—it was incredible to hear what came out of her mouth, like a sailor and a truck driver were having a competition—and I'm drenched in champagne—regardless of all that at that moment as I saw her face the only thing I could think was, how *bloody gorgeous* the woman was. She was absolutely stunning."

The next week Walter Chiari performed his concert in Melbourne, received a rubber check for his efforts ("He deserves it," said Ava, when Hanna relayed the news. "He's a sucker"), and left for the airport. Reporters came to record his departing words, less a press conference than a Hamletic monologue:

"This time it is really good-bye. Ava and I have parted and come back together many times, but this time it is final. I know what I'm doing. No one has to feel sorry because they think I've been hurt. I know when I'm hurt and I know how much hurt I'm willing to take. . . .

"I suffer because I love Ava, and I love her because I understand her, because I know she is so good and defenseless and because I know she suffers. If I could say just one thing to people, and especially to the press, I would say: 'Be kind to Ava. Because this is the only way to make her realize that people see in her more than she thinks they do.' "

She began making telephone calls to the man she so often ached to talk to at the lonely and restless moments in her life. Long distance calls to Los Angeles and Palm Springs and Las Vegas. They had begun calling each other regularly since the divorce—it was his need as much as hers—sometimes once in a month, sometimes several times a week. The conversations might go on for hours, intimate, far-ranging, comforting. Unpleasant memories were unremembered. She had come to think of him as the one person in the world who understood her, who wanted nothing from her, who cared only for her friendship and her happiness.

One night at her place in Yarra she was on the phone to him thousands of miles away, and he was telling her about a concert he had just done, and she said to him that she wished she had seen it and then that she wished she could see him.

He said, "So why don't I come down there and sing to you?"

She said, "I would love that, baby."

"Then you got it," he said.

The next time they talked he told her to leave some time for him on her dance card, he was on his way. It had taken a couple of hours to make it happen. He called the promoter he knew in Australia, an American guy named Lee Gordon. They booked it immediately. He was on his way. He traveled light, no orchestra, flying over with the great jazz combo he had been performing with in the States, the Red Norvo Quintet (Norvo, Jimmy Wyble, Jerry Dodgion, Red Wooten, John Markham) and pianist Bill Miller. It was an extravagant gesture, calculated to impress. But why the visit had to be in the form of a very brief, professional engagement neither Frank nor Ava seemed to consider. They would be happy to set eyes on each other, and they would leave it at that.

The local press interest in Sinatra's visit was enormous, of course, raised higher still by the presence in Australia of his former wife. Ava told David Hanna how she wished she could go to the airport and meet his plane the way ordinary people did. Hanna told her, "So do it. Just forget you're Ava Gardner and go to the airport and meet him." She looked at her manager in shocked disbelief, as if he had suggested she go to the airport naked, on the back of a mule.

She sat in the front row at the concert. He sang "All of Me" to her and they locked eyes like in the old days, as if there was no one else in the stadium. The scene afterward was chaos and invective. Sinatra bodyguards played rough with the local rubberneckers. The singer's imprecation to a photographer was widely reported: "Take another picture and I'll ram that camera down your throat. You stink!"

She went with him in the limousine to his hotel, a dangerous chase as a fleet of reporters' cars followed them, everyone moving at high speed, and Sinatra screaming for his driver to run them off the road. They went up to Frank's suite, and had some food sent up and drank champagne and talked and looked at each other and they went to bed.

In April, after nearly four months, she left Australia. The press was there at the airport to record her departure—though a fraction as many as had greeted her in January. Then it had been like the arrival of some dazzling monarch, huge crowd, cheers and smiles all around; now, in April, it resembled the hunched exit of a deposed monarch. A farewell statement to Melbourne: "Miss Gardner does not feel like talking today." For a week before she left the country, waiting only to know that her vocal dubbing was completed, she had barely left her rooms in the little building near the St. James. A reporter asked David Hanna about a story a resort hotel was putting around, that Ava was treating all her friends from the movie to an expense-paid beach holiday. Hanna joked to himself, "What friends?"

Australia would be the end of the line for David and Ava. The news of his termination had not come to him as much of a surprise. They had argued too often of late, and Ava's list of grievances and suspicions had grown too long for them to continue. Always uncertain of her place in the world, she was ever on the lookout for betrayal, Hanna believed, and age and fear and liquor had made it all the worse. Made it for him, at times, unbearable. You could be her greatest, most trusted friend one moment and treated like a barely tolerated servant the next. Often she had dropped hints that she suspected him of various corruptions, taking kickbacks from hoteliers or restaurants, tipping off photographers to her whereabouts for a share of the spoils, that kind of thing. Then she would do something so kind or generous or adorable, behave with such sympathy or honesty, that he would be back in her corner again, devoted. "I know how awful I can be," she said to him once after he had turned in a letter of resignation at the end of a particularly awful weekend in Paris. "But you know I don't mean it. . . . I'm sorry a minute afterward and at night I cry myself to sleep."

In Los Angeles a press conference was scheduled to publicize the opening of *The Naked Maja*. She had told someone at Metro she would be there, but she didn't go. It didn't matter: Nothing, no one was going to help—the film had disaster painted all over it.

She returned to Spain briefly then abruptly left. She was restless, dissatisfied, lonesome, but lonesome for what she wasn't sure.

Through the summer of 1959 she drifted. No plan, no itinerary. She would stay somewhere for days or weeks. One morning she would head for the airport again. She went to San Francisco, Palm Springs, Florida, and Haiti. She lay in the sunshine and swam in the palm-shaded pool at a hotel in Petionville, above the capital. She moved on by taxi to Cap Haitien, a dusty, spine-breaking five-hour drive. Her stay is well-remembered at the Hotel Mt. Joli, if not pleasantly so. Two rooms were taken (numbers 25 and 26) at the rate of eight dollars each, meals included. Miss Gardner drank at the bar till she fell asleep, to be carried to her room, say those who recall the brief but formidable visit. Late in the night she cried for the kitchen to be reopened for her dinner; she stayed up drinking till dawn. Her idiosyncratic schedule continued all the next day: She wanted breakfast at noon, lunch in the evening, supper after midnight. Ava and the management sparred. On the third day Madame Bussenius, the owner, requested that she look for lodging elsewhere. The hotel keeper's English was not so good, and there was some confusion regarding her request.

"What did you say to me?"

The request was repeated with elaborations, mostly in French. Ava picked out the repeated use of the word "*merde*." She cried out, "*That* I understand!" The two women began shouting at each other across the lobby while other guests looked on. As Yvette Bussenius recalled it, "She launched forward, wanting to attack me . . . she screamed, battled, kicked and called me all sorts of names." Only staff members rushing up to restrain the two women prevented physical injury.

The guest's checkout was expedited, Madame Bussenius closely observing her departure from the hotel. She recalled that Ava Gardner wore no shoes.

She moved on to Cuba. In January, Fidel Castro and his revolutionary army had seized control of the island. The dictator Batista had fled for his life. The political prisoners rotting in the colossal stone prison were freed, and fresh new political prisoners were invited to take their place.

At the Hotel Nacional she took a small suite on the second floor with a view of the *malécon* and the sea. Havana showed the signs of the recent upheaval in the shuttered shops, abandoned businesses, and patrols of khaki-clad, rifle-toting *barbados*, but the city was otherwise much as she remembered it, full of sun-tanning tourists, beggars, rum, rhumba, sin. The daiquiris at the Floridita remained ice cold, perfect.

Like everyone else in the summer of 1959, Ava had been fascinated by the stories and pictures of Cuba's charismatic, bearded liberator. And the *comandante*, as it turned out, had a similar interest in the *yanqui* movie star. A meeting was arranged at the Havana Hilton, the general's base of command. Castro greeted her with extravagant Latin gallantry. He took her on a tour of his headquarters, high up in a former VIP suite, now transformed into disheveled office space he shared with his brother Raul and Che Guevara. They sat on the balcony overlooking the whole city, drank Cuba libres, and Castro told her about the revolution and his dream of a prosperous and equitable future for his nation. She'd had no idea how tall he was—perhaps six-foot five in his combat boots, one of which was untied (also, his socks did not match). She thought him a compelling personality and very attractive, even the beard. ("She spoke very highly of Castro when she got back," said Betty Sicre. "She was very impressed with him. Said he was full of good ideas.") Ava wanted to know if it was true that he hated Americans. Fidel told her no. He hated only Richard Nixon. Some Americans, Fidel told her, he found very sympathetic.

What more occurred between the two is unclear, though Ava's attentions were evidently sufficient to enrage Castro's beautiful nineteen-year-old German translator-mistress, Ilona Marita Lorenz. "Gardner was after him," Lorenz would recall to writer Ted Schwarz, the "middle-aged woman" sending him numerous notes that the mistress claimed to have intercepted before Fidel could see them. The two rivals at last came face to face in the lobby of the Hilton, and it was an ugly scene. Ava was staggeringly drunk, said Marita, and called the girl "a little bitch" for hiding Fidel from her. Ava followed her into the elevator and then, said Marita, slapped her hard in the face. A Castro bodyguard named Captain Pupo, also in the elevator, drew his pistol from its holster and told everybody to cool it.

That night Fidel reassured his mistress he had rid himself of the movie star. "He had fixed up Ava Gardner with an aide," Lorenz claimed, "who was to satisfy her in a suite at the National Hotel, compliments of Cuba."

Ava flew to New York in late August. Frank loaned her the run of his new luxury pied-à-terre in Manhattan. She haunted the jazz clubs. She went to see Miles Davis at Birdland. She went every night. Pee Wee, the midget emcee, would introduce her from the bandstand. Ava and Miles became friends. "She was a stunningly beautiful woman," the trumpeter would remember in his autobiography, "dark and sensuous. . . . Man, she was a hot number." Some nights after the show at Birdland they would go out somewhere together. "We didn't get down or nothing like that. She was a nice person, real nice, and if I would have wanted to we could have had a thing. I just don't know why it didn't happen, but it didn't, even though a lot of people swear that it did."

One night at a party, Miles Davis said, she started kissing him. She had a beautiful full mouth, said Miles, "soft as a motherfucker."

In September she went to North Carolina, to Raleigh and then Smithfield and Brogden, visiting with each of her sisters and her brother in turn. There were new members of the family to meet each time she came, it seemed, nieces and nephews marrying and having kids. Their lives went on and prospered, all within a few miles of Johnston County. There were parties and barbecues, and the young people would pester her with questions, and the older sisters would scold them to stop making such a fuss over the girl and let her eat.

One day in the last week of September she boarded the Atlantic Coast Line train out of Selma and returned to New York City. On the night of her arrival she left for Europe.

In Madrid changes were coming. Beatrice would be going away, leaving her for America—leaving her for love. She had found a guy, a fella in the business, Art Cole, a veteran prop man who had come to Spain for a picture and returned to Hollywood. They had gone around together, fallen for each other, and wanted to give marriage a try. Bappie was no less devoted than ever, but she was nearly sixty years old and craved a little time to have some kind of life that did not involve her baby sister. Bappie had been her protector, booster, and the closest thing to a restraining influence (though some observers considered her quite the opposite) for twenty years, and now she was not going to be there anymore. And Reenie Jordan, Ava's trusted servant, would soon be missing as well. They were more like sisters, too, than employer and employee, but Ava was always the sister who paid the salary and had the last word in any argument. For Reenie the time had just about come to see if there really was a world out there without Ava Gardner. With her support system missing, Ava would find continued life at *La Bruja* more difficult and lonely, and soon what roots she had planted at the house in Moraleja would be pulled back out.

Later that autumn she flew to Rome to begin a new picture, *The Angel Wore Red*. Titanus, despite the debacle of *The Naked Maja*, had sought out Ava for their next international production (pursuant to the modest hope that lightning strikes once). Again it would be an Italian operation with MGM as mostly silent partner, once again a film with a Spanish setting shot in a Roman studio, the project barred from Iberian locations by the controversial subject matter (the Spanish civil war). As with *The Naked Maja*, the direction (and script) would be by a Hollywood veteran, this time Nunnally Johnson, a celebrated screenwriter (*The Grapes of Wrath*) and producer for decades at Twentieth Century–Fox and of late—and reluctantly—a director, with middling result, his heart still back in a warm room alone with his typewriter. It was the story—per Johnson—of "horny priest and virgin-type prostie"—a heroic cleric, that is, pursued by the forces of evil, taken under the wing of a luscious, gold-hearted hooker. Cast as the priest was Dirk Bogarde, Britain's fifties matinee idol, now in the course of revealing himself as a serious and daring screen actor. Unlike *The Naked Maja*'s mishmash of a script, *Angel*'s screenplay by Johnson had some coherence and the character of Soledad seemed compelling on the page. "It was," Bogarde told the *Evening Standard* in 1961, "a magnificent part for Ava. It would have done for her what *Two Women* did for Sophia Loren. She really put her heart into it."

Also unlike *The Naked Maja*, filming of *The Angel Wore Red* at least began with efficiency and a sense of purpose. Ava found Johnson wonderful company; he adored her and made her laugh; they were fellow Southerners who tried to outdo each other with tales of their humble beginnings ("Where I come from," said the Georgian Johnson, "Tobacco Road people are the country-club set"). The good times ended fast, however. Seeming to embrace the deglamorization process that had begun in *On the Beach*, Ava's physical interpretation of the role called for an earthy, Gypsy sensuality, sans makeup or underwear. A glimpse of the first footage shot and word came down (from Hollywood, according to Dirk Bogarde): This would not do. The higher-ups claimed the footage showed her with bags under her eyes and her ass spread all across the screen. This film stared Ava Gardner not Anna Magnani, they squawked. She was ordered into makeup and a girdle, *prontissimo*. Said Bogarde, "The life went out of Ava after that."

Before the production's end, she vowed never to make another movie. Enough was enough. She was going to collect her final fuckin' paycheck, she grumbled, and when the check cleared she was out of business, retired, for good.

Johnson, too, soured on the job at hand (it would be his last as a director). Used to the whipcrack efficiency and vast infrastructure of big-studio filmmaking, he became mired in the elusive ways of the Italian system. (Johnson: "In Italy you shoot from twelve o'clock to eight. That's in theory. But at noon they break for lunch, so you really start at one, if you can get them back. It's a very loose organization.") There were problems with the Mafia-organized extras, problems with the Vatican, and the director's job requirements included keeping a running count of the number of Communists versus Catholics the production employed. "The day I finished the photography," Johnson told biographer Tom Stempel, "I was given a ticket to leave town. I never saw the final cut. I've never seen the picture. I don't know what happened to it."

"It opened," wrote Dirk Bogarde, "apparently to ten Eskimos in North Alaska, closed the next day and sank without trace."

On the Beach opened in mid-December. With his editors working all during production, Kramer had been able to have an initial cut of the film completed while he was still in Australia. Screened for his production staff and invited guests, that first cut had run three hours and ten minutes. By the time of the film's commercial release, fifty minutes had been removed, possibly under some pressure from United Artists. "At three hours ten, it was a great, great movie," said assistant editor Alan Harkness, one of those who had seen the first cut back in Melbourne. "What got taken out were all these little scenes that had humor and drama and ordinary people, and he left in every scene that repeated the message about the stupidity of mankind in destroying itself, and in so doing he took out too much drama and left in too much message. It actually felt longer and slower at two hours and fifteen than three hours ten. When I went to the premiere I was the most disappointed person in the theater because I knew what was missing."

Kramer's arrangements for the film's opening displayed both inspired showmanship and his prideful belief that *On the Beach* was—at any length—a profound creation, the movie that was going to save the world. On December 17, 1959, after painstaking planning, the film had an unprecedented simultaneous "global premiere" in sixteen cities and on seven continents (Berlin, London, Moscow, Paris, Rome, Stockholm, and Zurich, in Europe; Johannesburg in Africa; Tokyo in Asia; Melbourne in Australia; Los Angeles, New York, and Toronto in North America; Caracas and Lima in South America; and Little America, in Antarctica). Gregory Peck attended the premiere at the Domkino in Moscow, while Ava Gardner appeared in Rome's Fiamma Theater where those in attendance included the Italian president and his entire cabinet. After the film's stark conclusion—a montage of empty Melbourne streets signifying mankind's end—audiences around the world responded with standing ovations (presumably an endorsement of the film's antinuke ethos and not of human annihilation)—though in Tokyo, it was reported, a large portion of the audience sat weeping at the end and stayed long after the lights had gone up in the theater (accounts of the Antarctic premiere have not been uncovered). The reaction of reviewers, a breed rarely accused of trying to save the world, was more reserved, many acclaiming the film for its lofty aim and dramatic impact but others deriding Kramer's "radiation romance" as preachy, defeatist, and/or dull ("How," asked one critic, "can the spectacle of the civilized world dying in front of your eyes be so strangely unmoving?"). The film's initial newsworthiness soon faded, and in the end *On the Beach* did not become the momentous event or lasting statement of Stanley Kramer's dream, slipping into its general release and vying for the public's coins like any other movie of that atomic age.

The mixed reaction to *On the Beach* as a whole muddied a greater appreciation of Ava's wonderful and touching performance, and what many had at first expected to be an award-winning triumph for the actress did not come to be. She *was* widely praised in the reviews, though the commendations sometimes included a blurring of the line between the thirty-seven-year-old performer and the bruised, blowsy character she portrayed. One critic declared that she had never acted better or looked worse. It was an inevitable comment regarding a woman whose very name had for so long represented physical perfection and desirability. Pepe Rotunno's soft, shaded images presented her with sympathy and care, and her bewitching eyes and the sublime crescent curve of her mouth were never more hauntingly captured on celluloid. But the camera did not turn back the clock, and the screen gave damning evidence: The goddess was mortal.

ELEVEN

"Love Is Nothing . . ."

She lived now without plan or purpose, escaping the past, evading the future. Happiness had proved elusive. Love didn't last. Beauty and fame and success were not all they were cracked up to be. She wanted to forget everything, said a friend, wanted only "to drink and dance and screw." She refused the tourists who came up for an autograph on the street. "Aren't you Ava Gardner?" they would say and she would answer, "No, I just look like her." Wanting it to be true.

On her return to Spain early in 1960 she put the house at La Moraleja up for sale. The place she had once thought would be her home for life was barely five years old, and she was through with it. It had always been a headache to manage, after all, something always falling apart, a phone connection impossible, the toilet flushed properly only on special occasions, repairmen like permanent residents, bills never ending, and now there were annoyances like the American jets from Torrejon flying too low, the increasing construction around the area changing her once-isolated enclave into a suburban hub. In the spring she moved out of *La Bruja* for good. While the house awaited a buyer it would be rented out on short-term lease, mostly to visiting movie stars and directors. Tenants complained of rats (seen sipping at the pool) and gossiped about the mirrored ceiling above the bed.

It suited her needs to live in the center of things, within the comforting embrace of a city where the nights went on forever, she would say, "if you knew your way around." After living out of hotel rooms for a few months she settled on a new permanent residence, a modern duplex apartment with terrace at 11 Avenida Doctor Arce in a discreet neighborhood of villas, apartment houses, and embassies off the Plaza de la Republica Argentina.

The dissolute life she sought in her newly declared retirement was not difficult to effect. She was now without responsibilities—no family, no work, no lover worth a second look. There was no one to answer to, and she herself was not asking any questions. Impulse and indulgence became guiding principles. By day, like a beautiful vampire, she did little other than sleep; with nightfall came the drinking, and with the drinking came the taste for blood. These years—the early 1960s—played out like a very long lost weekend. There were scenes, reckless liaisons, unfortunate misadventures. She left a trail of legend throughout Spain, her exploits disseminated like modern myth from Chicote's to the Barrio Chino. There was the night she was found wandering in the Reforma park, disoriented, wearing only bra and panties, and the incident—so they said—with a rejected young lover who tried to kill himself, and the wrecked cars, the wild parties. She could be literally dangerous to know. Old friends, out of self-preservation, faded from her life. She cultivated a new entourage from the Gypsy gangs who wandered the bars performing for tips. They came home with her to dance and play till the sun rose and beyond, feral characters among them who did not let her hospitality prevent their routinely stealing anything not locked up or nailed down. Sometimes she would wander off with a group of them, disappear for days, sojourns that were—all for the best—forgotten upon their conclusion. Esther Williams, MGM's Technicolor mermaid and a friend of Ava's since the 1940s, had moved to Spain with her husband, Fernando Lamas, in the summer of 1961, and in Madrid the old studio sisters would cross paths on several occasions. Williams remembered the young girl she had known in Hollywood long ago, the sweetest person in the world back then. Now, in Madrid, Ava's "halo of stardom" had dissolved. "She had gone from famous to infamous to notorious and was now regarded as something of a menace to polite society," Williams wrote. She would recall an impressive encounter with Ava in the company of her new playmates ("the ne plus ultra of trailer trash," according to the mermaid) at a party in the home of Luis Miguel Dominguín and his wife, Lucia Bose. The decorous gathering had been suddenly crashed by the actress and her Gypsy friends, all of them drunk, and the uninvited gang began to perform a flamenco, Ava stepping up onto a wooden table to dance, guitars and song and clapping hands and stomping feet merged in percussive assault on cringing guests. Facing Luis Miguel she danced with a wicked fury, her skirt raised high above her legs, revealing to the awed matador and to everyone else that she wore nothing underneath.

Her regimen encouraged unreasoned behavior, wicked moods. She burned bridges, usually from midstream. Restaurants and nightspots that had been honored by her presence five years before came to dread the star's business and the inevitable outbursts of imperiousness and para- noia, the cursing, the ugly scenes. At a number of her haunts she was banned outright, including Horcher's, long her favorite place for dinner. Loudly dissatisfied with the "cheap Spanish gin" in her martini, she had poured the drink down the owner's trousers. She was most notoriously barred from the Hotel Ritz, where one unfortunate night of drunken in- sensibility she had openly urinated in the vestibule between the reception lobby and the bar, witnessed by startled staff and passing guests. As a re- sult she was forbidden to ever reenter the hotel, an edict that in their rage the Ritz management had extended to any and all movie people, the pro- scription more or less enforced for years to come. (Director Billy Wilder claimed he had once pleaded with the manager for special dispensation— "I swore to God I would not pee in the vestibule.") Once in a while— longing to revisit that favorite bar with its cozy elegance and excellent bartender—she would attempt to test the hotel's resolve. Ben Tatar, for a time Ava's personal secretary, recalled, "She came in to me one day and said, 'Get dressed, we're going to the Ritz. I'll show those bastards they can't keep me out!' She had us both get all dressed up and we went there, and she was not allowed into the hotel. They stopped her from entering. There was an annex where we could sit and have tea outside but that was as close as they let us come. And she'd stare at the building, calling them all bastards, and trying to figure out how to get back in."

Testimony to the daunting scale of her hard living: It awed even Robert Mitchum, Olympian debauchee. "He was in Madrid making a movie," remembered Betty Sicre. "He and I were sitting in the lobby of the Hilton Hotel. I was waiting to meet Ava, but I hadn't mentioned it to him yet. We were just chatting about Madrid and about working there. I saw Ava come into the hotel then, and I said to him, 'Oh, there's Ava. Let me go get her.' And Mitchum jumped up and said, 'Ava Gardner! No, no—don't tell her I'm here! *If I get together with Ava I'm done for . . .*' And he sort of backed away and ducked behind a palm tree and ran off. He seemed very afraid of her bad influence."

When she grew bored with her Madrid routine, she would travel, often on no more than a couple of days' planning, sometimes without a plan at all. It was a short drive to Barajas, after all, and there was always a flight leaving for somewhere. She would fly off to New York or London or New Orleans or Monte Carlo for a few days or weeks. Once on an impulse she had gone to Las Vegas by herself to surprise Frank on the first day of an engagement at the Sands. She arrived to learn that he was hosting his first wife and his children for the occasion; without telling him she was there she checked out of the hotel immediately and took a taxi back to the airport. In any place she visited, the scene was the same: a suite at the finest hotel, bags of luggage sprawled in *deshabille*, close attendance by room service, a recruitment of acquaintances old or new, dinner, dancing, a club crawl till whatever hour the local laws allowed, and then figuring out a way to go on for hours after that. An expatriate friend from Madrid, Betty Wallers, remembered a weekend jaunt to London that began at a Covent Garden ballet among the formally dressed royals and high society and ended in a raucous dance joint, Ava sweeping through the nightclub in white chiffon gown, diamonds, and tiara. Heading straight into the ladies' room, Wallers recalled, "Ava lifted her dress and wriggled her girdle off. After more contortions she got off her undies. Then she took off the tiara and the diamond bracelets. The whole lot was stuffed in our handbags. Ava shouted, '*Thank God I'm me again.*' And wriggling happily she went back into the club. Later on she took the entire band home with her when the club closed."

A reporter dogging her trail in the fall of 1961 logged the itinerary of a typically manic visit to New York City: Ava "showed up at the Chateau Madrid with Tony Pastor's son, Guy . . . stormed out when a flamenco dancer started snapping pictures. . . . went to Count Basie's opening at Birdland and laughed until there were tears in her eyes when Jerry Lewis borrowed the baton and led the band . . . danced the pachanga with bandleader Pupi Campo . . . showed up at Jilly's with a bunch of unidentified men at closing time . . . 'I'm Ava Gardner,' she said, 'and I've brought along my own piano player!' . . . brought four men to a party by fashion photographer Bill Helburn. One of her escorts stood on his head on the floor to amuse her, but she was only bored . . ."

She went to Hawaii one winter. Tempest Storm, another fabled sex symbol, a striptease artist of legend, living in Honolulu in those days and married to Ava's old pal Herb Jeffries, befriended her there. "She was a great person and a great friend," Tempest Storm remembered. "And she was a wildcat, I'll tell you that! My husband introduced us. As a matter of fact, I *think* she and Herb had kind of hit it off once, they had a little thing going.* But I never questioned him about it. Let sleeping dogs lie. That was before he knew me. Ha! I said, 'It's great you can still be friends.'

"She was in Hawaii sort of on a holiday. She was with someone when we met. I think he was a bullfighter. She had a knack for collecting those. She was still a great beauty. Still flirty. Flirted with a lot of guys, of course. We used to play tennis together. I was staying at the Colony Surf, and I think she was maybe at the Ilikai, I'm not sure. I was working at the Forbidden City in Honolulu. She came to see the show. And we all went out to have breakfast after at a place called Coffee Dan's. It was late at night. I remember she couldn't seem to get her order correct with the waiter, and she had a little 'misunderstanding.' And all of a sudden she picks up her plate and throws a plate of eggs into the waiter's face. I said, 'Oh my God, Ava! I'm so embarrassed!' And she said, 'Well, he couldn't get my breakfast right.' To her it was no big deal. Well, you had to say, 'That's Ava,' you know. Always kind of wild. I think she had had a couple of drinks. And then I heard a story the next night she was at the Red Vest and they threw her out bodily when she was giving them a bad time over there! But basically I found her to be a very nice person. We had a lot of fun together playing tennis.

"She wanted to know what it was like to be an exotic dancer, a stripper. We kind of talked about it. She said, 'You know, I think I could do that. What do you think?' I said, 'Well, Ava, it's not as easy as it looks. It takes a lot of work to do it right and with a lot of class. But I could be a good teacher if you want to try it.'

---

*To reiterate an earlier statement: In our conversation, Herb Jeffries denied any intimacy with Ava Gardner.

"Well, then no one saw her for three or four days. And the rumors were really flying about her. She was holed up in a hotel with some black singer, I don't remember who the singer was, someone performing there. I took it with a grain of salt, you know how rumors start.

"Basically I have to say I liked her very much. She was a great gal, you know, and I considered her a friend. Still a great beauty, I'll tell you. Time was being kind to her. We had a lot of fun. She was an original."

In Madrid now her staff consisted of a battery of maids and kitchen help, her driver, Manolo (in charge of her bargelike American convertible), and for a period of time a series of live-in personal secretaries. The secretaries were American or English, and all were male ("They can be trusted more than a woman," she told Sidney Skolsky), some homosexual and some not, some unavoidably—if briefly—becoming involved with their employer on a more intimate level. All would quickly find themselves in something other than a business relationship, caught in the silky, sometimes sticky web of the boss's high-strung existence, an attachment that was nonetheless often abruptly terminated after some imagined or esoteric betrayal of her trust (one secretary was supposedly fired over the unaccountable absence of two golf balls). One year the secretary's position was filled by a young aspiring actor named Ben Tatar. "I had heard about the job through Gene Kelly," Tatar remembered. "I had worked for him on a picture, and at that time Reenie was Kelly's maid in Paris. Then Reenie was back with Ava in New York. But Reenie did not go back with her to Spain. This went on all the time with them. Ava would go into a fit and throw her out, and then she would call and apologize and Reenie would go back.

"Ava interviewed me for the job in New York. When she opened the door it took my breath away: She was much more beautiful off the screen than on. She asked whether I would be interested in taking a trip around the world as her secretary. She said she needed a letter written turning down the governor of North Carolina, who had invited her to a testimonial dinner. I did the letter and she liked it. I was hired. And that was the last secretarial work I ever did. The trip around the world never happened. Once we got to Madrid, I just became a part of the family, part of her strange life.

"When we got to Spain there was a guy there living in the apartment.

An American, an air force major. He might have been an old boyfriend, but I can't swear to it. He had been living there and looking after the apartment, and then finally she threw him out. She didn't make a film when I was there. I was sorry about that; I would have liked to have been involved. She was sent scripts all the time. They didn't interest her. There were only a couple of people left whom she was willing to work with, otherwise she didn't want to know. She was thirty-eight or thirty-nine at that time. She had fallen off a horse, damaged her face; she talked to me about that. She said that after the accident she had lost her looks. I couldn't believe she thought that. I had never seen anybody who looked as beautiful as she did.

"My job was basically to keep her company. After she got up we might go to play golf over by the U.S. air base. She was not a bad golfer, much better than I was. She knew someone on the base who gave her a pass to come and go. We would play golf, and then we would go to the clubhouse and play the slot machines. If she lost at the slots she would get upset. Every Thursday and Sunday we went to the bullfights. Sometimes the bullfighter would dedicate the bull to her. And when a bullfighter dedicates a bull to you, you have to do something in return, and so she would invite him to dinner that night, if he lived. Many nights we had flamenco parties, with the Gypsies. This is something she did almost every night, actually. We had many of them at the apartment because she was banned from a lot of the flamenco clubs. The parties went on all night, dancing, music, drinking. Every night. We'd have dinner at six in the morning. Ava loved to dance, not only flamenco. We used to dance at home. It came over her: she *had* to dance. She'd put some music on and we'd dance a little bit in the foyer of the apartment, and into the living room. The bossa nova was popular at the time, and we would dance the bossa nova. She played a lot of Frank Sinatra's records. She had every record he ever made. He called the apartment sometimes. I got the feeling they were still in love with each other. The first time I answered the phone when Sinatra called he said, '*Who the hell are you?*'

"We didn't involve ourselves that much with people. She didn't keep close friends because she'd usually thrown them out when she got on a binge. She was a great person until she got drunk, but she started drinking almost from the time she woke up. She was a lonely woman. She didn't have a boyfriend when I was there. Her romances never survived. I think alcohol was the main culprit.

"We had our own liaison, which I won't talk about. It wasn't romantic. It just happened.

"Yes. She was a great person. . . ."

Not long after moving into the duplex apartment in town, Ava found herself with a new downstairs neighbor. Juan Perón had been the president-turned-strongman of Argentina from 1946 to 1955, his notoriously idiosyncratic populist-nationalist dictatorship a success at first thanks to the help of his charismatic, platinum blond spouse, Eva Duarte de Perón, the *Evita* of West End–Broadway renown. Following Evita's death from cervical cancer, the dictator's job approval rate flatlined, and a violent coup d'état sent him into hiding. After some time on the run, Perón accepted a gracious personal invitation from Francisco Franco and settled in Madrid, and as a gesture of sentiment a place was found for him off the Plaza Argentina and on the street named after Perón's former ambassador to the United Nations (where Dr. Jose Arce was once known for his spirited defense of the Franco fascist regime, bringing it all back home). Perón was delighted to learn the identity of the woman who lived above him. He had been an admirer of the actress for many years and had tried to meet her during her visit to Buenos Aires on the publicity tour for *The Barefoot Contessa* in 1954 (she was steered clear, something to do with Perón's virulent anti-Americanism and his open-door policy for escaped Nazi war criminals).

Ava did not think much of her new neighbor's politics, but he was an old man now, and they were both occupying the same plot of land in Franco's Spain so she tried to be friendly. Perón had two dogs and a new wife, Isabel, from whom Ava learned that El Presidente was mad for women in showbiz. His Evita, with the Lana Turner dye job, had been a star of radio soap operas. He had met the beautiful *new* Mrs. Perón (his mistress until pressure was applied by Franco's Catholic advisers) when she was performing in a Panamanian nightclub. Isabel made *empanadas* that were out of this world, and Ava would sometimes go downstairs and eat them in the Peróns' kitchen while Isabel would sit and chat, speaking without jealousy about how the late Evita remained the most important woman in her husband's life. The ex-presidente longed to be reunited with Evita's perfectly preserved body (the cadaver had been embalmed to a permanent, astonishingly lifelike condition and remained in Perón's care until it was abducted during the military coup, sexually violated numerous times, then buried in an anonymous grave in Milan, Italy; eventually Perón was able to retrieve Evita's body and bring it to Madrid, where it would lie in its coffin inside the Peróns' apartment). Ava characterized Isabel as a "dumb broad" and never knew how much to believe of the odd things she heard about her. Mrs. Perón dabbled in the occult and at some point brought home to live with them her own warlock, a male witch (he was formerly a doorman) who performed macumba ceremonies in the living room. Isabel was also a big movie fan, became very excited when she learned that Ava was making a film with Charlton Heston, her favorite star (she had seen *The Ten Commandments* seven times), and wanted to know all about him. "Well," Ava told her, "he wears a wig."

Eventually the good relations turned sour. Perón complained that he couldn't sleep due to Ava's predawn—and postdawn—parties, the loud music and pounding flamenco dance steps on the ceiling. Ava, wanting to return fire, complained of the noise from his "yipping" poodles (though her own dogs were not exactly stoic). One day she was hosting a get-together with eight or ten of the young American pilots from Torrejon air base, and Perón's pets had apparently gotten loose and were making a racket in the hall. "So I said to my two corgis, one of which was blind, 'Go get those two little mutts!' " She swore no lasting damage was done to the Perón dogs, but the Argentines were outraged, called in a complaint to Franco, and soon a contingent of Guardia Civil arrived at the apartment house with orders to arrest Ava and everyone else in her apartment. The presence of the uniformed Americans complicated things, and the guards went away for new orders. Ava and the Peróns avoided any further contact after that, or at least friendly contact. Ava claimed that the ex-dictator often stood on his balcony and made speeches to an imaginary crowd of supporters, and that she and her maid would go out on their balcony as genuine hecklers, shouting, "Perón is a faggot!" in Spanish. Not very neighborly, perhaps, but after all the man had once given safe passage to Josef Mengele.

In July 1961 she heard shocking news: Ernest Hemingway had taken his own life. Driven into turmoil by physical and mental ailments, a shotgun blast through the head. She had enjoyed their friendship, their times together in Spain and Cuba. His books were among her favorites, and his characters were people with whom she could identify, for better or worse. She had taken pride in her association with his work on-screen, however mixed the results, and took to heart the compliments he had offered for her performances.

Ava's friendships with writers were among the most prized relation-ships in her life. They became a validation of sorts for her intellectual in-securities and a window onto a world of articulate thinking. With Robert Graves she continued to visit and to exchange notes and letters. She wrote to him often at low points in her life, with intimate confessions of her fears and disappointments. He would send her words of advice or comfort, sometimes a small poem, often with a little drawing beside it. "Getting your letters makes up for all the motion picture crap," she wrote him. "In-stead of feeling dirty and useless I felt very strong and worthwhile . . ."

She visited him at Deya in Majorca and in England, and went with him to Oxford to attend his final lecture as professor of poetry at the univer-sity. At the reception afterward she chatted with *Lord of the Rings* author J. R. R. Tolkien, who found her "easy and agreeable" but otherwise had no idea who she was.

There were other writers she counted as friends: Budd Schulberg, James Baldwin, Henry Miller. Miller, the author of *Tropic of Cancer*, which Artie Shaw had put on her reading list during their marriage ("Holy shit, what a dirty book!" she had reported to her husband), begged for an introduction to Ava from George Cukor. The old Brooklyn roué thought her the sexiest female he'd ever seen. They exchanged letters, and she sometimes called him for a chat at his Pacific Palisades home. He sent her autographed copies of his latest works. A print he sent her of his wa-tercolor *Three Heads*, signed and inscribed to "*Divine Ava*," hung in her London residence for many years.

"She liked being with writers, I think that was true," said Budd Schul-berg. "She tended to look down on her own work. She didn't think what she did anyway was much of an accomplishment and thought maybe that hanging around with writers was going to do more for her mind than hanging around with movie actors. There was a feeling in her of 'self-improvement,' wanting to expand her sense of the world, to talk about art and politics and things besides the movies."

In mid-1962, after two and a half years of professional inactivity, becoming fearful about her bank balance, Ava was at last persuaded to return to work. There had been no swell of nostalgic or creative compulsion impelling her before the camera, no longing for the old camaraderie and shared adventure of a film production. Far from desiring to end her early retirement, she would later speak of those wholly inactive years as like a wonderful float in warm water, sadly interrupted.

She accepted an offer from Samuel Bronston to play the female lead in something they were calling *55 Days at Peking*. The prospect of acting again was made slightly less annoying by the fact that the film would be shot not far from home, in and around Madrid. Bronston was a Bessarabian-born film producer who had left Hollywood after a career of no great distinction and in the late 1950s established headquarters in Spain, promoting investments from a hodgepodge of private speculators and distribution companies to bankroll a series of historical epics: *John Paul Jones, King of Kings*, and *El Cid*. He saw himself as a potentially great independent mogul in the tradition of Sam Goldwyn, making what he hoped were high-quality grand-scale motion pictures with international appeal. He borrowed heavily and spent freely for talent and production value. He leased vast acres of Spanish land for his sets, employed craftsmen by the hundreds, extras by the thousands, and for battle scenes most of the foot soldiers in Franco's army. What Bronston lacked was the iron will or the eagle eye of a Goldwyn, and his films were generally produced in an atmosphere of disorganization, middle-level corruption, and creative chaos. *55 Days at Peking* would be no exception.

The project came into being as no more than a historical subject—the Boxer Rebellion of 1900—dangled before the ranking king of screen epics, Charlton Heston. Bronston's de facto creative chief, Philip Yordan, and designated director, Nicholas Ray, talked Heston into signing a contract without a story or script written (screenwriter Bernard Gordon said Yordan "threatened to throw himself out the window of the hotel room unless Heston yielded"), and with nothing more than a title and a star Bronston presold *Peking* around the world and began reconstructing the Forbidden City (the royal Chinese enclave, not—see above—the Honolulu strip joint) on a field outside Madrid. Six weeks before filming the principal roles besides Heston's (set to play a rugged U.S. marine) were yet to be cast. The script, quickly written by Gordon (a Hollywood exile, victim of the blacklist), then written a second time when Yordan found the first draft too complex for the popcorn-eating masses, centered around the foreign legations in the capital city under siege by angry nationalists. The feminine "love interest" was a Russian aristocrat, a worldly adventuress who finds romance amid the insurgency, but just barely, before catching a fatal Boxer bullet. Bronston hoped to give Deborah Kerr the part (she was unavailable), while Heston favored Jeanne Moreau or Melina Mercouri. It was Nicholas Ray who suggested Ava Gardner, and Bronston endorsed the choice, certain his far-flung network of distributors would be pleased with a star known to even the most remote box offices of the world. Bronston offered her five hundred thousand dollars to portray Baroness Natalie Ivanof in *55 Days at Peking*, and she took it. Also hurriedly added to the cast were David Niven as the British ambassador, Flora Robson as the Empress Ts'u-hsi, and John Ireland as a marine sergeant. The hundreds of ethnic Chinese needed for bit parts and extra work would be press-ganged from all over Europe, many literally hired out of Chinese restaurants and laundries.

Things began pleasantly enough. Late in June Ava hosted a cocktail party for some of *Peking*'s personnel and that night she was in top form: charming, interested, funny. The skeptical Heston was favorably impressed: "She has a softer quality than you get on the screen," he noted in his diary, "more accessible, vulnerable." There was chitchat about Hollywood and some of the films in current release. Ava realized how far she had fallen out of touch with the picture business. She had never even heard of some of the new hits or stars. There was talk about the film they were about to make, and someone offered up a nugget of research about Chinese court life, not as yet in the script: how the empress dowager—*55 Days at Peking*'s villainess—made visiting diplomats kneel down in tribute and kiss her pudenda. Ava declared that the empress was her kind of gal and demanded Bronston recast her in the role.

A few days later, at a script conference in Nicholas Ray's villa, things went less well. Those gathered began to offer their views of the screenplay and the characters. Ava sat curled up, shy and tongue-tied until she had downed a second stiff vodka and tonic, then unleashed an angry assertiveness, complaining and cursing about the "fucking lousy" script and her unspeakable dialogue. The fury of her rhetoric made some turn away in shock. People looked to Nicholas Ray—legendary director of *Rebel*

Without a Cause and *In a Lonely Place* (as well as Bronston's *King of Kings*)—to bring the discussion to order but the director seemed curiously at ease, accepting the star's rant. The bitter discussion continued for most of an hour. Heston sneaked away and didn't come back (his diary entry: "A macabre evening").

After her corrosive behavior at the script conference an atmosphere of anxious expectation surrounded the actress's first day before the camera, a scene to be shot on one of Bronston's soundstages, broiling in the heat of a Madrid summer morning. Everyone was relieved to find her, per Heston, amiable, if edgy, and while she was seen to need "kid glove treatment" from Ray, she performed the scene perfectly. Alas, there would not be many such good days to come. "We had a great deal of trouble with her on that picture," recalled Philip Yordan, who had known Ava in the forties and as screenwriter and associate producer of *Whistle Stop* had played some part in her early steps toward stardom. "She didn't really want to work. I don't know. Maybe she needed the money. She had trouble concentrating at times. She was late. She didn't know her lines. She was very afraid of being photographed. How can you be a movie actress and be terrified of someone taking your picture?"

"She was drinking all the time," said Bernard Gordon. "You heard a lot of stories about her in Madrid, how she had been kicked out of the Ritz Hotel, all of that. She was in decline, I think, no longer at the top of the heap. I had the impression she was a troubled, lonely woman who was squeaking out the end of a long career. I don't know if she didn't care or didn't understand that she was making life difficult. I know that one time on the set she spoke to Paul Lucas, who was playing the doctor in the thing, and asked him if he knew how they could make their scene play better, and Lucas looked at her and said, 'Yes, it would help if you stop drinking before noon every morning.'"

Only Nicholas Ray, whose burden of responsibilities was made still heavier by his star's increasingly erratic behavior, remained firmly supportive. "Ray particularly enjoyed directing Ava Gardner," wrote Bernard Eisenschitz, Ray's biographer, "with whom he formed an alliance of outsiders. She was, indeed, almost unanimously detested or considered impossible: her lateness and her outbursts on the set were soon legendary."

The troubled, unpredictable side of her nature that caused anxiety for everyone else excited Ray as an artist. He was—platonically, aesthetically—smitten, saw in Ava a fellow traveler in nonconformity, a fellow free spirit. Like Lewin, Cukor, others before him, he imagined the great possibilities in their collaboration, the exploration of her persona, the artful unbridling of the qualities only vaguely required by the *Peking* script: dark passion and sensuality. Most of this was wasted daydreaming—like so many of the director's thoughts for the production—inappropriate to the task at hand (sensuality in a Charlton Heston picture!). The kind of poetic realism and idiosyncratic characterization that Nicholas Ray's unique gifts could bring to the screen were simply uncalled for among the cardboard-cutout archetypes and rampaging Chinese rebels of *55 Days at Peking*. "Ray was a great talent," said Bernard Gordon. "This was not his kind of thing. He should have been doing personal stories like *Rebel Without a Cause*. But Nick had his own problems with drinking and drugs and what have you, and he needed a job. He wanted to make this work for him, but he was not very successful at it." (According to some sources, Ray's vices in these years included the use of amphetamines and heroin.)

In August the company moved to the Marqués de Villabragima's rancho at Las Matas, thirty minutes outside Madrid, where a sizable portion of Imperial Peking had been built, much of it to actual scale (all who saw these sets agreed that the finished film never did justice to the truly spectacular nature of Bronston's ersatz China, less than a third of it ever exposed to a camera). A merciless sun made the outdoor work an endurance test for everyone. The pace was sluggish, tempers flared.

The script remained in contention, a work in progress, long past the time when it should have been set. Phil Yordan would commute daily from the sets to Bernard Gordon at his typewriter, with orders for line changes, a new action sequence, a soul-searching monologue suddenly required for David Niven. Fresh blood was flown in at great expense to tweak the odd page with "additional dialogue" (one of these imports being Robert Hamer, the brilliant writer-director of *Kind Hearts and Coronets*; on arrival seen to be in the shocking last stages of alcoholic self-destruction, sent back to London immediately). "If rewriting the script was for the purpose of making the picture better, you didn't mind," said Gordon, "but a lot of it was to keep the stars happy, who were all prima donnas, like spoiled children. If Ava Gardner didn't like something you were supposed to adjust the script so that it would be suitable and acceptable to her. And Heston—who I thought was about as animated as a block of wood—when he found out somebody had a scene rewritten he had to have a scene rewritten. And Niven, too. He refused to work at one point until he got a big speech for himself. Nobody cared if it made no sense to the picture as long as it fed their vanity."

The edict to keep the proceedings big, crowded—"epic"—as often as possible made even simple scenes full of complications and extras and kept everything moving at a crawl. The size of it all made it more likely for things to go wrong, and there were frequent technical mistakes and production miscalculations, forcing them to reshoot pages of script that were thought to be behind them. Director and stars floundered, sunbaked amid the looming fake Peking, drifting into an assortment of private hells, Heston alone remaining diligent and professional, though even he had begun to lose hope. Ava's behavior continued to be erratic, troublesome, until the first week of September, when it crossed over to what some considered the outright irrational. One day, at close to noon, the unit was preparing an elaborate, time-consuming shot involving Gardner and Heston trading lines while hundreds of Chinese, playing refugees, rushed through the gates behind them. Ava arrived on the set very late, increasing the tension as Ray and an assortment of assistants struggled to keep all the elements in order. During a lull in the activity, just before the first take, one of the Chinese extras in the crowd took out a small Brownie camera and snapped a picture of the stars as a keepsake. Ava spotted the man, turned red, cried for a halt to everything. Her reaction, according to Heston in his memoir, "made the Dowager Empress of China seem like your favorite aunt. . . . She insisted the offender be found, fired and stripped of his film. I'm surprised she didn't have him skinned as well."

Ava abandoned the set for her dressing room, exhausted by the ordeal. It would be two or more hours before she agreed to return. Ray and his team wearily worked to put the difficult shot back together: dialogue, crowd, camera movement. They were at last again ready to shoot and—incredibly, it happened again.

"I heard a camera . . . someone's taken a picture," Ava whimpered.

"No . . . Ava, darling, please," said Nick Ray.

"I heard it!"

And that was it, she couldn't work. They had to find who did it, take the film away from him. Heston and others believed that this time it simply had not happened; no picture had been taken; she had imagined it. And no culprit was found. But the result was the same. The shot had to be postponed, she had to go back to her dressing room and calm down from the ordeal.

There was no one else to blame for her seeming complete professional breakdown a few days later while shooting her most difficult—and potentially rewarding—dramatic scene in the film, the death of her character, the baroness, in the legation hospital. A rehearsal had gone well but by the time the set was lit and they were ready to roll, Ava, lying in a hospital bed, could no longer remember her lines. They started, stopped, tried again. She complained that the camera, above and below her as she lay on her back on the bed, had to be making her look horrible, double-chinned. They tried rearranging the angle. She still could not play the scene. Ray tried breaking the shot up, tried feeding the lines to her one at a time from off-camera, but even this seemed beyond her capacity. The director had shown a limitless patience until now, but after hours of Ava's intransigence and impenetrability he was exhausted. The towel was thrown in, the scene was eventually reworked, and most of Ava's lines were somehow given to Paul Lucas to speak instead. The death scene would later be tricked up in the editing room, using pieces from another sequence and an insert of a sheet being pulled over Ava's presumed body, though it seems she was not even in the bed at the time that shot was filmed. "Yordan said she had just disappeared, and they did it without her," recalled Bernard Gordon. It was her big scene and it would end up looking like what it was—unfinished, a mess.

It had been an ordeal for everyone there, and a mystery—no one could fathom the actress's motive. Heavy drinking was too common to credit entirely for her disruptions and distractions. Away from the set she was often seen to be relaxed, untroubled. In the same period she played delightful host to some relatives from Carolina and even granted a couple of reporters private interviews without incident. It was clear only that her heart was not in the job of acting. She had come back to making movies too soon, perhaps—or too late.*

The next day Ava was in her dressing room waiting to be called to the set when Charlton Heston came by and grimly informed her that Nicholas Ray had just collapsed, suffering what appeared to be a heart attack. White-faced and gasping, he had been carried to a car and taken to the hospital in Madrid.

Ava was shaken, Heston remembered, and her response seemed to him to assume at least some responsibility for what had occurred. Heston didn't know what to think. Her behavior had been very bad, but he also felt Ray had not been up to the responsibility he'd taken on. Ray, he decided, was a loser. Others were even less sympathetic. Yordan believed there had been no heart attack, that Nick had faked one as an excuse to quit the picture. But Ray did recover and according to some sources was ready to come back, and Bronston said, "I don't want him back." In any case he did not return, remaining in his house in Madrid while others completed the picture. Nicholas Ray would never direct another feature film.

Andrew Marton, generally a specialist in second-unit action sequences, with notable credits on *Ben Hur* and *The Longest Day*, took over for the remaining work, except two intimate scenes with the leads for which Heston had them import from Hollywood a director he admired, Guy Green (they had worked together on a scenic melodrama called *Diamond Head*). Whether Ava had become sobered and focused by the turn of events with Ray or somehow responded better to Green, these scenes were completed without incident. In the last week of September there were still two months of filming left, for Heston and the hundreds of Chinese waiters, but Ava's work was finally done. On the twenty-ninth she attended a birthday party for one of the Bronston executives and looked spectacular in a white satin evening gown and layers of emeralds. Ava and Charlton

*Almost simultaneously with Ava Gardner's seeming professional devolvement in Spain, Marilyn Monroe, Ava's presumed successor as Hollywood sex goddess, working on the Fox lot in California making a movie called *Something's Got to Give*, had evidenced a remarkably similar inability to perform. After weeks of Monroe's disappearances and difficulties, the filming was halted and the actress dismissed. On August 5, Marilyn Monroe was found dead from barbiturate poisoning. Whether her demise was caused by accident, suicide, or murder remains in dispute, though it was certainly at least in part a death by stardom.

Heston found themselves at first awkwardly seated together, watching as others at the party danced. Heston had been exasperated by her for many weeks—he would forever after call it the worst behavior he had ever seen by a professional colleague. But now it was all over and as they sat and chatted, he became aware again of vulnerability and sweetness beneath the sound and fury. It was difficult, he seemed to feel in the end, not to feel sympathy and a certain mystified awe for Ava Gardner's chaotic journey through life. Exiting the party just behind her, he caught a last, exemplary glimpse of his costar in the Madrid street, beautiful and alone, standing in traffic, looking for a taxi, she had taken up the pose of a matador and was making *veronica* passes with her red evening cape as the cars rushed by. "It was unforgettable," wrote Heston. "My most vivid memory of that extraordinary lady."

When *55 Days at Peking* opened in London in early May 1963, the *Daily Express* ran a feature by longtime Ava Gardner admirer Leonard Mosley. He had been eagerly charting her career for more than a dozen years: first with barely disguised salaciousness, then with growing respect; now he seemed to have composed her professional obituary. The piece was headlined: IS THIS THE TWILIGHT OF A GODDESS? And it began: "I hate to be cruel to a beautiful woman whose proud profile and rich body have quickened my pulses in film after film . . . my dream and idol of the female at her most exotic. . . . But yesterday I saw her in a film called *55 Days at Peking* and my heart instead of yearning for her, bled. Is this the last film Ava Gardner will ever make as the most exquisitely attractive femme fatale that has been seen on the screen?" Mosley listed a series of physical and spiritual flaws in his favorite sex symbol: There were bags, shadows, folds of flesh, she looked tired, acted tired. "She has a world weary attitude towards her performance," he wrote, "which seems to say: 'Oh Lord, if they ask me to do this scene again I shall scream.'"

Legendary status is too rare a commodity to be easily dismissed. Despite her age—the big four-oh in December 1962—despite what some observed as a decline in her appearance, despite her costly and debilitating behavior during the production of *55 Days at Peking*, still she could not deter more offers of work. Soon after finishing her job for Bronston she was approached about a part in a film Blake Edwards would be shooting in Italy in the coming winter, *The Pink Panther,* a farce-thriller that would introduce to the world the character of Parisian policeman Inspector Clouseau. Already cast were David Niven, Robert Wagner, Claudia Cardinale, and, in the role of Clouseau, Peter Ustinov. Edwards and producer Martin Jurow wanted Ava Gardner to play the inspector's chic and chronically unfaithful wife. "All audiences had to do was take one look at Ava's gorgeous pair of lips," according to Jurow, "and they'd understand why Clouseau believed every lie they spoke."

Ava, of course, could not simply be hired for the role. She had to be wooed. Jurow was dispatched to Madrid and put through days and nights of cajoling, flattering, begging, led on a chase through the city's nightlife, picking up the bills for Ava's hungry, thirsty entourage, drinking with Gypsies and doing an improvised flamenco with a restaurant tablecloth tied around his waist. At last, after much annoyance at the fact that Blake Edwards would not relocate his production to Madrid instead of the dreaded, paparazzi-ridden Rome, and with Jurow's consent to a list of costly perks demanded—a villa and staff in Rome, a twenty-four-hour limousine and two drivers, a particular private cook from a certain small Italian village, hairdresser Sydney Guilaroff flown in from Hollywood— Ava agreed to do the movie. Further sweetening the pot, Jurow arranged for French *couturier* Yves Saint-Laurent to provide her a custom wardrobe for the film, though she expressed aggravation on hearing that Saint Laurent would not abandon his spring collection to come to Madrid for her fittings. She flew to Paris, where Jurow and his minions had already done much to try and make her visit a luxurious one—a suite at the Plaza-Athénée, flowers and champagne awaiting her arrival. Unfortunately word had leaked to the press of Ava Gardner's visit, and the presence of photographers at the airport set off a temper tantrum of such foul-mouthed intensity that it left Jurow feeling stained. "There was Ava . . . with swiveling hips and vulgar expletives. . . . She cursed the photographers, only to be jeered at in return. She cursed me prolifically . . . she cursed the driver and the luggage carriers, who were simply doing their jobs and had nothing to do with what she perceived as a betrayal."

Jurow escorted her to the hotel without speaking to her and then called Blake Edwards and apprised him of their star's performance. They were only two weeks from the first day of filming. But the portents of a troublesome shoot ahead were too plain to ignore. Jurow waited till the middle of the night, then tiptoed up to Ava's suite and slipped a note under her door: Thanks, it more or less said, but no thanks.

The next day she would make furious phone calls, fifteen hundred dollars' worth, to the William Morris Agency in Los Angeles, demanding her salary, threatening to sue. But the matter fizzled. A few columnists took brief notice of the veteran actress's dismissal. For *The Pink Panther* she was quickly replaced by a starlet from Charles Feldman's stable, one of his many sometime bedmates, Capucine, whose obscurity relative to Ava Gardner led Peter Ustinov (apparently under orders from his real wife) to withdraw from the production, which led in turn to the last-minute hiring of Peter Sellers for the role of Inspector Clouseau—and thus, one might say, a legendary franchise was born, thanks to the lost temper and colorful vocabulary of Ava Gardner.

"I ran into her one day in Madrid at the Hilton," recalled Marc Lawrence, the actor and veteran Hollywood tough guy, who had moved to Europe in the blacklist period and in the sixties worked for Phil Yordan in Spain. "She was gorgeous, oh, Christ! She had nothing better to do and we were having a party, so I invited her to come up. We were going to have American hot dogs, and she liked that. You couldn't always get that kind of shit from back home. So she came. She didn't stay long. There were a lot of younger women at the party, and I don't think she liked the competition. We were talking, bullshitting. She was drinking a vodka or something. I said to her, 'How's your love life these days, kid? You in love with anybody?' She says, 'Love!' And she swallows the rest of her vodka. She says, 'Honey, love is nothing but a pain in the ass.'"

She had tried to avoid another serious romance, like an addict trying to stay clean. It was bad for her but it felt so good. There were brief flings, people she met—a Spanish film producer, a medical officer from the American air base—people she let pursue her for a few days at a time. There were one-night stands here and there: in Los Angeles with a young Steve McQueen—he complained to friends that she had all but assaulted him. In New York a one-week reunion with Walter Chiari who was making a disastrous debut in a Broadway musical. There was Sinatra, once in a long while in person, mostly on the phone, their conversations a mixed blessing. They were supposed to act like buddies, could tell each other anything, that was the deal, but sometimes there would be a hint of cruelty in the way he'd mention some chick in passing, some funny thing she'd said, and Ava knew that he wanted her to know that he and the chick were lovers and all the fun he was having without her. She would think about him and wonder about the possibilities, and then something would remind her that it was never going to work, and it would leave her upset for the rest of the day.

Friends and relatives sometimes tried to find her a new boyfriend. "I remember Bappie had somehow arranged a date for Ava with Rock Hudson," said Betty Sicre. "Nothing came of it, but Bappie was hopeful. Bappie and I were together then, and Bappie said, 'Oh, they make such a nice couple.' "

When Ava went to visit Princess Grace in Monaco, the princess wanted to "fix her up" with the Greek shipping magnate and her husband Rainier's patron, Aristotle Onassis. Grace—who Ava felt had grown bored in the confines of her little principality and was desperate for some thrills like in the old days, even vicarious ones—excitedly confided that Ari had a reputation as a very forceful lover and the rumor was that he enjoyed whipping his women before he had sex with them. A meeting was arranged, an intimate dinner party at the palace. Ava found the saturnine, late-middle-aged Onassis highly unappealing, whispered to Grace that not even a good whipping could make her change her mind, and slipped away.

In Paris at the time of the *Pink Panther* misunderstanding, she had gone one night to La Tour d'Argent on the quai de la Tournelle, the fabled four-hundred-year-old restaurant considered one of the finest in the world. Oblivious to normal dining hours observed outside Madrid, she had arrived at close to midnight, asking to be fed. The restaurant was empty, the cooks had all gone home. It was Ava Gardner, though, and deference was paid. The restaurant's owner and host, the tall, dashing Claude Terrail, came forth to greet her.

"Do you remember me, Claude?" Ava said. "I came here once long ago."

"I remember very well," said Terrail. "You came with Frank Sinatra."

He explained the unfortunate circumstances of the hour, the cooks all gone, but if she would care for a steak, Terrail told her, he would turn the stove on and cook it for her himself. And so he did, a filet mignon with fresh herbs.

When she had finished her meal Terrail returned again to the table. Ava looked up at him, sighed, smiled.

"Claude," she said, "that was without doubt the worst steak I have ever had."

They agreed to go out for a drink. They sat somewhere and talked and drank till five in the morning, then strolled along the Seine and back to Terrail's apartment below the Tour for a nightcap.

"Just for a drink," recalled Claude Terrail. "But we met again the next day. And again. And she returned to Paris a week later and then . . . for seven months, eight months, all over the world I went with her. My fantastic time with Ava, the most divine person I have ever met."

Claude Terrail was no naif, no stranger to glamorous women or to the eccentric lives of show-business celebrities. He was a playboy of some renown and for a time a resident of Hollywood, where he had been the son-in-law of mogul Jack Warner. He had known every sort of person in the course of his colorful life and he had never—in Paris forty-one years later, his assessment remained the same—known anyone like Ava Gardner. Everything about her would prove to be formidable, exceptional, extreme: her beauty, her generosity, her passion, her anger, her fears.

"Such highs and such lows, this was Ava. Nothing between. Like a queen one moment, a scared child the next. At times so romantic, so sweet, like a girl of seventeen years old. For my birthday a check on which she has written words: *for you . . . in the amount of a million kisses.'* Such lovely thoughts she had. Late at night, coming home to find these small notes she has written and left in a trail—it was like the story of the boy who leaves the stones that lead him home—notes of love across the floor leading to where she is waiting. . . . She was very romantic, a strange, romantic creature. The things she did were not those of an ordinary person. For instance, she was still very close to Frank Sinatra. She still had the greatest praise for him, and she would do something I found to be extraordinary. She would put one of his records on and have a private talk with him, as he was singing. She would sit and listen and say, *'Yes, yes, I know . . .'* or another song and she would say, *'No, don't say that . . . you must forget . . .'* She would have a talk with the record itself. It was something almost mystical. It was really something to see."

Terrail would remember a "dream girl"—from breakfast to nightfall. But then the drink and everything could change. A dream could become a nightmare. Like Jekyll and Hyde, Terrail would recall it. The alcohol made the difference. *Voilà!* Then came the fighting, the suspicions. Imagining that everyone was after her, the newspapers were her enemies—everyone, the chauffeur, or some strange man walking on the street. There were fits of fury. She would throw anything at hand: "Rare porcelain and fine crystal would meet the same fate." Being a person of discerning tastes as she was, said Terrail, the destruction of such beautiful objects would leave her all the more upset when she regained her temper. "In the night she could behave very badly. But if you waited, if you remained faithful, the Ava you loved would return; if you could stay awake to four or five in the morning she would come back from this angry place, back to being the sweetest woman again and saying the most tender things in the world."

It was a jet-set romance: each weekend a flight to one or the other's city, getaways in Europe, America, the Pacific. "Always she liked to go," said Claude Terrail, "to run, run, run. Keep on running." Travel with Ava Gardner, whatever the destination, was no ordinary holiday, more a journey to a surreal landscape where Ava alone possessed the road map. A trip to the south of Spain in her big American car. Ava, Claude, a maid, and chauffeur, a long drive to the coast, to Marbella. In bed at the hotel, Ava suddenly frightened, angry. A shadow in the garden outside their window. She was certain it was a photographer, slithering around in the darkness. They were out there, after her, nothing could convince her otherwise. Everyone had to awaken, pack their bags, they were leaving Marbella at once! They would go to Seville instead, hours on the dark roads, the chauffeur nodding off with his foot pressing the accelerator pedal to the floorboard, the car weaving across lanes, Ava in the back drinking an entire thermos of gin. Arrived in Seville, directing the driver to a club she knew, Ava wanted a flamenco, demanded they bring out the singers, but everyone had gone to bed, even the Gypsies. They drove on to the Alfonso XIII. The night clerk refused to find them rooms. The others could go find another hotel if they liked, Ava said, but in Seville she could stay only at the Alfonso, and then, barefoot, gliding through the lobby, curling up on a plush couch like a child, and going to sleep.

"I would sometimes say to myself, 'Enough!' " Claude Terrail remembered. "But I was too much in love, and she was too beautiful. One time she had been drinking all night and mad at everybody. I thought, I will awake early and I will look at her. I'm going to have a good look at her in the morning, no makeup on her face, after a night like tonight, and I will see the *true* Ava and that will be enough for me to say, 'Forget it!' *Not at all!* I looked at her in the morning and she was the same—*gorgeous, gorgeous*. There was no escape from it."

They traveled to Hawaii together. "We stayed at a villa. In Waikiki. A lovely house. A great time and also terrible. There is a wonderful drink in Hawaii—a mai tai. She loved mai tais. One is perfect. Two, okay. Three, four, too many. She would become unhappy, always fighting. We would be in front of the ocean. She said, 'Well, if you're not going to be nice to me, I'm leaving!' 'Where are you going?' I said. And she looked at the ocean. She said, 'I'm going to China. Leave me alone, I'm going to China.' I said, 'Well, all right, *go* to China!' She tried to get on the raft that was there, and of course she sank. And she said, *'See! See! You want to kill me!'* I said, *'I don't want to kill nobody!'* I said, *'I just want my life to get back to normal!'*

"In Hawaii every night Frank Sinatra called. It was difficult. He did not speak well of me. He would say to her, 'What are you doing there with that son-of-a-bitch? Do you know what I have heard about him?' There is something funny about that part. Later, back in France, I learned that my best friend, Porfirio Rubirosa, and his wife had been a guest of Frank Sinatra in Las Vegas at that time while he was saying such bad things about me to Ava. Sinatra asked him about me, and Rubirosa said, 'Who?' 'You know, your friend Terrail.' And Ruby said, 'Oh, let's not say *friend*. Let's just say I know him.' In Paris I went to him. 'Ruby, why did you not defend me in front of Sinatra?' He said, 'Oh, Claude, think. I am just starting my wonderful time in Las Vegas and suddenly you are starting problems with my host. I did not want to ruin my vacation!' So I said, 'Okay, Ruby. That's all right, then.' "

The holiday in the Hawaiian sun continued on its lyric and explosive course until one more terrible argument. A sudden accusation: Terrail was having an affair with the maid, she was sure of it! The restaurateur turned and started packing. "I said, 'Don't talk to me like that, I'm leaving.' And I left. It was over. I went to a big hotel in Honolulu and I began to call people, friends in Hollywood, New York. I said, 'I've left her. I'm coming back. Please, let's get together for some good times, introduce me to some new people.' And in the middle of my conversation to Hollywood the line was cut off, and suddenly Ava's voice was there instead. *'Claude, you have to come back.'* I said, 'No, I'm not going back with you. You are too rowdy, you're just a drunk.' Etc., etc. I hung up. I called a friend in New York. Same thing. The line interrupted, and Ava is speaking. I don't know how she did it—she had the telephone operator cut into the line for her each time. It was extraordinary. And then! A knock on the door. It is the hotel manager with two very large Hawaiians. The manager says, 'Please, sir, will you pack your bags. I must ask you to leave the hotel at once.' No explanation. I had no choice. I packed my bags, and they took me downstairs. When I crossed the lobby the people looked at me leaving with these two big men at my sides. 'Jesus, he must be a gangster or something. They are arresting him.' And they take me outside to a limousine and open the door. And there is Ava, sitting inside the limousine smoking a cigarette in a long holder. 'Now, Claude, do you see you can't get away?' She had kidnapped me!"

It had to end, of course. "To go on like this was impossible. I had to return to reality. I mean, I had to work, I had responsibilities. My behavior was rather cowardly, but when something like this is so strong, so big, it is the only way, I had to drop it completely. I never saw her again, I never tried to. She came to the Tour once more, I heard. I wasn't there. She said, 'Too bad.' And said, 'Give the bill to Mr. Terrail when you see him.' For her dinner. That was all right. She left a note. She said, 'Thank you for the meal.' Just that. And that was the end.

"Let me tell you, my friend, she was a wonderful woman. I want to always remember the good memories, and not the bad. She was lovely. She had class. She had something beyond anyone."

In June 1963 she returned to America, to New York City. To Frank. Their phone conversations in the preceding months had been frequent, lengthy, and tender. Past disagreements, disappointments, forgotten again. Whoever they were seeing, screwing—however antic their real lives—the voices traveling continents to murmur in each other's head could yet convince of a common emptiness and need. Call by call they led each other back into the old dream. In Manhattan this time, reunited, they were enraptured. For a few hours, anyway. They came together at Frank's East Side apartment and the next time anyone saw Sinatra he was walking on a cloud of bliss. "We're back, baby," he told his gathered lackeys. "It's on. All the way."

They lay around the apartment, making love, nestling, warming to each other in a way they hadn't done in years. Frank wanted to talk about a future. He told her it was time to come back home, and Ava admitted that her devotion to Spain was waning. They could live in New York, Frank said. Or get a nice place on the ocean or an estate in Connecticut, whatever the hell she wanted.

There was—had to be—a fly in the ointment. On this occasion it was an insectile fellow by the name of Momo Salvatore "Sam" or "Mooney" Giancana, a leader of the Chicago Outfit and one of the most powerful crime bosses in the world. Frank Sinatra considered him a good buddy (or a passing acquaintance, or didn't know the guy, depending on who was asking) and in the last few years especially, the two had spent much time together in the pursuit of certain interlinking mutual interests: Cal-Neva, the White House, the passed-around *goumada* Judy Campbell. Ava had met the fierce, gnomelike gangster on a number of occasions in her time with Frank, as she had met many others of his ilk, of variously greater and lesser couth, well-tailored, dead-eyed mob big shots who delighted in her ex's company, and he in theirs. Often in the past she had found herself surrounded by them at her table in a club as she waited to watch Frank perform somewhere, or backstage where she'd see them swarm around their favorite singer kissing and grab-assing like—she'd tell him—so many gravel-voiced fags. It was one more thing for them to argue about. Frank thought the mobsters had style, guts, took no shit from anybody. Ava thought they were slobs and psychopaths who spent a lot of their adult years in jail. Many times through their marriage and after she had spoken against his fraternization with such people. She didn't know much that went on between them and didn't want to know, but she was sure it wasn't healthy.

Now Giancana was in town with his current girlfriend, singer Phyllis McGuire, sexy centerpiece of the big-haired, harmonizing sibling act known as the McGuire Sisters, appearing that week on the *Ed Sullivan Show*. So naturally Frank wanted Sam to join them when they went out on the town. And when Dolly Sinatra demanded they come to Jersey for dinner at the fancy new home her son bought for her (a few minutes and a hundred grand from the old house in Hoboken), Frank had her invite Sam and Phyllis as well. (Dolly remained an Ava booster and during the evening grabbed her former daughter-in-law by the forearm, asking, "So when you two gettin' married again?") Back in New York, Frank took Ava to Jilly's, his hangout on West Fifty-second Street, and naturally Giancana joined them, taking a place at Frank's elbow. Ava resented having the mobster foisted on her like this, spoiling what had been shaping up as a dreamy reunion. She didn't like him, and in so many words and icy looks she let him know it. (The feelings were mutual; Giancana told people he thought Ava Gardner was "a crazy bitch.")

"Hey, lighten up with Sam!" Sinatra squawked when they were alone. "What the man ever do to you?"

"How about what he does to other people?"

"The guy's a businessman. He's a good guy. Ask Phyllis."

"You and your fucking gangsters."

"Ava didn't like those types of people at all," Phyllis McGuire told writer Kitty Kelley. "She hated the image. It wasn't just Sam, either. Frank had others around him all the time and when Ava found out . . . she really gave him hell."

As a member of the retinue in New York told it to Randy Taraborrelli, that night at Jilly's Ava had suddenly had enough and got up from the table where Frank and Giancana were gazing fondly at each other and went wandering off to the other side of the room, where she stopped and sat with a stranger who was by himself having a drink. Sinatra and Giancana stared in open-mouthed disbelief as Ava chatted and flirted with the man and then when she got up and moved over and sat her rear end—the rear end that Sinatra worshipped nearly as much as he adored her beautiful face—sat it far back on the man's lap, Giancana's jaw dropped to the tabletop like an anvil, and Sinatra's face did a Tex Avery complete with steam-whistle sound effect. In a flash Frank crossed the room to them, yanked his ex-wife to her feet, and grabbed the stranger by the collar.

"Are you *crazy*?" Sinatra shouted into the man's face. "You want to *die*? Because I'm the guy to make that happen, chump!"

He took Ava by the arm and hurtled her back to their table. Ava then reached down to the glass in front of Sam Giancana, pulled it from his hand, and tossed the contents in Frank's face. She snarled, once at Frank, and once at the underboss of the Chicago Mob, then exited Jilly's without looking back. According to the witness Sam Giancana "laughed riotously" at Sinatra standing there with a gin-and-tonic dripping from his chin. "Buddy boy," said Mooney, "I ain't never seen anything like that. That was *classic*."

They made up—barely. And then Frank insisted they see still more of Momo. Giancana wanted to throw a little celebration for Phyllis and the sisters after their Sullivan gig on Sunday night. Ava refused to go; Frank insisted, *demanded*. Fuming, she went. At the party, in a Polynesian restaurant on Broadway, they snarled and spit at each other like two alley cats. No one knew what it was about, no one wanted to know.

"Dumb broad bitch!"

"Fucking guinea!"

The gangsters and girl singers sipped their Virgin Sacrifices and tried to look the other way. The next morning, as Frank sat around his living room expounding to some acolytes, a limo driver came to the door and Ava, without warning, emerged from the bedroom, had her bags taken downstairs, and departed for the airport. Frank stared after her, speechless, while his friends in the living room squirmed with empathy.

She spent the rest of the summer with Bappie in California and made another movie in her spare time. It was hard to believe, but she had not done a picture in Hollywood since *Ride, Vaquero* at MGM more than ten years before. It was fine with her if she never worked there again in her life, but the offer by producer-star Kirk Douglas of a six-figure salary for just six days of her time was all but impossible to refuse. *Seven Days in May* was a political thriller about an attempted military overthrow of the U.S. government by a right-wing general, based on a recent, controversial bestseller by Fletcher Knebel and Charles Bailey II. The prospective film had been refused cooperation by the insulted generals at the Pentagon, but President Kennedy personally endorsed the production and offered Douglas permission to shoot some exterior scenes on the grounds of the White House. In addition to old acquaintance Kirk, the film's cast included two of Ava's colleagues from *The Killers*, Burt Lancaster and Edmond O'Brien. Ava's part was that of another world-weary elegant lady with a spotty past, the conspiring general's former mistress now enlisted by Douglas to help foil the coup d'état with some incriminating love letters. There was a sharp script by Rod Serling and the director was the dynamic John Frankenheimer, two veterans of the hectic years of 1950s television. With Frankenheimer's experience putting together "live" ninety-minute broadcast dramas, Ava's tight schedule did not at first seem worrisome: they would simply work at television's killing pace. And with only a single week to do everything there would not be any time for her to lapse into the desperate boredom and confusion she had experienced while making the endless *55 Days at Peking*, in other words, no time to do anything crazy. It was a good theory, anyway. In reality, with such a short schedule there was much greater pressure on her to get it right—and right away. Almost at once Ava was plagued by anxiety. "She was exquisite. She was just so beautiful," Frankenheimer would remember. "A lovely person but at times difficult to work with." She drank, had trouble with her lines, reported late. Frankenheimer was compassionate, but with his youth and ultra-adrenalized personality (and short schedule) he had difficulty slowing down and connecting with Ava's enigmatic sensitivities, and Kirk Douglas, already feuding with the director, seemed reluctant to get involved. Agitated by the pressure to perform, Ava made each day an ordeal, for her and everyone else. There were the usual obsessions to distract her. One day a studio photographer arrived on the set to take publicity pictures. Ava recognized his name from *Life,* a magazine she hated for some past betrayal.

"You people promised me no press on the set!" she shouted. "Fucking *Life* magazine!"

And she ran to her dressing room and would not come out. The photographer was made to go to her and plead his case. After suffering a startling assault in four-letter words—"I mean, I couldn't even repeat it," the

photographer would recall—he was finally allowed to explain the innocent circumstances of his employment and his disassociation with a peri-
odical she despised. The man's abjectness mollified her, and eventually
she returned to work.

The shooting was somehow completed on schedule, but the six days
went by like a thousand. In the end, for everyone's trouble, she had given a
superb performance, the character's faded glory perfectly, poignantly
caught in a few minutes of screen time. It was a small part and might easily
have been satisfactorily handled by a character actress or minor leading
lady, but the producers had paid extra for something more and they had
gotten it, an *aura* not contained by the limited screen time, the instant glamour and embedded history of a star. What Ava herself saw of the work left
her aghast. Perhaps it was the director's or cinematographer's style, or the
speed with which they had to work, or maybe it was a covert reflection of
their exasperation with her, but the sharp-focused black-and-white camera
work seemed mercilessly to highlight her every wrinkle, her every swell.
She told people not to dare go to see the movie. "I look like shit."

Once again she declared herself closed for business.

But another offer arrived and this one at least had to be dignified with
consideration. It came in mid-1964, from John Huston, one of the men—
with Mark Hellinger and Robert Siodmak—who had, eighteen years ago,
enabled Ava Gardner to become a star. Huston, after that under-the-table
scripting of *The Killers* at the end of the war, had resumed his directorial
career and soon had several brilliant and award-winning works to his
credit, including *The Treasure of the Sierra Madre*, *The Asphalt Jungle*,
and *The African Queen*, that established him as one of the greatest talents
of the era. There had been successes since then, and many flops and mistakes, but even Huston's failures were invested with his adventurer's
spirit, jagged humor, and artist's eye. A maverick in the assembly-line
world of the big studios, he, like Ava, had turned his back on Hollywood
and gone to live in Europe, settling in a restored Georgian manor house in
county Galway, Ireland, (stocking it with modern abstract art, ancient
Bhutanese bronzes, an entire Japanese bath complete with shoji screens,
and select mistresses, screenwriters, and jockeys). Huston had not seen
much of Ava since the inebriated 1946 weekend at his ranch in the Valley,

but she had remained a lively memory, and now at last there came an opportunity for them to work together, a part for her in his film version of Tennessee Williams's play *The Night of the Iguana.* The play (which would prove to be the last of Williams's long string of major critical and popular successes) had opened on December 28, 1961, at Broadway's Royale Theatre, starring Bette Davis, Margaret Leighton, and Patrick O'Neal. A typical Williamsian study of desire, dysfunction, and emotional crises, *The Night of the Iguana* was set in a frowzy Acapulco hotel where defrocked, alcoholic, horny minister, now tour guide, the Reverend T. Lawrence Shannon haphazardly battles for his salvation, aided and abetted by lusty innkeeper Maxine Faulk and wandering spinster Hannah Jelkes. Film rights were purchased by an agent turned producer, Ray Stark, who correctly believed that *Iguana*'s mix of soul-searching, melodrama, and lowlife exotica would capture the interest of John Huston.

Stark and Huston agreed on Richard Burton for the role of the loquacious, boozing Shannon, Deborah Kerr for the gentle Miss Jelkes, and Ava Gardner to play earthy widow, Maxine. Huston was hardly unique in associating the Southern actress's feline sensuality with one of Tennessee's hot-blooded ladies. Through the years she had been mentioned in regard to several adaptations of the playwright's work, and Metro had begged her to play Alexandra del Lago in *Sweet Bird of Youth* (she was "retired" at the time, and anyway the role of the washed-up, pill-popping, man-hungry movie star had appeared way too close for comfort). Tennessee Williams had written the role of Maxine Faulk, and Bette Davis had played it onstage, as blowsy and loud, Davis with a red dye job, lots of jiggling cleavage, and a harpy's screech. Huston believed the playwright's characterization of Maxine revealed his fear of women and, by the play's conclusion, his disdain for "a woman's place in the love life of a man." Huston had a different view of the part, reshaped it in his script and cast it accordingly. His Maxine was lovable, sexy, profane, funny, flawed, romantic. She was *Ava.* Stark and Huston arrived in Madrid to make their pitch. Ava took the pair out for several exuberant, exhausting nights on the town, but always deflected any attempt to discuss the proposed film job. No way she could do the thing they were offering. A part Bette Davis had created? Davis was Ava's idea of a real actress, a legitimate star (she had seen her in person once, rushed up, introduced herself, and told Davis how thrilled she was to meet her; Davis eyed the younger movie star imperiously, said,

"*Of course you are,*" and went on her way). Huston, though, observing Ava in her element, her mature allure, her blend of sexiness, sadness, and rowdiness, saw the exact Maxine he wanted and was not to be put off. The nocturnal pursuit went on for almost a week.

"Dear Ava," said Huston at last, "I know damn well you're going to do this part and so do you."

The script—by Huston and his old *Killers* collaborator Anthony Veiller—opened up the stage play to include several settings in addition to the seaview hotel, and the director looked forward to shooting them all on authentic locations along the tropical Pacific Coast. Huston was put in contact with a Mexican architect and entrepreneur named Guillermo Wulff, who claimed to hold a long-term lease from the Indians for some undeveloped beach and jungle property on a stretch of the Bay of Banderas known as Mismaloya. It was proposed that said land would be the perfect place to shoot much of *The Night of the Iguana* while at the same time laying the groundwork for an investment in the future, constructing lodgings, dock, roads, plumbing, and more that could have subsequent use as the infrastructure of a holiday resort. The exact nature of the deal the two men concocted would become a bit fuzzy with passing time ("The whole thing," Huston would say years later, "certainly appealed to my sense of chicanery"). Like many of the characters in his films, Huston was often in hope of securing his fortune through unconventional schemes, but, as in a Huston picture, this quest for loot in Mexico would end ironically, the gold blowing away like dust in the wind.

The cast and crew of *The Night of the Iguana* started gathering in Mexico City in late September. Ava arrived on the twenty-first, accompanied by Reenie Jordan, her long-serving maid having returned for another tour of duty. The following day saw the arrival of Richard Burton and his inamorata, Elizabeth Taylor, whose love affair, begun on the sets of *Cleopatra* in Rome, had made them the most scandalous and talked-about adulterers in the world (both were still married to other people at the time), the Frank-and-Ava of the 1960s. A day later came Sue Lyon, the sultry seventeen-year-old blond, playing *Iguana*'s troublemaking nymphet, typecasting after her debut the year before in Stanley Kubrick's *Lolita*. An aura of anarchy began to gather around the production even before the actors had all checked into their hotel rooms. There were riots at the airport with the landing of the Hollywood movie stars, and the press laid siege to the hotel and the entrance to Churubusco Studios. Huston had gone missing for days, sequestered somewhere with Tony Veiller trying to complete the screenplay (their collaboration at the Irish manor house that summer having been subject to distractions and sidetracks, such as the days genially wasted rewriting the ending to their script for *Moulin Rouge*, a film that had been shot ten years earlier). And proving something of a recurring disruption was *Iguana*'s indigenous "standby director" (a position imposed on foreign productions by the local film guild), Emilio "El Indio" Fernandez. Huston's choice for the mostly no-show job, Fernandez was an actor (he later portrayed Mapache, the vicious general in Sam Peckinpah's *The Wild Bunch*) and filmmaker (*La Perla, La Cucaracha*), and a certified *loco hombre* who generally went around in a cowboy hat or sombrero and carried a pair of six-guns strapped to his belt. Fernandez was currently at loose ends, having been blacklisted in the Mexican film business for shooting a producer. "He once told me he didn't know how many people he had killed in his life," recalled Bayard Veiller, Anthony Veiller's son, "because he didn't count Indians. He was really quite something. My father said the first time they went to see him at his place in Mexico City he was in the living room practicing the bullwhip on a cowering young girl. There always seemed to be fifteen-year-old girls nearby him wherever he was."

Fernandez had terrified Burton and Taylor at the airport during the press riot by stampeding onto their airplane with his guns drawn, an ostensible rescue attempt, grabbing Elizabeth and attempting to lead her away. Burton had pulled him off, screaming, "Let go of her! Someone take this maniac away!" Most of all the Mexican was causing distress for Ava. From the moment he had set eyes on her, El Indio had become infatuated with the American actress, stalking her movements and refusing to leave her side whenever she appeared at the studio or a dining room. He flirted and flattered, attempted to impress her with tales of his various bloodthirsty adventures and the number of young women and whores he had bedded. He also offered to shoot anyone who bothered her or came between them. Ava pleaded with Huston to take him away, but the director and others were amused by the sight of the ferocious, slobbering Fernandez's courtship and the way he gazed upon Ava with puppyish adoration. Eventually Huston made El Indio's crush the subject of one of his practical jokes, planting a story with one of the visiting reporters that would end up in many of the world's newspapers: that Ava and Emilio Fernandez had fallen in love while making *The Night of the Iguana* and were going to be married. (For example, the *Hollywood Citizen-News* declared: "Ava Gardner May Marry on Saturday. . . . Fernandez said that he was going to Los Angeles on Saturday and that the wedding might take place there or at Puerto Vallarta, or Guadalajara, or in the village of Mismaloya.")

In Mexico City, Ava reported for several days of wardrobe and hair tests. Though she was not allowed to have her own costume designer (as usual she wanted the Fontana sisters for the job) the producers did permit her to import Sydney Guilaroff from Hollywood to spend all of five minutes creating Ava's *Iguana* hairdo: pulled up, with a few strands left dangling in the back. Filming proper began on September 26, shooting Burton's pulpit breakdown at a seventeenth-century church in the village of Tepozotlán. As Huston had decided to shoot the entire film in continuity, from first script page to last, Ava was not needed before the camera for a while. She was encouraged to make a visit to a local health resort, where it was hoped she would drop some weight and lose what one of Huston's assistants Thelda Victor described as "huge dark bags under her eyes." Assigned to take care of her, make sure she returned on time, was Ray Stark's young assistant, Sandy Whitelaw.

"I was terrified," Whitelaw remembered. "A nervous wreck meeting her again. I had a whole thing with Ava before *Iguana*. I had been sent over to see her in Madrid about her doing a movie. It was an Irwin Shaw novel they were going to make, I forget the title—it was a girl's name [*Lucy Crown*]. I went to see her about doing this film, and it was most bizarre, the whole meeting. She lived opposite the dictator Perón then. We went out. We had a long night on the town which ended up completely weird. We had an excellent time at first. But she acted very strange. We would go into restaurants, and she would storm out over something. We would go to a nightclub, and then she became very angry. Maybe the drummer was not keeping very good time. Or there were people shadowing her. When she drank she became very paranoid. She had all this hostility and fear. She would get up suddenly, saying, *'We've got to get out of this club!'* Or she would tell a taxi driver to stop and she'd jump out of the cab. *'I'm not letting him drive me!'* she would say. And I'd have to jump out and go after her on foot. She was very fussy about the strangest things. She could turn nasty. She told me a woman once came up to her and said, 'For a moment I thought you were Ava Gardner. You are so lucky that you're not that awful woman.' It ended up badly between us. We had been having a very good time, but I was there to do a job. And at some point she got very pissed off because she thought I was more interested in getting her to commit to this movie—which *was* what I was there for—than in being nice to her personally. And it ended up very badly with her scream-ing, 'Why are they always sending *faggots* to see me all the time!'

"So now I had taken the job with Ray Stark as an associate producer, and I'm terrified of meeting her again. We're in Mexico and the time came to see her, and I expected I would be fired the next day. She extends her hand and says, 'So nice to meet you.' She had no memory of meeting me before in her life. I was supposed to keep an eye on her, go over her lines with her, and get her ready. We went to this place in Mexico, sort of a spa, where people went to dry out and get in shape. She brought her black maid with her who was very sweet, and Ava treated her more like she was her girlfriend. And at this spa there were a lot of racist Texans, Southerners, who couldn't believe how she acted, like this black person was an equal. I remember one of them actually offered me fifty dollars if I could do something to have the quote unquote *spook* sit somewhere else away from them. But Ava was just 'up yours' to people like that. And she was great. We became very good friends. She was not my type, and I was not tempted to mix business with pleasure with her, but I liked her very much. She still couldn't remember meeting me before. We would be sitting around talking and she would say something like, 'You have to come visit me in Madrid. There's this amaz-ing guitarist I want you to see.' And I'd say, 'Yes, Ava, I know, his name is Paco.' And she'd say, 'You know Paco?' And I'd say, 'Yes, Ava, you took me to see him last year.' It was a blank. We remained friends from then on, though at the location I didn't see much of her away from the set. I ended up hanging out more with Burton and Taylor. Ava went off to live very separately from the rest. She had her own interests there. The rumor was that she was getting to know some of the local beachboys."

———

On October 1, chartered planes began flying *Iguana* personnel to the Pacific Coast town of Puerto Vallarta (the vaguely existent road from the interior through the rain forest was considered unreliable due to landslides and bandits). A colonial creation at the foot of jungled mountains, onetime port for the silver dragged down from the Sierra Madre mines, it was an attractively tumbledown place of whitewashed adobe buildings and cobblestone streets, fronted by seaside promenade and golden beach, populated by an affable Spanish/mestizo community and a small complement of American expatriates (remittance men, retirees, gay divorcées), the better heeled among the latter residing in villas in the eastward section known as "gringo gulch." (From this expat colony Huston would recruit several women to play some of the long-suffering ladies in Rev. Shannon's tour group; others the director spontaneously cast as hapless teachers for the tour bus were his assistants Gladys Hill and Thelda Victor and his actress friend Eloise Hardt.) The company filmed on the streets and outskirts of Puerto Vallarta until late October, then moved seven miles south to Mismaloya, where production was to be centered for the final six weeks. Everyone was transshipped to reside in the just-barely completed lodgings at the mountainside compound built by Guillermo Wulff, except Ava and Burton (with Taylor) and Deborah Kerr, who would remain in the relative comfort of private homes in town and commute each day to the location. Ava's villa on the hill, the Casa de la Luna, was enclosed by a stucco wall and thickly overhanging foliage, the living space within largely open-air in the tropical style. The villa also sported a rare air conditioner, but it worked only erratically and there was often no electricity on the block at all. At night bats swooped down across the courtyard, and large rodents and thick-shelled scorpions skittered along the bedroom floor. Each morning Ava would be taken from the house and down to the Playa Los Muertos (the Beach of the Dead), where she waded into a dugout canoe and was paddled across the surf and lifted aboard a waiting motorboat for a half hour commute along the coastline to the peninsula at Mismaloya. From the new floating dock at the edge of the beach she climbed a steep 134 steps cut through the overgrowth to where the ground leveled off high above the bay and the dense tropical forest had been cleared for a series of bungalows, a kitchen, a commissary, two bars, and at the highest point, the primary set: the lush grounds, stone patio, and main building of Maxine Faulk's Costa Verde Hotel. (Pursuant to Huston and Wulff's plans for post-*Iguana* property development, the set had been built in full working order and was intended to be the centerpiece of their would-be resort.) Here, in extreme heat and humidity, without fresh water, and constantly pursued by biting insects, Ava would work six days a week until December.

It was John Huston's delight to film under such circumstances, to bring a group of interesting people to an inhospitable, sweltering locale and watch the result. The actual stress and discomfort of the cast added to the reality of the film, and besides that it was fun to observe. From the start *Iguana*'s gathering of volatile and scandal-prone personalities promised an amusing time, a prospect further guaranteed by the steady arrival of friends and family from the outside world: wives, mistresses, ex-husbands, an opium-smoking nanny, and Tennessee Williams, along with his boyfriend and his promiscuous poodle. Among those at hand awkwardly linked by a web of not necessarily friendly personal histories were Michael Wilding, Liz Taylor's former husband and now the agent of her lover; and accompanying his new wife, Deborah Kerr, Peter Viertel, who had once had an intricate relationship with Ava during the making of *The Sun Also Rises* and was also the author of the novel *White Hunter, Black Heart*, with its distinctly negative portrait of John Huston. Viertel also had a delicate link to Ava's and Burton's visiting friend Budd Schulberg, having married Schulberg's first wife, Jigee, upon her split with Budd. Everyone, said Huston, was "expecting at least one murder." Enjoying the perceived tension, the director contrived a commemorative gift for the principal actors on their first day together at Mismaloya. "I gave them all gold-plated derringers," he would recall, "the kind of little pistols that the card sharps used to wear up their sleeves. Then I also gave each one five bullets with the names of the other members of the cast on them."

There might have been a shot heard round the world had Ava followed an early impulse regarding Richard Burton. There was one story that could probably generate more public interest than the Burton-Taylor affair: the breakup of the Burton-Taylor affair by Ava Gardner. She was quickly alert to the appeal of her hypermasculine, hard-drinking, poetry-spouting costar. As the pair were sweatily in close quarters at the torpid Mismaloya location, there appeared a certain spark of mutual interest. Observers twittered about the meaningful eye contact between the legendary sex symbol and the lustful Welshman. "She is livelier and lovelier around him," wrote Thelda Victor in her journal. But Liz Taylor was obsessively in love with her guy and in hot pursuit of a wedding ring, and she could recognize a proximate seductress as she could her own face in the mirror. Almost immediately she became a presence on the Mismaloya set and thereafter came every day without fail. What's more, she came dressed for battle: ripely armored in sultry outfits, a series of tiny custommade bikinis or bikini bottom with loose top and no bra (Victor: "You literally could see the complete upper structure"). She would stand just behind the camera during filming and then move in between takes, kneeling over Burton, whispering in his ear, fussing with his hair (often to his evident displeasure). Ava got the message, averted her eyes when the camera stopped. Besides, she liked Liz well enough. They had too much in common to become enemies now, the two femmes fatales, survivors of the MGM trenches made equally unfit for normal life.

Ava and Richard Burton had at least one thing in common. Burton's intake of liquor was legendary, astonishing. There was a great deal of drinking at Mismaloya, some of it disruptive to the work at hand. Burton drank at all hours. Ava generally abstained until lunch at midday or afternoon (but not always; there were sometimes cocktails on the morning boat ride). Terry Morse, second assistant director on *Iguana*, recalled, "If we got her into makeup and got her up on the set without a drink, then we'd have her most of the day. If she started in the morning it was bad news. We just didn't get a lot of work with her after lunch." By late afternoon both stars might begin to slur their lines; sometimes no one heard until later when the rushes came back from the lab in Los Angeles and then they would have to reshoot or throw away an otherwise superior take. Huston was accepting. He had too much respect for the magic in alcohol and the vagaries of creativity to impose a prohibition on his actors. For some performers booze was crucial to a truthful performance. *In tequila veritas*. "Huston just rolled with the action," said Morse. "He was wonderful that way. He could just roll along, and if she was too drunk he'd go on and do another scene." "He didn't give a shit," said Tom Shaw, the director's longtime first assistant. "He never bothered them. He'd never say anything about that. He might be as drunk as they were."

It was left to Shaw and his team to figure out how to keep on schedule despite the stars' proclivities. Since no one, drunk or sober, really wanted to do much after the midday break, with the sun blazing even hotter and the Pacific waters beckoning, for a while it was arranged to begin shooting a couple of hours earlier in the morning and go on through the lunch break, and then everyone could have the afternoons off. The shortened hours were welcome but did not discourage the feeling that they were all there not to work but to enjoy a tropical holiday. Some days Ava would finish a scene and go direct from the set to the beach, where a hired speedboat would be waiting to take her waterskiing across the shark-infested bay or riding up the coast to some isolated beach where she would swim and lie in the sun. Her aquatic chauffeur, a young Yaqui Indian named Ramon, kept the boat stocked with the items from a long list she had provided. "Always it was a lot of ice, and plenty of beer, and tequila, and gin—a lot of gin," Ramon told journalist Bruce Porter. "Sometimes she would drink it with an olive, or mix the gin and the tequila and pour it into a coconut with ice and stick in a straw."

"She was having a good time," Budd Schulberg remembered. "Everyone was drinking quite a bit. Richard hit it very hard. And Huston always did. And Ava, yes, she was pretty good, too. I stayed out with Richard Burton several nights. It would be past three in the morning, and he would be in his cups and want to talk about Dylan Thomas or—he was a big fight fan—we'd be yakking about the fights. And Elizabeth would come storming out in her bathrobe looking for him, giving him hell—'What do you think you're doing, you've got to work in the morning!' They were all having a good time. It was a happy company. You couldn't believe they were making a movie."

By night Puerto Vallarta's population swelled with *Iguana* personnel taxied by flotilla from Mismaloya, filling the small selection of restaurants and bars to overflowing. The visitors were also a boost to Vallarta's underground economy, giving brisk trade to the local prostitutes and purveyors of marijuana and of a local moonshine known as *raicilla*, made from a variant agave plant peculiar to the state of Jalisco, a ninety-plus-proof mescal Burton endorsed but Ava decried as "cactus piss." The scene in town was hectic, made even more so by the influx of gawkers, celebrity chasers, and journalists (many of dubious provenance) drawn by the publicity the production was receiving. Puerto Vallarta had seen nothing like it since the conquistadores had traipsed through four hundred years before. Most locals seemed to enjoy the excitement and the spike in commerce, but there were those who complained about the hedonistic ways of the foreign invaders. Church sermons and newspaper editorials denounced the amorality, skimpy clothing, drug use, and homosexuality (even Tennessee Williams's dog, Gigi, came under fire, due to a propensity for running away from her owner and getting humped by local mutts on the public beach).

"It was a very sensuous location," recalled Eloise Hardt. "It was like never-never land. Everyone was on edge from the heat and the sickness. Scorpions and iguanas hopping on your bed. You never knew if you were going to be bitten by something or stranded by a storm. There were all these emotions and egos. Everyone got a bit desperate, everyone wanted to be loved or to love. I often thought of the Sadie Thompson story, where the preacher goes to the tropic island and loses control. It got to be ridiculous. If you wanted to get in a sexy mood, just go to the malécon and listen to the waves. Even if you didn't want it, your body felt it, the atmosphere was so primeval."

Ava was constitutionally unlikely to be immune to all this sensuousness. On arrival she entered into a brief romance with one of Guillermo Wulff's handsome relatives, who was collaborating on the project at Mismaloya, but she soon abandoned him to enjoy the less complicated attentions of the fun-loving boys from the *playa*. It was that curious phenomenon striking again, real and screen lives beginning to morph, blending into one. In the script hotel keeper Maxine's bellhops were a pair of bare-chested young men who were clearly kept around for more than their ability to tote luggage. Now, as if in a walking rehearsal, Ava was to be seen going about Vallarta with her own entourage of sinuous young attendants. She threw parties many nights, and the beachboys would fill the villa—drinking, smoking marijuana, and dancing the twist. "They all wanted to be with her, of course," said Nelly Barquette, Guillermo's wife. "She was so beautiful, so sexy, you know? And she was taking water-ski lessons. She loved to water-ski. And that was how she met Tony. He was teaching her to water-ski. And one thing led to another. Tony . . . he was about twenty-two, twenty-three years old. He was not so handsome. I don't think so. Very skinny. Maybe she liked this kind of person. Cheap looking. She wanted to be with him, and he moved into the house with her."

It looked to most like a frivolous fling, an amusing way to get through the night, but others thought there was considerable passion between the two. There was certainly some of the volatility of past romances. James Bacon, the Hollywood columnist, witnessed Ava and one of the beach-boys having a violent argument down by the ocean one afternoon: "They were going at each other, and the kid started hitting her. It was right in front of the tourists, and he was slapping her around pretty good. And she was taking it."

Richard Burton thought the beachboy a hustler and advised her to get rid of him. "He bleaches his hair," Burton told her. "And any man who does that is trouble."

"I don't know how serious it was, but you know, Ava had a tendency to get caught up in these things," said Angela Allen, the script supervisor (who had known the actress since the days of *Pandora* and the now-long-forgotten Mario Cabre). "He was just a boy she'd picked up. A Mexican beach bum. And I don't think he was very nice to her, but who knows what went on? I remember she threw a birthday party for him, and she was looking forward to it. And then the boy didn't show up. He was very late. And she was very disappointed. I remember saying to him when he finally got there, 'She's organized this party for your birthday, and it's very rude of you to be so late!' I tried to make him go and say to her, 'I'm sorry,' but he was in his early twenties and selfish and didn't care about her feelings, I suppose. She was drunk by then, and I thought, This is going to end up in a very messy thing, and I don't want to be here mopping up the blood! So I decided I was not going to hang around, and I got out."

There *was* a movie being made during all this. In fact, it had been rolling along quite well. Everyone was pleased with what had been put on film. Though skittish and uncertain of herself as usual, Ava was pleased to hear the widespread praise for her own work. Her Maxine was a charismatic, funny, bittersweet creation. The performance had a raw, nervous energy, a quirky authenticity. She was offering a vision of herself in the caustic, ro-mantic Maxine, more revealing in some ways than anything she had ever done. Huston had drawn it from her in his easy, sly way. His was an open, amused approach to the job. He offered an actor time and freedom to find the way to a performance. He was certainly capable of being displeased, and his sarcasm and cold shoulder could be withering, but with Ava he never showed impatience or disappointment (not even when for more than a dozen takes she persisted in blowing the same line, saying "My husband *Frank*" instead of "My husband *Fred*"). "It was sheer magic," she told writer Lawrence Grobel. "John put you in the mood, got you to feel you could do the right thing, and then let you go."

For the first time in years Ava really wanted to be good—not that she could promise it would be easy. When the time came to shoot one of Ava's showy scenes, for instance, a distraught Maxine spiting Rev. Shannon by rushing into the ocean to cavort with her two beachboys, she had become sick with fear—of the physicality of the scene (how could she not look bad falling around in the water with her hair all soaked?), the sexuality of it (the two boys roaming all over her body as the surf rolled across them), and the physical exposure (the scene called for her to be wearing a skimpy bikini). Huston told her in that case, kid, they would rewrite and shoot the scene at night and with minimal lighting. As she continued to feel uncertain about the bikini, Huston suggested she simply go into the water in her clothes (Maxine's ubiquitous poncho top and toreador pants). "It'll look more natural like that anyway," the director said. While they were preparing to shoot Huston waded into the water with her (they had had a drink or two together first) and held her hand till they were ready. Then he directed the scene in his shorts, dripping wet. It was not that he had asked her to do something so difficult or daring, but for her moments like this often became a kind of test of the director's allegiance. Was he really listening, looking out for her? She had wanted the special attention, and Huston gave it to her, and in return she gave him all that she could. The scene was done, beautifully, in a single take.

Some speculated about ulterior motives for the favored treatment, although Huston was there with his girlfriend, Zoe Sallis, and their baby son, Danny. But no, he had simply grown devoted, protective. She was a kindred spirit, an extraordinary character. The more he knew of her the more he was moved by her life's predicament, what he saw as the ironic, even tragic aspect to her physical blessings. He told Deborah Kerr—who counted herself a great fan of Ava's ("she is funny and rich and warm and human")—what a disadvantage it could sometimes be to be so beautiful, like a curse from the gods. "It has been so for Ava, and she has well and truly paid for her beauty."

By late November *Iguana*'s jungle location had lost its charm for nearly everybody. For the hundred and more members of cast and crew who lived there full-time, in the bungalows strung down the hill below the Costa Verde set, the discomforts had accumulated like clockwork. The heat, the humidity, the stinging insects were a constant. Then the bungalows proved to be infested with termites and spiders. And they were falling apart. The ancient actor Cyril Delevanti, playing "the world's oldest living and practicing poet" in the movie, had the roof of his residence cave in. The lack of potable water at Mismaloya, and the usual susceptibilities of gringo *turistas*, left nearly everyone with a running case of amoebic dysentery, aka the "Aztec two-step," a whole company with loose bowels. Tempers frayed. Lovers fought. There were injuries, on-set bruisings and falls. The portable generator that provided the only source of electricity began to break down with increasing frequency. Sue Lyon developed a bad case of pimples. Richard Burton was nearly electrocuted. A significant scene had Shannon, in a symbolic gesture, cutting loose the rope of a captured iguana. The iguana refused to run away when the rope was cut and so an electric wire with a 110-volt charge was used to get the lizard moving. Something went wrong with something, and Burton was touching the iguana as they shocked it. Burton's whole body felt the charge, and he was lifted straight into the air and crashed to the stone floor.

One day Burton had dozed off for a few minutes while sitting in a camp chair waiting to do a scene. An assistant woke him. His eyes opened, and he looked around uncertainly.

"Where am I?" he said.

"Mismaloya," said the assistant.

"God, no!" Burton cried.

Ava's main source of misery was the ever-increasing presence of visiting reporters and photographers. Media interest in the filming and the personalities involved was enormous, and producer Ray Stark and his appointed publicists eagerly exploited it, encouraging the dozens of requests from the press for on-site visits and interviews (and Huston, the would-be resort magnate, had his own reason for allowing them). Each day the single flight from Mexico City would be packed full of journalists from the United States and Europe. Ava mostly ignored the reporters or greeted them with an obscene dismissal, but the interlopers with cameras were more difficult to avoid and caused her the usual waves of anxiety. Gjon Mili, a photojournalist of some repute, had been sent to the set on assignment and was shooting both posed and candid shots of the stars. Ava had cooperated for the formal shots, but when Mili continued snapping afterward she shouted at him to quit. The photographer ignored her and went on taking pictures, at which point Ava charged at him and kicked him solidly in the stomach, so hard he fell over gasping for air. He abandoned his assignment and left Mexico the next day.

Ross Lowell was a young documentary filmmaker who had been hired by the production company to shoot a 16 mm behind-the-scenes promotional short.* "I got down there, and it was a pretty interesting bunch of people," Lowell remembered. "When I got to Mismaloya the first place you passed was a bar they had built there, and John Huston's adopted Mexican son was sitting there with another Mexican, a pretty dynamic guy who was holding a firearm [Emilio Fernandez]. There was a lot of drinking going on, and Huston had to work around a lot of problems, but he was holding it all together. He took things very casually. He was an extraordinary person. I met Deborah Kerr, who was just such a lovely lady. And Burton and Elizabeth Taylor were pretty wonderful. Burton was very friendly and insisted I have some beers with him. This was after he'd sobered up enough in the fresh air to consume some more alcohol. And Ava Gardner was very sweet when she was sober. But I was advised to be awfully careful with her after noontime. She was at that point in her life where she was very much concerned about her appearance. And one afternoon I was filming her, and I guess I got on the wrong side and she had a fit. I was trying to frame a shot of her through some flowers, and she must have thought I was trying to sneak some shots of her, I don't know. But she saw it, and she blew up and went off the set and didn't come back.

*On the Trail of the Iguana, with Lowell's color footage of the production, offers a lush contrast to Gabriel Figueroa's sharp, stark black-and-white cinematography; Huston later concluded that he should have made The Night of the Iguana in color.

She went off to her room and held up production long enough that I became very upset. I went to Huston and told him what I had done, and I said that I would leave the job if he thought that was what I should do. Huston had a world-class sense of humor and knowledge of people. He said no, he didn't want me to leave over this. He said, 'We knew what the problems were when we hired her, and we're willing to live with them.' I asked if he objected to my going and apologizing to her and he said, 'Not at all.'

"So I went to see her. And she agreed to see me and I apologized. I think she took it well. But she was pretty busy crying."

The low point of the filming, and a near tragedy, occurred on the night of November 20. They were shooting now from sundown to late in the night, some of the final scenes in the picture. Ava had been having problems getting her performance right. She would go away and drink, and when she came back the problems were worse. It went on like this for many hours, and finally around two or three in the morning assistant director Tom Shaw told Huston, "I don't think she's going to get it. We better call it a day." The company was dismissed, and everyone straggled to their beds. "It was a long night, shooting exteriors on the porch there where they had Burton tied up in the hammock," Terry Morse remembered. "I headed back to my place. We were all living in these houses they had built, the ones they were hoping to sell as condos. Huston . . . I don't know who was involved. And they were already starting to fall apart. Tom Shaw was up in his place on the second floor when I came by. It was about three, four in the morning. And he was sitting on the balcony, and he said, 'Come on, sit down for a minute, we'll talk about tomorrow's work.' "

Shaw: "I'm telling him, let's make sure so-and-so and so-and-so, about the next night, and I don't know, I must have leaned too hard on something and down that son-of-a-bitch went. . . ."

Morse: "I just sat down and the whole building seemed to give out, just crumble. The building came down. And the two of us went flying over backwards down twenty feet onto our heads. I landed right on my head, and it was just luck that I wasn't killed. I came to and Deborah Kerr was looking at me, holding my head up. They thought Tom Shaw might have been dead."

"Yeah," Tom Shaw recalled, "I threw my back out on that thing."

Unconscious and bleeding, Shaw was taken down the mountainside to the dock, put onto a motorboat, taken to the town, Huston and some others carrying him to the beach through deep water with the surf over their heads. An airplane was hired and flew Shaw away that morning to a hospital. His back was broken, and there were threats from internal bleeding. The doctor, when Huston managed to make contact, couldn't be sure if Shaw would make it. (He lived, and after a lengthy period of recuperation went to work on Huston's next picture.)

It was believed that the cement used in the bungalows at Mismaloya had been made with seawater instead of fresh because of the difficulty and expense of bringing freshwater to the jungle, and that this had left the cement unstable in the humid climate. After the injuries to Tom and Terry, Huston lost all interest in the potential jungle resort, wanted nothing more to do with it. (Forty years later a sprawling superresort does operate above the Mismaloya beach just beside the old *Iguana* location, and the rotting remains of the bungalows can still be found scattered over the jungle peninsula; the Costa Verde, constructed of better materials, is intact, currently operating as a restaurant and bar, with photographs of Richard Burton and Ava Gardner indicating the men's and women's lavatories.)

Some thirty-six hours after the accident with Shaw and Morse had shaken the company, there came more bad news. On November 22, it was learned, via the ship-to-shore radio on Ray Stark's yacht, that President John Kennedy had been assassinated. "Everyone was in a state of shock, of course," remembered Ross Lowell. "And there was a lot of disbelief and waiting to get confirmation because communication down there was so terrible. The radio was full of static."

Ava, like everyone else, stood about, feeling helpless, numb. After a time Huston gave a somber speech to all who were there. It was decided that they should try to keep working.*

---

*Small world that it is: Ava had crossed paths with both JFK, her former swain, and his avenger; Jack Ruby, the assassin of the assassin, in a rambling testimony to the Warren Commission not long before he died, would distractedly recall a morning in Havana in 1959 when he had bumped into the beautiful movie star, Ava Gardner herself, having breakfast right before him; a pointless happy memory of a better day.

Filming concluded at the end of November. A wrap party was thrown on the last day of the month. It began at four in the afternoon and ended twelve hours later. Cast and crew and two hundred Mexican townspeople attended. There were locally made dishes as well as a planeload of American items Ray Stark had flown in from a Los Angeles delicatessen, and cases of fine wines and spirits for which Stark had also provided passage (there were also bottles of tequila and *raicilla* contributed by the local citizenry). Ava arrived, turning all heads, wearing a bright-patterned Pucci harem suit, a gift from the producer. A twenty-piece mariachi band played, and people danced.

With the work done, nearly everyone was eagerly moving on, to return to home, family, the next job. Ava felt nothing, no one, drawing her away. She decided to stay on a while longer, for a little more of the sun, the waterskiing, the beachboy.

One day in December the police came to the villa to tell her that Frank Sinatra's son—nineteen-year-old Frank Junior—had been kidnapped (a gang of three having snatched the kid from a Lake Tahoe hotel room). How they came to deliver this information to her is not certain. Perhaps Frank himself had wanted her to know. Nelly Barquette, Guillermo Wulff's wife, had translated for her, and now Ava, who was very upset, asked Nelly to stay with her for a little while and talk. Nelly had never liked Ava much, and the two had never become friends. Ava was a wild person and acted too much like a big movie star, Nelly thought—what she would call a diva—always ordering people around as if they were all her servants. But now, in the Casa de la Luna, as they sat together and had some drinks, Ava seemed like another person, more of a human being. She was very upset, Nelly remembered, and she cried because of the boy who had been kidnapped. She cried out, "That boy . . . he could have been *my son!*" She had never had a child, she said, and for this she felt much regret. She could have had one with Frank Sinatra, she said. And she cried some more, and it seemed like she was no longer crying for the boy who had been kidnapped but for herself and the things in her life that she had done wrong. And she told Nelly Barquette that she was still in love with Frank

Sinatra and it hurt so much to be in love with someone you could not have.

"Yes, she said this to me many times. She was in love with him. She would always be in love. And it hurt so much."

PART FOUR

TWELVE

Venus Falling

She celebrated her forty-first birthday in Hollywood in a brawl at a nightclub called Basin Street West. A photographer bored in on the film star and an unidentified "young male escort," said the papers the next day. The camera went off, and the escort grabbed for it, shouting, "You can get your head broken for that!" The two men scuffled, Ava running out, the escort catching up, a Cadillac sedan screaming out of sight. A visit to Elizabeth Arden's Maine Chance in Scottsdale, Arizona, for her sins mummified in seven pounds of crystalline paraffin. To New York with Bappie and the corgis, Rags and Cara, a suite at the St. Regis, a limousine at her disposal courtesy of Ray Stark, long nights of Broadway, jazz, and booze, holding court for old friends like Larry Tarr (still running the family photo shops where it had all begun), and new ones like the Birminghams, Stephen and Nan.

Stephen was a young magazine journalist, one of those sent down to report the goings-on in Puerto Vallarta; he had slipped under the barrier chain she held up to reporters, become a drinking companion, she'd taken him under her wing. "I want to marry you," he would remember her telling him somewhere. "We'll worry about your wife later." Nan was a homemaker and mom in suburban Westchester. "I got the phone call one day, telling me, 'I've been here a week, and Ava Gardner and I have been inseparable,' " she remembered. "Well, for a relatively young bride that was a bit terrifying. Ava Gardner: That's pretty stiff competition. I mean, that was scary. Then he got home. And he'd had a ball, I can tell you that.

And I heard some of the stories of what went on down there. It was the closest thing to real decadence. The bottles open by eight in the morning. Ava with her Mexican hunks. People banging anything that came by, male, female, in between. Two legs, four legs. Then Ava began calling Stephen from all over. She was at the place in Arizona where you went to dry out. She was wandering around. And I took one of the calls and she says, *'Hey, hon, I'm just dying to meet you!'* Ha! She was coming to New York and wanted to take us out on the town. So, if you can't fight 'em, join 'em. We went to meet her in Manhattan. And this was very glamorous for me. I wasn't the biggest square around, but I was a housewife taking care of kids and this was going to be a very glamorous evening for me. My God, glamorous! By the time it was over I'm doing things like lugging the corset off of Ava Gardner's drunk elderly sister and scooping up dog poop from the floor of the St. Regis Hotel. . . . The start of what I call the Ava Gardner Period of my life.

"She was a raging beauty. That was first. I never saw anybody so beautiful. Maybe Elizabeth Taylor. Maybe on a very good day Elizabeth Taylor. She was like an animal, Ava. The sex thing. I've known a few women like that. It's like something's sprayed, like a bitch in heat. You can't get to the end of the block with women like this where five guys aren't following, falling over themselves. Guys and girls following, too. And these women know, they understand it about themselves. I'm not one of them, so I don't know how it works. Ava had it times a hundred. She could seduce anyone in two split seconds.

"She was the most charming person in the world. Until she had too much to drink, and then she could be your worst nightmare. We had a fight right at the start. We were in the taxi. She was drunk, and she wanted to go to another club. It was already late. I told her we had to get back and get our car before the garage closed. We had to go home. 'Don't tell me what to do!' 'Ava, I'm not telling you what to do, I'm telling you we have to go home.' She was furious with me. Nobody told her she couldn't do something she wanted to do. 'Take me back to the St. Regis. I'm going to take my dogs for a walk.' I said, 'Ava, I hope you take off that emerald necklace first, you won't last twenty seconds in Central Park.' We get up to her suite, and she goes stumbling into her bedroom and slams the door. Her sister is stretched out, passed out cold, and there was dog doo all over the floor. I called down to the front desk to have them take the dogs out.

She came storming out finally in her slacks and loafers. 'Where are my dogs? What have you done with my dogs?' I said, 'I've had someone from the hotel come to walk them. You're in no condition.' This was too much. This was *High Noon* time. She was like a tiger coming at me. My husband's fallen asleep, and she's coming at me. I thought, if she hits me I'm going to hit her back! I was terrified, actually. She looked ready to kill me. But when she got within a foot the whole rage melted away. She said, "*Oh, hon, I just love you.*' And she collapsed against me. And I said, 'Well, Ava, I love you too.'

"From then on she was really very very dear to me. Maybe it was the fact that I had stood up to her, I don't know. I don't know if a lot of thought went into anything that she did. We became friends. She trusted me, and she didn't trust a lot of people. I became like the old sorority sister she never had, who didn't want anything from her, never asked for anything. And she was very generous. Always trying to give you presents. She'd give me a fistful of jewelry. The good stuff. I'd put it back. She'd say, 'You never let me give you anything!' A lot of the time I played the caretaker. There had to be somebody in the group who knew where the car keys were or how to get home or what city you were in. You wouldn't believe how much these people drank. Drunks and total nuts who survive have a knack for finding people to look after them. . . ."

And Ava needed a lot of looking after. She could lose her shoes in two minutes. Has anybody seen Ava's shoes? If she went to the bathroom someone had to go along or you didn't know if she would ever come back. The Birminghams would get the call when Ava hit town. What are you kids doing? Come on over! It was like a trip through the looking glass when you went to visit Ava. You never knew what would happen, who you were going to meet. There was one afternoon at the Regency Hotel— she'd been banned from the St. Regis by then—Ava in bed with the flu, her room covered in blackout curtains, not a splinter of light, Bappie tiptoeing in the dark. Ava, honey, are you feeling any better? Can we get you anything? and Ava moaning, Oh, she was so sick, just bring her a big glass of vodka. And all day long the visitors popping in. Tony Curtis. James Baldwin—Jimmy wanted Ava to come and join him picketing outside Arthur Miller's play *After the Fall* because it was so mean to Marilyn Monroe. Salvador Dalí dropping by. Dalí brings a rhinoceros horn at the tip of which is a candied violet for Ava. Some of that surrealism. Ava takes the candied violet and eats it. And so on through the afternoon. Ava at last well enough to get dressed. Then downstairs to the bar. Ava says she's feeling like a Manhattan. That sounds good to me, Bappie says. Manhattans for everybody!

"Then there was the time," Nan Birmingham remembered, "we're all together at the hotel and Ava says, 'Francis is coming.' Just like that. Sinatra! He's coming by. And this was a magic night. Five or six of us are there. And he arrived. By himself. Just came over to see Ava. He brought her some flowers and one of his new record albums or something. And there they were. Their relationship with each other was just charming. They were so cute together it was hard to imagine what I had heard about them, the fights, the crazy arguments, throwing ketchup at each other and all this stuff. The two of them sat together and Sinatra told stories. He told some story about how he'd been out at Lake Tahoe with the Rat Pack. And they'd gotten somebody dressed up in a bear costume, somebody's valet or somebody, so they could scare the drunky one, Dean Martin, and the bear jumped out and chased Dean Martin screaming into the woods. It was pretty damn silly, but it was Frank Sinatra telling the story with these big blue eyes, and this guy had a magic about him that was unbelievable (I mean, when he looked at you it was like you were sure you were the cutest thing that ever came down the pike; I mean it was a very heady trip being in his presence, even with his ex-wife in the room). But they were something together. And when he was leaving, she was seeing him to the door of the suite and he put his arms around her and pulled her really close to him. And he slides his hands down into her trousers to her backside. And I heard him say, 'I love your . . .' I don't remember what word exactly but the message was clear. And he said, 'There's one more reason we should get back together.' You could see he was still mad for her.

"Oh, Ava. God she was fun. Not just the decadence. Ava had a great *sense of fun*. She was funny and fun and exciting. But exhausting. It was a strenuous job being around her. I scooped up a lot of dog doo during my Ava Gardner Period. I couldn't go on with it for long. I said, 'Stephen, if you want to go, take Ava out, she needs an escort, do whatever you want, I can't handle it.' Who had the energy? I had to get three kids off to school every morning at seven."

In May, Ava accepted an invitation from Betty and Ricardo Sicre for a Mediterranean cruise on their motor yacht *Rampager*. It was foremost a chance to get to know one of her heroes, the brilliant, twice-defeated candidate for U.S. president and now ambassador to the United Nations, Adlai Stevenson. A day late, missing the departure, she joined them at Capri, coming by helicopter from Naples. "She admired Stevenson, talked about him many times and how he should have been president," Betty Sicre would say. "They got along well, became real friends, though she didn't stay with us long. He liked her, too. They talked about politics, literature. She was at her most personable with him. No, there was no hint of romance. She was on her good behavior. They did turn some heads when we were in port. I remember Ava and Adlai were walking a bit ahead of us and an American couple passed them, and they both sort of fell over when they saw them. And by the time they passed us I heard the wife saying, 'That was Ava Gardner with Adlai Stevenson!' and the husband saying, 'No, it couldn't be.' "

They swam, lay in the sun, anchored off Stromboli with its smoldering volcano. Stevenson kept a journal. He was intrigued, a little perplexed by the admiring movie star. One night in port he awoke, long after midnight, and he saw her outside, all alone, walking away toward the sleeping village, disappearing in the dark. The next night he wrote this in his journal: "Dinner a splendid pasta with sausages and meat balls and glorious sauce very piquante cooked by Ava, who then went to bed afraid, anxious about our reaction! Strange, lovely, lush girl."

The pressure to perform, to impress, grew too strong for her. On edge, she had a row with someone over something one day, and in a sulk she abandoned the *Rampager* at the next port of call. Stevenson was evidently not put off by the whiff of temper, inviting her to visit him at the UN later that year, a very happy occasion for Ava. "We saw her after she left him," recalled Nan Birmingham, "and she never looked so proud and thrilled. She really adored Adlai Stevenson." She looked forward to the friendship blossoming, Stevenson becoming another wise man—father figure like Robert Graves, but it was not to be, the sixty-five-year-old ambassador dropping dead of a heart attack in London the following summer.

Ava returned to New York to attend the July 10 charity premiere (one hundred dollars per seat) of *Night of the Iguana* at the Philharmonic Hall, bringing as her guests the Birminghams and a visiting relative and two friends of the family from Johnston County. In the auditorium Ava sat beside Tennessee Williams, whose guest was his beloved mother, Edwina (wearing a startlingly weathered muskrat stole). Soon after the lights went down, Tennessee—or it might have been his mom—produced a bottle of Wild Turkey, and the two of them and Ava passed it back and forth in the dark, sipping the Kentucky nectar till the movie's end. The audience responded to the film with enthusiasm, and perhaps most happily of all to the raucous, poignant performance of Ava Gardner. For many among the social and media elite in attendance who had not gotten out to catch such less-than-de-rigueur entertainments as *55 Days at Peking* or obscure vehicles like *The Angel Wore Red*, there was the exciting feeling of seeing a legend returned from what seemed like limbo, older and a little haggard now, but with an increased honesty and depth to her work. (The image of the actress seen in the film was mitigated by a glimpse of her in the flesh that night, stunningly glamorous in an aqua satin creation by Balenciaga.) A long roar of applause greeted the film's fragile happy end, the fade-out on a moment of tenderness and hope: *Iguana*'s battered souls, Shannon and Mrs. Faulk, agreeing to try and make a life together, him tentative, her yearning, the pair in a two-shot against the open window, the hotel keeper suggesting they go down to the beach for a swim before it gets too hot.

"I can . . . get down the hill, Maxine, but I'm not too sure about getting . . . back up."

"I'll get you back up, baby . . . I'll always get you back up."

After the screening there was much praise for her performance, and Ray Stark declared that they would do what was needed to get her an Academy Award nomination. Ava dismissed the compliments. She'd thought she had done a good job, she told people, until she saw the goddamn thing. "I was embarrassed—I was false and fidgety."

She skipped out on the clamorous premiere party—the buffet featured

Beef Puerto Vallarta—and led her entourage to a club downtown to see Miles Davis.

Whether or not her disappointment in her *Iguana* performance was genuine (or merely the usual defiant professional self-deprecation), Ava appeared only pleased when offered another chance to work with the man she now called her "favorite and only director." While still in Mexico, John Huston had agreed to take on a project of Italian mogul Dino De Laurentiis, *The Bible*, a large-budget filming of a half-dozen stories from Genesis i–xxii. De Laurentiis had originally planned for each segment of the screenplay by Christopher Fry (with additional dialogue by the Lord Almighty) to be given to a different major director—Robert Bresson, Luchino Visconti, Orson Welles were consulted—but in the end Huston alone got the job (and then assigned himself additional employment as an actor in the role of Noah—after the part was turned down by Chaplin and Alec Guinness—and as the mellifluent, baritone voice of God). The last and lengthiest story in the film would be that of Abraham and his wife, Sarah, the barren woman who with God's blessing gives birth to a son at the age of ninety, becoming "mother of the Jews," "matriarch of all nations." It was the role of Sarah that Huston offered to Ava Gardner.

"Whatever else, it would be another adventure for us," he told her. "It's not just that I think you can speak the lines beautifully—but I'd get to see you on the back of a racing camel all swathed and bedizened. . . . No, on reflection I don't suppose that's the real reason, either. The truth, dear Ava, is simply I want you to be in every picture I ever make."

Shortly after receiving the screenplay she reported back with enthusiasm. She felt such sympathy for Sarah, she joked to Huston's assistant Gladys Hill, "I almost believe in circumcision. And by God I'm beginning to think that—at forty-one—I can produce a child. . . . Please tell our boss I love the script but more than the Bible and the script I love him."

She arrived in Rome in midsummer, when filming had been under way for months. Among sequences already in the can were Creation (partly the work of photographer Ernest Haas, who had gathered footage from wilderness areas around the world), the Garden of Eden (with Michael Parks and Ulla Bergryd as a naked American Adam and Swedish Eve gamboling on the grounds of an Italian count's summer palace), Cain and Abel (Richard Harris and Franco Nero, respectively), and the Tower of Babel (Stephen Boyd as Nimrod, that shoot disrupted when Egyptian extras staged a bloody rock-throwing riot). And next up was the story of Abraham and Sarah, with filming to be done at the De Laurentiis studio followed by location work in the Abruzzi mountains and in Sicily.

On the afternoon of Ava's arrival Huston had called from his suite in the Grand Hotel a few floors below her own. "Honey," he said, "I want you to come down and meet George."

Playing the part of Sarah's hundred-year-old spouse, Abraham, was George C. Scott, the brilliant thirty-six-year-old stage and screen actor from Virginia and Detroit, in movies since 1959, his work including acclaimed appearances in *Anatomy of a Murder*, *The Hustler*, and *Dr. Strangelove*. Scott had a craggy, broken-nosed face, a gravelly voice, a powerful physique (he had been a U.S. Marine for four years). On film he conveyed sharp intelligence, contempt, coiled anger, a screen presence that was intense and rather unpleasant. In movies he had been typed to play the antagonist, a smart bad guy or a creep, until John Huston had given him his first lead, casting him against type as the pukka English detective hero of his retro mystery, *The List of Adrian Messenger*, released in 1963. For *The Bible*, Huston found Scott a perfect choice to capture the gravitas, strength, and mysticism of the Old Testament patriarch.

In Huston's suite Ava met her costar. Scott seemed friendly, low-key, complimentary but not effusive, looking forward to working with her and all that. They left together. Out in the hall, out of Huston's view, sort of an afterthought: "Ava, perhaps . . . if you're not busy. . . . Would you like to have dinner? Talk about the script."

They had a good evening out. Yes, she looked forward to working with him, too. Nothing happened at once. He had a wife—the actress Colleen Dewhurst—and a baby son residing with him in a villa across town. There was that. For a while Scott hovered at the periphery, friendly, interested, but nothing more. Then they began to act together, and they were enjoying the experience, Scott very much. They huddled on the set, had lunches. By this time Ava had started up a thing with Stephen Grimes, Huston's personable art director and another veteran of Puerto Vallarta.

It was an on-location thing, a nice guy, some company for the night. Then one evening, without warning, Grimes discovered that he was out and George C. Scott was in. Suddenly the two performers were inseparable. Ava found George smart, sardonically funny, sensitive. They talked politics and books and poetry. He declaimed to her like a broken-nosed Cyrano, snatches of Shakespeare and Walt Whitman. Scott thought show business was rubbish, but he was passionate about acting and language and the theater and film. And now about Ava Gardner. His ardor flared white hot. Within days of their affair starting up, he was overwhelmingly in love. And Ava in turn responded at once to his intense passion, she was intrigued, flattered, captivated.

It had seemed a good idea at the time.

"That was a bad, bad relationship," Betty Sicre recalled. "He was not good for her. And she was bad for him too."

Scott had a drinking problem. Big time. Booze, in the right dosage, unleashed in him darkness and demons—paranoia, violent jealousy, rage. He had gotten the liquor habit in the marines, a response, he would say, to a depressing, haunted detail overseeing the bodies for burial at Arlington Cemetery. From his days as a struggling actor in the 1950s there would be rumors, tales told of a "Jekyll-Hyde" personality, a propensity for violence when he got into the liquor and particularly violence toward women, including the account by a longtime girlfriend with whom he had a child out of wedlock (while his then-wife was also pregnant) and whom he twice attempted to kill, once with an iron barbell and once in a thwarted murder-suicide. With success and the desire not to do anything to screw it up, perhaps along with some sense of responsibility or fear for his wife and children, Scott had tried to clean up his act, to stay away from alcohol, and to keep his demons at bay. Now, swept up in an affair with Ava Gardner, this was not going to be possible.

"He had been on the wagon for years," said Betty Sicre. "She got him drinking again."

"Oh, yeah," remembered Nan Birmingham. "She said he'd been on the wagon. But she said he sure wasn't staying on there."

Ava had seen indicators of his potential in the fury with which he argued and roared his sudden jealous complaints, but her temper was nothing to be taken lightly either, when the vodka was flowing. Shouting and slap-ping and throwing things were not unknown activities in her life and no reason to interrupt what had become a divertingly passionate relationship. Then came a night, on location in the Abruzzi, in the village of Avezzano. They had come back to his hotel room. They were drinking. It was said to have been a mention of the name Frank Sinatra that triggered the argu-ment this night. There was screaming, four-letter words thrown back and forth. Scott became increasingly threatening, inflated with rage. Though she was probably in no condition for entirely rational thought herself, Ava decided she'd heard enough, told him she was leaving, and headed for the door. Scott charged at her, flung her back, and punched her on the side of the head so hard she spun in a circle and dropped to the floor. The power-ful, furious ex-marine hovered, held her down, and punched her again, again, again. She felt her skull ringing, blood on her tongue. It went on till he released his grip suddenly, turned away for a moment, muttering curses, and she scrambled to the door and was gone.

In the morning he was lying in wait. Her face bruised, red, and swollen, she rushed past him. He shuffled alongside, head bowed, like a cur.

"Ava, my God! I'm so sorry . . . I don't know how I could do such a thing . . . Forgive me, please, I'm so ashamed." He whimpered and grov-eled. *"Ashamed . . . I beg you to forgive me!"*

"Fuck you, you bastard!"

The makeup department did what they could to make her presentable. Word of what had happened spread through the company. There was a sense of shock, sympathy for her, disgust with George C. Scott. "I re-member Peter O'Toole wanting to go right away and give Scott a beat-ing," said Tony Huston, a visitor to his father's set (he had acted with Scott two years before in *Adrian Messenger*). "Dad intervened before things got out of hand. But no one was very happy with George after that. He had a drinking problem, but Dad came to feel that was just an excuse, that he was essentially a coward. The drink was there to cover up some es-sential flaw in him as a man. Hitting women was part of it."

Ava was not the sort to call in the cops, and while she gave some thought to quitting the picture she felt she owed it to Huston to carry on. Scott remained with his tail between his legs, begging to be forgiven. Some say she taunted him by turning to other men at hand, including a very brief encounter with a guy from the De Laurentiis office.

The unit was headed south to the next location. She had a long week-end off and Frank was in Italy making a movie, *Von Ryan's Express*. He was going to come see her, then he wasn't. The press rats were all around, he told her. They had a bounty out for a picture of the two of them to-gether. He wasn't giving them the satisfaction. She flew to Rome, and a couple of his bulky underlings took her from the airport to his Twentieth Century–Fox–provided digs outside the city, an eighteen-room villa complete with heliport (from which he was flown each morning to the *Von Ryan's* mountain location at Cortina d'Ampezzo), walled off and guarded like a despot's fortress. Frank was affectionate, sentimental. There was some of the old talk about them getting back together. But there was a sense of strain in the air. There was no sex that weekend. Brad Dexter, Sinatra's sidekick at the time, told biographer Randy Taraborrelli, "Frank was still trying to revive the relationship, but she had started to hit that bottle and it was painful for Frank to see the woman he adored destroying herself with booze."

She returned to *The Bible*, which was shooting now at desolate locations around the Gulf of Catania in eastern Sicily. She felt stressed and lonely on her return, and the atmosphere at work did not help. A malaise had set-tled on the huge, tiring production. Huston's low threshold of boredom had been reached, his growing disengagement apparent—one morning nearly a thousand people stood around waiting for direction while he sat working on a crossword puzzle. Ava declared that this one would be her last movie. A visiting journalist, Peer Oppenheimer, got her (in her lone-liness perhaps) to speak to him for a few minutes. She was "as tense as the spring of a tightly wound watch," he reported. "If anything," she grum-bled, "I hate making films more than ever. The only exception was *The Night of the Iguana* . . . thanks to Richard and John. No—thanks mostly to John. He's wonderful to work with. It was John who talked me into playing Sarah in *The Bible*. But I'm already sorry I accepted. It's such a big picture with so many people in it. You sit around, and you really aren't close to anyone." Huston, speaking with the same reporter, offered his own mixed feelings: "I don't really know her. I don't think anyone does. I wanted her for *Night* because I thought she had always been miscast and had never been given a chance to show what she could do as an actress. I think she showed it in *Iguana*, and I think she will be as good again as Sarah."

Every day she had to work with George Scott. He was at all times considerate, supportive. He asked her once more to forgive him, and then one day she did. They began going to dinner again. She began going back to his room. He told her he was more in love with her than ever, begged her to marry him. The ugly night of violence was nearly forgotten. Then, another night, one drink too many and back came the demons. It was like a horror movie transformation, suddenly the deep breathing, the eyes bugging out, the filthy names, the slapping, strangling, punching. In the hotel bar one evening he came storming through the entrance looking for her, like the Frankenstein monster on a rampage.

"I'll kill you, you fucking bitch!"

Huston ran forward to intercept him, leaping on his back and locking arms over his face. The actor was too powerful to bring down, and he lurched and twisted across the barroom with the director wrapped around his shoulders, knocking over chairs and bottles, Huston digging in as if he were riding an ostrich. Some others joined the battle and pulled him over and subdued him, and Ava was hurried out of sight.

He was taken to a hospital—"a nuthouse with bars" according to Ava—and pumped full of tranquilizers. The moviemakers were looking at a potential catastrophe if Scott could not return—his part ran through nearly one-third of the picture, half or more to be shot again if he was replaced. "Without George," said Huston in his voice of God, "we're *fucked*."

It was, naturally, Ava who would be called on to lure the crazed star back to work in one piece. And so she did. The show must go on. And George remained devoted to her, when he wasn't trying to murder her. One day three Sicilian bruisers came and took Scott for a ride. He refused to talk about it; some believed they were three Mafiosi sent by Sinatra to deliver an ultimatum, others that Huston had hired them from central casting for the same purpose. There was nothing logical about what went on, nothing rational. The affair continued, the drinking continued, the violence continued, *The Bible* got made.

Stephen and Nan Birmingham had gone to Spain that year. Ava had finished her movie in Italy, and she invited them to have Thanksgiving dinner at the duplex. They were in Madrid then and Ava called, asking them to meet her flight and take her home from the airport. She had been to see a doctor in England that day and was flying back, wanted to dodge the press. "We said, 'Sure thing, Ava,' and we went to get her," Nan Birmingham remembered. "Ava arrives, and I see that she has an arm in a sling. That's why she'd been to her doctor. She's got the arm in a sling. And then I see there's a bald patch on the back of her head. We had no idea what this was all about. 'Oh,' she said, 'George and I had a fight.' She'd gotten a dislocated shoulder . . . or a broken collarbone, one of those. And he'd torn a chunk of hair from her head. I didn't know how to react to that. It must have been some fight." (Some say the broken bone was a result of whiplash from a misplaced punch thrown at Scott by Ava.)

"Then, a couple of days later, we went over to her place. It was a small gathering she was having. And now George was on the scene. We met George C. Scott. Ava introduced us. Ava was not drinking. And George wasn't either. She was eating an apple. I think George was eating an apple, too. He seemed very relaxed. He was charming, simply charming. But the thing you couldn't help noticing was George's face—it looked terrible, all red and burned, like he'd been in a fire. And Ava gives me one of her signals, *'Psst! Woo-hoo!'* And I go with her and she whispers, 'Did you see George's face?' She said he had been drunk the night before and he had thrown himself into the fireplace and he had smashed his head in it, beaten his own head on the hot coals or the hot fire grille. Oh, boy. And I looked over at him and, jeez, his face did look pretty terrible, I'll tell you that. But there was George sitting and talking away like everything was normal, just eating his apple. And then Ava said, 'Come on upstairs, Nan, I want to show you something.' So I went upstairs to her bedroom. And she shows me the door to her clothes closet, and there was a great big hole in it. She said, 'Look what he did!' She said Scott had put his head through the door. She said they were fighting, and George was coming after her. She went into her bedroom and wouldn't let him in, and he kicked the door in and she went hiding in her closet and barred the door or something, and he literally smashed his head through the door. I don't know how Scott ever survived all this. I don't remember the whole itinerary, whether his head went into the closet first or into the fireplace! Ha! But it seemed like a pretty strange relationship and a miracle that they both survived."

Thanksgiving dinner was served. Ava's mood had declined by then. They were not going to have a fucking turkey, she told the guests, they were going to have a fucking chicken. "There isn't," she said, "a fucking turkey in all of Madrid."

And they went into the dining room, and Ava went over to where the meal was all set out, and she picked up a chicken leg and hurled it across the room. For why no one knew. Who was she throwing it at? No one knew. The *world*. And then she stormed upstairs and that was the last anyone saw of her.

The affair with Scott went on into the next year, 1965. No one who knew Ava could explain it, not with a great deal of certainty or understanding. She was a magnet for mad situations, some said, or addicted to high drama or turned on by violence, or it was her upbringing ("redneck," said Stephen Birmingham, "where men beat up women"), or it was just that crazy little thing called love, only this time very much too crazy. The turning point in the affair—though, unfortunately, not its climax— occurred in London. They had gone to the theater to see *Othello*. Reenie Jordan thought that was definitely the wrong play to see with George C. Scott. They were drinking afterward, and Scott's demons had begun to surface. By the time he and Ava returned to the suite at the Savoy, he was out of control. He began slapping and punching her. She ran from him, but Scott blocked the way out of the suite and she retreated and hid in the outer bathroom off the foyer, calling for help. When Reenie attempted to go to her, Scott threatened her, dared her to try and get past. Reenie left the suite through a bedroom door, found a busboy to help her, and got Ava out through a transom. Hotel security came. Then the police. Scott was charged with "disturbing the peace" and spent the night behind bars. Ava and Reenie were checked out and gone before he could be released. She swore she would never see him again. It had to end before someone's head got cut off.

But Scott's passion for her continued. For some time he tried all methods to reach her, declaring his love, begging for a last chance. He sent word he was seeking a Mexican divorce from his wife, Colleen, so that he and Ava could be married. It went on like that, and she went on avoiding him until at last it seemed he had gotten the picture and faded away.

She was in Los Angeles then, late in 1965, visiting Bappie and her husband (their marriage remained a modest success). She was staying in a bungalow at the Beverly Hills Hotel above Sunset Boulevard. In bed sometime after midnight, she was awakened by a racket at the back door. There was a sound of a window shattering, things cracking and crashing. And the next moment George C. Scott was in the room with her. He was heaving with rage, his flesh dank with whiskey sweat.

"I love you! Do you hear me?"

He held a bottle of booze in his hand and he smashed the neck and waved the jagged glass under her eyes.

"I won't give you up! I'd rather see us both dead!"

She pleaded for mercy, for the sake of their love, said whatever lies he needed to hear. It took forever to wind him down. It was a little before dawn when she convinced him he needed something "for his nerves," she would call somebody they could trust, she said, and she phoned her physician and friend Dr. Smith, while Scott sat there watching her, shaking with rage, his eyes popping. The doctor arrived, calmly assessed the situation, gave Scott a powerful sedative, then went off to alert the hotel and phone Bappie. Scott dozed while Ava and a security guard, and then Bappie, debated what to do next. Suddenly, Scott woke up, stared at them for a moment, then got up and disappeared out the back door.

She would never understand it. Love was supposed to be such a wonderful thing. How could it cause so much unhappiness? Why did love always have to mean a broken collarbone, 50 ccs of phenobarbital, and somebody fleeing in the night?

On July 19, 1966, Ava got a call from Las Vegas. It was George Jacobs, Frank Sinatra's longtime valet. On his boss's instructions he was calling to say that Frank was about to marry Mia Farrow. Mr. S. had not wanted her to find out about it after the fact in the papers or on television. Mia was the young star of the TV soap opera *Peyton Place*, the daughter of Maureen O'Sullivan and director John Farrow. A slender, fawnlike blond, she epitomized the flower-power youth culture, a believer in macrobiotics and rock music and the Maharishi. Their relationship had been in the papers over the previous year, but mostly it had been the subject of jokes, the hippie and the old Rat Packer. She was twenty-one years old, Sinatra was fifty. Said Mia of her mature boyfriend, "He's groovy, he's kinky, and above all he's gentle." And now, after a quickly planned ceremony inside the Sands Hotel Casino, they were going to be husband and wife.

Ava had wanted to be untouched by the news. Later people would hear the tough-broad wisecracks (playing on the new Mrs. Sinatra's stick figure and ultrashort haircut): that Mia was "a fag with a pussy," and how she'd always known Frank wanted to go to bed with a boy. But she had not been able to hold it together that first night, and the sense of loss had overwhelmed her. She cried and could not stop crying.

An examination at the Chelsea Hospital for Women in London had detected the likely presence of a fibroid tumor in her uterus. Her mother's early death from uterine cancer had haunted Ava for more than twenty years. Any gynecological problem she ever experienced had provoked anxiety, and she would imagine a harbinger of that killing disease. Now, with little consideration, she elected to undergo a hysterectomy.

She had grown tired of Spain, bored with the life she had created for herself there. A dozen years had passed in her adopted home, and now what wonderful experiences there had been seemed long ago and faded in her mind and she had come to think of her time there as mostly wasted. What had she done with the years? Why had she ever come there in the first place?

And Spain, it could be said, had grown tired of her. The local press printed derisive stories, unflattering photos. Her neighbors filed complaints about the noise and the unsavory visitors (Gypsies wandering about Doctor Arce at dawn). A local actor was quoted in an article, circa 1965: "I don't know who started all that about how popular she is in Spain. She's too unfeminine for the Spaniards. They like women to behave like women."

Lately she had come under the government's scrutiny. It was rumored that Franco himself had warned the U.S. ambassador to keep her under control. One day she was paid a visit by an auditor from the revenue department. There was a discussion of back taxes owed, perhaps—*Quien sabe, señora*, they were still investigating—a million American dollars or more.

To a woman who might give away a fortune in jewelry on a whim one day and obsess about a missing golf ball the next, any formal questions about her financial history were strictly gobbledygook. Ricardo Sicre would try to help, and her money managers from Los Angeles would fly in carrying bags full of paperwork, but the problem lingered on without resolution.

She began to talk of moving to London. She had been there so often in recent years it was already a home away from home. She loved the city, the people, the good manners. She liked the tiny shops and the parks where you could walk your dog. And the rain. A person could have too much fucking sunshine.

She arranged to sublease the Park Lane flat of Robert Ruark, the North Carolina–born columnist turned best-selling, Hemingwayesque author, who at fifty had recently dropped dead from alcohol abuse. For two years she shifted back and forth between residences in Spain and Britain until settling permanently in London in 1968.

After the completion of *The Bible* in the autumn of 1964, she did not work again for more than three years. The offers continued to come, but no longer with the frequency or the urgency of before. The most significant film she did *not* make in this period was the epochal coming-of-age hit of 1967, *The Graduate*. "Ava was the person they had wanted for the role of the mother, Mrs. Robinson," Betty Sicre would recall. "She was still living in Madrid then and she threw the script over to me and said, 'Take a look and see if you think I should do this.' I read it in a couple of hours and brought it back to her. I said, 'Ava, this is great!' She read the script and agreed to do it. They brought her to meet Mike Nichols, the director. Ava claimed that Nichols had booked her into a hotel and that their rooms were connected by a door. She was very insulted. She came back to Madrid and she said, 'Oh, I turned it down because Nichols was coming on to me, and he expected me to unlock the doors.' But I doubt Mike Nichols would do that. Why would he do that? I think probably what happened was she just got drunk in their evening interview and he decided she'd be too iffy to work with. I think she blew it herself there. I don't think she could do it at the time."

Mike Nichols's version of the encounter cast him in the role of an inno-cent, disconcerted Benjamin to Ava's seductive, scary Mrs. Robinson, summoned for an appearance at her New York hotel suite. "She was Ava

Gardner," he would recall to the Associated Press, "and my heart was pounding . . . the source of a million fantasies." When the two were alone in the suite, Nichols said, "She did all the things you prayed would and wouldn't happen."

The exact nature of these prayers Nichols would leave unrevealed. As to the prospective film, with its mature themes and sexy scenes, Ava declared, "I strip for nobody. I want to make that clear." She then told Nichols, "I can't act . . . they've all tried, but it's hopeless."

"Miss Gardner, you're wrong," said Nichols. "You're an excellent actress, I love your acting."

"You're very sweet," Ava said. "But I can't act."

Instead of *The Graduate*, her return to the screen would be in the 1968 remake of *Mayerling*, the venerable historical confection about star-crossed romance among the Hapsburgs. Enacting the part of the Austro-Hungarian empress Elisabeth to James Mason's Franz Josef, she was paired with a man she had first worked opposite eighteen years before, Pandora to his Flying Dutchman. Then they had been the romantic leads in Albert Lewin's passionate fantasia. Now they played support to more bankable mad lovers, Omar Sharif and Catherine Deneuve as the doomed Crown Prince Rudolf and his mistress, Marie Vetseia. For the temperate, dapper director Terence Young she worked without difficulty, offering a seductive and convincing performance full of imperial hauteur, glamorous, worldly, and assured. She and Mason, the old-timers, the supporting players, would receive the best notices upon the film's unspectacular release. (The approval of Ava Gardner in the role of historical European royalty was fresh testimony to the distance she had traveled from Grabtown and from rival Love Goddesses like Turner and Monroe.)

Sharif, the handsome Egyptian then at the height of his period of international stardom, was just ten years younger than the actress portraying his mother, and he did not respond to Ava Gardner as anyone's mom but as a woman, very beautiful and "infinitely feminine." They struck up a friendship—"a rather ambiguous," he would write in his memoirs, "highly pleasurable camaraderie, one that bordered on romance."

For three months on Austrian locations Sharif would be her affectionate squire. He found her fascinating but so troubled—full of sorrows, unfulfilled desires, only alcohol easing the distress. "Terrific guys have been in love with her," he wrote, "but they couldn't satisfy her need for the absolute and Ava was always disappointed. She has known glory, wealth, but never love in the sense that she understood it: total giving shared in passion."

Omar's insights had to warn him of inherent dangers in a more intimate relationship with his complicated new friend. The two did not cross that border to a romance. "I didn't want to do anything to ruin our wonderful friendship."

Frank had sent notes, good wishes, a phone call on her birthday. He wanted her to know, he said, that he was still there for her. Anything, anytime. Talking on the phone to him, she had bitten down on her lip till the skin bled. "Say hi to Mia for me," she told him.

But the marriage did not go well. Frank and his swami-loving child bride had turned out not to be compatible after all. A year and a little more after their wedding there began to appear items in the gossip columns, reports of discord, by autumn 1967 a separation. Frank filed for divorce. "Maybe it bothered him not being young," Mia reflected. "My friends from India would come into the house barefoot and hand him a flower. That made him feel square for the first time in his life."

Ava grappled with her reaction. There was undeniable relief in the news that Frank and Mia would not be going on together, happily ever after. But there were no more jokes. She knew what it felt like to have a marriage die.

Work was finishing on *Mayerling*, the crown prince and his gal dead and buried in the name of love, when a call reached her from Florida.

"Mrs. Sinatra?" the voice on the phone said. "It's Frank. He's sick. He's got the pneumonia. It don't look so good, I got to be honest. He keeps asking for you. Just keeps saying your name over and over. I would come pretty quick if you know what I mean."

She flew to him at once. Frank had been in Miami to make a private-eye picture (*Lady in Cement*) in the daytime and sing in the Hotel Fontainebleau's La Ronde Room by night. "He was pushing himself so hard, and that whole divorce thing, it was too much, he couldn't take it," Jilly Rizzo told her. "The poor guy."

She was taken by private elevator to his inner sanctum at the top of the Fontainebleau, behind sprawled layers of hangers-on, yes-men and three hundred-pound gorillas—Frank's mouth-breathing *cuadrilla* he now took with him wherever he went.

"You glad to see me, baby?" Frank said.

"They told me you were dying, Francis," she said. "I've been traveling for 24 hours to get here."

He'd had a virus in the lungs, it was bad, not quite bad enough to go to the hospital and lose his penthouse view. But when Frank got sick he needed a lot of people at his bedside, praying. She remembered that time in Lake Tahoe when the stooge, with tears, told her Frank was at death's door and she had to turn around and rush back from Los Angeles at dawn. In Miami, stressed from worry and jet-lagged, she screamed at him for being a selfish prick.

"Hey, lady, I been sick. What you come here for if you're gonna give me a hard time . . ."

It didn't get much better than that. Frank was in a cranky mood, and now that she had come to see him he seemed to have little interest in the two of them being together. He didn't want to leave the hotel so he sent her out to enjoy Miami in the care of Joe E. Lewis, the raunchy nightclub comic whose throat had once been sliced by gangsters (Sinatra had portrayed him in *The Joker Is Wild*). When she was with Frank it was all tough talk and dirty jokes and rants about the hippies ruining the country, playing to his goons, whom she hated. A couple of the hangers-on pushed a piano through a window, and Frank said something about her looking old. Ava went back to her suite, packed her things, and flew away.

He would make it up to her. In time the relationship returned to something like what it had been before the coming of Mia, they went back to the phone calls in the night, the affectionate notes, Frank generous in small ways and large. There was, however, no return to the sexual relations they had—prior to his remarriage—enjoyed, intermittently but intensely, in many of the years since their own formal separation and divorce.

In London she lived at the luxury flat on Park Lane with Reenie and her corgi Cara (Rags, her first "baby," had died after a long and pampered life). She brought few of her things from Spain, most of the furniture and other large items shipped to the states and a storage facility in New York where they were forgotten for decades and finally sold at auction. She did bring her antique brass and lace-covered bed from Madrid but eventually replaced it after she heard someone describe it—because it was too narrow for two—as a "pessimist's bed."

In London she was setting out to make a new life. To make a new Ava Gardner. In departing from Spain she had wanted to leave behind the furies that had directed her behavior for so long. "By that time in her life she was really very tired of stardom," said Spoli Mills, Ava's close friend for the last thirty years of her life. "It had overwhelmed her. She started out a very shy person, and a lot of what had happened to her she found very embarrassing. When she came to London she really just wanted to become a normal person again, an anonymous person. She wanted to walk down the street and not be bothered. She wanted peace. She didn't want to think about being beautiful, about having to live up to that legend. She wanted to walk her dog in the park and not give a damn about how she looked."

In the cooler, less tempestuous climate of England she went about constructing a more reticent existence. There were to be fewer all-night club crawls and more evenings at the opera and the ballet. Tennis tournaments took the place of the bullfights as her spectator sport of choice. There were to be no more public brawls or broken bottles, or far fewer, anyway. No more cursing at journalists (not to their faces). No more mad love affairs, not after the nightmare with George Scott (although she knew very well this promise to herself would be the hardest to keep if and when temptation came). There would be men who caught her eye, always, men with whom she would flirt and toy in the years ahead (and, gossip had it, a few women, too), but she would remain cautious in her personal affairs, keep out of harm's reach. In public she would occasionally be seen and photographed on the arm of a handsome escort—the gossip columns might hint at a new "love interest"—but most of these were homosexuals. Her physical needs she would satisfy for a time in occasional, and discreet, liaisons, including one long-running relationship with a young man (an eighteen-year-old messenger boy delivering a package to her flat when they first met) with whom she arranged clandestine visits at a hotel in Knightsbridge.

In pursuit of her new self-image she would even give up alcohol, at least temporarily. Once or twice a year she would go for a week to Grayshott Hall Health Farm in Surrey, south of London, and diet and exercise and not touch a drop. Other times she would check in at a local private nursing home, where they would keep her away from liquor for a twenty-four-hour period, enough, apparently, to set her straight without further treatment. She could stay completely sober for three or four months at a time before she would begin drinking again.

Contentedly she went without work for a year and a half after *Mayerling*, and would have remained unemployed but for the pleading of a new friend, Roddy McDowall.

McDowall was the doleful child star of the 1940s, returned to movies in the sixties as an eccentric, spritely leading man and character actor. Early in 1969 he had promoted himself to his first job as a feature director with a project known as *Tam Lin* (the most lasting title of the many it would assume in a long and bumpy history, including *Toys, Games and Toys, Tamilin, The Devil's Widow,* and *The Ballad of Tam-Lin*), from a story by Gerald Vaughan Hughes, based on a Scottish Borders ballad by Robert Burns. Adapted as a kind of horror movie fable set in a contemporary mod Britain, it told of a wealthy, older woman, demonic godmother to a band of swinging, stoned young wastrels; a witch in fact, she takes a terrible, uncanny vengeance on the man who spurns her love. To play the lead role of Michaela Cazelet, the deathless bitch-goddess, the "devil's widow" of the piece, McDowall needed an actress with the qualities of "glamour, maturity and mystery." His list of cinema divas of a certain age quickly narrowed to one legendary name, a woman he had met—only briefly—when he was a boy at MGM and with whom he had remained fascinated ever since. It was a strong, juicy part, a rare central role for a woman of middle age, and was so well suited to Ava Gardner it read in places like an occult reflection of her own life, this story of the legendary, aging but glamorous "witchy" woman, Michaela, and her "coven" of mooching layabouts (not unlike the Gypsy bands who once filled Ava's living room in Madrid) and her young lovers, and her tempestuous temper.

As usual, Ava did not want to go back to work. McDowall pursued her. He was a rare character in the picture business of that time: a veteran Hollywood insider who was also a movie buff, deeply knowledgeable of film history, a collector of autographs, posters, and 35 mm prints. He was the first prospective director Ava had met who appeared able and eager to talk to her with a thorough knowledge of her past work, surprising and flattering her with aesthetic appreciations of her performances in *Pandora* and *Bhowani Junction* and others. And beyond that McDowall was an engaging and empathetic person. They became friends. Coming to know her—"this gouache of remarkable qualities," he would write, "deeply appealing, heartbreakingly moving . . . a study in contradictions"—he wanted her for the film more than ever. But Madame Cazalet was the longest and, Ava thought, the most complicated part she had been offered in many years, too much trouble, and she had never before worked with an inexperienced director. McDowall persisted. At last, with the producers getting restless, she came around. His sympathy for her was all-apparent, and she liked him very much; she agreed to do *Tam Lin* for Roddy, more than anything to help make sure his dream of directing a movie came true.

In London, Roddy McDowall picked his other actors and technical crew. To support Ava's central role he cast a mix of old and new names, venerable Cyril Cusack and Richard Wattis (late of the popular *St. Trinian's* comedies, now to steal scenes as Michaela's mordant Jeeves), rising new leading man Ian McShane, and an assortment of teenagers and twenty-somethings, some to make their one and only film appearance in *Tam Lin*, others at the very start of what would be long careers in movies and television, including Joanna Lumley, Stephanie Beacham, Sinead Cusack, and Bruce Robinson (future writer-director of the transcendent *Withnail & I*). To photograph the film McDowall chose Billy Williams, the brilliant young British director of photography whose other credit that year would be for Ken Russell's *Women in Love*. "Roddy wanted to work with someone of his own generation, a cinematographer who was not set in his ways but would be willing to experiment, to try out new ideas," Billy Williams would recall. "He was a very stimulating person to work with, had a great deal of interest in the composition and the color and the effects, and we had a lot of fun finding ways to shoot certain scenes, like the drug scene, trying to find unique imagery to express someone high or crazy on drugs.

"There was a launch party for the film at a lovely restaurant in Covent Garden, and that was where I met Ava Gardner for the first time. She had that legendary very beautiful face and an extraordinary presence, a bearing that I can only describe as regal. She had a long body, her legs were not long, but with this long body and the wonderful carriage she had she appeared very tall when she was sitting down. There was a quality about her, this poise and elegance that told you at once she was a star. Just to see it commanded your respect."

The principal location, where filming began in mid-July, was in the wooded lowlands of the Tweed Valley in southeastern Scotland. Arrangements were made to shoot on the grounds of the tenth-century Traquair House, former home of the Scottish kings. Cast and crew were put up nearby at the Peebles Hydro Hotel, a capacious Edwardian health spa, a rather staid establishment in those days, full of dour old Scottish ladies who had come every year since they were children and who regarded without cheer the arrival of Ava Gardner and an international film unit. ("They were quite unable to cope with us," Billy Williams would recall. "At the restaurant we all ordered off the à la carte menu, and I don't think they had ever gotten an order off the à la carte in sixty years.")

It was at the spa hotel the first night where one of *Tam Lin*'s young cast members, Joanna Lumley, met the American movie star. The twenty-three-year-old Lumley was a beautiful blond actress at the beginning of what was to be a notable career, her own stardom on television a few years away. "I was just starting out, and it was a small part, but I was very happy to be in this exciting film," Joanna Lumley would recall. "I was to play one of a coven of twelve, who all had one or two lines, some parts slightly larger than others. All of us in this younger group traveled up to Scotland together, and we'd all made friends with each other. We were staying at this tall, grim hotel called the Peebles—I'm sure it's lovely now, but it was fairly Spartan in those days—and Ava was there. And there was this tremendous tension and excitement about meeting Ava Gardner and seeing her for the first time ever, the sense of extreme excitement that we were going to be working with a Hollywood diva. And she was quite tense about it, too, I learned that later.

"It was the evening before the first day's shoot, and I went out walking on the hillside and it was summertime and there were briar roses on all the hills, and I picked a mass of wildflowers to bring back to my room. When I got back I thought, Don't be selfish, give some of them to Miss Gardner. So I knocked on her door and her maid, Louise, came to the door and I handed her the flowers, saying, 'Would you please give these to Miss Gardner and say they're from Georgia'—which was my name in the film. I went back to my little room and hardly got inside before the phone rang. It was Ava Gardner's voice on the line, and she said, 'Georgia, this is Big A. Won't you come down and have a drink with me, honey?'

"I went back down immediately just as I was. Her maid, Louise, showed me in and I met Reggie, Ava's secretary then, and he was a darling man, and beyond was Big A—as she had us all call her on the film—sitting with bare feet, legs tucked up under her on the sofa, with her face completely unmade-up, hair just pushed back from her face, and looking marvelous. She greeted me warmly and gave me a drink and we talked in that typical hopeless-new-person-to-madame-film-star way. We had a drink or two. She loved gin, and I remember one thing she said, 'Gin tasted better from the bottle.' That was one of her sayings I remembered and treasured, and another was that she said she liked men hot and sweaty from the bullring! Then she asked if we could read some lines from the script so she could hear them. She said, 'We've got this scene tomorrow, darling. I'd so like it if you and Reggie would read through it.' So Reggie read Ian's lines in a wonderful, slightly camp voice and me sounding completely English, read Ava's. And when that was done she said, 'Wonderful. Now let's go for a swim.'

"The people at Peebles Hydro had this big old-fashioned indoor swimming pool in the basement—for an American I'm sure it looked very grim. And because it was Ava Gardner, the manager immediately went and opened the pool, and we went down. We went down, the three of us, Big A, me, and Reggie holding the towels. And she had her little dog with her, her corgi, Cara. And Ava and I jumped in the pool. Ava dived in and she swam beautifully. And then the dog came in, and the dog paddled and yapped and splashed about with us. And we got out and Ava by mistake took my towel, and she used it to dry the dog. She said, 'Oh, darling, don't you have a towel?' I said, 'Oh, no, no.' I couldn't say, 'You used it to dry the dog.' So I chucked on my clothes on my wet body, and we went upstairs and had some more to drink. Eventually, very reluctantly—because I didn't know how you excuse yourself from royalty—I left her and went to my room, walking on air, because I'd made friends with her. And, you know, in a funny way, I think she was also pleased because you get a case of the nerves when you're starting, and she got to see a familiar face among the crowd of strangers she was working with next day. (I remember her first line for the camera, as she stood on a parapet sipping champagne; it was one word directed at all of us lounging below her: 'Scum!') Anyway, everyone soon became her friend and just magnetically enthralled by this extraordinary, legendary woman."

It had been almost two years since Ava had last gone before a camera. When she viewed some of the first day's work on *Tam Lin* she was dismayed to see how much older she now appeared, a condition she thought only accentuated by the on-screen proximity of so many healthy, attractive young people.* "I thought she looked wonderful," said Billy Williams. "But she was forty-seven years old [in December], and there was no question that her skin texture wasn't anything like as lovely as it must have been when she was younger. And drinking also showed in the skin tone and color. I had never worked with a big star who was aging like that. It became obvious to me that she would need particularly careful lighting. I had to light her very carefully and use quite a lot of diffusion on the lens. I was able to do this easily in the studio because in the studio you can have absolute control of the light. But on exteriors, with changing weather conditions, particularly with overcast light, this was more of a problem. Quite early in the shooting I was made aware that Ava was not happy about the way she was looking in exteriors. I did want her to look her best and to be happy. So what I had to do was find a way to stop the natural light overhead and fill in with a more favorable illumination. I was quite a young cinematographer, you know, just kind of finding my feet then. It was a learning process for me. What I did, when I could shoot her close enough to do it, I began putting up a canopy over the top of her head, black, twelve feet square, which cut out all of the top light, and then I lit her from over the top of the camera, which smoothed things out very nicely. It was the first time I'd had to go to those lengths to protect someone. And she saw how that looked, and she was happy with it. But now and again as we went on, she would say something, and you knew she was quite conscious of the fact that the years had gone by. It was rather sad.

---

*The adored Cara sat in Ava's arms whenever the actress came to a screening of the *Tam Lin* dailies, and the dog was known to go into a barking frenzy at the moment her mistress came on-screen.

One day she said to me, out of nowhere, 'You know, I was very beautiful once.' I didn't know what to say. I thought of her earlier films I'd seen. I said, 'Yes, Ava, I know.' "

From the outset McDowall as director lavished his star with interest and affection, but he found his efforts at first undermined by her self-doubts. "She was a wonderful actress," he wrote, "and she never believed it." She was also clearly bored with the moviemaking process. It was her living, it gave her money, she would say. He worked to awaken her interest, to make her feel a part of the entire creative endeavor. He would sit with her in her dressing room and talk about his ideas for the film while she smoked one of her sixty cigarettes for the day and played with the corgi, or he would walk her around the set and behind the camera and explain the shots he was trying to make, something she could not remember any director ever before taking the time to do. It was a show of respect for her talent and intelligence to which she began to respond warmly, as Roddy hoped, giving him her concentration and devotion.

The part of Michaela was not an easy one, wriggling as it did from realism to theatricality and fantasy, requiring large shifts in style and extravagant emotional displays. There were scenes for which she needed much coaching and many takes and many glasses of champagne. The part also called for her entry to the brave new world of cinematic permissiveness, something about which—inculcated with Papa Mayer's Old Testament views—she had great reservations. In *Tam Lin* the veteran sex symbol at nearly forty-seven had to perform her first (at least vaguely) coital love scene and appear en suite with an unclothed Ian McShane. The day of filming the latter sequence she was extremely nervous in advance, and she complained to Roddy: Was it quite necessary for the boy to be actually bare-assed naked? When they did finally get to shoot the scene, however, she rather seemed to enjoy it. (Ava grew fond of the twenty-year-younger, darkly handsome actor who played her on-screen lover. "He looked beautiful then, like a black-eyed Gypsy, and Ava quite fastened her eyes on him," recalled Joanna Lumley. "I don't know that anything happened between them or not, but we all at the time assumed and hoped that it did!")

They shot for two weeks in Peebleshire, then returned to London and Pinewood Studios for the interior sequences. There was a great deal of hard work and in Ava's mind an uncertainty that the film itself was adding up to anything good, but Roddy and the people she'd come to know on the production had made it a pleasure. The young people in the cast she had initially feared for their youth and unsullied flesh became her beloved brood—"my babies," she called them. She had grown so fond of the dozen guys and girls in Michaela's original "coven" that when they came to a scene that called for her to administer to them a brutal verbal thrashing, she was filled with dread. "I can't tell them off," she pleaded to the director. "I love them!" When he had seen how their energy and the familial ambiance kept Ava happy and *up*, Roddy encouraged the group to hang around the sets for the duration, long after there was anything for them to do. "I used to cram all of us 'children' into my ancient 550-quid Rolls-Royce," Joanna Lumley would recall, "drive down to Pinewood and everybody would tumble out. And we'd spend all day with Big A. It was like a gang, and she was our leader. She was so much fun, the opposite of the grand star, so easy to talk to, but we all respected her hugely, and nobody ever took liberties with her.

"At the very end of the shoot I decided to give a party at my flat. The party was going to be just the 'children' and some of the second assistants, but none of the 'grown-ups' as we called the important people on the film. I mean, I had a very tiny, very humble place two stories up in a very old house, not a place to which you would invite film stars and directors. Well, Big A found out about it, and she said, 'Hon, ain't you inviting me to your party?' I said, 'Oh! Of course, Big A, of course!' And then Roddy wanted to come, and this one and that one, all the grown-ups ended up coming. Once the party started I realized that the drinks were going to run out. And the people were running up and back to the local pub and the off-license to bring back more drink, and we were never keeping up with the demand. And finally there was a ring of the bell, and it was Big A downstairs. She came up the stairs with her secretary, Reggie, before her, and Reggie carried a basket in which had been put every kind of drink you can imagine, brandy, whiskey, gin, vodka, rum—you name it. And Reggie arrived with this basket and behind him came Ava, dressed like a Spanish princess with a cinched eighteen-inch waist and a great flower in her hair and smelling just like paradise with the scent of tuberose all around her. And she entered this fourteen-pounds-a-week humble little place and she made it look like a palace. She said, 'Do you have some kind of big bowl or big jug or something?' I said, 'Sure,' and I pulled out this big old-fashioned Victorian jug from a bath set. And Ava started pouring in all these bottles she brought, everything mixed together, rum, whiskey, gin, vodka. 'Mommy's Little Mixure,' she called it. It was the most lethal kind of cocktail. And everybody got a tooth mug of this mixture. We all drank with Ava, and the party just took off, it was just fantastic. I don't know what kind of party I had expected it to be, but I didn't expect it would go on until six the next day.

"I really speak with unreserved affection for her. Knowing her, making the film, was really one of the happiest experiences in my life. It came at a time when I was just beginning my career and at a terribly impressionable age. And I learned from Ava; she set an example for me. And it so affected me that I've gone out of my way always to make sure I respected and spoke to people who had the tiny parts or the extras because I can't ever forget how it made me feel that she treated all of us like that.

"I saw her only once more many years later. It's a terrible thing about this business, really, you don't keep up. We get so close to each other in such a short period of time, depend on each other, share the long hours and the lack of food, get trucked around like cattle, do amazing things and see beautiful places together. And then it ends, and we look in each other's eyes and exchange addresses and kiss each other like best beloveds, and then everyone heads in different directions and we're like terrible old tarts, in someone else's arms the next day.

"It's a bittersweet business."

The result of Roddy McDowall's first—and only—directorial effort was an elegant curate's egg; dreamlike, imaginative, at times inane. It captured on film a last gasp of swinging England, an air of instant curdled decadence, and in Ava Gardner's full-throttle performance a strange, memorable portrait of a sacred monster, arrogant, vulnerable, terrifying, deepened by the resonant echoes of the star's real life. No one saw it. Not for years, anyway, and then in a considerably diminished version. The production company found itself in financial difficulty and *Tam Lin* went into limbo. Ava was forced to take legal action to obtain her unpaid salary. The film remained on the shelf until 1972, by which time its mod mannerisms already looked vintage. A.I.P. (American International Pictures) in

America gave the butchered cut a brief release; most of the few who saw it then did so from behind the windshields of their automobiles at drive-ins in the Southwest.

She spent the last night of the 1960s at home, cooking New Year's Eve dinner for herself and Reenie and getting "quietly pissed."

She had come to London for a more orderly existence, and she had gotten it. And now: What to do with it? She walked her dog. She went to the theater. She hosted small dinner parties and larger ones at Christmastime and on the Fourth of July. Most nights she was in bed by midnight, with a book and a bag of Maltesers. She would sit in the park and chat with pensioners and Jamaican nannies. When she went around in simple clothes and no makeup, few people recognized her. It was nice to note the English respect for privacy, but she could sense that a part of it was her fame slowly fading away.

"I went to see her in London after she had settled there," Budd Schulberg would recall. "I was passing through town and I went to see her. We sat, and she drank champagne, and we talked about people we knew. I sensed a loneliness in her. I know that when other people would come through London she would sort of grab onto them and say, 'You've got to come right over.' She wanted to reminisce. She was becoming very nostalgic, wanted to talk about the old days, the glamorous days of the past."

Eloise Hardt, Huston's friend, was another American in London in the early seventies, having abandoned Hollywood after a terrible personal tragedy. She had taken a job with a public relations company, trying to lose herself in work. "I would run into her. I remember there was a publicity party at a hotel. She was alone; she was looking kind of sad. That seemed to be her state of affairs then. There had been no normal in her life for so many years that now I think she was paying a price. She seemed to have a dim view that it had all gone wrong, but there was no way to fix it. I don't doubt that she wanted to get off the bandwagon and have a quiet life. But there was no one left to build a life with. She didn't know many people in London. She seemed to me like such a complete Americana and here she was in England and had been there for a while. I said, 'Why don't you just go home?' Well, she wasn't up for that kind of discussion, and we quickly changed the subject."

"She was lonely at times and unhappy, yes, but we all have those times in our lives," Spoli Mills would say. The daughter of the Russian composer Mischa Spolianski and the wife of Paul Mills, the former publicity chief at MGM's London office, she had known Ava since 1957 and would become her closest friend in the later years, in some ways taking the place of Betty Sicre in Spain as the wise, level-headed chum and confidante. "Paul and Ava had known each other since *Mogambo*, and he had sometimes been her escort," Spoli Mills recalled. "And I remember after we met she said to me, 'I was prepared to hate you for taking away my escort. But I find that I like you. We're going to have a lot of fun together.' And we did. When she moved to London we became the best of friends right to the day she died. Ava was such a funny, fascinating person and a joy to be with, and when she wasn't—well—you had to get through it with her because she was worth it.

"She had regrets in her life, of course; we all do. You get in a melancholy mood, and you think about the mistakes. She would have liked things to have lasted with Sinatra. But it didn't work. She said that together they were like bringing a lighted match to TNT. Or to find someone else to take his place. But, you know, you reach a point of no return. She just never found anybody who she could love like that again.

"She would occasionally say to me, 'Jesus, honey, you've got everything I would have loved to have had.' I had a husband and two children, and she felt very close to my two sons. But how serious she was I don't know. Sometimes she would admit, 'I wouldn't have been a good mother anyway, with my life, wouldn't have been able to cope.'

"And, you know, she had her family, really. It would be wrong to think of her as alone in the world. She was very much a part of our family, we thought of her that way, and she had Bappie who was really like Ava's mother, and she was always in close touch with her. She was an extraordinary person, too—Bappie, a tough Southern broad—and she had really looked out for Ava all those years. They beat the hell out of each other; there were lots of arguments, Bappie was not such a paragon of virtue either, but there was great love between them. And then Ava had Reenie, lovely Reenie, who had been with her for years and years. And that was a fiery relationship, too, but they were very close, like sisters. Reenie came and went, but she was always there if Ava needed her. These were people she had around her most of her life and they loved her and she loved them.

And then came the last member of the family, really—Carmen, who was as devoted as a daughter and was there with Ava at the very end."

Carmen Vargas was a pretty, raven-haired native of Ecuador, resident in England for several years when she arrived at Ava Gardner's London flat to interview for the job of housekeeper. The position had become a nuisance to fill as several women in a row had not gotten along with Cara, and some of them had been chased off before they had quite come through the doorway. "She was frightened because that dog bite everyone," Carmen Vargas would recall. "It tear up everyone who go there. The ladies used to come to interview and the dog pulled the bags, bite the ankles. They say the dog bite, and they say, 'Oh, Miss, I'm sorry I cannot live in a house with this dog!' She said it was very bad. Miss Gardner said to me, 'I'm afraid the dog bite you.' I said, 'I think maybe I change my mind to come here.' I don't want to be next for the dog to bite. She said, 'I think I will give up to find someone. Then I will just do everything myself. I will mop the floor myself and everything. But what else can I do? I cannot put the dog to sleep just to have a housekeeper!' I see she is sad about this, so I come into the house and we sit down. The dog came in then. Name was Cara. And the dog came right to me, sat next to me. The dog looks peaceful. I want to pet her. Miss Gardner is very afraid. 'Oh, please, no!' she says. 'Don't touch!' But the dog want me to pet her. And I scratched the ears of the dog. Miss Gardner, she just look at me and the dog and she didn't say anything she just look. Then she say, 'Carmen, let me show you the house.' I tell her, 'Okay.'

"She told me to think about it. The third day I call, I say, 'I take the job.' In the morning I started working for her. I started working that first morning and after a few hours she said to me, 'Carmen, I have to meet someone for lunch. I will be back around three or four.' And she go away, leaving me alone in the house. And I saw that she had very valuable things everywhere. I was so surprised. I had to ask her when she come back. 'How is it you are so trustful? To leave a person who just start working a few hours and leave her in your home with all these valuable things?' She laughed. She said she knew I was special. Then in the evening she said, 'Carmen, we're not going to cook tonight. Let's go out. Come on, I'm treating you.' We went to have dinner at a very nice Italian restaurant, Montpeliano. And I think to myself, 'It must have been somebody crazy to leave this job.' I was so happy. I feel straightaway like I am with my own family.

"Another day she says to me, 'Carmen, how you cook?' I said, 'Miss Gardner, I cook a little, not too much.' She said, 'Okay, you don't have to be cordon bleu, lady.' She said, 'I do a lot of cooking. You can watch what I do.' And I said, 'Okay, you will teach me, and I will follow you.' And I learn many things from her. She taught me to cook Chinese food and Italian and Southern fried chicken. She was a fantastic cook. Every gravy she made, believe me, so good, *mmm*! On Sunday she liked to prepare a special dinner, a big dinner, roast beef or roast lamb. She would put it in the oven and then go to do ironing. Yes, she used to love to iron. She would iron every little thing, my little apron, everything. I would say, 'Miss Gardner, you don't want me to do ironing?' She said, 'No, I enjoy it.' She would iron and watch the television. She liked to watch cartoons or any old movie while she ironed the clothes.

"For three months I was working for her, and I did not know who I was working for. I did not know who was 'Ava Gardner.' My friends say, 'Where are you working?' I say, 'It is an American lady. No husband. She comes in and out. Some people come. I never pay attention what they're talking about. She is very nice.' One day she says to me, 'Carmen, I would like you to come with me. I have to go to . . .' *Someplace*, some country, maybe it was Mexico. I was nervous. I said, 'I will think about it.' She said, 'Don't think about it. We will have a good time.' I said, 'Miss Gardner, why we have to go to this place?' She said, 'I have to go work, baby, it's my job.' I said, 'You have a job? What kind of job do you do?' She started to laugh. She started to laugh very much. Then she says, 'Carmen, *for heaven's sake*, don't you know I'm a lousy movie star?' "

Once again Ava's presence had been requested by John Huston. In the autumn of 1971 he was making *The Life and Times of Judge Roy Bean*, starring Paul Newman in the title role, an episodic and highly fanciful account of the self-appointed 1890s Texas hanging judge, the legendary "law west of the Pecos." As scripted by John Milius and then revised and recon-

ceived during filming by Milius and the director, the film was to be another Hustonian venture in subversive storytelling, a violent, absurdist
black comedy that mocked the notion of Wild West heroes and legends
while ultimately offering a heartfelt, haunting lament for their passing. A
leitmotif throughout was Judge Bean's obsession with a British theatrical
superstar of the time, Lily Langtry, a woman Bean would never meet but
in whose honor he named both his Texas town and his saloon. For the
film's finale, the actress, on an American tour, would make a brief visit to
the windblown whistle-stop and to the shrine created by her number one
fan, the long-dead Judge Bean. To play the part of the "most beautiful
woman in all creation" in her one brief but significant scene, Huston could
think of no one better than the great beauty of his own acquaintance, and
a woman for whom he had felt something of a Bean-like adoration for
nearly thirty years. In September he sent her the script with a brief note
("Ava darling . . . you'll see that it's a must. Much love"). In October she
joined the *Judge Roy Bean* company at Tucson, Arizona.

She was needed for just three days of filming, but it was time enough to
cause some commotion and show them all that living legends had not died
with "the Jersey Lily." At the party given to welcome her she arrived two
hours late. "And she didn't walk into the room, she came in like a cat," actress Victoria Principal told Lawrence Grobel. "I had never seen a woman
move like that or have that kind of presence, before or since. I've never
seen a woman electrify a room sexually like she did. You were aware that
she was on the prowl."

Ava had been looking forward to meeting Paul Newman (by now she
regretted turning down the chance to work with him years before in *Sweet
Bird of Youth*), but in Tucson she found the man—for reasons that are not
clear—less than simpatico. ("One of my unfavorite actors," she would
say later.) She drank too much one night, had words with somebody,
glasses were broken, she disappeared. John Milius, the young screenwriter
on hand, was drafted to go find her where she had wandered into the
desert. He refused the assignment. She was too old, he'd say (to Grobel),
unappealing, "predatory."

Out there in the desert was even more potential trouble. Over the next
tumbleweed from *Roy Bean*, directing himself in a film called *Rage*, no
less, was George C. Scott. When Huston learned that Scott and Ava had
been in contact (What was she thinking? Not with her head, anyway) he

paid two stuntmen to keep her under watch until her scenes were completed. The reunion became no more than a brief, calm conversation.

Her filmed entrance to Langtry by rail was staged in a long single take, Miss Lily coming down the steps of the train, greeted by the few residents, and walking off to see the town as the craning camera moved before her. Playing the part of the stationmaster who leads Lily Langtry from the train was Billy Pearson, a Huston crony, former jockey and sometime pre-Columbian art smuggler, whose real job was to keep the director amused. As the much rehearsed and elaborate shot started, Pearson stepped up to Ava, doffed his stationmaster's cap, and, with his back to the camera, said, "Welcome, Miss Langtry . . . And on behalf of the entire railroad let me jes' say . . . *I would be honored if you would let me eat your pussy!*" He continued in this vein or worse as they played out the whole lengthy shot, but Ava refused to react, only remaining perfectly in character to the end, at which point everyone exploded with laughter, Huston with tears in his eyes. It would mean an hour on the clock before anyone could work again, but, as it was explained to the producers, who could put a price on a good joke?

Heading home, she made a brief visit to New York City, staying at Frank's apartment in the Waldorf Towers (he had given her an open invitation to use any of his many apartments and vacation homes when she was traveling or on holiday, and she did so happily; when he got rid of his Las Brisas property in Acapulco, Mexico, she was heartbroken). Also staying at the Waldorf apartment when she arrived was Tina Sinatra, Frank's youngest child. She had been born only a year and a bit before Ava and Frank had gotten together. She was in her early twenties now, a dark-haired beauty. The girl seemed to hold no ill will about past events, and Ava was happy to find that the two of them got along very well. As they spent time getting to know each other, she saw something of herself in Tina, and there was a physical resemblance as well, a notion she considered confirmed when they were out on Fifth Avenue together and someone mistook them for mother and daughter. It was an amusing and then saddening mistake.

Ava's flat in the high-rise at Park Lane was in time exchanged for a large town house on Alexander Square in Kensington. The five stories plus wine cellar were difficult to keep up, the rooms with their thickly barred windows never felt very cheering, and the neighbors objected to Sinatra and Maria Callas recordings played loud after midnight. Early in 1972 she sold it and moved once again, this time to a large second-floor flat with balconies in a converted Victorian house with a pillared entrance at number 34 Ennismore Gardens. The new place was in a quiet, graceful part of the city, looked out on a private park, and was a short walk from Hyde Park and Harrod's. She found it a comfortable fit, enjoyed the space, the neighborhood, the neighbors. Much time and expense were given to the design and furnishing of the large, light-filled rooms, early on under the guidance of George Alfred Stacey, the American "decorator to the rich and famous." He filled the flat with pristine eighteenth- and nineteenth-century antiques, rare Chinoiserie, towering old oil paintings, and gilded mirrors. There would be few mementos—some pictures of friends and relatives and a framed photo of Frank—certainly no items to directly commemorate her life in the movies (unless one counted the original, framed Man Ray photograph of her as a sixteenth-century maiden seen in *Pandora and the Flying Dutchman*). The apartment looked like the residence of a veteran ambassador—visitors would remember thinking—or a well-off, widowed contessa.*

In the early years at number 34 there would be occasional talk about moving on again, heading to the next place, back to somewhere warmer, somewhere on the beach this time—Hawaii or one of the Virgin Islands or the Spanish coast—especially when the rain did not stop or she felt a cold damp in her lungs, or the time there was no hot water to be had in her building and she had to scurry across the street in a terry-cloth robe and

---

*At Ennismore Gardens an inventory of her drawing room alone would include the following items: a circa 1785 Louis XVI giltwood *canapé* (divan), a pair of circa 1750 Louis XV flower-carved *fauteuils*, two late-eighteenth-century Venetian parcel-gilt armchairs, a nineteenth-century gilt-carved Pietra Dura circular chess table, four eighteenth-century footstools, nine eighteenth-century decorative Chinese painted panels, a pair of large nineteenth-century French gilt-bronze candelabra, a George I giltwood overmantel mirror, two nineteenth-century Japanese red lacquer tables, a circa 1760 Meissen gilt-metal-mounted tobacco jar, a giltwood Lambrequin-carved coronet, a Regency-era painted cabinet on simulated bamboo stand, a nineteenth-century brass and steel basket grate with fan–spark guard raised on brass monopodia (of course!), an ebonized Napoleon III brass-and-ivory-inlaid *bonheur-du-jour*, a circa 1920 red-ground-lacquer mah-jongg set, and an antique U-shaped bronze Japanese gong; partial list.

wet hair to use a neighbor's bath ("God bless the English," she said, "they pretended not to notice me"). But such talk faded after a while. Ennismore Gardens became, finally and forever after, her home.

All Ava's periods of negative energy, which Reenie Jordan summed up simply as "movie-starrish," meaning the bad behavior and self-indulgence and self-destruction, were going away. In London now, freed of the violent passions and many of the fears of the past, her generous, positive spirit—often dormant—took charge. She was to be a much loved and admired addition to her new neighborhood, made many chums. Though she was still shy with strangers, it became easy enough to break the ice with her, especially if you were an animal lover; a person who was seen to be affectionate with their dog was soon among the flock and in receipt of an invitation, welcome for coffee or a drink. When neighbors became sick she brought them flowers and books. She went to sit with an elderly woman who suffered a stroke or took her for a walk every day until she was feeling better. "Miss Ava was very generous," Carmen Vargas would say. "She would worry about all the people. She did not like to see someone in trouble. If she saw someone homeless or sick, she would bring them home to give them something to eat, or send them in a taxi to her doctor. I say to her, 'Oh, Miss Gardner, you cannot bring everyone here you don't know. Maybe they will rob or kill us!' She say, 'Oh, Carmen, I could not leave them like that.' " For her Christmastime birthday parties she would invite people from every walk of life. Oblivious to the class consciousness of some of her well-heeled neighbors, she entertained local housekeepers and workers, people who had never expected to be the guest of a Hollywood legend. "I remember one nice old lady come to the party," said Carmen, "she was caretaker of some building, she say to me, 'Carmen, I will never forget this as long as I live!' Miss Ava make her so happy."

Many actors and people from the film industry lived in the Knightsbridge neighborhood, and she would often run into acquaintances from her cinematic past, people with whom she had shared adventures twenty and thirty years before, perhaps last seen at some back-of-beyond location. One day there was Eva Monley, veteran of *Mogambo* and *Bhowani Junction*, now living a couple of blocks away. "I was walking along the street, and suddenly I see a face popping out of the door. 'Eva! Come up! Come up! Coffee! Coffee!' And there was Ava. 'My dear! And how are things in Pakistan?' " They would sit and reminisce. They would remember the Christmas in the jungle under the stars, cranky John Ford, and the beautiful blue-black Congolese singing carols, and the drunken cameramen dancing on the dinner tables, mad dogs and Englishmen, and the time John Huston introduced them to each other—"Eva meet Ava," he had said—when they had already been through Africa together, silly man, and the bat in the room at Faletti's in Lahore, and Ava running around without a stitch, and fussy George Cukor afraid to get ill and eating nothing every day but boiled eggs.

There would be new friends, too, among the show-business professionals who lived on Ennismore, some as starstruck by the American movie actress as any of the "civilians." "I knew she lived in the neighborhood and I had thought how wonderful it would be to meet her sometime," recalled Peter Blythe, the stage and television actor (well-remembered as Sam Ballard in the long-running *Rumpole of the Bailey* series). "Late at night, returning from the West End, I would take my dog Herky, a Rhodesian ridgeback, out for his p.m. walk and one night a woman who was walking a small dog saw me and stopped, obviously nervous. I said, 'It's all right, I'm just walking my dog, too.' The woman relaxed, came closer, and asked, 'What kind of mutt do you have?' And there was Ava Gardner. And I was very thankful for that casual meeting because had I been formally introduced to her, I know I would have stammered away. And she was wonderful. We became friends, to my delight. I would see her nearly every day on her walks or striding up the street with a towel under her arm (she liked to go for a swim in the nearby university pool). I liked her very much . . . I remember one day she came by our place to show off her new dog. She knocked on the door, and it was Ava with a puppy in her arms. 'Just come to let you meet my new mutt!' she said, and after mutual agreement that the mutt was magnificent, she said, 'Something smells good.' It was a Friday, my day for cooking my specialty— though I say it myself—very good fish-and-chips. I invited her to have some, and she did. She must have enjoyed it, because from then on she frequently found something she simply had to tell me or show me that brought her by just exactly at lunchtime on a Friday. She was a wonderful person, full of life, could party with a stamina I envied, and I was so delighted to know her."

Another neighbor and one she became especially close to was Charles Grey, an actor best known for playing smugly sinister villains in the movies including—twice—James Bond's nemesis Ernst Stavro Blofeld. He was a frequent drinking companion, partner in card games, and comrade in arms for various jaunts through the city and to the theater. Together, and in their cups, the two were said to have made a quite amusing team. Alistair Cooke, who once spent an afternoon with them after they abducted him from a London book-signing appearance, likened the two together to "a sort of raucous Nick and Nora from the *Thin Man* movies," although it was strictly a platonic "marriage" in this case, Grey a very gay Nick Charles.

Ava's "local" was the Ennismore Arms, a tiny pub tucked away in the nearby mews. She bought the place its first jukebox, then directed it to be filled with Frank Sinatra records.

Thanks to the wise investments made by her financial planners, she could afford to live a very comfortable life without ever acting again. "I'm wealthy," she would explain, "just not 'stinkin' rich.' "

She did continue to work in the movies, but now with the secure conviction that such employment was no more than a vague sideline. If her name, her face, were still worth something to someone she might act again, but only for immediate practical reasons, to afford some desired extravagance like an expensive addition to the apartment, or as a favor to a friend or as a paid vacation. With no emotional or professional stake in what she did, no great pressure to work or not to, she could now almost enjoy her old profession. When producer Jennings Lang visited London in the chill winter of 1974 to offer her a part in his next film, *Earthquake*, the prospect of a salaried three-month stay in sunlit Southern California was sole and sufficient motivation; she told him to send the air tickets, she could read the script when she got there.

Lang, a Universal executive and overseer of the recent *Airport* sequels, had personally experienced a mild but thought-provoking earthquake one night in Beverly Hills, and this had led him to decide the subject for the next great entry in the expanding, popular Hollywood genre known as the "disaster movie." *Earthquake* was going to chronicle, with spectacle and vivacity and tons of breaking glass, a "big one" shaking apart the city of Los Angeles. Lang would assemble a vast team of craftsmen, model makers, audio technicians, and special effects wizards to create many and various scenes of destruction, earth splitting, dam bursting, skyscrapers tumbling, and much more, all accompanied by what was hoped would be an exciting sound-track effect they were going to call Sensurround (a sonic rumble intended to simulate the vibration of a quake and felt by audience members through the floor and the seats). To let the audience get to know some of the people the buildings were going to fall on, a screenplay was written by Mario Puzo and George Fox. This followed the stories of a dozen or so characters all more or less interwoven as a result of the calamitous quake. Ava's assigned role was that of a shrewish, pill-popping, hysteria-and-suicide-prone wife of a long-suffering architect husband (to be played by her old *55 Days in Peking* comrade Charlton Heston), whom she drives into the arms of a kittenish young mom (to be played by kittenish French Canadian actress Geneviève Bujold). The earthquake and its aftermath puts both women in mortal peril, but in the end—as originally scripted—the wife is washed away to her death and her husband is left free to return to his pouty young girlfriend.

Ava arrived from London at the end of February, moving in with Bappie at her house high in the Hollywood Hills, and two days later reported for work at Universal in the Valley a short drive away. Costumer Edith Head fitted her for her wardrobe, which consisted mostly of variations of the same cream-colored suit, each one more torn and stained than its predecessor, indicating the increasing ravages of the disaster (unlike on many previous jobs, Ava would not be asking to keep her clothes from this film at the end of production).

Earthquake renewed Ava's friendship with Monica Lewis, the sultry blond singer-actress she had known at Metro nearly twenty-five years before. Now Monica was the wife of Jennings Lang, and a mother. She had taken a small part in the film, playing the secretary of Lorne Greene, who played Ava Gardner's father. "It was great to see her after so many years, and we became very pal-sy all over again," Monica Lewis would recall. "I thought she looked fine, but she was older—we all were. She had thickened. I think she was worried that maybe she didn't look that good. Jennings told her, 'Don't worry about it, Ava. We'll make Lorne look older or we'll make Heston look worse.' "

Directing the film was Mark Robson. He and Ava had last worked together at Cinecittà in Rome making *The Little Hut*. He was a nice man, but she had not found him very inspiring in Italy and did not expect much from him now at Universal City. There was some tension in the air at the reunion with Chuck Heston, who was understandably wary after their time together in Spain. He was relieved to find her less visibly troubled on this picture, anyway less troublesome. She seemed, he wrote in his autobiography, "to have lost some of the fiery core that had been so much a part of her persona." In his diary, though, he took note of her nervousness, her need for many takes, and her distracting tendency only to "approximate the exact text." Their first dramatic sequence together, an early-morning domestic crisis, they performed with their usual lack of on-screen chemistry, and—thanks to Robson's slack hand, perhaps—gave the appearance of working in two separate movies, Ava's raw, gutsy acting something out of *Who's Afraid of Virginia Woolf*, Heston's overarticulated humorlessness more redolent of *Plan Nine from Outer Space* (*"Of course I'll induce vomiting!"* he shouts into the telephone after his wife has apparently attempted to kill herself). Anyway, it mattered little—the real stars of the film were the miniature models and the high-decibel sound effects.

By April they had gotten down to the bruising business of dodging girders, falling into rubble, and shimmying through sewer pipes. For many shots in the earthquake sequences, ranging from the uncomfortable to the dangerous, Ava refused the services of a stunt person and did the action herself. It was the tomboy in her coming out, she explained, a chance to roll about in the muck the way she did as a little girl. "She was very game," said Monica Lewis. "Always ready to get right in there. Totally professional. And some of the scenes were difficult."

Earthquake's climax involved her character and Heston's becoming trapped in a storm drain and overcome by a torrent of water set loose by a bursting dam, being swept away to their deaths (Heston had demanded a change in the script—a noble if unhappy ending for his character—instead of survival; now he would give up his life trying to save his "bitchy wife"). Ava again agreed to do the risky shot herself. A floodgate released a pressurized flow of 360,000 gallons per minute that rushed across them like an express train, the wig she was wearing ripped from her head, and her body pounded against the concrete, leaving her black-and-blue for a week. She was brought out at last, looking as glamorous as a drowned rat, shivering, and walking with a limp. The crew applauded her effort. She said, "I don't think you could call that acting."

"She led a quiet life out here when she wasn't at work," Monica Lewis would remember. "We spent a lot of time together. She wasn't interested in seeing many people. She hung around with her sister and with us, at my house. She had some friends who were not in the business, and she went to see them, too, a wonderful massage person and his wife, who had been a dancer in England. At night Ava used to go running. And she had a lot of guts, running down the road at night all by herself. I remember one night she was very excited because Maria Callas was singing somewhere. She said, 'I'm going, I don't care if I only get to sleep for three hours, I gotta hear Maria.'

"And then, on the set, we'd sit around in her room and talk. Ava had a very eclectic and curious mind. She knew about many things. She wasn't trying to impress anyone. She had taught herself about things because she wanted to *know*. And she'd play Frank Sinatra records, and she'd sing along . . . *'Is it an earthquake, or simply a shock?'* And she'd say, 'Sing it for me, Monica, sing it!' And I'd say, *'He's in a different key, honey.'*

"We had a very good time on that picture."

Late in April Metro-Goldwyn-Mayer celebrated its fiftieth anniversary. Nearly every media report on the milestone focused on the golden past, the time of Mayer's factory of stars, Gable and Garbo, Crawford, Harlow, Gardner. What else could you focus on? Under the leadership of James Aubrey the studio had sold most of its heritage at auction to the highest bidder and had essentially forsaken moviemaking for hotel management in Las Vegas. In the year 1974 there were just five new films bearing the MGM logo, one of them a low-budget Israeli musical comedy. One of the four others was the company's spearhead for its birthday celebration, a documentary tribute to itself called *That's Entertainment*. Naturally the film focused on an earlier, better chapter in the studio's history, primarily the golden age of the Metro musical. The company's new owners desired to restore some of the old luster to a tarnished name, and hopes were riding high on the documentary's joyful display of the MGM legacy. There was to be a gala world premiere and press event, and invitations were sent out to all the stars and major contract players from the studio's heyday who were still alive and to a few who were not. Ava's old friend and Metro's onetime chief hairstylist, Sydney Guilaroff, insisted she go, it was an honor and a duty he said, MGM was her alma mater for better or worse, it was history, probably the last chance anyone would ever have to see many of the people who would be there, and so she went, Guilaroff her date. A large, loud mob of gawkers had come out in force for the uprecedented gathering of classic Hollywood notables. The black limousines moved up one after another, and onto the red carpet at the Beverly Theater the stars emerged—Fred Astaire, Gloria Swanson, Jimmy Stewart, Ginger Rogers, Gene Kelly, Myrna Loy, Howard Keel, Janet Leigh, Eleanor Powell, Marge Champion, Cyd Charisse, Roddy McDowall, Jackie Cooper, Elizabeth Taylor, the one and only Tarzan, Johnny Weissmuller, and on and on. At Ava's appearance an electric surge of recognition went through the mob—some among the autograph hounds and cinephiles knew she had not been to a premiere in Hollywood in more than two decades—and pockets of enthusiasts began chanting her name louder and louder, some screaming for her recognition. She turned pale, hissed to her escort, *"I'm scared to death!"* and dug her nails so hard into Guilaroff's arm that the hairdresser nearly let out a scream himself. Inside the theater, the lion roared, she saw the footage of old Culver City driveways and soundstages, too many bad memories, bitter feelings never gone away, telling Sydney she wanted to leave, but then staying to watch the clips of old friends showing their stuff, seeing how the studio had sometimes gotten it right, all the great talent (and here and there some just getting by, but beautiful), old friends, old lovers, and old husbands, Frank wonderful singing and dancing with Bing Crosby, and Mickey, his time on-screen a startling reminder to her of how very gifted he was. The film went on, unreeling before its once-in-a-lifetime audience as half testament, half three-strip Technicolor home movie. There was applause and cheering from beginning to end, loud laughter, inside jokes, pride, trauma. Some in the darkened theater who watched themselves on-screen were heard to sob quietly, tears for what had been and was no more.

In the early months of 1975, as a favor to her friend Paul Mills, she made *Permission to Kill*, a warmed-over spy movie starring another of her 1960s leading men—and a sympathetic one—Dirk Bogarde. From the Bristol Hotel in Vienna they ventured off each day to the various Austrian locations. Bogarde, in his memoir, *An Ordinary Man,* could recall the experience as little more than countless hours of freezing in snow and biting wind and nothing to eat or drink all day but stone-cold tea and boiled spaghetti on a sagging paper plate. Ava left as soon as possible, telling an envious Bogarde that London was calling her, "quite desperately."

Then, another favor. George Cukor had agreed to make a film of Maeterlinck's children's fantasy, *The Blue Bird,* in an unprecedented co-production deal between American interests and the Soviet Union, to be shot entirely in the USSR. It was a time of a thawing Cold War, and Cukor felt invested with a historic cultural assignment. To raise the film's commercial prospects he sought notable "guest stars" for cameo and small roles, and obtained the services of Elizabeth Taylor, Jane Fonda, and Cicely Tyson. There would be not much salary to speak of, George explained, just deluxe accommodations and some expenses—he told Ava to think of it as volunteer work for a good cause, the way Audrey Hepburn helped out the United Nations. She arrived in Leningrad to find the production, already in progress for five months, a disaster, mired in inefficiency, bureaucracy, despair. Nearly everyone was ill, Elizabeth Taylor thought to be at death's door for a time. Ahead was an unpleasant experience. Scheduled to work for three weeks, Ava ended up being there, off and on, for more than three months. She found the Russian actors and crew uniformly the saddest and most depressing people she had ever met. The elevators at the hotel never worked, and she hated the glaring floor attendants—worse than the Roman paparazzi the way they followed you around with their eyes. And her rooms, so she'd been advised, were probably bugged with hidden mikes and cameras; it was like dating Howard Hughes again. In lipstick she scrawled a homemade sign, KEEP OUT, and hung it on the door as a statement of principle. She hated the food—even the delicacies flown in from Fortnum & Mason tasted like cold potato soup by the time they were served. The security officials wanted none of the visiting film people to go off on their own but boredom got the better of her one night and she found a friendly Russian cabdriver to take her out on the town. They drank vodka and danced together at a little jazz club until security agents finally found them just before dawn and escorted her back to the hotel (and the driver to Siberia, no doubt). Cukor, at age seventy-five, was full of vigor, but the project wore on his nerves. He was frequently nasty. One day he snapped at her—for the first time ever—and again, with no apology to follow. She completed the job, refused even to say good-bye to him, and flew home. She stayed mad at him for a year or so; then one day she watched one of his old pictures on television, *Pat and Mike*, and she sent him a cable with her regards, writing about the movie (*Pat and Mike*, not *The Blue Bird*), "They don't make 'em like that anymore." Cukor cabled back at once: "Ava, they don't make 'em like you anymore."

On July 11, 1976, Frank Sinatra was in the news again. At the estate of newspaper magnate Walter Annenberg in Rancho Mirage, California, he had gotten married for the fourth time. His new wife, Barbara, was a blond and beautiful former Las Vegas showgirl, ex-wife of Zeppo Marx (brother of Groucho et al.).

For Ava it was, anyway, easier than the last time. She had made her peace with things. She and Frank had what they had. She didn't expect that would change now. He would go on calling, checking in with her; she would know she could turn to him whenever. But then after a while, it was said, Barbara began to let it be known that whatever it was Frank and Ava had, they possibly had too much of it. A man was entitled to one wife at a time, after all. It had been good enough for Zeppo Marx, and it ought to be good enough for Frank Sinatra. Over time, the calls and notes from Frank became fewer. He was still out there for her, but he was a little farther away.

In the garden of Frank's home in California there had stood for more than twenty years the magnificent marble statue of Ava that had been created for the opening scene in *The Barefoot Contessa* and that Frank had purchased from the movie company and had transported across sea and ocean and land from Italy to the western coast of America. One day in 1976 a truck came and hauled the statue away, and that was the last anybody has ever seen of it.

In London, as she lived her quiet life, it sometimes seemed that the past was another, very far off country indeed. One day she opened the newspaper to read that her old downstairs neighbor Isabel Perón was the president of Argentina. Husband Juan had finally staged a comeback, gotten ill, pronounced his wife the country's new leader, and died. How odd the course a person's life could take. Ava remembered Isabel, the sweet, simple, former exotic dancer in her kitchen in Madrid and could not easily picture her as a head of state. The woman did cook a very good empanada, you had to give her that.

Then there was the day she ran into Artie Shaw. Artie, who had abandoned his musical stardom ages ago. He had put the clarinet down and never picked it up again, wandered around Europe, married Evelyn Keyes, dumped her, lived in a motor home for a while, became a gun collector, thought of himself as a writer now, published something every twenty years or so. They had seen each other in Spain and then not again for many years. She had run into him recently: a stooped, bald character with tufts of hair in his ears and an unpleasant white mustache. Where the hell was the sleek, sexy bastard she had been so crazy for, with whom she had once been so wildly, emotionally, and erotically obsessed? No way it could have been this fuzzy old man.

And Howard. Dead in the spring of 1976. The news reports of the man she had once known so well read like a ghastly horror story, an atrocity report: shrunken to ninety-four pounds, lost in insanity and addiction, his atrophied body studded with shards of broken syringe needles, an open wound where a tumor had been scratched from his head, the richest man in the world. She remembered the last time she saw him. Autumn in Palm Springs, before the *Barefoot* jaunt to Tokyo. He had called her late at night, said he was flying in with important news for her, landing for a few minutes only before he had to rush on to Washington or somewhere. She had gone out to the airport to meet him. The airport was closed but a dozen drivers with black limousines had been summoned to line up in formation along either side of the landing strip and to illuminate it with their headlights. It was like the memory of a dream, the cars lined up and the headlights blazing a trail in the dark desert. Howard had come down out of the black sky, walked to her with his lanky stride, in his dirty flying clothes, carrying a small box under his arm. What was the important news, Howard? What was all the fuss? A movie, Howard said. A great new project for the two of them. He would make the deal with Metro but he wanted to come and tell her in person and give this to her. And he had opened the box under his arm—an old shoe box it was—and inside were stacks of loose cash, thousand-dollar bills, a quarter million dollars in cash. A bonus for her, in advance, he told her. It was to show her how much he looked forward to it, how much she meant to him. And she had laughed and knew there was no movie, just another crazy attempt to buy her interest, her affection. Howard, she told him, I don't want your money. And Howard said: There must be something you want. And then the wind had picked up and blown across the open shoe box and lifted some bills off the top, four, ten, a couple dozen thousand-dollar bills whipped up and fluttered off into the desert night.

She continued to work, once a year or every two years. Most of the things she was offered had little to recommend them in advance but a paycheck and her best guess that the director was not going to be a pain in the ass. They were in some cases the 1970s equivalent of the bottom-of-the-bill pictures in which she had started her career, though at least in the old days those movies had been guaranteed a release. The most visible of her later feature film appearances would be in *The Cassandra Crossing*, shot in 1976, and *The Sentinel*, made the following year. Filmed largely at Cinecittà and featuring an ensemble cast of her fellow faded stars—Burt Lancaster, Sophia Loren, Richard Harris—*The Cassandra Crossing* was another disaster film, this about a runaway train carrying a deadly plague. It was a pleasant, uneventful time. ("Is yours a good part?" reporter Roderick Mann asked her. "No, just some old broad," she replied.) The days of the old location adventures were over. No more haunting the Roman night, touring brothels, car chases, and battles with the photographers. Now she liked a good night's sleep after a day on the set, and on the weekends whenever possible she flew back to London, like any commuter wanting to get home from the office, pet the dog, and watch some telly. The job ended up being more trouble than it was worth. The Italian authorities, on a vendetta against wealthy tax dodgers, accused producer Carlo Ponti, his wife, Sophia Loren, and various *Cassandra* stars, including Ava Gardner, of violating the nation's currency laws and charges were made, warrants issued. Sophia was briefly put in custody, and Ponti was sentenced to two years in prison in absentia (he had wisely taken a hike from his native land). Like the producer, Ava stayed far away from the court proceedings, but unlike Carlo she was eventually acquitted.

The Sentinel was a horror movie, a lurid haunted-house story about a portal to Hell in a Brooklyn brownstone. The filmmaker was the prolific and lively Michael Winner. A great movie buff from an early age, he often tried to cast in his productions some of the veteran stars who had been the idols of his youth. Ava Gardner, he would say, he had first met in the 1940s, "transfixed by her beauty in the little cinemas where I got my education." An MGM publicity photograph of her in a one-piece bathing suit had hung on the wall of his room at school. Now he was offering her a small part as the agent for the story's infernal real estate, and he went to her home not far from his own to talk to her about it.

"She lived very comfortably, had a lovely apartment," Michael Winner would recall. "I immediately hit it off with her. I had told her, 'Ava, you know, the government in America is now going to make you pay tax even if you're living abroad.' So she immediately rang her accountant. He was at lunch, and she insisted they give her the name of the restaurant. So she rang the restaurant. And she made them find this accountant, and she gets on the line with this fellow in the middle of his lunch and gives him a long spiel about this tax thing. When she put the phone down I said, 'Ava, are you a Capricorn?' She said, 'How did you know?' I said, 'Because that's exactly what Capricorns do—when they want something they don't wait a second, they don't care, they'll phone you in the middle of the night. . . .' She enjoyed that. And we hit it off. I thought she was lovely. Incredibly shy, always interesting, a great sense of humor.

"We made the movie. She was very good. She didn't think she was. She had a very key line in the movie, the line that told the audience this girl in the house was in terrible trouble. And she did it very, very well. She was a very underrated actress, I think. She was a big crowd puller on location. If you walked the streets of New York with Ava Gardner you got very big crowds. She was like Sophia Loren—you walk with them on the streets, you're mobbed. But put them in a movie and nobody goes! Just a fact of life, isn't it? She was very professional, down-to-earth, a person first and a star next. She was late one day and I told her off, I gave her a big bollocking. She said she had been to some restaurant in Brooklyn where she used to go with Frank Sinatra. She said, 'I just wanted to go there and remember things.'

"We became close friends. In London we went out to dinner occasionally, though she was becoming quite a recluse by then. She was shy but occasionally she opened up to me about things in her life. She was very outgoing if she trusted you. She was a lovely person. A very nice person, really. Of all the people I've known, maybe the nicest.

"We talked on the phone all the time. She'd ring me up. She might be a bit tipsy. She was coherent, but a bit sloshed. She did crossword puzzles a great deal, and she'd often ring me and ask for help with a crossword puzzle. She'd say, 'What's a seven-letter word for ephemeral?' "

In the spring of 1978 she returned to the States to see her family. First her sister in Los Angeles. Bappie was a widow now, living alone in the house in the hills, with a corgi of her own (though they both knew it was really so Ava could walk him when she was in town). She would be seventy-five years old in the fall, but she was still feisty, ready to take on the world for her baby sister. Ava had Bappie come along to a thing George Cukor was throwing for a bunch of foreign movie directors. Bappie blew out a tire on the car just below the grand Cukor estate. A long sedan came by and stopped to see what the problem was. In the backseat, poking their heads out the window were George and the third Mrs. Sinatra, Mia Farrow. She and Ava exchanged pleasantries. "You two must have a lot to talk about!" Cukor giggled. He had to hurry on to his party, George said, but he would send someone to fix the flat tire. He sent Katharine Hepburn, and she did a good job of it.

Ava arrived in North Carolina in time for an event she had reluctantly agreed to attend. She and the governor, Jim Hunt, would be the special guests at the ceremony for Rock Ridge Day in the town where she and her mother had gone to live thirty-nine years earlier. People smiled and applauded with prideful exhilaration to see the movie star who had once walked among them as a mortal. Smithfield might have given her life, but Rock Ridge had given her a diploma. Asked in advance to say a few words, she had tried to write down what she would say and had made a mess of it, so instead she just said what came to mind, remembering things and people she had not thought about in many years. In the crowd was Alberta Cooney, long ago Ava's best friend. The other most beautiful girl at Rock Ridge High. They had exchanged letters once in a while through the years, but it had been a long time and Alberta hardly thought she could impose herself on such an occasion. But then Ava had seen her, and she was making the policemen open the way so she could get to her. And she cried, "Alberta!" And the two embraced and Ava wouldn't let her go. She wanted Alberta to come to Smithfield so they could talk, but it seemed to Alberta that was for family and she couldn't impose; they promised to write each other, and then the troopers were getting Ava out of there and into the limo and driving away.

She stayed at her brother Jack's house on Vermont Street in Smithfield. Jack, who had bounced around in various lines of work over the years, oilman and salesman and restaurateur, had finally found a calling for his intelligence, charisma, and social concerns in the world of politics and had been elected a representative to the North Carolina General Assembly. He was still her hero, Ava told him, just as he had been when she was seven.*

By evening the others arrived at the house for a big reunion—the sisters and in-laws and nieces and nephews and their children, and now their children as well.

In 1980 her beloved Cara died. It was nothing less than the death of a child. The dog had been such a part of her heart—at the flat there were stacks of scrapbooks and photo albums containing thousands of pictures of Cara, more coverage than a supermodel; when Ava had to be away from her she would call home day and night just to hear the dog bark, and she had even written letters to the pooch—the caretaker in place was expected to read them aloud to her. The grieving went on for months.

"Such a wonderful baby," Ava would say. "She would bite photographers at the airport, just like her mistress."

---

*Brother Jack would die of a heart attack in Raleigh in 1981, at the age of sixty-nine, only hours after being sworn in for his second term of office.

In time came a pup, a Pembroke Welsh corgi (of course) with snow white paws. She named him Morgan (after Jess, her longtime financial adviser and pal in Los Angeles) and rushed around the neighborhood introducing him to everyone. This dog liked to bite even Ava, but she pampered and praised him with unbridled enthusiasm. Soon more scrapbooks began filling up with photographs. "It was like she had adopted a new child, it's true," said Spoli Mills. "And all was right with the world again."

Wanting something to do with herself after Cara's death, she took a job. *Priest of Love,* a screenplay by Alan Plater, based on the book by Harry T. Moore, chronicled the turbulent wanderings of tubercular, controversial D. H. Lawrence and his wife, Frieda, in the 1920s. Director Christopher Miles offered Ava the role of the American heiress and sybarite Mabel Dodge Luhan, who for a time was the writer's devoted patron, bringing him to live at her ranch and sometimes in her bed in Taos, New Mexico. Lawrence said of the four-times-married Dodge, "She collects money, great artists and husbands." Ava found the character not sympathetic but the part well written, and the lead role of Lawrence was going to be played by an actor Charles Grey assured her was brilliant—Ian McKellen, fresh from a West End theatrical triumph in the play *Bent* and now to make his first film as a star. She went to be introduced to her castmates at a party in the Mayfair home of the film's producer, Stanley J. Seger.

McKellen would write of their meeting, "I knew from her neighbor, Charles, that she liked cards and liquor and, I gathered, men—she flirted playfully, offering fun and a good time rather than sex. After a couple of drinks she hauled off her shoes and danced to music that Stanley had written for the film."

At the party Ava met actress Penelope Keith (cast as Lawrence's hapless admirer the Honorable Dorothy Brett), who would become a good London friend in the years ahead.

Two weeks later they were all in Oaxaca, Mexico (substituting for Taos). She was thought by some in the cast to be a bit remote on the location, disappearing at the end of the day, taking her meals in her hotel room with her maid while the others would go out at night to eat and explore the town. It was just the usual desire for privacy and shyness around new people and feeling a bit out of the circle of the younger English actors. Carmen Vargas remembered that Ava was also not enjoying the hot, humid weather, and that she and many with the company suffered at times from the tourist's lament—what Maxine Faulk would have called the old Aztec two-step.

"We was uncomfortable with the stomachs," said Carmen. "Oh my God, I thought I was going to die there!"

The production amenities were haphazard, the Mexican pickup crew not very disciplined. Ava and the other actresses had to change and make up in a single small, broiling trailer, joined now and then by men from the crew squeezing by to use the ladies' toilet. Limited transportation was provided from the rural location back to Oaxaca, and Ava would find herself finished for the day and stuck in the heat and the dust for many hours until a car was made available. One night she called Frank in the States and told him of the miserable conditions. He told her to try to get a good night's sleep. The next morning—and each morning thereafter—a chauffeured limousine was waiting to take her to the location and bring her back when she was ready.

Many credited Ava with a fine performance, but the film as a whole was not well received. *Time Out* magazine called it "interminable," "twee," and "high in the running for the year's dumbest art movie." A bit harsh— there were good things in it, a penetrating incarnation of Lawrence by McKellen, evocative production design and costumes. Appropriately provocative as an account of the author of *Lady Chatterley*, the film would bear the distinction of being the first mainstream English-language movie to represent a male erection on-screen, though McKellen was to confess humbly that it was not his own but the work of a dildo and much sticking plaster.

There was one more feature film appearance, in an obscure, low-budget endeavor called *Regina,* shot in Rome in the summer of 1982. It was a ponderous, four-character piece (starring a top-billed Ava plus Anthony Quinn, Ray Sharkey, and a virtually mute Anna Karina), about an elderly couple spending an evening with their son and his girl. It had the look of a very underfunded television program and was shot entirely on a single, badly lit set (it may indeed have been intended for sale to television in some markets). Startlingly, Ava's acting was like nothing she had ever done before, a kind of go-for-broke, raw emoting one might more normally associate with Anna Magnani or Shelley Winters. It was proof that there were aspects to her talent still to be explored, but this odd and cheap production was not a worthwhile place to explore them. It was the unfortunate—and fortunately barely seen—end to her forty years in the movies.

Any acting she did from now on would be for television. She had held out all this time, turned down many offers through the years, a movie actress loyal to the old school, defending the bulwark between the big screen and the very tiny; Mayer would have been proud. And now, wherever he was, he had to forgive her at this late date for taking a few welcome paydays in the upstart, cut-rate medium in which the glamorous names of the past were still a welcome currency in the "all-star" miniseries and the popular "nighttime soaps" that laced their cast lists with former matinee idols and femmes fatales. She played devilish ancient Roman matron Agrippina, Nero's mother, in *A.D. (Anno Domini)*, a miniseries shot in Tunisia that ran a cumulative half day in all its parts; an exotic grand dame of the white-slave racket in *Harem*; a senior Southern belle in a TV version of the honeysuckle melodrama, *The Long Hot Summer*, starring Don Johnson (a sexy boy Ava seemed pleasantly to remember getting to know briefly—very briefly and very pleasantly—long ago, introduction by her chum Sal Mineo). In the winter of 1984 she signed to make six episodic appearances in the CBS series *Knot's Landing*, a long-running, Southern California spin-off of *Dallas*, playing scheming Ruth Galveston (mother of the show's star William Devane, and the widow of a character who had been played by Ava's long-ago boyfriend Howard Duff). She was treated well, gave a rousing performance, and was asked to do more episodes, but she begged off. It was simply too much of a disruption at this stage in her life. "Those people work eighteen-hour days," she told Spoli Mills. "And they're all eighteen years old."

She appeared before the camera once more, in the pilot for a proposed female private-eye series set in London, *Maggie*, with Stephanie Powers.

Turning sixty: It was fine, she told people. Fifty had been the hard one. That was when you knew there was no turning back. She didn't mind people knowing her age. "I'm one hell of an old broad," she would say. "It's undignified to lie about it."

She put herself on the wagon in anticipation of a birthday celebration, just to lose weight. There was a gorgeous new red dress she had bought for her party, and she was determined to get into it. On December 24 they could start pouring the champagne again. Sixty years old. For that one, she said, they were going to have one hell of a ball.

The press had been calling her a recluse for years. Oddly, in her sixties, as her life had become truly more circumspect—cocooned in her cherished home, venturing far from her neighborhood only rarely and then to visit personal friends or to catch them in a new play, traveling abroad only when necessary for work—she had let herself become increasingly accessible to members of the press. There had always been a few favored journalists she would occasionally meet for a chat and with whom she had established a rapport (they tended to be good-looking or at least charming males). Now, asked to promote some of her television work especially, she began seeing any number of reporters, feature writers, and photographers dispatched by the various papers and magazines eager to get some copy from the legendary, long-unavailable star. She welcomed them to number 34, introduced them to Morgan, offered a cup of tea or (her voice rising hopefully) a drink, perhaps? Maybe she felt obliged to her employers, or lonely, or simply had gotten over and beyond the old fear and disdain of such meetings. They frequently became a chance to set straight some of the errors of the past, the mistaken notions that the newspapers and the public had gotten about her.

"The trouble was that I was a victim of image," she would explain. "Because I was promoted as a sort of siren, and played all those sexy broads, people made the mistake of thinking I was like that off the screen."

It was good to have all that straightened out at last.

She made her last journey to Spain in 1984, to Seville and Madrid. It was a country she would always love, though now with a certain reserve, as toward a seducer who had led her astray. "I stayed there far too long," she would say. "I don't know why."

"I was in Spain doing a film . . . had two fabulous lunches with her," actress Susan Tyrrell would recall of the time of Ava's final visit. "She had saddlebags of vodka on the sides of her eyes. But what a beauty. You're just in awe, it's like taking in the Taj Mahal of beauty. But she was a real girl. 'Honey honey' and smoking smoking and the beauty of this face and drinking and laughing our asses off. She was trying to get me out of Madrid. She said I had to get out of there—get the fuck out of the country. And she leaned over the table, and she said, *'You need to get the fuck out of Spain, because the guys all have little dicks and they'll fuck you in the ass before you can get your panties off.'* I loved her so much. We laughed so hard. . . . What a genius. She held a lot of vodka in her, boy, that's for sure."

The year 1986 had begun, and she did not feel well. She mourned the loss of her beloved friend Robert Graves, and she lay in bed for much of January, suffering with a cold and congestion. Winter became spring and she was still run down, losing weight, and with a hacking cough that got only worse. She smoked too much, but it was too hard to stop, even with the coughing. By the autumn she was feeling pains in her chest most of the day, and her breathing was not good. Her London physician saw the possibility of a grave illness and ordered her to the hospital for testing, including a test for lung cancer. Frightened, she flew at once to Los Angeles, on October 6 checking into the St. John's Hospital and Health Center in Santa Monica (she had previously favored British medical facilities while living in Spain; now, living in Britain, she preferred to put herself in the care of specialists in California).

The tests showed no cancer. The diagnosis was pneumonia.

Treatments were administered. She got better. A week after entering the hospital she was permitted to eat normally and to get out of bed.

"I talked to her in the hospital," said Monica Lewis. "She had pneumonia, and she was down to 110 pounds. From 140 or something. You know, she was a very robust girl, healthy. Maybe 120 would be okay, but 110 for her was very low. I told her I was coming to see her. She said, 'No, no, don't come here. You'll get sick with what I've got.' "

The nurses doted on her. She told them funny stories, some involving famous people, some that left the nurses' mouths hanging open. A nice young orderly brought her fast-food burgers and hot dogs and Cokes. The room filled with flowers. From Frank. He called many times to check on her.

One day she opened her eyes and Stewart "Jimmy" Granger was giving her a kiss. He was white-haired now, but otherwise as handsome and dashing as ever. He pulled a chair close, and they talked and laughed, and Jimmy launched into some of his usual outrageous, arrogant opinions of the world. An awful man, she thought, and wonderful.

On her eleventh day in the hospital she awoke with severe headache. The left side of her body was without feeling, and when she tried to sit up she fell back with a nauseating dizziness. Blood vessels had ruptured in the brain. A stroke, perhaps more than one. The left side of her body was partially paralyzed, a hemiplegia, and her face was twisted into thick knots and drooping downward. She could speak, but her contorted mouth made the words all but impossible to understand.

Tests were done to determine the extent of the injury. There appeared to be no marked cognitive problems, no damage to judgment, attention, memory. She lay in bed, medicated, taking oxygen, wired up, closely monitored for signs of a recurrence.

Frank would call, and the nurses would hold the phone to her ear. She tried to speak, but it was hard to make herself understood, and so she just listened to his voice.

"I love you, baby," he told her. "It stinks getting old."

Then she heard no more from him for some time. In early November, while Ava lay in her hospital bed in Santa Monica, the seventy-year-old Sinatra entered the Eisenhower Medical Center in Palm Springs with a case of acute diverticulitis and, barely escaping death, underwent an eight-hour operation during which twelve feet of infected intestine were removed from his body. (By the end of the month he was performing again in Las Vegas.)

On November 28, Ava was released from St. John's. "I told her she had to give up smoking and drinking," her physician, Dr. William Smith, remembered. "She laughed and said she would try. She was a very fun-loving individual, and she wasn't about to give up things easily."

The hemiplegia of the left arm remained, and her face was still swollen and contorted. She needed medication, rest, exercise. With a stroke there was no certain timetable, no way to predict exactly when or if full recovery might occur, and much depended on the diligence and determination of the patient. It was considered unwise for her to go back to England just yet, to the damp English weather. Bappie's home was thought too remote and cramped, and it was arranged for her to stay at the home of a friend from her days with Frank, the criminal attorney Paul Caruso.

Returning to London early in 1987 she began a course of poststroke rehabilitation. A therapist came to the flat several times a week, working to increase her mobility. A visiting nurse monitored her vital signs and mental response. She was able to walk on her own again in time, with a slight impairment, and her speech improved, but her arm remained problematic.

"She called me to let me know how she was doing," Monica Lewis remembered. "Her voice was slurred. I'm quite familiar with a stroke, having taken care of my husband, Jennings, for thirteen years after he had his. And she was having difficulty speaking. It was hard. But she hadn't given up, and she hadn't lost her humor. She said, 'Lady, if you happen to know anybody who could use a has-been actress with a wasted arm, a drooping lip, and a reconstructed Southern accent, then I'm their gal!' And I fell apart. That was Ava for you. She could still laugh at herself. She was great."

Writer and translator Lucia Graves, Robert Graves's daughter, and a friend of Ava's since their first meeting in Majorca when she was a schoolgirl, visited her at Ennismore Gardens. "We sat and talked. Always with Frank Sinatra playing in the background! It was after she'd had her stroke and one arm wasn't working. But she wasn't letting it get her down, and she could joke about it. She told me of how she had been to a dinner party and she had been seated next to a man who had also suffered a stroke and lost the use of one arm. She said, 'Between us we couldn't get a bite of food into our mouths.' She was very funny."

A few months out of the hospital, she was becoming bored and frustrated. Though still distressed by her physical condition she was eager to do something besides recuperate. She entertained an offer from Michael Winner to appear in another movie, a part chosen to accommodate her reduced capacity since she could do the whole thing in a wheelchair.

"It was called *Appointment with Death*," Winner would say. "An Agatha Christie story. The part was of a crippled woman. She decided she wanted to do it. We talked about it, we agreed on everything.

"It was nearly time to start. And then she rang me. She said, 'Michael, can I come and see you?' I thought, This is very rare that she wants to come around. So she came over to my place to see me. We went out and sat in the garden. You could see her face was slightly distorted and her movements slightly disjointed. But only slightly. It would have been fine. And there was no effect to her mind. She was absolutely bright. She said, 'Michael, I hate to let you down, but . . . I'm just not up to it.' I said, 'It's okay, Ava. I understand.' She was the most gracious person, a very sensitive person."

"She was afraid to be seen after the stroke," said Spoli Mills. "Afraid of the camera. She had a limp, and the left arm was weak. She saw the drop in her face. I didn't really see it but she did. . . . Well, that's wrong, *of course* I saw it. I mean, I wasn't blind. But I wanted to help her not feel too badly about it. But she did feel badly about it. And then she had this lupus disease which began to weaken everything."

Lupus erythematosus: a difficult-to-diagnose systemic autoimmune disease affecting mostly women. It is a progressive disease that essentially causes the body to attack and weaken itself, making it vulnerable to destructive bacterial and viral organisms. Probable symptoms were evident for some time, such as a sudden acute sensitivity to the sun, which she had begun to experience a year or so earlier. The disease—if lupus is what she had, because some difference of opinion existed—was likely the root cause of her stroke. The root cause of lupus was—is—unknown, but various genetic and environmental influences were assumed. Friends, some of them, suspected that no matter what you called what was happening to her, it was likely the cumulative, corrosive effects of drinking that had set in motion her health crisis; that Ava had over the years damaged her body's ability to function properly and to fight back when something went wrong.

Throughout the year she was often in pain or discomfort. Her condition was subject to what the doctors called flares and remissions. She would begin to feel better, but what seemed like progress became only the upside of a cycle. She suffered with flu symptoms, pain in the muscles and joints, labored breathing, fatigue, malaise. Her medication was the probable cause of swelling and weight gain.

She spent much of the time in her apartment, venturing out only to take Morgan for his walks. Her contact with the outside world was through the telephone and the handful of friends who visited in person. Zoe Sallis had known Ava in Puerto Vallarta when she was living with John Huston and had played Hagar to her Sarah in *The Bible*, but they had become close friends only much later in London. "She never acted starlike at all," Sallis remembered, "just very down-to-earth. She was a very funny, warm, generous person. I didn't know her during her wild days. When we became friends in London she was a different person: quiet, and often lonely. But she stayed busy. We'd go to lunch and dinner, take walks in the park, go swimming or take exercise together. She did a lot of exercise, wanted to keep herself trim and together. And then she became ill, and she couldn't keep up. Every day she had different illnesses and different pains. First she didn't go out much. Then it progresses. You don't go out, then you don't see people, and then you don't walk the dog. She became hermitlike, not wanting to be seen. She had been so beautiful, and now she was seeing it all slipping by."

She would lie in bed and watch old movies on the television. And she would catch some of her own, some for the first time. It felt like the first time she had seen any of them. They all now seemed imbued with good memories and a kind of magic that had not been there for her before. She watched *The Barefoot Contessa* one night, and she felt only fondness and awe for Bogart and for Joe Mankiewicz, men she had held a grudge against for years, her reasons now forgotten. When Mankiewicz was to be honored with a lifetime achievement award (the *Leone d'Oro alla Carriera*) at the Venice Film Festival in 1987, she alone among the major stars he had directed agreed to make a contribution, a taped message of congratulations that played through the festival hall. "Hi Joe," she said, "this is your barefoot contessa speaking. . . ." Mankiewicz was visibly moved. "Is that Ava?" he asked. "I always thought . . . she didn't like me."

Some nights, in the middle of watching one of her old pictures, she would reach for the phone and call someone who had made the movie with her, Greg Peck or Katie Grayson or Stewart Granger, wanting to share with them her epiphany. She would watch *Bhowani Junction* by herself, late at night, and call Stewart Granger in Los Angeles.

"Were we really that beautiful, honey?" she would ask him.

And white-haired Stewart Granger would say, "You were, my sweet. You still are."

Sometimes she would lie in bed and take out the letters from Frank. They were all sorts and sizes, from all over the world, notes, postcards, long letters of many pages. She would take out each one and read it from start to finish, then put it back in the envelope and go on to the next one. She would read one and it would make her feel misty, then another that would have her laughing or cursing him on the page. Then she would pack them up again and put them away.

Another winter came to London. Ava began to have trouble with her breathing, and with the new year the problem worsened, seeming to be a recurrence of pneumonia. Again it was decided that she go to California for treatment, and this time a private jet was chartered for the flight. It landed in Los Angeles after midnight on January 6, and she was transferred by stretcher to the ambulance that brought her back to St. John's in Santa Monica.

She remained at the hospital for two weeks of treatment and testing.

Various old friends called to wish her well. But she did not hear from Frank.

"Do you think he knows I'm in here?" she asked Bappie.

"I don't know, hon," her sister said. "I'll look into it."

But Frank's only contact was through an intermediary. His attorney made a call to Jess Morgan, Ava's financial manager in Los Angeles, saying Frank had wanted to help her out. There was talk about the great cost of the chartered jet and the medical expenses. Sinatra's man said Frank would certainly want to help her out there.

But there were still no visits to the hospital or phone calls.

Ava said, "It's that fucking wife of his."

Bappie said, "Baby, she is so jealous of you."

Bappie went out and found a reporter waiting to ask about her sister's condition. Bappie told him, "It's such a shame that Frank won't be able to come see Ava after all they've meant to each other. She's having such a tough time and could really use the support. Last time he was so sweet, calling her and sending flowers, she really appreciated it. I don't know why he hasn't called her, I really don't. I mean, it's on the news all over the world that Ava is in the hospital. I guess he must be the only person doesn't know."

When Jess Morgan told Ava of the donation Sinatra had made to her expenses—reportedly a check for fifty grand—she was not feeling overly appreciative. "She didn't think it was enough," Morgan would recall. "So yes, she had a caustic comeback."

One of the tabloids published a story the following week, headlined: SINATRA MISSING FROM BEDSIDE OF STRICKEN EX AVA. It quoted Bappie many times, giving her take on Frank's "conspicuous absence." The piece included an uninflected statement relayed from Sinatra's representative: "He has just returned from a trip to Australia and is at home in Rancho Mirage."

"Bappie did not want her to go back to England," said Betty Sicre. "She thought that climate was not good for her health. She stayed with Bappie for a month, and she was doing really well. Bappie thought that if she had stayed with her in California and not gone back to that London damp and fog she would have gotten strong again and she would have lived a lot longer."

She was by most standards still a wealthy woman, with investment dividends, a sizable pension from MGM, and perhaps a million dollars' or more worth of personal possessions—art, antiques, jewels. But Ava's rising expenses and the end of her supplementary income from motion picture and television work had put a strain on her resources. She would say she had been offered a gentle ultimatum: that it would be wise at this time, for the sake of liquidity, either to sell her jewelry or to agree to write her memoirs. She had sworn countless times that she would never under any circumstances be willing to sell her life story, and it would be the apex of hypocrisy for her to agree to divulge for money the secrets of her private life and those of the people she had known and loved. And yet, she was very fond of her jewels.

A deal was made for the autobiography of Ava Gardner. It was not a difficult sell. Publishers had been pleading for her to do such a book for ages. A collaborator or ghostwriter was found, Peter Evans, a journalist and author who had previously written a biography of Aristotle Onassis and knew Ava socially.

The first sessions did not go well. But then Ava began drinking more while she talked, and the drink made her more expansive, funnier, and less "discreet." There suddenly loomed the prospect of an entertaining book. Ava, however, when she was sober, recalled enough of what she had said in her uninhibited state to know that as far as she was concerned not a word of it was going into any goddamn book. The work up to then was destroyed, the collaboration ended.

Michael Winner would recall, "I talked to her one day, and she said to me, 'You know, I'm doing my autobiography.' I said, 'Well, Ava, you've had the most incredible life; it will be the most wonderful autobiography, as long as you tell the truth.' She said, 'Well, I'm certainly not going to tell the truth!' "

Another writer was found to work with her on the book, a veteran author named Alan Burgess. The two would sit together for two or three hours at a time and talk into a tape recorder. A version of Ava's life story was eventually put together based on the transcribed interviews and delivered to Bantam Books in New York. "The manuscript that was turned in," said Genevieve Young, the book's editor, "was very boring, it didn't say anything, and she left out large swatches of her life."

A third ghostwriter was hired, this one in Los Angeles and this one to have no contact with the subject, constructing the missing pieces of Ava's life story out of quotes and information in archival sources and melding these with the usable sections of the Burgess-Ava collaboration.

"She was in poor health all that last year," Spoli Mills would remember. "The lupus got worse and worse. She was in pain. Her joints felt so bad. She would cry to me, *'I ache, I ache.'* There were rashes and swellings. I mean, it was not a happy time. She had medicines and painkillers to take, but, you know, she was going to different doctors, and she would take too much of the medicine, and you mix it with drink. It was just a rotten situation. She wasn't supposed to drink or smoke, but at that stage she just thought, What the hell's the difference?

In October 1989 she arranged to sell a selection of her jewels at auction. She had no more use for them, she said. They were disposed of at Sotheby's in New York: the emeralds and the diamonds and the gold and the pearls and the Kashmiri sapphires, gone to the highest bidder, all with their secrets and stories never to be told.

"I was on my way to Africa, and I stopped in London to call on her," said Gene Young of Bantam Books. "I had to meet with her to pick the pictures for her book. So I went to her lovely apartment overlooking a park. I met her very nice housekeeper and a dog named Morgan. Ava was not recognizable. Her friend Steve Birmingham had warned me about her changed appearance. He said that if you passed her on the street you would not recognize her. And that was absolutely true. She had gotten fat, she told me, because she had been on steroids because of her illness. She was barefoot and somewhat disheveled. She was clearly in a state of depression. She was very, very depressed. She was cordial, she was sweet, you know. But she did babble, not always coherently, about what had happened to her, what bad shape she was in, about her past. She couldn't do anything, she couldn't exercise, she was fat, she didn't feel well.

"We sat and had tea. And then we looked over the pictures for the book. And she looked them over, very wistfully. There were a couple of pictures of her with Burt Lancaster very early in her career, the two of them exercising on the beach. She said, 'I used to be quite an athlete.' And there was another picture of her from years ago, and she sighed. She said, 'I used to be very beautiful.'

"I left her then. I got quite distressed. I thought I ought to talk to Jess Morgan about this. I called him and said, 'Look, this woman is very depressed. She's up there talking about her father, who died of pneumonia. And she's frightened. And she's facing another winter in London. And I think maybe we ought to get her out of there. And I think she also needs some psychological help.' Jess was very concerned. He was very protective of her. So I called a friend of mine, a neurologist, who had a psychiatrist friend who was going to London. He was also a doctor. And he agreed to call on Ava. He called on her and spent three hours with her. And then, two days later, he sent her a bill for three hundred dollars—which made her furious. She told me, 'Here I spent time with this guy and gave him tea and he sends me a bill!' But the psychiatrist saw that she was ill and needed treatment. He said that she was not going to live if she stayed there. And so they arranged to have her flown to Los Angeles, to get treatment and to get out of the cold weather. And it was my understanding that they had a plane ready with a doctor and a nurse and she wouldn't go."

Michael Winner: "When I rang her to wish her Happy Christmas, she said, 'They want me to go to Los Angeles for treatment. I'd rather die in my own bed, here."

"She love England, she love her apartment," said Carmen Vargas, "she have her dog. She did not want to go anywhere else."

One day in December, Ava called her friend and erstwhile collaborator Peter Evans and asked him what he knew about EXIT, an organization that assisted the terminally ill and others to commit suicide. She told him, "I hear they give you a bottle of brandy and the necessary pills and it takes you out. When I go, I don't want to make a mess of it."

"She wasn't religious," Zoe Sallis said. "Every time I tried to talk to her about it, she would say, 'Oh, it doesn't exist.' She was an atheist, or perhaps she had become disillusioned with life. If you get a little of that, you lose faith. But when John died, John Huston, she gave me a lovely rosary as a present. He had given it to her, she told me. She said, 'I want you to have it now.' It was a very old rosary from Italy or somewhere. She must have thought there was something to religion to do that, don't you think?"

On Christmas Eve, her sixty-seventh birthday, two cakes were baked, one chocolate and one coconut, just as one it was done the day she was born. Her mother had taught her the secret recipe, and she had taught it to Carmen Vargas. Bappie, eighty-six years old now, was ill herself in California and could not travel to be with her sister.*

"The last time I saw her was not long before she died," said Lucia Graves. "And I remember looking up at her from the street, seeing her through the window of her flat without her seeing me. I remembered how she had once been, and I could not help feeling sad that she had lost her wonderful beauty. But, you know, the moment you were with her and she spoke to you—when you heard the affection in her voice and her sense of humor, her sense of life—you saw that nothing had really gone away, nothing was lost, she was still beautiful."

"Miss Ava, she used to say, 'Oh Carmen, I think I'm dying, I'm going to Chicago.' I say, 'No, no, no say "I'm dying!" I tried to know what she was meaning. She say, 'I think I go to Chicago.' She mean that she is going away to die. She say, 'Carmen, I only want to ask you one favor.' She say, 'Please, wherever you go, will you stick with my baby?' Morgan, the dog, she mean. 'Wherever you go, whatever you do, please hang on with my baby. Then I can go, and I will be at peace. Then I will go to Chicago in peace.' I don't know why she talk so funny. I say, 'Don't go to Chicago, Miss Gardner, please, it is too cold there!' "

One day she called to Carmen. She held in her hand a wrapped package. She said, "Carmen, take this and if something happens to me I want you to destroy it. I don't want anyone to open it or see inside. Will you do that for me?"

*Bappie was to die in Los Angeles on November 6, 1993.

Carmen took the package. She did not know what was inside, maybe letters, she thought, but she did not try to open it or see inside. "I respected her wishes. She trust me fully. I did what she asked."

"She was suffering," said Spoli Mills. "She had pneumonia again. It was very bad. We spoke on the telephone the night before. She said, 'I feel so awful, Spoli.' And she was going to try to go to sleep. And I was so sad, but I didn't want her to hear it. And she said, 'Spoli, I just don't think we'll ever have any more fun together.' And I said, 'We will, Ava, we will. I'm going to get you right and we will have fun again.' And those were the last words I spoke to her."

On the morning of January 25, 1990, Carmen Vargas brought a breakfast tray to Ava Gardner where she lay in her canopied Chippendale bed. When the housekeeper returned for the tray a little later Ava looked up and smiled at her. She said, "Carmen, I'm tired."

Tributes and lengthy obituaries appeared all over the world. Headlines variously described the passing of the Screen Beauty, Sultry Film Star, Legendary Femme Fatale. *People Weekly* in America pronounced her "The Last Goddess . . . the most irresistible woman in Hollywood." With a somber enthusiasm writers pondered her ravishing looks, spectacular glamour, tempestuous private life. They counted up the stormy marriages, paying particular attention to the third (the Romance of the Century, as some were valuing it), tabulated an assortment of the also-rans, bullfighters, and playboys, and billionaires. Regarding her professional achievements, some were perhaps encouraged by Ava's denigrating self-assessments, but others described a fine actress given too few good opportunities in a career lasting more than forty years (in itself a rare tribute to her professionalism). She was, said the *London Times*, "certainly one of the most striking and genuine stars of her time . . . her great beauty and, even more, the sheer personality shining through even the most indifferent vehicles."

Reporters and television crews solicited remembrances from Ava's colleagues: Gregory Peck, Burt Lancaster, Joe Mankiewicz, among those offering words of affection and admiration.

The media sought comment from Ava's three famous former husbands.

Mickey Rooney said: "My heart is broken with the loss of my first love. The beauty and magic of Ava will forever be in all of our hearts."

Artie Shaw refused to comment. But a few months later, realizing that he had passed up one more opportunity to sound like a coldhearted prick, he offered this: "What are you going to say about something that represents a part of your past you don't recognize anymore? I don't even know who she is. There's nothing to talk about. She ruined her life. She killed herself—I mean, by smoking and drinking and carrying on."

A statement was issued on behalf of Frank Sinatra: "Ava was a great lady and her loss is very painful."

He had heard the news, it was said, and he had slumped down and his eyes had filled with tears. He had turned red with anguish, and he cried out, "Why wasn't I there for her? Why wasn't I there to help her?"

His daughter Tina would recall that he had gone into his room and he sat there alone all night and all the next day and when he spoke to her at last he could not raise his voice above a whisper.

Ava had wanted to be buried beside her mother and father in the family plot at Smithfield. Carmen accompanied the coffin from London to North Carolina. The Reverend Francis Bradshaw delivered the graveside eulogy at Sunset Memorial Park just at the edge of town. It began to rain during the ceremony, and umbrellas were opened, and it seemed to some that it was very much like the funeral of Maria in *The Barefoot Contessa* except that the color was not as pretty as in the movie, when the sun came back out.

Carmen returned to London, and when she entered the apartment at Ennismore Gardens and understood that no one was there she felt shock and sadness again as if for the first time. She was permitted to stay on at number

34 until the place was finally closed down in August. She had to take care of Morgan—that was a promise to Miss Gardner, and she had wondered what she was going to do with the two of them because who would hire a housekeeper with her own dog? Then Gregory Peck had asked her to come and work for him and his wife in California. Gregory Peck liked the dog very much and said it brought back good memories of his friend. The dog lived to the age of fifteen and was buried behind the house under a weeping elm. The stone marker reads: MORGAN GARDNER VARGAS.

SOURCES

INTERVIEWS

Berdie Abrams
Angela Allen
Diana Altman
Robert J. Anderson
James Bacon
Nelly Barquette
Kathleen Beckett
Turhan Bey
Nan Birmingham
Johnny Blowers
Peter Blythe
Keith Botsford
Phil Brown
Joe Bushkin
Waller Bussenius
Jack Cardiff
Marge Champion
Esme Chandlee
Betty Comden
Alistair Cooke
Alberta Cooney
Luther Daughtry, Jr.
Steve Dunleavy
Milton Ebbins
Marge Edwards

J. M. Fordham
Leatrice Gilbert Fountain
Raul Garcia
Murray Garrett
Richard Goldstone
Bernard Gordon
Johnny Grant
Lucia Graves
Virginia Grey
Pete Hamill
David Hanna
Eloise Hardt
Alan Harkness
John Hawkesworth
Skitch Henderson
A. E. Hotchner
Cici Huston
Tony Huston
Christopher Isherwood
Herb Jeffries
Neil Jillett
Howard Keel
Evelyn Keyes
Mickey Knox
Frank Laico

Marc Lawrence
Margaret Lee
David Leeming
Janet Leigh
Monica Lewis
Michael Logothetis
Ross Lowell
Sid Luft
Joanna Lumley
Joseph L. Mankiewicz
Francis Matthews
Virginia Mayo
Ann Miller
Mitch Miller
Spoli Mills
Eva Monley
Terry Morse
Nan McGlohon
Mike Oliver
Dale Olson
Roy Parkinson
Kathleen Parrish
Bob Rains
Jess Rand
Gene Reynolds

Betty Rose	Donald Sinden	Carmen Vargas
Ron Rosenberg	William Smith	Bayard Veiller
Ann Rutherford	Robert Stack	Imogen Wheeler
Zoe Sallis	Mokie Stancil	Sandy Whitelaw
Budd Schulberg	David Stenn	Ann Williams
Artie Shaw	Austin Stevens	Billy Williams
Tom Shaw	Tempest Storm	Michael Winner
Vincent Sherman	Ben Tatar	Clarence Woodell
Betty Sicre	Claude Terrail	Jimmy Wyble
George Sidney	Roma Tomalty	Philip Yordan
Arthur Silber, Jr.	Candy Toxton	Genevieve Young
Sheila Sim	Tony Trabert	
Jeanie Sims	William Tuttle	

ARCHIVES AND SPECIAL COLLECTIONS

USC Cinema-Television Library, Los Angeles, California

Margaret Herrick Library of the Academy of Motion Picture Arts and Sciences, Beverly Hills, California

Los Angeles Public Library

Lincoln Center Library for the Performing Arts, New York City

British Film Institute, Library, London

Heritage Center, Smithfield, North Carolina

Ava Gardner Museum, Smithfield, North Carolina

Smithfield Public Library, Smithfield, North Carolina

BOOKS

Allen, Bunny. *Second Wheel*. Clinton, NJ: Amwell Press.

Alpi, Deborah Lazaroff. *Robert Siodmak*. Jefferson, NC: McFarland, 1998.

Altman, Diana. *Hollywood East*. New York: Birch Lane, 1992.

Annakin, Ken. *So You Wanna Be a Director*. Sheffield, England: Tomahawk Press, 2001.

Arden, Eve. *Three Faces of Eve*. New York: St. Martin's, 1985.

Bacall, Lauren. *By Myself*. New York: Knopf, 1978.

Bacon, James. *Hollywood is a Four Letter Town*. Chicago: Regnery, 1976.

Bartlett, Donald L., and James B. Steele. *Empire*. New York: Norton, 1979.

Bernstein, Walter. *Inside Out*. New York: Knopf, 1996.

Bogarde, Dirk. *An Orderly Man*. New York: Knopf, 1983.

Bogle, Donald. *Dorothy Dandridge*. New York: Amistad, 1997.

Botsford, Keith. *Dominguín*. Chicago: Quadrangle, 1972.

Bradford, Sarah. *Princess Grace*. New York: Stein & Day, 1984.

Bragg, Melvyn. *Richard Burton*. Boston: Little, Brown, 1988.

Brion, Patrick. *Albert Lewin*. Paris: Bibliothèque du film, 2002.

Brown, Peter Harry, and Pamela Ann Brown. *The MGM Girls*. New York: St. Martin's, 1983.

Brown, Peter Harry, and Pat H. Broeske. *Howard Hughes: The Untold Story*. New York: Dutton, 1996.

Buford, Kate. *Burt Lancaster*. New York: Knopf, 2000.

Cahn, Sammy. *I Should Care*. New York: Arbor House, 1974.

Callow, Simon. *Charles Laughton: A Difficult Actor*. London: Methuen, 1987.

Cannon, Doris Rollins. *Grabtown Girl*. Asheboro, NC: Down Home Press, 2001.

Cardiff, Jack. *Magic Hour*. London: Faber, 1996.

Clarens, Carlos. *Crime Movies*. New York: Norton, 1980.

Clase, Pablo. *Porfirio Rubirosa El Primer Playboy del Mundo*. Santo Domingo, R.D., Taller, 1989.

Chilton, John. *Roy Eldridge, Little Jazz Giant*. New York, Continuum, 2003.

Clarke, Gerald. *Get Happy*. New York: Random House, 2000.

Clooney, Rosemary, with Joan Barthel. *Girl Singer*. New York: Doubleday, 1999.

Cohen, Mickey. *Mickey Cohen: In My Own Words*. Englewood Cliffs, NJ: Prentice-Hall, 1975.

Daniell, John. *Ava Gardner*. London: Comet, 1984.

Davis, Miles, with Quincy Troupe. *Miles*. New York: Simon & Schuster, 1989.

Davis, Sammy, Jr. *Hollywood in a Suitcase*. New York: Morrow, 1981.

Davis, Sammy, Jr., and Jane and Burt Boyar. *Why Me?* New York: Farrar, Straus & Giroux, 1989.

Dominguín, Pepe. *Rojo y Oro*. Madrid: Alianza, 2002.

Douglas, Kirk. *The Ragman's Son*. New York: Simon & Schuster, 1988.

Douglas, Melvyn. *See You at the Movies*. Lanham, MD: University Press of America, 1986.

Eames, John Douglas. *The MGM Story*. New York: Crown, 1976.

Eisenschitz, Bernard. *Nicholas Ray: An American Journey*. London: Faber, 1993.

Eyman, Scott. *Print the Legend*. New York: Simon & Schuster, 1999.

Falacci, Orianna. *The Egotists*. New York: Tempo Books, 1969.

Farber, Stephen. *Hollywood on the Couch*. New York: Morrow, 1993.

Farrow, Mia. *What Falls Away*. New York: Doubleday, 1997.

Felleman, Susan. *Botticelli in Hollywood*. New York: Twayne, 1997.

Fishgall, Gary. *Gregory Peck*. New York: Scribner, 2002.

Flamini, Roland. *Ava*. New York: Coward, McCann, 1983.

Ford, Dan. *Pappy*. Englewood Cliffs, NJ: Prentice-Hall, 1979.

Fordin, Hugh. *The Movies' Greatest Musicals*. New York: Frederick Ungar, 1984.

Fowler, Karin J. *Ava Gardner: A Bio-Bibliography*. Westport, CT: Greenwood, 1990.

Freedland, Michael. *All the Way*. London: Weidenfeld & Nicolson, 1997.

Gardner, Ava. *Ava: My Story*. New York: Bantam, 1990.

Geist, Kenneth L. *Pictures Will Talk*. New York: Charles Scribner's, 1978.

Gordon, Bernard. *Hollywood Exile*. Austin: University of Texas Press, 1999.

Granger, Stewart. *Sparks Fly Upward*. London: Grenada, 1981.

Graves, Robert. *Steps*. London: Cassell, 1958.

Grobel, Lawrence. *The Hustons*. New York: Scribner, 1989.

Grunwald, Henry. *One Man's America*. New York: Doubleday, 1997.

504 • *Sources*

Guilaroff, Sydney, as told to Cathy Griffin. *Crowning Glory*. Santa Monica, CA: General Publishing Group, 1996.

Guiles, Fred Lawrence. *Tyrone Power: The Last Idol*. New York: Doubleday, 1979.

Gussow, Mel. *Don't Say Yes Until I Finish Talking*. New York: Doubleday, 1971.

Hack, Richard. *Hughes*. Beverly Hills: New Millennium, 2001.

Hammond, Paul. *The Shadow and Its Shadow*. San Francisco: City Lights, 2000.

Hanna, David. *Ava*. New York: Putnam, 1960.

————. *Sinatra: Ol' Blue Eyes Remembered*. New York: Gramercy, 1997.

Harris, Radie. *Radie's World*. New York: Putnam, 1975.

Hayes, David, and Brent Walker. *The Films of the Bowery Boys*. Secaucus, NJ: Citadel, 1984.

Hernan, Luis Miguel, and Ignacio Adellac. *Ava Gardner: El Mito*. Madrid: Wizen, 2000.

Herreros, Enrique. *Hay Bombones y Caramelos*. Madrid: EDAF, 2000.

Heston, Charlton. *The Actor's Life*. New York: Dutton, 1976.

————. *In the Arena*. New York: Simon & Schuster, 1995.

Higham, Charles. *Ava*. New York: Delacorte, 1974.

————. *Howard Hughes: The Secret Life*. New York: Putnam, 1993.

Hillier, Jim, ed. *Cahiers du Cinema: The 1950s*. Cambridge, MA: Harvard University Press, 1985.

Hoad, Jenny, and Jack Pollard. *My Life with Lew*. Sydney, Australia: HarperCollins, 2002.

Hopper, Hedda, and James Brough. *The Whole Truth and Nothing But*. New York: Doubleday, 1963.

Horne, Lena. *Lena*. New York: New American Library, 1965.

Hotchner, A. E. *Papa Hemingway*. New York: Random House, 1966.

Huston, John. *An Open Book*. New York: Knopf, 1980.

Hyams, Joe. *Mislaid in Hollywood*. New York: Peter Wyden, 1973.

Jacobs, George, and William Stadiem. *Mr. S.: My Life with Frank Sinatra*. New York: HarperCollins, 2004.

Johnson, Nora. *Flashback*. New York: Doubleday, 1979.

Johnson, Nunnally. *The Letters of Nunnally Johnson*. New York: Knopf, 1981.

Jurow, Martin. *Marty Jurow Seein' Stars*. Dallas, TX: Southern Methodist University Press, 2001.

Kass, Judith M. *Ava Gardner*. New York: Jove, 1977.

Kelley, Kitty. *His Way*. New York: Bantam, 1986.

Knox, Mickey. *The Good, the Bad and the Dolce Vita*. New York: Nation Books, 2004.

Koszarski, Richard, ed. *Hollywood Directors: 1941–1976*. New York: Oxford University Press, 1977.

Kuralt, Charles. *North Carolina Is My Home*. Guilford, CT: Globe Pequot Press, 1998.

Lamarr, Hedy. *Ecstasy and Me*. New York: Fawcett, 1966.

Lambert, Gavin. *On Cukor*. New York: Capricorn, 1972.

Lassiter, Tom J. *Smithfield's 200 Years: 1777–1977*. Smithfield, NC: Hometown Heritage Publishing, 1977.

Lassiter, Tom J., and T. Wingate Lassiter. *Johnston County: Its History Since 1746.* Smithfield, NC: Hometown Heritage Publishing, 2004.

Laurence, Frank M. *Hemingway and the Movies.* Jackson: University Press of Mississippi, 1981.

Lawford, Patricia Seaton, with Ted Schwarz. *The Peter Lawford Story.* New York: Carroll & Graf, 1988.

Lazar, Irving. *"Swifty."* New York: Simon & Schuster, 1995.

Levinson, Peter. *September in the Rain.* New York: Billboard, 2001.

———. *Trumpet Blues.* New York: Oxford University Press, 1999.

Levy, Emanuel. *George Cukor, Master of Elegance.* New York: Morrow, 1994.

Linet, Beverly. *Star-Crossed.* New York: Putnam, 1986.

Long, Robert Emmet, ed. *George Cukor Interviews.* Jackson: University Press of Mississippi, 2001.

Lord, Graham. *Niv.* London: Orion, 2003.

Lorenz, Marita, with Ted Schwarz. *Marita.* New York: Thunder's Mouth Press, 1993.

Madsen, Axel. *Stanwyck.* New York: HarperCollins, 1994.

Maheu, Robert, and Richard Hack. *Next to Hughes.* New York: HarperCollins, 1992.

Man Ray. *Self Portrait.* Boston: Little, Brown, 1963.

Mann, William J. *Behind the Screen.* New York: Viking, 2001.

Martin, Pete. *Hollywood Without Makeup.* New York: Bantam, 1948.

Marx, Arthur. *The Nine Lives of Mickey Rooney.* New York: Stein & Day, 1986.

Marx, Samuel. *Mayer and Thalberg.* New York: Random House, 1975.

McBride, Joseph. *Searching for John Ford.* New York: St. Martin's, 2001.

McGilligan, Patrick, ed. *Backstory 2.* Berkeley: University of California Press, 1991.

———. *George Cukor: A Double Life.* New York: St. Martin's, 1991.

Meredith, Burgess. *So Far So Good.* Boston: Little, Brown, 1994.

Milne, Tom, ed. *Godard on Godard.* New York: Viking, 1972.

Monder, Eric. *George Sidney: A Bio-Bibliography.* Westport, CT: Greenwood, 1994.

Morley, Sheridan. *The Other Side of the Moon.* New York: Harper & Row, 1985.

Mormorio, Diego. *Tazio Secchiaroli.* New York: Abrams, 1999.

Mosley, Leonard. *Zanuck.* Boston: Little, Brown, 1984.

Munn, Michael. *Sinatra: The Untold Story.* London: Robson, 2001.

Niklas, Kurt. *The Corner Table.* Los Angeles: Tuxedo Press, 2001.

Nogueira, Rui. *Melville.* New York: Viking, 1972.

Petkov, Steven, and Leonard Mustazza, eds. *The Frank Sinatra Reader.* Oxford, England: Oxford University Press, 1995.

Porter, Bruce. *Blow.* New York: HarperCollins, 1993.

Pratley, Gerald. *The Cinema of John Huston.* Cranbury, NJ: A. S. Barnes, 1977.

Prats, Juan Carlos. *Ava Gardner: La Diosa Descalza.* Madrid: Ediciones JC Clementine, 2000.

Previn, André. *No Minor Chords.* New York: Doubleday, 1991.

Price, Victoria. *Vincent Price: A Daughter's Biography.* New York: St. Martin's, 1999.

Reed, Rex. *Do You Sleep in the Nude?* New York: New American Library, 1968.

Reynolds, Debbie. *Debbie: My Life.* New York: Morrow, 1988.

Riehl, Karen Truesdell. *Love & Madness*. Alpine, CA: Sands, 2003.

Robinson, Jeffrey. *Rainier and Grace*. New York: Atlantic Monthly Press, 1989.

Rockwell, John. *Sinatra: An American Classic*. New York: Rolling Stone, 1984.

Rooney, Mickey. *I.E.: An Autobiography*. New York: Putnam, 1965.

———. *Life Is Too Short*. New York: Villard, 1991.

Ross, Lillian. *Picture*. New York: Limelight Editions, 1984.

Sakol, Jeannie, and Caroline Latham. *About Grace*. Chicago: Contemporary, 1993.

Server, Lee. *Robert Mitchum: Baby, I Don't Care*. New York: St. Martin's, 2001.

Sharif, Omar. *The Eternal Male*. New York: Doubleday, 1977.

Shaw, Arnold. *Sinatra, Twentieth Century Romantic*. New York: Holt, 1968.

Shepard, David, and Ted Perry. *Henry King Director: From Silents to Scope*. Scarecrow Press?

Silber, Arthur, Jr. *Sammy Davis Jr.: Me and My Shadow*. North Hollywood: Samart, 2003.

Simon, George T. *The Big Bands*. New York: Schirmer Books, 1981.

Sinatra, Nancy. *Frank Sinatra: An American Legend*. Santa Monica, CA: General Publishing Group, 1995.

Sinatra, Tina, with Jeff Coplon. *My Father's Daughter*. New York: Simon & Schuster, 2000.

Skolsky, Sidney. *Don't Get Me Wrong—I Love Hollywood*. New York: Putnam, 1975.

Spada, James. *Grace*. New York: Doubleday, 1987.

———. *Peter Lawford*. New York: Bantam, 1991.

Spoto, Donald. *Stanley Kramer: Film Maker*. New York: Putnam, 1978.

Stack, Robert, with Mark Evans. *Straight Shooting*. New York: Macmillan, 1980.

Stempel, Tom. *Screenwriter Nunnally Johnson*. San Diego, CA: Barnes, 1980.

Taraborrelli, J. Randy. *Sinatra: Behind the Legend*. New York: Birch Lane Press, 1997.

Temple, Shirley. *Child Star*. New York: McGraw-Hill, 1988.

Thomas, Bob. *Golden Boy*. New York: St. Martin's, 1983.

Thompson, Verita. *Bogie and Me*. New York: St. Martin's, 1982.

Tormé, Mel. *It Wasn't All Velvet*. New York: Viking, 1988.

Tornabene, Lyn. *Long Live the King*. New York: Putnam, 1976.

Truffaut, François. *The Films in My Life*. New York: Simon & Schuster, 1978.

Turner, Lana. *Lana*. New York: Dutton, 1982.

Tynan, Kenneth. *The Diaries of Kenneth Tynan*. New York: BloomsburyUSA, 2001.

———. *Show People*. New York: Simon & Schuster, 1979.

Viertel, Peter. *Dangerous Friends*. New York: Doubleday, 1992.

Wayne, Jane Ellen. *Ava's Men*. New York: St. Martin's, 1990.

Whiteside, Jonny. *Cry: The Johnnie Ray Story*. Fort Lee, NJ: Barricade Books, 1994.

Williams, Esther, with Digby Diehl. *The Million Dollar Mermaid*. New York: Simon & Schuster, 1999.

Wilson, Earl. *Hot Times*. Chicago: Contemporary, 1984.

———. *Sinatra*. New York: Macmillan, 1976.

———. *The Show Business Nobody Knows*. Chicago: Cowles, 1971.

Winecoff, Charles. *Split Image*. New York: Dutton, 1996.

Winner, Michael. *Winner Takes All.* London: Robson, 2004.

Winters, Shelley. *Shelley II.* New York: Simon & Schuster, 1989.

————. *Shelley, Also Known as Shirley.* New York: Morrow, 1980.

Yablonsky, Lewis. *George Raft.* New York: McGraw-Hill, 1974.

Young, Freddie. *Seventy Light Years.* London: Faber, 1999.

PERIODICALS, ETC.

"$455 Mil Fines Asked in Loren-Ponti Case." *Variety*, Dec. 4, 1978.

"$455 Million Fines Asked for Sophia Loren, Ponti." *Los Angeles Times*, Dec. 3, 1978.

" 'All a Gag,' Says Ava." *Daily Mail*, May 16, 1950.

" 'Amber' Writer, Shaw Marriage (?) Tangled." *Hollywood Citizen-News*, Oct. 31, 1946.

" 'Well,' Said Frankie, 'We Finally Made It.' " *Life*, Nov. 19, 1951.

"50G Ava Gardner Suit Versus Commonwealth." *Variety*, Sept. 8, 1970.

"A Film Fright." *Grimsby Evening Telegraph* (England), June 6, 1950.

"A Rare Pic of Two ex-Mrs. Sinatras." *Photoplay*, July 1978.

"A Simple Service for Ava Gardner." *Smithfield Herald*, Jan. 30, 1990.

"A Slimy 99 Degrees in Manhattan" *Time*, July 10, 1964.

"Actor Mickey Rooney Inducted into U.S. Army." *Los Angeles Times*, June 15, 1944.

"Actress Ava Gardner." *Los Angeles Times*, Oct. 28, 1986.

"All Is Not Harmony with Ava, Frank Sinatra Says." *Los Angeles Times*, Oct. 7, 1952.

"Along the Johnston Wayside." *Smithfield Herald*, May 14, 1985.

"An Open Love Letter to Actress Ava Gardner." *Raleigh News and Observer*, May 11, 1980.

"Angry Frank Leaves Ava to Bullfighter." *Long Beach Independent*, May 18, 1950.

"Army Takes Film Actor Rooney." *Los Angeles Examiner*, June 15, 1944.

"Artie Shaw Gets 'Amber' as Wife No. 5." *Los Angeles Daily News*, Oct. 29, 1946.

"Artie Shaw Weds Actress at Home of Judge Mosk." *Los Angeles Times*, Oct. 18, 1945.

"Artie Shaw, Ava Gardner Still Together, He Says." *Los Angeles Times*, June 28, 1946.

"Artie Shaw." *Top Secret.* N.d., circa 1953.

"Artie Shaw's Ava Gardner Asks Divorce." Aug. 16, 1946.

"Ava 'Nervous,' Tossed Out of Brazil Hotel." *Hollywood Citizen-News*, Sept. 9, 1954.

"Ava and Her Times." *Newsweek*, Nov. 24, 1952.

"Ava and Mario Lunch Together." *Manchester Daily Dispatch* (England), June 6, 1950.

"Ava and Sinatra Will Carry Out Divorce Plans." *Los Angeles Times*, Nov. 27, 1953.

"Ava Blames Row on Anti-Americans." *Los Angeles Daily News*, Sept. 16, 1954.

"Ava Confirms Separation from Movie Husband." *Smithfield Herald*, Sept. 11, 1942.

"Ava Could Have Danced All Night." *Los Angeles Times*, July 23, 1975.

"Ava Denies Divorce Suit in Mexico." *Los Angeles Examiner*, May 5, 1957.

"Ava Denies Plans to Wed Italian Actor." *Los Angeles Times*, Feb. 7, 1957.

"Ava Denies Plans to Wed Rubirosa." *Los Angeles Times*, July 11, 1956.

"Ava Denies Sinatra Romance." *London Star*, Aug. 14, 1950.

"Ava Ducks Camera in Nightclub Fracas." *Los Angeles Herald Examiner*, Dec. 28, 1963.

"Ava Ejected by Hotel After Rio Welcome." *Los Angeles Times*, Sept. 9, 1954.

"Ava Eludes Newsmen." *Raleigh News and Observer*, Dec. 5, 1968.

"Ava Flies to Spain." *Nottingham Guardian* (England), Apr. 15, 1950.

"Ava Gardner at 44: Still the Most Beautiful Woman in the World." *Evening Standard*, Feb. 20, 1968.

"Ava Gardner Buys Spanish Home." *Los Angeles Examiner*, Dec. 23, 1955.

"Ava Gardner Coming Home." *Smithfield Herald*, June 5, 1942.

"Ava Gardner Completely Free of Artie." *Los Angeles Daily News*, Nov. 15, 1947.

"Ava Gardner Divorces Shaw." *Los Angeles Times*, Oct. 25, 1946.

"Ava Gardner Divorces Sinatra." *Los Angeles Examiner*, July 6, 1957.

"Ava Gardner Dropped in Film Row." N.p., circa Dec. 1963.

"Ava Gardner Facial Injuries Reported." *Los Angeles Mirror*, Jan. 3, 1958.

"Ava Gardner Gave Us Reasons to Be Proud." *Smithfield Herald*, Feb. 2, 1990.

"Ava Gardner Hints She Bathes 'Sans Costume.' " *Show Business*, Apr. 20–27, 1950.

"Ava Gardner Hospitalized for Respiratory Ailment." *Raleigh News and Observer*, Jan. 13, 1988.

"Ava Gardner in British Hospital." *Los Angeles Times*, Jan. 13, 1966.

"Ava Gardner Injured in Bull Ring; Denies Plastic Surgery Is Needed." *Los Angeles Times*, Jan. 4, 1958.

"Ava Gardner Is Too Unbelievable for My Novel." *Good Housekeeping* Press Release, Feb. 21, 1961.

"Ava Gardner L'Indomptable." *Paris Match* Tribute, Feb. 8, 1990.

"Ava Gardner May Marry on Saturday." *Hollywood Citizen-News*, Oct. 3, 1963.

"Ava Gardner Out of Hospital." *Los Angele.s Herald Examiner*, Nov. 29, 1986.

"Ava Gardner Plays the Gypsy." *Collier's*, July 23, 1954.

"Ava Gardner Posts 'Do Not Disturb' Sign in Caracas." *Los Angeles Times*, Sept. 11, 1954.

"Ava Gardner: Random Notes for a Tintype." Glenn Rose Public Relations, 1964, Margaret Herrick Library.

"Ava Gardner Released from St. John's Hospital." *Variety*, Dec. 2, 1986.

"Ava Gardner Romance Is Over, Italian Says." *Los Angeles Times*, Feb. 7, 1959.

"Ava Gardner Rome-bound sans Frankie" *Los Angeles Daily News*, Nov. 23, 1953.

"Ava Gardner Sees No Hope for Marriage." *Los Angeles Daily News*, Nov. 28, 1953.

"Ava Gardner Set for Roy Bean." *Hollywood Reporter*, Oct. 5, 1971.

"Ava Gardner Shops in Church Street." *Kensington News*, July 21, 1950.

"Ava Gardner Stars in 'Toys.' " *Hollywood Citizen-News*, July 14, 1969.

"Ava Gardner Still Determined to Divorce Sinatra." *Hollywood Citizen-News*, Nov. 23, 1953.

"Ava Gardner Stricken on Set in Africa." *Los Angeles Times*, Nov. 25, 1952.

"Ava Gardner Suffers Stroke in Hospital." *National Enquirer*, n.d., circa 1966.

"Ava Gardner Tagged Screen Siren of This Decade." *Smithfield Herald*, Jan. 30, 1951.

"Ava Gardner to Star 'Tam Lin.' " *Hollywood Reporter*, May 12, 1969.

"Ava Gardner Was in St. John's Hospital." *Los Angeles Times*, Jan. 13, 1988.

"Ava Gardner, a hometown girl . . ." *People*, Oct. 21, 1984.

"Ava Gardner, a Londoner in recent years . . ." *Variety*, Apr. 4, 1980.

"Ava Gardner, the actress, made a rare . . ." *Times* (London), Jan. 23, 1986.

"Ava Gardner." *Current Biography*, May 1965.

"Ava Gardner." MGM Files, July 1948.

"Ava Gardner." MGM Publicity Dept., 1942.

"Ava Gardner." MGM Publicity Dept., 1956.

"Ava Gardner." Obituary, *Daily Telegraph*, Jan. 26, 1990.

"Ava Gardner." Obituary, *Times* (London), Jan. 26, 1990.

"Ava Gardner." Paramount Publicity, July 1963.

"Ava Gardner." Universal Press Release, June 25, 1974.

"Ava Gardner: Biography." Stanley Seger Presents, Publicity Dept.

"Ava Gardner: One of Hollywood's Great Ladies." *Woman's Home Journal*, Oct. 1976.

"Ava Gardner: Studio Denies She's 'Hot Potato.'" *People Today* (England), June 6, 1951.

"Ava Gardner: Too Much Spice?" *Quick News Weekly*, Apr. 30, 1951.

"Ava Gardner's Appearance at Club Reported." *Los Angeles Times*, Oct. 19, 1951.

"Ava Gardner's seductive beauty . . ." *Newsweek*, Oct. 21, 1974.

"Ava Gardner's sister, Bea . . ." *Variety*, obituary, Nov. 19, 1993.

"Ava Gardner's Treasures Come Home." *Us*, Sept. 18, 1979.

"Ava Gardner—Beauty." *Vogue*, Feb. 1, 1954.

"Ava Gets the 'Goddess Build-up.'" *Daily Express*, Mar. 22, 1950.

"Ava Has Idyllic Outing with Soon Free Frankie." *Binghamton Press* (NY), May 31, 1951.

"Ava Here for Romulus Film." *Cinema*, Mar. 29, 1950.

"Ava in Cement Mum on Frank." *Los Angeles Examiner*, Oct. 22, 1952.

"Ava Leaves Rio by Air for N.Y. After Hectic Visit." *Los Angeles Times*, Sept. 10, 1954.

"Ava Married to Sinatra in Pennsylvania Rites." *Los Angeles Times*, Nov. 8, 1951.

"Ava on the Mend." *Los Angeles Herald Examiner*, Nov. 1, 1986.

"Ava Poses for Sculptor; Frankie Heads for U.S." *Los Angeles Times*, Jan. 3, 1954.

"Ava Rents Lake Tahoe Home in Move to Divorce Sinatra." *Los Angeles Examiner*, June 13, 1954.

"Ava Returning Home; Plan to Wed Hinted." *Los Angeles Times*, Mar. 21, 1960.

"Ava Returns; Mum on Plans to See Frankie." *Los Angeles Examiner*, Sept. 8, 1953.

"Ava Sees Power Play." *Sunday Graphic*, July 23, 1950.

"Ava Statue Dedicated in Spain." *All About Ava*, Spring 1999.

"Ava Talks to Frank, Still Plans Divorce." *Los Angeles Times*, Nov. 22, 1953.

"Ava to Ditch Sinatra for Bull Fighter." *Los Angeles Daily News*, May 26, 1954.

"Ava to Return in January and Seek Divorce." *Los Angeles Times*, Aug 1, 1956.

"Ava Visits Mother Here." *Raleigh News and Observer*, Dec. 20, 1942.

"Ava, Frankie Back Home from Mexico." *Los Angeles Times*, Aug. 8, 1951.

"Ava, Sinatra Settle Property Before Divorce." *Hollywood Citizen-News*, July 31, 1956.

"Ava's Face Said Scarred in Mishap." *Hollywood Citizen-News*, Jan. 3, 1958.

"Ava's Family Thanked for an Open Funeral." *Smithfield Herald*, Feb. 2, 1990.

"Ava's Goodbye to Hollywood." *Daily Express*, July 19, 1955.

"Ava's Latin Hair-Dos." *United Artists Publicity Dept.*, Jan. 12, 1959.

"Ava's Remarriage Reported Having Sinatra's Okay." *Hollywood Citizen-News*, Dec. 31, 1956.

"Ava's Return." *Parade*, Nov. 7, 1971.

"Ava's Story Reveals Her Love, Pain." *Long Beach Press Telegram*, Oct. 4, 1990.

"Back Home in Carolina." *Photoplay*, June 1949.

"Beauty by the Inch." Eros Film Publicity, June 21, 1950.

"Biographical Information." MGM Files, 1956.

"Biography of Ava Gardner." United Artists Publicity Dept., 1959.

"Birth Certificate: Ava Lavinia Gardner." North Carolina State Board of Health, Dec. 24, 1922.

"Bullfighter in London with Odes to Ava." *Morning Herald* (Australia), June 3, 1950.

"Bullfighter Is Jilted." *Daily Graphic*, May 24, 1950.

"Bull-Fighter Mario Is Jilted." *Evening Standard*, May 24, 1950.

"Bullfighter Rival of Sinatra Quite Sure of Ava's Love." *Los Angeles Times*, May 13, 1950.

"Bull-fighter Says It in Verse." *Manchester News Chronicle*, June 3, 1950.

"But What About Frankie?" *Los Angeles Examiner*, Sept. 8, 1952.

"Chicote." *El Mundo*, Mar. 16, 2003.

"Cinema." *Time*, Apr. 6, 1959.

"D.A. Undecided on Shaw-Winsor Marriage Action." *Hollywood Citizen-News*, n.d., circa 1946.

"Decree." *Los Angeles Times*, Oct. 24, 1946.

"Did the Barkeep Dream About Ava?" *Celebrities Answer to the Scandal Magazines*, July 1957.

"Dire Drama on the Death of the World." *Life*, Nov. 30, 1959.

"Dominguin, 69, Bullfighter in Hemingway Chronicle, Dies." *New York Times*, obituary, May 9, 1996.

"Duke Meets Stars." *Los Angeles Times*, Dec. 11, 1951.

"Earthquake." MGM Pressbook.

"East Side, West Side." *Daily Variety*, Dec. 13, 1949.

"Enter Ava—So Quietly." *Daily Express*, Nov. 11, 1962.

"Every Kiss Carved His Name on Another Bullet." *The Killers* advertisement. *New York Times*, Aug. 25, 1946.

"Excerpts Morning Newspapers 'Bhowani Junction . . .'" Strickling, MGM Publicity Dept., May 25, 1956. Margaret Herrick Library.

"Fat and 54—It's Ava Gardner." *National Enquirer*, Mar. 9, 1976.

"Film Actress Ava Gardner Spends Four Days Here." *Smithfield Herald*, Sept. 29, 1959.

"Flamenco, Flamenco!" *Leicester Mail* (England), May 15, 1950.

"For Better or For Worse?" *Hollywood Yearbook*, 1952.

"Frank Misses Gentle Ava's Pink Sunset." *Daily Mirror*, Jan. 30, 1990.

"Frank Sinatra and Ava Gardner." *People: The Greatest Love Stories of the Century*, Feb. 12, 1996.

"Frank Sinatra Glum as Spain Visit Ends." *Stockton Record* (CA), May 15, 1950.

"Frankie And Ava Merge Sniffles." *Los Angeles Daily News*, Dec. 29, 1953.

"Frankie and Ava to Return, Denies 'Quickie' Divorce Plan." *Los Angeles Herald Express*, Aug. 3, 1951.

"Frankie and Ava: Desperate, Dramatic and Doomed?" *Hollywood Romances*, Aug. 1951.

"Frankie Came in . . . and Out Went the Bullfighter." *Daily Herald* (England), May 15, 1950.

"Frankie Changes His Tune; Hunts Crosby in Paris." *Wilmington Press-Journal* (DE), May 18, 1950.

"Frankie Denies Mario Gave Him Bull's Rush." *Brooklyn Eagle*, May 22, 1950.

"Frankie Giving Ava Necklace." *Redding Record-Searchlight* (CA), May 15, 1950.

"Frankie Takes Home Gift for Wife Nancy." *Oxford Mail* (England), May 23, 1950.

"Frankie The Voice Is Looking Upset." *Daily Herald*, July 8, 1950.

"Frankie, Ava in Hide-away Honeymoon at Miami Beach." *Los Angeles Daily News*, Nov. 8, 1951.

"Gable Kissed Her." *Los Angeles Times*, Aug. 24, 1947.

"Gardner 'Knots' debut." *Hollywood Reporter*, Jan. 15, 1985.

"Gardner Never Found Eden." *Los Angeles Herald Examiner*, Dec. 19, 1982.

"Gardner Recuping At St. John's." *Variety*, Jan. 13, 1988.

"Gardner's Biography Arrives." *Hollywood Reporter*, Oct. 4, 1990.

"Gerrard 2504 . . ." *Cinema*, Mar. 29, 1950.

"Ghosts on Loose Slimsy Material." *Hollywood Reporter*, June 9, 1943.

"Ghosts on the Loose." *Daily Variety*, June 9, 1943.

"Green Gardner." *People*, Oct. 20, 1980.

"Grouchy Sinatra Meets Ava Gardner in Spain." *Los Angeles Times*, May 12, 1950.

"Hail! Hail, Ava's Gang's All There." *Los Angeles Daily News*, June 10, 1954.

"Happily Ever After?" *Modern Screen*, Dec. 1951.

"Harlow Wanted." *Yorkshire Evening Post*, May 27, 1950.

"Haunted." *Photoplay*, Oct. 1959.

"Hearth & Home." *Time*, circa 1950.

"Hearts & Flowers." *Time*, Aug. 13, 1951.

"Hen-Party Phone Drive Versus Ava Gardner as 'Runaway' Heroine." *Variety*, Sept. 28, 1960.

"Here Comes Mario." *London Star*, June 2, 1950.

"Hollywood Stars Snub Ava's Funeral." *Evening Standard*, Jan. 30, 1990.

"How Ava Gardner Fooled Hollywood." *Photoplay*, Oct. 1951.

"How to Win Friends with Ava and Frankie." *Movie Time*, June 1952.

"Huston's Gospel." *Newsweek*, Oct. 3, 1966.

"In the Priest of Love . . ." *Hollywood Reporter*, Mar. 4, 1980.

"Intimate Diary of Ava Gardner." *Filmland*, Dec. 1953.

"It's Lies, Says Ava: Mario Here Next Week." *Manchester Daily Dispatch* (England), May 26, 1950.

"Italian Press Say Walter Next for Ava." *Hollywood Citizen-News*, Jan. 3, 1957.

"Italian Stage Actor Asks Ava's Hand." *Hollywood Citizen-News*, Dec. 28, 1956.

"J.M. (Jack) Gardner." *Los Angeles Times*, Jan. 19, 1981.

"J.M. Gardner." *Variety*, Jan. 20, 1981.

"James Mason Gives England Away." *Sun* (Australia), June 7, 1950.

"James Mason Has Plans." *Morning Herald* (Australia), June 1, 1950.

"James Mason to His Ship Visitors—KEEP OUT." *Daily Express*, Apr. 21, 1950.

"Joe Smith, American." *Daily Variety* Jan. 7, 1942.

"Johnston Girl Gets 7 Year Movie Contract." *Smithfield Herald*, July 25, 1941.

"Just for Variety." *Variety*, Jan. 26, 1990.

"Just Married." *Los Angeles Examiner*, Oct. 18, 1945.

"Kid Glove Killer." *Daily Variety*, Mar. 11, 1942.

"Knot Young Anymore." *People*, June 10, 1985.

"L. Dominguin; Famed Spanish Bullfighter." *Los Angeles Times*, Obituary, May 9, 1996.

"Lead Role in Film Scripture." *New York Daily News*, July 7, 1964.

"*Life* Article Planned on Johnston Natives." N.p., Mar. 25, 1949.

"Loren Charged with Illegally Exporting Art." *Los Angeles Times*, Apr. 15, 1978.

"Lovely Ava Gardner." *Los Angeles Examiner*, c. 1946.

"Machine-made Film Star." *Autocar*, Aug. 11, 1950.

"Magic That's Forever Ava!" *Daily Mail*, Feb. 18, 1985.

"Magnificent Jewelry." Sotheby's Catalog, New York, Oct. 25–26, 1989.

"Maisie Goes to Reno." *Daily Variety*, Aug. 11, 1944.

"Maisie Goes to Reno." *Hollywood Reporter*, Aug. 11, 1944.

"Male Call." *Newsweek*, July 5, 1965.

"Mario Flies Here with Ode for Ava." *Daily Express*, June 3, 1950.

"Mario Has New Hat for Ava." *Glasgow Citizen*, June 2, 1950.

"Mario Terms Dancer's Beef Publicity Stunt." *New York Daily News*, May 24, 1950.

"Mario's Acting Left No Time to Show Poems." *Daily Graphic*, June 6, 1950.

"Mason Says 'No,' Slams the Door." *Evening News*, Apr. 21, 1950.

"Matador Mario Has Poem for Ava—'But She Doesn't Love Me.' " *Daily Herald* (England), June 3, 1950.

"Meat, 2 Veg for Ava And Mario." *Daily Mail*, June 6, 1950.

"Mellow actress Ava Gardner . . ." *Daily Mail*, Feb. 28, 1980.

"Mexican Divorce Asked by Ava." *Los Angeles Examiner*, June 15, 1957.

"Mickey Rooney and Young Actress, Ava Gardner, to Be Married Soon." *Los Angeles Examiner*, Dec. 10, 1941.

"Mickey Rooney Eager Beaver." *Look*, May 13, 1947.

"Mickey Rooney Visits Bride in Hospital." *Los Angeles Times*, Feb. 19, 1942.

"Mickey Rooney Wed in Village." *Los Angeles Times*, Jan. 11, 1942.

"Milestones." *Time*, Feb. 5, 1990.

"Mogambo." MGM Pressbook.

"Morning Report." *Los Angeles Times*, Nov. 23, 1990.

"Mrs. Mickey Rooney to Leave Hospital." *Los Angeles Examiner*, Feb. 19, 1942.

"Mrs. Shaw Sues Artie for Divorce." *Los Angeles Daily News*, Aug. 16, 1946.

"Navy Enacts Hoax on Ava-Sub Used in Underhand Trick." *Los Angeles Examiner*, May 6, 1952.

"New Light on Ava." *Life,* April 12, 1954.

"Newsmakers." *Philadelphia Inquirer,* Jan. 30, 1990.

"No Ole for Ava." *Modern Screen,* Mar. 1954.

"No romance in Sagaro." *Daily Graphic,* May 16, 1950.

"Notes on Ava Gardner." Samuel Bronston/Allied Artists Studios, Apr. 29, 1963. Margaret Herrick Library.

"Nothing Between Us, Says Ava." *Daily Herald* (England), May 26, 1950.

"Nothing to Say." *News Review,* May 18, 1950.

"Old Wife's Tale." *Newsweek,* May 2, 1966.

"Once a Star, Always a Star!" *Clayton Star,* Apr. 29, 1986.

"One Minute Interview With Ava Gardner." 20th Century–Fox Press Dept., circa 1952.

"One More Time." *Los Angeles Herald Examiner,* July 7, 1988.

"Oriental War on Plains of Spain." *New York Times,* 1962.

"Pandora Unit in Spain For 5 Weeks." *Cinema,* Apr. 19, 1950.

"People." *Time,* Mar. 11, 1985.

"Pillow Talkers." *Los Angeles Herald Examiner,* Mar. 7, 1983.

"Ponti Guilty, Miss Loren Acquitted in Money Shift." *Los Angeles Times,* Jan. 24, 1979.

"Pretty Ava Gardner In Limelight as Mickey Rooney's 'Latest' Girl Friend." *Smithfield Herald,* Oct. 3, 1941.

"Publicity-shy Star Meets the Press." AVCO Embassy Pictures Publicity Dept., 1979.

"Red-Headed Film Star . . ." N.p., circa May 1950.

"Relaxed." *News Chronicle,* May 16, 1956.

"Remembering the poet and the actress . . ." *Classic Images,* Apr. 1986.

"Representative Jack Gardner Dies." *Smithfield Herald,* Jan. 16, 1981.

"Rift." *Los Angeles Examiner,* Aug. 16, 1946.

"Save Her, It's Ava!" *This Week,* Oct. 16, 1956.

"Sayings of the Week." Weekly Scotsman, Mar. 30, 1950.

"Says Sinatra: 'Romance? No, I Like Spain.' " *Evening Standard,* May 18, 1950.

"Scherzo di carnevale." *La Domenica Del Corriere,* Feb. 22, 1959.

"Shades of Ava Gardner!" *New York Daily News,* May 20, 1963.

"Shelley, Ava Brawl Denied." *Los Angeles Mirror,* Aug. 26, 1958.

"Sick Bay." *Los Angeles Herald Examiner,* Oct. 28, 1986.

"Simon Lagarcia Puts Barefoot Ava on Ice." *Los Angeles Daily News,* Sept. 9, 1954.

"Sinatra and 'Angel' Ava Vacationing in Mexico City." *Los Angeles Daily News,* Aug. 2, 1951.

"Sinatra and Ava Celebrate to Wee Hours." *Los Angeles Times,* Dec. 27, 1953.

"Sinatra and Ava Stroll Barefoot on Frigid Beach." *Los Angeles Times,* Nov. 9, 1951.

"Sinatra Attacks Music Czar." *Daily Express,* Sept. 29, 1956.

"Sinatra Booed When Ava Fails to Appear at Show in Naples." *Los Angeles Times,* May 16, 1953.

"Sinatra Departs, Ava Blows Kisses to Bullfighter." *Hollywood Citizen-News,* May 17, 1950.

"Sinatra in Sulks, Toreador Phones, Ava Plays Field." *Humboldt Standard* (England), May 16, 1950.

"Sinatra Leaving Field to His Rival." *San Francisco News*, May 16, 1950.

"Sinatra Leaving Spain, Ava for Visit to Paris." *Hollywood Citizen-News*, May 16, 1950.

"Sinatra Missing From Bedside of Stricken Ex Ava." *Star Weekly*, n.d., circa 1988.

"Sinatra Reunion Plan News to Her, Ava Says." *Los Angeles Times*, Nov. 20, 1953.

"Sinatra Shocked by Noel Coward First Night Scene." *News Chronicle* (England), July 8, 1950.

"Sinatra Tosses a Pooh at 'Rival.'" *New York Journal-American*, May 22, 1950.

"Sinatra, Ava Get Marriage License." *Los Angeles Times*, Nov. 3, 1951.

"Sinatra-Ava Boudoir Row Story Buzzes." Clipping, Constance McCormick Collection, USC, Oct. 21, 1952.

"Singapore." Universal-International Publicity Dept. 1947, *Universal Collection*, USC.

"So-Sad Ava Steps Out to a Party." *Daily Express*, Nov. 17, 1982.

"Spain Suits Sinatra." *London Star*, May 15, 1950.

"Spanish Flame Spurns Sinatra's Love Rival." *New York World-Telegram and Sun*, May 23, 1950.

"Speaking of Pictures." *Life*, Oct. 18, 1954.

"Squared-circle Sidelight." *Hollywood-Citizen News*, Sept. 19, 1946.

"Star on the Horizon." *Smithfield Herald*, July 25, 1941.

"Studio Says Ava Still to Shed Frankie." *Hollywood Citizen-News*, Nov. 24, 1953.

"Studio Work Under Way on 'Pandora.'" *Cinema*, June 28, 1950.

"Telling Ava's Fortune." *This Week*, Nov. 16, 1958.

"The $1,000,000 Voice." *Manchester Daily Dispatch* (England), July 3, 1950.

"The Best Performance by a Celebrity." *Soap Opera Digest*, Jan. 14, 1986.

"The Blue Bird of Détente." *Vogue*, Nov. 1975.

"The Hucksters." *Daily Variety*, June 26, 1947.

"The Killers." *Daily Variety*, Aug. 7, 1946.

"The Killers . . . Ava Gardner." Universal Studio Publicity, May 31, 1946, *Universal Collection*, USC.

"The Life and Times of Judge Roy Bean." Pressbook.

"The Man Who Wouldn't Look at Ava Gardner." *Look*, Oct. 6, 1953.

"The Naked Maja." MGM Pressbook.

"The Real Ava Gardner—Uncensored." *Vue*, Sept. 1955.

"The Screen Was Silver in Her Day." *Time*, Mar. 11, 1985.

"The Story Behind the Photos." *Parade*, Nov. 16, 1996.

"The Truth About Ava's Rough Romance." *Modern Screen*, n.d., circa 1966.

"The Woman Who Took Mia's Place." *Modern Screen*, Aug. 1968.

"There comes a time . . ." *Newsweek*, July 3, 1972.

"They'd Rather Fight Than Smooch." N.p., circa 1966.

"Thieves Take $16,800 of Sinatras' Jewelry." *Los Angeles Times*, Dec. 11, 1951.

"Three Faces of Ava." *Smithfield Herald*, Jan. 30, 1990.

"Throat—Not Heart—Trouble." *Northern Daily Telegraph* (England), May 16, 1950.

"Tooter Artie Shaw Toots Sour Legal Note in Wedding." *Los Angeles Daily News*, Oct. 30, 1946.

"Tragedy of Lidice Poorly Re-enacted." *Hollywood Reporter*, June 9, 1943.

"Travels in Spain." *Derby Evening Telegraph*, May 26, 1950.

"Wave from American film actress . . ." *Bournemouth Echo* (England), Apr. 18, 1950.

"Welcome Ava!" *Film World* 2, no. 6, 1950.

"What Ava Gardner Wants from Marriage." *Screen Guide*, Dec. 1951.

"What Bob Ruark Wrote About Ava's Home Town." *Smithfield Herald*, Nov. 17, 1953.

"What I like about London . . ." *Newsweek*, Nov. 1, 1976.

"What Makes Ava Run?" *Movieland*, Apr. 1955.

"Where did 27-year-old Hollywood star go . . ." *Daily Mail*, Mar. 27, 1950.

"Wife Divorces Artie Shaw as 'Utterly Selfish.'" *Los Angeles Examiner*, Oct. 24, 1946.

"Will Career Trouble Kill the Sinatra-Gardner Marriage?" *Movie Land*, Feb. 1953.

"Will Sinatras Luck Last?" *Screen Guide*, Nov. 1951.

"Wilson Girl in Movies." *Raleigh News and Observer*, July 24, 1941.

"With Omar Sharif." *Time*, Dec. 8, 2003.

"Zinnemann, Cast, Chertok Show Class." *Hollywood Reporter*, Mar. 11, 1942. 24, 1950.

Albelli, Alfred, and Neal Patterson. "Divorces Illegal, Still Wed to Ava, Artie Tells Amber." Aug. 7, 1948.

Archerd, Armand. "Ava Gardner—Hollywood's Loneliest Wife." *Filmland*, Apr. 1953.

Ardagh, John. "Huston in Eden." *Sight and Sound*, Autumn 1964.

Arons, Rana. "New Flavor for Ava." *Photoplay*, Oct. 1976.

Aulis, Jack. "Ava Gardner May Return." *Raleigh News and Observer*, Feb. 19, 1973.

Baer, Atra. "Along Came Frankie." *Los Angeles Herald and Express*, Oct. 15, 1953.

Banker, Fred. "Speed Cameraman." *American Cinematographer*, Oct. 1948.

Battelle, Phyllis. "Ava Chases Romance." *Daily Sketch*, Nov. 27, 1956.

Beckett, Kathleen. "Prime Time for Ava." *US*, Mar. 11, 1985.

Bhutta, Samiya. "Lt. Gen. Shah Rafi Alam 1932–2004." *Lahore Daily Times* (Pakistan), April 9, 2004.

Biderson, Lina. "Beautiful Ava Gardner Says She's 'Old Broad.'" *Entertainment Today*, Feb. 11, 1977.

Bledsoe, Jerry. "Pretty Student Graduates to Films." *Greensboro News and Record* (NC), July 30, 1982.

Block, Maxine. "Ava Gardner." *Screen Guide*, circa 1950, Constance McCormick Collection, USC.

Bosquet, Jean. "Star in Will-o'-Wisp Hunt for Happiness." *Los Angeles Examiner*, May 22, 1960.

Botham, Noel, and David Wright. "Ava Gardner Was Obsessed with Ex-Hubby Sinatra Until the End." *National Enquirer*, Feb. 13, 1990.

Bowers, Lynn. "Gable Fable." *Movie Show*, 1947, Constance McCormick Collection, USC.

Boyd, James. "When the Band Played On—Up In Ava Gardner's Room." *Confidential*, Sept. 1957.

Boyle, Hal. "Ava Gardner Wants to Change Her Public Image." *AP Newsfeatures*, Oct. 5, 1966.

Brady, James. "With Ava Gardner." *Parade*, Oct. 15, 1989.

Brady, Thomas F. "New Hollywood Enterprise." *New York Times*, Jan. 9, 1949.

————. "Gable's Back (Again) and Metro's Got Him in 'The Hucksters.'" *New York Times*, Jan. 19, 1947.

Breen, Joseph. Letter to Maurice Pivar, Mar. 13, 1946, Mark Hellinger Collection, USC.

Bretton, John. "There's No Place Like Home." *Picturegoer*, July 8, 1950.

Brown, Bob. "Ava Rushes to His Side." *Motion Picture*, July 1968.

Buckholder, T. C. "Mobster Mickey Cohen Squeals on Mob's Crime Life." *National Tattler*, Apr. 15, 1972.

Burns, Sally. "Tragic Triangle. *Photoplay*," n.d., circa 1950.

Caldwell, Rowena. "Twilight of a Goddess." *Ladies' Home Journal*, July 1972.

Calloway, James. "Back Roads Lead to Ava Museum." *Raleigh News and Observer*, Aug. 6, 1982.

Cannon, Doris. "Barefooted Ava Drops In." *Smithfield Herald*, May 16, 1978.

————. "Big Sister Dynamic Force Behind Film Star's Career." *Smithfield Herald*, July 24, 1987.

————. "Frank Cared Lovingly for Ava." *Smithfield-Selma Sun*, May 21, 1998.

————. "Who was Ava Gardner?" *Smithfield Herald*, Jan. 30, 1990.

Carlile, Tom. "The Truth About Ava Gardner." *Photoplay*, Jan. 1951.

Carroll, Harrison. "Frankie Visits 'Lone Star' Set." *Los Angeles Evening Herald Express*, May 24, 1981.

Cassandra. "What Is a Native Land?" *Daily Mirror*, June 1, 1950.

Castro, Tony. "Ailing Ava Gardner Tells Her Friends: I'll Die Happy." *National Enquirer*, Mar. 17, 1987.

Cerio, Gregory. "Notes from Underground." *Newsweek*, Feb. 5, 1990.

Champlin, Charles. "Ava Gardner—Image of a Bygone Era." Los Angeles Times, Jan. 26, 1990.

Chaplin, Charles. Note to John Huston, July 21, 1964. John Huston Collection, Margaret Herrick Library.

Chinigo, Michael. "Ava May Get Proxy Decree in Mexico." *Los Angeles Examiner*, Nov. 22, 1956.

Clarke, Susan. "Why They Are the Battling Sinatras." *Look*, Sept. 23, 1952.

Coleman, John. "Mayerling Mould." *New Statesman*, Oct. 25, 1968.

Connard, Avril. "Over on the Small Screen." *Today*, Apr. 11, 1986.

Conniff, Frank. "Two Men and a Girl—An Old Publicity Stunt." *New York Journal-American*, May 22, 1950.

Connolley, James. "Ava's Off Beat Taste in Men." *Sir*, Apr. 1957.

Conway, Harold. "Where Is Our Vera-Ellen?" *Evening Standard*, May.

Costin, Glynis. "The Original Paparazzo." *W*, Sept. 3–10, 1990.

Craven, Charles. "Byways of the News." *Raleigh News and Observer*, Dec. 6, 1968.

Crowther, Bosley. "Violence Erupts Again." *New York Times*, Sept. 1, 1946.

Cullum, Paul. "My So-Called Rotten Life." *Los Angeles Weekly*, Nov. 3, 2000.

Curran, Bob. "Has Frankie Had It?" *Motion Picture*, July 1952.

Dacre, Paul. "Ava . . . Still the High Priestess of Love." *Daily Mail*, May 27, 1980.

Darnton, Charles. "Wed Early, Too, Rule of Rooney." *New York Herald-Tribune*, Jan. 18, 1942.

Davidson, Bill. "Stormy Love with Ava." *Daily Herald*, June 8, 1957.

Davis, Emma Lee. "Ava Reports Wonderful Time Visiting Smithfield." *Smithfield Herald*, Dec. 6, 1968.

Davis, Victor. "I'm Not in Bad Nick for an Old Broad." *Mail on Sundays*, Sept. 21, 1986.

Donoghue, Quinn. "Ava—Beauty in Exile." *Hollywood Studio Magazine*, Oct. 1979.

Drew, Frances Huggins. "Smithfield and Its Ava Enjoy Native's Return." N.p., circa 1948, Heritage Center Collection, Smithfield, NC.

Dunne, Dominick. "Ava Now." *Vanity Fair*, June 1984.

Engle, William. "The Forever Amber Story." *American Weekly*, Feb. 2, 1947.

Epstein, Florence. "That Girl Ava." 1955.

Evans, Peter. "All Beautiful Women Should Smash Their Mirrors Early." N.p., circa 1990, British Film Institute Collection.

Faris, Clint. "It Was a Folksy Day at Rock Ridge." *Wilson Daily Times* (NC), May 1978.

Fink, Hymie. "I Was There." *Photoplay*, Dec. 1951.

Fitzgerald, John. "Lies Still Hurt Tired Ava." *Gazette*, Sept. 25, 1978.

Folkart, Burt. "Ava Gardner, Sultry Film Star, Dies at 67 in London." *Los Angeles Times*, Jan. 26, 1990.

Fowler, Raymond. "Howard Hughes." *Psychology Today*, May 1986.

Frank, Stanley. "Hollywood's Fabulous Brat." *Saturday Evening Post*, Dec. 6, 1947.

Franklin, Olga. "AVA—the beauty who rejected him." *Daily Sketch*, Aug. 16, 1956.

———. "Beaten Up—By the Cops He Hated." *Daily Sketch*, Aug. 18, 1956.

Frazier, George. "Mickey Rooney Comes of Age." *Coronet*, Oct. 1948.

Friedman, Favius. "Future Indefinite?" *Screen Stars*, n.d., circa 1957, Constance Mc-Cormick Collection, USC.

Gardner, Ava. "Ava Gardner Admits Love Has Let Me Down." *The People*, Mar. 16, 1958.

———. "Ava Gardner on the Snares of Stardom." *The People*, Mar. 30, 1958.

———. "Confessions of an ex-Playgirl." *Modern Screen*, n.d., circa 1949, Constance McCormick Collection, USC.

———. "Honeymoon with Ava Gardner." N.p. Mar. 23, 1958.

———. "Subbing for Hollywood Columnist; Ava Writes of Women in Africa." *Smithfield Herald*, Sept. 17, 1954.

———. "Take My Word for It." *Modern Screen*, Feb. 1954.

———. "The Role I liked Best." *Saturday Evening Post*, Oct. 23, 1948.

———. Letter to Clara Whitley. June 1936. Heritage Center File, Smithfield, NC.

———. Letter to George Cukor, Aug. 16, 1958. Margaret Herrick Library.

Gibbons, Ed. "Ava Gardner—Beauty and the Bullfighters." *Climax*, Apr. 1961.

Graham, Roy. "Ava Gardner: The Bullfighters' Delight." *Confidential*, circa 1956.

Graham, Sheilah. "Busy Britisher." *Hollywood Citizen News*, Mar. 27, 1970.

————. "Hollywood's Best Known Mystery." *Modern Screen*, Apr. 1949.

Grant, Jack D. "Gable, Deborah Kerr Commanding Team." *Hollywood Reporter*, June 26, 1947.

————. "The Killers." *Hollywood Reporter*, Aug. 7, 1946.

Graves, Robert. "Toast to Ava Gardner." *New Yorker*, April 26, 1958.

Green, Michelle, Doris Bacon, et al. "Many Passions, No Regrets." *People*, Feb. 12, 1990.

Gris, Henry. "Ava Gardner: The Lady is Tough." *Cosmopolitan*, July 1976.

Grunwald, Henry. "Witness." *Time*, Mar. 9, 1998.

Hagerty, Bill. "Shy Ava Loves the Quiet Life." *Daily Mirror*, Feb. 5, 1977.

Hamilton, Sara. "Heartbreak for Mickey Rooney." *Photoplay*, Dec. 1942.

Hanna, David. "Ava Gardner . . . the Runaway Star." *Los Angeles Herald Examiner*, Dec. 2, 1962.

————. "What Happened to the Girl Who Had Everything." *Cosmopolitan*, Nov. 1962.

————. "Will Ava Gardner Steal Burton from Liz?" *Confidential*, Nov. 1963.

Harris, John. "Ava Gardner on Films and Love." *Los Angeles Herald Examiner*, May 1, 1976.

————. "Ava on Come Back Trail." *Los Angeles Herald Examiner*, Mar. 17, 1975.

Harris, Radie. "Broadway Ballyhoo." *Hollywood Reporter*, Apr. 23, 1971.

Hastings, Peter. "Frankie wooed with diamonds and Coke." *Sydney Telegraph*, May 21, 1950.

Hauptfuhrer, Fred. "Ava Gardner Is Back." *People*, Jan. 11, 1982.

Hawkins, Robert F. "Inside a 'Little Hut' in Italy." *New York Times*, Sept. 9, 1956.

Henry, Al. "Glamour People." *Classic Images*, Summer 1980.

Hildred, Stafford. "Screen Beauty Ava Plays a Beast." *Star*, Dec. 4, 1986.

Hirshberg, Jack. "Amador de Los Rios No. 6." Jack Hirshberg Collection, Margaret Herrick Library.

Holman, Gordon. "Sinatra Talks—But Not of Ava." *Evening Standard*, July 3, 1950.

Holt, Paul. "This Gardner's Good." *Picturegoer*, Feb. 7, 1953.

Hopper, Hedda. "A New Ava Rises from Filmy Past." *Los Angeles Times*, n.d., circa 1951.

————. "Ava Gardner Notes." Hedda Hopper Collection, Margaret Herrick Library.

————. "Ava Gardner to Do Film for Bronston." June 11, 1962.

————. "Ava Will Meet Attorney; May Ask Sinatra Divorce." *Los Angeles Times*, Oct. 28, 1953.

————. "Ava's Life is Frantic Hunt for Happiness." *Los Angeles Times*, Aug. 18, 1957.

————. "Ava's Unpredictable Future Is Still More Unpredictable." *Los Angeles Times*, n.d., circa 1952, USC.

————. "Culture, Not Love, Her Aim Now, Says Ava Gardner." *Los Angeles Times*, Aug. 24, 1947.

————. "Frank Talks Back." *New York Daily News*, May 25, 1950.

————. "Mickey Rooney's Wife to File Second Action for Divorce." *Los Angeles Times*, Apr. 30, 1943.

——. "Metro Lets Ava Gardner Have Choice of 3 Films." *Chicago Tribune*, Aug. 5, 1960.

——. "Mickey Rooney and Wife Part." Feb. 5, 1943.

——. "Torchy Ava Gardner Croons 'Where's the Right Man?' Tune." *Los Angeles Times*, May 15, 1949.

——. "Why Can't Ava Stay Married?" *Chicago Tribune Magazine*, Aug. 18, 1957.

——. "Why Nancy Sinatra Agreed to Divorce Frank." Hedda Hopper Collection, Margaret Herrick Library.

Hotchner, A. E. "Star Bullfight." *This Week, Los Angeles Times*, Aug. 8, 1954.

Howe, George L. "Small Town Girl." *Weekly Film News*, n.d.

Howe, Herb. "Christmas Eve." *Photoplay*, Dec. 1948.

Hoy, Michael J. "Ava Gardner Confesses." *National Enquirer*, Aug. 10, 1976.

Hoyle, Bernadette. "Ava Returns Here to Visit Relatives." *Smithfield Herald*, Jan. 7, 1949.

Hudgins, Morgan. "Bivouac on the Trail of 'Mogambo' in Africa." *New York Times*, Dec. 1952.

——. "Logistics of a Bivouac on the Liffey River." *New York Times*, 1953.

Hunter, William. *Glasgow Herald*, Jan. 3, 1985.

Huston, John. Letter to Charles Chaplin, July 16, 1964, John Huston Collection, Margaret Herrick Library.

Huston, John, and Anthony Veiller. "The Killers." Draft script pages, John Huston Collection, Margaret Herrick Library.

Hyams, Joe. "Ava Gardner: In Search of Love." *Look*, Dec. 11, 1956.

——. "My Men." *The People*, Dec. 16, 1956.

——. "That Old Devil Jealousy." *The People*, Oct. 23, 1956.

——. "The Private Hell of Ava Gardner." *Look*, Nov. 27, 1956.

——. "The Private Hell of Ava Gardner." *The People*, Dec. 9, 1956.

International News Service. "Nev. Official Challenges Sinatra Wedding." *Los Angeles Evening Herald and Express*, Dec. 6, 1951.

Italie, Hillel. "Mike Nichols reflects on *The Graduate*." Associated Press, Mar. 2, 1997.

Ivey, John Mark. "Chairman of the Board Retires." N.p. Summer 1998.

Jackson, Ray. "The Day Ava Gardner Sneaked 400 Gs in Cash Out of the USA." *Top Secret*, Oct. 1959.

Jaffe, Rona. "The Private Demons of Ava Gardner." *Good Housekeeping*, 1961.

James, Antony. "Ava's Secret Pact with Liz." *Whisper*, Jan. 1964.

Jamison, Barbara Berch. "You Can't See the Jungle For the Stars." *New York Times*, 1952.

Johnson, Erskine. Column. *Los Angeles Daily News*, Dec. 19, 1951.

Kael, Pauline. *New Republic*, Oct. 22, 1966.

Kaplan, Peter W. "From Clark Gable to J.R. with Ava Gardner." *New York Times*, Feb. 25, 1985.

Kauffman, Stanley. "On the Beach." *New Republic*, Dec. 14, 1959.

Kaufman, Joanne. "Ava My Story." *New York Times Book Review*, Nov. 18, 1990.

Kennedy, Paul P. "The Sun Also Rises South of the Border." *New York Times*, May 5, 1957.

Kobal, John. "A Memory of Ava Gardner." Sotheby's Catalog, Nov. 21, 1990.

Kramer, Stanley. "The Many Moods of Ava." *American Weekly*, Jan. 24, 1960.

La Barre, Harriet. "Ava in Pakistan." *Cosmopolitan*, March 1956.

Lane, Lydia. "Ava Gardner Confides Glamour Tricks in Caring for Lips and Tired Eyes." *Los Angeles Times*, July 29, 1951.

Lassiter, Tom. "Fan Makes Her Home a Museum. *Smithfield Times*. N.d.

Lawrenson, Helen. "Shooting 'The Sun' With Ava." *Esquire*, Oct. 1957.

———. "The Nightmare of the Iguana." *Show*, Jan. 1964.

Layng, Rosemary. "Honey Chile." *Modern Screen*, 1947, Constance McCormick Collection, USC.

Levin, Robert J. "The Strange Exile of Ava Gardner." *Redbook*, 1960.

Lewin, David. "She Can't Act, She Can't Talk, She's Terrific." *You Magazine*, Dec. 5, 1985.

———. "Ava Gardner Flies Here." *Daily Express*. Mar. 27, 1950.

———. "Ava to Divorce Sinatra." *Daily Express*, Oct. 30, 1953.

———. "Ava, a True Goddess." *Daily Mail*, Jan. 26, 1990.

———. "Mario Flies Here with 18 Poems for Ava." *Daily Express*, June 1950.

———. "Mario Goes Bull-Fighting—Sinatra Stays with Ava." *Daily Express*, May 15, 1950.

———. "Spotlight." *Daily Express*, May 17, 1950.

Lightman, Herb A. "The Killers." *American Cinematographer*, Dec. 1946.

Loring, Charles. "Photographing the Bible in Dimension-150." *American Cinematographer*, Feb. 1965.

Lu, Adrienne. "Screen legend pays tribute to first love." *Raleigh News and Observer*, Apr. 27, 2001.

Mackay, Ian. "An Open Letter to Frank Sinatra." *News Chronicle*, July 5, 1950.

MacPherson, Virginia. "Ava in Best Film." *Los Angeles Herald Express*, Feb. 13, 1951.

Madigan, Dan. "Remembering Ava." *All About Ava*, Spring 1999.

Mann, Roderick. "A Few Rotten Hands, But Game's Rarely Dull." *Los Angeles Herald Examiner*, Mar. 24, 1968.

———. "Ava Finds Beauty Can Be a Drawback." *Sunday Express*, Mar. 10, 1968.

———. "Ava Flourishes in Her Own Way." *Los Angeles Times*, July 6, 1975.

———. "Ave Ava: A Maverick's Homecoming." *Los Angeles Times*, Feb. 17, 1985.

———. "Films, Privacy and Ava Gardner." *Los Angeles Times*, April 20, 1978.

———. "How Fame Can Help—By Ava." *Sunday Express*, Sept. 28, 1969.

———. "How the Leader Ruled the Rebels of the Clan." *Sunday Express*, Mar. 28, 1971.

Manners, Dorothy. "Ava Gardner's Ultimatum." *Los Angeles Herald Examiner*, May 2, 1975.

———. "Ava Gets Down to Business on Set." *Los Angeles Herald Examiner*, May 20, 1974.

———. "Sad Visit for Ava Gardner." *Los Angeles Herald Examiner*, Sept. 1, 1976.

Martin, Pete. "Tarheel Tornado." *Saturday Evening Post*, June 5, 1948.

Martland, John. "Franks for the Memories." *Stage*, May 27, 1998.

Maxwell, Elsa. "The Gardner-Sinatra Jigsaw." *Photoplay*, July 1951.

McBride, Joseph. "Ava Gardner Dies of Pneumonia." *Variety*, Jan. 26, 1990.

———. "Screen Beauty Ava Gardner Dead." *Variety*, Jan. 31, 1990.

McClay, Booker. "Earthquake." *American Cinematographer*, Nov. 1974.

McHarry, Charles. "The Wedding." *Hollywood Yearbook*, 1952.

McKenna, Kristine. "Altered Chords." *Los Angeles Weekly*, Nov. 12, 1999.

Miller, Burton. "Earthquake." *American Cinematographer*, Nov. 1974.

Mooring, W. H. "Question Mark for Ava." *Picturegoer*, Oct. 1, 1949.

Morris, Ted, and Jane Morris. "The Amazing Ava!" *Movieland*, 1949, Constance Mc-Cormick Collection, USC.

Morrison, Bill. "The Quintessential Star." *Raleigh News and Observer*, Jan. 27, 1990.

Mosby, Aline. "Aline Mosby in Hollywood." *Beverly Hills Newslife*, Nov. 16, 1953.

———. "Ava Refutes Rumors on Marriage Break." *Hollywood Citizen-News*, Nov. 14, 1953.

———. "No Chance of Patching It Up with Sinatra, Ava Reveals." *Los Angeles Daily News*, Nov. 21, 1953.

Mosley, Leonard. "Ava Saw a Way to Stardom." *Daily Express*, Nov. 25, 1949.

———. "Ava Tames Them All." *Daily Express*, Oct. 30, 1953.

———. "Bhowani Junction." *Daily Express*, Aug. 30, 1956.

———. "I Hate to Be Cruel to Ava." *Daily Express*, May 7, 1963.

Muir, Florabel. "Ava and Frankie." *Photoplay*, n.d., circa 1953, Constance McCormick Collection, USC.

———. "The Truth About Dope in Hollywood." *Photoplay*, Dec. 1948.

Murphy, Nicola. "Selling Fruits of Gardner's life." *Times* (London), June 12, 1990.

Musel, Robert. "Without Frankie." *Motion Picture*, Jan. 1954.

Nash, Roy. "Life and Love—By Ava Gardner." *Star*, Jan. 6, 1955.

Nepean, Edith. "Round the British Studios." *Picture Show*, Aug. 26, 1950.

Nolan, Patricia. "Ava Gardner Regrets: 'I Failed as a Wife.'" *Women's World*, July 23, 1985.

Nolan, Tom. "Still Cranky After All These Years." *Los Angeles*, May 1990.

Norman, Barry. "Now That Someone's Said 'No' to Ava." N.p., Dec. 1962.

O'Neill, Enid. "Gardner the Rebel." *Picturegoer*, Aug. 26, 1950.

Oakes, Peter. "Oh, Ava! How Could You Do It?" *People*, Oct. 27, 1968.

Oppenheimer, Peer. "Ava Gardner Can't Forget Frank Sinatra." *Family Weekly*, May 31, 1959.

———. "Ava Gardner: The Woman Who Could Have Had Everything." *Family Weekly*, Feb. 28, 1965.

Osborne, Robert. "Rambling Reporter." *Hollywood Reporter*, Jan. 26, 1990.

Parsons, Louella O. "Actor's Bride Today Consulting Lawyer About Divorce." N.p., July 1942.

———. "Ava Denies Retirement." May 15, 1950.

———. "Ava Gardner Undergoes Emergency Operation." *Los Angeles Examiner*, May 25, 1952.

————. "Ava Pauses in Vegas to See Sinatra, But Nancy Is Visiting Him." Los Angeles Examiner, Feb. 7, 1961.

————. "Ava's Plan to Marry 'Surprise.'" Los Angeles Examiner, Dec. 28, 1956.

————. "Ava . . ." Los Angeles Herald Examiner, June 28, 1963.

————. "On my desk . . ." Los Angeles Examiner, Jan. 25, 1958.

————. "Retakes Delay Rooney Nuptials." Los Angeles Examiner, Jan. 7, 1942.

————. "Schary Picks Ava Gardner for Remake of 'Painted Veil.'" Los Angeles Examiner, Apr. 18, 1955.

————. "Surgery Undergone by Ava." Los Angeles Herald Examiner, Jan. 20, 1963.

————. "In Hollywood with Ava Gardner." Los Angeles Examiner, n.d.

————. "Sinatra-Ava Make-Up Real." Los Angeles Examiner, Oct. 30, 1952.

————. "There has been so much talk about Ava Gardner's beautiful face . . ." Los Angeles Examiner, Jan. 10, 1958.

Peer, Robert. "I Want to Get Married!" Movie Stars Parade, Dec. 1948.

Pegler, Westbrook. "Pegler Says: Frankie and Ava Do London!" Los Angeles Examiner, Dec. 20, 1951.

Perkins, V. F. "The Cinema of Nicholas Ray." Movie 9. 1963.

Pinsky, Mark. "Where Ava Grew Up." Los Angeles Times, Nov. 3, 1986.

Proctor, Kay. "It's Marriage for Mickey." Motion Picture, circa 1942.

Prowler, Paul. "The Real Truth About Ava Gardner and Sammy Davis, Jr." Police Gazette, May 1955.

Puig, Claudia. "Peoplewatch: Celebrities Bid Farewell to Gardner." Jan. 30, 1990.

Purnell, Tony, and Ian Black. "Sinatra Weeps as His Ava Dies Alone." Daily Mirror, Jan. 26, 1990.

Quillin, Martha. "Ava Gardner Laid to Rest in Soil that Nurtured Her Tar Heel roots." Raleigh News and Observer, Jan. 30, 1990.

Reddy, Thomas. "Ava Gardner Again to Seek Career." Los Angeles Examiner, Apr. 23, 1944.

Redelings, Lowell E. "The Hollywood Scene: One Minute Interviews." Hollywood Citizen-News, September 19, 1952.

————. "The Hollywood Scene." Hollywood Citizen-News, May 27, 1959.

Reed, Rex. "Ava Finds Peace at Hometown Family Reunion." New York Daily News, 1978.

————. "Ava: Life in the Afternoon." Esquire, May 1967.

————. "The Road Gets Tough for the Barefoot Contessa." GQ, April 1983.

————. "Ava, What a Dame!" Talk, Dec–Jan, 1999–2000.

Reynolds, Oliver. "The 8 Secret Sins of Ava Gardner." Hush-Hush, Nov. 1961.

Rickey, Carrie. "Ava Gardner's Vivid Life." Philadelphia Inquirer, Jan. 26, 1990.

Robinson, David. "Wiener Blut." Times, Oct. 24, 1968.

Rochlen, Kendis. "Candid Kendis: Author Shaw Speaks." Mirror-News, Sept. 12, 1956.

Rogers, Kiley. "Ava Gardner's Wild Parties." Police Gazette, Jan. 1965.

Ross, Frank, and Leeds Moberley. "Bullfighter a 'Nice Guy' to Sinatra." New York Daily News, May 22, 1950.

Rotella, Mark. "Simply Red." *New York Times*, Aug. 10, 2003.

Rothman, Cliff. "Artie Shaw's Solo Boat." *Vanity Fair*, June 1999.

Samson, Leonard. "Meet a Matador." *Answers*, n.p., Aug. 19, 1950.

Sandilands, John. " 'Oh Gahd,' said Ava Gardner." *Nova*, June 1968.

Saroyan, Aram. "Ava's Loves, Ava's Life." *Los Angeles Times*, Jan. 28, 1990.

Saunders, Marsha. "We Finally Made It." *Modern Screen*, Feb. 1952.

Schallert, Edwin. "Ava Gardner May File Early Divorce Action." *Los Angeles Times*, May 11, 1957.

———. "Film Roles Belie Her Real Self, Says Ava." N.d., cira 1950.

Schwartz, Dan. "Ava Gardner: My Movie Career Was a 'Life of Slavery.' " N.p., n.d.

Scott, John L. "Little Ava Goes Back to Learnin'." *Los Angeles Times*, June 30, 1946.

Scott, Vernon. "Ava." *Ladies' Home Journal*, Nov. 1974.

Screencomber. "Close-Ups." *Kinematograph*, May 25, 1950.

Shearer, Lloyd. "Mickey Rooney Tells All." *Parade Magazine*, 1991.

———. "What It Means to Be One of Mickey Rooney's Six Wives." *Parade*, June 29, 1967.

Sheffield, Dewey. "North Carolina's Shining Star." N.p., n.d., circa 1978.

Sher, Jack. "From Hut 67 to Hollywood." Clipping, fan magazine, circa 1948.

Shipman, David. "In the Picture." *Radio Times*, (England), Mar. 27, 1982.

Skolsky, Sidney. "Hollywood Is My Beat." *New York Post*, June 2, 1950.

———. "Tintypes." *Hollywood Citizen-News*, Jan. 7, 1942.

———. "Tintypes." *Hollywood Citizen-News*, Oct. 15, 1953.

———. "Tintypes." *Hollywood Citizen-News*, July 19, 1951.

———. "Tintypes: Ava Gardner." *Hollywood Citizen-News*, Oct. 17, 1964.

Sloan, Robin Adams. "DON'T INVITE . . ." *Los Angeles Herald Examiner*, June 24, 1975.

———. "Gossip Column." *Los Angeles Herald Examiner*, Jan. 10, 1975.

———. "Gossip Column." *Los Angeles Herald Examiner*, Jan. 26, 1975.

———. "Gossip Column." *Los Angeles Herald Examiner*, Oct. 26, 1971.

Smith, Alan Braham, Noel Botham, and Barbara Sternig. "Sinatra's Wife Furious over His Devotion to Ex-Wife." *National Enquirer*, Mar. 8, 1988.

Smith, Liz. "Ava Gardner, one of the . . ." *Los Angeles Herald Examiner*, Dec. 15, 1988.

———. Column *Los Angeles Times*, May 29, 1991.

Smith, Robert G. "Ava Predicted 'Awful Storm' Would Announce Her Death." *National Enquirer*, Feb. 13, 1990.

Speck, Gregory. "Ava Gardner." *Interview*, Dec. 1986.

———. "Ava Gardner." *Cable Guide*, Dec. 1988.

Speers, W. "Newsmakers." *Philadelphia Inquirer*, Jan. 31, 1990.

St. Johns, Adela Rogers. "The Hollywood Story: Ava and Mickey." *American Weekly*, Sept. 9, 1951.

———. "The Hollywood Story: Ava Gardner's Rising Star." *American Weekly*, Aug. 26, 1951.

————. "The Hollywood Story: Problems of Frankie and Van." [*sic*] *American Weekly*, Sept. 16, 1951.

Starr, Jimmy. "Ava Gardner to Get Big M-G-M Build-Up." *Los Angeles Evening Herald and Express*, Feb. 8, 1951.

Sterling, Bill. "A Millionaire's Strange Love for Ava Gardner." *Whisper*, Nov. 1961.

Stevens, Brac. "Human Side of a Heavenly Body." *Screenland*, 1949.

Streete, Horton. "What Makes Ava Run for Sammy Davis, Jr." *Confidential*, March 1955.

Swift, Orla. "Dutch Artist Bequeaths Ava Gardner Treasures." *Raleigh News & Observer*, May 2, 2002.

Taylor, Russell. "Encounter with Siodmak." *Sight and Sound*, Summer-Autumn 1959.

Taylor, Vestral. "Thanks for the Memories." *Big Reel*, Feb. 1986.

Thomas, Carson L. "How Sick-sick-sick Can Frankie Get?" *On the QT*, Jan. 1956.

Thornton, Michael. "All About Ava." *Daily Express*, Dec. 13, 1982.

Todd, R. "Did Ava Gardner Strike Out with Roger Maris?" *Photoplay*, Jan. 1962.

Tomkies, Mike. "Hollywood's Runaway." N.d., circa 1963.

Tuohy, William. "Ava Gardner—Still That Certain Something." *Los Angeles Times*, May 9, 1976.

Tusher, Bill. "The Strange Loves and Times of Ava Gardner." *Silver Screen*, Apr. 57.

————. "What Ava Wants Ava (Seldom) Gets." *Silver Screen*, Oct. 1955.

United Press. "Actress Gets Rest from Film." *Los Angeles Herald Express*, May 13, 1950.

————. "Ava Doesn't Write; Toreador's Love Cools." Los Angeles Times, Jan. 19, 1951.

————. "Ava Hints Crooner's the Man—If Divorced." *Los Angeles Times*, May 15, 1950.

————. "Ava Tells Off Policeman." N.p. clipping, Aug. 1951.

————. "Bullfighter Rival of Sinatra Quite Sure of Ava's Love." *Los Angeles Times*, May 14, 1950.

————. "Grouchy Sinatra Meets Ava Gardner in Spain." *Los Angeles Times*, May 12, 1950.

Usher, Shawn. "Sinatra: His Way." *Daily Mail*, Dec. 16, 1995.

————. "Sinatra: His Way; Part Two." *Daily Mail*, Dec. 18, 1995.

Vallance, Tom. "Better Than She Knew." *What's On in London*, Feb. 7, 1990.

Van Deusen, Charles. "Artie Shaw Graduates Another Wife." *American Weekly*, June 5, 1955.

Victor, Thelda, with Muriel Davidson. "The Drama the Cameras Missed." N.P., n.d.

Vincent, Mal. "Ape Over Ava." *Virginian-Pilot*, Aug. 8, 1980.

Voland, John. "Film Femme Fatale Ava Gardner Dies." *Hollywood Reporter*, Jan. 26, 1990.

Wade, Jack. "Can Ava Gardner Be Herself?" *Modern Screen*, Nov. 1949.

Wallers, Betty. "Ava, Sinatra Play Game of Heartache." *Los Angeles Examiner*, May 1, 1960.

————. "Torrid Star's Wild Parties." *Los Angeles Examiner*, May 15, 1960.

Wandworth, James. "The Strange Case of Gardner-Sinatra." N.d., circa 1951. Constance McCormick Collection, USC.

Wansell, Geoffrey. "Star in a Leafy Square." *Sunday Telegraph Magazine*, July 8, 1984.

Warren, Jill. "New Name for Happiness." *Photoplay*, Feb. 1952.

Waterbury, Ruth. "Ava Gardner's Dry Tears." *Photoplay*, Apr. 1957.

————. "Film Roles Belie Self, Ava Insists." *Los Angeles Examiner*, Oct. 19, 1952.

————. "The Life and Loves of Ava Gardner." *Photoplay*, Feb. 1952.

————. "Think of Her with Tenderness . . . She Needs It!" *Motion Picture*, n.d., circa 1959, Constance McCormick Collection, USC.

————. "Untamed." *Photoplay*, Apr. 1973.

Watson, Bob. "Haunted." *Photoplay*, Nov. 1959.

Weatherby, W. J. "The Myth and Lucy Johnson." *Guardian*, Jan. 26, 1990.

Whitcomb, Noel. "The Answer to Frankie's Wrath Was in the Negative." *Daily Mirror*, July 8, 1950.

Whitley, Reg. "They Got Tough with Ava!" *Daily Mirror*, Aug. 31, 1956.

Williams, Jay. "Ava: She Wows 'Em and Wrecks 'Em." *Confidential*, May 1954.

Wilson, A. E. "Cries and Sighs." *London Star*, July 11, 1950.

Wilson, Cecil. "Mogambo." *Daily Mail*, Apr. 9, 1973.

Wilson, Earl. "Ava Boiling Mad over Harsh Letters from Sinatra Fans." *Los Angeles Daily News*, Mar. 25, 1950.

————. "Ava Speaks of Love to Wilson!" *New York Post*, June 26, 1950.

————. "Frankie and Ava Striving to Avert Marriage Crack-up." *Los Angeles Daily News*, Oct. 6, 1952.

————. "Sinatra Bullish in Toreador War for Ava's Love." *New York Post*, May 19, 1950.

Wilson, Liza. "Don't Cry over Me." *American Weekly*, Sept. 8, 1957.

Wiltshire, Maurice. "Coward Comes Back with a Bang." *Daily Mail*, July 8, 1950.

————. "Says Mason: I don't feel guilty about becoming American, British in Hollywood cut pathetic figure." *Daily Mail*, May 31, 1950.

Winner, Michael. "My Beautiful Pal." *Evening Standard*, Jan. 26, 1990.

Wollman, Lisa. "Tribute to actress stems from childhood." *Clayton News* (NC), July 24, 1984.

Wooten, Lynn. "Popularity Continues After Death." *Goldsboro News*, Mar. 20, 1991.

VIDEO/TELEVISION

Tam Lin, introduction by Roddy McDowall. VHS. Republic Home Video, 1988.

"Ava Gardner: Hollywood Diva," *Lifetime's Intimate Portrait*, Lifetime Network.

Seven Days in May, commentary by John Frankenheimer, DVD. Warner Studios, 2003.

"Frank and Ava." *20/20*, ABC.

Strange Testament. 1941. MGM. Exec. producer: Richard Goldstone. Director: Sammy Lee. (Passing Parade short subject.)

Fancy Answers: What's Your I.Q.? 1941. MGM. Exec. producer: Richard Goldstone. Director: Basil Wrangell. (Short subject.)

We Do It Because. 1942. MGM. Exec. producer: Richard Goldstone. Director: Basil Wrangell. (Short subject.)

Mighty Lak a Goat. 1941. MGM. Director: Herbert Glazer. (Our Gang short subject.)

H. M. Pulham Esquire. 1941. MGM. Producer-director: King Vidor. Screenplay: Elizabeth Hill, King Vidor. Cast: Hedy Lamarr, Robert Young, Ruth Hussey, Van Heflin. (AG uncredited.)

We Were Dancing. 1941. MGM. Producer: Orville O. Dull, Robert Z. Leonard. Director: Robert Z. Leonard. Screenplay: Claudine West, Hans Rameau, George Froeschel. Cast: Norma Shearer, Melvyn Douglas, Gail Patrick, Lee Bowman (AG uncredited.)

Joe Smith, American. 1941. MGM. Producer: Jack Chertok. Director: Richard Thorpe. Screenplay: Allen Rivkin. Cast: Robert Young, Marsha Hunt, Darryl Hickman. (AG uncredited.)

This Time for Keeps. 1941. MGM. Producer: Samuel Marx. Director: Charles Reisner. Screenplay: Muriel Roy Bolton, Rian James, Harry Ruskin. Cast: Ann Rutherford, Robert Sterling, Guy Kibbee. (AG uncredited.)

Kid Glove Killer. 1942. MGM. Producer: Jack Chertok. Director: Fred Zinnemann. Screenplay: Allen Rivkin, John Higgins. Cast: Van Heflin, Marsha Hunt, Lee Bowman. (AG uncredited.)

Sunday Punch. 1942. MGM. Producer: Irving Starr. Director: David Miller. Screenplay: Allen Rivkin, Fay Kanin, Michael Kanin. Cast: Jean Rogers, Albert Lundigan, Guy Kibbee. (AG uncredited.)

Calling Dr. Gillespie. 1942. MGM. Producer: Jerome S. Bresler. Director: Harold S.

Bucquet. Screenplay: Willis Goldbeck, Harry Ruskin, Kubec Glasmon (story), based on characters created by Max Brand. Cast: Lionel Barrymore, Philip Dorn, Donna Reed, Philip Brown. (AG uncredited.)

Reunion in France. 1942. MGM. Producer: Joseph L. Mankiewicz. Director: Jules Dassin. Screenplay: Jan Lustig, Marvin Borowsky, Marc Connelly. Cast: Joan Crawford, John Wayne, Philip Dorn. (AG uncredited.)

Pilot No. Five. 1943. MGM. Producer: B. P. Fineman. Director: George Sidney. Screenplay: David Hertz. Cast: Franchot Tone, Gene Kelly, Marsha Hunt. (AG uncredited.)

Du Barry Was a Lady. 1943. MGM. Producer: Arthur Freed. Director: Roy Del Ruth. Screenplay: Irving Brecher. Cast: Red Skelton, Gene Kelly, Lucille Ball, Virginia O'Brien. (AG uncredited.)

Ghosts on the Loose. 1943. Monogram. Producer: Sam Katzman. Director: William Beaudine. Screenplay: Kenneth Higgins. Cast: Leo Gorcey, Huntz Hall, Bobby Jordan, Bela Lugosi, Ava Gardner, Rick Vallin, Minerva Urecal, Stanley Clements.

Hitler's Madman. 1943. MGM. Producer: Seymour Nebenzal. Director: Douglas Sirk. Screenplay: Peretz Hirschbein, Melvin Levy, Doris Malloy. Cast: John Carradine, Patricia Morison, Alan Curtis, Ralph Morgan. (AG uncredited.)

Young Ideas. 1943. MGM. Producer: Robert Sisk. Director: Jules Dassin. Screenplay: Ian McLellan Hunter, Bill Noble. Cast: Susan Peters, Herbert Marshall, Mary Astor. (AG uncredited.)

Lost Angel. 1943. MGM. Producer: Robert Sisk. Director: Roy Rowland. Screenplay: Isobel Lennart. Cast: Margaret O'Brien, James Craig, Marsha Hunt. (AG uncredited.)

Swing Fever. 1943. MGM. Producer: Irving Starr. Director: Tim Whelan. Screenplay: Nat Perrin, Warren Wilson. Cast: Kay Kyser, Marilyn Maxwell, William Gargan, Lena Horne. (AG uncredited.)

Three Men in White. 1944. MGM. Producer-director: Willis Goldbeck. Screenplay: Martin Berkeley, Harry Ruskin, based on characters created by Max Brand. Cast: Lionel Barrymore, Van Johnson, Marilyn Maxwell, Keye Luke, Ava Gardner.

Two Girls and a Sailor. 1944. MGM. Producer: Joe Pasternak. Director: Richard Thorpe. Screenplay: Richard Connell, Gladys Lehman. Cast: June Allyson, Gloria De Haven, Van Johnson, Tom Drake, Jimmy Durante, Henry Stephenson, Ben Blue, Frank Sully, Donald Meek, Frank Jenks, Gracie Allen, Harry James and Orchestra, Xavier Cugat and Orchestra, Lina Romay, Ava Gardner.

Maisie Goes to Reno. 1944. MGM. Producer: George Haight. Director: Harry Beaumont. Screenplay: Mary C. McCall Jr. Cast: Ann Sothern, John Hodiak, Tom Drake, Marta Linden, Paul Cavanagh, Ava Gardner.

Music for Millions. 1944. MGM. Producer: Joe Pasternak. Director: Henry Koster. Screenplay: Myles Connolly. Cast: Margaret O'Brien, Jose Iturbi, June Allyson, Jimmy Durante, Marsha Hunt, Hugh Herbert, Harry Davenport. (AG uncredited.)

Blonde Fever. 1944. MGM. Producer: William W. Wright. Director: Richard Whorf. Screenplay: Patricia Coleman. Cast: Philip Dorn, Mary Astor, Felix Bressart, Gloria Graham, Marshall Thompson. (AG uncredited.)

She Went to the Races. 1945. MGM. Producer: Frederic Stephani. Director: Willis Goldbeck. Screenplay: Lawrence Hazard, from a story by Alan Friedman and De-Vallon Scott. Cast: James Craig, Frances Gifford, Ava Gardner, Edmund Gwenn, Sig Ruman, Reginald Owen, J. M. Kerrigan, Buster Keaton.

Whistle Stop. 1945. United Artists. Producer: Seymour Nebenzal. Director: Leonide Moguy. Screenplay: Philip Yordan, from the novel by Maritta Wolff. Cast: George Raft, Ava Gardner, Victor McLaglen, Tom Conway, Florence Bates, Jorja Cartwright, Mack Gray.

The Killers. 1946. Universal. Producer: Mark Hellinger. Director: Robert Siodmak. Screenplay: Anthony Veiller (John Huston, uncredited). Cast: Burt Lancaster, Ava Gardner, Edmond O'Brien, Albert Dekker, Sam Levene, Phil Brown, Donald MacBride, Charles McGraw, William Conrad, Vince Barnett, Jack Lambert, Jeff Corey.

The Hucksters. 1947. MGM. Producer: Arthur Hornblow, Jr. Director: Jack Conway. Screenplay: Luther Davis, from the novel by Frederic Wakeman. Cast: Clark Gable, Deborah Kerr, Sydney Greenstreet, Adolphe Menjou, Ava Gardner, Keenan Wynn, Edward Arnold.

Singapore. 1947. Universal. Producer: Jerry Bresler. Director: John Brahm. Screenplay: Seton I. Miller, Robert Theoren, from a story by Seton I. Miller. Cast: Fred Mac-Murray, Ava Gardner, Roland Culver, Richard Haydn, Spring Byington, Thomas Gomez.

One Touch of Venus. 1948. Universal. Producers: William Seiter, Lester Cowan. Director: William Seiter. Screenplay: Harry Kurnitz, Frank Tashlin, from the play by S. J. Perelman and Ogden Nash, music by Kurt Weill, from a story by F. Anstey. Cast: Robert Walker, Ava Gardner, Dick Haymes, Eve Arden, Olga San Juan, Tom Conway, James Flavin.

The Bribe. 1948. MGM. Producer: Pandro S. Berman. Director: Robert Z. Leonard. Screenplay: Marguerite Roberts, from a story by Frederick Nebel. Cast: Robert Taylor, Ava Gardner, Charles Laughton, Vincent Price, John Hodiak, Samuel S. Hinds.

The Great Sinner. 1948. MGM. Producer: Gottfried Reinhardt. Director: Robert Siodmak. Screenplay: Ladislas Fodor, Christopher Isherwood, from a story by F. Dostoyevsky. Cast: Gregory Peck, Ava Gardner, Melvyn Douglas, Walter Huston, Ethel Barrymore, Frank Morgan, Ludwig Stossel, Agnes Moorehead.

East Side, West Side. 1949. MGM. Producer: Voldemare Vetliguin. Director: Mervyn LeRoy. Screenplay: Isobel Lennart, from the novel by Marcia Davenport. Cast: Barbara Stanwyck, James Mason, Van Heflin, Ava Gardner, Cyd Charisse, Nancy Davis, Gale Sondergaard, William Conrad, Beverly Michaels, William Frawley.

My Forbidden Past. 1951 (produced in 1949). RKO. Producers: Polan Banks, Robert Sparks. Director: Robert Stevenson. Screenplay: Marion Parsonnet, from the novel by Polan Banks. Cast: Robert Mitchum, Ava Gardner, Melvyn Douglas, Lucille Watson, Janis Carter, Clarence Muse.

Pandora and the Flying Dutchman. 1951. MGM/British Lion. Producer: Albert Lewin, Joseph Kaufman. Director: Albert Lewin. Screenplay: Lewin. Cast: James Mason,

Ava Gardner, Nigel Patrick, Sheila Sim, Harold Warrender, Mario Cabre, Marius Goring, Pamela Kellino.

Show Boat. 1951. MGM. Producer: Arthur Freed. Director: George Sidney. Screenplay: John Lee Mahin, from the stage musical by Jerome Kern and Oscar Hammerstein II, from the novel by Edna Ferber. Cast: Kathryn Grayson, Ava Gardner, Howard Keel, Joe E. Brown, Marge Champion, Gower Champion, Robert Sterling, Agnes Moorehead, Adele Jergens, William Warfield, Frances Williams.

Lone Star. 1952. MGM. Producer: Z. Wayne Griffin. Director: Vincent Sherman. Screenplay: Borden Chase. Cast: Clark Gable, Ava Gardner, Broderick Crawford, Lionel Barrymore, Beulah Bondi, Ed Begley, William Farnum, William Conrad.

The Snows of Kilimanjaro. 1952. 20th Century–Fox. Producer: Darryl F. Zanuck. Director: Henry King. Screenplay: Casey Robinson, from the short story by Ernest Hemingway. Cast: Gregory Peck, Susan Hayward, Ava Gardner, Hildegarde Neff, Leo G. Carroll, Torin Thatcher, Marcel Dalio, Ava Norring.

Band Wagon. 1953. MGM. Producer: Arthur Freed. Director: Vincente Minnelli. Screenplay: Betty Comden and Adolph Green. Cast: Fred Astaire, Cyd Charisse, Jack Buchanan, Oscar Levant, Nanette Fabray (cameo appearance by AG).

Ride, Vaquero! 1953. MGM. Producer: Stephen Ames. Director: John Farrow. Screenplay: Frank Fenton. Cast: Robert Taylor, Ava Gardner, Howard Keel, Anthony Quinn, Kurt Kasznar, Jack Elam, Ted de Corsia, Percy Helton.

Mogambo. 1953. MGM. Producer: Sam Zimbalist. Director: John Ford. Screenplay: John Lee Mahin, based on the screenplay *Red Dust* by Mahin and play by Wilson Collison. Cast: Clark Gable, Ava Gardner, Grace Kelly, Donald Sinden, Philip Stainton, Eric Pohlmann, Laurence Naismith.

Knights of the Round Table. 1954. MGM. Producer: Pandro S. Berman. Director: Richard Thorpe. Screenplay: Talbot Jennings, Jan Lustig, Noel Langley. Cast: Robert Taylor, Ava Gardner, Mel Ferrer, Anne Crawford, Stanley Baker, Felix Aylmer, Maureen Swanson, Gabriel Woolf.

The Barefoot Contessa. 1954. United Artists. Producers: Joseph L. Mankiewicz, Angelo Rizzoli, Robert Haggiag. Director: Joseph L. Mankiewicz. Screenplay: Joseph L. Mankiewicz. Cast: Humphrey Bogart, Ava Gardner, Edmond O'Brien, Marius Goring, Valentina Cortese, Rossano Brazzi, Elizabeth Sellars, Warren Stevens, Mari Aldon, Franco Interlenghi, Bessie Love.

Around the World in 80 Days. 1955. United Artists. Producer: Michael Todd. Director: Michael Anderson. Cast: David Niven, Cantinflas (cameo appearance by AG).

Bhowani Junction. 1956. MGM. Producer: Pandro S. Berman. Director: George Cukor. Screenplay: Sonya Levien, Ivan Moffat, from the novel by John Masters. Cast: Ava Gardner, Stewart Granger, Bill Travers, Francis Matthews, Abraham Sofaer, Marne Maitland, Peter Illing, Edward Chapman, Freda Jackson, Lionel Jeffries.

The Little Hut. 1957. MGM. Producers: Mark Robson, F. Hugh Herbert. Director: Mark Robson, Screenplay: F. Hugh Herbert, from the play by Andre Roussin and English-language adaptation by Nancy Mitford. Cast: Ava Gardner, Stewart Granger, David Niven, Walter Chiari, Finlay Currie, Jean Cadell, Henry Oscar.

The Sun Also Rises. 1957. 20th Century–Fox. Producer: Darryl F. Zanuck. Director: Henry King. Screenplay: Peter Viertel, from the novel by Ernest Hemingway. Cast: Tyrone Power, Ava Gardner, Mel Ferrer, Errol Flynn, Eddie Albert, Gregory Ratoff, Juliette Greco, Robert Evans.

The Naked Maja. 1959. Titanus/MGM. Producer: Goffredo Lombardo. Director: Henry Koster. Screenplay: Giorgio Prosperi, Norman Corwin, Oscar Saul, Albert Lewin. Cast: Ava Gardner, Anthony Franciosa, Amedeo Nazzari, Gino Cervi, Lea Padovani, Massimo Serato.

On the Beach. 1959. United Artists. Producer: Stanley Kramer. Director: Stanley Kramer. Screenplay: John Paxton, James Lee Barrett, from the novel by Nevil Shute. Cast: Gregory Peck, Ava Gardner, Fred Astaire, Anthony Perkins, Donna Anderson, John Tate, Harp McGuire, Lola Brooks, Guy Doleman.

The Angel Wore Red. 1960. MGM/Titanus. Producer: Goffredo Lombardo. Director: Nunnally Johnson. Screenplay: Nunnally Johnson, from the novel by Bruce Marshall. Cast: Ava Gardner, Dirk Bogarde, Joseph Cotten, Vittoria De Sica, Aldo Fabrizi.

55 Days at Peking. 1963. Samuel Bronston. Producer: Samuel Bronston. Director: Nicholas Ray (uncredited: Andrew Marton, Guy Green). Screenplay: Bernard Gordon, Philip Yordan. Cast: Charlton Heston, Ava Gardner, David Niven, Flora Robson, Paul Lucas, Leo Genn, Robert Helpmann, Elizabeth Sellars, John Ireland, Nicholas Ray.

Seven Days in May. 1964. Paramount. Producer: Edward Lewis. Director: John Frankenheimer. Screenplay: Rod Serling, from the novel by Fletcher Knebel and Charles W. Bailey II. Cast: Burt Lancaster, Kirk Douglas, Fredric March, Ava Gardner, Edmond O'Brien, George Macready, Whit Bissell, Hugh Marlowe, Andrew Duggan.

The Night of the Iguana. 1964. MGM/Seven Arts. Producer: Ray Stark. Director: John Huston. Screenplay: John Huston, Anthony Veiller (uncredited: Tennessee Williams) from the play by Tennessee Williams. Cast: Richard Burton, Ava Gardner, Deborah Kerr, Sue Lyon, Grayson Hall, Cyril Delevanti, James "Skip" Ward, Emilio Fernandez, Mary Boylan, Gladys Hill, Eloise Hardt, Thelda Victor, Bernice Starr, Dorothy Vance, Liz Rubey, Barbara Joyce, Betty Proctor, Roberto Leyva, Fidelmar Duran, C. G. Kim.

The Bible. 1966. 20th Century–Fox/De Laurentiis. Producer: Dino De Laurentiis. Director: John Huston. Screenplay: Christopher Fry, also Jonathan Griffin, Ivo Perilli, Vittorio Bonicelli. Cast: Michael Parks, Ulla Bergryd, Richard Harris, John Huston, George C. Scott, Ava Gardner, Peter O'Toole, Zoe Sallis, Franco Nero, Eleanora Rossi-Drago.

Mayerling. 1968. Associated British/Warner-Pathé. Producer: Robert Dorfmann. Director: Terence Young. Screenplay: Terence Young. Cast: Omar Sharif, Catherine Deneuve, James Mason, Ava Gardner, James Robertson Justice, Genevieve Paige, Fabienne Dali.

Tam Lin (aka *The Ballad of Tam Lin, The Devil's Widow*). 1972 (produced in 1969).

Commonwealth United. Producers: Alan Ladd, Jr., Stanley Mann. Director: Roddy McDowall. Screenplay: William Spier. Cast: Ava Gardner, Ian McShane, Richard Wattis, Cyril Cusack, Stephanie Beacham, David Whitman, Sinead Cusack, Joanna Lumley, Jenny Hanley, Madeleine Smith, Michael Bills, Hayward Morse, Julian Barnes, Bruce Robinson.

The Life and Times of Judge Roy Bean. 1972. National General. Producer: John Foreman. Director: John Huston. Screenplay: John Milius. Cast: Paul Newman, Jacqueline Bisset, Ava Gardner, John Huston, Stacy Keach, Roddy McDowall, Anthony Perkins, Tab Hunter, Victoria Principal, Ned Beatty, Anthony Zerbe, Steve Kanaly, Billy Pearson.

Earthquake. 1974. Universal. Producers: Jennings Lang, Mark Robson. Director: Mark Robson. Screenplay: George Fox and Mario Puzo. Cast: Charlton Heston, Ava Gardner, George Kennedy, Lorne Greene, Geneviève Bujold, Richard Roundtree, Marjoe Gortner, Victoria Principal, Lloyd Nolan, Walter Matthau, Monica Lewis, Gabe Dell.

Permission to Kill. 1975. Warner/Sascha. Producer: Paul Mills. Director: Cyril Frankel. Screenplay: Robin Estridge, from his novel. Cast: Dirk Bogarde, Ava Gardner, Timothy Dalton, Frederic Forrest, Bekim Fehmiu, Peggy Sinclair.

The Blue Bird. 1976. 20th Century–Fox/Edward Lewis/Lenfilm. Producer: Paul Maslansky. Director: George Cukor. Screenplay: Hugh Whitemore, Alfred Hayes from the story by Maurice Maeterlinck. Cast: Elizabeth Taylor, Jane Fonda, Ava Gardner, Cicely Tyson, Will Geer, Mona Washbourne, George Cole, Patsy Kensit.

The Cassandra Crossing. 1976. AGF/International Cine/Avco Embassy. Producers: Lew Grade, Carlo Ponti. Director: George Pan Cosmatos. Screenplay: Tom Mankiewicz, Robert Katz, George Cosmatos. Cast: Sophia Loren, Richard Harris, Ava Gardner, Burt Lancaster, Martin Sheen, Ingrid Thulin, John Phillip Law, Lionel Stander, Ann Turkel, Alida Valli, O. J. Simpson.

The Sentinel. 1977. Universal. Producers: Michael Winner, Jeffrey Konvitz. Director: Michael Winner. Screenplay: Michael Winner, Jeffrey Konvitz, from the novel by Jeffrey Konvitz. Cast: Chris Sarandon, Cristina Raines, Martin Balsam, Ava Gardner, John Carradine, Arthur Kennedy, Sylvia Miles, Deborah Raffin, Eli Wallach, Christopher Walken, Beverly D'Angelo.

City on Fire. 1979. Astral-Bellevue-Pathé/Sandy Howard. Producers: Sandy Howard, Claude Hewroux. Director: Alvin Rakoff. Screenplay: Jack Hill, David P. Lewis, Celine La Freniere. Cast: Barry Newman, Susan Clark, Shelley Winters, Henry Fonda, Leslie Nielsen, James Franciscus, Ava Gardner.

The Kidnapping of the President. 1980. Safel. Producers: George Mendeluk, John Ryan. Director: George Mendeluk. Screenplay: Richard Murphy, from the novel by Charles Templeton. Cast: Hal Holbrook, William Shatner, Van Johnson, Ava Gardner, Miguel Fernandez.

Priest of Love. 1981. Filmways/Enterprise. Producers: Christopher Miles, Andrew Donally. Director: Christopher Miles. Screenplay: Alan Plater. Cast: Ian McKellen, Janet Suzman, Ava Gardner, Penelope Keith, Jorge Rivera, John Gielgud, James Faulkner.

Regina. 1982. Bognor/Spiritus/Galla Int'l. Producers: David Amiri, Serge Roux. Director: Jean-Yves Prate. Screenplay: Pierre Rey. Cast: Ava Gardner, Anthony Quinn, Ray Sharkey, Anna Karina.

A.D. 1985. International/Procter & Gamble. Producers: John A. Martinelli, George Jensen, Jack Wishard. Director: Stuart Cooper. Screenplay: Anthony Burgess, Vincenzo Labella. Cast: Anthony Edwards, Ava Gardner, John Houseman, Colleen Dewhurst, Ian McShane, James Mason, Jennifer O'Neill, Richard Roundtree, Richard Kiley, David Hedison. (Multipart for television.)

The Long Hot Summer. 1985. Leonard Hill. Producers: Leonard Hill, John Thomas Lenox, Dori Weiss. Director: Stuart Cooper. Screenplay: Rita Mae Brown, from the story by William Faulkner and screenplay by Irving Ravetch and Harriet Frank, Jr. Cast: Don Johnson, Jason Robards, Jr., Judith Ivey, Cybill Shepherd, Ava Gardner, Wings Hauser, William Forsythe. (For television.)

Knot's Landing. 1985. Lorimar. Producer: Lawrence Kasha. Cast: Ted Shackelford, Joan Van Ark, Don Murray, Michele Lee, Donna Mills. (AG, five appearances in long-running television series.)

Harem. 1986. Highgate/New World. Producer: Martin Manulis. Director: Billy Hale. Screenplay: Karol Hoeffner. Cast: Nancy Travis, Art Malik, Omar Sharif, Ava Gardner, Sarah Miles, Cherie Lungie, Yaphet Kotto. (For television.)

Maggie. 1986. Warner Bros./Karoger. Producer: William Hill. Director: Waris Hussein. Screenplay: Katherine Craddock, Rod Browning. Cast: Stephanie Powers, Ava Gardner, Herb Edelman, Jeremy Lloyd, Ian Ogilvy. (Episode for television.)

ACKNOWLEDGMENTS

I am very much indebted to the many people, in a dozen countries, who have generously contributed knowledge, memories, energy, and friendship to the creation of this book.

For interviews, conversation, and correspondence I want to thank the following: Berdie Abrams, Angela Allen, Diana Altman, James Bacon, Nelly Barquette, Kathleen Beckett, Turhan Bey, Nan Birmingham, Johnny Blowers, Peter Blythe, Keith Botsford, Phil Brown, Joe Bushkin, Jack Cardiff, Marge Champion, Esme Chandlee, Betty Comden, Alistair Cooke, Alberta Cooney, Luther Daughtry Jr., Steve Dunleavy, Milton Ebbins, J.M. Fordham, Leatrice Gilbert Fountain, Raul Garcia, Murray Garrett, Richard Goldstone, Bernard Gordon, Johnny Grant, Lucia Graves, Virginia Grey, Eloise Hardt, Pete Hamill, Alan Harkness, John Hawkesworth, Skitch Henderson, A. E. Hotchner, Cici Huston, Tony Huston, Christopher Isherwood, Herb Jeffries, Neil Jillett, Howard Keel, Evelyn Keyes, Mickey Knox, Frank Laico, Marc Lawrence, Margaret Lee, David Leeming, Janet Leigh, Monica Lewis, Michael Logothetis, Ross Lowell, Sid Luft, Joanna Lumley, Joseph L. Mankiewicz, Francis Matthews, Virginia Mayo, Ann Miller, Mitch Miller, Spoli Mills, Eva Monley, Terry Morse, Nan McGlohon, Bill Newman, Mike Oliver, Roy Parkinson, Kathleen Parrish, Bob Rains, Jess Rand, Gene Reynolds, Betty Rose, Ann Rutherford, Zoe Sallis, Budd Schulberg, Artie Shaw, Tom Shaw, Vincent Sherman, Betty Sicre, George Sidney, Arthur Silber, Jr., Sheila Sim, Jeanie Sims, Donald Sinden, William Smith, Robert Stack,

Mokie Stancil, David Stenn, Austin Stevens, Tempest Storm, Ben Tatar, Claude Terrail, Roma Tomalty, Mel Torme, Candy Toxton, Tony Trabert, William Tuttle, Carmen Vargas, Bayard Veiller, Imogen Wheeler, Sandy Whitelaw, Ann Williams, Billy Williams, Michael Winner, Clarence Woodall, Jimmy Wyble, Philip Yordan, Genevieve Young. Although not everyone here has been quoted directly, all have contributed insights and recollections of Ava and her world. I must give an extra line of appreciation to Betty Sicre, who shared with me so many memories of her great friend; and to Angela Allen, a uniquely close witness to so much of the history of the movies, who not only gave freely of her memories of filmmaking but also helped me with access to a number of people who were important to Ava Gardner's life and career.

Some quotes and information from firsthand sources predate my official research, and these prior interviews, associations, and random encounters are an unintended benefit. An interview with Christopher Isherwood in California shortly before his death; a conversation with Mel Tormé, including the tale of Ava in the MGM commissary, at a bizarre birthday party for Mel in the basement of Sam Goody's record store in Manhattan; during a week in the company of the wonderful George Sidney, in Las Vegas, while plotting out a collaborative project (alas canceled by his death), we often spoke of Ava G., one of George's favorite "success stories." Time spent with the late Joseph Mankiewicz, in New York City and at his home in Bedford, New York, touched on many items in his long career including *The Barefoot Contessa*; if only I had anticipated this project then, we would have spent far more time talking about Ava Gardner and less about the writing of the movie *Sooky* or the comedic skills of Wheeler and Woolsey. Many of the tales in the preceding pages I first heard from David Hanna, a friend and employer of mine for several years, and Ava's publicist and manager in the 1950s. David did not name-drop readily but when the conversation warranted it he could lean back in his office chair and tell a story: "One time with Ava, we were flying in to Rio . . ." Some of the things he recalled were startling, revelations he had not put in his own writings about her, but he never spoke with scorn or derision, only amusement and amazement.

For access to archival collections and library materials, I thank the British Film Institute, London; the Library of Congress, Washington, D.C.; the Heritage Center in Smithfield (much gratitude to the wonderful

Ms. Margaret Lee); the Houston Library Research Center, Houston, Texas (Joel Draut); the State Library in Raleigh, North Carolina (especially Steve Massingill and Alan Westmoreland); Denise Jones and Paul Magann at the *Raleigh News & Observer*; Los Angeles Public Library, Main Branch; the New York Public Library, Lincoln Center Branch; the Cinemateque Francaise, the Academy of Motion Picture Arts and Sciences, Beverly Hills; the Cinema Library at the University of Southern California, Los Angeles; the *Daily Times*, Lahore, Pakistan. I wish to thank two individual archivists for their great skill, helpfulness, and charm: the all-knowing Barbara Hall at the Margaret Herrick Library in Beverly Hills, and the remarkable Ned Comstock at USC, the best in the business.

Much thanks and gratitude to Susan Huxley, a researcher both skilled and inspired, who blazed a trail across Britain in pursuit of Ava associates. To Arlene Hellerman, writer, researcher, incisive interviewer, an invaluable support in any endeavor. To Joan Cohen, another highly skilled researcher.

For their generous support and encouragement I cannot begin to thank the following, colleagues and friends, wonderful writers, and historians all: Pat McGilligan, Scott Eyman, David Stenn, Peter Levinson, Tony Crawley, Tom Weaver, Diana Altman, and Ted Schwarz. Buy their books. For his generous help through the creation of this work I also thank Nigel Algar, great documentary maker now at the BFI; ditto to my friend Down Under, the film producer Richard Brennan, who went above and beyond to unlock doors for me in Melbourne and Sydney. A *merci* to Bertrand Tavernier in Paris for sharing with me his Burt Lancaster story. For help all along the way, thanks to friend Patrick Shields in California; and to my composer buddy in Australia, Norma Martin. Great thanks to journalist Paul Cullum and actress Susan Tyrell for giving me access to their memorable conversation. To Gary Goldstein for his help in tracking the story of Ava's autobiography. For assorted translations, thanks to writer and linguist Sara J. Welch. For their assistance in preparing research, transcribing interviews, and other work I am very grateful to: Carol Hardin, Jeannie Gosline, Colomba Johnson, Joanna Sondheim, Cat Tyc, Cynthia Sullivan, and Sean Bronzell. In London again, thanks to Allen Eyles and BAFTA for putting me in touch with some of Ava Gardner's performer friends. And in Connecticut to A. E. Hotchner for conversation and for permission to use his photo of Ava, Dominguín, and Hemingway. In New York City, the same to Diana Altman, who shared with me some of her father's work.

For providing a mighty long trail of Ava lore I owe a debt of gratitude to the hundreds of authors and journalists who have written about the actress over the past sixty-some years. Of obvious particular interest were Ava's autobiography, and the previous biographies of Ava Gardner by Charles Higham, Roland Flamini, and Doris Rollins Cannon; also the comprehensive works on the life of Frank Sinatra written by Earl Wilson, Kitty Kelley, and J. Randy Taraborrelli.

Another big thank-you to all of the following for various contributions and forms of assistance during the research and writing of this biography: In Smithfield, North Carolina: Miss Lee and staff at the Heritage Center; the Ava Gardner Museum; the Super 8 Motel; the Howell Theater; Café Monet and Smithfield Barbecue; all the friendly people of Smithfield and Brogden, including Mokie, Luther, Clarence. In Madrid: the Wellington Hotel and staff; the Ritz Hotel; Juan Tejero and Co. at T&B Editores; Chicote's Bar (and Museo de la Cocktail). In Palm Springs, California: Mark Graves at Palm Springs Desert Resorts; Stephen Zapantis of Time and Place Homes for the tour of the Sinatra home, "Twin Palms"; the Spa Casino Resort. In Puerto Vallarta, Mexico: Los Tules; the Rio Hotel; Nelly Barquette; Maurizio at Casa Kimberley; La Jolla Mismaloya; John Huston's Sunset Bar; The Sets of the Night of the Iguana Restaurant; the Four Seasons Punta Mita; the Oceano Bar; Ramon the Tailor. In Acapulco: Mike Oliver; Adolfo Santiago; Los Flamingos Hotel; Raul Garcia and family. Also: the Viceroy Hotel, Santa Monica; the Tour d'Argent; the Sofitel Bercy; St. Mark's Poetry Project, New York City; Sorelle Fontana, Rome; Walter and Nicolas Bussenius at Hotel Mt. Joli, Cap Haitien; the Michigan Hemingway Society; Oficina de Turismo de Tossa de Mar; Sahara Hotel, Las Vegas; the Dorchester and the Sofitel St. James, London; Lily Devlin at the Portaferry Library in Northern Ireland; the Hotel de Paris and the Hermitage, Monte-Carlo; the JW Marriott Starr Pass Resort, Tucson, Arizona.

And my gratitude to the following: Robert Server; Helen Smith; Walter Donohue; Corinne Sidney; Tisha Sterling; Scott Gould; Alan Rode; Sal Ceravolo; Stuart Wolff; Patricia Alisau; Gordon van Gelder, Heather Florence, Jorg Jaramillo at AP; Sandy Silverman; Bruce Serlen; Marcy at the

New York Post; Vincent Alonzo; Carol Martinez at LA Inc.; Don Salkaln; Maggie Hurt at the British Film Institute; and Dixie Evans (curator: Striptease Hall of Fame, Helendale, California).

Many thanks to Elizabeth Beier, my editor at St. Martin's, who has blessed this project with her talent, enthusiasm, insight, and patience. And to Michael Connor at St. Martin's Press, Mary Morris at Bloomsbury, and to copy editor Sue Llewellyn for all of their help and great editorial contributions.

At Bloomsbury, I am very happy and very grateful to have an editor as wise and sympathetic as Alexandra Pringle, from the beginning offering all the support and freedom any author could desire.

I am beholden to two wonderful agents: To Roslyn Targ in New York City, my longtime friend and associate, always there with advice and care, keeping the light burning. And to Mary Clemmey in London, with her diligence and discernment and great ideas and instincts.

I send my love to Elizabeth Server, always and forever.

And to Terri, collaborator, spiritual adviser, press agent, femme fatale.

Blessings on Ava Gardner, where it all began.

Have I forgotten anybody? Well thank you, too.

Lee Server
LServ500@aol.com

INDEX

A NOTE ON THE AUTHOR

Lee Server is a writer, biographer and chronicler of popular culture. His previous book, *Robert Mitchum: Baby I Don't Care*, was hailed by the *Sunday Times* as the 'film biography of the year'.